'At last a book on costume that truly answers th
ars ask themselves on a daily basis. It must surel
on theatrical costume this decade.'
— **Scott Ande**

CW01509648

WHAT IS THE ROLE OF COSTUME IN PERFORI
HOW DOES IT PRODUCE, REINFORCE OR DECONSTRUCT IDENTITY?
WHAT CAN IT TELL US ABOUT THE THEATRE EVENT?

This wide-ranging collection of readings examines costume from a variety of perspectives in order to take account of its multi-layered presence onstage and backstage.
Exploring costume in the contexts of key historical periods, artistic movements, people and performances, Ali Maclaurin and Aoife Monks consider the major theoretical
and practical approaches to the craft.

Underpinned by a series of new practitioner interviews, reference to important
texts and suggestions for further reading, this diverse resource weaves a rich tapestry of experience and perspective that will be invaluable for students, practitioners
and researchers alike.

ALI MACLAURIN is a freelance designer and lecturer. She set up and led the degree
in Costume Design and Construction for Queen Margaret University, Edinburgh, UK.

AOIFE MONKS is Reader in Theatre Studies, Queen Mary University of London, UK.

READINGS IN THEATRE PRACTICE

Series Editor: Simon Shepherd

Published:

Ross Brown: Sound

Jon Davison: Clown

Penny Francis: Puppetry

Ali Maclaurin and Aoife Monks: Costume

Scott Palmer: Light

Simon Shepherd: Direction

Forthcoming:

Jane Boston: Voice

Joslin McKinney: Construction

Readings in Theatre Practice
Series Standing Order ISBN 978–0–230–53717–0 hardcover
Series Standing Order ISBN 978–0–230–53718–7 paperback
(*outside North America only*)

You can receive future titles in this series as they are published by placing a standing order. Please contact your bookseller or, in the case of difficulty, write to us at the address below with your name and address, the title of the series and the ISBN quoted above.

Customer Services Department, Macmillan Distribution Ltd, Houndmills, Basingstoke, Hampshire, RG21 6XS, UK

Costume

Readings in Theatre Practice

Ali Maclaurin

and

Aoife Monks

First published 2015 by
PALGRAVE

Palgrave in the UK is an imprint of Macmillan Publishers Limited,
registered in England, company number 785998, of 4 Crinan Street,
London N1 9XW.

Palgrave Macmillan in the US is a division of St Martin's Press LLC,
175 Fifth Avenue, New York, NY 10010.

Palgrave is a global imprint of the above companies and is represented
throughout the world.

Palgrave® and Macmillan® are registered trademarks in the United States,
the United Kingdom, Europe and other countries.

ISBN 978–1–137–02949–2 hardback
ISBN 978–1–137–02948–5 paperback

This book is printed on paper suitable for recycling and made from fully
managed and sustained forest sources. Logging, pulping and manufacturing
processes are expected to conform to the environmental regulations of the
country of origin.

A catalogue record for this book is available from the British Library.

A catalog record for this book is available from the Library of Congress.

Typeset by MPS Limited Chennai, India.

Printed in China

Contents

List of Illustrations

Acknowledgements

Aoife

Huge thanks go to the many colleagues and friends who have sustained and supported the writing of this book. My long-suffering parents, brother and Sam the Dog, the Mick Chicks in London and friends all over the world have been deeply tolerant of my lifelong interest in dressing up and all that this entails. My colleagues at Birkbeck, University of London, particularly Louise Owen, Fintan Walsh, Isabel Davis, Laura Salisbury and Adam Smyth, have been a huge influence on my thinking around 'things' and 'stuff'; colleagues at the London Theatre Seminar, not least Joe Kelleher and Bridget Escolme, have helped me think through questions of craft, working and wearing, and colleagues internationally – Erin Hurley in Montreal; Patrick Lonergan, Lionel Pilkington and Charlotte McIvor in Galway; Mary Ann Bolger in Dublin; Mark Phelan and Aoife McGrath in Belfast – have helped me think through this material in various sustaining and exciting seminars, debates and dinners. My editorial team at Contemporary Theatre Review offered their usual invaluable support, particularly Maria Delgado and Dominic Johnson. The Research Fellows at Birkbeck, particularly Christopher Cook, sustained me spiritually and with wine. Colleagues at the Critical Costume conference at Edgehill University and at the TaPRA conference in Glasgow offered invaluable feedback and encouragement. Some of this material was developed through archival work at the Harry Ransom archives, Austin; the New York Public Library, Lincoln Centre; the British Library and the V&A Theatre Archives. The support of Ruth Frendo at the Globe archives has been invaluable. Many thanks to Simon Annand, Lois Weaver, Lez Brotherston, Tina Bicat, Jenny Tiramani and Dawn Wood for agreeing to be included in the book and for giving me their time. The support of Jenni Burnell and Lucinda Knight at Palgrave Macmillan has been as superb as ever, as has been the guiding hand of Simon Shepherd. Finally, of course, huge thanks go to my co-author, Ali Maclaurin: I hope this book has marked the beginning of a long friendship.

PERMISSIONS

Photographs

Daniel Day-Lewis backstage at *The Futurists*, National Theatre, 1986 (Simon Annand, photograph, by permission of Simon Annand, featured in *The Half* [Faber and Faber: 2010]).

Dancers and audience members at Punchdrunk's *The Masque of the Red Death*, Battersea Arts Centre, 2007 (Steve Forrest, photograph, by permission of Steve Forrest).

Ali

Thanks to John Bloomfield for the best careers talk ever; to drama staff at Loughborough University, particularly Mick Mangan, Elaine Aston and Christine White who gave me advice and encouragement when I first realized I might need to write a book on stage costume more than fifteen years ago; to Yvon Bonenfant, for whose singular work I have designed costumes that have stretched my thinking on both function and aesthetics; to Jessica Bowles for her initial collaboration and ideas; and to all friends and colleagues over the years with whom I have discussed 'the book'. The National Library of Scotland and the British Library have both sustained me wonderfully through this long project and their staff has been unfailingly helpful. Many thanks also to Stewart Laing, Alex Rigg, Mark Thomson and Jenny Tiramani for giving their time and expertise so generously in interview; to Simon Shepherd and Jenni Burnell for their endless patience and support; to my long-suffering husband and son; and to my co-author, Aoife Monks. I wish all collaborations were so easy and so pleasurable. Finally, I remember my parents with the deepest love and gratitude: my mum who taught me to sew and my dad who encouraged my curiosity and inspired my love of a matching sock.

PERMISSIONS

Photographs

Alex Rigg in *Feather Mammy at Shambellie House*, National Museum of Costume, 2009 (Xander Gisby, photograph, by permission of Alex Rigg).

Audience member in *The Salon Project*, directed by Stewart Laing, Traverse Theatre, Edinburgh, 2011 (Tommy Ga-Ken Wan, photograph, by permission of Tommy Ga-Ken Wan).

Emma Cunliffe, Malcolm Shields and Robin Laing in Shakespeare's *As You Like It*, directed by Mark Thomson, Lyceum Theatre, Edinburgh, 2005 (Douglas McBride, photograph, by permission of Douglas McBride).

Series Preface

This series aims to gather together both key historical texts and contemporary ways of thinking about the material crafts and practices of theatre.

These crafts work with the physical materials of theatre – sound, objects, light, paint, fabric, and – yes – physical bodies. Out of these materials the theatre event is created.

In gathering the key texts of a craft it becomes very obvious that the craft is not simply a handling of materials, however skilful. It is also a way of thinking about both the materials and their processes of handling. Work with sound and objects, for example, involves – always, at some level – concepts of what sound is and does, what an object is and does … what a body is.

For many areas of theatre practice there are the sorts of 'how to do it' books that have been published for at least a century. These range widely in quality and interest but next to none of them is able to, or wants to, position the *doing* in relation to the *thinking about doing* or the thinking about the material being used.

This series of books aims to promote both thinking about doing and thinking about materials. Its authors are specialists in their field of practice and they are charged to reflect on their specialism and its history in order, often for the first time, to model concepts and provide the tools not just for the doing but for thinking about theatre practice.

The series title 'Readings in Theatre Practice' uses the word 'reading' in the sense both of a simple understanding or interpretation and of an authoritative explication, an exegesis as it were. Thus, the books first gather together people's opinions about, their understanding of, what they think they are making. These opinions are then framed within a broader narrative which offers an explanatory overview of the practice under investigation.

So, although the books comprise many different voices, there is a dominant authorial voice organising the material and articulating overarching arguments. By way of promoting a further level of critique and reflection, however, authors are asked to include a few lengthy sections, in the form of interviews or essays or both, in order to make space for other voices to develop their own overviews. These may sit in tension, or indeed in harmony, with the dominant narratives.

Authors are encouraged to be sceptical about normative assumptions and canonical orthodoxy. They are asked not to ignore practices and thinking that might question dominant views; they are invited to speculate as to how canons and norms come into being and what effects they have.

We hope the shape provides a dynamic tension in which the different activities of 'reading' both assist and resist each other. The details of the lived practices refuse to fit tidily into the straitjacket of a general argument, but the dominant overview also refuses to allow itself to fragment into local prejudice and anecdote. And it's that restless play between assistance and resistance that mirrors the character of the practices themselves.

At the heart of each craft is a tense relationship. On the one hand there is the basic raw material that is worked – the wood, the light, the paint, the musculature. These have their own given identity – their weight, mechanical logics, smell, particle formation, feel. In short, the texture of the stuff. And on the other hand there is theatre, wanting its effects and illusions, its distortions and impossibilities. The raw material resists the theatre as much as yields to it, the theatre both develops the material and learns from it. The stuff and the magic. This relationship is perhaps what defines the very activity of theatre itself.

It is this relationship, the thing which defines the practice of theatre, which lies at the heart of each book in this series.

Simon Shepherd

Introduction

Aoife Monks

On 8 January 2013, the UK's *Grazia* magazine ran a story entitled '[...] The Dos and Don'ts of Stage Door Chic'. Referring to the post-show appearances of actors like Katie Holmes and Jessica Chastain, the magazine offered its readers 'a list of easy-to-follow rules for successful stage door dressing'. With advice like 'DO get noticed in bright red' and 'DON'T wear sunglasses at night' (*Grazia*, 2013), the magazine failed to notice that what they termed the 'the vintage hipster look' of the British actor Anna Friel was in fact a clear reference to her leading role in the West End (London) production of Chekhov's *Uncle Vanya*, from which she emerged nightly to the frenzy of the paparazzi. Friel, wearing heavily embroidered dresses, fake fur wraps and Cossack-style boots matched her backstage appearances with her onstage persona while ensuring that, according to the *Daily Mail* newspaper, she looked: 'every inch the star' (*Daily Mail* Reporter, 2012). Attention to the backstage appearance of actors is nothing new. By the end of the nineteenth century, with the emergence of the mass media, reports of the fashion worn by actors at the stage door, or on the street, began to emerge as a companion narrative to descriptions of actors in costume onstage. For Friel to dress herself in contemporary fashion backstage with resonance for the period costume she wears onstage is to maintain the cultural status of the actress as a 'trendsetter and role model' (Schweitzer, 2009, p. 8). We might ask, however, what the relationship is between Friel's street clothes and her costume, and what exactly it is we are looking at when we see an actor dressing up at the theatre.

This photograph of Friel raises some interesting questions about the peculiar work that costume does at the theatre. Often overlooked by scholars and critics as an important aspect of both acting practice and scenography, costume works as a bridge between the actor's body, the environment of the stage and the spectator in the auditorium. Costume most obviously forms the interchange between actors and the fictional characters they play, but, as we've seen with Friel, it may work simultaneously to frame and reinforce the actor's own star persona or association with previous roles. At the same time, the costume also works as a link between the actor and the scenographical environment of the stage, situating performers within a series of aesthetic and spatial structures. These scenographical choices may also function to place the actor's body within a particular historical milieu, or position the actor's body within a broader set of ideas about the nature of the 'body' and embodiment more generally. Finally, the costume may also work as a bridge between the actor and the audience in how it situates the actor within systems of fashion, categories of social identity (such as gender or class) or social relations of power. By focusing on costume for this Reader, we are really probing how the various languages of the stage and the systems of belief and value in the auditorium meet within the object of costume. Examining costume, then, means understanding the interchange between the work of the performer, the design and craft of the costume designer, and the experience of the audience at the theatre.

It's important to emphasize, however, that these various aspects of costume don't present themselves sequentially onstage. Rather, a single stage costume is capable of enabling all of these exchanges between actor and character, actor and scenography, and scenography and audience. Returning to Anna Friel in *Uncle Vanya* can help us to trace out the multiple ways in which costume works at the theatre. In an onstage photograph of Friel in role, we see her wearing a long white lace dress and gloves in the style of the 1890s, with her hair up, holding a cream parasol and the ropes of a swing. The image suggests that Friel is in character, playing the role of Yelena, the young second wife of Aleksandr, a professor, and the object of love and desire for the other male characters in the play. We also see her wearing a costume that is claiming a certain kind of historical authenticity, positioning Friel's body within the milieu that the play is set in, and providing a visual pleasure that may retain an autonomy from the fictional narrative – we may enjoy looking not only at Yelena in her everyday dress but also enjoy looking at Friel dressed up in an appealing costume that has been designed based on 1890s fashion, playing into forms of nostalgia and longing for the past, emphasizing the role that costume plays in providing visual pleasures at the theatre, pleasures that are often tied to nostalgic longing for other times.

If we look at a photograph of Friel leaving the stage door after the show has ended, we see a kind of 'negative' image of her onstage costume, with Friel now dressed in a heavily embroidered short black dress, with a fur collar and her hair down. While the dress is clearly contemporary it also makes reference to a generalized 'Russian' aesthetic of embroidery and fur. Here we see the actor using clothes to present her 'real self' after the show has ended. But the fact that her modern clothes are ghosted by the period costume that she wore onstage and the fact that she is being photographed by paparazzi after the end of the performance make reading her appearance more complicated. It's clear that her star persona is being formed through her choice of clothing – she becomes the means to stage the clothes, while at the same time the clothes stage her celebrity status as an icon that forms its own sort of spectacle. The 'Russian' styling of her clothing also suggest that Friel might want us to see her as infected by her costume and character, rendering her body decorative and appealing through its connection back to the pictorial qualities of her stage role. Friel's 'real' clothes turn out not to be 'real' at all, but are in fact working as an extension of the logic of costume by organizing the actor's body within hierarchies of celebrity and past performance.

The poster publicizing the show demonstrates another function of costume, in how it organizes Friel as a member of an ensemble of actors. With the headline of the poster describing the show as 'the theatrical event of the season', Friel is shown from the shoulders up, with long straight hair in black modern dress, surrounded by her fellow actors. The image clearly delineates the performers as individuals, with the names of each star performer (Friel, Samuel West, Ken Stott, Laura Carmichael) listed above the play's title on the poster, while also organizing them as a collective through their shared use of modern costume. The show's poster, in its focus on the actors' faces, seems to want to emphasize the personalities of the actors, rather than the characters, asserting the presence of the actors over the story by Chekhov, or the vision of the director or scenographer. Nonetheless, the fact that the actors have been styled to look uniform in their shared colour palette and composition also indicates that their bodies are organized in relation to each other, that they will be bound as a collective by a coherent and unified stage picture. The work of costume to produce visual coherence within a scenographical logic emerges here as another function of the clothing worn by Friel.

The contrasts and connections between these three images raise some important questions about the nature and role of theatre costume. They prompt some consideration of what historically accurate clothing is imagined to achieve onstage, asking us to interrogate the relationship between the actor's body, the fictional world of the play, the social milieu in which the play was written and the pictorial pleasures that the presentation of this milieu might provide for the audience. The use of a collective styling for the four actors in the ensemble might also ask something about the role that costume plays as a function of the mise en scene. This leads to a consideration of the work of the director and scenographer in producing a 'unified' stage picture, in which costume works to render the actor's body a form of visual spectacle or a function of the broader scenic concept.

Costume then may become variously the means to situate an actor as the vehicle for a fictional character, the means through which an imagined historical authenticity can be accessed or a key aspect of how a scenographic vision for a production is made manifest. Of course, within these various and interlinking modes of costume can be found the work of the designer, maker, dresser, props-maker and all the labour it takes to produce the fabric, lace, buttons, etc., that make up these costumes. The role of these workers in producing the costume that Anna Friel embodies as Yelena may not be foremost in the experience of the audience, however. Rather, the costume may be received as 'inevitable', as fictional as Chekhov's character, rather than being literally material, produced by hard work and expertise backstage, and

performed with hard work and expertise by Friel herself. The material qualities of the costume, and the work that it takes to make that costume, may be
disavowed within the experience of the audience watching the performance.

Of course, we can also see the work that costume does in producing and
depicting identity onstage. We can see here a performed version of gender,
in which the character of Yelena and her clothes, and the body of Friel and
her costume, produce and imagine forms of femininity and class privilege.
But there is also another identity being produced here, which is that of
'Anna Friel'. The costume determines how Friel's celebrity 'self' is being
presented and reinvented by her appearance in the play. Friel's previous
roles: her scandalous turn as a lesbian character in the British television soap
opera *Brookside*, her previous appearance at the Theatre Royal Haymarket as
Holly Golightly in *Breakfast at Tiffany's* (2009), her longstanding appearances
in the gossip columns of the British tabloids, these previous personae are
remoulded and consolidated by presenting her as a decorative love object in
period dress in Chekhov's play, enabling a further interchange between the
system of costume on the stage and the system of fashion that Friel enters
when she leaves the theatre.

MAPPING THE BOOK

This example of Anna Friel in costume onstage and off suggests that
costume should not be viewed merely as clothing for characters. Rather,
costume plays an intricate role in organizing the relationship between the
actor's body and the character's body, the audience's historical moment and
the moment of the fictional world and the actor's persona and the ways in
which that persona might be reimagined or remoulded through the performance. These varying modes of embodiment often require a disavowal of
the actual labour it takes to make these costumes and indeed to wear them
onstage. An actor appearing in costume onstage may enact a disjunction
between the material conditions of producing the stage illusion and the
audience's experience of consuming the costumed body in the auditorium.
Equally, costume may function to organize the actor's body in relation to a
mise en scene that acts as a screen for the director or scenographer's vision,
controlling the stage environment through the principles of visual coherence. Costume may also be a means for theatre artists to renegotiate images
of the body in order to critique the bourgeois theatre system's imbrication in
systems of fashion or to offer new visions of embodiment or new versions of
identity to its audience. The systems through which costume is produced,
as well as how it is worn, tell us much about the politics and meanings of
the theatre event, and this book aims to investigate these various forms of,
and approaches to, costume. The book therefore engages with costume from
multiple perspectives, thinking about its relationship to historicism and
modern dress; examining its role onstage for actors and backstage in the

'craft' work of designers; thinking about the work it does to produce, reinforce or deconstruct systems of identity; and considering the role it played for designers of the twentieth century in renegotiating ideas of embodiment and structures of power.

This book is written from two perspectives: the approach of the costume designer, Ali Maclaurin, and the approach of the theatre scholar, Aoife Monks. We hope that these combined perspectives will open out the complicated web of functions, meanings and forms of work that theatre costume constitutes onstage and off. Intermixed with chapters on costume are interviews with a range of theatre artists: designers, makers, performers, directors and photographers. These voices help to offer further perspectives on the wide range of approaches to designing, making, wearing and photographing costumes.

The first chapter, written by Ali, offers an overview of the relatively limited books, articles and resources available for the study of costume design. In Chapter 2, she investigates the role of costume within the stage picture. Even as costume may appear to be indelibly and uncannily fixed to the body of the actor, indeed constituting the actor's and character's body for the duration of the performance, as Ali outlines, the role of costume in producing a unified stage picture varies considerably. Modern dress productions, for example, carry with them a freight of ideological values that may be rendered invisible by the 'natural' and taken-for-granted qualities of modern clothing. By contrast, historically accurate costume may play into forms of nostalgia for the past, or alternatively may offer audiences a distanced position from which to examine the implications of the play and its performance, denaturalizing hidden assumptions about power relations and identity.

The third chapter, written by Aoife, traces the varying 'appearance' of costume within the different frames of the theatre event. Examining the uncanny status of costume as a material object that works to produce apparently immaterial effects, the chapter takes the specific example of Mark Rylance's performance as Hamlet at the Globe theatre in 2000, in order to think about how costume is understood and used differently by critics in the auditorium, by actors in the rehearsal room, by dressers, stage managers and prop makers backstage and by the designer Jenny Tiramani and the numerous costume makers that she works with in the wardrobe. The chapter investigates the categories of 'virtuosity', 'technique' and 'craft' to suggest that, while the classical Shakespeare tradition in Britain often imagines backstage labour as working in 'service' to an evanescent and immaterial illusion, in fact the work done by makers and actors also retains a system of values that is independent from the audience's experience of costume in the auditorium.

The fourth chapter, also by Aoife, focuses its attention on the body of the performer, in order to consider the role that costume may play in reflecting, imagining and consolidating hierarchies of identity through the production of stereotypes in performance. Focusing largely on nineteenth-century theatre, the chapter acknowledges the role of costume and make-up

in constructing stereotypes such as the blackface minstrel and the stage
Irishman. However, the fixity of these images can also become destabilized
by the fluid relationship between the performer's body and the costume that
they wear to produce these images of identity on the stage. The chapter goes
on to consider the modernist critique of theatre stereotypes in the work of
the Irish-American playwright Eugene O'Neill and the ways in which the
postmodern theatre company, The Wooster Group, reimagined his work
in the 1990s by suggesting that theatrical representation has become an
inescapable reality.

The fifth chapter, by Ali, moves from the actor to the auteur in the role
that modernist and avant-garde costume designers played in reimagining
the body and the ensemble in the nineteenth century. Examining the ways
in which these experiments in costume worked to conceal the actor's body,
or eradicate it altogether, the chapter moves on to look at the ways in which
groups of bodies can be organized through the use of costume.

Throughout the book, we offer a series of interviews with theatre artists
who represent a very wide range of theatre forms and design practices. The
book starts with Jenny Tiramani, the head of design at Shakespeare's Globe
Theatre, whose intricately researched and designed Renaissance costumes
are discussed in Chapters 2 and 3. By contrast, Mark Thomson, the artistic
director of the Royal Lyceum Theatre in Edinburgh, offers a sense of costume
as character-driven and centred on a modern dress aesthetic. Simon Annand
discusses his longstanding project of photographing actors backstage in their
dressing rooms and the kinds of insight this brings into the actor's relationship to costume and work. The performance artist Alex Rigg views costume
as a productive obstacle, in which choreography is produced through the
artist's struggle with the object of costume. Lois Weaver, part of the feminist-
lesbian duo Split Britches, offers another approach to costume in the 'found
object', where the DIY aesthetic of her work functions in conversation with
its gender politics. Lez Brotherston's approach to costume emerges from
an entirely different aesthetic tradition, with his designs for the large-scale
dance pieces choreographed by Matthew Bourne, giving a sense of how
budget and time limitations become a productive set of constraints in the
collaboration between choreographer and designer. Finally, Tina Bicat discusses her designs for the site-specific theatre company Punchdrunk, particularly emphasizing the collaborative relationship between her work and
that of the performer. The similarities between her designs on *The Masque of
the Red Death*, where audiences wore masks and cloaks, and Stewart Laing's
work with Salon Project, which costumes the audience in full period evening dress, finish the book with the question of what audiences wear to the
theatre. This image of the audience dressing up leaves us with the overall
questions of this Reader: when audiences sit in the auditorium and watch
an actor in costume, what exactly do they experience? Who has made the
costumes and why? And what are the multifarious, complicated and often
contradictory roles played by costume at the theatre?

Chapter

1 Writing about Costume

Ali Maclaurin

Readers of this book will inevitably have different reasons for reading it and different purposes they need it to fulfil. There is nothing more disappointing than standing in a library staring bleakly at a shelf because the book you need does not seem to exist and when I began writing this book I was of the opinion that, although there were a number of books written about costume history, costume making, and the process and product of costume design, there was almost nothing written about how costume works on the stage. Potential and practicing designers and makers may question why they need to know more than who wore what, when or how it was cut (difficult enough in itself!) particularly when they are working to a tight deadline. All I can say is that as a designer I reached a point where I wanted to understand the context of what I was doing, to consider the practices and opinions of other eras and practitioners in order to find different ways of approaching my work. Undoubtedly, this is an under-researched area possibly because of the view that clothes are frivolous and ephemeral, or because the work of costume is difficult to unravel from the work of the actor (Monks, 2010, pp. 10–11). However, in researching this book I have discovered many sections and chapters tucked away in books that appear to be about other subjects, such as the theatre of particular periods and genres, or fashion history or art, so that I am left of the opinion that it is not only the paucity of material but also the variety of contexts in which costume is considered that makes material quite difficult and time-consuming to track down. Part of the purpose of this book is to allow easier access to some of this writing though inevitably my choices will be subjective and cannot be definitive. I would encourage potential scholars and practitioners to treat printed resources like an untidy props store, and go much further than the display shelf, by checking chapter headings and indexes for relevant data. It is worth the trouble. Studying not just what stage costume looked like, but the particulars of how it was used and received during a specified period can reveal much about the period, about costume and about how theatre works.

For the purposes of order, I have divided the books reviewed into separate areas. Inevitably there is some fluidity, for example, books primarily focussed on making costume may also provide valuable historical information, so the sections should not be considered as discreet.

ENCYCLOPEDIAS AND HISTORIES OF COSTUME

This section provides a brief summary of books that have a bearing on stage costume. Anyone more broadly interested in dress history should begin with Lou Taylor's comprehensive summary in *Establishing Dress History* (2004). In the Renaissance period, with its urge to collect and catalogue, and its legal emphasis on clothing as a social indicator, it is not surprising that encyclopaedias of costume began to be compiled for the use of scholars and artists. From about 1520 onwards there were a number of contemporary print collections available on world costume, and by 1590 the first printed books on the subject, some of which included costumes of the past copied from paintings or statues. Much of this material was not strictly accurate, nevertheless examples such as Vecellio's *De Gli Habiti Antici et Moderni di Diverse Parti del Mondo* (*Clothing Ancient and Modern from All Parts of the World*) written in 1590 (Vecellio, 1590) are a useful window into the world of late sixteenth century Venice reflected through contemporary eyes. In this large volume, the woodcuts are probably copied from previous drawings as shown by their awkward drapery. The book was clearly used by artists of the time such as Inigo Jones as shown by Orgel and Strong through their visual comparison (Orgel and Strong, 1973). There is very little explanatory text, just titling, and the rather unsystematic 'ancient dress' illustrated includes, for example, an 'Ancient Roman patrician' (Vecellio, 1590, p. 2), 'Mediaeval garb of young nobleman out wooing' (ibid., p. 12), and 'Another old costume for unmarried young women' (ibid., p. 21).

The mid to late eighteenth century saw an increase in such books as appreciation for social history grew. According to De Marly (De Marly, 1982, p. 54), Garrick had a number of books on world and historical costume in his library, such as Thomas Jefferys 4-volume work, *A Collection of the Dresses of Different Nations, Ancient and Modern*, published between 1757 and 1772. Jefferys was 'geographer to his Majesty' (Jefferys, 1772, p. 1) hence the emphasis on world rather than historical costume. In volume 4 the plates include 'the Habits of the Principal Characters of the English Stage' (ibid., p. 1). Mainly of the mythological and allegorical variety such as Circe or Hope and dressed in essentially contemporary costume with symbolic additions such as a padlocked bodice for Secrecy, these engravings, Taylor suggests, were aimed at masquerade participants and, although they may have stirred interest in costumes of the past, were not concerned with historical accuracy (Taylor, 2004, p. 34). In contrast, Joseph Strutt published the first edition of *Complete View of the Dress and Habits of the People of England from the Establishment of the Saxons in Britain to the Present Time* in 1792. This book is probably the first scholarly chronological work published on historical costume in Britain, and, as such, is very important. It comprises precisely detailed descriptions of garments worn, as well as a series of beautifully engraved and coloured plates. Strutt assures his reader that the pictures are, 'faithfully copied from the originals, without an additional fold being made to the drapery' (Strutt, 1792, Address to the Public). The seriousness with which he regarded his research is indicated by comments such as, in the chapter on gowns,

I have often considered myself, when engaged in the abstracted researches of antiquity, in the situation of a traveller who has lost his way in a country unknown to him … and never did I feel the force of this similitude more than in the compilation of this present chapter'.

(Ibid., p. 17)

He goes on to admit his ignorance of the names of ladies' garments and beg forgiveness for any impropriety!

Strutt's work was greatly respected by later Victorian scholars of costume, such as J.R. Planché (see Chapter 2), whose *Costume of Shakespeare's Historical Tragedy of King John* (1823), was used by the great exponent of researched historical costume, Edmund Kean. Planché wrote the preface to an 1842 reprint of Strutt's book in which he stated, 'notwithstanding the great improvement of taste and the consequent increase of anxiety on the part of English Authors, Painters, Sculptors, and Actors, to acquire sufficient knowledge of costume … no publication has subsequently appeared … so full of information on the general subject of costume'. Planché's *History of British Costume* (1834) was, according to Taylor, 'the first serious dress history book to be marketed to a popular rather than an elitist public' (Taylor, 2004, p. 37). Strutt was also much admired by another influential antiquarian and writer of the time, F.W. Fairholt. His *Costume in England* (1846) again faithfully copied from contemporary sources, was followed by other similar volumes, many of which mention him and his work with great reverence.

The public became more and more interested in historical costume and by the middle of the nineteenth century the popularity of leisure activities such as costume balls began to rise. As the trend developed, so did books with a different emphasis. As opposed to a serious scholarly quest for faithful accuracy, Debenham and Freebody, a major department store, published *Fancy Dresses Described, or What to Wear at Fancy Balls* by Ardern Holt (written and published between 1880 and 1896). '"But, what are we to wear?" laments the introduction, "This is the first exclamation on receipt of an invitation to a Fancy Ball, and it is to assist in answering such questions that this volume has been compiled"' (Holt, 1887–1896, p. vii). The book is full of entertaining suggestions all of which are categorised as best for 'Brunes' or 'Blondes' and, judging by the illustrations, were based firmly around the silhouette favoured at the end of the nineteenth century with some appropriate trim, for example, 'Druidess. Long flowing cashmere robe bordered with embroidered oak leaves and mistletoe' (Holt, 1887–1896, p. 71). Hovering somewhere between scholarship and celebrity fanzine, the picturesque *Costume: Fanciful, Historical and Theatrical* (1906), by the fashion writer and gossip columnist Eliza Davis Aria is worth mentioning for its title alone. Besides chapters on historical periods it has sections on fancy dress, occupational dress and a final chapter, 'Of Theatrical Dress' (Aria, 1906, p. x). The work is dedicated 'To the dear Memory of Sir Henry Irving by whom I was inspired with a love of all things beautiful' (Aria, 1906, p. v) and the theatrical chapter is written in an entertainingly anecdotal style, for example, 'Macready ... carried his sense of the importance of costume to such a point during the rehearsals of *Henry V* that he went to bed in his armour, ... I recollect Sir Henry Irving quoting this fact, when telling me that he himself always followed the practice of wearing the clothes for a new part a few days previous to assuming them on the stage' (Aria, 1906, p. 238).

In the twentieth century one of the most prolific writers on dress history, including the stage, was James Laver who worked in the Prints and Drawings department at the Victoria and Albert Museum, now generally known as the V and A, for many years and wrote numerous histories of costume and fashion such as *Taste and Fashion* (1937) and *A Concise History of Costume* (1969). His work was descriptive more than analytical but there is no doubt that he did much to popularize the study of costume and fashion and was described in his obituary as 'the man in England who made the history of costume respectable' (Gibbs-Smith, 1976). He also wrote the well-known *Costume in the Theatre* (1964) (see section on stage costume). Janet Arnold too observes in her book, *A Handbook of Costume* (1973) that 'over the last ten years more people than ever before seem to have aquired an interest in costume' (Arnold, 1973, p. 7) and her book 'is intended to provide a guide to the ways in which people interested in costume can obtain information for themselves' (ibid.). It comprises detailed and precise lists of a wide range of sources for all types of costume, including the stage, it has an extensive bibliography and it forms an invaluable record of the resources available at that time.

Since the 1970s, the quantity and quality of such books has grown until now there is a huge choice of books on period costume often with good photographs or reproductions of original sources. Boucher's *A History of Costume in the West* (1987) is a broad chronology well illustrated with contemporary paintings. The V and A publish a wide series of books concerning their collections, such as the classic *400 Years of Fashion* (1984), the *Costume in Detail* Series, and catalogues linked to fashion exhibitions. In terms of costume history through photographs of original garments, the Kyoto Costume Institute's collection *Fashion: A History from the 18th to the 20th Century* (2005) is unbeatable, although it must be noted that it is indeed high fashion, worn by the richest and most up to the minute strata of society. The resources available to study original garments through photographs allow more and more understanding of the skill of early costume makers and the beauty of the garments produced. They allow a study of the shape, appearance and detail of clothes which can only be bettered by looking at the clothes themselves.

What these books are generally not written for is to offer any suggestions as to the 'why' of clothing and fashion, of how clothes are linked to social and economic history. For a re-contexting of clothes in the past, Christopher Breward's *The Culture of Fashion: A New History of Fashionable Dress* (1995) which the author describes as 'an introductory guide to the cultural significance of fashion' (Breward, 1995, p. 4) with an intention to 'highlight the potential of clothing as a creative medium for expressing social change and cultural value', (ibid., p. 38) is a well-illustrated chronology with chapter headings that suggest readings of the development of costume as a social and cultural signifier, for example, the Renaissance chapter is characterized as 'The Rhetoric of Power' (ibid., p. v). As an interesting parallel strand in the cultural history of dress, Naomi Tarrant's *The Development of Costume* (1994) examines changes in costume and fashion through the relationship of what people wear to available materials, tools and tailoring skills. 'Cloth production, or the raw materials for its manufacture, have been the staple of most of the European economies at some time. It was also the main motivator behind the technical innovations which led to the industrial revolutions of the Mediaeval period and of the eighteenth century. Dress should not therefore be seen as a wholly frivolous concern,' she suggests (Tarrant, 1994, p. 2). Her book is not a straightforward narrative of the history of costume but uses examples from the dress collection of the Museum of Scotland where she worked, such as Inuit parkas and tartan trews. In content, it moves between discussing a garment's cut (with accompanying pattern drawing) and its cultural and economic significance. This is a history book written by someone with an understanding of both historical context and the construction of the objects themselves and deserves to be read more widely.

BOOKS ON MAKING PERIOD COSTUME

As the interest in historical costume grew in the nineteenth and early twentieth century, both for stage and for 'dressing-up' events such as fancy dress balls, the previous academic histories of dress made way for more populist works, including the first that contained some kind of period pattern.

Talbot Hughes' *Dress Design* (1913) is a scholarly work in the series, 'Handbook on Artistic Crafts', written by a well-known painter and collector of historic dress, and includes both patterns and photographs of garments in his collection. Fernald and Shenton's *Costume Design and Making: A Practical Handbook* (1937), on the other hand, is described by its authors as 'a practical guide to the making of period costumes for stage purposes' (Fernald, 1937, p. 9) and comprises descriptions and reproductions of some contemporary portraits as well as a series of cutting diagrams with instructions. According to the publication, *The Lady*, quoted on the flyleaf, the book should be 'a boon to theatrical producers, especially of the school and amateur kind' (ibid.,

1937), and this type of book may well be linked to the rise in popularity of amateur dramatics between the wars.

In contrast, Janet Arnold was an exceptional costume historian who had no personal links with theatre till late in her career (see interview with Jenny Tiramani). She began her research in the 1950s and spent her life painstakingly examining, measuring and drawing all the period clothes she could lay her hands on in museums and private sources. It was through her that many misunderstandings were unravelled, such as quite how a farthingale worked, and her contribution to historical research cannot be underestimated. Although two of her *Patterns of Fashion* series were given a small print run in the mid-1960s, they were not widely known or used by stage costume makers until the late seventies and early eighties when they were republished by Macmillan.

In a very short introduction, Arnold writes, 'so much has already been written about costume that I feel some explanation is due for producing yet another work on the subject. There are already a few books containing some patterns of women's costumes ... but there is very little available about pattern cutting and the construction of dresses. This book ... is a practical guide to cutting period costumes ... and is not intended to be a complete history of women's costume of the period. I hope it will prove useful for craftwork in schools and colleges, ... for students of dress and historic costume and those working in the amateur and professional theatre' (Arnold, 1964, p. 2). Her books reflect her love and respect for the makers and garments of the past and show, in meticulous detail, how a series of original garments were cut, constructed and finished. The earlier volumes are illustrated solely with her delicate and precise line drawings while the latest in the series, assembled after her death by Jenny Tiramani and her team and published in 2008, contain photographs where appropriate. The publication of more of Janet Arnold's work, much of which is still in manuscript form, is under discussion. Tiramani has continued and developed Arnold's approach with two recent books published through the School of Historical Dress in association with the Victoria and Albert Museum, *Seventeenth Century Women's Dress Pattern 1 and 2.* These visually fascinating books use detailed close-up and X-ray photography to give a unique insight into the creation of a series of surviving garments.

Everyone interested in historical dress should study, if not own, a book by Janet Arnold since inevitably they will learn something new while being inspired by the beauty and skill of the work illustrated and reminded of why they first became interested in clothes. On a practical level, however, some find the detail of her work too much and prefer a more generalized approach to making, as illustrated in books such as Norah Waugh's *Corsets and Crinolines* (1954), *The Cut of Women's Clothes* (1968) and *The Cut of Men's Clothes* (1964) and Jean Hunnisett's series, *Period Costume for Stage and Screen.* Norah Waugh taught in the 1960s at the Central School of Art and Design, having been in charge of Michel Saint-Denis' London Theatre Studio in the late 1930s (faber.co.uk/authors, accessed 9/12/13) and so came from a solid theatre background. She too studied actual clothes as well as visual sources, judging from the sources she lists but she does not seem to have made any drawings of them. However, her awareness of their importance is demonstrated in the preface to her earliest work where she writes, 'It is impossible to appreciate the design of the clothes of the past, and certainly quite impossible to reproduce them accurately, without understanding the shapes of these artificial foundation garments' (Waugh, 1954, p. 7). Her books, all of which span at least three hundred years, contain drawings and instructions, contemporary references and basic patterns. Jean Hunnisett had a similarly theatrical background and taught for many years at the London College of Fashion. She writes in *Period Costume for Stage and Screen: Patterns for Women's Dress 1500–1800* (1991) that her books are 'not a history of costume as that subject is covered by other people far more learned than I. The dating is not precise but accurate enough for general use in the theatre. Anyone making recreations should consult other forms of reference, original sources or museum textile departments … Many people fall into wardrobe work because they can sew and find themselves faced with a production of a *Man for All Seasons* requiring the reproduction of Holbein's paintings and drawings. The art of the costume now comes into its own and can either make or mar the production' (Hunnisett, 1991, p. 6). She too has contemporary references and pictures in her books but the patterns are easier to reproduce and are accompanied by clear instructions for making up. Each series of books by these three authors have become classics in the field of period cutting and it would be hard to find a historical maker who does not use at least one of them.

Of course there are other books on making period costume, such as an excellent pair on seventeenth and eighteenth century men's wear by Ron Davis and *The Tudor Tailor* by Ninya Mikhaila and Jane Malcom-Davies, which is particularly notable for its information on middle- and lower class clothing and with the founding of Jenny Tiramani's School of Historical Dress, it is hoped that there will soon be more.

'HOW TO' BOOKS ON DESIGNING FOR THE STAGE, RUNNING A THEATRE WARDROBE AND COMMON THEATRICAL TECHNIQUES

One of the largest and most easily accessible categories of books concerned with stage costume records more general approaches to designing costumes and creating a historical wardrobe for stage purposes. Although books on historical costume increased in the early part of the twentieth century, few costume books did more than mention the stage until around 1930 when a number of published books on historical costume began to include a page or two, perhaps even a short chapter, about the stage context offering advice on colour and light and sometimes practical tips on construction. Barton's *Historic Costume for the Stage* (1935) follows this form, written by

American maker and teacher Lucy Barton who was notable for setting up an early college qualification in stage costume. The preface justifies the publication by quoting her students, 'If only you would write a book like your lectures, expanded!' (Barton, 1935, p. vii). Her book includes descriptions, line drawings and a final chapter entitled, 'Some Notes on the Construction of Costume' (ibid., p. 569), which gives advice on patterns, materials, the effect of light and the making of unusual articles such as chain mail. The shift of emphasis from the insistence on complete accuracy of the Victorian era is noticeable in these publications. In Nevil Truman's *Historic Costume* (1936) the producer writing the preface comments, 'It is right that these data should be available to the theatre in as accurate a form as possible, though I would venture to suggest that for stage purposes, there are few instances of plays in which the very strictest historical accuracy is necessary' (Truman, 1936, p. vii). Iris Brooke's beautifully illustrated *Western European Costume and Its Relation to Theatre* (1939) serves a similar purpose and makes a similar point 'So many truly lovely costumes', she says, 'have been dwarfed and rendered inconspicuous … by too much attention to small detail and not sufficient concentration on shape and colour – the two most important factors in theatrical production'(Brook, 1939, vol. 2, p. 18).

This type of book developed in the 1950s through authors such as Jeanetta Cochrane, a stage designer and teacher at the influential Central School of Art and Design. Because there is now such a selection of these books, it is often a matter of personal choice and particular emphasis that selects one over another. *Designing and Making Stage Costumes* was written in 1964 by the three women designers that comprised Motley. The group Motley comprised three women: Margaret ('Percy') Harris, her sister Sophie Harris and Elizabeth Montgomery. They met at art school in the 1920s and went on to design costumes (and later, sets) for many leading directors such as Sir John Gielgud. Their style was broadly authentic in feel but always 'theatrical' in its sensitivity to each individual production. In the late 1930s they taught at the London Theatre Studio (as did Norah Waugh) creating the first design course attached to a drama school in the UK (Mullin, 1996, p. 58). Their book is still, I believe, the best combination of inspiration and practical advice on both costume design and construction and should be on every costume designer's bookshelf. However, others such as Sheila Jackson's *Costume for the Stage: A Complete Handbook for Every Kind of Play* (revised 2001), Ingham and Covey's *The Costume Designer's Handbook: A Complete Guide for Amateur and Professional Costume Designers* (1983) and *The Costume Technician's Handbook* (2003) and Thorne's *Designing Stage Costumes: A Practical Guide* (2001), and Bicât's *Handbook of Stage Costume* (2001, 2006) in the more recent *Croward Practical Guide* series are all clear, informative and well-illustrated texts.

For information on costume drawing and preparing costume illustrations for presentation and use, *Costume Character Figure Drawing* (2004) by Tan Huaixiang is a straightforward, well-illustrated introduction to what is needed.

COSTUME ON THE STAGE: HISTORY AND ANALYSIS

In 1931, Theodore Komisarjevsky, a theatre director, published *The Costume of the Theatre*. Although an avowed Modernist with a contempt for theatrical realism, he saw clearly that costume choices revealed more than just personal decisions. 'The stage costumes, merely accentuating those fashions worn in life, or interpreting period dresses in the modern spirit, express the theatrical attitude of the world with even more intensity than the everyday life costumes themselves' (Komisarjevsky, 1931, p. vii). Although the book is a chronological survey, it is told through the pen of an opinionated director of theatre with a wide theatrical knowledge and a lot of practical experience. It is a thought-provoking read, if rather biased on the side of a non-naturalistic approach. It was not until the early 1960s that the costume historian James Laver wrote a similarly structured survey *Costume on the Stage* (1964), a work without Komisarjevsy's theatrical experience, but benefitting from Laver's extensive knowledge and access to the prints and drawings of the V and A. The book broadly describes and illustrates the type of costume that each theatrical era from the Ancient Greeks to the 1930s put on the stage. His writing does tend to 'treat actors as living paper dolls, rather than fully interrogating the uses and reception of costume' (Monks, 2010, p. 8). Nevertheless, the book is invaluable for its images and for acknowledging differences between clothing on and off the stage. Hollander's *Seeing through Clothes* (1975) deals with representations of dress in Western art, and has a long chapter on stage costume. Her historical summary of clothes on stage is useful, particularly on periods well recorded through images such as the eighteenth century, although her approach is clearly art historical. She is particularly thoughtful and observant on the way clothes transform on the stage and on attitudes to and assumptions about historical dress on stage. Diane De Marly's 1982 *Costume on the Stage*, a dense but informative read, is more descriptive but deals analytically with elements such as costume's connection to technical developments in theatre and its relationship with the wider economics of the time. Besides these two books and the occasional chapter in fashion books such as 'Theatrical Dress: Costume or Fashion' in Valerie Cumming's *Understanding Fashion History* (Cumming, 2004) there are no summaries of the history of stage costume in the same way that there are variety of summaries of historical costume with different emphases and approaches.

Beyond this there are several excellent books that deal only with the history, the dress or the theatre of a particular period, which include stage costume, the details of which will be found in the bibliography. These are often scholarly, observant and informative but only if the information is what you want. Costume seems to be found more often as an accompanying chapter in a book principally about something else that in a book devoted to itself, as if it is best or more easily analysed if set against the context of a Stuart Masque or a Victorian director. Perhaps this is because, more than anything else, it is embedded within the live performance of a particular text and disappears when the actors leave the stage. The set can be studied without them, so can the script, but the clothes really make no sense without the bodies of the performers to bring them to life.

COSTUME ON THE STAGE – PICTURE BOOKS

There are many inspiring picture books on stage costume. These range from pictorial surveys such as *World Scenography* (2012) to monographs on influential figures such as Bakst, Motley, Koltai and Mnoushkine. Most are lavishly illustrated and have some commentary. As an example, two books on the director and designer, Julie Taymor, illustrate different aspects of her work. *Playing with Fire* (1995) describes her early work and the evolution of her ideas through working on islands such as Bali. *Pride Rock on Broadway* (1998) reveals the creative processes behind the making of her musical version of *The Lion King* and includes notes on costume construction, working drawings of masks and countless practical details that link the making of meaning with the theatrical crafts through which they are carried out. There are also books on particular contexts, such as Roy Strong's *Designing for the Dancer* (1981) or which contain interviews with designers and reproductions of their designs, for example, Lynn Pecktal's *Costume Design: Techniques of Modern Masters* (1999). Many such books contain little commentary and although they are an inspiring and important record and resource they do not necessarily deepen our theoretical understanding. The Society of British Theatre Designers publish a catalogue to accompany their Quadrennial exhibition linked to the Theatre Design exhibition in Prague which, although they serve primarily as a showcase for designers, in format and subject matter attempt a more exploratory tone, looking at how designers research, the relationships with directors or ways of seeing. This is reflected in their titles, for example, *2D>3D* (2002), *Collaborators* (2007) and *Transformation and Revelation* (2011). Again, they are not exclusively about costume but contain a multiplicity of designs, sketches, thoughts and photos which reveal much about a designer's process.

SCENOGRAPHY AND FASHION THEORY

It was not until the 1930s, with thinkers such as Komisarevsky (*The Costume of the Theatre*, 1931) and Robert Edmund Jones ('Some Thoughts on Stage Costume' in *The Dramatic Imagination*, 1941) that costume began to be written about as part of the scenographic and theatrical experience considering such issues as its function and reception instead of simply as a historical succession of choices. Jones' viewpoint is clearly that of a practitioner and, at times, verges on the mystic. 'If we are to create in the theatre', he writes, 'we must first learn to put on this creative intention like a mantle of rainbow feathers' (Jones, 1941, p. 91), but at the same time he acknowledges the importance of costume and recognizes the need to understand how this important element works in order to make the best use of it. His mantras are precise individuality, theatricality and appropriateness (Jones, 1941, pp. 94–96), and all are still relevant today. Roland Barthes' essay, *The Diseases of Costume*, (1955) comes from a very different standpoint, that of a philosopher watching from the auditorium. In the essay he contextualizes costume and analyses its function and meaning by identifying three potential diseases, (1) 'the hypertrophy of historical function, or archaeological verism' (Barthes, p. 42), which he finds unsuccessful because it is *too* accurate to feel true on stage, (2) 'the hypertrophy of formal beauty' (ibid., p. 44) as a distraction from the play and its internal meaning and (3) 'money, the hypertrophy of sumptuosity or at least its appearance', as if, he suggests, the cost of the costumes reflect the worth of the production (ibid., p. 45). In place of these he suggests that *the costume must be an argument* (ibid., p. 46) and that *it must create a humanity* (ibid., p. 48). The points made by Barthes are as true now as they were in 1955 when the essay was written and it is worth reading by anyone interested in costume and how it functions.

A few directors have also continued to think and write about stage costume as a concept rather than simply as a problem to be solved on every show, such as Peter Brooke in his books *The Empty Space* (1970) and *The Shifting Point* (1989). Darwin Reid Payne deserves an honourable mention for *The Scenographic Imagination* (1974), which fall somewhere between a 'how to be a designer' and an analytical scenography text. He treads a fine but commendable line between skills teaching and provoking ideas and questions through excerpts from the writings of directors such as Stanislavski and designers such as John Bury and Mordecai Gorelik.

It was not really until the 1990s, though, that both fashion theory and scenography began to emerge as significant academic disciplines with accompanying publications. *Fashion Theory: The Journal of Dress, Body and Culture* (Berg) began to be published at about this time and continues to publish significant theoretical articles on clothes in context. The Berg publishing house specializes in work on clothes and fashion and its two volumes published in 2003, *Fashion Foundations: Early Writings on Dress and Fashion* and *Fashion Classics from Carlisle to Barthes* are an invaluable resource for early theoretical writings on dress by authors such as Veblen, Flugel and Simmel. Lou Taylor's *The Study of Dress History* (2004) and Valerie Cummings' *Understanding Fashion History* (2004) both analyse a possible series of approaches to studying and theorizing dress in particular contexts which offer possible parallels for stage costume researchers. I would also recommend *Addressing the Century: 100 Years of Art and Fashion* (1998) the catalogue of a remarkable exhibition at the Haywood Gallery that contains excellent photographs and several good essays, particularly Judith Clark's 'Kinetic Beauty: The Theatre of the 1920s' (Heywood, 1998, pp. 78–87); and Radu Stern's *Against Fashion: Clothing as Art 1850–1930* (2005) which covers aesthetic, reformist and avant-garde dress and contains an invaluable section of original writings on dress by artists and scholars such as E.H. Godwin, Oscar Wilde, Balla, Stepanova and Sonia Delaunay.

For a more theatre-centred approach, Kennedy's *Looking at Shakespeare* (1993) is large in scope, excellently researched and written. As well as being an extensive and detailed history of the staging of Shakespeare throughout the twentieth century, Kennedy also analyses the scenographic solutions of successive eras in a way which, through his broad knowledge of art and theatre history, links their decisions to the social and cultural milieu in which they existed. Unusually, he writes vividly and clearly about the function, power and reception of not just the staging but the costume too and his words are well supported by a wide range of original photographs.

In 2002, the redoubtable 'visual artist of the theatre', Pamela Howard published *What Is Scenography*, a groundbreaking book in Routledge's *Theatre Concepts* series which manages to combine a very personal approach gained through years of work in many different theatrical contexts, with a systematic yet poetic analysis of the elements of performance on stage. Although only some of it is explicitly devoted to costume, its holistic approach makes it useful reading in understanding costume within the performance. Since then, writing on scenography has become a growing field from which I would pick two excellent and well-contrasted general books on the subject. McKinney and Butterworth's *The Cambridge Introduction to Scenography* (2009) outlines the ideas of pioneer scenographers such as Appia and Craig and goes on to consider scenographic processes and reception in a useful and accessible way. In contrast, Collins' and Nisbett's *Theatre and Performance Design: A Reader in Scenography* (2010) republishes key texts relevant to scenographers by a diverse selection of scholars and practitioners. They divide the work into sections on looking, space, the designer, bodies, making meaning and semiotics and offer a short analytical explanation for each section and each piece of writing. Again, although neither of these books are specifically about costume, they offer numerous possible ways of thinking about costume within the theatrical process.

Finally, Aoife Monks' *The Actor in Costume* (2010) seeks to find ways to discuss how costume functions on stage, presenting a 'concise and considered meditation on the interrelationship of performer, costume and audience' (Dorney, 2011). It is a book that is centred on costume alone with a theoretical but accessible approach to costume on stage using recent productions as examples and should be on everyone's booklist.

OTHER RESOURCES

The V and A, home of the Theatre Museum, holds many resources related to costume and fashion, both material and paper based and the website has much good basic information and reading lists for particular subject. The Mander and Mitchenson collection is an extensive archive housed at Bristol

University which is in the process of digitization. The National Theatre and the Royal Shakespeare Company also hold extensive archives for the student who has a focused research area and time to spare, and have useful exhibitions from time to time. The National Theatre website (www. nationaltheatre.org.uk) houses an excellent series of video clips on all sorts of relevant stage practices, and publishes a series of *Platform Papers* which include well-known designers such as Jocelyn Herbert and Alison Chitty talking about their approach and methods either in general or in response to a particular text.

Online resources, such as *Digital Theatre*, are growing fast and allow researchers to witness filmed versions of productions they have not seen, although this never quite replicates the live experience. It does however make the analysis of clothes on stage, up till now such an ephemeral practice, easier and more possible which can only be a good thing. Costume research is a small field but a growing one with a richness of resource to be tapped into as long as it can be accessed.

AN INTERVIEW WITH JENNY TIRAMANI

Ali Maclaurin

Introduction

Jenny Tiramani has worked as a costume and set designer in the theatre since 1976. She is probably best known for her role as Director of Theatre Design at Shakespeare's Globe Theatre from its opening in 1997 until 2005, where she established the concept of 'original practice' productions that dressed actors in handmade clothing based on the evidence of surviving clothes, inventories, wills and pictures contemporary with the production. In 2003, she received the Laurence Olivier Award for Best Costume Design for the Globe production of *Twelfth Night*. She also has a long-standing relationship with the Theatre Royal Stratford East where she still designs the sets for the pantomime each year. Jenny is the Principal of The School of Historical Dress (theschoolofhistoricaldress.org.uk) which was established in 2009 to promote an object-based study of historical dress and to teach the skills necessary to design and make historical clothing for the theatre.

Jenny Tiramani = JT, Ali Maclaurin = AJM

AJM: Tell me about your time at the Globe when Mark Rylance was Artistic Director there.

JT: The Globe was a complete watershed for me because before that I'd had a really up and down relationship with Shakespeare. I was nine when I fell in love with the theatre. I only knew about acting and wanted to be a actress. My dad took me to the Victoria and Albert Museum when I was twelve to look round. There was a little exhibition of Claud Lovat costume designs from the 1910s. They were obviously influenced by Bakst, very graphic, colourful and strong. I asked my dad what they were and he explained. I told him that I wanted to do that and I never changed my mind. I've always loved set design. The problem now is that because I'm seen more publicly connected to costume the set design gets left behind. I did spend twenty years doing it. I trained at Nottingham Trent and loved it. It was very small and very eccentric, all in an old primary school, with so much space and three amazing tutors: Stephen Doncaster who used to be the wardrobe supervisor at the Royal Court, Judith Park who was all about costume and Robin Linklater who did props and scenic building. And then Malcolm Griffiths came which was just what I needed. I was passionate about political theatre and Malcolm was a good friend of John McGrath who came to teach us as a freelancer. After graduating, I got a job as assistant designer to David Ultz at the Theatre Royal, Stratford East, and I'm still working there now. That is my home. The Globe was never my home. It's at the Theatre Royal where I do most stage design now with my partner in the School of Historical Dress, Hattie Barsby, doing costume. I still do stage and costume design for the occasional big opera production but generally speaking, I feel I've done enough costume design now, I don't feel like I *have* to do it any more. I love the stuff I'm doing, really big operas or Shakespeare that allow me to have the money I need for the School but they do take a long time to create. I'd rather give others the opportunity.

AJM: So how did you get from there to the Globe?

JT: After all sorts of work in the 1970s and 80s, I met Kenneth Branagh through my agent and spent three years with his Renaissance Theatre Company, which has almost disappeared in everyone's memory now. No one had ever asked me to do Shakespeare before and it was all very exciting because the company was young and got lots of attention. I think they were very lively productions but design-wise they are really corny to me now. We never had any money and there were always actors direct-ing and they only ever wanted to do more modern dress than the time of Shakespeare. The first three shows were at Birmingham Rep and we had to use their stock a lot so we did nineteenth century, basically. The last couple of shows were very conceptual. There was a *King Lear* where everyone was in bright red except the French in blue, which I just want to go away!

When I was working with Ultz I'd made a cocktail dress for Mark Rylance to play Madame in a Shared Experience production of *The Maids*. We' d kept in touch and when he started Phoebus Cart Theatre Company and had the idea to do *The Tempest* at the Rollright Stones I designed it. Then Sam Wanamaker asked us to do it on the Globe site and we did, on the concrete foundations that flooded daily, but it was magical! Mark played Prospero. It was a great production, I'm very proud of it, all modern dress with an alchemical Druidic colour scheme, although you wouldn't know that unless you knew. After that we did more Shakespeares together including our infamous *Macbeth* in a sort of Hare Krishna cult. We always did modern dress. We couldn't even imagine doing Shakespeare in a non-contemporary way.

AJM: Why not?

JT: We thought what a weird thing to put people in funny clothes. Mark had done stuff at Royal Shakespeare Company (RSC) in a big romantic shirt and trousers tucked into boots (JT smirks here) and he had also done Peter Greenaway's *Prospero's Books*, for which he had been dressed in clothes where they had looked at portraits and done a very stylized version and he didn't like it at all – he felt fake – and he thinks it's a terrible performance because of that. So we had both got to the point where we were loving working with modern dress because we could control it and we could be subtle with it and we could afford it. We wanted to make Shakespeare's plays come from our world; so when we did *As You Like It* in New York it was natural to say Rosalind and Celia were going to escape to a North American forest because they've got them big time and they come back to New York with a deer on the bumper of the 4 × 4. It's part of the culture in the US and for a story like that it's really helpful. So, to do *Macbeth* you think, well, this often happens in a cult. When we did it David Koresh had just happened but we didn't want to make it him because we were doing it in England, so we thought about the Hare Krishna thing here in the late 70s. One of them did go crazy and behead another member of the sect and we were always trying to base things on reality. But in 1995 our *Macbeth* was controversial. It had a lot of press. Some of the Scottish education boards banned the teachers taking school children to see it. It divided the critics but it was compelling. Then Mark got the Globe job and he said, looking really scared, 'I think they want us to do the odd show in Elizabethan dress, if I get you a bit of money could you go and research it?' He sent me off with three research questions: (1) find out what Elizabethans wore, (2) find out what Elizabethan actors wore in the plays and (3) find out what is in the hire departments all round the country and how much would it cost. And right up there (she points to a file marked 'Costumes at the Globe') that's my report full of photos of all the things I found in the BBC, Angels, the National Theatre and RSC stores. And I found out what Elizabethans wore through Janet (Arnold). She helped me. I'd never thought about approaching her before all through my career and nor did many other theatre designers and she loved the theatre.

AJM: There was an exhibition of her work the V and A around the time she died.

JT: That's right, there was an exhibition in the September after she died. I planned it with her but she didn't make it. She got me into museums, you can imagine, 'she seems to think she's going to do hand made clothes, … she's crazy …' and I bought her books. I never realized that there were really Elizabethan clothes left and that are so beautiful. The first time I held a real ruff in my hand I remember just getting tearful. I said to Mark, 'let's have a go'. It took us two years to persuade a director.

AJM: Why was that?

JT: I think because period dress had such a terrible reputation; trousers in boots and lumpy ill-fitting ugly clothes that people didn't understand.

AJM: Does making it as it really was made, what you call 'Original Practices', does that make a huge difference to what it looks and feels like?

JT: Everything. How it moves, how it is on the body. 1600 is pretty much the height of tailoring, it's the point at which there is the most extraordinary structure and understanding of shape. It's the end of the Renaissance, there's a mathematical geometric system for everything on the upper body and everything fits perfectly. It has to fit in order to work. And if it's got the right technology in it actors look like real people in clothes and it loses that sort of naff quality.

AJM: Is it a completely different way of drafting?

JT: The Renaissance Period is, yes. You can see the use of compasses. You go from just drawing freehand, to a system that really reaches its height in the 1620s. The shapes are stunning; and then it changes, all the tailoring softens out and comes back in the eighteenth century. Then the minute you hit the Industrial Age, they start drafting patterns in straight, parallel lines, a grid system that I think is quite different.

AJM: Do you think actors like it?

JT: I don't think it, I absolutely know they love it. Stephen Fry went on the Jonathan Ross Show last year after acting in *Twelfth Night* and Jonathan Ross had to stop him talking about his clothes. He said, 'I'll do anything to do one of these every five years'. I've hardly met an actor who doesn't love it, except perhaps the occasional one who's very set in their ways and can't be bothered.

AJM: Are you still working at the Globe?

JT: I have a difficult relationship with the Globe. It's very sad for me the way it's set up now. The director is not at all interested in costume. He just finds it gets in the way really. He's great at commissioning new plays but is putting all the money into quantity and new writing. Now that's fine, the Shakespearean companies originally spent all their money on new writing…… (pause, stage whisper) AND CLOTHES! But it means the enquiry we were making has stopped. We went back last year and did two shows for Mark Rylance and now we are taking them to Broadway.

AJM: Do you work like this on anything other than Shakespeare?

JT: I've done a series of operas these past few years and the last ones I've done in accurate historical dress. In France it's really easy because the French are so far ahead of us. I've had superb work done there. They don't always hand sew the long seams but that is the first compromise you make. You must use the right materials always, the period appropriate pattern drafting as much as I can teach people. In Paris the people I use also do Haute Couture work so they are in a different sort of culture. They've got great costume schools. They have collections of real clothes in the schools that they seriously use. And it's a different culture. In Italy too, Piero Tosi at the *Centro Sperimentale di Cinematografia* in Rome is teaching dress beautifully, and he is making costume design students learn it so they know what is at the heart of, what their craft is and what they are asking other people to do. I think the British are falling behind in a sad way. When I designed *Anna Bolena* in 2011 at the Met (the Metropolitan Opera House) in New York it was tough but incredible, particularly their men's tailoring department. The singers just loved it, and their dressers loved dressing people in it. Suddenly it's not a mystery. They like understanding what they are wearing – it's helpful.

AJM: So they're kind of stepping into the period slowly as they put their clothes on.

JT: That's it. They don't do that for every show there but they seemed to love it.

   We even got invited to do a lecture at the Metropolitan Museum. We dressed a young singer in his costume based on clothes at the court of Henry VIII and I gave a talk about it and we sold 750 tickets. If you dress people live, people love it. At the Apollo in the autumn the actors, including Stephen Fry got dressed on stage. They came out in their linen smocks and shirts and dressed in front of the public.

AJM: so it becomes part of the performance.

JT: Yes, That's a thing Mark started having seen it in Mnouchkine's work (Ariane Mnouchkine, Director of *Théâtre du Soleil*). We aren't saying that Shakespeare's actors did that but it's helpful to our modern audiences sometimes.

AJM: I read an article about you at the Globe that used the word 'Authentic'…

JT: There's no such thing. You won't see me ever using it except to say there's no such thing as authenticity. All there is for me is as close an interpretation as you can do. It's a conversation – an experiment with history. I feel I sometimes get really close to the cut of something. I can get fairly close to the fabric although that's the hardest thing of all because that's not dependent on labour. For example, Mark Rylance's gown for Olivia in *Twelfth Night*; there's a fragment of a silk velvet from about 1590/1600 and we had a velvet woven by Giuseppe Gaggioli who is the silk weaver that we've been working with outside Genoa. Handwoven, cut and uncut velvet in the pattern that is period appropriate, in black. Now it's hand woven, but it's hand woven on a jacquard type loom with punch cards. The design which I hand drew from the original piece is quite like one that in the sixteenth century someone would give a silk weaver, but Giuseppe gave it to a guy who works on a computer so it became rather pixelated whereas the real thing the lines would be unbroken. It doesn't have nearly as many picks per inch so it's not quite as dense as a real one and the silk for it is not hand spun or plied and it's not naturally dyed black … so what's authentic? There's a hat here that's nearly authentic, but it's not. Authentic is the thing, it's not a version of the thing. This hat is a project, not a theatre project. It's part of an outfit I made for a historian at Cambridge University. It is an interpretation of a 1530 bonnet or cap, worn all over Europe and for Rachel Frost who made it, it was a labour of love.

AJM: Is it hand felted?

JT: It's knitted. She took the wool off the sheep, she spun it herself into a knitting yarn and it's naturally dyed by the most common method of getting a good over-dyed black. It's hand knitted in the round but the two tabs were knitted on two needles so it's got the right methods. It probably should have a silk lining. She felted it by hand. We know that it's not as brushed as it probably should be. Originally they made them look like velvet, so the sheep were probably not the right kind of sheep. This is from an outfit a young man had in Augsburg, Germany and he was called Matthäus Schwartz. He was a high-up accountant to the Fugger Bank and he had himself painted a hundred and twenty seven times, every time he got a new outfit. And there is this old black and white book published of his miniatures. I made one for Ulinka Rublack who wrote a book about dressing up in the Renaissance. Its on YouTube and the BBC website.

AJM: What are you working on at the moment?

JT: I've been doing my own work and I'm designing *Andre Chenier*, an opera set in the French revolutionary period for the Royal Opera House, Covent Garden.

AJM: Are you doing that by hand?

JT: Yes. The workshops seem terrified of me, it's like a big factory there and it may be difficult.

AJM: Does the workroom change when you're working by hand?

JT: It gets quieter. It's takes about three times as long. You can do a lot while you sit and watch the telly with a sewing pillow; it's really quicker to do things like that. It's a different process.

AJM: Do you find that design in Britain is very set led?

JT: Yes, and the supervisor and assistants end up doing a lot of it even if they don't want to

AJM: Is that because designers don't know enough about costume?

JT: Costume isn't introduced in the right way and it isn't being taught very well. You need to teach people about fabrics. They need to understand the history of fabrics and you can teach that in quite exciting ways. It doesn't need to be dull. What chance do students have if they don't know the difference between cotton, linen and wool. That's a basic! I do think costume has been the poor relation for too long. At least there are some designated courses now. American design students always specialize in one or the other. Their theatres generally employ two people, ours don't. You have to be at the top opera houses or the National or RSC to get two designers on board. We don't have that tradition here and it gets shunted. For me theatre starts with an empty space and an actor. What the actor is wearing kind of comes first simply because he or she can operate in that empty space.

AJM: It would be interesting to track why in Britain costume is the poor relation and not in other countries.

JT: And why are people shocked and say how expensive my clothes are on the big shows when they haven't got a clue what things cost under the stage and will accept if it's big and metal that it's OK if it costs a lot of money. I know the difference. The audience love to see people dressed up. They don't like to see badly fitting clothes made out of nasty fabric and all our Globe stuff gets better as it gets older. It doesn't degrade like cheap costume. A well-worn beautiful old jacket is still gorgeous fifty years later.

AJM: The stuff you made for the Globe that is only cleaned by brushing – has it lasted?

JT: Yes. That outfit there (she points) was worn two years running and did an American tour. It has never been dry-cleaned and it's fine. You air things and wear a linen or cotton shirt underneath. I don't think dry cleaners are good for clothes.

AJM: Do you draw your designs?

JT: I never draw. The way I work, which I don't advocate for everyone, if I want something to be historically accurate I won't draw because my hands are twenty-first century hands. What I seem to do is very little… 'oh, she just photocopies things and cuts them out of books' (JT gets an A3 Manila file down to show me). They'll shock you because there is nothing there, so I'm doing it in my head. When you're twenty-five you probably can't do that, but I think that comes with experience. I can imagine. Also, I want the thrill of not knowing quite what it will be like till it's there. I was never very good with producing complete pictures because then I'd get that thing from performers of 'Don't tell me what I'm going to wear'. Some are fine and some are not and I was no good at being persuasive so what I do now is look at portraits or photos of real clothes with them so the performers feel that we are making it up together. I usually do know what I want to do and have colour schemes in my head. I think that's a trick, a designer's trick, not dishonest, just not full disclosure.

AJM: What would you do if someone said they didn't like the costume.

JT: Well, no one has ever quite said that. I think I'm good at getting performers' trust at the beginning. With opera, the first time you may meet the singer is at the first fitting. So I try and get in there and talk to them immediately, often apologizing that I've had to go ahead with some decisions already. They don't expect that so anything is a bonus. I did *Anna Bolena* at the Met (the Metropolitan Opera in New York) and David McVicar (the director) wanted to do the whole thing in black. It's quite accurate, I've got the wills of Henry VIII's Courtiers. The wonderful lead soprano Anna Netrebko didn't want to start in black. She didn't really want to wear black at all, so I changed some details and added a red dress in the middle of the opera. I though it worked really well, a deep red silk velvet, it was beautiful, and she loved it. I added white fur and a cloth of gold forepart to her first outfit and she was very happy. It's about relationships.

  Look, let me just show you, if I'm doing an opera I will produce lots of sheets of real things (JT opens an A3 folder).

AJM: So good-quality reproductions of contemporary images.

JT: I'll just keep finding more and more references and pictures of real surviving clothes so lots and lots of sheets and when I have photos and ages and measurements I choose who wears what for a chorus. Everyone will be different.

AJM: So it depends what the performers look like?

JT: Yes, it's not a preconceived idea.

AJM: And you're dressing them as people.

JT: Yes, you get everything from small children to soldiers. Hundreds and hundreds of drawings.

AJM: And they are beautifully mounted and presented on nice paper. Is that important?

JT: Yes, of course. It's partly to show that I've really thought about it and about the detail and about really choosing what I put together and also these have to last over a year. If I want you to cut that dress I'll give you a

Janet Arnold pattern if I have one, maybe even an unpublished one, and I'll talk through it exactly but no drawing because you'll change it.

AJM: So you are working with individual makers, then?

JT: Yes, and I spend a long time with them. I collect fabrics and I go shopping with the supervisors and I make folders of swatches beforehand. It takes so long to build up a great range of fabrics. If you leave it till the last six weeks you are going to have problems and a more limited range. If I'm doing other things I just pick up stuff.

On the other hand, we did do a giant rabbit in our panto last Christmas made of crocheted baby blankets!

AJM: … and I thought you just did Elizabethan clothes by hand.

JT: Well, I think that's because we like to put people in pigeonholes. I hope I'm not a one-trick pony although I'm happy to have specialized. I do think the Globe has made all my work better, it gave it a rigour, a system, it's like a Mantra: materials, cut, construction. In a way it's that simple. Those things are not given their importance.

AJM: Tell me about your new school, I'm interested you call it the School of Historical Dress. You haven't aligned yourself with anything theatrical.

JT: No, I haven't, I think very astutely because I don't want us to be seen as competitive. I want it to be complimentary, but of course I know and you know that eighty percent of theatrical costume is based on historical dress. It's what we all do whatever we think we're doing, whether we acknowledge it, however we interpret it. My big thing is if you know what the real thing is like then you can fly with it; you can do whatever interpretation you want whether it's accurate or very conceptual, because you understand.

AJM: So it's like grammar really?

JT: It's exactly like that, it's the language. What depresses me is that the last few times I've taught in colleges I've come across the use of modern pattern blocks for drafting historical patterns. Even when I went to Nottingham in the early 1970s we were taught to work with modern blocks, which then were from the 1950s. We were taught to cut everything for men's legs from a 1950s trouser block which didn't go anywhere near men's legs generally! But we were taught that if there was a Janet Arnold or a Norah Waugh pattern we were to use that. The teachers wanted us to make things really real. They didn't talk to us a lot about pattern drafting which is of course the big thing. Nothing is really published on it that I consider to be worth it. There are no studies of historical pattern drafting methods so it's all a bit of a mystery and I know that many people just photocopy the patterns and blow them up.

AJM: Is there evidence? Does someone just need to research it?

JT: Oh yes, and some of us have researched it, we just haven't published anything but we do teach it. We started teaching certain methods last year on our short courses.

Over the last year we've had five tutors from costume design courses coming with money from their colleges for training. I love that because they can go back and their methods of teaching can be improved and spread. I think that's a very good pyramid system. I can't bear that costume is so far down the pile and it still is to some extent, although it's getting better. Here we are hoping to stick to small classes and specializing in what the other colleges can't teach. I hope it will develop but it's important for me to get historical dress as an idea out there. And colleges need to teach students to sew. They aren't learning it from Granny any more. You just have to hammer in basic skills in the first three weeks, it's really not rocket science, but you *can't* leave a course with a BA in Costume and not know how to do a hem properly!

AJM: So finally, here's an end of the interview question. What would you like to be your professional legacy?

JT: That people dress performers better. I've set the school up because I want to be able to go to the cinema and just enjoy the story and not be looking at horrors. I think that film, TV and theatre largely dictates how we see history, the way we see ourselves and where we come from is through the media, so I think there's a responsibility to be as accurate as possible when depicting history. I'm a free artist – I can do whatever I like. However, we are doing our ancestors a great disservice if we lose sight of what mattered to them and don't try to understand their lives well. I think that matters a lot.

AN INTERVIEW WITH MARK THOMSON

Ali Maclaurin

Introduction

Mark Thomson has been the Artistic Director of the Royal Lyceum Theatre in Edinburgh since 2003. Before that he was the Artistic Director of the Brunton Theatre, Musselburgh between 1997 and 2003 during which time he directed twenty productions, including nine World Premieres and built a tradition of directing accessible and originally staged productions of Shakespeare's plays. He continues this at the Lyceum, where he directs, and sometimes writes, a wide variety of plays (see Figure 1).

Figure 1   Emma Cunliffe, Malcolm Shields and Robin Laing in Shakespeare's *As You Like It*, directed by Mark Thomson, Lyceum Theatre, Edinburgh, 2005
Source: Douglas McBride, photograph, by permission of Douglas McBride.

MT = Mark Thomson, AJM = Ali Maclaurin

AJM: When you start to think about a play, say it's a classic, how do you start to think about it, about your concept? And where does costume come into that?

MT: Well, the first thing to say is that I think if you start with the idea that you need a concept it's very often that you start from the outside of a play. You are starting from a point that this piece of work and set of ideas and words needs dressing up in order to be fit for purpose or fit to be seen any more, or that somehow it reflects some kind of inner lack if you deliver it as it is. What I tend to do is just get into the text and think around what I think it's about. I get my own personal relationship with it through what I see and what I get excited about in it – the politics of it, a relationship in it, the metaphysics of it. Once I start to understand my own relationship with it I start to understand how I might develop that relationship. That said, I think when you are doing classics now what you're looking to do as an artist is to make that relationship an intense and specific enough one that your production and your version will make it feel fresh......and to a degree unique, although what constitutes unique I don't know. The great danger of having too strong a concept, and I've found this with some of the things I've done even when I've thought they haven't been highly conceptual, is you start to change the play slightly because it doesn't quite fit and you want it to work. For me, particularly with Shakespeare, my starting point is that within them is great wisdom about how human beings work and how the world works in relationship with society and that they still have things to reveal to now. My job is to create a conversation that is a lively one visually and verbally so that the play can communicate its contents like it has never been spoken before.

AJM: How does that come to you visually, or do you work with a designer to find what the visual side of that is?

MT: There is no one way it happens for me. Sometimes there is a very clear picture but very often, and I think this is why I love working in theatre, I will work with a designer who will have a very strong influence on how those ideas or insights, how I want to tell the story will be visually manifest. And that is a good and lively conversation that goes backwards and forwards as we try to articulate it. So the relationship with the designer is very important because if there's a taste issue then you can get into trouble with both being unhappy and not finding the way forward. It does differ. Sometimes I'll be very definite about the period I want it to be in, sometimes the designer will say, look, I think this is, say, the Thirties. That happened with *Othello* with Frances O'Connor where he showed me some pictures from the period and it made sense of why I liked the play. There are other times like *The Merchant of Venice* where I just knew that one of the drives of the play was the city, the way deplorable things were happening in the city. I wanted there to be as little barrier between it and our time as possible and it was very recognizable as people doing business and buying shares. I was looking for a little bit of a lift in terms of costume, but I think it was pretty naturalistic. The background was this piazza where everything took place, meetings, fights, everything. It was all mirrors so there was a burnished feel.

AJM: In terms of time, it wasn't particularly specific, was it?

MT: For me, the costumes were relatively besuited and fairly contemporary.

AJM: It's interesting, this idea of fairly contemporary, there's a sense where it's recognizably modern in a kind of post nineteenth century way.

MT: Yes, trousers, cut of jackets … yes, for years I used to think, let's go for timeless, then I thought, hang on, what's timeless? Timeless??!! So I try not to do too much of that. There are clever designers who can make it sit at roughly twentieth century, but with that I think I did make it pretty nowish.

AJM: Yes, my memory is sort of fairly modern but the women had a bit of an eastern twist.

MT: There was an otherness.

AJM: Was that research that was done specifically?

MT: No, it was an idea. What we felt about the piece was that it veers between a thriller and a fairy tale. When you are in 'casket land' and when Bassanio goes at the end to marry Portia it's like a kind of fairy tale. Shakespeare does this quite a lot, he does it with *As You Like It*, he does it with *A Winter's Tale*, he creates an argument. Shakespeare always thinks antithetical. He explains the world by looking at two opposites and the key to doing his plays is finding that relationship and making it work. One side might reflect and comment on the other, or they are two parts of the same equation but they don't look like they are, they seem disparate, so we wanted to make that feel slightly fairy tale like.

AJM: Was there a sense that you didn't want the costumes to be recognizable?

MT: We wanted a slightly timeless ethereal, fairy tale feel. The truths that live in the market place were eternal more than to do with the now and the appetites to do with the now.

AJM: So how important is costume to you in relation to set?

MT: I find it very important. It's probably, and I'll be very frank here because as you well know my partner is a costume designer, I usually have quite a lot to say in costume, but it might well be the area I am least confident in. I need an interpreter. What I do is comment a lot. I'll say, no, that's the wrong story. It's character for me, character, character, character. At the moment we're doing a piece called *Union* which is set in 1707, and Megan's doing it, [Megan Baker, a costume designer and Mark Thompson's partner] it's the first time I've worked with Megan for 17 years. I always thought it was a wee bit inappropriate. A costume designer and a video designer, that's the team, because I think the costume is really important and we want to sit it in its period costume wise, and maybe play with it a bit...... or maybe not. You've got to wonder why you are playing with things. I get rather fed up with oppressive symbolism in costume. I think 'OK, thanks for just throwing that at me! That's it on a plate'. There's no poetry to it, no ambiguity, no engagement and if I believe that theatre is a conversation then it must be sophisticated. If someone is telling me the complete story visually there's nowhere to go. It might look gorgeous, or not, but for me the set and costume must engage, be eloquent .....

AJM: If you are using period costume do you think it is not saying anything other than its period, and......... ?

MT: ... and then the play can unfold through character. And here's the thing, I think some people think that is easier than it really is. I think they think it's a bit dull, but an audience isn't thinking that. An audience is thinking, 'I am completely in that world you have conjured'. So, it's good to be creatively restless and to find new ways of telling stories, but if you feel there is some kind of cultural ringmaster in the critical sense whipping the ground going, 'Jump, jump, different, different, different', then actually that has got nothing to do with art. Art is about your voice, your response to the world. What I am sensing at the moment in theatre and maybe in other forms is there is almost an oppressive ringmaster who is providing an external force to try and make you jump and I'm not sure that's the best way to forge an individual's creativity and voice. All the best artists have influences, of course they don't live in bubbles, but actually the uniqueness of their voice was formed by and large by how they perceived the world, not with someone standing in front of them going, 'You can't do this, do that. You should really think of this'. I don't think I've ever done a period Shakespeare here [at the Lyceum Theatre in Edinburgh]. Everyone of my Shakespeare's has been shifted, changed, because that's the way I think you should tell the story.

AJM: So it comes from the text, it's not about being 'clever'?

MT: For me it does ... and if it were about being clever, we're all doomed because Shakespeare is always cleverer than us. Whenever I'm directing a Shakespeare, thinking about the ideas, I say to people that it's like having the best car service imaginable. Your mind couldn't be more tuned because of what he asks of you. Cleverness is absolutely imperative. If you are dumb you are going to dumb down Shakespeare. It's the wrong kind if cleverness when you put yourself in front of him. If you do that you better have something special to say because his richness of thinking will be diluted by an inferior mind.

AJM: What about costume as a tool for an actor, is that important to you?

MT: Oh, yes. The amount of actors that you spend four weeks in the rehearsal room with exploring approaches and then they put the costume on and say, 'Right, I get it!' There are times, and I don't mean just in period costume, when I will try and get something in the rehearsal room that's close to it because it can make people feel differently, not just in terms of how people move, it becomes essential to them, it's their skin effectively.

How different designers work with actors has always interested me. Wherever possible I try and get a dialogue going between the designer and the actors so that there is not an imposition but a sharing of ideas. Because you might get an actor who for four weeks is concentrating on one characteristic and the costume needs to reflect that. But if it's something period or you've got thirty in the cast sometimes it's made before you arrive and then it's critical that the costume designer takes an inspirational role.

AJM: What happens when an actor puts a costume on and says it doesn't feel right?

MT: It does happen ... it's a dialogue, rather like 'I don't know if we should be together any more'. It's part of a conversation that can get very defensive very quickly because the actor knows the costume is made. There are various outcomes. One is that the costume goes – the director will get involved in that – or it will be amended, or you say 'Actually, you've got to make this work; it's an eighteenth century costume, we're up next week, we're in a practical business … I know you're not fond of a Nissan Micra but we can't afford the BMW.'

AJM: Your part of that, then, is your response to the actor. Will it depend on how you think that costume works in the play, not what the actor thinks?

MT: I wouldn't dismiss the actor because at the end of the day he's playing Hamlet for three and a half hours, he's taking the metaphysical journey. If he feels wrong in this balloon costume I have to say, what is the most important thing here? Do I hold with the costume? I will do what I think is best for the production and that has a different answer every time. The only thing that matters to me is getting the best result and that will mean that sometimes I make a designer unhappy, or an actor …

AJM: Do you think that there are some periods or styles that audiences find more difficult than others?

MT: I think there is a little bit of a leap needed before trousers came in … I think there are ways of dealing with it, but there is a visual bump. There is an element of the exotic which is pleasing and a sense that you are somewhere else. It doesn't alienate, but there is a distancing, so I have to figure out how to get over that. It's the play.....if you are in a toga, you will still manage if the play is good enough, but there is an oddness or an exoticness.

AJM: I think robes can be particularly difficult …

MT: They're kind of alien …

AJM: ..... or funny, especially if they are short.

MT: What you'll find is that people will move it up a few years. Designers will want to do that too, to shift into something more familiar.

AJM: Is the distance sometimes useful?

MT: Well, it depends what you are trying to achieve. If you want to tell a love story then anything that alienates is probably working against you. It's all possible. It can be to do with where you place people on stage and that's about craft, which sometimes gets downgraded in favour of the 'Different'.

AJM: Have you ever done a period Shakespeare?

MT: The ironic thing is the last thing I did with Megan was *The Duchess of Malfi* in a pub in London and we did that in period costume. I think that's the only Jacobean play I've ever done in period.

AJM: Why did you do that in period?

MT: I think it because I wanted to go right to the core of what Marlowe was saying and doing. That's as an exploration for me, an act of devotion about those Elizabethan writers and I didn't want anything to get in the way. The set was very non-naturalistic so.....

AJM: Was it to do with it being in a pub and the juxtaposition with that?

MT: I'd love to say so but I don't know that it was. In retrospect I don't think it was the right thing. In a pub you shouldn't do that, it looked odd. Megan did a great job but I don't think I used that, I don't think I was as sophisticated as that.

You mentioned *as You Like It*, I loved that play, it's one of my favourites....

AJM: I found the way you did really interesting.

MT: I found there was an extraordinary feminine wisdom and I just thought it was one of the most female of all Shakespeare plays. The fact is you couldn't really write for women then because there were no women on the stage and he was writing for guys playing women, but the Rosalind character and the harsh world that was my starting point, the prevalence and wisdom of the feminine in harsh angles and black squareness …

AJM: It started with that really shallow stage.

MT: And lots of men in black suits, where have we seen that before …

AJM: It was very striking, especially with that change into …

MT: Tellytubby land! White mounds, so sensual, and big circles, all soft, that was very much *masculine and feminine.*

AJM: You really felt the change in texture.

MT: Yeah, it was very visceral. Think it was a very simple but strong thing and Greg Smith managed to find an articulation that was wonderful.

Now I tell you the nearest I've got to concept theatre, it was at the Brunton, [the Brunton Theatre in Musselburgh where Thompson was artistic director] and I did '*Twelfth Night*'. What I did was, I set it in a fashion house, the House of Belch. So when they are hiding behind the trees watching Malvolio, it was a clothes rail, simple things. It was playful but I didn't think it got in the way. When I started looking at the play, two things interested me – identity and a group of people going on a journey to discover themselves … so it was about how we dress ourselves and each other up because we think we are one thing but actually we are not. I suddenly thought this is fashion, this is what we do, we play with who we are.

AJM: Costume must have been fun.

MT: It was great fun, great fun. You got Malvolio with his stockings and things like that. Edward Lipscombe did it and had great fun with the costumes.

AJM: It sounds like a costume designer's dream!

MT: I suppose that might have looked like a concept but it came from the play, from my relationship with it and what I was interested in.

AJM: That makes sense. There's a quote by Peter Hall about not believing the costume unless it looks like the language. What do you feel about that? How do you make the language and costume work?

MT: It's interesting ... ambiguous ... but in the end it's subjective ... I did a *Macbeth* in khakis and I got letters saying, 'It's not the Balkan wars, there are no guns in Shakespeare, only daggers'. For me, if you create a world that bumps rather than provokes an interesting and sophisticated response in an audience where the visual is meeting the words, if they are having a horrible messy tussle, then that's not interesting. If you've got something that becomes part of the richness of the play, then that is. Sometimes you can get an idea that just troubles the play and troubles the audience and sometimes that might be seen as a success ... which is interesting – 'oh, well, at least something happened' – but I'm not sure about that. The audience won't come back!

AJM: So do you think audience expectation is one of those things you have to manage?

MT: The truth is that everyone's different. Some people don't want me to put it in suits, they say 'Just do the play', and others love not knowing what they are going to see. You've got to allow yourself be fired. I don't know what the job is otherwise. If I'm chasing my audience expectations then I am working as externally as the ugliest side of concept theatre. I must do what I want to do and be prepared to be fired or hated. That's my job.

Chapter

2   The Stage Picture

Ali Maclaurin

A theatre wardrobe, like the museum of costume, conjured up by Elizabeth Wilson is an eerie place where the empty garments 'like souls in limbo … wait poignantly for the music to begin' (Wilson, 1985, p. 1). Whether pulled from such a wardrobe, specially made, bought or borrowed, a stage costume is not fully 'made' until it is assembled on an actor's body and put to use onstage. The journey each garment has made to reach the stage varies considerably and the act of changing clothes to perform may entail getting out of one pair of jeans and into another or involve an extended act of transformation requiring dressers, make-up and wigs. The garments themselves may be part of a specially made unified group of garments controlled by an individual artist or may appear haphazardly from an actor's suitcase. But since the earliest times of which we have evidence there is a sense that clothes worn to perform in are different from everyday clothes. As Hollander puts it, 'Dressing up meaningfully to perform a rite is as old an institution as religion itself' (Hollander, 1975, p. 238).

In his witty essay, *The Diseases of Costume*, the philosopher, Roland Barthes is more specific. He writes,

> The costume is nothing more than the second term of a relation which must constantly link the work's meaning to its 'exteriority'. Hence everything in the costume that blurs the clarity of this relation … is bad … in all the great periods of theatre, costume has a powerful semantic value; it was not there only to be seen, it was also there to be *read*, it communicated ideas, information or sentiments.
>
> (Barthes, 1972, p. 42)

Our knowledge of the history of stage costuming is often scant and unsatisfactory, gleaned through interpretation of written descriptions, partial lists, paintings of unclear provenance and posed photographs, but what we can see, both then and now, is that the way we choose to costume our plays, whether as individuals or as societies in time and space, reflects what we wish to communicate.

To examine this more specifically, I will take as examples two common but opposing practices, the use of 'modern dress', and that of 'historical costume'. Modern dress productions, first exemplified in the early modern period (defined very broadly as 1500–1800), use clothing of the same era as the play's audience, regardless of the time in which the play may have been set or written. In doing this, they are able to tap into that audience's understanding of its own dress codes. Those using 'historical costume', that is, costume based on what people wore in the past, may realize it in different ways and for different reasons. Here, I contrast Victorian 'historicism', in which the desire was to recreate the narrative of the play in realistic detail as if it were history itself, with the (re-)rebuilt Globe's use of 'original practices' in the 1990s, a practice which in a glorious theatrical contradiction, practised as far as possible the manner and method of Elizabethan 'modern dress' in a context in which audiences saw it as historical costume. An examination of these different 'ways of doing' will form the basis of this chapter in order to consider why such choices have been made and what they bring to the performance. As Bridget Escolme writes, in her excellent chapter on costume in *Shakespeare and the Making of Theatre*, 'the most obvious work that costume does onstage is to create a cultural and historical world for the audience. But costume can also highlight the socially and theatrically constructed nature of that world, the class, gender and racial relations within it and the ways in which we are always in the process of producing and reproducing the past' (Hampton-Reeves and Escolme, 2012, p. 130).

1 MODERN DRESS: HAND-ME-DOWNS AND HAUTE COUTURE

When I was about ten and fascinated by historical costume, my mum took me to York Theatre Royal to see Shakespeare's *Richard III*. It was the late 1960s and the production was played in 'rehearsal clothes', mostly jeans, T-shirts and desert boots. I remember my mum commenting on her disappointment that 'there weren't any proper costumes', that is to say, the costumes did not entertain or enlighten her. As a modern designer, I find the idea difficult that I am required by my choices to entertain, but my mum's comment makes clear that part of our impulse to go to the theatre is a visual and sensual one, and that impulse is not always fulfilled by the production. Modern dress, particularly of the everyday utilitarian kind, can easily be seen as dull by an audience and is, as Hollander writes, 'that most subtle kind of costume' (Hollander, 1975, p. 265). In 2011, for example, I designed a community opera set in a modern domestic dream world that hovered mysteriously between night and day. The children all wore pyjamas and I wanted the thirty or so adults to wear clothes that seemed of this world but that echoed the ethereal quality of the music and the twilight colours of the lighting. Inevitably, on a small budget, the wardrobe supervisor and I spent a long afternoon in Primark, matching floaty handkerchief cardigans and long T-shirts with leggings and soft skirts in blues, greys, creams and lavenders. The costumes were a great success both to wear and to look at, but prompted two interesting responses. The cast all wanted to take their outfits away to wear at home, while several audience members commented on how well the community cast had chosen their own clothes to work in the stage setting. Apparently, modern dress is so familiar that its transformation into stage costume may render it invisible, but to actor and audience this may be either 'dull' or exciting, depending on the clothes. When in 1975, Terry Hands played the opening scene of his production of *Henry V* in jeans 'the actors attempted to persuade Hands that this lack of costume made the audience see "them and nor their character"', while others worried about the queen, who was due to attend, watching actors in their jeans (Kennedy, 1993, p. 168).

However, modern dress can work very differently. Let's consider it first in the context of a very different world, that of the early modern playhouse at the time of Shakespeare (1564–1616) and his contemporaries. There is a general, if rather vague, understanding that early modern plays were costumed mainly in clothes of their own period, most of which were hand-me-downs. This assumption is based on scattered written evidence and one contemporary image, known as the Peachum drawing, which may show a scene from the play *Titus Andronicus* in a version which may be by Shakespeare. Laver writes, 'We find in this drawing the mixture of clothes of various styles and periods which audiences of the time took for granted. Other indications are almost non-existent except for a few literary references to 'gorgeous and sumptuous' apparel. It is thought that the courtiers sometimes passed on their fine clothes to the actors' (Laver, 1964, p. 96). De Marly quotes at length from the costume lists in the diary of Philip Henslowe, an entrepreneur who also financed the Rose and the Globe theatres, but does not consider such costume's use or reception (De Marly, 1982, p. 29). Hollander, an art historian, prefers to pass over costume in the playhouses and concentrate on the contemporary but much better documented masque costumes (Hollander, 1975). It has been left instead to cultural and social historians, more used to the close reading of early texts than the study of images, to give us a better understanding of early modern costuming in context.

It appears to be true that, during the early modern period, many of the clothes worn on common stages were bought, given or borrowed and had once belonged to the rich. The significance of this is made clear in an exceptional chapter in 'Renaissance Clothing and the Materials of Memory' on 'Staging Clothes' (Jones and Stallybrass, 2000). The authors explain that clothing, in an era with no mechanization, was a precious commodity continually reworn and reworked. Buying a new outfit was an investment more comparable today with buying a house and so there was an accepted circulation of rented, inherited and second-hand clothing not just on the stage but off it. 'A play usually cost about £6 to put on' they write, while in an inventory made by the actor, Edward Alleyn, he 'lists a single, admittedly expensive "black velvet cloak with sleeves embroidered all with silver and gold"' which cost more than £20' (Jones and Stallybrass, 2000, p. 178). The inventory, made in 1598 with Philip Henslowe, seems very small for the company's known repertoire and leads the authors to the conclusion that 'theatres, like the society as a whole, turned money into clothes and clothes into money' (Jones and Stallybrass, 2000, p. 184). It also adds weight to the idea that actors may have collected their own stock of costume as a resource important both to their craft and their cash flow. Despite the fact that they were only expected to provide accessories such as hats and hose, sharers, that is full members of acting companies, are recorded as buying, selling, borrowing, lending, pawning (and stealing!) clothes. According to Macyntire, though, the interchangeability of clothes and cash made it impossible 'to discriminate between a sharer's investment in a company (much of which went for costumes), his personal apparel, and his privately owned stage costumes' (Mackintyre, 1992, p. 76). The cost of these costumes coupled with the speed of repertoire change in early modern companies resulted in continual reuse of the same costumes. We are accustomed today to the reuse of costume in different plays, but perhaps not on the scale it was done in the sixteenth and seventeenth centuries. The role of costume as material spectacle to be admired and enjoyed put a continual pressure on the companies; using old costumes for a new play brought complaints from the audience and could result in its failure (De Marly, 1982, p. 31). In contrast, particular costumes might be received so well that they were reused the following year. For example, in 1664, Aphra Behn brought special feathered garments back from her travels in South America for Dryden's play *The Indian Queen*. Such was their popularity that he revived their use in his sequel *The Indian Emperor* and noted in the prologue,

> The scenes are old, the Habits [clothes] are the same We wore last year, before the Spaniards came.
>
> (Dryden, 1677, prologue)

Not surprisingly, items that were this valuable were worth treating properly and so 'the professional companies employed specialists, in the form of wardrobe keepers and tiremen' (Jones and Stallybrass, 2000, p.178) or 'attire men' who functioned as dressers. Both were usually tailors or apprentices to tailors who did the mending and sometimes made simple costumes, such as a witch's gown. Henslowe also, 'made payments on behalf of the actors to tailors, mercers, a milliner, lacemakers and a "sylke man"' (ibid., p. 178). It is easy to see, in this context, why powerful guild members from clothing trades were so involved in the economy of the playhouses of the time. Jones and Stallybrass convincingly list the Tudor theatre financiers: John Rastel – theatre owner, clothing hirer and playwright; Philip Henslowe – member of the Dyer's Company, financier of the Rose and Fortune Theatres, fripperer and pawnbroker; Francis Langley – member of the Draper's Company, financier of the Swan Theatre, woollen cloth inspector (ibid., p. 179). It is also clear that, although using second-hand clothes was the cheapest option at the time, it was not by any means a cheap one.

So we understand that the costumes were a playhouse's most important commodity, many covered in real gold thread, precious jewels and fur. De Marly writes, using the evidence in Henslowe's diary, 'The Admiral's Men […]

owned a black velvet gown trimmed with white fur, one of crimson striped with gold and faced with ermine, one of cloth of gold, another of cloth of gold for actor Cavendish and one of cloth of silver for W. Parr' (De Marly, 1982, p. 29). However, their stage value lay not just in their monetary value, but in the controlled status of these garments within the tight class hierarchy of the early modern period. In 1574, Elizabeth I's Sumptuary Laws or 'Enforcing Statutes of Apparel' state,

> The excess of apparel and the superfluity of unnecessary foreign wares thereto belonging now of late years is grown by sufferance to such an extremity that the manifest decay of the whole realm generally is like to follow (by bringing into the realm such superfluities of silks, cloths of gold, silver, and other most vain devices of so great cost ...) but also and particularly the wasting and undoing of a great number of young gentlemen
> That
> 'None shall wear in his apparel:
> Any silk of the colour of purple, cloth of gold tissued, nor fur of sables, but only the King, Queen [and other royalty].
> Cloth of gold, silver, tinseled satin, silk or cloth mixed or embroidered with any gold or silver: except all degrees above viscounts'.
> (Elizabethan.org., 2013)

In this context, we learn from Thomas Platter, for example, that

> [T]he actors are most expensively and elaborately costumed; for it is the English usage for Lords or Knights at their decease to bequeath and leave almost the best of their clothing to their serving men, which it is unseemly off the latter to wear, so that they offer them for sale for a small sum to the actors.
> (Williams, 1937, p. 167)

Jones and Stallybrass suggest,

> There were real limits to what frippers [sellers of second-hand clothing] and pawn-brokers could do with the most splendid of the clothes that they had acquired, because of the Sumptuary Laws, ineffectual as they were, that regulated what specific classes could wear. But the professional theatres were founded upon the flouting of sumptuary laws and upon the circulation of clothes from aristocrats to commoners.
> (Jones and Stallybrass, 2000, pp. 187–188)

Lublin places the emphasis slightly differently. He writes, 'The theatres proved to be the one place where sumptuary laws largely succeeded in determining the apparel that people wore. There, it was essential that the clothes worn by an actor clearly represent his character's social standing' (Lublin, 2011, p. 43). In other words, in Elizabethan times, people's status was still understood by what they wore even if they did not always stick to the rules. Everyone knew that only royalty were allowed to wear purple and ermine, therefore a stage king would conform to the sumptuary laws in order to be understood. For example, he quotes the character of Tamburlaine who begins the play as a shepherd dressed in sheepskin and simple worn clothing. Then he moves into the armour of a warrior and finally to the clothes of a king which, in Henslowe's Diary are recorded as 'Tamberlanes breches of crimson vellvet' and his 'cotte with coper lace' (ibid., p. 54). The sumptuous fabric, expensive red dye and precious lace all represent the clothing of royalty. It is only the use of copper, as opposed to gold lace, that indicates the garment may have been made for the stage as opposed to being handed down from a real king. Indeed, copper was used so often as a cheaper substitute for gold onstage that actors were sometimes identified as 'copperlaced' (Jones and Stallybrass, 2000, p. 191). Conversely, in 1664 after the Restoration, King Charles II watched *Henry V* played in his own coronation robes, legitimately borrowed under licence as part of the royal household.

For many Puritans such ostentatious costume was ungodly at best and seditious at worst and several commentators wrote pamphlets railing against the playhouses that encouraged its use. In the middle of the day under natural light, the sumptuousness of the garments could be observed in all their glorious detail, and the act of watching them was a visual feast, especially to a middle and lower class audience who demanded to be entertained by the materiality of what they saw onstage. The way clothes were acquired meant that a king might be played not just as he would have looked, but in the actual clothes he had or at least might have worn, complete with real jewels and even ermine, the ultimate symbol of royalty. When 'Harry ye VIII gowne' was listed by Henslowe in 1598, Henry had already been dead for fifty years, and by the time Cromwell sold off his remaining garments in 1649 he had been dead over a hundred years. It was the status of such clothing that contributed to its significance while its longevity and availability allowed its continued use, creating, according to Jones and Stallybrass, 'a circulation of clothes that unstitched apparel from social status, an unstitching that theatre both staged in its fictions and encouraged in its audience' (ibid., p. 192). Lublin concedes that some writers have interpreted the way theatres used the sumptuary laws as subversive. However, he believes that,

The theatre, far more than the rest of society, respected the social semiotics whereby the audience could understand the characters on sight. Although the actors wore apparel onstage that was outside the realm of their social station, the characters they played carefully observed the dictates of social decorum. Moreover, those who failed to follow the dictates of social decorum were most often punished for their transgression. Thus, within the walls of the playhouses, social order was observed even more carefully than it typically was in normative society. And if an actor walked beyond the walls of the playhouse in his costume, he left himself vulnerable both to punishment for failing to obey the sumptuary laws and to a stiff fine for breaking the strict rules of the theatrical companies that forbad actors from leaving with their social apparel.

(Lublin, 2011, pp. 56–57)

There are no surviving costume designs for early modern plays, as there are for court masques, nor any evidence that costumes were considered in the kind of unified artistic way that would have required them. Although there are countless references to clothing within the plays of Shakespeare and his contemporaries, the references refer to the custom and practice of the time and the evidence we have points to a costume hierarchy identical onstage to off. What we do not see, however, is the sense of a coherently designed stage world. This may have been to do with the prohibitive cost of sets of costumes given the speed at which new plays came in and out of repertory. However, it is also to do with the different role and expectation. Stella Mary Newton and others have argued through close study of pieces of visual art, that the Early Moderns did have a 'sense of the historic past' (Newton, 1975). They certainly wrote about it, as evidenced by extant works such as Raphael Holinshead's *Chronicles of England, Scotland and Ireland* which was used extensively by Shakespeare (Kewes et al., 2012). Yet there is little evidence that an audience required to see such history onstage, nor that they expected costume to perform this task. The Peachum drawing, because of its unique status, has been the centre of much speculation, some of it around the awareness of 'historic' costume. Yet the drawing's very unique-ness, coupled with its sketchy style and unclear context, make it a constantly unreliable source in a period where written records, though sparse, seem to give more clarity.

In terms of how costume functioned at this time, there were generally eight to twelve full 'sharers' in an early modern acting company plus three or four boys and perhaps some hired players. Plays at the time could have twenty to thirty written parts as well as disguises, so doubling was an accepted convention and a change of costume generally denoted a change of character. Indeed, Macintyre goes so far as to state that 'the number of characters a small company could play was limited not so much by how many belonged to it as by how many costumes it owned' (Mackintyre, 1992, p. 31). Because clothes were difficult to remove quickly, rapid doubling or disguise was often achieved by means of a cloak, a versatile cover-all garment worth spending money on as evidenced by the number in Alleyn's inventory. De Marly writes, 'among the cloaks were one of scarlet decorated with silver lace and buttons, a short velvet cape-cloak embroidered with gold and gold spangles, a damask cloak faced with velvet, a scarlet cloak faced with blue velvet and trimmed with gold buttons, one of scarlet faced with black velvet, and one of worsted decorated with gold lace' (De Marly, 1982, p. 29).

Beyond the draped fabric to indicate 'Roman and/or hero' (as seen in contemporary masque costume and in the Peachum drawing) and pos-sibly turbans for 'moors' and robes for 'Persians' as seen in illustrations of contemporary masque costumes, we have little evidence of clothing unique to the stage in the early modern playhouses, only of clothes such as Alleyn's expensive cloak, which was newly made to be worn onstage but of a style equally at home off it. However, that costume was important and its use well-considered is evidenced by the continual reference to clothing in plays of the time, and a close reading of the plays reveals a significant use of clothing conventions that would be understood by the audience, including the idea that dress reflects morals or can make a moral point. Writes Mackintyre, 'A different dress may show that a character has abandoned good for evil or evil for good,' (Mackintyre, 1992, p. 13). While in Shakespeare's *Hamlet*, Styan tells the reader, the hero makes a telling point to a contemporary audience by wearing black, the colour of mourning, at his mother's wedding to Claudius, an occasion where convention dictates that all should wear their best (read brightest) apparel (Styan, 1996, p. 142).

Styan, in the passage referred to, successfully conveys the feel of contemporary drama onstage through staging and costume, but occasionally reveals his twentieth-century viewpoint; he writes, 'The wardrobe no doubt saved costs to some extent by keeping its costume for the most part contemporary' (ibid., p. 101). This comment seems misleading on two levels, pointing to an intentionality in rejecting historicism of which we have no evidence and confusing 'contemporary-ness' with 're-usability' in clothing both on and off the stage. What is clear is that in order to really understand the choices made in stage costuming, it is necessary to understand not just the play involved, not even just the accompanying stage practises, but also the economy, politics and wider culture in which such choices are made.

What is also written into the very structure of early modern texts is a solution for the practicalities of how outfits were put together; upper class clothing consisted of complicated layers of garments tied and pinned to themselves and each other, requiring time, care and help, and certainly not conducive to a quick change. In *Lingua, or the Combat of the Tongues*, the satirical play written by Thomas Tomkis, the audience hears the account of a dressing scene,

> 5 hours ago I set a dozen maids to attire a boy like a nice gentlewoman; but there is such doing with their looking glasses, in pinning, setting, unsettling, formings and conformings, painting blew veins and cheeks; such stir with sticks and stones, castanets, dressings, pulls, falls, squares, husks, bodies, scarves, necklaces, carantes, rebatoes, borders, tires, fans, palisades, puffs, ruffs, muffs, cuffs and pusles, fusles, partlets, for islets, bandlets, fillets, crosslets, pendulets, amulets, annulets, bracelets and so many lets (ie hindrances) that yet she is scarce dressed to the girdle; and now there is such a calling for fardingales, kirtles, busk points, shoe ties etc., that seven pedlars shops-nay, all Stourbridge Fair-will scarcely furnish her: a ship is sooner rigged by far, than a gentlewoman making ready.
>
> (Tomkis, 1607, act IV, sc. VI)

When discussing character development in Shakespeare's plays, Styan explains, 'Shakespeare often allows for three costume changes for his principals and these flag the dramatic progress of the character through his play, even in comedy' (Styan, 1996, p. 143). This is no doubt dramatically true, but what is also true is that the middle costume of all three, Malvolio, Hamlet and Lear, is a state of undress; for Malvolio, a nightgown; for Hamlet a 'doublet all unbrac'd' and 'stockings fouled'; and for Lear an onstage undressing. With a sense of the workings of clothes of the time this has another very practical function; what better way to facilitate a tricky costume change than to make the middle 'costume' an undress as opposed to a dress? Suddenly the hectic scene in the tiring room is brought to life and we can see how dramatic action is inextricably linked, if not led, by the practicalities of staging.

In summary, we can see from detailed examination that although choice of costume may have been limited, it was highly significant. Because the clothes were part of a recognizable system, they could make clear statements about status and power, yet the very familiarity of this system allowed its manipulation to function playfully around status and gender with characters using and abusing sartorial customs that the audience would recognize; and although changing clothes was complicated it was important and interesting enough to become a part of many plays. There was little sense of staging the past in the costumes, but instead a fascination with highlighting the development of characters and the shift of relationships through changing costume.

The first notable use of modern dress as a self-conscious practice in traditionally historical plays did not emerge until the early twentieth century. There is evidence to suggest that the director, Max Reinhardt, attempted both a Moliere and Shakespeare's *Hamlet* in modern dress before 1920, but the best known and best documented examples of historical plays, by playwrights such as Shakespeare and Ibsen, staged in modern dress took place in the 1920s at the Birmingham Rep under Barry Jackson (Cochrane, 1993, p. 97). In 1928 his co-director, H.K. Ayliff vividly stated 'I think, then, when our modern dress in a play does not offend the sensitive dignity of our scholastic learning, we ought by all means to retain it … all the wrestling and bending and fighting and falling in a strange costume we may understand, but we do not feel' (ibid., p. 97).

Jackson agreed, suggesting that in Shakespeare, the 'sublime unnaturalness of blank verse', the strangeness of the costumes and the conventions of Shakespearean acting 'interpose a veil between [the man in the street] and the author's intention and [he] comes away with an increased feeling of almost superstitious awe' (ibid., p. 105). Jackson, in complete contrast, wanted the audience to feel that they were 'witnessing a real conflict of credible human beings'.

Cochrane, painting a picture of how modern dress can be so effective, writes,

> The prompt-book tells us that the actors on the stage laughed and probably the audience with them, as Polonius advised Laertes that 'the apparel oft proclaims the man'. 'Proclaiming the man' was achieved with great care, revealing people of flesh and blood in characters formerly smothered by their ornate costumes. Polonius, (A. Bromley-Davenport) usually played as a tedious old clown, emerged

as a dapper elder statesman first seen in white tie and tails. For his farewell to his son, he wore a formal dark three piece suit, winged collar and bow tie as he eyed his son's casual light tweed suiting. Later in morning coat, striped trousers and spats he fumbled with a pince-nez as he struggled to read Hamlet's love letter. To the critic of the Liverpool Weekly Post he looked 'like the elderly and worldly wise French count of musical comedy' (29 August 1925), especially when he ogled the girls in the players' company. Ophelia was not, as some newspapers reported, an ultra-modern flapper which might have made her submission to her father seem rather improbable. The intention was to emphasize her extreme youth and inexperience; indeed Muriel Hewitt celebrated her eighteenth birthday during the run of the production. Alan Bland, Jackson's publicity manager, explained 'Ophelia is just a girl fresh from school with a fussy father and a prig of a brother and a dress suitable to such a young person …' (Evening News, 22 July 1925). Muriel Hewitt's hair was not shingled but remained long, plaited and wound in 'winkles' round her ears. She wore a plain cream satin frock which reached to just below her knees and 'nude' stockings.

(Cochrane, 1993, p. 108)

Shelving's costumes were reviewed in detail both because they revealed new depths of character and because they came from the most expensive and fashionable shops. As in Shakespeare's own era, modern dress was not necessarily a cheap option, and yet these expensive couture gowns were not chosen solely for their glamour and allure. However, the production gained much publicity and coverage in the fashion magazines as extensive as that of the 'fashion plays' of Wilde and Pinero discussed later in the chapter. The outfits were carefully selected to create characters recognizable to the audience as from their own time but subtly and realistically enough to allow the actors to develop their characters within them. The actors were profoundly affected and sometimes felt very exposed, as Frank Vosper explained during his run as Claudius, 'I long to feel the re-assurance of robes about me, to know that even if I am looking pompous and theatrical, at least I am looking decorative' (ibid., p. 10). Actors' delivery and their gestures changed and the Vogue critic wrote, 'king, queen and courtiers stopped being clothes props to become suffering human beings like ourselves' (ibid., p. 116). Even the great Elizabethanist, Poel, wrote, 'I don't think that a nearer approach to an Elizabethan rendering of the play on the stage has before been reached by a producer' (ibid., p. 118). And yet it is difficult to know quite how close in intention it did come. The play had a designer of set and costume who interpreted the characters and chose the costumes, however modern they were. These were not costumes chosen for status or through custom, they were designed individually to give insight into the character of each of Jackson's 'suffering human beings'. So on the surface, the convention may seem similar, although the way it was put into practice reflects the differences between the eras.

What this account does make clear though is that when modern dress is done with accuracy and wit on an appropriate play, it can allow the audience to see it with fresh eyes. Yet, Jackson himself was alive to its limits and worried that he had 'created a mechanical monster far more powerful than he dreamed' (ibid., p. 130). On hearing of modern dress versions of, for example, *The Rivals*, he 'worried about reported attempts to present the precisely defined social milieu of Goldsmith and Sheridan in modern dress and was anxious that audiences should not be robbed of the enjoyment of beautiful period clothes. He feared that too much trivial modern detail would prove a distraction which would lead to more ridicule poured on what were serious artistic experiments' (ibid., p. 130). His fears seem to reveal a prejudice about the frivolity of modern fashion and a bit of intellectual snobbery that somehow others following might trivialize an idea which he instigated as an innovation.

There is no doubt that modern dress in a play normally staged in period costume can allow the audience the chance to read the costumes at a more detailed level and this means that it is not a 'one-stop shop' as historical dress might be. Most theatre goers are unlikely to distinguish between, say, slightly old-fashioned and cutting-edge design in an Elizabethan doublet without the designer resorting to more generic or stereotypical (modern!) signifiers. In modern dress, the nuances of status and subculture are better understood and it is this, presumably, which makes its use so popular. Yet a scenographic interpretation needs to allow its audience to understand not just the clothes onstage but also the play better through the clothes. As Escolme puts it, again using Shakespeare's plays as the example,

> Modern dress, then, shifts its meanings depending on physical environment and cultural context, and powerfully serves the need to read 'now' into 'then'. It can be used to insist on Shakespeare's 'relevance' and, simplistically, suggest the cultural and political concerns of a Shakespeare play are identical to our own; or it can provoke nuanced comparisons between historical periods. It can be an easy universalizing trope or produce challenging disjuncture and distanciation.
>
> (Escolme in Hampton-Reeves, 2012, p. 135)

Theatre costume and fashion are inexorably linked when modern dress is used since the audience will inevitably view and judge the clothes both as costumes for the character and as garments they might wear themselves. In the nineteenth century genre that contemporary critic William Archer called 'the fashion play' (Kaplan and Stowell, 1995, p. 1), already mentioned in relation to Jackson's use of modern dress in Shakespeare, newspapers would have whole columns devoted to the fashions seen on the West End stage, and plays by playwrights such as Wilde and Pinero allowed middle and working classes audiences to watch the upper classes at play. Ibsen's plays were severely held back by what was seen as their suburban nature and lack of cutting-edge fashion and Pinero's society comedies, such as *The Second Mrs. Tanqueray*, characterized as 'Ibsen adjusted for Mayfair markets' (ibid., p. 49) were much preferred. In plays such as Oscar Wilde's *Lady Windemere's Fan*, the leading lady would be costumed by her favourite dressmaker or couturier who often treated the performance like a catwalk show. Wilde was interested enough in dress to embrace the Dress Reform Movement and to write widely on clothes and costume. He used dress codes and conventions of respectability to comment on the characters in his plays with his typical black humour, for example, Mrs. Ehrlynne in her final line in *Lady Windemere's Fan*, comments, 'and if a woman really repents she has to go to a bad dressmaker, otherwise no one believes her' (ibid., p. 17). Actresses such as Mrs. Patrick Campbell were as wealthy as the characters they played and dressed as glamorously. Such was the identification between clothing on and offstage that actresses might be identified with the excess of their characters even if their own lifestyle did not reflect it. The actress Constance Collier, for example, in her memoir *Harlequinade* written in 1929 recounts that in one play she had eight costume changes including a set of magnificent sables. The firm had lent them to her, she admits, 'for the sake of advertisement ....' Their worth became so exaggerated and the public so disapproving that she was almost murdered by one of the costume assistants (Collier, 1929, p. 127).

2   HISTORICAL DRESS AND 'SPECIAL STAGE CLOTHES'

Peter Brook writes, in a thought-provoking passage on stage costuming in *The Empty Space*, that 'everyday clothes' are 'usually inadequate as a uniform for performance' but that accurate historical costume is not the answer because 'an actor whose work seems real in rehearsal clothes easily loses this integrity when dressed in a toga copied from a vase in the British Museum' (Brook, 1970, p. 115). In the sixteenth and seventeenth centuries in Britain theatre costume might reflect, or even construct, gender, class, status and role, but it was not, I believe, really concerned with showing history. Yet from the nineteenth century onwards, historical costume onstage has been such a preoccupation that, in her interview, Jenny Tiramani suggests 80% of theatre costume is historically based. The gradual emergence of period costume onstage through the eighteenth and early nineteenth centuries relates to the complicated interplay of changing fashions, cultural advances in fields such as archaeology and technical developments. The actor-manager Garrick in the 1760s was the first to move the audience off the stage to create an uninterrupted stage world with which it was more difficult for the audience to interact. Throughout the next hundred or so years the contraction of the stage apron, the invention of gas and then electric lighting gradually widened the distance, both physical and psychological, between actor and audience. When, around 1880, Henry Irving began the custom of turning down the house lights, the stage became even more like an independent world to be examined from a distance, reflecting a Victorian society with a growing concern for the study of its own history and identity.

'Unless what's on stage looks like the language, I simply don't believe it', writes Peter Hall in 1989 'Ruritanian or modern or eclectic costumes are all very well – I can see why people do that – but if you are speaking

Elizabethan English, to me there is always a war between the two' (Brown, 2008, p. 141). For him then, possibly controversially, it is the language of the play that determines the costume style. However, for a growing number of producers and directors in the nineteenth century it was the location of the play in time and space that needed to be shown accurately through detailed historical sets and costumes. As, during the nineteenth century, the director's power grew, the use of complete theatrical environments became a way of exerting control over every aspect of a play as well as giving the audience a history lesson.

As has already been noted, the only common use of historical dress of which there is evidence in the early modern period is the style 'a la romaine' or 'in the style of a Roman', a knee length draped cloth representing a Roman toga. In the Stuart masques of Inigo Jones we see the convention used to personify the leading noble, whether king, prince or duke, as a classical hero, the highest accolade in post-Renaissance Europe. In this sense its use is more about status and respect than a desire for historical accuracy. By 1663 though, there is evidence of change. After attending the Roman play, *Heraclius or the Emperor of the East* at the Whitehall Palace Samuel Pepys, apparently enjoying and praising the historical accuracy of the stage picture, wrote, 'At the beginning, at the drawing up of the curtain, there was the finest scene of the emperor, and his people about him, standing in their fixed and different postures in their Roman habits, above all that ever I saw at any of the theatres' (De Marly, 1982, p. 20). By the mid-eighteenth century, the influential French philosopher, Diderot, was suggesting that actors should study the clothing styles in portraits of historical figures (Hollander, 1975, p. 279). In contrast, Goethe's opinion, as distilled by Hollander, was 'that reality was not the point of staging and acting; art makes a controlled representation, not imitation of life – and so should drama' (ibid., p. 289). Nevertheless both agreed that, in art and dress, simplicity and truth should be sought over display and splendour. In 1738, Pompeii and Herculaneum began to be excavated and engravings of the findings were available in Europe from about 1750. From the mid-eighteenth century, 'truth in the form of dramatic believability was also invoked for the first time' (ibid., p. 276) and some of those working in theatre began to consider the idea of historical costume onstage.

This new way of thinking took time to permeate public consciousness. Since performers were expected to costume themselves with whatever they could get by whatever means, many actors wore gifts from patrons or second-hand clothes and were more concerned with fashion and glamour than historical accuracy. Some actor-managers, however, whether through conviction or in the search for an audience, began to use artists to conceive a total scenic world and to experiment with innovative ways of costuming familiar characters.

The first record we have of the idea of costuming a complete cast with historical accuracy is by Aaron Hill in his play, *Athelwold* staged in 1731, a time when, according to Gerrard, there was a 'vogue for all things Saxon' (Gerrard, 2003, p. 154). Hill wrote,

> To say nothing as to the impropriety, in the custom of dressing characters, so far back in time, after the common fashions of our days, it weakens probability, and cuts off, in great measure, what most strikes an audience; for it relaxes the pomp of tragedy, and the generality being led, by the eye, can conceive nothing extraordinary when they see nothing uncommon.
>
> (Hill, 1760, p. 90)

Hill even created his own costume drawings although it is not clear whether these were ever constructed. The play, however, was a complete flop. What is interesting in his observations quoted above is his belief that distancing the audience from the world onstage will allow them to see more than they might if the piece were in the more familiar modern dress. It indicates clearly his understanding that how a play is presented visually will affect the way the audience receive and understand it, and he takes an early stand in the continuing debate over realism or stylization that still continues.

The actor-manager David Garrick was one of a group who began a significant change to the stage picture. He was the first to banish 'stage sitters' in 1762 in order not to interrupt the unity of the stage world and from 1772–1776, he employed the French artist Loutherbourg to achieve 'absolute fidelity to historical fact and setting' (Baugh, 1990, p. 18). Loutherburg, billed as 'designer' and not 'painter of scenes', designed both sets and costumes and strove for visual unity and truth. In 1785, he designed *Omai or A Trip Round the World* in which it was recorded that 'The dresses and scenery were done from drawings of Mr. Webber, the artist who made the voyages with Captain Cooke' (ibid., p. 47). Garrick had a library of books on historical costume and, in 1750, produced *Edward the Black Prince* with the whole cast dressed 'in the habit of those days' (De Marly, 1982, p. 52). Although we have no reason to think that the costumes were any more fourteen century than the accepted style of court coronation robes, it is significant that the whole cast were included, not just the principals. Garrick's use of historical costume was inconsistent, however, and may well have been chosen for its novelty in order to encourage an audience. Komisarjevsky claims (without accompanying evidence), 'When he appeared as Romeo … he looked like a young Englishman of the eighteenth century. As Hamlet, he wore the same but in black … When playing an ancient Greek, Aegis, in 1758, he wore the costume of a Venetian gondolier, on the ground that the majority of Venetian gondoliers of the time were of Greek origin' (Komisarjevsky, 1931, p. 130); and, just to indicate his love of novelty, when he played Hamlet, he wore a wired wig that was designed to stand on end through the clever pulling of strings when he saw Banquo's ghost. Alas, it failed to work (Baugh, 1990, p. 74). De Marly suggests that Garrick's part in the rise of accurate historical costuming has been overemphasized (De Marly, 1982, pp. 54, 57). However, he did own a number of books on the subject, including the works by Jeffries and Strutt mentioned in Chapter 1 and there is no doubt that his desire, sometimes at least, to create an accurate historical stage picture in set and costume, while it may not have succeeded to modern eyes, was a significant step on the way to the consistent stage worlds that are now the norm. An engraving of 'Venice Preserv'd' (1765) shows the actors looking, according to Baugh, like the 'fashionable well-dressed inhabitants of the Covent Garden Piazza area which, at the time, they really were'. He continues, 'The greater and more detailed the information which describes the actuality of the eighteenth century, the greater appears the discrepancy between this and the emotional effect which the performances had upon their contemporary audience. The stage photograph … which begins a hundred years later, illustrates clearly the wide gap … between the recorded reality and the contemporary received impression' (Baugh, 1990, p. 13).

The height of Victorian historical pictorial theatre was undoubtedly the later years of the nineteenth century, and Komisarjevsky writes in characteristically vivid language that 'until the last quarter of the nineteenth century, nearly every production of what is known onstage as a "costume play" was a sort of Bedlam as regards dress' (Komisarjevsky, 1931, p. 135). However, 'historicism', with its emphasis on history above all else and its claims to precise recreation of the historic past, was actually being staged on a grand scale from 1823. This was when the actor-manager Charles Kemble produced Shakespeare's *King John* with costumes designed by J.R. Planché, previously a writer of melodramas and other popular theatre forms, now a herald and Fellow of the Society of Antiquaries. Planché was 'determined that the year would see the most accurate reproductions of mediaeval clothes that the theatre had ever seen' (De Marly, 1982, p. 69). He studied contemporary manuscripts and surviving statues to ensure the correctness of the costumes and published his designs in a book, *Costumes of Shakespeare's Historical Tragedy of King John* even before opening night. The book reproduces his designs with notes on sources and colours. There are no notes on fabrics or construction which was plainly not his concern. The actors are recorded as finding their costumes odd and being worried about their reception (Booth, 1981, p. 44), but when the play opened it was a great success and the costumes were applauded.

The avowal of absolute accuracy in Kemble's *King John* must be seen as a precursor to the series of 'spectacular' and allegedly historically accurate stagings of plays by Shakespeare which followed in the later nineteenth century, all huge in scale, designed both to entertain and inform, reflecting the Victorian taste for richly detailed panoramic art which extended through all classes. Writes Booth,

> If there is any age in which visual taste has been less abstract, it is the Victorian. The general public and the theatre audience included in that public, craved concrete images of historical and contemporary reality in the book and magazine illustrations, prints, magic lantern slides, panoramas and paintings they

saw. Legend and history had to be actualised and made visually familiar and accessible.

(ibid., p. 14)

This pictorialism was taken so far that sometimes well known paintings would be incorporated as tableaux, for example, Douglas Jerrold's play, *Rent Day* (1832) began with a staged version of David Wilkie's similarly named picture.

Even then, there were those who did not approve. H.G. Tomlin wrote in 1840, '"correctness of costume" was a phrase invented to excuse pageantry' (Nicoll, 1930, p. 41) and Hollander plainly agrees, writing 'The success of *King John* made "historical authenticity" a fad, and all spectacular effects thereafter tended to be "historical" and have programme notes about their "correctness."… the public was, however, also being trained simultaneously to think of the whole past as spectacular and of all spectacle as authentic' (Hollander, 1975, p. 291).

The same play, *King John*, was taken up by another actor-manager determined to recreate scenes from history, Charles Keane, again using Planché's designs, first in 1846 in New York and then from 1851 at his own theatre, the Royal Princess. Keane worked with the costume historian, Charles Hamilton Smith and his daughter and assistant, Emma, to develop Kemble's production. It is recorded that Emma did further research using Planché's sources and found many more knights' costumes than featured in the play so she encouraged Kean to add more characters – which he happily did! According to Schoch, this led to a kind of theatre more concerned with accurate re-enactment of events from English history than with interpreting the original play and its characters as written (Schoch, 1998, p. 79). Comments from actors of the time support this idea, one complaining that he had been cast 'for my damned archaeological figure' rather than his acting talent (ibid., p. 89) and some critics despised Keane's tampering with the play. However, middle-class audiences were delighted with these so-called pictorial dramas and flocked to see them.

Throughout the 1850s Kean created a series of epic literal realizations of particular worlds, rebuilding ancient Athens for his version of Shakespeare's *A Midsummer Night's Dream*' (1856) peopled by 'scores of faeries' (De Marly, 1982, p. 79) and recreating Mediaeval London for his *Richard II* with six hundred costumed extras. The emphasis on education as well as entertainment allowed audiences to feel that they could enjoy the visual feast while learning about a 'real' episode in history. According to De Marly, 'Kean's vision was infected by the Industrial Age and his sets seemed as big as railway stations, which meant that the impact of the costume was reduced' (De Marly, 1982, p. 79), but even within such a scale, the sheer numbers created a startling scene. Evidently though, period shape was a real problem for the women. In a wonderful portrait photograph of Mr. and Mrs. Charles Keane, as *Lord and Lady Macbeth* (1858), she wears a kind of striped mediaeval robe but clearly cannot dispense with her crinoline. 'Throughout the history of historical costume, every generation of actors (sic) even the naturalists at the end of the nineteenth century, dressed themselves according to *their own* conception of a certain epoch,' wrote Komisarjevsky (Komisarjevsky, 1931, p. 69).

As the popularity continued, actor-managers vied to outdo each other in scale and effects. Henry Irving's version of *Macbeth*, staged in 1888 but set in the eleventh century, took a month of research in the British and the Victoria and Albert Museums by the antiquarian and designer, Cattermole, in order to design the four hundred and eight costumes needed. Costumes on such a scale were too much for individuals makers or even theatre wardrobes and hiring houses began to spring up in this era. Nathan's, for example, was started by a tailor in 1790 and by 1845 had become a hiring house calling itself 'Court and Theatrical Costumiers and Fancy Dress Makers'.

In 1910, another impresario, Henry Beerbohm Tree produced *Henry VIII*, designed by Percy Macquoid, with nearly four hundred costumes made by B.J. Simmons, Historical Costumiers. Parker, the assistant producer, told the *Daily Express* (27 July 1910) that 'we have ransacked every authority and obtained the most astonishing exactitude' (Booth, 1981, p. 132). Such authority included books, historical portraits and effigies but did not seem to involve any investigation of real period clothing. Several photographs of the production remain, including a magnificent portrait of Tree as Wolsey in his glistening robes and long train, one leather gloved hand held aloft. The robe was made from a silk specially woven in Lyons of a specially chosen red so bright as to stand out from all the other costumes (ibid., p. 142). The photograph of Anne Boleyn's coronation scene shows over a hundred extras crammed onto the stage wearing acres of velvet and white fur as well as dressed dummies at the back of the stage and more figures painted on the backdrop. To modern western eyes, the stage looks crowded and uncomfortable but the Victorians enjoyed it hugely.

The Victorian quest for accuracy required the costumes to follow the interpretative vision of its pioneering antiquarian researchers such as Planché, Hamilton Smith, Godwin and Alma-Tadema and showed scant regard for period cutting or appropriate fabric. However, they made-up for this in scale and detail. As styles changed, the twentieth century saw a loosening of Victorian realism into the varied and eclectic styles we see today. An essay written in 1941 by the American director and designer, Robert Edmund Jones, reveals a viewpoint on the workings of stage costume totally at one with his era and his position as a pioneer in the 'New Stagecraft' which espoused a unified simplicity and symbolism over complicated realism onstage,

A stage costume is a creation of the theatre. Its quality is purely theatrical and taken outside the theatre, it loses its magic at once. It dies as a plant dies when uprooted. Why this should be I do not know. But here is one more proof of the eternal enchantment which every worker in the theatre knows and feels. The actual materials of which a stage costume is made count for very little. Outwardly it may be nothing more than an arrangement of shabby velvets and cheap glass 'glits'. I remember Graham-Robertson's description of a costume worn by Ellen Terry as Fair Rosamund:

'She looked her loveliest in the rich gown of her first entrance, a wonderful Rosettian effect of soft gold and glowing color veiled in black, her masses of bright hair in a net of gold and golden hearts embroidered on her robe. ... The foundation was an old pink gown, worn with stage service and retrieved for the occasion from the rag-bag. The mysterious veiling was the coarsest and cheapest black net, the glory of hair through golden meshes was a bag of gold tinsel stuffed with crumpled paper, and the broidered hearts were cut out of gold paper and gummed on. The whole costume would have been dear at ten shillings and was one of the finest stage dresses that I have ever seen.

The wardrobes of our costume-establishments are crammed with hundreds of just such costumes. I can see them now, with their gilt and their fustian and their tinsel and their bands of sham ermine. ... in the theatre a miracle takes place. The dramatic imagination transforms them. They become dynamic. They become a surprise, an adventure, a reminder of things we once knew and now remember with joy. The actors wearing them become ambassadors from that bright other world behind the footlights.

(Jones, 1941, p. 93)

For Jones, it is the conjuring of the stage through deception and deft use of technology that is the stuff of theatre and he rejects both the historical reality of the Victorians and the material reality of the Elizabethans. In the 1950s and 60s the influential designer, John Bury, who worked first with Joan Littlewood at Stratford East and later with Peter Hall at the Royal Shakespeare Company, described another kind of reality in an essay entitled *Against Falsehood*, written around 1965. He wrote,

I wanted to use the real materials, not transmute everything into the fairy-tale unreality of canvas and scenepaint ... I wanted to take the fancy dress out of costumes. But attempts to produce a 'timeless' costume were failures-I think you nearly always end up with variants on the spaceman or superman-with-a-helmet image. What we try to do now is remain true to the period in silhouette, but by use of tailoring techniques, choice of materials, modern parallels, to reduce the historical identity down to essentials and to create a costume which is truly functional in telling us as much as possible what we want to know about the wearer. Again, in costume, it is essential that approximation and indication is avoided and the image must be precise and organic-in fact they must be clothes, not costumes.

(Bury in Payne, 1974, p. 36)

In total contrast to this, the most remarkable quest for historical accuracy onstage in the recent past emerged at the Globe under the actor-director, Mark Rylance and his resident designer or 'master of clothing, properties and hangings at Shakespeare's Globe', Jenny Tiramani, between 1997 and 2000 (see interview and Chapter 3). Tiramani's and Rylance's aim was to use 'recreated clothing rather than theatrical costumes' as part of an experiment into 'original practices'. Tiramani believes these original practices are necessary so that today's audiences can witness what the Elizabethans really wore. She abhors what Hollander describes as the 'whole fake history of costume, almost entirely composed of stage conventions, [which] has come to exist, if rather nebulously, in the public consciousness' (Hollander, 1975, p. 303). Instead she prefers a more accurate, although probably much more unfamiliar, stage picture. This accuracy owes much to the research of the costume historian, Janet Arnold, who, in the 1950s began to examine and draw as many surviving historical clothes as she could find, in a quest to really understand historical dress. Her books are referred to in Chapter 1 and her research has probably extended our understanding of what people wore in the past more than any other person. The costumes worn at the Globe in plays that are realized according to such 'original practices', then, will be modelled on an original, and cut according to period methods. As far as possible they will be made by hand from the correct fabrics and dyed with the correct dyes. Escolme describes these practices as 'historically researched *restrictions*' (Brown, 2008, p. 408). For example, not only was everything made according to period cut, there were no modern concession such as quick change fastenings or lycra underwear. Tiramani, in conversation with Irene Cottis, felt that 'this was the most useful way of finding a group understanding of the Elizabethan world' (Eynat-Confina, 2000, p. 100).

> To that end they used 'natural' rather than man-made fabrics-silk, linen and wool, natural dyes such as madder (reds and browns), indigo (blues) and saffron (yellow) … hand embroidery … authentically constructed linen underwear, points for fastening rather than zips, careful hand sewing everywhere: all, as far as possible, made using the patterns and techniques of sixteenth century tailors … the underclothes and shirts are hand washed frequently, because linen is absorbent and actors tend to sweat: but the sumptuous outer garments in silks and velvets are deliberately not washed or dry-cleaned but beaten … and sprinkled with sweet herbs … these outer garments are also, in proper Elizabethan manner, used by other actors in later plays. … the first serious attempt was for *Henry V* in 1997 when a team of seamstresses, all female unsurprisingly, constructed in a mere eight weeks forty five Elizabethan outfits, including underwear and the all-important hats … the fabrics were organically dyed, the ruffs made of yards of cartridge pleated linen, were starched and held in place only by pins, the doublets were laced to the hose with points, the underwear was linen and shoes handmade.
> (Eynat-Confino, 2000, p. 103)

According to Tiramani, most actors enjoyed this way of working. There is no doubt that it took time for them to find ways to achieve any necessary quick changes, by leaving some fastenings undone, for example, but they liked the sense of changing, with as much material authenticity as possible, into the era in which the play was written. Tiramani, quoted here in interview, describes how Stephen Fry was so enamoured of his costume that on Jonathan Ross' TV show he had to be coaxed into talking about anything else. The audiences, though, did not always find such clothes so comfortable. The clothes on the Globe stage, 'did not conform to the taste for the subtle and the muted, characteristic of much late twentieth-century theatre design. These clothes refused to signify the pre-consumerist functionality or faded grandeur offered by many heritage sites. They were newly made clothes ...' (Brown, 2008, p. 409). The unfamiliarity and lack of stage conventionality of such clothes meant that their reception was mixed and wrongly identified. One early critic even referred to 'plastic armour' (Eynat-Confino, 2000, p. 104). Cottis, on examining some early press notices in 1999 wonders if the authentic costuming was even noticeable and whether such effort is 'worth it'. Escolme's article, using later plays performed under similar conditions, contradicts this idea. The effect she describes is that the experiment made its audience look at a different kind of costuming, a kind of costuming that audiences today find unfamiliar. Escolme suggests that the costume style was akin to the style of playing that she calls an 'honourable showing off'. She describes Rylance playing *Cleopatra*, 'The effect was of an actor standing up for as well as standing in for his character, very different from that produced by the naturalistic actor in a space intensely focused by stage lighting.' These new brightly coloured richly decorated costumes disturb both a modern convention of how costume should perform onstage and a modern assumption about what clothes looked like in the early modern period. As costume, they are anything but invisible.

AN INTERVIEW WITH SIMON ANNAND

Aoife Monks

Introduction

Simon Annand is a British photographer who has been making images of theatre productions onstage, and off, for the past thirty years. Annand's work covers a breadth of theatre forms and also pictures a range of moments within the theatre process. He takes production photos for performances onstage and in rehearsal; he documents costumes for the Royal Shakespeare Company and the Globe Theatre (photographing actors backstage in between their scenes); he takes actors' headshots; and he has also sustained a thirty-year project of photographing actors in their dressing rooms before the performance has begun.

This project, entitled *The Half*, is named for the shorthand used by the theatre profession to describe the thirty-minute period where actors are required to be in their dressing rooms before the curtain goes up. As Michael Kustow acknowledges in the introduction to the book in which these images are published: 'the half is a tense and vulnerable time [...] This journey, from person to persona, is a private one; it is rare for a photographer to be admitted' (Kustow, 2008, p. ix). These images function as an archive of theatrical production on the main stages of British theatre over the past thirty years. Some actors, now familiar from their star status in cinema and television, appear shockingly young in these images, recorded by Annand while they prepare to play one of their first-stage roles in one of their first professional costumes, later reappearing as old hands, their experience etched into their bodies and demeanour.

Annand's photographs do remarkable work in exposing the peculiar qualities of dressing-room life and tell us a lot about the relationship between actors and their costumes. At first glance, Annand's pictures seem invested in the image of the virtuoso, offering us the charisma, individuality and spirituality of the actor. Performers are often pictured alone averting their gaze from the camera, suggesting that dressing-up in costume may involve forms of thinking and inner change, as well as outer transformation. The psychological activity of acting is at the forefront here, giving a sense of performance as a serious and potentially risky activity.

At the same time, as Annand suggests in this interview, the actor's work getting dressed backstage can also be read as a mundane activity in his photographs: dressing-up is part of the actor's job and costumes sometimes appear as little more than work clothes. Even when picturing the mundane, however, these photographs offer an oddly melancholic sense of the stakes involved in acting, the precariousness (economic and emotional) and vulnerability that structure the actor's experience. Kustow acknowledges: 'the images' underlying gravity, even when the actors are apparently letting off steam, playing cards or the guitar, or sleeping' (Kustow, 2008, p. ix). This gravity may explain the litter of objects that surround these actors in their dressing rooms, the ways in which performers shore up their existence with postcards, props, first-night gifts and even possibly objects of superstition: talismans that must be appeased and maintained to ward off the vulnerabilities of exposing oneself to the stage and the gaze of the audience.

Nonetheless, Annand's images also tell us something about the fun involved in dressing-up: the pleasures and fantasies that emerge from applying make-up, warming up, and 'playing'. While many of the images are of individuals, we also see actors in communal changing-rooms laughing, fooling about, or offering each other comfort and support. We see the individual work of performers against the backdrop of professional structures of identity and community. Dressing-up at the theatre, it turns out, involves a lot more than changing clothes (see Figure 2).

Figure 2 Daniel Day-Lewis backstage at *The Futurists*, National Theatre, 1986
Source: Simon Annand, photograph, by permission of Simon Annand, featured in *The Half*
(Faber and Faber: 2010).

S = Simon Annand, A = Aoife Monks

A: Why did you begin working on *The Half?* What attracted you to photographing actors backstage?

S: I became a photographer when I was working at the bar at the Lyric, Hammersmith and I was so bored with what I was doing, that when Yuri Lyubimov was commissioned to do *Crime and Punishment* (1983) I asked could I take pictures of his rehearsals and he let me in every day for six weeks. Then five years later I wrote to Jonathan Miller and said 'how about having a resident photographer in the Old Vic?' So he took me on board. In the meantime, I had been doing dressing room pictures as a way of learning, meeting the actors to learn their point of view, since they're on the front line after the director's gone: they're what theatre is all about. That was my education.

A: Were you learning from them how to take better pictures, or was taking pictures a way to learn about the theatre?

S: Both. The pictures were a means to an end. When I photographed Griff Rhys Jones onstage in *Charley's Aunt* (1983), everything he was doing was getting a huge laugh. So I bought my first camera and I took a picture of what was probably his biggest laugh, pouring the milk into his father-in-law's top hat. And I asked him if I could take a picture of him from offstage, on his entrance, which got another big laugh. And then I just thought 'let's go to the dressing room' and discovered a total contrast, because while he was playing a very ebullient character onstage, in the dressing room there was an atmosphere of melancholy, and I thought that this was something I could explore. So I kept on doing it. I was making it up as I went along, but I knew I wanted to avoid what you would normally think was a dressing room photograph: people putting on lipstick or eye make-up or something. I was more interested in getting inside the head of the man or woman who happens to be an actor, who might be famous, who is basically dressing-up every evening. It was showing that theatre work must be made and repeated every day, the actors have to go through it, there's no escape and no bluffing …

A: You went backstage to learn something about the theatre and something about acting. I'm wondering what you learned and whether that changed over time?

S: I used to put them on a pedestal, which I don't anymore, because I see acting more and more as their job. The point at which you're seeing them during the show's run is important. I tend to try and do the photograph towards the end of the run.

A: Why is that?

S: Partly because they're so used to what they're doing onstage, but also because they've absorbed the character day after day. For example, Charles Dance when he was doing *Good* at the Donmar (1999), I think I photographed him in the last week, and what fascinated him about playing a Nazi was very much in evidence, and ten days later when he'd had a holiday he would go back to being the affable Englishman, Charles Dance. I'm not trying to make people look like actors, I'm looking for why this person's interested in that part and I don't ask many questions.

A: What's very exciting about the pictures is the opportunity to think about actors as workers who dress up. It's a lovely way of describing what actors do. I'm wondering if there's a variety of different relationships to costume that you've come across?

S: It varies. One extreme is that actors find their performance because of an item of costume: the green shoes, the red umbrella, whatever it is. And the other extreme is that they're having to fight against a costume designer's concepts and it doesn't help their performance. You tend to see that a lot in opera.

A: Do you come across actors having to technically master wearing the costume?

S: Certainly if you've got big costumes and a raked stage. And complex timing as well. I was thinking today, for example, in the rehearsal [of Jez Butterworth's *Mojo*, currently playing at the Harold Pinter Theatre], that the actors were extraordinarily strong at this point in the process, partly because of what they were wearing. It seemed to me that they had chosen really specific '50s clothes, the jeans or the shoes or ties or things to help them get into the character. I asked the costume person at half-time, 'Are they all wearing their costumes?' And she said, no, they weren't. It's curious: they'd all had haircuts, and the difference I was seeing from when I photographed them two and a half weeks before was huge. I went in there and I was just amazed just by the haircuts. They all had this spiv stuff going on and it was amazing. I mean the really clever actors use their costumes to help them work.

A: Can I ask you about make-up? You have some beautiful pictures of actors making-up their hands and I'm wondering why you like those moments?

S: The way people use their hands anyway is interesting and if you're actually making-up your hands to be the hands of somebody else I think it's lovely. I'm taking the pictures when you're seeing the two things together. When they go on the stage you're just seeing the fictional character's hands …

A: You also have those photos of actors smoking. I wonder whether there's something about the activity that makes the actor absorbed in a task and makes them interesting to look at?

S: Yeah, they may be concentrating or they may be trying to distract themselves, so it goes back to the idea of whatever they've done during the day, as a father, a mother, friend, they have to come into the theatre, and whatever they're feeling they have to either use it, or contain it. It's one or the other, every day, every single day, towards what the character is onstage. And so all these tasks might help them to do that. I mean I took pictures of Rory Kinnear the other day, I let the mundane be the theme, so I just took pictures of him eating and phoning and reading, which are mundane tasks, which I think, given that he's playing Iago, might be a way for him to distract himself. He said he threw on the costume, he said he didn't want to think about it too much, he threw on the costume right at the end and then walked on and it kept him fresh, which is quite the opposite of what someone like Michael Sheen does, of getting in the zone, of spending quite a long time getting ready before he walks on the stage. But they're equally brilliant actors and their performances are equally good.

A: You have talked before about being more interested in photographing actors before they go onstage, rather than after, because of the intense focus beforehand.

S: Yes, it's the wind-up of the springs, because once they come offstage they just want to go to the pub …

A: What is the difference between photographing actors in rehearsal and backstage and onstage: they may be in costume but are they in costume in different ways?

S: In rehearsal they're developing their relationship to costume. That's why I attend rehearsals; to just let it seep into my mind without having to make too many decisions about where I'm going to take a photograph, so I'm not scared shitless by just turning up at a dress rehearsal and seeing how impressive it looks. But the thing about costume is that, whether it's theatre or fashion, it's the flesh and bones that are inside it that matter. When I did the Viktor and Rolf fashion show in the Tuilleries in Paris, it was just alarming the degree to which the job of the women was to make themselves as neutral and abstracted from their own personalities in the costume, even though they might be really intelligent or beautiful, and it was heartbreaking to see that. Of course, in theatre it's completely the opposite. Photographing somebody backstage in mid-performance is somewhere halfway: they're not on the stage, they're not fully in the fictional character, they revert to the potential of being themselves. My job, when I'm shooting them on the stage, is to make a big show look like itself. So I've got to try to understand what the writers are doing, so the difference between a Strindberg, Chekhov and Ibsen, and what the director's trying to achieve, and what the actors are trying to achieve, and how to make that show look like itself. The dressing room is different for me because I'm not taking pictures of other people's work, it's actually my own work, so the way I'm feeling that day comes into play as well, whereas I can't afford for that to happen quite so much when I'm taking pictures of productions.

A: I'm interested by the vulnerability that you find backstage: that seems to be the quality that you're attracted to?

S: My definition of vulnerability is someone who's open to emotion. It doesn't make them melancholic or weak but they're open to it and where it's going to take them. In my photograph of Glenn Close in her dressing room (2001), she's 92% Blanche, because she's made-up that way, but she's still 8% Glenn Close because she's not onstage. Vulnerability is really important for an actor, because their instrument is within themselves, and the moment they go into the half hour before the show, it's really at its greatest. And it's very photogenic. For me, the dressing room work is like street photography.

A: What is it you're trying to capture?

S: It goes back to the thing of seeing anybody, whether you're a dancer, a writer, a director, a sculptor or a painter, they're men and women first, that's what I mean about street photography. Everyone on the street, you don't actually know what they do, they're just men and women, you might go around Paris, taking pictures like they did in French photography. So when I get into the dressing room, I'm not trying to make them look like actors. When I go and see Anthony Hopkins doing Lear (1986), I'm not fooling myself that I'm seeing Lear, I'm watching a man called Anthony who's a Welshman etc, who's chosen to play Lear, that's what I'm watching.

A: Have you found a difference in photographing opera singers or dancers backstage, to actors?

S: Costumes are so much more heightened in dance and opera that they don't go into huge internalizations, because they have a lot of things to do; they have to put things on. Like Hanna Waddingham's work: she came to prominence as the Lady of the Lake in *Spamalot* and she played the Wicked Witch in the *Wizard of Oz*, she was Kate in *Kiss Me Kate*. And she's one of the most fun people to photograph. She just loves putting on as much costume as possible. She's very good looking, but she's chosen a part (in *Wicked*) which trashes her beauty, and I find that interesting. So, the more interesting your costume is, the more the actor has got to pull it off. Even being ugly is quite a challenge.

A: I wanted to ask about the term 'craft'. Do you think of photography as a craft?

S: Unfortunately, if it is a craft, then I'm useless at it because I hardly know anything about cameras. I've had the same camera for ten years, I never change it. My pictures are made in my head, in the relationship between my head and my heart. When I'm taking a picture it's like writing a text in one twenty-fifth of a second. The craft of the photographer is relatively simple. I don't think it's nearly as complicated as learning to dance or to paint. It's the same with costume. You've got to give the audience their money's worth, but it's the person inside the costume that counts. The actors, the flesh and blood come first. I think they're on the front line.

AN INTERVIEW WITH ALEX RIGG

Ali Maclaurin

Introduction

Alex Rigg, an artist who refuses to be categorized, has been making live events since 1982 with his company Oceanallover. These can take any form, but often take place outside and involve a mix of performance, music and non-naturalistic costume. Alex leads the whole process including devising, design and construction of all kinds. According to the website, 'If there a common thread to the style and content of these events then it must be a strong need to push boundaries around, to set foot on unknown soil and generally to play with our concepts of art outside its accepted form' (www.oceanallover.co.uk, accessed 13/12/13). He is currently working on a project entitled Polleniser which looks at the battle for blue between indigo and woad in Europe (see Figure 3).

Figure 3　Alex Rigg in *Feather Mammy* at Shambellie House, National Museum of Costume, 2009
Source: Xander Gisby, photograph, by permission of Alex Rigg.

AR = Alex Rig, AJM = Ali Maclaurin

AJM: I'd like to start with a quote. You write in a document for *Polleniser* that your work contains ' … a continued play between costumed exuberance and performative rigour'. Can you just unpick what you mean by that?

AR: So….. in first year at art college you are encouraged to try lots of different things. I tried as much as possible and one of my tutors said, 'Well, you'll be fine Alex, once you decide what it is you want to do' and I thought, 'Naaah, that's not right' so I just carried on doing, *doing* whatever I thought was needed. If I have an idea then I use what medium or what material or what artistic form it requires without being restricted.

AJM: What do you mean by an idea?

AR: So, don't exclude any possibilities at all, it might be just to meet someone and chat, there's that kind of freedom of approach at the beginning. Obviously, it has to get narrowed down fairly quickly because of practicalities. But then after that, whatever you do you have got to do it well. So that means if it's going to involve visuals then they have to be well conceived and well made so they're good up close. I'm quite happy to work with rubbish like bits of scrap, so it's not that it has to be perfectly manicured all the time but if you are doing something that's meant to be perfectly manicured it has to *be* perfectly manicured. That's a fine art process, it's a useful training. If you are going to do something there is honestly of materials. I don't try and make something look different from what it is, although that's not very theatrical, I know. Actually it helps in my performance practice – if you're working with a broom, then it's a broom, or if you are making period costume then make it properly and then the same technique in performance. I am interested in things that are quite rigorous in their intellectual approach so there's a very strong work ethic which has to run through the whole thing with an emphasis on access to personal content during performance.

AJM: When you say personal, do you mean to each of the people involved in performance or personal to you?

AR: Both. I'm not a fan of people divulging horrible intimate secrets, either performer or public. I don't mean that, I mean emotional content. If I'm feeling strongly about something or if the intention of the work is to have a particular emotion in it, to try and access that emotion. So it's using some kind of performance technique which gives you a strong back foot to stand on but then adding a content which is much more emotional and wobbly. An analogue is between consciousness and unconsciousness, or order and chaos. There's a line which I try and find in my performance work and then I walk along it. I'm quite happy to drop off either side but not to fall without trace.

AJM: So is that line concerned with the second part of the quote where you refer to 'difficult work presented within a visually arresting skin'?

AR: Yes, it's using the costume and live music and any kind of visual things as an access point, so that once the audience is drawn in, what they are actually watching, if you took away that skin, is quite difficult work. So that means that although it's difficult work, as long as I'm careful about things like explicit content it's accessible to anybody including children because there is this other layer. It's a sort of disguise for them so they can watch the pretty thing, or the alarming thing … and then wonder later what it was all about.

AJM: How did that develop, that way of working?

AR: The first theatre stuff was quite conventional, youth theatre, stuff like that. Then, after studying archaeological drawing I was working in Orkney. I started doing sets for amateur drama and I just did what I wanted. I tried some fairly odd things. They are quite broad-minded up there!

AJM: And how did that move into costume?

AR: Well, I was designing costume and set for Shakespeare, not particularly well, I don't think, although the sets were more interesting than the costumes. Then I came down to art college in Glasgow and at that point in 1998 any companies that were brought into the city were obliged by Glasgow City Council to give a workshop which was available with subsidy to students. I went to lots of workshops with lots of different dancers particularly. I did a lot of butoh and related things, [with] Masaki Iwana and Lindsay John. Through Lindsay and through Angus Farquar (now director of the large-scale performance company, NVA) and Test Department I got involved with performing and costume for big outdoor events and performances and then I started making my own work. I was still in college so I had a visual idea of it as well as a physical idea. I continued making my own work and work for other people, calling it design. I did teach a module at the RSAMD (now the Royal Conservatoire of Scotland) for the contemporary practice course for a couple of years also called design, where I actually got them to design and make their own performances.

AJM: How did your work with costume develop?

AR: At first the costume was very minimal because the body was the ultimate form of expression so we wore as little as possible …… hardly anything, in fact! And, then, I did the charity shopping version for a while, old suits and that kind of thing. Probably only in the last four years or so, I have started getting seriously into sewing. So last year I worked with Scottish Opera, well, not *with* them, they just let me go and be a lackey for a few weeks while they were working on *The Magic Flute* and *Hansel and Gretel.* I was making a project for myself, the *Last Supper* which was based in the same century, the same end of the century, so I was going home and making period costume, well, period-related costume and then working with them on the real McCoy, sewing on buttons and stuff.

AJM: So does that mean that every project, then, develops in a different way?

AJM: Yes, and depending on what I've got in my shed. So I've got a lot of this non-woven geotextile, which is fab, and I haven't run out of things to do with it yet.

AJM: It looks like stiffener, like Vilene …

AR: No, it's not. They use it for gardening and road building.

AJM: It's almost like paper, paper you can sew.

AR: Basically it's plastic felt. There are lots of different kinds. I've got lots of it and I'm working my way through it because it can do big visual shapes. I also have some pretty hefty sewing machines, old treadle powered leather machines, that sort of stuff.

AJM: The costumes have a very specific shape … is that to do with that fabric? They look as if they are either pleated or layered.

AR: Ah, yes, to go back in the story then, in 1995, Lindsey John attempted to start Glasgow Carnival as part of the West End Festival. He's from the Caribbean, went to school in Trinidad. We went out there and had a look at how they organized themselves and looked at the way costume is there. Costume there is sculptural, each costume is a piece of art, it's not related to everyday clothes. They have some very big sculptural pieces which is what we were looking at. I made stuff for Glasgow carnival for several years running and I found a pile of that geo-textile in a skip. It was a stage set which got dumped at the back of Tramway [a performance venue in Glasgow] so I chopped it up and made that kind of gill-like costume and then last year I thought I'd make some more.

AJM: So the costume developed from the material and your experience in Trinidad? … or could you have made it with something else?

AR: Yes, I could. I used it because it didn't cost anything and it fitted the idea. It could have worked with canvas.

AJM: Could you say a bit more about how you made these and why they developed in the way they did?

AR: Again, coming from a fine-art background, it seems just as valid to reach for a staple-gun, glue-gun or pop-riveter as it does to head for the sewing machine. I found the material and then found a way to work with it, in that order.

AJM: And do you ever get others to make costumes for your pieces?

AR: I try to make everything myself … great idea but seldom a reality. If time is restricted then I will work on a prototype and hand it over to a making team to make multiples. Occasionally I need to give the design directly to a maker, but this is fraught with difficulties and so I try to avoid it. Usually ends up being disappointing … my own fault!

AJM: How do you start a piece?

AR: I do a lot of drawing. I also start making, but separately from drawing. For years, I just did drawing and then got on with it but recently I've been making little scraps of things and trying ideas out; seeing how things stick together, or what that shape looks like when you cut it out.

AJM: So does the costume evolve along with the work?

AR: Well, there are several approaches and it entirely depends who I am working with. Personally where I get the chance I like to make a costume, to rehearse somebody and then not give them the costume till just before the show. The costumes are very awkward so they are constrained. Performers agree that they will attempt the choreography and the work is then a struggle.

AJM: So you want that struggle?

AR: Yes, I do.

AJM: And does that mean that sometimes the choreography looks really different from what you designed?

AR: Yes, intentionally so. Although there are exceptions to that, like with the gilled skirts we were talking about, they only work if you rehearse in them because they need to look graceful, but that is an exception. Quite a lot of time I like to give people things fresh, like Joey hasn't worn that mask before and he's got to sing in it. [Joey is sitting behind us rehearsing on a harmonium with a large beaked leather mask beside him waiting to be put on.]

AJM: That's so different from theatre. What do you like about not putting people in the costume before the performance itself? What do you gain?

AR: Personally, I'm learning about it in front of the audience which is an interesting process. And what they see isn't an accomplishment, it's something else. It's not about a gymnastic achievement.

AJM: So it's not about doing something as well as you possibly can?

AR: Yes, it is, but you have to do it in a blindfold or some other simple adjustment so that people are so busy psychologically that they don't have time to worry about what they look like.

AJM: When you're performing in your costume, is there any element of playing a character or is it more about costume as moving sculpture?

AR: It depends on the performance. I quite often have amateur and professional people mixed up in one performance. I have my own cast, then I have some students, or retired ladies, and the training they get is different. I have to give them much more fundamental instruction. I give them a series of exercises that lead directly into what I want without too much time for them to think, 'How am I going to do that? I have to, because then they have got this thing I gave them to do and there is a lot to think about. Then afterwards the common reaction is, 'I see what you mean'. So they have to do it in order to understand what it is.

AJM: And are they very physical instructions?

AR: Yes. There are two ways. Depending on the group, I give them simple choreographic instructions like move from there to there. It might involve some physical moves. It might involve specific actions with the costume or set and then on top of that there are a series of emotional landscapes that I construct for them. They're sort of dream images but not a dream where it's all floaty; more the kind of dream where you wake up in it and you are wide awake and some very strange things are happening to you. So they have got to deal with that and the costume and the other people.

AJM: A lot of the time you work outside. Is that important to what the work looks like?

AR: That's been a deliberate effort to avoid authority. It's just sneaking off and doing things in a field because you don't have to ask particular people permission. Whereas in the gallery system and the established theatre world you have to ask, 'Please can I put this on?' and they say, 'Oh, no, I don't think so.' Theatre space is such a specific thing that being outside appears easier to students initially but it's not. When you go outside to rehearse for the first time concentration just disappears. It's like if you do a drawing indoors and then you look at it in daylight it looks awful. You have to work much harder.

AJM: The way you talk about it the choice to go outside was a political one, not a visual one.

AR: Yes.

AJM: Is it different inside?

AR: It's not often inside. I did Al Seed's show, *Last Orders* a couple of years ago as an actor and also designed the show. I really enjoyed it. I'd like to do more of that.

AJM: Do you repeat events?

AR: It doesn't happen very often but that's not deliberate. This show tonight is a transmutation of something I've done once and will do again. We have a show called *The Tide Machine* which we did several times each. I built two different versions and did them four times each.

AJM: And were they very different?

AR: Yes, because if you are working outside you have to adapt to the space you are in and if you don't it doesn't work so you have to change it.

AJM: Do you like the fact that it changes?

AR: I like the idea of doing a run, I think, but I know I would get bored.

AJM: Do you make your costumes to last?

AR: I do, actually. They're made from a pretty hefty thread and they're quite chunky. That's partly aesthetic.

AJM: So to do with the look not the practicalities?

AR: It is just the idea that things need to be strong. Maybe it's from my dad or something. I make buildings sometimes. Doing the willow stuff, the metal frames have to be picked up by cranes without falling apart so they have to be pretty strong.

AJM: If stuff gets damaged in performance, do you mend it?

AR: It depends. I quite like things getting worn, but I don't like them looking unintentionally ripped. Wear is OK, but things looking as if they are falling apart because they weren't made very well is not acceptable.

AJM: There's a political dimension to your work; how does it work with the way you use costume?

AR: Well, for example, thinking about a new work, I read that in the Americas if a plantation owner wanted to buy a slave, they exchanged indigo pound for pound with flesh …so now I'm thinking about that. I think work has to cross boundaries and be inclusive, not in grant application speak but in reality so that it's socialist but not in a political way; anti-nationalist and anti-capitalist but not making a big statement about it, just because it is. The idea that the only people who can afford an orchestra are people with a lot of money gets my back up.

AJM: So it's similar to why you want to perform outside.

AR: Yes, you need to have something to work against.

Chapter 3

Virtuosity, Craft and Technique in the Work of Costume

Aoife Monks

When Samuel Pepys visits the King's playhouse in 1665, while it is undergoing renovations and is lying empty, he makes his way backstage to satisfy his curiosity about the workings of the theatre that he so loves. Here, Pepys is confronted by the peculiar mix of objects and costumes that form the detritus of leftover performance. Pepys has a remarkable emotional response to this 'stuff', seeing:

> [H]ere a wooden-leg, there a ruff, here a hobby-horse, there a crown [that] would make a man split himself to see with laughing. And particularly Lacy's wardrobe, and Shotrell's. But then again, to think how fine they show on the stage by candle-light, and how poor things they are to look at now too near hand, is not pleasant at all. The machines are fine and the paintings very pretty.
>
> (Pepys, 1665, n.p.)

Pepys' initial laughter at the absurdity of the unused props and costumes backstage turns into melancholy. His experience is one of discomfort and loss, betraying a sense of disappointment at the mundane and material qualities of the things that it takes to make the theatre happen. In its *memento mori* structures, we might even go so far as to see his response as peculiarly of the mid 17th century: just as these objects once seemed alive and fine by candlelight, they now appear lifeless, their magic having evaporated once the performance has ended. In the litter of objects backstage, Pepys is confronted by the evanescent qualities of the theatre event itself.

Pepys' disappointment emerges from his confrontation with the theatre event as a historically situated set of material practices, bound to the time and space of the stage. To be faced with the mundane reality of this stuff is to undergo a discomfiting moment of alienation. In this, we might imagine Pepys to have suffered the experience of the 'uncanny', an experience Sigmund Freud defined three centuries later as 'nothing new or alien, but something which is familiar and old-established in the mind and which has become alienated from it only through the process of repression' (Freud, 2003, p. 148). In other words, Pepys is faced with the knowledge of the materiality that underpins the theatrical illusion, knowledge that he has repressed while watching performances in the auditorium.

The fact that it's the empty costumes of the actors Lacy and Shotrell that particularly amuse him in their peculiarity is important here – these costumes, hanging lifeless backstage confront him with their incompleteness, containing the trace of the bodies they once appeared to constitute. In doing so, they remind Pepys of the work that Lacy and Shotrell had to undertake in order to produce the fantastical and fine bodies that gave him so much pleasure *and* the work of the tailor, seamstress, weaver, dyer etc. in producing these clothes. Pepys experiences a mismatch between the appearance of these costumes onstage and their presence backstage, so that, even while he looks behind the scenes 'to see the inside of the stage and all the tiring-rooms and machines', the costumes that he confronts don't seem to be willing to reveal to him the mysteries of how the illusion was really made.

We might want to ask why it is that costumes in particular inspire such discomfort in Pepys, to investigate why they have such an uncanny affect. Pepys seems to want to retain the illusion of personhood that the costumes present to him onstage, to maintain the ways in which they appear laminated to the personae of Lacey and Shotrell. However, the fantasy of a seamlessness between actor in costume, a sense of the inevitability of their appearance, is disrupted by the disembodied nature of the clothing backstage which begins to reveal the other ways it might be read. Now costume can be understood as that which constructs the personae of these actors rather than being seamless with them, or it can be seen as a product of the labour of other backstage workers. Costumes, in their status as brute matter and the outcome of work, disrupts the illusion of inevitability, and the apparent inevitability of illusion, that Pepys so enjoys on the stage.

I've argued elsewhere that costume can't quite be understood as an autonomous object, that is distinct from actors, and simply worn by them. From the perspective of the audience, costumes are more often perceived as enmeshed with actors' bodies, indeed costume can be understood as constituting the actor's body for the duration of the performance. Here, I understand the 'body' as an emergent set of social practices, rather than as a prior objective fact, and I argue that costumes should be understood as 'bodies that can be taken off'. It is this apparently seamless yet removable aspect of stage-dress is what makes it so uncanny when unworn – peculiar and disembodied in the costume-store or the dressing room (see Monks, 2010, p. 11). The work that costume does in making the actor's body possible and available to the spectator's view, places the actor's work in an interdependent and uncanny relationship to the labour of the designer and maker of the costume. To see costumes without bodies in them forces Pepys to confront the uncannily embodied nature of clothing. After all, actors do their job in part by dressing-up, and yet, while it's the actor that turns the costume into a working body, actors do not (usually) make the object of clothing themselves. The costume backstage therefore also functions as a trace of other absent bodies, the other workers that constructed the costume. And yet these workers don't actually appear to Pepys, and are not actually discernable in the object of clothing. To confront empty costumes backstage, then, is not necessarily to confront the 'reality' of theatre behind the scenes, but to be faced with the materiality and evanescence of backstage labour.

I've written elsewhere about the allure of the backstage and the wardrobe in how they are imagined by audiences as the place in which the 'real' work of the theatre can be discovered. In depictions of dressing rooms, green rooms, rehearsals and the theatre wings in novels, paintings and photographs, we see the fantasy that the structures of how the illusion was made will finally be revealed (ibid., 2010, pp. 14–19). This is a fantasy that often ends in disappointment, as Alice Rayner has argued (Rayner, 2002, p. 540). In fact, as Rayner suggests, this reality was always-already apparent onstage, evident in the objects and costumes made for the performance, in the gestures, movement and speech of the actors and in the work of stagehands. However, this reality is hidden in plain sight, both visible and inaccessible to the experience of the audience, as Rayner argues, '[the backstage] world is in some sense even more hidden precisely because it is so obvious; its pragmatic functions make it seem transparent' (ibid., p. 540).

This backstage work – the immediate work of the dressers and stage managers backstage, the prior work of rehearsal by actors and construction and design in the wardrobe – is often presented by theatre workers within the framework of 'service', describing their practices as 'serving' the work or the illusion. This idea of service presents the idea of an immaterial 'work' (usually a play) that exists beyond the purview of the stage, which is served and made manifest by the material structures of theatre: actors' bodies, costumes, sets, music, lights etc., but is somehow not 'of' these structures – as if the illusion is capable of transcending the material conditions in which it is made. The materials used to make the illusion are therefore imagined to serve it, but are somehow not of it, working within a system of value that 'consigns the real labor of theatre to servitude', as Rayner argues (ibid., p. 544).

Even while the idea of 'presence' is often invoked in relation to live performance, in fact, the relationship between the materials of the stage and the illusion is structured around absence, as William B. Worthen argues: '*Performance* dramatizes the complex, concrete decisions made to produce the immaterial work in a given material state. [...] Performance signifies an absence, the precise fashioning of the material text's absence, at the same time that it appears to summon the work into being, to produce it as performance' (Worthen, 1997, pp. 16–17, emphasis in original). Here, Worthen suggests, specifically of Shakespeare production, that there is a distinction made in some theatre systems between the actual physical printed copy of a play (the material text) and the idea of the 'play' in an ideal sense, which is imagined to transcend and exist beyond the limits of this concrete object. In this we see a fantasy of Shakespeare that is clearly influenced by the Romantic desire for a sublime transcendence of the material world, including even Shakespeare's texts themselves.

This chapter probes the idea of costume as working 'in service' at the theatre, by examining the particular case of Shakespeare's Globe Theatre in London. The Globe, a theatre famous for its approach to staging Shakespeare, offers a particularly intense set of relationships between the materials of the stage and their service to the illusion. The work of Jenny Tiramani, a costume designer, and Head of Theatre Design at the Globe, has drawn plaudits for the remarkable depth of research and the quality of detail in her costumes. There has been much fascinating scholarship published on the particular approach to history and historical accuracy at the Globe (see Gurr, 2000; Carson and Cooper, 2008), but for the purposes of this chapter, I want to focus on the role that Tiramani's costumes play in the onstage performance of actors (and the auditorium-based work of theatre critics), and also in the backstage work of dressers, stage managers, designers and makers in order to understand the varying modes of working with costume at the theatre and to suggest that 'service' is only one of the functions that costume fulfils in performance.

Tiramani herself presents costume as doing service to the actor's work and the 'play' and the 'story'. She is critical of design that is not 'helpful to the unfolding narrative of the play' (Tiramani, 2008, p. 60) and praises costumes that work 'to pull the audience towards [the play]' (ibid., 2008, p. 62). In her writing on costume, we see Tiramani maintaining the hierarchies of theatrical production that imagine the theatre as serving an evanescent idea of 'the play'. Tiramani's use of the term 'play' is echoed in Worthen's notion of 'the work', which he, paraphrasing Barthes, defines as: '[T]he vehicle for authorized cultural reproduction, a 'signified' approached through interpretation' (Barthes, 1997, p. 6). Indeed, Tiramani's view of design is bound up with questions of authority and hierarchy in the theatre system, imagining costume to serve as a manifestation and interpretation of a 'play' that is external to the theatre production but which governs it from afar (a system that Roland Barthes describes as 'theological' in its structures [ibid., 1977, p. 146]). Here we see a form of theatre that relies heavily on the concrete practices of the stage, while discursively repressing and disavowing their material nature. Furthermore, this discursive construction of theatre-making as a form of service produces a set of hierarchies within the construction of the stage illusion, with stage managers and dressers imagined to be serving and mediating the vision of the costume designer (also served by makers, cutters, dyers, etc.), which is thought to serve the actor's performance, and the director's vision, and thought to be serving the immaterial illusion that manifests the authority of the 'play'. This hierarchy is replicated in the forms of attention given by theatre critics to the theatre event (who often focus on writers, actors and directors with usually only a cursory glance at the scenographic features of the performance), and, indeed, by theatre scholarship which has paid little attention to the 'craft' elements of the theatre event until recently. The theatre profession itself often presents the performance event as ideally immaterial but served by a hierarchy of makers whose function is imagined to be more material the 'lower' down the scale they go.[1]

However, the Globe's archives tell a slightly different story. The documentation of Tiramani's design process: stage-management notes, financial records, correspondence, costume designs and notes, and health and safety notices, suggest that backstage uses of costume don't solely function in service to the onstage 'play', or to the actor serving it. In these notes, we see how the struggles of actors with their costumes in the rehearsal room do not only serve the eventual representation of *Hamlet* or *Richard II*, and how the expertise and craft of costume makers and designers doesn't only contribute to the audience's eventual experience in the auditorium. Rather, these practices of creating and working with costume are asymmetrical, each occupying their own conditions of signification and representation, each maintaining forms of autonomy from the work of the illusion. It's not that they are any more or less immaterial backstage. Rather, the qualities of their materiality shifts depending on their status and use within a range of practices and uses within the rehearsal room, wardrobe, props store and in the theatre wings.

In other words, backstage, costume does not stop performing, but performs differently. Onstage, the costume may function to provide the illusion of character for the audience, to constitute the actor's body and to become the grounds for the actor's expressive virtuoso powers in performance. Costume may also serve the work of theatre critics by enabling them to assert their identity as professional theatre historians. Backstage, costume functions as a precarious and untrustworthy environment for actors to extend (and constitute) their technique, in order to act, interpolating the actor's body within a disciplinary regime of bodily relations and communities of practice. For stage managers and dressers, costume functions to mediate between the actor's body and the time and space of the performance. It also constitutes, for the stage-management team, the means to the repetition of the theatre event: costumes and actors must be protected in order that the performance can take place nightly. For the wardrobe, the props department, and actors, costume functions as a material obstacle to, and facilitation of the appearance of effortlessness and immateriality in performance – in other words, costume paradoxically provides the solution to itself throughout the rehearsal process. In the wardrobe, the process of designing and making the costume works to dismember and re-member the actor's body,

---

[1] It's worth noting here that this hierarchy is historically and geographically variable and will also be distributed differently depending on the aesthetic traditions and practices of the performance. My focus here is on the British classical tradition, which is particularly invested in this hierarchy of 'service', centering around a rhetoric of fidelity and authenticity that imagines that, as W.B. Worthen argues: '[A]ll productions betray the text, all texts betray the work' (Worthen, 1997, p. 21). I'm focusing on this example because it seems to articulate the question of service with such intensity.

revealing the 'presence' of the performer as in fact constituted by a series of intricate substitutions. The process of costume design equally functions as the expression of expertise, and the discovery of new forms of knowledge, among the community of designers and makers, transmitting insight to an inner circle of expert 'audience' members.

Looking behind the curtain at costume backstage then doesn't reveal the costume's 'reality' beyond the theatrical illusion. Rather, these varying contexts reveal further forms of representation, expressive practices and audiences. We could breakdown the varying appearance of costume into three main categories: (1) in its role in supporting and producing virtuosity onstage, (2) in its function as the grounds for the practice of technique in rehearsal and (3) in the emanation and expression of the values of craft in the wardrobe. For the rest of the chapter I'm going to focus mainly on the Globe's production of *Hamlet* in 2000, which starred Mark Rylance in the lead role. Mark Rylance is an apt figure to consider in relation to the question of virtuosity. For the past twenty years, he has been hailed as one of the greatest actors on the British stage, renowned for his performances of key Shakespearean characters such as Cleopatra (1999), Hamlet (2000), and Richard II (2003) during his reign as the actor-manager of the newly established Globe Theatre in London. Since his departure from the theatre in 2005, Rylance became known for his dazzling performances in shows such as *Boeing Boeing* (2007), *Jerusalem* (2009) and *La Bete* (2010).

Described by critics as charmingly eccentric with other-worldly qualities, Rylance's performances are often imagined to exceed technique, infusing familiar and well-worn characters with virtuosic spontaneity and novelty. The virtuosity attributed to him by critics presents costume as tethered to the expression of his genius, which is itself imagined as tethered to the genius of Shakespeare. I will take a look at the varying roles that costume played backstage in this production, drawing occasionally on other examples of Globe performances, in order to think about the relationship between the concepts of 'virtuosity', 'technique' and 'craft' at the theatre. Throughout, I want to argue that costume does not only function to serve the immaterial 'play' rather, it also authorizes other forms of expression, expertise and knowledge throughout the theatre building.

REVIEWING VIRTUOSITY

When Mark Rylance played Hamlet on the Globe stage in London in 2000, critics were full of praise for his daring, seemingly spontaneous performance. Likened to an athlete, a musician and a magician, Rylance was lauded for his risk-taking approach to performance. Indeed, Rylance pulled off such acts of daring that critics imagined his performance as to be imbued with magical powers. I want to consider how costume appeared and disappeared in Rylance's stage presence, functioning not as an expression of the backstage work that produced it, but rather serving the authority of writer, actor and theatre critic at the performance.

Rylance first entered the Globe stage as Hamlet and began to speak with his back to the audience, not turning until the seventh line of his first speech.[2] Bridget Escolme reads this moment as a blurring of character and actor in which Hamlet begins by 'appearing absorbed in his own inner world', but in his turn and direct address to the audience, Hamlet began to address the audience 'as though abashed by such a great crowd' (Escolme, 2005, p. 66). Hamlet then, the character, appeared present and capable of direct communication with the audience, moving from an inward examination of conscience to a reluctant and embarrassed communication with the spectators present at the theatre. However, this moment of Hamlet's hesitancy presented itself as simultaneously an instance of supreme theatrical confidence. Rylance pitted his technical skills of vocal range against the outdoor space, and brazenly asserted his command of the audience, daring them to listen to him even when he didn't look back. In doing so, Rylance competed not only with the conventions of the outward facing actor, but equally with the acoustic challenges of the theatre space: the sound of planes overhead (constantly referenced in reviews) and the rain falling lightly on the raincoat-clad groundlings in the auditorium. Rylance revealed the acoustic possibilities of a relatively uninvestigated theatrical space, while also demonstrating that he could exert his technical abilities 'beyond the odds' (States, 1984, p. 119). The reluctant, abashed character of Hamlet was ghosted by the technically sophisticated daring actor Rylance, a common affect of virtuosity that promotes and maintains the star system in performance, where audiences experience a double performance. Critics maintained the sense of this distinctiveness by repeatedly pointing to this moment as evidence of his greatness as an actor, claiming that 'he is audible as he is emotionally truthful' (Nightingale, 2000, p. 22), and declaring that 'if acting were a contest, the game would have gone to Rylance' (Fay, 2000, p. 6).

Costume was one way in which the production ensured that Rylance as Hamlet stood out from the rest of the cast. The costumes for this production were designed to follow Elizabethan styles from 1600. The scenographic landscape of the stage was colour-coded according to the allegiances of the characters – the colours of the court were painted through fabrics that ranged from rusty browns, dark reds, to pink mixed with gold (which matched the painted 'marble' of the pillars onstage). By contrast Rylance-as-Hamlet first appeared dressed in black and white, while the actor playing Horatio was wearing a costume that mixed greys with blacks. While these colours indicated the characters' emotional and class status, drawing on the logic of Hamlet's state of mourning from the text, the palette employed by the

---

[2] I base my description of this performance on having attended the show during its original run, and reviewing it on video at the Globe Archives in 2013.

designer also meant that although the techniques of construction and fabric were based on Elizabethan techniques, the scenographic sensibilities were distinctly of the twentieth/twenty-first century. The concept of a visual coherence that underpinned and served the narrative drew on a post-Wagnerian legacy of a consistent scenographical environment. Rylance, dressed in black and white, was distinguished from the norm – as character *and* actor. This meant that, even before his first moment of audience-address, the character of Hamlet was established from the outset as isolated, lonely and distinct from the conventions of the court; while Rylance was established as a 'star' and as a virtuoso performer through his visual separation from the ensemble.

Here we see a staging system that was designed to serve two figures at the same time: the figure of Hamlet the character who is of central importance to the fictional narrative, and the figure of Rylance who is of central importance to the stage action. Costume played an important role in serving this system, being, as Tiramani described, 'helpful to the unfolding narrative of the play' (Tiramani, 2008, p. 60). But the picture is a little more complicated here – it's not only the narrative of the play that is being served but also perhaps the narrative of individualist, heroic, transcendent actor: a narrative that Judith Hamera describes as the 'communal organizing fiction' of the virtuoso (Hamera, 2011, p. 41).

Gabriele Brandstetter argues that the idea of virtuosity as a category of performance emerged in the late eighteenth century when the authority of the performer began to be contested at the theatre. While it's perfectly possible that the charisma of actors was viewed as problematic before this period, it was the emergence of Romanticism, which elevated the notion of an individual authorial genius at the heart of an artwork that began to present the virtuoso actor as a particular problem. The excessive charisma and presence of the virtuoso was seen as a threat to the primacy of the writer, whose 'ownership' of the meanings of the production were beginning to be asserted in this period. The idea that performers might have their own autonomous powers, beyond their service to the play or score began to be viewed by some eighteenth century critics as a threat to the sanctity of the fictional narrative and the theatrical illusion, setting up 'a field of conflicting authorities: the authority of the text on the one hand and that of the performer (or interpreter) on the other' (Brandstetter, 2007, p. 182). Virtuoso performance therefore constitutes a competing authority with the 'play' and its realization through the theatrical illusion, by introducing a rival narrative of actorly presence through 'the ethos of the person displaying their individuality' (ibid., p. 185). In this, Hamlet's costume and Rylance's costume might be imagined to be competing with each other for prominence and authority on the stage, even as they are actually constituted by the same items of clothing.

Indeed, the ambivalent role that costume played in staging Rylance's stage prowess can also be seen in the newspaper critics' response to his performance. While critics often described Rylance as a virtuosic performer, this was sometimes employed as an ambiguous soubriquet. Some reviews expressed a sense of breathless delight at Rylance's theatrical abilities, as one review headlined: 'Fresh and Daring, Rylance's Prince Creates a Rapport That Nears Genius' (Taylor, 2000, p. 7). On the other hand, some critics expressed an abiding sense of suspicion that Rylance might be competing with the authority of the work, with the *Metro* critic complaining that 'his sheer physical presence tends to overshadow the rest of the cast' (Metro, 2000, p. 21), while Alistair Macaulay in the *Financial Times* commented: '[P]erhaps I should call him daring for trying to deliver several speeches with his back to the audience – but to what purpose?' (Macaulay, 2000, p. 26). On the one hand critics praised Rylance for the qualities of genius, but on the other hand we see a suspicion that his presence onstage competes with the coherence of the 'play' and may constitute empty trickery.

As Susan Bernstein outlines of Romantic thinking about virtuosic performers in music, critics implicitly hold two different categories of virtuosity in view when judging Rylance's performance. On the one hand, there is the idea of the 'bad' virtuoso, described with 'the disparaging tone of "mere" skill that is less than art' (Bernstein, 1998, p. 12). Critics take up this idea of mere skill as an apparent threat to the sanctity of the work. Rylance is seen to compete with this spirit, embodying the actorly equivalent of the musician when 'the "mere" instrument is brought into focus by the "mere" player, who begins to dominate the picture with details of the concrete materiality of the body in direct contiguity with the thing-like qualities of the instrument' (ibid., 1998, p. 59). In other words, by visibly relying on and grappling with the materials of the stage, such as the acoustics of the space, Rylance is imagined to disrupt the desired immateriality of the ideas and vision of the play.

On the other hand, reviewers are often gushing in their praise for what they imagine as Rylance's 'good' virtuosity, where, as Bernstein puts it: '[T]he instrument disappears in the face of what it reveals' (ibid., p. 74). In these moments, Rylance is imagined to transcend technique, where he does not assert a competing authority or autonomy from the play, but rather 'give[s] up the authorial model of proper expression' (ibid., p. 86). In these moments, however, critics tend to reach for the language of the supernatural to explain his effect, suggesting that Rylance does not in fact rely on the material conditions of his work, but imagines that he somehow transcends them. It is when the actor's work and technique are imagined to be surpassed, that Rylance is seen to serve the 'play' through his own transcendent powers.

It's notable that the costumes in this production tended to be overlooked by critics, apart from the occasional nod to the visual sumptuousness of the Elizabethan style. This reiterates the tendency of reviews to follow the hierarchy of 'service' in which it is Rylance's support (or not) for the ideal 'play' that is given the most attention. However, many critics did mention one choice of costume: the nightgown worn by Rylance during the 'antic disposition' scene, which appeared to be stained with faeces. The critics read this costume not as the work of Tiramani, but as an authorial intervention by Rylance himself. Critics thought of the costume as functioning to comment on the character's incipient madness, as Robert Gore-Langton put it: '[W]hen he goes mad, it's real soiled shirt madness' (Gore-Langton, 2000, p. 57). Almost every review mentions this costume: '[H]e wears a dirty nightshirt and shakes his bottom at Polonius' (Margolies, 2000, p. 21); he is described as 'reeling about in a nightgown streaked with ordure' (Nightingale, 2000, p. 22); and Charles Spencer describes how 'he takes to the stage in an excrement-smeared nightshirt, and paces it like a caged neurotic lion in the zoo' (Spencer, 2000, p. 5). Even when dismissing Rylance's performance, Nicholas de Jongh seized on the costume as evidence of his poor interpretation: '[W]hen he appears in a night smock, which looks as if it is heavily stained with excrement, [he] veers towards the grotesque rather than fearful or disturbing' (de Jongh, 2000, p. 67). Either way, the dirty nightgown is taken up by critics as evidence of Rylance's interpretive vision. The costume is laminated onto his authority as the mediator of the character's body: in a sense there are two Rylances being imagined here, the Rylance who embodies the image and wears the costume, and the Rylance who commentates on this body and its relationship to Shakespeare's vision.

In the nightgown, then, we see costume being imagined as an instrument of virtuosity that is foundational to the interpretive job of the actor in service to the play. Furthermore, I wonder whether the virtuoso figure is in fact a means by which a collective sense of critical identity is being articulated by theatre reviewers? Critics used the nightgown to sketch out a theatrical genealogy, positioning Rylance within his own performance history, tracing it back to Rylance's last appearance as Hamlet at the RSC in 1989, as Robert Gore-Langton put it: '[L]ike all great improvisors, Rylance riffs on all his own repertoire, building on the Hamlet he first gave in a pair of pyjamas' (Gore-Langton, 2000, p. 57). Paul Taylor read the nightgown as 'a mischievous nod to the legendary pyjama-clad Hamlet he gave a decade ago' (Taylor, 2000, p. 14); while Carol Woddis viewed it as an 'odd throwback to his more radical reading' (Woddis, 2000).

Here, the costume enabled theatre critics to articulate their own memory and experience of performance – costume became the connective tissue between the performance of two Hamlets, functioning simultaneously to draw together the proof of Rylance's power, and to establish the status of theatrical criticism as a form of professional theatre history. Susan Bernstein points out that the early nineteenth century was not only a moment in which the virtuoso emerged as an important category of performance. This period was also marked by the emergence of the mass media and a concomitant concern about the nature and affect of journalistic language, which was often dismissed as morally bankrupt: '[J]ournalism comes under attack as the discourse governed by inauthentic and debased standards' (Bernstein, 1998, p. 11). As she suggests, the suspicions about the authority of the virtuoso chime with suspicions about the transient and ephemeral nature of journalistic writing. The connection here is not only one of similarity, however. As Bernstein suggests: '[T]he virtuoso emerges as a counterpart to the journalist, displaying the same evanescence and instability of purpose. The virtuosi provided the cultural reporter with subject matter, while the virtuoso's success is a function of journalistic advertising and good press coverage' (ibid., 1998, p. 11).

Bernstein's claims can be seen being played out in how the critics take up Rylance's costume as a means to stage their own theatrical knowledge, establishing a lineage of performance that shores up the status of the actor *and* the professional identity of theatre reviewing. His costume is read as both the expression, and material guarantor, of his accumulated status as a virtuoso, but his virtuosity can only be established or 'proven' in its reception. In this, then, virtuosity cannot be said to take place only on the stage, rather, as Judith Hamera argues, virtuosity 'offers an especially fertile field for interpersonal, vicarious, intimate conversations between artist and spectator/critic' (Hamera, 2011, p. 39). At the Globe production of *Hamlet*, costume functioned to mediate between reviewer and actor, enabling virtuosity to make an appearance and allowing the theatre critics to sustain the status of their profession. In all of this conversation, Jenny Tiramani's role was entirely effaced.

This sense that the virtuoso is distinguished from the ensemble onstage through the illusion of supernatural ability that is expressed with an authorial control over costume, arranges the audience's attention in such a way that it is possible to fantasize that the figure of the virtuoso occupies a stage environment that has been produced without work. The effacement of Tiramani here is a case in point. However, the pleasures of the virtuoso are fraught with ambiguity and contradiction. After all, even as the virtuoso's activity is apparently effortless, it is necessary for us to understand that the actor must be working in order to take pleasure in the idea that they appear not to be. Even as the actor seems unbound by gravity, acoustics or breath, we can only admire their daring by knowing in some way that they are in danger of falling or suffocating. In fact, virtuosi, by their very nature, are defined by their reliance on the material conditions of performance – this is what differentiates them from the supposedly immaterial work of writers and this may in fact constitute the central problem presented by a performer like Mark Rylance. The experience of virtuosity requires that we know that the actor is working hard, even as it promotes the idea of the individual exceptional genius that rises above the materials of the stage. The myth of the virtuoso promotes a profoundly ambivalent attitude to stage work.

The ambiguities at the heart of the work of virtuosity may explain why theatre costume looks so different when we approach it through the frames of 'technique' or 'craft'. I want to re-imagine this production of *Hamlet* now through these two frames, moving to the rehearsal room, the props store, the wings and the wardrobe to attend to how Rylance and his work emerge very differently once these frames are applied to his Hamlet in costume. Like

Pepys we will peer backstage, to confront the uncanny affects of costume behind the scenes. Unlike him, however, the aim is not to discover the 'reality' of costume, so much as to engage with its multiple performances and functions backstage in order to argue that costume doesn't only serve the work of actors, or the ideal 'play', it also lays claim to a potential autonomy from the illusion onstage.

COSTUMING TECHNIQUE

We have established that the myth of the virtuoso 'genius' emerged through the figure of Mark Rylance onstage, a myth that emphasized him as a heroic, individual, transcendent figure. However, the rehearsal records begin to sketch a different image of him and the other actors in the performance. The notion of an actor as an individual genius morphs into a very different picture, in which the work of the actor is precariously dependent on the skill and knowledge of other workers at the theatre. The identity of the actor flickers on and off and takes on a collective, rather than singular, aspect. The stage-management notes that make requests for objects and costumes, that organize the actor's body backstage, timing dressing and performance, reveal the work of the actor to be often mundane and repetitive. The illusion of individuality and transcendence produced by the virtuoso turns out to be comprised of logistical struggles, accurate timing, collective repetition and hard work. Costume constitutes both the obstacle and the solution to this process.

A stage-management note of Saturday, 6 May, for example, notes the need of Joanna McCallum, playing Gertrude, for 'some advice about how to fall while wearing her costume. [...] Is there anyone available?' (Globe Stage Management, 2000, note 19). In a note within the following day's records, the solution is presented: 'Miss McCallum has arranged with Viktor to have falling tuition' (Globe Stage Management, 2000, note 20). It turns out that acting, at least partially, comprises learning how to fall well in costume. Not only this, but the actor's work in adapting, modifying and transforming her body in order to adapt to the needs of the costume (and the role) are achieved not through magic or transcendence, but through practice, training and Viktor's expertise. Costume is presented here as the obstacle that must be overcome and understood by the actor through the acquisition and practice of technique.

Technique offers a very different idea of acting to the notion of the virtuoso actor, who is imagined to somehow transcend the technical in the realization of the aesthetic realm. Unlike the virtuoso's individualism, technique situates actors within a community of embodied practices that has a history. Training then organizes the body through technique in relationship to its stage environment (in which costume plays a constitutive role) and in relation to inherited acting practices and traditions, in order to become readable and pleasurable to a range of spectators – co-workers and audience members.

As Judith Hamera argues: '[T]echnique is [...] simultaneously constituted by an overarching ideal vision of the subject-ed body, and through the micro practices which actually inscribe this vision onto specific bodies with varying degrees of success and failure' (Hamera, 2011, p. 19). Technique situates the actor's body historically – not within the historical period of the costume (whose management by an actor is always inevitably contemporary to the time of the performance), but within the historical moment in which the rehearsal takes place. The particular modes of embodiment expressed by actors through the means by which they wear their costume emerge through inherited forms of bodily practice taught by one practitioner to another, functioning, as Hamera puts it, as 'a preexisting conversation between bodies, histories and desire' (ibid., 2011, p. 4).

Hamera imagines technique as a collective set of practices that form community. On the other hand, Worthen points to the ways in which the classical training system asserts the idea of the actor as a servant to the work by naturalizing a host of disciplinary regimes of training, a system that

> links the propriety of performance to the right expression of Shakespearean authority. [...] 'Shakespeare' becomes a powerfully naturalizing trope, used to justify the battery of techniques applied to the performer's body to make its performance readable in the theatre. Actor training [...] produces agents, whose behavior is fully involved in representing and reproducing the ideology of the subject. Acting evokes deep, even invisible commitments to the fictions of nature, origin, and identity, fictions sustained by the ghostly hand of 'Shakespeare', writing the body of the modern performer
>
> (Worthen, 1997, p. 98).

Worthen suggests that acting technique that is presented as 'neutral' or trans-historical covers over its ideological foundations, which sustain the hierarchies of service at the theatre and also discipline and regulate the actor's body to 'appear' in ways that shore up dominant norms of bodily conduct and identity. This approach to technique imagines the actor's body as a passive object that is the locus of disciplinary regulation and situated within a system of servitude.

However, the Globe's emphasis on original practice may counter this passivity and servitude somewhat, even as the notion of serving 'the work' is maintained and asserted. Tiramani outlines her aim to 'help our actors understand the way in which Elizabethans wore their clothes and use them in the appropriate manner according to surviving evidence' (Tiramani, 2008, pp. 61–62). Actors are being trained then, not just within the received notion of 'Shakespearean' acting. They are also being inducted into a form of historical research that is being transmitted from one body (Viktor) to another (McCallum) via the object of costume. This mode of performance might be likened better to the idea of 'craft' than the notion of servitude, or indeed the system of virtuosity. Richard Sennett, in his book, *The Craftsman*, suggests that inspiration, individuality and genius are far less important features than imitation and repetition within the traditions of craft work: '[D]eveloping one's talents depended on following the rules established by earlier generations; that most modern of words – personal 'genius' – had little meaning in this context. To become skilled required, personally, that one be obedient' (Sennett, 2009, p. 22). In this model, costume becomes a key means to frame acting not as an autonomous form of genius, nor necessarily as a passifying regime of discipline, but through a system of inheritance and mentoring within a collective set of practices that may not only work to serve the illusion, but which may also articulate a network of relationships and practices of identity. Falling over in costume, it turns out, constitutes the practice of technique through historical modes of inherited embodiment that might be understood to constitute the collective 'craft' of acting.

ANXIOUS EFFORTLESSNESS

The fact that acting can be framed as activities like learning to fall in costume offers the same kind of uncanny affect that Pepys sees in the empty costumes of Lacy and Shotrell. This affect is one that Rayner locates in the 'asymmetry of the relationship between the conceptual and the material practices' of theatre (Rayner, 2002, p. 545). This asymmetry becomes particularly apparent for *Hamlet* when the difficulties with staging death emerge in the backstage records. I've written elsewhere about the specific challenges of costuming ghosts and the ways in which these challenges constitute an historical problem in which belief, technology and audience response converge (Monks, 2010, pp. 119–137). Here, though, I want to suggest that we can trace out the ways in which costume operates as both the obstacle to and solution for, a production that is profoundly anxious about the status of its own materiality.

Early in the process of rehearsing *Hamlet*, the question of immaterial labour takes a particularly theatrical turn: '[W]e would like the ghost to move as quietly as possible, can the armour be made in such a way that it is not very noisy?' (Globe Stage Management, 2000, note 5, 7 April). Here we see the production team confronting the problem that ghosts shouldn't have bodies, producing an anxiety that, as Stallybrass and Jones have suggested, emerges in the nineteenth century in the threat of laughter at the ghost's appearance (Jones and Stallybrass, 2000, p. 245). Here, the anxieties caused by the system of service, in which there is a mismatch between the materials of the stage and the immaterial work of Shakespeare, come fully to light. For a ghost to wear noisy armour is for the costumed actor to insist on his own materiality, potentially interrupting the production's impulse towards a transcendence of the stage. Indeed, it appears that as John Gielgud bemoaned, there is no such thing as silent armour (see ibid., 2000, p. 246) and the Globe did not find a solution to this problem, at least according to Susannah Clapp's review of the performance, where 'the ghost clanks across the stage in heavy-duty black armour. Got up in doublet and hose of mustard and crimson, the male members of the cast look like pear drops' (Clapp, 2000, p. 26).

In subsequent rehearsals, the stage-management notes trace how these attempts to manage the material assertions of costume emerge in the problem of sound itself: the mechanics of producing the ghost's speech: 'we will need 4 lengths of plastic drainpipe for Act I Sc 5, for the understage ghostly voice' (Globe Stage Management, 2000, note 20, 7 May). And these logistical challenges then translate into acting problems: 'Mr Preece is concerned about entering through the doorways in his armour, particularly the height as he does not want to duck when he makes an entrance (Globe Stage Management, 2000, note 21, 11 May). The need for drainpipe (that it must presumably be ordered, purchased and assembled by a Globe staff member), and the difficulty of high helmets and low doorframes performs a set of theatrical struggles with the materials of the stage. Captured in these struggles we see the production attempting to realize what Nicholas Ridout describes as the bourgeois spectator's fantasy that 'a realm of human experience might be possible that does not depend upon human labour' (Ridout, 2006, p. 26). The desire for the ghost to appear to have no body, to make no sound, to not be bound by the time and space of the stage has its corollary in the myth of the transcendent aesthetic figure that the virtuoso embodies. These stage management notes trace the theatre's attempts to maintain the fantasy of the absence of labour and materiality onstage, while simultaneously recording the effort that it takes to produce this fantasy backstage. After all, even as the materiality of the stage is the obstacle to the ghost's presence, it's also in the end, the solution to it. It's the drainpipes, adjusted helmets, and actor's body that eventually supply this illusion of effortlessness on the stage. In the end, costume presents the solution to itself.

Finally, we can see how this asymmetry between the material stuff that makes the performance and the ideal 'play' that is imagined to be transcendent and immaterial at the theatre also contributes to the peculiarly repetitive aspects of the theatre event: the fact that it must take place nightly. In this, the material dimensions of the performance must be protected and made safe in order to guarantee the survival of the illusion that serves the play. Again, we see the effort to protect the illusion from its own materiality noted in the production meeting minutes on 2nd May, in which:

RH [Richard Howey] asked about the hole in the arras for the death of Polonius [...]. There were also safety concerns regarding the proximity of SM and actors to the sword when it was thrust through the arras.
(Globe Production Meeting Minutes, 2000)

That Hamlet's sword thrust through the arras might be a danger for the Polonius *and* the actor that plays Polonius *and* the stage management crew that organize and care for the actor, plays out the mismatch between the illusion and what it takes to produce this illusion – in other words the materials of the performance must be protected from the 'play'. The fact that the sword endangers both character and actor, but that Polonius must be murdered while the actor who plays him must not be injured, is not only a health and safety problem, but also a protection of the illusion from its own materiality. The actor who plays him mustn't be killed, so that Polonius *can* be killed night after night.

THE DISMEMBERED ACTOR

So far, I've suggested that once we visit the uses of costume backstage, we begin to see how costume is one of the means through which the theatre grapples with its own materiality, all the while maintaining certain forms of collective practice that may not only be 'serving' the illusion. Once we move to the stage-management props table and the wardrobe, we begin to see a further dismantlement of the individualist myth of the virtuoso, and a further sense in which the hierarchy of service may emerge differently and be inadvertently undermined through backstage practices.

Addressed to the props department and the wardrobe, the stage management notes of the 20 April for the rehearsals of *Hamlet*, read:

> *Mr. Rylance* would like different clothes for the play within the play [...]
> *We* will need a bloody shirt for Hamlet in Act 3 Sc 5 [...]
> *Hamlet* would like to have a bloodied meat cleaver for Act 2 Sc 5.
>   (Globe Stage Management Notes, 2000, note 13, 20 April, emphasis mine)

Within a single set of notes, the demands for costumes and props switch from the actor, to the ensemble, to the character. In these shifts, we see a faint echo of the records of Phillip Henslowe and those of his contemporaries in the guild performances during the Renaissance. Peter Stallybrass and Ann Rosalind Jones have traced the ways in which Renaissance costumes retained 'the vivifying magic which attaches both to a theatrical part and to the figure which the part embodies' (Jones and Stallybrass, 2000, p. 177). They note, for instance, moments in which fees are paid by the guilds to the role rather than the actor: 'The Chester records of the Smiths, Cutlers and Plumbers for 1575 record payments to "litle god" of 20d. and to "oure marye" of 18d.' (ibid.). This effect of the role existing before the actor they argue, is also an effect that inhabits the costume stock 'because the costume can endure after the performance is ended [...] it can take a curious precedence over the actor' (ibid.). Stallybrass and Jones also note the ways in which the actor-manager Philip Henslowe framed costumes in his records for the Elizabethan Rose Theatre as if the character still resided within them, suggesting a clothed quality to the repertory system of performance in which costumes preceded the actors who wore them.

We must be suspicious of laminating the similarities between the Renaissance onto this moment of rehearsal at the contemporary Globe theatre too easily. Clearly, there are specific historical conditions at play in the Renaissance: a complex blend of belief, theatrical practice, a particular relationship to costume; the high value of clothes etc., that determine the ways in which character and clothing are imagined to be enmeshed. In these contemporary stage management notes for the Globe, the emergence of Hamlet himself as an agent within the rehearsal process is a slip made easily, when the illusion and the worker combine anecdotally within rehearsal shorthand. But Hamlet as a 'real' figure in rehearsal, who makes requests for objects and costumes, also speaks to the contemporary historical moment in which the character and actor precede the costume at the theatre: a moment in which costumes are made specifically *for* actors. Both actor and character are imagined to be agents within the creative process who have needs, demands, and for whom costume is made, but who must also accommodate, use and learn the costume in order to emerge in performance. Rylance then is only one of many figures, alongside the character of Hamlet, the ensemble, the costume makers and the designer, who will produce this final role. Hamlet-the-character plays a role in the rehearsal process as he does in The Mousetrap: a participant in the staging choices that will then constitute the illusion that produces him.

This multiple aspect of the figure of the actor comes to light too in the documentation of the costume design and making process in which it becomes clear that the costume designer's job is to dismember and re-member the actor's body. While the critics viewed the appearance of Rylance's body in his nightgown as an inevitable emanation of his personal genius, these very ordinary records of the process of making Hamlet's costume begin to deconstruct the myth of the transcendent virtuoso body. In Jenny Tiramani's costume bible for *Hamlet* and other productions, such as *Richard II*, Rylance's body is first fragmented and then reorganized through objects and costume. We begin by viewing Rylance's body as a series of measurements:

Under knee	13 3/4
Thigh	16 1/2
Knee	16/12
Calf	15 1/2
Calf height	15
Knee height	22 1/2
Shoe size	8

Source: Table transposed from Globe *Hamlet* Costume Bible notes, 2000.

Rylance is turned into a series of anatomical components. The costume bible then supplies a list of the clothes and objects required for Hamlet to appear onstage and through this list we see Hamlet/Rylance rebuilt through costume:

Doublet	Black velvet inkle braid (dye green) – Julie
Cloak	Black melton
	Hainsworths, lined in taffeta and textured
Stockings	Gina – black
Shoes	Andrew Fr
Boots	Mark Beaby long black leather
Gloves	Dawn
Shirt	Lucca
Hat	Plush low crown – dye it. Kate D.
Collar	Blackwork – Lesley – integral to shirt

Source: Table transposed from Globe *Hamlet* Costume Bible notes, 2000.

However, of course, this imagined composite body of Hamlet/Rylance is not simply reconstructed through clothes. Each item is annotated with the labour it requires and the maker who will undertake this work, noting implicitly the range of forms of expertise in dyeing, leatherwork, millinery, lacework, etc., that are required to build the character's body. The actor's body then becomes re-membered via a series of substitutions comprising objects of clothing that have been made by another set of bodies. The actor is fragmented and recomposed through costume and labour.

The costume designer continually takes apart the actor's body, only to piece it back together through a range of 'translations' – turning it into objects, costumes, workers and financial values which simultaneously produce the character's body through objects. This re-membered double body – Hamlet/Rylance – is always uncannily incomplete, and yet forms a significant aspect of what appears to the audience as the image of character/actor – for them, the cloaks, stockings, hats and shoes *are* a substantial aspect of Hamlet/Rylance's body: not simply exterior decoration, but the grounds in which Rylance's performance is made possible and available to view. Similarly, as we have seen, these objects, this half-rendered body is also the grounds in which Rylance works, functioning as an environment for his labour, an instrument for his work and an obstacle to be overcome in the expression and extension of his technique.

Furthermore, actors are not the only theatre workers who perform or grapple with costume. There is also the mirroring performance of the dresser, who inserts the actor into the space and time of the performance through the addition or subtraction of items of clothing. The notes made by the dresser for *Hamlet* articulate the schedule of the performance, marked by costume changes. The bloody shirt that we saw earlier being requested in rehearsal, is now an object to be added and stripped from Rylance as he moves between stage and offstage, noting the exact minutes at which these changes will be made:

> Act One Sc 2 Hamlet 7–11 (blk velvet). […]
> Act Three Sc4 (+ Sc5 + Sc 6) Hamlet 74–81 (change bloody shirt).
> (Dresser's Notes, Globe *Hamlet* Costume Bible, 2000)

As Barbara Hodgdon notes of Ian McKellan's performance of *Richard III*, 'the dresser's notes […] reveal a precisely articulated shadow performance, a sequence of timed actions making up an invisible spectacle that runs alongside the prompt script' (Hodgdon, 2012, p. 380). Here we see again a sense of Rylance's body being produced and reproduced again by a series of objects and workers, each 'making' parts of his body, or transforming that body and inserting it into the space and time of the performance.

Far from being an individual figure who exerts his expressive powers, transcending the materials of the stage, Rylance now emerges as oddly absent, figured almost as a form of negative space that is filled out with the projections of theatre critics, the collective 'body' of technique, the objects and items of clothing made by other workers and the mirroring performance of the dresser who matches his onstage performance with backstage timing and costume. These counter performances not only undo the myth of the virtuoso but they also point to the ways in which backstage work may constitute its own kind of performance that certainly emerges through Rylance onstage, but which also retains a kind of autonomy from how the audience experience the 'play'. I want to turn finally to the concept of craft to think about the ways in which the work of the wardrobe may not always articulate its work in relation to actors at all.

CRAFT, AUTONOMY AND RE-ENACTMENT

The ideals of craft have clearly underpinned the development of the work of the Globe since its inception. This idealist framework has informed the development of original practices costume design and making by Jenny Tiramani. In this, Tiramani has worked with a range of expert workers to produce costumes and objects based on the fabrics, construction techniques, iconography, shape and pattern and practices of wearing clothing from 1600. As we have seen, Tiramani frames her designs as functioning in service to the immaterial 'play'. However, the records of the process of designing for *Hamlet* and *Richard II* not only enable us to trace out these practice but also express forms of professional pride and identity, a particular relationship to the past as a form of re-enactment rather than representation, and the production of new knowledge. I want to suggest that these approaches may give theatre craft work a certain degree of autonomy from its service to the illusion, the actor, the director and 'the play'.

In a letter to Tiramani, Dawn Wood, (a glove maker) asks:

For the posh gloves I meant to ask do you want them to have the extra long fingertips which were [stiffened] padded, and the gauntlets were stiffened with paper (handmade) which I can do?

(Globe Correspondence, 2000)

Wood's question concerns her practice of making gloves with the techniques of early modern practices of glove-making, determining the level and quality of detail that Tiramani desires for the production of costume. This question has very little to do with the role that the design of these gloves could play in the production of illusion for the audience. It seems unlikely that any audience member, other than a few groundlings perhaps, could possibly see that the fingertips of the gloves were extra long, let alone know that the paper used to stiffen them was handmade. The work involved in producing these gloves cannot then be understood to work entirely in the service to the audience's experience at the theatre, but rather assumes the autonomy of a 'job done well for its own sake', which Richard Sennett suggests is the very definition of craftwork (Sennett, 2009, p. 9).

In this, just as with the Elizabethan underwear famously worn by the actors during Mark Rylance's term as artistic director, there is a rhetoric surrounding the Globe practice that imagines that the hidden authentic details of the costume will infuse the actor's work with an energy that will produce novelty and innovation. This secret aspect of the costume is imagined then to have a Stanislavskian dimension in functioning as a catalyst in the actor's inner world so that the audience are imagined to access the underwear or the overly long fingertips indirectly through the force of the actor's performance. In this way then, the costume appears to the audience in a similar form to that of the virtuoso, concealing its seams, eliding the labour that produced it by appearing inevitable, and yet functioning to engage the audience in the experience of astonishment and awe *indirectly* through the actor's performance. It isn't only then that the actor is made possible by the labour of others, it's also that the actor might be said to be the final worker in the realization of the costume.

Nonetheless, it isn't clear that the handmade paper produced by Wood will be visible to the actors or necessarily discussed with them. It's possible that the standard of accuracy to which Wood works serves nothing but the realization of the object itself. While the historical exactitude of Globe practices has its own specificity, it also stands as an expression of the care and expertise that characterizes the work of many theatre designers and makers. Tiramani's facilitation of craft takes on a kind of autonomy that stands apart from its service to Rylance and to the play itself, but this autonomy remains a secret, hidden in the fingertips of gloves, articulated only between craft workers.

The use of expert language by these costume makers and designers chimes with Hamera's discussion of technique, language that functions to bind people together through a shared vocabulary of expertise, working to communicate not only the tacit knowledge of practice but also to articulate forms of community. We can see these modes of community enacted in a note from Tiramani to Mark Wheeler, a maker at the Globe:

Dear Mark
Please could you pink these sleeves for Laertes with tiny cuts like the Essex photocopy. The tacked outlines are the finished sleeve <u>without</u> seam allowance.
Speak soon,
Love Jenny xxx.

(Globe Correspondence, 2000) (underline in original)

In this correspondence, Wheeler's tacit knowledge of cutting practices, traditions of making, and relationships to tools like scissors, and materials like fabric, are articulated and assumed. Wheeler is asked to practice this knowledge in relationship to a photocopy: documentary evidence of historical practice that he is asked to reproduce through his application of this knowledge to those materials through these tools. The language used by Tiramani does not instruct him on how to do this, the *how* of pinking and seam allowances has already been learned by Wheeler, probably not through language alone, but through forms of imitation of mentors and through practice itself. In this, then, the language used does not produce practice but rather gestures to a community of practices that are not being described. As Hamera argues, technique can be understood to work as an act of translation between bodily practices and vocabularies: '[A] common "mother tongue" to be shared and redeployed by its participants: a discursive matrix, a vocabulary and a grammar, to hold sociality together across difference and perpetuate it over time' (Hamera, 2011, p. 19). Like other craftwork at the theatre, making costumes gains an autonomy that produces its own 'texts' and forms of knowledge that remain contained within interactions among the communities of workers that produce the costumes, not necessarily always serving other forms of work at the theatre.

What is striking about much of the correspondence in the Globe records is how these makers imagine the performance of the play not as a representation of the past but as a re-enactment of it. Their concern with the accuracy of items of clothing imagines that the actors wearing these costumes will, as Rebecca Schneider describes of American Civil War re-enactments, 'put [...] themselves *in the place of* the past, reenact [...] that past by *posing as if* they were' (Schneider, 2011, p. 9, emphasis in original). This approach to re-enactment sees the costume and the actor who wears it as a substitution for, rather than an imitation of, the historical past. This means that the production of costume is focused not on the representation of a fictional milieu or work but rather on the imagined access to a real historical moment. Schneider describes this logic of re-enactment as the fantasy that 'if they repeat an event *just so*, getting the details as close as possible to fidelity, they will have touched time and time will have recurred' (ibid., 2011, p. 10).

This sense of makers like Wood as contributors to the re-enactment of an historical moment renders them the curators of an archive that they sustain by making objects. What we see in their correspondence is how historical insight can be produced through practice: forms of knowledge are articulated, communicated and sustained by making things at the theatre. Again, the historical project of the Globe is a particularly intense example, but it might be possible to suggest that all designers and makers are 'knowing' by doing. And this knowledge does not necessarily serve the illusion, indeed, at times, it might actually offer an alternative or competing narrative to the realization of the 'play', performing as a form of re-enactment of the Elizabethan. Rather than as a representation of Shakespeare's *Hamlet*.

The ways in which the forms of knowledge that inform craft might challenge the authority of text or actor, can also be seen in a programme note for *Richard II*, written by Tiramani, that informs the audience of the research it took to make the costumes and props onstage, including the pedigree of the fabric used in the costumes (from Zoagli near Genoa); the visit to 'Bayerisches national museum in Munich and the Germanisches national museum in Neuremberg to study their extensive collections of late 16th-Century garments' and the fact that the throne onstage was constructed using '16th Century furniture-making techniques'. Tiramani even describes the training that the team undertook to produce these costumes and objects, 'by the City and Guilds London Art School in the use of pigments and late 16th Century fine artists' techniques' (Tiramani, 2003).

The programme note makes backstage work public, pointing to the extensive research that undergirds the costume (this is one of many programme notes articulating the theatre's broader craft-based historical practice). Importantly, Tiramani's authorial intervention in the programme note, does not describe her scenographical interpretation of (and service to) Shakespeare's text. Instead, her note insists on the scholarly underpinnings of craft, suggesting that making things at the theatre can contribute to and produce knowledge of its own kind, rather than purely serving and interpreting the authority and knowledge of others. This authorial intervention was parodied by Lloyd Evans, the theatre critic for *The Spectator*, who described how:

A wardrobe full of tailors was punted across the Rhine. From there, navigating by starlight, they journeyed south to [...] study the fashions of the 16th Century. Their colleagues were borne in litters across the snow-bound Alps. Overcoming fatigue and harsh weather, they gained the gate of Genoa where they purchased rolls of taffeta and plain-weave velvet. [...] Back in England, a confederacy of woodcutters pondered the problem of Richard's throne.

(Evans, 2003, p. 74)

Evans then asks: '[A]nd the result? The result of all this heaving, throbbing, ant-like industry? The result is a triumph' (ibid., 2003, p. 74). Evans makes fun of the apparently excessive and peculiar work of the Globe design team for their pre-modern modes of labour *and* for asserting this labour as a form of scholarly activity that can produce its own forms of knowledge and insight. He treats Tiramani's work as a special case, but perhaps the only difference between this production and the work of many designers and makers, is that Tiramani asserts the status of her work in narrative form in the programme. It may be that the laughter provoked in Evans is not at the excessiveness of Tiramani's work, but has emerged because he has been forced by the programme note to understand costumes as work at all. We might see in his response an echo of the belief that Nicholas Ridout describes as the bourgeois idea that 'there is something improper and shameful in the theatrical apparatus and […] this impropriety and shame is somehow linked to labour' (Ridout, 2006, p. 28).

CONCLUSION: INVISIBLE WORKERS

At the end of the last performance in the run of *Hamlet*, Mark Rylance emerged 'out of character' to address the audience directly in the role as artistic director of the theatre. Still in costume, jumping up and down enthusiastically onstage (as if to say that he could repeat this grueling three-hour performance happily and effortlessly), greeted by screams of appreciation from the audience, Rylance proceeded to pay homage to those who had worked on the show. Speaking tentatively in rhythms uncannily identical to those of Hamlet's, Rylance congratulated the cast for their work, telling the audience that the space was difficult for actors to perform in, and that the daylight conditions of the Globe theatre forced the cast to see the audience up close 'and some of you ain't pretty' (Globe *Hamlet* DVD, 2000). Rylance then invited the crew to come onto the stage to take a bow. Filing onstage awkwardly, the crew in their modern dress and un-choreographed bows looked profoundly uncomfortable. Underlining their hard work, noting 'it takes a lot of work to dress us and undress us' (ibid.), Rylance then pointed out Jenny Tiramani, the designer, in the audience, congratulating her for her work, describing her as the person 'who made all these clothes for us and who persists in struggling …' (ibid.).

Here we have a moment that might have satisfied Pepys: the reality of the backstage world finally makes its appearance onstage. Now, it seems, the audience will finally understand how the illusion was made. However, inevitably perhaps, the event of the bow was profoundly disappointing. In the end, the actors, in Elizabethan dress, looked far more 'real' on the stage than the crew, whose contemporary dress matched that of the audience, but not that of the iconography of the Globe space. Not only this, the crew were clearly not qualified by technique or role to submit their bodies to the gaze of the audience – their bows were embarrassed and awkward. Furthermore, while the material workers that produced *Hamlet* were made visible, literally embodied by workers in the 'wrong' place (Rayner, 2002, p. 538), even then, the real conditions of their work, its distinction from and service to the illusion, was inaccessible.

Rylance's framing of the crew's labour in the guise of the artistic director, using that strangely familiar voice and body that had once been Hamlet's (and still partly was), meant that the workers were being presented as less real than the fictional characters the audience had only just seen. It was the crew's work that was in fact presented as the illusion, the fiction: only imaginable through Rylance's narration of it as something invisible and mysterious, rather than the 'true' events that had played out before the audience by actors in proper period dress. Putting the crew onstage and making them 'visible' only served to further distance the idea of work from the spectacle. In the end, the backstage visited the audience, and the experience was once more one of melancholy and a little laughter.

AN INTERVIEW WITH LOIS WEAVER

Aoife Monks

Introduction

Lois Weaver is an American performance artist and theatre maker who co-founded the theatre troupe Split Britches with Peggy Shaw and Deborah Margolin in New York in 1980. The company describe themselves as producing 'vaudevillian, satirical gender-bending performance', which they term feminist and lesbian: 'feminist because it encourages the imaginative potential in everyone, and lesbian because it takes the presence of a lesbian onstage as a given' (Split Britches Website, 2013). Prior to her work with the troupe, Weaver was a co-founder of Spiderwoman Theatre in 1976, a collective that explored gender in relation to Native American traditions and identity, while Shaw first performed with the theatre drag company Hot Peaches. Split Britches went on to make twenty-one performance pieces, including their first production, *Split Britches* (1980), the film noir influenced *Dress Suits for Hire* (1987, written by Holly Hughes) and *Belle Reprieve* (1990), a pastiche of Tennessee Williams' *Streetcar Named Desire* in collaboration with the British male drag company BLOOLIPS. The company's most recent projects are *Miss America* (2008) and *Lost Lounge* (2009). Weaver has also made theatre work with women in prisons in the UK and Brazil as part of the People's Palace Projects' *Staging Human Rights* series.

In this interview, Weaver discusses the aesthetic and political practices that inform the company's approach to costume as a 'found object'.

Emerging out of the downtown New York avant-garde of the 1960s and 70s, the Split Britches were influenced by the approach to objects, spaces and costumes that come from a 'poor theatre' aesthetic. As Weaver points out, however, this approach is also informed by a feminist do it yourself (DIY) view of theatre-making, emphasizing the importance of these artists being able to exert control over their own means of production, and making work that responded to the social and domestic milieu of their lives. As Sue Ellen Case puts it, they: 'do not presume technical support. For years, they turned on the light that catches them, or turned to change costumes from their own upstage trunk. They assume responsibility for their own housework' (Case, 1996, p. 11).

In tandem with this aesthetic is the company's emphasis on the 'fabulous': on costume's role in enabling fantasy, erotic pleasures and the investigation of identity. In this, Split Britches engage in forms of drag that don't necessarily involve cross-dressing, if cross-dressing is taken to mean crossing from one gender position to another. Rather, viewing costumes as drag enables these performers to access fantastical aspects of butch-femme lesbian experience. As Weaver points out, the line between stage costume and real life here is porous: clothing doesn't only function to express 'real' identities, but shows that identity can be performed and constituted by dressing-up. Theatre performance becomes a means for these performers to articulate a sense of self not only through what they wear, but also through the very process of finding and wearing costume.

AM – Aoife Monks, LW – Lois Weaver

> *AM*: I'm interested by the systems of production that your work is situated within: the fact that you don't necessarily work with a designer, that you often make your own costumes. Where do you start with costume?

> *LW:* Costume comes from two places in our work. One is the idea of found art: what we find, we use. The other thing for me, and I think this is part of our feminist methodology, is that a big part of our making work is about performing fantasy. We ask, 'what is it that you want to be onstage? Who do you want to do onstage?' Some of that comes out of our drag roots, certainly Peggy's drag work with Hot Peaches. I came out my work with Spiderwoman, and they are the ones who said, 'what do you want to be, who do you want do, what can we put together that makes you feel fabulous, whatever that fabulous might be?' Of course, that fabulous might be a sort of torn clown, or a bag-lady, which is one of the first roles that I played, which was just to put on as many clothes as I could. So I think the root of our work with costume is desire; what do you want to wear onstage? And for Peggy and I in our early days, of course that 'what do

you want to wear' is really located in butch-femme culture. I want to be high femme, she wants to be stone butch onstage. And I think that what's interesting for Peggy is that her desire to wear the suit on the stage is really translated into her desire to be that in life. Whereas for me, my desire to be high femme onstage has slowly translated into the opposite in life, and I think that is partly because it's so high maintenance.

AM: Can we go back to the idea of 'found' objects? What does that actually mean? Does that mean that it happens to be in the room you're in, or that you come across it in charity shops? Is 'found' is also about looking?

LW: We were constantly on the prowl for fabulous pieces of costume. We always went to the charity shop; that was the first place we went when we started a performance, to see what we could find, and that was for our music as well. We found old recordings, and sometimes the costume inspired the performance, or inspired the text, or inspired the piece. Finding has a lot more looking attached to it than just what you find in the room. It's is about going to the charity shop, or going into your closet, or recycling the costume. Sometimes it was finding it on the street, you'd be in the rehearsal room and say, 'Oh my God, I'd really like to wear a tuxedo for this', and then you're going down the street and there's one in the garbage. That happened to us several times. Or you find something in the garbage that you realize that you can make into the costume that you've been looking for. So it isn't about just using what's there, it's about going and looking for a specific look. And it's a little magpie-ish, it's about what's glittery, it was what helped me represent that 1950s subverted femininity – that combination of my mother and Marilyn Monroe.

AM: What does it mean to feel fabulous? What's that like?

LW: I think again, in the early days, for me and for Peggy, what made us feel fabulous was also inspired by drag. And that early '70s feminist where you weren't supposed to wear make-up, and you weren't supposed to wear push-up bras and boas and high heels. To give myself that theatrical permission to do this, that made me feel fabulous.

AM: The simplistic thing to say would be that somehow you were expressing your 'real selves'. But I wonder if there's something much more complicated going on there because it sounds like the dressing-up onstage works to articulate who you start to be in your lives and that there is a real blurring of the boundaries between performance and life?

LW: We knew that the costume represented and celebrated a butch-femme identity and for both of us who came from working-class environments this was something that we romanticized. And it was at the same time an identity that was being rejected by feminist culture as repressive and het-eronormative. So we knew that by performing those identities onstage we were reclaiming them, almost from a class perspective and celebrating them. But also we were really conscious of the theatrical effects. Peggy tells this great story about when she joined Hot Peaches, she wasn't a performer, and the way she learned to perform was realizing that whoever had most sequins and the highest heels, was the best performer. So the quality of performance was dictated by the costume. We didn't go down that route. We always asked, how do we dress the couple? So it wasn't just what makes me feel fabulous and what makes Peggy feel fabulous but also what would make us look like a fabulous pair? And that question was always informed by popular culture: Neil Diamond and Barbara Streisand, or Tammy Whynot and George Jones. So we always looked at double acts. But, I'll say this too, is that for me, being fabulous meant that I didn't have to be perfect. There was an element of not quite making it in the costume. Not so much as someone like David Hoyle, but a performance where I could be totally done up with unshaven legs, or dirty finger nails, or a wig that I'd never combed. That allowed us to feel like that we weren't playing the game, that we were playing against the game.

AM: So you weren't being forced to turn into the image that you were enjoying making?

LW: It's something I learned from working with the company Spiderwoman, who were named after a Hopi Indian goddess of weaving, and her philosophy was that you had to leave a flaw in the design so that the spirit could come out. So that was our philosophy very early on in performance, and that, along with fantasy, that's one of the things that I inherited from working with them. And also the costume should never be totally finished because we were not trying to be actors, we were trying to be performers. And we wanted the audience to be able to see us through the costume, to not hide behind the costume.

AM: Obviously the company name, Split Britches, is named after an article of clothing. So can you tell me about a show where you started with costume?

LW: I'll just say something about the show, *Split Britches*, since you mentioned it. When I moved to New York, and I saw bag women on the streets, they wore layers and layers and layers of clothes. Sometimes out of necessity, sometimes out of desire, because that was what they wanted to wear. And then I saw *Grey Gardens*, which had a similar use of clothing and a kind of anti-establishment way of living. And both felt extremely similar to these three aunts of mine who lived in one room of an eight-room farmhouse, and wore all of their clothes. I thought, what is that about women who reject this idea of the single family home, or are rejected from it, so that they wear their clothes this way? And so in a way *Split Britches* the show began from that idea. On the other hand, *Dress Suits for Hire* didn't actually begin from a specific costume. But it did begin from the idea of clothing, because there was a tuxedo shop in the East Village that was derelict with a sister still lived in the building, and the tuxedos were still in the window, and it had a sign saying 'dress suits for hire' in neon. We tried to rent it for a lesbian club but she wouldn't let us have it. And then we got interested the idea of ghosts: what happens to the clothing that speaks to these massive events in people's lives? The clothes must carry those stories. And the other thing was this rumour, that the sister's sister was killed in the shop and there was some kind of underworld crime connection with the strip joint across the street. So, those two things were the starting point for the show. But it was really came down to our fascination with how clothing features in lesbian culture. The way clothing can be a presentation of something, of sexuality, I guess.

AM: How do you think clothing works in lesbian culture?

LW: The funny thing is, the lesbian look is jeans and a black T-shirt, and there are several lesbian looks that are not associated with tuxedos and gowns at all. But our language was, not camp in a gay men way, but being camp and fabulous in a lesbian kind of way. We did loads of concert balls and debutante balls, we had a Freudian Slip Party, where everybody wore slips.

AM: What do you think the difference is between male and female drag? Thinking about *Belle Reprieve*, for example, and your work with BLOOLIPS: do you think there is something different going on?

LW: Well, BLOOLIPS is another kind of kettle of fish altogether. One of the reasons we worked with them is not because they were drag queens but because they were men who liked frocks. So they never wore breasts. Ever. And they made the most imaginative costumes, into fabulous gowns. Betty Bourne had a gown made of clear plastic knives and forks as a fringe all the way down a dress. And Lavinia reversed these umbrellas, and made a whole outfit out of umbrellas. In one scene, they came out dressed as cheeses. Every time they came out onstage you'd go, 'I can't believe I'm looking at this'. So that's what they called drag, but it wasn't drag like wearing tits and impersonating women, and being all sort of, camp fabulous. I think for Split Britches, our version of camp, was to take those elements of fabulousness and downgrade them just slightly, and play with them, not with the attempt to *be*, but with the attempt to not be.

AM: It's obvious that the costume is doing lots of work for you that audience members couldn't know about. I'm wondering what sort of work it does for you as a performer?

LW: Peggy has this funny line that we wrote for her last show, and she says when you look at a video of the show, you realize you don't look so much like James Dean as you thought you did. That's what the costume does. It makes you *feel* like Marilyn Monroe, it makes you feel like Stella, it makes you feel like Gilda, Rita Hayworth, or it makes you feel like Tennessee Williams – I did some male drag. I got that masculine, Southern thing from wearing the costume.

AM: And how does it give you that experience?

LW: I think drag is really sexy, and I think that we use clothing for erotic purposes. I think that the actual interaction between your body and the clothing has a charge, it's almost like a sexual charge. Like how cross dressers, who just do that for their sexual pleasure, must feel. We did this piece called *Little Women: The Tragedy* (1988), where I started naked and reversed stripped into Louisa May Alcott. So what we give the audience is our own relationship to the costume. It's not serving a purpose for the play, it's not serving a purpose for the playwright, it's not that final piece of the puzzle of the character. We get to let you know how we feel about wearing this, and I think that invites the audience into a kind of pleasure; who these characters are, what their aspirations are, that sort of thing. Because there is a real self-consciousness about, 'I'm in this dress, I'm in this wig, I'm in this suit'. I think that's part of it, we let you in and you can do it too, you know. You can be in this, because all it is, is a dress.

AM: It sounds like playing with dressing-up boxes?

LW: Working with the women in prison, dressing-up boxes were the key that unlocked our process. We wanted to get them to talk about human rights abuse. But we were getting: 'why should they talk about all this', and finally we just brought in the costumes, and that was it. We guided them into becoming these kinds of fantasy characters, and through those voices came their stories. Because they could step back from them. So we started calling it our dressing-up box. I just like playing. I think that's what our butch femme was, we're playing at being straight, and we wanted to say, 'You could have fun with this, it doesn't have to be so serious'.

AM: Can you talk to me about your character Tammy? She emerged quite early on in your career. How did you find her, and has her dress sense changed over the years?

LW: I made Tammy in 1978 when I was with Spiderwoman. I'm sure you've heard me tell the story about when Spiderwoman were on tour with a piece called *'Women and Violence'* so we were really in these sort of downtrodden costumes: that's when I was playing the bag-lady. And our costumes went missing and we ended up having to do that show in costumes borrowed from the Hot Peaches drag show. This informed our next piece, which was called *The Lysistrata Number*: it completely marked how we decided to dress that show, so we became these fabulous women, and we consciously used drag. I was 'Lampito', one of the Spartan women, who was not so bright. So I decided to turn her into a Country and Western singer and I called myself Tammy Why Not. So that's where she came from.

AM: Why did you turn her into a country and Western singer?

LW: Well, I am Southern, so the identification with that sort of representation of country people as stupid is something that I have lived with. And I hated country music. I didn't realize it then, but it's definitely something

I denied, in terms of it being part of my background. So it was like a subversion of that shame: it was a good clown for me. I didn't bring her out again until *Upwardly Mobile Home* (1984), and then I used her a lot for MC-ing. So she started as this strident real two-dimensional clown, literally with platform shoes. And then in *Upwardly Mobile Home* I was influenced by the film *Nashville* at that point and the vulnerability about that kind of woman, and I wanted to bring that into Tammy, and then she became a little bit more confident and ballsy when she became an MC … and that's when her hair grew.

AM: So her wardrobe has changed accordingly?

LW: She had a short high blond hair when I first came here in '97. In that interim also, she used to do a lot of gowns, like Dolly Partonesque gowns, and mostly orange or pink. And now I'm into this uniform where I have the same country shirt, the same long wig, the same shoes, the same pants, because it's easy. And also 'cos she just fits in a bag, and I just say, "Here's Tammy", and then I get dressed. And I often do that actually, I start out as me and then I get dressed.

AM: It sounds like you keep her in the dressing-up box and she comes back to life when you put the clothes on, so she is *in* the clothes.

LW: She's definitely in the clothes. I had a radio interview years ago, as her, and I couldn't do it without the wig. They said 'you don't need to put the wig on, it's radio', I said, 'Yes I do'.

AM: Can I ask you about the relationship between feminism and things like housework, home-made clothes, craft, the domestic, those kinds of qualities?

LW: I think our practice was probably what they call the DIY aesthetic now. I think that's what we were doing then, and I do think there's this kind of feminist impulse in that. I think a lot of what we do is to play with what we got, so we just made it with what we had. Maybe that's a class thing, maybe it's a woman thing, I don't know. But I think that's the confidence that it gave us: that we could do this ourselves. And I think that confidence was essentially feminist.

AM: So you had a kind of ownership over it, over the means of production?

LW: Yes. For me the greatest compliments that we can receive after a performance is for someone to come up to us and say, 'Wow, you really made me feel like I could do that'. And I think there is a kind of empowerment around the idea that you *could*. You totally could. We would raid each other's dressing-up box and do something that we'd never done before that night, and that was how we all came up into this performance world.

AN INTERVIEW WITH LEZ BROTHERSTON

Aoife Monks

Introduction

Lez Brotherston is a well-known theatre designer, best known for his long-time collaboration with the choreographer Matthew Bourne. He has also worked extensively with Christopher Gable, director of Northern Ballet Theatre, and has designed for Manchester Royal Exchange, opera and film. His design work spans sets and costume and his work is largely located in the area of dance theatre. Dance theatre is a performance form that emerged out of German expressionism in the 1920s, and which, as Roland Langer outlines: 'refers to a performance form that combines dance, speaking, singing and chanting, conventional theater and the use of props, set, and costumes [...]. It is performed by trained dancers. Usually there is no narrative plot; instead, specific situations, fears, and human conflicts are presented (Langer, 1984, p. 1). While Langer's description applies well to the work of a choreographer such as Pina Bausch, in Brotherston's work with Bourne we see a slightly different sensibility.

The work of Bourne's New Adventures Company (formerly known as Adventures in Motion Pictures) is influenced by cinema, popular culture and forms of camp and kitsch, and places storytelling at the heart of the production. Here, Brotherston discusses his role in designing costumes that function to enact the narrative and to depict character: often having to do much more work than theatre costume might to communicate narrative in a performance form without any verbal text. Brotherston also outlines the ways in which constraint functions in his work: the ways in which the budgetary limitations of a production may enable a particular scenographic vision to emerge, and the way in which costume may provide a useful starting point for the development of choreography, restricting and channelling the dancer's movement. The role of costume in producing an ensemble of dancers, serving the uniformity of movement that comprises the corps de ballet also emerges as the particular demands of the form.

Brotherston speaks at length about his work designing Bourne's *Swan Lake* (1995), a production that caused such a sensation at its debut that it earned the misnomer of the 'all-male' performance. In fact, as Brotherston points out, it is only the swans who were recast and performed by male performers, reconfiguring the ballet as an expressionist depiction of repressed desire, combined with some very funny parodies of the British Royal family and a profoundly camp pastiche of classical dance. Brotherston's costume designs were crucial for how the production restaged and reclaimed the ballet, remodelling the swans as highly athletic and often threatening figures, asserting forms of masculinity that recalibrated the visual pleasures of the dance.

Lez Brotherstone= L, Aoife Monks = A

A: Where do you start as a designer? Do you start in different places depending on the project and the particular genre that you're working on?

L: Not particularly, because everything I do, or everything I'm involved in, has always been driven by the narrative and by character. Matt [Matthew Bourne] and I work very much from the story. Once you're telling the story, then you only have to answer certain questions and it becomes a much more specific way of designing.

A: Do you see costume as a form of storytelling?

L: Yes, well it has to be, particularly if you're doing something that's non-verbal. We only have a character moving onstage and somehow in the visuals you have to be able to know who they are, what they are, and something about them. With all the stuff I do with Matthew, and the stuff I used to with Christopher Gable [of Northern Ballet], those choreographers were interested in dance theatre as opposed to pure dance, so they were using acting techniques to inform the movement as well, and when you're doing that then it's second nature that the clothes have to in some way reflect what the people are.

A: Do you start to design costumes before the performers are cast?

L: Certainly before the performers come in because the way theatre works in Britain is that we just don't have time. It took six months to design *Edward Scissorhands* (2005) and it wasn't cast until much later. If you work in Germany where you have a twenty-three week rehearsal period it's different, but normally we get four weeks or five weeks and there isn't time to design, and have made, and put the costumes onstage, in that time.

A: Would you rather design while the performance is being developed?

L: No. It's good to work on a concept first, otherwise you end up designing by committee where you get a whole load of ideas and nothing strong. At least if you start with a director and a designer, then you have two people working on a vision of what the piece might be. That's not to say that when the actors get involved there isn't any discussion, because there very often is, but it's not as inclusive as some people would like to pretend it is, because a lot of it has to be decided well in advance. Part of the job of a designer is to take the actor with you on a journey for a character without making them feel cornered into it. If you say, 'You're wearing blue because I like blue', that's not good enough. You have to say, 'This is why this character's wearing blue, they're wearing blue because of this line or because of this feeling …' You bring them with you on the journey.

A: It sounds like your primary collaboration is with the director then?

L: Always. I think when a collaboration works at its best, the line is completely blurred. Together you research, you exchange ideas, and it sort of cross-fertilizes. A play is slightly different in that it exists, but things like *Play without Words* (2002) and those kind of dance pieces, there was nothing. We sat down with *Play without Words* and we knew that we had five weeks to create it at the National Theatre and we had no music, we had no story and all we knew was that there was a whole series of 1960s films that we quite liked and we wanted to do something that had a flavour of those films.

A: It sounds like your primary responsibility is to tell stories. Are there any other considerations?

L: Budget. Budget is a fantastic consideration. For instance, when I did *Giselle* (1997) at Northern Ballet Theatre they had thrown away their existing *Giselle* costumes by mistake. They only had a revival budget to put on a new *Giselle*. And so I sat down with Christopher and said, 'OK, if you've only got this much money, I have to be able to buy the clothes, which means that the concept *has* to be twentieth century because I can buy thirties or forties, or fifties clothes but I can't buy nineteenth century costumes and it's going to have to be much more rigorously narrative than *Giselle* might usually be because it's got to be poor as well. What it can't be is 1940s couture fashion, it's got to be something poor and shoddy'. So that drove what I think was a very good concept. It wasn't a hindrance, in fact it ended up, I think, being a particularly good concept for *Giselle*. So budget is not necessarily a hindrance, but it does shape things.

A: How do you work with an audience's expectations around classical ballet, particularly their expectation of lovely frocks?

L: In ballet, I can get very bored with the lovely frocks because ultimately, if you do one of the white ballets, if you do the *Sylphides* or you do the *Swan Lakes*, and *if* they're done with the original steps and *if* they're staged how you'd expect classical ballet to be staged or to look, then it's: 'Oh, a white tutu's a white tutu' – it becomes about who can make the best white tutu as opposed to 'who is Odette?' and that, for me, is not very interesting.

A: Could you talk about where you started with the male swans for *Swan Lake*?

L: It was really, really simple. Having made the decision that the swans were going to be played by men, you then say, 'well, why is it they're

being played by men? What is it we're trying to achieve by men dancing the role as opposed to women dancing the role?' If men are dancing
the role, the movement can be more aggressive, it can be more athletic,
it's not about beauty. In the original of *Swan Lake* you never see swans
because by night-time they take the form of women. In our version they
were animalistic, so I wanted to give them costumes that weren't human.
We also had to think about what was important in the choreography and
a lot of the shapes that Matthew uses are the classical shapes. Then it
becomes about uniformity because you can only see those shapes if
everyone's *sort of* the same. We had a big mixed race cast and what you
did notice when they were dancing was that when the black dancer came
round or when the Asian dancer came round or the guy with dreadlocks
came round you noticed them, you didn't see the whole thing. So then
we said, 'OK, we have to kind of white them all down'. The choice was to
make them pale and interesting. And then the next choice was that their
hair should be the same and we crew cut all their hair so they became
like cobs. ... I did a piece called *Highland Fling* (1994) just before and the
costumes owed a bit to the sylphs in *Highland Fling*. They were like little
sylphs, they had little wings, they were animalistic. They were pale, they
had black eyes and they all had lots of rags tied in their hair so they looked
like weird, naughty children. And they were inquisitive and they were odd.
And to a certain extent I suppose that fed into the swans. And if you look
at the movements, the movement in *Highland Fling* informs the movement
in the swans because we're a company and the previous work informs
the work we're doing next. I had twelve years with Matthew Bourne,
working with dance theatre in a contemporary vocabulary.

A: It must be very rich to work that way.

L: It gets better and better. I don't know any designer who wouldn't say
that: the thing we all hope for is a long-term relationship with a director.

A: Do you consciously draw on tradition to inform your work?

L: In *Swan Lake*, in the cod ballet there is a point of reference which is
Sadler's Wells Royal Ballet, circa 1943, when it was just painted cloths
and it wasn't particularly visually arresting. Matt was drawing on the
Bournonville Ballet, and Bournonville used to put men in little tiny shorts
and great white legs and so they looked fine at the time but come across
as funny now. So we chose the smallest man in the cast to play the
huntsman and when he comes jumping in, in a pair of green lederhosen
that are a bit too short and big white legs, it's funny.

A: Do you think the swans were cross-dressed in *Swan Lake*?

L: No. They're men. They're *male* swans. They were always meant to be
male swans. The joke is, it's become known as the gay Swan Lake. It was
never intended to be a gay Swan Lake. It was *never* a love affair between
two men. The swan was an idea of freedom and of being able to do what

you wanted to do and in some way being accepted and loved. Which are all the things denied to the Prince from when he was a little boy. For him, the swan is freedom. When he decides to commit suicide and he goes into the park, he goes into an outside space where the swan shows him something he wants to be. It's not cross-dressed. People sometimes call it, 'the all-male Swan Lake', which it's not, there's about fifteen women in it. Indeed, when the Princesses come on, I've heard people in the audience go, 'They look fantastic, those men don't they?' But they're women! No, the swans weren't cross-dressed ... they were always male swans. That was the *point* of why they were dressed in that way.

A: In the end, for you, costume supports the moment and the story and the character. What about how the performer feels when they're wearing it? Do you ever make costumes that means that the performer can only use their body in restricted ways? Does costume motivate movement?

L: It does motivate movement. For instance, in *Scissorhands*, he's got scissors on his hands: we made the hands very early and we put them into rehearsal. And what Matt found interesting were the limitations. If you begin choreographing and you can do anything you want, that's really hard. If he has to work with a pair of hands then he's asking, 'Well, what can you do with these hands? Can you hold her? Can you catch her? Oh, no you can't, watch her eyes ...'

A: So it's the beginning point for a certain kind of choreography?

L: It can be an anchor point for a choreographer to go: 'What can we create with this?' Problem-solving is easy. If the budget requires this, or that, then it sort of narrows your choices. And in narrowing your choices it then forms what you're trying to do in performance.

A: What's the difference between designing for film and the stage?

L: I think you've got a lot more people between you and the film, like producers and people. That's why I like working in theatre. I like working in theatre because I have almost complete control over what an audience sees

A: So do you enjoy the opportunity to design both set and costume together?

L: Yeah, always, always. For me it's always about a character in a world. Whether you start with the world first and put the character into it or you start with the character and build the world around them. And that world needn't necessarily be naturalistic but it's about finding a theatrical language to tell whatever it is you're trying to tell.

Playing the Body: Costume, Stereotypes and Modernity in Performance

Aoife Monks

In 1867, the critic John Ruskin went to see a pantomime performance of *Ali Baba* at Covent Garden Theatre in London. His experience was one of vertiginous and multiple crossings:

> The Forty Thieves were girls. The Forty Thieves and their forty companions were in some way mixed up with about forty hundred and forty fairies, who were girls. There was an Oxford and Cambridge boat-race in which the Oxford and Cambridge men were girls. [...] The forty Thief-Girls proceeded to light forty cigars. Whereupon the British public gave them a round of applause.
>
> (Ruskin cited in Senelick, 2000, p. 263)

The pantomime provides Ruskin with a host of scenes from British imperial life: Orientalist Arab thieves, the elite and male world of Oxbridge, and fantastical and probably sentimental depictions of magic and fairies. Ruskin's rather sardonic description enables us to enjoy the fact that these figures are all played by 'girls', presumably scantily clad chorus girls, hired for the visual and erotic pleasures they provide onstage, even as they also depict a range of other identities. The costumes that they wear to perform these roles, therefore, are designed as much to display their body for erotic pleasure, as they are to depict the fictional 'Other' identity that they represent.

The peculiar work that costume does in producing and imagining bodies onstage is captured in this description. The pantomime enables its audience to enjoy the spectacle of a series of foreign bodies through the medium of the girl's body. Costume produces the representation of 'other' identities, such as masculinity, class and Orientalism, and the performance of femininity in the fairies via the bodies of the chorus girls. The spectator therefore vacillates between two kinds of costume – the costume that produces the imaginary body of the represented Arab or Oxford student, and the scanty costume that displays the 'real' body of the girl. However, of course, this shift isn't quite so clear-cut, since these two forms of costume are contained in the same object of clothing. The erotic display of the girl's body inevitably mediates and determines the nature of the representation of the Arab or the Oxford student, while the Arab and the Oxford student become the staging-ground for the erotic display of the girl's body through exoticism and cross-dressing. The real body of the performer and the represented body of the character therefore combine and produce each other. We can see moments though when Ruskin wants to distinguish between these bodies, when he describes the moment of cigar-smoking, for example, as 'an ugly and disturbing dream' (cited in Weltman, 2011, p. 31), evidently upset by the display of such unfeminine behaviour in female performers.

In this account of a spectator at the theatre in the nineteenth century, the peculiar nature of costume comes to light. The costume worn by the chorus girls works to produce a series of stereotypes on the stage: it 'fixes' the image of Arabs and upper-class students, making them instantly recognizable. The costume also delimits the female working-class performer's body, turning it into an object that provides spectacle and erotic pleasures for a male theatregoer. In this, we might see how the role of costume is to make bodies safe and recognizable on the stage, depicting (indeed, producing) fixed categories of identity. On the other hand, the fact that these stereotypes are being played out by the 'wrong' body, that of the chorus girl, has the simultaneous effect of unfixing identity by enabling female bodies to behave in unfeminine ways, such as smoking. Furthermore, the fact that the chorus girls play so many roles onstage, showing that they can shift between Arab, fairy and upper-class gentleman in such quick succession, also undercuts the fixity of the identities that they present: the role of costume is to render identity stable and fixed, but changing *between* costumes means that the performers keep on undoing the stereotypes that they produce onstage.

This conundrum of bodies that are fixed and unfixed all at once is nothing unusual onstage, but I want to argue in this chapter that it becomes a particularly intense paradox on the nineteenth-century stage. This is because this period had a particular investment in depicting idealized and denigrated bodies onstage through the production of stereotypes, in which costume played a crucial role in rendering identity and bodies knowable and readable. Furthermore, Ruskin's description of a cross-dressed stage is not exceptional: the nineteenth century was a period in which roles tended to be played by the 'wrong' body, opening out complicated relationships between the actor, the character, the costume and the audience. This, I argue, results from the convergence of a range of historical contexts: industrial modernity, which was at its peak in Ruskin's 1860s and which organized bodies in radically new relationships to time and space; British imperialism, which required the representation of 'other' bodies from around the world on the British stage; and the related interest in categorizing, describing and understanding bodies that emerged out of the burgeoning discourse of Social Darwinism. This mid-nineteenth-century moment placed huge pressure on the idea of authentic and real bodies, and required the theatre to act as a staging-ground for the spectacle of these bodies, in order that they could be understood, assimilated and controlled.

The cultural critic, Marshall Berman, defines modernity as the experience of: 'agitation and turbulence, psychic dizziness and drunkenness, expansion of experiential possibilities and destruction of moral boundaries and personal bonds, self-enlargement and self-derangement' (Berman, 2010, p.18).[1] Here, Berman describes the emergence of a form of modernity that crystallizes in the nineteenth century as enormous and rapid social change. Referring to the scientific discoveries of the enlightenment and the emergence of new forms of technology, Berman traces the effects of these innovations on the experience of space and time, arguing that this rapid social change creates 'new human environments and destroys old ones, speeds up the whole tempo of life, generates new forms of corporate power and class struggle; immense demographic upheavals, severing millions of people from their ancestral habits, hurtling them halfway across the world into new lives [....] and rapid and often cataclysmic urban growth.' (ibid., p. 16). In the face of this movement of people from rural to urban space and across national borders, who grapple with new forms of work and communication, an important question emerges: to paraphrase Richard Sennett, how can we tell who people are by what they wear? (Sennett, 1976, p.165).[2]

This may seem a trivial problem, but it in fact speaks to the emergence of the growing urban centre as a space that presents, as Sennett describes, the problem of: '*audience* – specifically, how to arouse belief in one's appearance among a milieu of strangers' (ibid., p. 38). Where interaction with strangers becomes the social norm, in the face of rapid urban growth, recognizing and understanding others through their clothing becomes more and more difficult. This difficulty was heightened further by the advent of mass-produced clothing in the early nineteenth century, which rendered appearance more and more homogenous. Sennett points out that this shift coincides with the greater scrutiny of appearance on the street: 'as the images became more monochromatic, people began to take them more seriously, as signs of the personality of the wearer' (Sennett, p. 164).

This close attention to the public appearance of the body that is less and less readable may have emerged from the historical disjunction that characterized the mid-nineteenth century, as Berman describes the experience of: 'living in a revolutionary age, an age that generates explosive upheavals in every dimension of personal, social and political life. At the same time, [being able to] remember what it is like to live, materially and spiritually, in worlds that are not modern at all' (Berman, 2010, p. 17). The nineteenth-century anxiety about the difficulty of telling who strangers are by what

---

[1] Here Berman traces out the qualities of Jean Jacques Rousseau's view of modernity in the eighteenth century, which he argues opens out the key identifying experiences of industrial modernity that emerge most strongly during the mid-nineteenth century.

[2] Sennett: 'How do you recognise a gentleman when you meet a stranger?'

they wear is an expression of anxiety linked to a still-remembered earlier period in which dress placed its wearer within a social hierarchy organized through recognizable codes and conventions. By contrast, the nineteenth century, in which identity and social relations were rapidly changing and 'looked' different, had profound implications for the structural relationship between embodiment, identity and appearance. Furthermore, given that national identity expanded beyond geographical lines through imperialism, the colonies provided new and deeply fraught sets of social relationships that were often understood and translated through visual codes of appearance. The newly emerging discourse of Social Darwinism worked to affirm and naturalize already existent social hierarchies of class, race and gender, but gave them a fixity through the scientific claims to objectivity and 'truth'. Working out who somebody was by what they wore carried with it the desire to decode modern forms of embodiment and to place them within a set of newly defined social categories.

In the nineteenth century, then, we can see the question of dress and appearance being related to the articulation of modern categories of identity, in which bodies were scrutinized, defined and organized through visual codes. While identity became more and more unreadable in the street, the theatre became a place in which costume could render appearance immediately comprehensible on the stage. As Sennett puts it: 'the public began to demand that, in art at least, one really could tell, and without difficulty, who someone was by looking at him or her' (Sennett, 1976, p. 174). One of the ways in which appearance became readable onstage was through the deployment of stereotypes in performance. These stereotypes, such as blackface minstrelsy's depiction of African American identity, the pantomime dame's representation of post-menopausal womanhood, or the Stage Irish comedian's depiction of Irishness worked to make identity instantly recognizable, through an easily decoded, repeated and recognizable costume. Costume then worked to reinforce and produce power relationships between the audience and the images onstage, making appearance and identity seamless.

The concept of the 'Real' is useful for understanding the role that theatre costume can play in producing stereotypes that mediate how the audience might feel able to read bodies on the street. The philosopher and gender theorist Judith Butler defines the Real as: 'a phantasmatic construction [...] – [an] illusion [...] of substance – that bodies are compelled to approximate, but never can' (Butler, 1999, p. 186). Butler suggests that the Real is a socially constructed ideal to which the spectator is expected to aspire or conform, thus moulding their own bodies in service to this ideal image. Rather than seeing bodies as somehow natural or 'outside' of culture, Butler proposes that our bodies are always in process, materialized *through* cultural discourse, through the conformity to, and repetitive performance of, social norms governing bodily appearance and identity. Butler argues that stable bodies are the illusory after-effect of this performance. Unlike theatrical performance, however, Butler argues that the repetitive nature of social gender performance on the street renders it invisible, giving gender and sex the appearance of being 'natural' and immutable (see ibid.).

However, even as Butler distinguishes between artificially produced identity onstage and invisibly produced identity on the street, the role that theatre costume plays in producing these ideal standards of bodily conduct remains important. The nineteenth-century stage can be understood as a place in which the Real is imagined and reinforced through the performance of stereotypes, and requires that we interrogate the function of costume in producing idealized and denigrated bodies. Costume, then, can be examined for its role in forming how spectators may imagine their own bodies, by constructing legitimate and illegitimate identifications with particular modes of embodiment on the stage. Costume not only helps to represent the hierarchies of identity in its social context but also contributes to, and shapes, those hierarchies. Costume can therefore be understood as a mechanism of the Real, a place in which legitimate and illegitimate bodies are invented, formed and produced.

So far, I've suggested that the huge social upheavals of the nineteenth century meant that appearance became ambiguous on the street, and required the stage to offer unambiguous fixed images of identity that were rendered readable through costume. What's more, costume may have played a role in organizing how spectators related to their own bodies and the bodies of others, by offering stereotypes that set up ideal or denigrated states of identity. However, I want to query here, whether stereotypes onstage can ever truly fix identity when they are played out through costume on the body of an actor? To raise this question, I want to draw on the work of the Indian scholar, Homi K. Bhabha, who investigates in his essay, 'The Other Question', how racial and ethnic stereotypes are based on the perceived stability and timelessness of colonial identity during Imperialism. He argues that the use of stereotypes to fix identity belies a profound anxiety about the unknowable otherness of colonial natives, 'the stereotype is a complex, ambivalent, contradictory mode of representation, as anxious as it is assertive' (Bhabha, 1994, p. 70). Bhabha also suggests that representation itself is (problematically) formative rather than imitative, examining how: 'the processes of subjectification [are] made possible (and plausible) through stereotypical discourse' (ibid., p. 67). Along with Bhabha, I want to suggest that the use of costume to render identity fixed and knowable onstage can also be taken as the expression of anxiety about the unknowable and fluid qualities of this identity. Furthermore, I want to suggest that even as costume fixes identity, as we've seen with Ruskin's chorus girls, the fact that the performer may perform in more than one costume and play out more than one stereotype in a performance also has the potential to destabilize identity, to undermine the apparently timeless and unchanging nature of the bodies being depicted.

In the following sections I want to consider how the stereotypes produced by costume in mid-nineteenth-century stage Irishness and blackface minstrelsy functioned to fix and delimit the possibilities of Irish and black identity, while at the same time betraying profound anxieties about the nature of this identity and becoming unfixed by their place in the malleable and contradictory space of the stage. I want to suggest that costume does complicated and ambivalent work in performance, and may fix and unsettle categories of identity all at once. The chapter will go onto consider the legacies of this theatrical period by examining the responses to these forms of theatre in modernism, specifically in the work of the Irish-American playwright, Eugene O'Neill, and will conclude by looking at a recent performance of his work by the postmodern experimental American collective, The Wooster Group, in order to think about the continuing and ever-changing configurations of performer, role, costume and audience in the possibilities of costuming the body at the theatre.

STAGE IRISHNESS

When Dion Boucicault (1820–1890) wrote *The Colleen Bawn* in 1860 for Laura Keene's Theatre in New York, his aim was to find ways to entertain audiences with a new version of Irishness embodied in the comic figure of Myles-na-Coppaleen. Boucicault, a Dublin-born playwright, actor and manager, could be viewed as the global celebrity of his day: he'd had numerous hits as a playwright and performer in London and now New York, made and lost millions of pounds as a theatrical impresario, had scandalized and incensed his critics with his daring elopement with Agnes Robertson (the young ward of Charles Kean), and had made a name for himself with numerous theatrical inventions (such as the Corsican trap and fireproof scenery) and his lobbying for the greater legal status of playwrights and their play-texts (see Fawkes, 1979, and McFeely, 2012). *The Colleen Bawn* was the first play that Boucicault had set in Ireland, and he based it on the true story of a young Irish peasant woman wooed into marriage by an aristocrat who murdered her so that he could make a more financially advantageous match.[3] Boucicault adapted the story so that Eily, the heroine, is saved from drowning by Myles Na Coppaleen, the comic hero, played by Boucicault himself. His success with *The Colleen Bawn* (his seventh work in seven months) was immediate and he brought the play to London where it had the longest run in the history of the English stage at the Adelphi theatre, its 230 performances making it *The Mousetrap* of its day (see ibid., 1979). Seeing that there was a market for plays set in Ireland, Boucicault proceeded to write and star in three further Irish melodramas: *Arrah Na Pogue* (1864), *The Shaughran* (1874) and *Robert Emmett* (1884).

---

[3] The story of the play is based on the novel *The Collegians* written by Gerard Griffin in 1829, which was itself based on a true story.

Against the backdrop of the scenic rural setting of Kerry, Boucicault appeared in the role of Myles in the traditional rags and stovepipe hat of the stage Irishman. His costume placed him firmly in the longstanding stereotype of the poor comical drunken Irish peasant that, as Richard Cave has suggested, has circulated on the stage since the Renaissance (see Richard Cave, 1991). It's true that the ragged stage Irishman has a long legacy, but I want to suggest that the rags worn by the comic Irish character played a particularly important role in Boucicault's Irish plays. The rags produced a fixed stereotype of Irishness, while becoming unfixed when performed in combination with Boucicault's celebrity persona, which offered an alternative and competing version of Irishness in performance. Furthermore, while Boucicault's ragged costume mimicked the anti-Irish polemical caricatures of the day, it nonetheless rendered Irishness inoffensive and safe, by offering audiences an escape from industrial modernity. Boucicault therefore used Ireland to enable audiences to feel nostalgia – homesickness – for a rural pre-modern Irish idyll through the figure of the comic Irishman, while at the same time employing truly modern production techniques to do so. As a result, nostalgia for the pre-modern was the surface style of a profoundly contemporary sensibility in his work, and the rags of Myles Na Copaleen were crucial in mediating these complex and contradictory emotional states.

While there had been a long line of comic Irishmen on the British and then American stage, the nature of their depiction shifted from a harmless figure on the eighteenth-century stage to a more menacing and violent character by the mid-to-late nineteenth century. An earlier amiable example can be seen in Tyrone Power's performance as Paddy Murphy in *The Happy Man* by Samuel Lover, written in 1839, set in a fantastical version of India. At the opening of the play, Paddy is discovered in British army uniform, but is:

> washing a small front of a shirt and a frill in the stream – his dress is rather tattered, and it must be apparent that he has no shirt; his musket and a drum lie beside a fallen column. [...]
>   Pat: well clane linen is comfortable, and though it's little I have, yet for the honor o' the service, I like to make it look as respectable as I can. [...] It's a hard thing that an Irishman, whose native land is the land of linen, should want a shirt – but that's the fate o' war

> (Lover, 1839, p. 9).

The plot revolves around the fact that the superstitious Indians think Paddy's shirt has special powers to make him happy – when they swap clothes with him, they discover he is just wearing a frill and no shirt and are even more impressed by how magically powerful a talisman his shirt can be. The play mixes the spectacle of exotic 'Indian' dress with the comedy of the stage Irishman's raggedness, even when in army uniform. The joke of the play is both on the Indians for their gullible superstition and on Paddy himself for his innocent happiness that renders him stereotypically principled, brave and rather stupid.

The theme of rags continues in the Irish-American playwright Bayle Bernard's play *His Last Legs*, which opened at the Theatre Royal Haymarket in 1839 with the lead stage Irishman O'Callaghan, played again by Tyrone Power. Wearing a 'black coat, buttoned up, black pantaloons, hessian boots, shabby bat, linen mantle and thick stick', O'Callaghan first enters 'in a shabby genteel suit, dirty from travelling' (Bernard, 1839, p. 8). Like many of Bernard's characters, O'Callaghan is a member of the Irish gentry, down on his luck, and his clothes become a testament to his straitened circumstances: 'This is the age of revolution, and you now see mine – a fellow who once set examples to dandies, destined henceforth to set copies to boys!' (Bernard, 1839, p. 10). In O'Callaghan having to move to England and become a teacher to pay his debts, we see the earlier stereotype of the Irish comic figure as a spendthrift, uneconomical, vainglorious member of the Irish gentry sunk low to his current ragged state. The effect of this loss of money has a major effect on his clothing, and O'Callaghan shows his guile in managing his poverty in his treatment of clothes:

> My wardrobe's in a very delicate state of health, and a brush would just now be a dangerous cathartic. I was obliged to have my coat turned for this journey; though that I didn't mind – I'm not the first man that's turned his coat to get into office. My trousers I resuscitated with a bottle of 'Scott's Reviver' – that's what I call being reduced to a dyer necessity.
>
> (ibid., p. 11)

O'Callaghan's rags reduce him to a figure of comedy and pathos – his poverty is a means to both malign him, mock him and feel pity for him.

Bernard offers another aristocratic figure in his play *The Irish Attorney: Or, Galway Practice in 1770* (1847), which was first performed at the Haymarket, 6 May 1840, with the central character of Pierce O'Hara played by Tyrone Power. This Irish play is set seventy years earlier than the time of the audience, and Power is costumed (in contrast to the usual rags of the Irishman), in the style of an eighteenth-century fop: 'scarlet gold-laced coat, cut in the fashion of 1770, turned up with green, buckskin breeches reaching to the calf, with bunches of black ribbons, white satin waistcoat, low-top boots, powdered head, conical hat, broad band and buckle' (Bernard, 1847, p. 1). The contrast between O'Hara's flamboyance and the dour Yorkshire lawyers' offices that he's been forced to work in due to his accumulated debts is marked through costume. The Yorkshire characters express disdain for O'Hara's exaggerated dress, violence and spendthrift tendencies – as Saunders the lawyer declares, 'why, he's more likely to break the law than keep it: those Irish gentry are such devils for fighting they call them fire-eaters' (ibid., p. 8).

But O'Hara's exuberance ensures that he is the most sympathetic figure onstage, with a better grasp of the codes of honour than the anachronistically nineteenth-century parsimony and economy demonstrated by his new employers: 'before I was fifteen I could nick a tail, and prick a vein, wing a snipe and worm a hound; I could draw a house, a horse and a game cock, tin a saucepan, rim a wheel, play the German flute, crack a skull, and cane a bailiff with any man in the county' (ibid., p. 15). Indeed, O'Hara's principles come right: the play shows that it is he who knows the difference between the law and true justice through the exertion of his wits, undergirded by the many typical qualities of the stage Irishman: gallantry, sentiment, drunkenness and violence, as he puts it: 'if drinking hard all night, and riding hard all day, can make a man a lawyer, by my honour, sir, though I say it, I'm qualified for the woolsack myself' (ibid., p. 15).

While in these earlier nineteenth-century plays, rags or flamboyant dress are worn by the stage Irishman as a form of sympathetic and harmless fun, connected to the dissipation of the gentry or the benignly shambolic conduct of Irish soldiers, the rags and red shawls that are worn by the Irish comic character later in the century presented a much more menacing version of Irishness. After the Fenian revolt of 1848 in Ireland and subsequent forms of violent agitation in Britain, such as the murder of a police officer in Manchester and the Clerkenwell prison bombing in 1867, the depiction of the Irish as harmless if idiotic peasants shifted considerably. L. Perry Curtis Jr argues that there was a significant change in how British cartoons represented Irishness: 'from a rather primitive, rustic, or simple minded peasant to a degenerate man and then an ape-like monster bent on murder or outrage' (Curtis Jr, 1997, p. xiii). The growing social and political unrest of nineteenth-century Ireland transformed the Irish into ragged menacing monkeys in British representation. Boucicault's Irish melodramas emerged during this period and, while they reiterated many of the stereotypes of Irishness, they also undercut and worked against the caricatures of stupid ragged peasants with simian features, by offering a safe and inoffensive version of Irishness onstage.

In the case of Boucicault's star turn as Myles na Coppaleen in *The Colleen Bawn*, his ragged costume enabled audiences the chance to ameliorate their status as modern city dwellers by offering them a pre-modern fantasy of Ireland. Spectators were drawn to the theatre to see Boucicault undertaking the sensational stage dive into the 'lake' in which Eily O'Connor (played by Agnes Robertson) drowned nightly (a lake produced by twenty small boys enthusiastically shaking blue gauze) (see Fawkes, 1979, pp. 112–133). But they also came night after night to access the idyllic, pre-modern world of Ireland. The scenery of Killarney allowed them to escape, even if just for the evening, the sooty, industrial, foggy London town for the wilds of Kerry. It's possible to see Boucicault's theatre as a form of escapism and wish-fulfillment for workers living in the most modern of cities. For them, the ragged Myles-na-Coppaleen embodied everything that is not modern.

Boucicault's character appeared onstage at a time when there was great anxiety about the proprieties of dress, where as Richard Sennett puts it: 'there arose […] a need to pay great attention to details of appearance and to hold oneself in, for fear of being read wrong or maliciously' (Sennett, 1976, p. 166). Myles's rags suggest a freedom from this constraint and he represents all that is alternative to the model modern city dweller: he speaks English badly, he drinks when he likes, he fights, he's lazy, he is emotional, he challenges injustice, he plays the fool and then undermines his foolishness by demonstrating himself to be just as clever as lawyers and aristocrats. The stage Irishman is always on the side of the poor against the middle classes: his triumphs over their harsh laws and their moralizing condemnation are triumphs on the poor's behalf. His combined raggedness and heroism enables a form of escapism and identification, while at the same time rendering Myles so simple and exuberant that the possibility of resistance or menace to British law and order is contained and made safe.

The working classes weren't the play's only audience, however. The repeat visits of spectators to the show can be found in the diaries of Queen Victoria who recorded on 4 February 1861 that: 'D. Boucicault and his wife [...] acted admirably as the ragged Irish peasant and the Colleen Bawn. The scenery was very pretty and the whole piece very characteristic and thrilling' (cited in Fawkes, 1979, pp. 122–123). She saw it three times in total and just like her, audiences flocked to the theatre to see the show over and over again. The Strand got blocked up with 'colleen cabs' (hansom cabs dressed up like Irish peasant wagons) outside the Adelphi theatre. The show even set off a trend in red shawls, with fashionable women dressing themselves up to look like Irish peasants (see Nicholas Daly, 2009, pp. 55–81). Nostalgia became a fashion choice: audiences were being primed to engage with the image of poor Irish peasants as the site of authenticity and longing, as alternatives to the modern city. And yet of course, in buying and wearing a red shawl, the privileged members of the audience organized themselves as consumers of an image of Irishness that had little real relation to the impoverished conditions of actual Irish peasants shortly after the Irish Famine. Rather, they indulged in the experience of nostalgia, the sense of homesickness for a place that they most likely had never actually visited, through the vehicle of Boucicault dressed in rags.

Of course, Boucicault's presence onstage complicated the attractions of the comic Irishman even further. Audiences watched a badly dressed, feckless, lazy, undisciplined and drunken Irish character onstage while also seeing a highly disciplined, skilful and hard-working Irish celebrity performing him. They saw an Irish character who is poor, ignorant and parochial, and a millionaire Irish actor-manager, who travels the world with his plays, prompting the faint suspicion that his characters might be strategically rather than authentically Irish. Boucicault was hounded by accusations of plagiarism throughout his career (accusations that appear to be entirely accurate in many cases – see Fawkes, 1979, and McFeely, 2012), but I wonder if this suspicion of inauthenticity and lack of originality might centre on the sense that his performances offered two, competing and contradictory, versions of Irishness all at once? Even as Boucicault rendered the Irishman instantly recognizable and knowable through the fixity of his costume, he also undid this fixity by offering a competing identity in the assertion of his celebrity persona. Admittedly this competing persona was connected to a publicly decadent lifestyle (as one American journalist put it: 'having seen, in the castle at Versailles, the famous bed-chamber of Louis XVI, I am prepared to say that the dormitory of Boucicault's was decidedly the most comfortable' [cited in Fawkes, 1979, p. 119]). Critics attributed to Boucicault an exuberant, spendthrift and flamboyant persona – situating his 'real' self in the earlier stage Irish tradition of the valiant member of the fallen gentry, rather than the more recent version of the roguish and menacing Irish peasant.

The fixed qualities of the comic Irishman, then, were undercut by the suspicion that this very pleasurable stereotype might not actually correlate with the reality of a much more fluid form of Irish identity. Boucicault's rural settings were just as calculated. As Nicholas Daly suggests, *The Colleen Bawn* might have been set in a nostalgic version of Ireland, but the logic of its production was entirely contemporary. The show's record-breaking long run and the simultaneous touring productions that Boucicault sent out across England reiterated his longstanding success at manipulating the market, drawing on the very contemporary principles of a market-led theatre system. Indeed, Boucicault's repeated diving into the lake' to rescue Agnes Robertson as Eily might be understood as a move from repetition (the nightly performance of the same show) to the logic of what Walter Benjamin described as 'mechanical reproduction' (Benjamin, 1968, pp. 214–218). As Nicholas Daly suggests, the fact that audiences returned nightly to watch him execute this daring stunt meant that Boucicault's performance took on the logic of the machine. Even as he offered a pre-modern rural setting for his plays, his performance relied on new visual effects of lighting, and split second timing. As Daly puts it: 'sensation drama produced a sort of "training" in modernity, acclimatizing people to the pace of industrial, urban life through homeopathic doses of shock and suspense' (Daly, 2009, p. 5). In effect, Boucicault smuggled in a distinctly modern sensibility under the cover of nostalgia, hiding within the pre-modern rags of the stage Irishman an induction into the experience of modern time and space. The Irish may have been rendered instantly recognizable in Boucicault's nostalgic forma-tion of the stereotype onstage, but the affect/effect that image had on its audience was by no means as simple as it might first appear.

PLAYING IRISH, PLAYING BLACK

On 20 November 1865, Dan Bryant, leader of the New York-based Bryant's Minstrels and the 'most famous expositor of that hop, skip and jump affair', sang a song in Gaelic, dressed as an African American field slave:

> Och! I wish I was on Butthermilk hill, Faix, an' I was there I would cry my fill, An' its every tear would turn a mill, Musha Slathereen ma colleen boucahal deelish.
> (Bryant's Minstrels, 1864, Vol. VIII, No. 51, p. 806)

An image of Bryant from circa 1865 gives us some sense of what he might have worn to sing this song: ragged trousers that were too short, collars that were too large, a straw hat, worn boots and, of course, a burnt cork mask, with his whitened lips distorted into a grimace that indicates his character's status as a clown. The image offers us a clear depiction of a racist caricature: Bryant is presenting a fixed representation of black identity that is part of a long theatrical tradition of white performers playing black on the nineteenth-century American stage. While the black make-up he wears can easily be understood as a mask, in fact his entire costume functions as a kind of mask: a presentational disguise that stands in for an entire racial category. This image is probably taken from the part of the show known as 'Plantation Darkies of the South', as described by one eye-witness:

> They were attired as field hands, checked shirts, with large collars, striped pants and big shoes. This consisted of plantation songs, grotesque dancing, banjo songs, 'Lucy Long,' 'Old Bob Ridley,' 'The Cachuca' dance, 'Banjo Lesson,' and wound up with a festival dance for the whole troupe, called a 'walk around.'
>
> (Dumont, 1914)

The picture is even more complicated when we see Bryant again, this time in 'whiteface' dressed as a familiarly ragged figure. With his large curly hair, courdroy trousers, ragged jacket and trousers, a hat full of holes, his clothes a tapestry of patches, holding a shillelagh and a bottle, Bryant embodies the ideal stage Irishman. Indeed, Bryant was famous both for his blackface minstrel routines and for his depictions of stage Irish characters like Handy Andy in 1863. His success was so great that he toured these roles to Europe, performing black and Irish characters for audiences in London, Liverpool and Dublin, even playing Boucicault roles, leading one critic to declare: 'Dan Bryant in Celtic characters had a great reception in Dublin and Liverpool in 1865 [...] He was a better Shaun the Post in *Arrah Na Pogue* at Niblo's than the author Dion Boucicault himself.' The playbills and programmes from Bryant's Minstrels make clear that Bryant appeared in the role of both blackface minstrel and stage Irish character in the same shows – performing laments (often with phonetic Gaelic lyrics as we've seen) while in blackface, and playing comic routines and songs while dressed as stage Irish.

The picture gets more complicated again when we take account of Bryant's own ethnic background. Bryant emerged as an important minstrel performer in Christie's Minstrels in the mid-nineteenth century. In 1857, changing his name from O'Brien to Bryant he formed Bryant's Minstrels with his brothers Jerry and Neil Bryant. The brothers came from an Irish family and their company included other Irish or Irish-American performers such as Daniel Donegan, J.J. Kelly, J.F. Hogan and Dan Emmett (composer of the song Dixie which Bryant's Minstrels first performed onstage in 1859). The formation of the company spanned the American Civil War, and in 1868 the company moved into a theatre based at Tammanay Hall, the seat of the Democratic Party in New York.

Here we have an example in which two stereotypes are in play onstage through the medium of one performer's body: that of the Irishman and the black man. In both cases these are crude, limited depictions of identity that are established through a very fixed use of costume and make-up. However, the Irish American identity of the performer playing these roles, and the fact that he switches between these roles begins to undo the fixity of the images. Rather, we see a complex interaction between actor and role, between the two roles played and the audience.

The role of the Irish in performing minstrelsy in the mid-nineteenth century has been investigated in detail by scholars such as Eric Lott (1993) and David Roediger (1991). I have written elsewhere about the complex ways in which blacking up became a means for Irish performers to gain whiteness through the structure of disavowal contained in the minstrel costume. The fact that the performer wants us to know that he is not who he plays becomes a crucial aspect in our imagining his 'true' white identity underneath the costume and make-up. However, as Anne McClintock points out: 'Ireland presented a telling dilemma for pseudo-Darwinian imperial discourse' (McClintock, 1995, p. 52), with the newly arrived Irish immigrants in America being viewed as 'coloured' and at the bottom of the racial scale next to African Americans. In other words, the whiteness that we imagine Bryant to possess 'beneath' the make-up is actually an after-effect of the make-up – his racist denigration of blackness allows us to imagine him as white, when his Irishness is actually far more ambiguously situated within the racial hierarchies of the mid-nineteenth century. We might imagine too, that the largely immigrant audiences attending his performances might also gain whiteness in their rejection of blackness through laughter and mockery.

Minstrelsy here might also be seen as a form of training in how to 'look' race at bodies on the street. Dan Bryant's blackened face and ragged costume became a means for audiences to reconfigure their own embodiment as white and modern, and to configure their view of black people after the performance had ended. The picture gets more complicated though, when we examine the relationship between the minstrel character and the stage Irish roles played by Bryant. Just as Bryant changed his name to appear less Irish, both of the roles he plays are clearly acts of disavowal – Bryant is distancing himself from the 'colour' attributed to Irish immigrants *and* from the stupidity, drunkenness, sentimentality, etc., of the stage Irishman. Indeed, the characters share many of the same qualities, and Bryant necessarily used very similar skills to play both roles: he wears rags to perform both characters, and in both cases he depicts a poor, stupid, badly spoken, drunken, violent, sentimental and superstitious character who sings, dances and tells jokes. Bryant shows himself to be a thoroughly modern city-dweller by the fact that he is *not* these characters: minstrelsy and Irishness are stereotypes that enable him to distance himself from the social qualities that he is imagined to possess as an Irish-American.

We might ask then why Bryant might have sung laments about homesickness in Gaelic while in blackface. Eric Lott points out that many of the minstrel songs concerned 'traumatic parting, distance, temporal and geographical breaks' (Lott, 1993, p. 198), suggesting that Irish-American minstrel performers in particular seemed drawn to the performance of loss and longing through singing sentimental laments, playing out homesickness beneath a blackened mask. With an enormous displacement of population during the Irish Famine in the 1840s, with emigrants to America often moving from agricultural contexts to the big industrial cities, singing a Gaelic ballad enabled these immigrant performers to mourn their own loss of a pre-modern, non-industrial agrarian existence and their own alienation in the modern city. They explored this experience through the surrogate figure of the black field slave – pasting their homesickness onto a figure that they simultaneously rejected.

On the other hand, Bryant did not generally sing songs of loss and longing while dressed as Irish. Rather, the repertoire of the company emphasizes the performance of comic songs while in 'white face' and a full 'Irish' costume. Performances of *Tim Finigan's Wake*, for example, played out the cheerful, drunken comic stereotype without the focus on longing and loss that the minstrel mask enabled. Instead we have the song about Tim Finigan, whose partiality for the 'drop of the creatur every morn' causes him to fall to his death. His wake ensues, in which his corpse is arranged with 'a barrel of pratees around his feet', while the guests 'laid into tay and cake, then pipes and tobacky and whiskey punch', a heady mix that ends when 'shillelah law was all the rage, and a rousing ruction soon began' (Bryant's Minstrels, Vol. VII, pp. 22–23). Here we see the wish fulfilment supplied also by Boucicault's comic heroes, in which drunkenness and disorder are celebrated and performed. But there is no trace here of the homesickness and sentimentality that characterizes Bryant's minstrel performances.

It seems, then, in order for Bryant in particular, and the Irish in general, to appear modern in 1860s New York, he must not be seen to miss home. Playing black is a way to disavow this longing and at the same time play it out 'under the cover of darkness'. If, as Svetlana Boym, paraphrasing Michael Kammen, suggests, nostalgia can be understood as 'history without guilt' (Boym, 2001, p. xiv), then the sentimentality and nostalgia performed in these laments enables a longing for home through a bizarre displacement onto a longing for slavery in the Deep South, without any recognition of the real conditions of that slavery. Instead, the costume of the slave becomes a space for fantasy through which these working-class performers could organize an affective relationship to their status as workers in a modern city like New York. As Eric Lott puts it: 'the spectator may have intermittently identified with black characters […] but he always knew what he was not: a slave whether of wages or the plantation' (Lott, 1993, p. 205).

On the other hand, the Irish costume also allows Bryant to displace the disorder, violence and drunkenness onto a stereotype that he also distances himself from, even as he is himself Irish, playing out the same deconstructive effects that Boucicault also produced in the dissonance between his own persona and that of the character. It's important, however, to point to the ways in which the minstrel and the stage Irish roles were not symmetrical in Bryant's performances: the lasting and deeply damaging effects of minstrel performance on African American identity shouldn't be forgotten here. As Ann McClintock warns, these interrelated identities should not be considered symmetrical or interchangeable (1995, p. 65). The question of power and hierarchy must always come under consideration when examining how multiple identities are constructed and formed on the stage.

In Bryant's work we can see how costume enables a performer to play out what he is not: to establish a gap between himself and the role, and to do this doubly: placing at a distance the blackness and stereotypical Irishness that characterized the depiction of Irish immigrants in New York in the nineteenth century. The peculiar thing about the use of costume here, however, is how Bryant distances himself from these qualities by embodying them. The stereotype then is both assimilated and rejected through costume. Equally, the minstrel mask and the stage Irish costume enabled Bryant and his audiences to access nostalgic longing disguised as a form of comic rejection: the costume worked as a kind of disguise for the expression of a homesickness that had no place in the public image of city dwellers anxious to prove their modernity in order to access work, social status and acceptance.

MODERN STEREOTYPES

So far, I've examined how costume can function to organize the spectator's approach to embodiment through the use of stereotypes, which produce idealized and denigrated bodies. However, I've also suggested that these modes of identification are complex and often ambiguous, offering a sense of identity as both static and unstable. These stereotypes emerge from the particular conditions of living in nineteenth-century cities and navigating new arrangements of class, ethnic and national categories. I want to turn my attention now to the critique of these modes of representation within the movement that can be described as modernism. As Marshall Berman suggests, modernism can be defined as the philosophical, political and artistic movements that approached the conditions of modernity and: 'aim[ed] to make men and women the subjects as well as the objects of modernization, to give them the power to change the world that is changing them, to make their way through the maelstrom and make it their own' (Berman, 2010, p. 16). I want to focus in particular on the modernist playwright, Eugene O'Neill, whose early work in the 1920s engaged with the stereotypes of the nineteenth-century popular stage, but who utilized these stereotypes in order to dismantle and critique them.

O'Neill, a New Yorker, was born in 1888 to an Irish father, James O'Neill, who made his name as an actor playing Shakespeare on the popular stage in America (having made his debut in a production of *The Colleen Bawn* in Ohio in 1867). In his early work with the Provincetown Players, Eugene O'Neill rejected his father's popular theatre and instead concentrated on developing an experimental and critical form of writing heavily influenced by the avant-garde experiments in Expressionism and Cubism emerging out of Europe. This interest in experimentation was aligned with an investigation of racial and class identity in America, emerging in the controversial casting of a black actor in a lead role in his 1920 play *The Emperor Jones.* Written in 1922 as a companion piece to this play, *The Hairy Ape* employs many of stereotypes of blackness and Irishness that we have seen emerging out of minstrelsy and Boucicault's work, but puts them to use in order to critique the modern conditions of work and alienation in modernity. In other words, O'Neill borrows the masks (as I've argued earlier, a full-body mask of costume and make-up) of these roles in order to critique the modern condition of social masking and the forms of alienation that emerge from it. Stereotypes are therefore crucial to, and rejected by, O'Neill's play. I want to investigate the use of costume and colour in *The Hairy Ape* to consider how a critique of modernity is played out under the mask of blackness. I will then go on to consider how The Wooster Group used the play in order to offer a meditation on the inescapable theatricality of costume in their 1997 production of the play.

Eugene O'Neill's *The Hairy Ape* is the story of Yank, a befittingly named American every-man, who works as a stoker on a transatlantic steam ship. Blackened by coal dust, Yank constructs his masculinity and class status through the relationship between his body and the ship he works for, giving him the unshakeable belief that 'he belongs' (O'Neill, 1998, p. 257). That is, until he is confronted by the ghost-like figure of Mildred Douglas, a wealthy heiress travelling on the top deck of the ship who, dressed all in white, pays a slumming visit to the stoke-hole. Mildred, aghast at the simian, blackened and truculent figure of Yank, faints dead away at the sight of him, and Yank's world is turned upside down. Yank sees himself through Mildred's eyes as a 'hairy ape' and his sense of his place in the world is destroyed. In a reverse love story, Yank 'falls in hate' (ibid, p. 275) with Mildred and sets out on a quest to get revenge, going onshore at New York in an attempt to find her. Yank finally makes his way to the zoo, where he releases the apes from their cage. He's hugged to death by one of the gorillas, and the play ends with O'Neill's epitaph for Yank: 'And perhaps, the Hairy Ape at last belongs' (O'Neill, 1998, p. 308).

O'Neill constructs an expressionistic mechanized universe in which a Darwinian notion of human evolution has been reversed. The machines of cultural 'progress' have reverted working-class men to the state of apes (see Zapf, 1988). The mechanization of the human spirit extends to the gendered identities of the characters, and O'Neill shows how Yank has internalized the structures of his own alienation and exploitation by turning them into an expression of his masculinity. Yank sees himself as a machine, his physical strength has become a testament to his masculine virility and the hardship of his world is a proof of his manhood: 'Hell in the stoke hole? Sure! It takes a man to work in hell!' (O'Neill, 1998, p. 260). Yank maintains the homosocial environment of the ship by feminizing the ship itself, which then becomes the standard against which he can prove his masculinity and virility. As C.W.E Bigsby argues, masculinity in this mechanistic world 'now goes into the service of the machine which becomes a substitute for a life giving feminine principle' (Bigsby, 1982, p. 61).

The mechanization and brutality of Yank's world also imprints itself on his body, and his blackened and simian features are simultaneously a corporeal expression of his degraded status, and a material marking of his body by the oil and dirt of the ship. Yank's blackness contrasts markedly with the whiteness of his antagonist, the upper-class Mildred Douglas, who lives aboveboard on the ship. Dressed all in white, with a 'pale pretty face', Mildred is as mechanized and artificial as the men in the stoke-hole. Mildred's class status is defined by a kind of translucence, she is semiotically encoded as 'pale', 'white' and 'delicate', and her power as an upper-class woman is theatricalized visually as 'white'. Mildred's pallor plays into a longstanding image that runs through art and theatre in the nineteenth century, what Nicholas Daly describes as: 'The woman in white. A vulnerable even ethereal figure who yet has the power to spellbind the crowd' (Daly, 2009, p. i). While Mildred's whiteness is a sign of her class status and her emptiness, it is also essential to O'Neill's vision of her femininity, the traits of which has traditionally been associated with 'whiteness', particularly within performance traditions such as melodrama and ballet. The play constructs a vision of whiteness which is an empty form of identity, formed only through its opposition to blackness and working-class identity, and formed by the absent figures of fathers and grandfathers who are the real source of Mildred's wealth, and are perhaps so 'white' that they are entirely invisible.

Class, gender and race are intertwined in Yank and Mildred's colour coding, and this is shown most clearly in the moment when they see each other in the stoke hole:

> He whirls defensively with a snarling, murderous growl, crouching to spring, his lips drawn back over his teeth, his small eyes gleaming ferociously. He sees Mildred, like a white apparition in the full light from the open furnace doors. He glares into her eyes, turned to stone. [...] As she looks at his gorilla face, as his eyes bore into hers, she utters a low choking cry and shrinks away from him, putting both hands up before her eyes to shut out the sight of his face, to protect her own.
>
> (O'Neill, 1998, pp. 272–273)

While this scene sets up the antagonism of these two characters, with a little adjustment it could easily constitute a romantic love scene: Her glowing presence, his sudden vision of her, their held gaze; the action in this scene is built along conventional heterosexual romantic lines. Mildred's appearance in the stoke hole throws Yank's world into disarray. Announcing 'I've fallen in hate, get me?' (ibid., p. 275), Mildred's presence forces Yank to go on a quest for self-discovery, functioning as a muse for his burgeoning self-awareness. However, unlike the life-affirming principles of the love story in which narrative closure is achieved, this quest results in the absurdity of Yank's death, the destruction of his masculinity, and the collapse of his world.

In the aftermath of Mildred Douglas's devastating visit to the stokehole, the Irish character Paddy tells Yank:

> 'Sure 'twas as if she'd seen a great hairy ape escaped from the zoo!
> Yank: [...] Say is dat what she called me – a hairy ape?
> Paddy: She looked it at you if she didn't say the word itself.
> Yank: Hairy ape huh? Sure! Dat's de way she looked at me, aw right. Hairy Ape!'
> (ibid., p. 277)

As David Roediger points out, this moment in the play offers the notion that: 'whiteness and non-whiteness can be "looked at" others' (Roediger, 1997, p. 37). Yank's body is reconfigured by Mildred's look, a look which Eric Lott might describe as the 'pale gaze' (Lott, 1993, p. 153). Receiving Mildred's objectifying gaze colours and reconfigures Yank's body. Her whiteness forces him to become aware of his 'blackness' – the way in which his body is marked by work and class. Her female presence in the stokehole also undermines the gendered binary between man and machine, and forces Yank to confront the gulf between the power of his body and the power he has in the world. While Yank sees himself as white and masculine, the power of Mildred's look forces him to confront the way in which he is marked by his social positioning and so he begins the journey towards his death.

O'Neill encoded Mildred as 'white' and Yank as 'black' in order to colour-code the class hierarchy of his play. However, in his portrait of Mildred, O'Neill also maintained many of the gendered stereotypes of his day. Mildred's emptiness essentializes her femininity just as Yank's inarticulate brawn fixes him within his gendered and class status. Even as O'Neill presented a social hierarchy, which is evidently constructed through economic and scientific ideologies, he simultaneously relied on the deployment of a limited depiction of working-class male identity and upper-class female identity both of which have been alienated and brutalized by industrial culture, but which are nonetheless essentially static. *The Hairy Ape* contains a central contradiction in its attitudes towards identity. Class and gender are both deconstructed and universalized, critiqued and then essentialized in the bodies of Yank and Mildred, manifested through costume and make-up.

This contradiction of simultaneous critique and essentialization can also be seen in O'Neill's positioning of the Irish character, Paddy, in the play. Yank rejects Paddy, saying: 'he's old and don't belong no more' (O'Neill, 1998, p. 260). But Paddy's yearning for the time before mechanization, when men could work with dignity on ships, when 'men belonged to ships [...] [when]

a ship was part of the sea, and a man was part of a ship and the sea joined all together and made it one' (ibid., p. 259), is the voice in the play that is closest to O'Neill's own form of modernist nostalgia. Through his indictment of the technological progress of modernism, O'Neill yearns for a utopian moment where men's minds and bodies could be free and he uses an Irish character as the mouthpiece for this nostalgia as a peculiar and inadvertent echo of Boucicault. While Paddy conforms to the stage Irish stereotypes of maudlin drunkenness and sentimentality, he also operates as the character whose yearnings coincide most strongly with O'Neill's, reiterating Boucicault and Bryant's undercover homesickness. As Paddy puts it:

> Oh, to be back in the fine days of my youth, ochone! Oh there was fine beautiful ships themdays – clippers wid tall masts touching the sky – fine strong men in them, [...] Oh the clean skins of them, and the clear eyes, the straight backs and full chests of them! Brave men they was, and bold men surely!

> (ibid., p. 258)

With Paddy's reference to 'clean skins', we can see how O'Neill organizes the visual environment of his stage through the theatrical lens of blackface minstrelsy. The stokers' bodies are marked by an indelible mask of soot and dirt, rendering their economic disenfranchisement visible for the gaze of the theatre audience. Unlike blackface, however, the coal dust on the men's bodies can never be fully removed. Even after the men have washed in preparation to go ashore, 'around their eyes, where a hasty dousing does not touch, the coal dust sticks like black make up, giving them a queer, sinister expression' (ibid., p. 274). The dust is un-removable, because the men are indelibly marked by their class positioning. As David Roediger argues: 'O'Neill fashioned tragedy out of a proletarian blackface in which "rivulets" of sooty sweat' could hardly be scrubbed out and ultimately helped kill Yank' (Roediger, 1997, p. 39).

O'Neill's play therefore evokes an eerie and ghostly presence of blackness while simultaneously configuring it through the lens of the white body. While power is figured and made material through colour in Yank's world, through degrees of whiteness and blackness, there are no black characters in the play. This has a similar effect to minstrelsy itself: the half-presence of blackness operating in a world that excluded black performers, both evoking and erasing the black body. In *The Hairy Ape*, O'Neill constructs a hierarchical world which is colour-coded in the absence of black characters, who form an invisible and ghostly absent referent in the play. Costume and make-up make visible in his play how modernization has limited life itself within the crude constraints of theatrical stereotypes, and longs for an alternative to modern masking.

POSTMODERN STEREOTYPES

When the Wooster Group performed O'Neill's play in New York in 1997, they set his text within the popular performance styles of his day, using the theatrical techniques of burlesque, vaudeville, melodrama and blackface minstrelsy. By using popular theatre styles in order to stage O'Neill's play, the Wooster Group constructed their own version of a Darwinian evolutionary system of theatre practice, tracing their inheritance of theatrical and performance traditions from O'Neill's time to their own. Examining how O'Neill's theatrical context had moulded and shaped his artistic vision, the Wooster Group ghosted O'Neill's modernist play with the popular theatre forms that O'Neill had rejected within his own practice. The use of melodramatic and vaudeville styles in the production demonstrated how unconsciously influenced O'Neill was by these forms, and the company's use of blackface, ballet costume and boxing gloves foregrounded the link between the workers' sooty faces and the popular performance forms that ghosted O'Neill's work.

The Wooster Group began life as the Performance Group in 1967, which was established by Richard Schechner to explore new forms of theatrical practice that 'would break down barriers: between art and life, between performance space and audience space, and between production elements' (Savran, 1988, pp. 2–3). In 1968, company purchased a disused garage in Soho in downtown New York and renamed it The Performing Garage, which has been their home ever since. In 1980, after a break with Schechner, the company renamed themselves The Wooster Group, with Elizabeth LeCompte as director. In 1981, The Wooster Group performed their first production under their new name, *Route 1&9 (The Last Act)* which was hugely controversial for its juxtaposing of Thornton Wilder's *Our Town* with blackface minstrel routines and a porn film. Their 1984 production of *LSD (... Just The High Points ...)* also attracted media attention, when Arthur Miller threatened to sue over their use of extracts of his play *The Crucible*, in combination with the life and times of Timothy Leary the LSD guru, and which also contained the use of blackface minstrelsy. The company continued its exploration of racial and gendered identity in its use of Orientalism in *Brace Up!* (1991) and in their production of Eugene O'Neill's *The Emperor Jones* in 1993, with Kate Valk (a founding member of the company) performing the title role cross-dressed in Japanese robes and blackface, while Willem Dafoe (the Hollywood actor, and another founding member of the company) in whiteface as Smithers the Cockney trader.

Deliberately performed as a kind of 'negative image' of their production of the *Emperor Jones*, *The Hairy Ape* featured Dafoe in the role of Yank in blackface, with Valk playing Mildred in a white ballet dress and giant ballet shoes. By framing O'Neill's play within the theatrical codes of his day and by making reference to vaudeville, music hall, ballet, strip tease, melodrama and blackface minstrelsy, the Wooster Group production implicated the representational structures of theatrical costume within the racial hierarchies of O'Neill's historical moment. The Wooster Group's use of colour in make-up and costume, therefore, was not simply a theatrical style; it also operated as a commentary on how the visual economy of representation can construct identity both on and off the stage. In other words, as I argued in the introduction to this chapter, the Wooster Group revealed the role that theatre costume plays in the construction of the Real, in disciplining and regulating racial and gendered identity through the production of ideal bodies onstage. I want to look at how blackface operated in the Group's production and then go onto consider how the binary of black and white interrogated the representation of gender in O'Neill's play, all the while implicating the visual economy of theatre masks in the construction of social hierarchies of identity. While O'Neill used masks onstage to critique social masking, the Wooster Group revealed the ways in which theatre masks may regulate the ways in which spectators feel able to perform their own identities after the performance has ended.

In the early scenes of the play, all the male actors onstage wore black make-up, apart from the character of Paddy. Their faces were painted a featureless black that evoked the minstrel mask without quite reproducing it. The monochrome use of black make-up suggested that the actors were marked in black not as a sociological statement on class or race, but as a theatrical statement on the unconscious context and roots of O'Neill's text. The use of blackface in the Wooster Group show acknowledged O'Neill's borrowing of minstrel conventions for his 'high art' play and therefore contextualized O'Neill's vision of class in the play as mediated through the practice of minstrelsy. Later on, following the text, the ensemble of actors washed off their blackface, leaving only the traces of soot in their eye sockets in a shower scene staged in view of the audience, suggesting that what we had seen was after all simply coal-dust. However, Willem Dafoe as Yank subverted and re-negotiated this sense of blackness, by having a make-up artist remove his blackface in full view of the audience, emphasizing its theatrical rather than sociological status. The blackface was asserted as a theatrical mask and reference once more, but also became a commentary on the relationship between performance and race, foregrounding the mechanics of minstrelsy itself where: 'minstrels claimed the right to turn black for as long as they desired and to reappear as white' (Roediger, 1991, p. 125).

The production therefore playfully combined several masks in its use of blackface: first blackface as a material mask of dirt from the ship, which could be washed off; secondly blackface as a mark of white working-class identity, which could not be removed, hence the coal dust left in the men's eye-sockets; and finally blackface as a theatrical mask which could be removed as make-up at the end of a show, giving white performers the opportunity to 'play black' and then resume their whiteness as they wished. However, the use of blackface also worked to establish the oppositional figures of Paddy in relation to Yank. The actor playing Paddy was not blacked up in the role (although his face was dirtied, which was closer to the original stage directions of the text). Furthermore, the actor played the character with an Irish accent, which contrasted with the evidently artificial rap and jazz style rhythms with which the other actors spoke their lines. The fact that the actor playing Paddy was less stylized than the other characters staged the character's nostalgia for a pre-mechanized past, but also functioned as a representative figure for Eugene O'Neill himself, a stage-Irish and simultaneously 'authentic' Irish figure, whose modernism operated in opposition to the industrial age which Yank so clearly endorses. Paddy's lack of blackface became the Wooster Group's means to imagine O'Neill's body as the outcome of his play.

The use of blackface was presented by the Wooster Group as a marker of gender as well as class and race, and was further destabilized by Kate Valk's performance as Mildred in the production. Kate Valk wore over-large white ballet shoes on her feet, and moved through a variety of melodramatic poses as she spoke. As with all the other performers, she spoke only through a microphone, and her voice was distorted to become 'Minnie Mouse-like' feminine. When Mildred demanded to see the stoke-hole, the stokers stripped her of her outer costume to reveal a diaphanous white ballet dress, offering a coy moment of burlesque which invoked the popular theatre of O'Neill's day. Valk wore white make-up, and her face resembled the Hollywood stars of silent film. As Ben Brantley described her: 'Ms Valk [...] brings an appetizing splash of burlesque intensity to the show's monochromatic canvas. Her face made up to suggest a silent movie siren [...] she minces (and on those giant feet) into Yank's world like a debutante from hell' (Brantley, 1996).

Valk's ballet costume and artificially posed body language, along with the distortion of her voice, offered a parody of the theatrical conventions of femininity. Mildred's femininity was as oversized as her ballet shoes, and Valk's performance offered a sense of gender itself as a construct, an artificial distortion. Valk's performance took the theatrical conventions of gender to a hyperbolic extreme, revealing the structures of class identity to be intimately bound up within questions of gender and colour. The use of ballet as a trope of Mildred's whiteness, class, and femininity seemed particularly appropriate, since classical ballet relies on the denial and erasure of the dancer's body in order to construct a transcendent aesthetic of femininity. The hyperbolic nature of Valk's performance framed O'Neill's vision of femininity within the performance codes of his day, showing the 'pale gaze' to be intricately bound up with the 'male gaze'.

Valk's performance and semiotic encoding performed the function of what Judith Butler calls drag, where: '[drag] reflects on the imitative structure by which hegemonic gender is itself produced and disputes heterosexuality's claim on naturalness and originality' (Butler, 1993, p. 125). While Valk was a female actor playing a female role, nonetheless the hyperbolic nature of her performance called into question the stability of the performance of femininity and demonstrated that the codes and norms of gender can be constructed by, and through, costume and representation. The Wooster Group exposed the theatre itself as a place that produces stereotypes, with costume constructing an idealized 'Real' that the spectators' bodies are expected to attain. Valk's parody of the performance conventions of femininity formed a critique of the gender stereotypes contained in O'Neill's play and created a 'cross-dressed effect' on the stage, undermining a naturalized notion of gender identity.

The production colour-coded the interlinked masculinity and femininity of Mildred and Yank throughout the show. Dafoe's performance of masculinity was as artificial and parodied as Valk's Mildred. Just as Valk used the performance trope of ballet to exaggerate her femininity, Dafoe used boxing to stylize his masculinity and class status. As Ben Brantley puts it: '*Ape* has here been conceived as a sort of boxing match between one man, the animalistic Yank, and the universe' (Brantley, 1996). Boxing and blackface became a means to underline the performative nature of Yank's masculinity and class, showing how Yank's work formed his masculinity and materialized his bodily identity. Both Valk and Dafoe destabilized gender through the performance disciplines of ballet and boxing and their exaggerated costuming and make-up and their colour-coding as white and black was therefore linked just as much with the gender of the characters as with their class status. Rather than the costume acting as a decoration or representation of character, here costume functioned to organize the actor's body within a set of gestural codes and behavioural conventions – the costume functioned both as the means to the actor's performance and as a critique of the social performance it depicted.

Through this interlinked relationship, the production offered a critique of O'Neill's essentialization of Mildred. Even while Mildred objectifies Yank with her Darwinian gaze, in O'Neill's play she also covers *her* eyes, warding off *his* gaze when they meet. The idea that Yank might look back might objectify Mildred through *his* fetishization of *her* femininity was a theme explored throughout the show. While in the text, Mildred does not feature again after fainting at the sight of Yank, in the Wooster Group production Valk fulfilled Yank's description of Mildred as a ghost by haunting Yank throughout his journey towards his death. Valk's uncanny laughter resonated via the microphones as Dafoe-as-Yank remembered the injuries she had caused him and the production extended her ghostly presence even further in the scene where Yank visits New York to attack the upper classes on 42nd street. Seeing the wealth in the shop windows around him, Yank ruminates on Mildred: 'she didn't belong. She belonged in de window of a toy store, or on de top of a garbage can, see!' (O'Neill, 1998, p. 292). In this scene, Valk sat behind a transparent screen, wearing furs and jewels. Mildred became a mannequin, reconfigured by the way that Yank sees her, sitting in the window of a toy shop for the rich. As Johan Callens points out, by positioning Mildred as an object, LeCompte examined the relationship between Mildred's class and gender, showing her artificiality to be a sign of the subjectivity denied to her by the social system she occupies (see Callens, 1999, p. 158). Mildred *is* a mannequin, an object that functions to display the wealth earned by her grandfather and father without any purpose of its own; a female body that is designed to be looked *at*, as well as to look. The production showed how the gaze between Mildred and Yank is reciprocal; just as Mildred objectifies Yank, her body is equally reconfigured through Yank's male gaze.

Gender identity was presented as evidently artificial and theatrical in this production. There was an obviously critical 'gap' between actor and role. The antagonistic relationship between Valk and Yank implicated the specular economy of theatre practice itself within the production of gender stereotypes, revealing how theatre can teach audiences to 'look' race, gender and class, materializing bodies through the pale and male gazes of theatrical representation. Whiteness was made strange in the Wooster Group's production of *The Hairy Ape*, and this was achieved in the absence of African American performers on the stage. The bodies of the actors were ghosted not only by the white spectre of Mildred but also by the white spectre of blackface minstrelsy, the performance tradition that unconsciously informed O'Neill's play and had done so much to materialize raced bodies in O'Neill's historical moment. Like O'Neill, the Wooster Group colour-coded class through the binary of black and white and furthermore exposed how O'Neill had also colour-coded and essentialized masculinity and femininity through the same tropes. Race, however, was erased in both play and production but still worked as the uneasy metaphor through which other identities could be examined and explored.

The Wooster Group's production deconstructed the representational politics of O'Neill's play, not only his text but also his theatrical context of the 1920s. In doing so, the Wooster Group revealed how the gaze of the audience itself, can, like Mildred, reconfigure bodies. Just as Mildred's aunt tells her 'be as artificial as you are I advise. There's a sort of sincerity in that you know' (O'Neill, 1998, p. 265), the Wooster Group created a sincerity through their clearly artificial employment of costume and make-up on the stage, raising important questions around the right to look, the experience of being looked at, and how vision can contain complex and contradictory relations of race, gender and class. Ultimately, even as the company utilized the theatrical vocabularies of blackface, stage-Irishness, music hall and boxing, the performance was filled with a despair at the inescapable theatricality of stereotypes: their formative effects on identity and the fact that, for the Wooster Group, there is nothing else.

The role that costume and make-up play in constructing identity is revealed by the Wooster Group to be deeply precarious. But in fact, examining the performances of Dion Boucicault and Dan Bryant also reveals that costumes may function to produce stereotypes and, in doing so, may discipline and regulate the possibilities of lived identity for the spectator after the show has ended. Nonetheless, the fact that these costumes are often worn by the 'wrong' body onstage, or that actors can assert a complex and contradictory relationship to that costume through their competing public personae, suggests that stereotypes are never quite fixed onstage and are always capable of shifting and undoing themselves. Costume may act as a social mask, but it is also capable of unmasking the very conditions by which identity is formed, performed and imagined on the stage and in the street.

AN INTERVIEW WITH TINA BICAT

Aoife Monks

Introduction

Tina Bicat is a well-known costume designer who has worked for the National Theatre in London, the English National Opera, the New York City Ballet and various regional companies and theatres around the UK. She also teaches costume design at St Mary's College, London. This interview focuses on her work with the theatre company Punchdrunk, whose site-specific work presents particular challenges for costume design. Founded in 2000, directed by Felix Barrett and choreographed by Maxine Doyle, Punchdrunk 'blend[s] classic texts, physical performance, award-winning design installation and unexpected sites' (Punchdrunk Website, 2013).

In shows by Punchdrunk, audiences are encouraged to move through large performance sites, engaging seemingly at random with different performance areas within the venue. In the company's performance of *Faust* (2006), audiences circulated within a vast disused warehouse in Wapping, the formerly industrial area of London. In *The Masque of the Red Death* (playing at the time of this interview in 2007), audiences moved through the extensive rooms and studios of Battersea Arts Centre. Most recently the company's production of *The Drowned Man* (2013) has been staged in a disused post office in Paddington, London. Audiences are often required to wear masks while promenading through these shows, and indeed, Bicat discusses her decision to cloak the audiences for the BAC production.

The genres of promenade and site-specific theatre have become more and more central to the landscape of theatre production in the UK. Here, Bicat offers an account of the processes, constraints and considerations of designing costume for performers playing to a mobile and non-cohesive audience. The production of *Faust*, that is the focus of this interview, combined Goethe's story with scenographic installations of cinematic levels of detail that invoked the work of the American painter, Edward Hopper. Against this backdrop, dancers moved through crowds of masked audiences, dressed in costumes that quoted rather than embodied American dress from the 1940s and 1950s. In this interview, Bicat also articulates the collaborative relationship that emerges between actors and designer, outlining the process of developing costumes through rehearsal and in response to the needs and vision of performers (see Figure 4).

Figure 4   Dancers and audience members at Punchdrunk's *The Masque of the Red Death*, Battersea Arts Centre, 2007
Source: Steve Forrest, photograph, by permission of Steve Forrest.

A = Aoife Monks, T = Tina Bicat

A: Where do you start when you're designing costumes?

T: I always start with the mirror. There's me and there's an actor and there's a mirror and we play with costumes. The dancers have to run in this show, and luckily my workroom was at the bottom of the marble staircase, so they'd just go out of the workroom and run up and down stairs...

A:– With you watching them?

T: Usually, yes. And it tells me a lot when people run, as to how comfortable they feel.

A: It sounds like there's a whole series of interrelated concerns for actors in how they feel about their role, how they want their body to feel. Are they showing you how they feel, rather than telling you?

T: Very often they don't know with words, they know it with their bodies. They often just wriggle, not really dance, you know, but wriggle. Just like children do when they've got a tight, itchy thing on.

A: So their bodies are telling you things and you're responding to that by re-using costume, trying out different formulations but also considering at the same time the larger framework of what the performers have to do and when they will the costume in certain ways. So what the costume looks like for an audience seems to be quite far down the list of priorities?

T: In the immediate work it's quite far down the list of priorities, but in my head I have a picture of the scene with all the performers like a film or something, and when I'm watching them run up the stairs I'm not watching them alone, I'm watching the person they're going to be running after and the person they're going to be running behind. So the picture of what I want the audience to see is very clear. If I'm trying to communicate what I see to the actor, I just draw it, And because I'm doing it when he's there, he'll say, 'YES!' or he'll say, 'no, no what I wanted … is this' … Whereas if I present someone with a picture, saying, 'this is how I see you', they're going to feel they have to fit their body into that picture, which wastes their own body and their own beautiful movement by forcing it into some pre-existing structure made by me.

A: Where and when does costume begin for Punchdrunk?

T: If you're doing a naturalistic Chekov, you design the costumes, you go to the production meeting with the designs. But with Punchdrunk, it's more like there's a heap of ideas: there's the actor who comes into the heap, there's me playing on the heap, there's this heap is created by all the research and the budget. The heap is like the raw material, the wood that you're going to build from, a palette of colour and texture.

A: How does it feel to design costumes with the knowledge that they will be seen in huge detail by some audiences and not at all by others?

T: Or seen running past for a second. … My job is to make the picture. You see a chap running across the balcony, and you see him in a flash, but that flash has to tell the audience who that person is, where they come from, what sort of class they are, what sort of power they have in their minds, where they fit. And the way the performers move does this, but the costume will help make that picture.

A: I wondered if I could ask you about the *Faust* costumes? It felt as if the costumes were from one world, the set was in a slightly different world and the actors' movement was in another world and there was a tension between those states that made the performance really interesting.

T: I was trying to make this world where you feel like you *know* you're in a dream but the people in the dream seem real. It isn't just the costume, it's also the lighting and the sound, not to mention the performance … For Faust there was the influence of film noir, the *Third Man*, Edward Hopper …

A: How did you put all those ideas together?

T: I started by talking with Felix and Maxine. Then there were all the *Fausts*: we read Marlowe's, we read Goethe's, we read a modern one, and they all seeped into this heap of ideas along with various painters and various photographs and images. Then the next step as far as I'm concerned is that I need to know about the style of the movement, the budget, the number of people, the venue, the time, where you're going to work, how long you have, how long the actors are employed for, do you have to pay them to come in for fittings, do the actors have to be fitted during rehearsal time, what's the Equity status, all that sort of stuff … the nailed down facts. There's these facts that you have to know before you let your imagination free because otherwise you get disappointed. You have to know *that* to know what your imagination's allowed to do because otherwise you can't let it go free. The ideas are in a way the easy bit. So if you've got all your constraints in place then you are free to go woozy: allow for mental play, with me wandering round car boot sales, going to fabric shops, going for a walk, going to look at pictures, listening to stuff.

A: Who you feel most responsible to? Is your duty to the audience, the performers, or the production?

T: I think it's a balance. I think all the time you're balancing what the audience will get from it, what the performers can give, and what the director wants them to give, which is what the story wants them to give. The mirror in my workshop lets me see it from both sides: that's why I work in the mirror all the time. The mirror stands in for the audience's gaze and that's why I can't work in a room without a mirror and I also can't work in a room with the door shut – I need to leave it open for the audience to come in even though they're not there!

A: It sounds as though a lot of your costumes emerge from problem solving, that it's about responding to the conditions of performance and finding useful solutions for actors?

T: That's particularly true for Punchdrunk. You have to get the problems sorted early because you can't have thirty-six people unable to move in their trousers just before the dress rehearsal, I mean what on earth do you do …?

A: Do you make, as well as design, the costumes?

T: Yes. I can say to someone, 'would you like to try this? Would you like to try it out, would you like to play with it?' And because I do the cutting myself, and the shopping, I can have it on them by the afternoon if we talk about it in the morning. Doing the cutting myself allows me to do exactly what I want in a way that designing and handing it over to a maker can never do for me. The thing I'm really good at is making performers trust me and making costumes for them that gives them something they didn't expect to find in their own performance. The actors come into the workroom and it's *their* space, it's not that they're coming into the wardrobe where people are going to tell them what to do. They're coming into a place which is *for* them.

A: Do you ever work with costume to produce an emotional affect in the actor?

T: There are endless, endless things you can do to help an actor make emotion from their clothes. I worked with the actor playing Roderick Usher in this show, who wanted to feel as if his body was slightly deformed. He wanted to *feel* it rather than for the audience to see it. We mucked about a bit by putting padding underneath his jacket and I didn't think it would work because I didn't think he would feel it enough. Then I had this thought about giving him trousers which had elastic under the soles, like ski pants, but using braces. We braced them very high, so he was conscious all the time of a tension between his shoulders and the soles of his feet. It was an elastic tension, he could move with it, but it was nonetheless there all the time. And then he wore them for rehearsal, just with his t shirt, and it worked really well and it made him feel a sense of deformity that padding wouldn't have achieved. Anything that gives actors a better experience is what you're there for. You can see the same affect if you give somebody a corset: it may be underneath the clothes and the audience can't see it, but it makes the way someone stands and moves completely different.

A: What about the idea of costuming the audience? Does giving the audience masks liberate them? Why did you start using cloaks in the *Masque of the Red Death*?

T: To make a picture in the space. When you put on one of those cloaks you do have the urge to play in it. You do have that faint feeling that you could if you dared, run up and down the stairs and feel it swirling out behind you …

A: You use the word 'play' a lot and I wonder what you think playing does for an audience?

T: Playing is physical communication, and for the audience wearing the masks and cloaks they are being given the chance to play, even if normally they'd be horrified at the idea of having to expose themselves in any way. The costumes make them feel safer. Or rather, freer. They give you permission to be something you aren't usually, that you don't usually show. The darkness allows you to play and I think the fact that you're an anonymous part of a gang allows you to play. The audience are seeing each other as part of the dream world of the show. And you see them suddenly clocking it: they look round the space and they see a hundred other people looking the same as they do.

AN INTERVIEW WITH STEWART LAING

Ali Maclaurin

Introduction

Stewart Laing directs and designs theatre and opera and makes his own work with his company, Untitled Projects, which he formed in 1998. Stewart originally trained as a theatre designer at Central School of Art and Design in London and started working as a director in 1993. He has worked extensively as a theatre designer throughout the world, winning a Tony Award in 1997 for his work on the musical *Titanic*. He recently designed *Peter Grimes* at La Scala, Milan and, with Untitled Projects, staged a reconstruction of Paul Bright's *Confessions of a Justified Sinner* (see Figure 5).

Figure 5 Audience member in *The Salon Project*, directed by Stewart Laing, Traverse Theatre, Edinburgh, 2011
Source: Tommy Ga-Ken Wan, photograph, by permission of Tommy Ga-Ken Wan.

AJM = Ali Macluarin, SL = Stewart Laing

AJM: How did the idea for *The Salon Project* come about?

SL: There's something really profound and fundamental about fashion, in that clothes for most people are how they present who they are to the world and for me that's not a trivial issue. Of course who you are is worth serious consideration, serious thought; and that reflects right through costume, through the whole theatricalization of what clothes and fashion are.

AJM: How did you come to that idea? What is your background and training?

SL: I trained in Theatre Design at the Central School of Art and Design in London. It was a theatre course, very much set and costume, taught as one discipline, and the reason I did that in London was that there was nowhere to do it in Scotland. I think that's still the case. I know that RCS [Royal Conservatoire of Scotland] offer a course but it's not an art school education and for me, it was really important that I was studying the subject in an art school environment.

AJM: What do you think makes that different?

SL: Because you then think of it as an art form rather than craft. I've got a lot of respect for craft but for me thinking about what you're doing in terms of what it means is the fundamental thing; the sense that what it looks like onstage informs the meaning that it might have. I think that the non-art school education is often about the craft of how to make things rather than the big thought processes.

AJM: So how did you move from being a designer towards creating your own pieces of theatre?

SL: My very first experience of working in theatre was here at the Citizens Theatre in the late 1970s. I joined the design team before I went to art school. I was on the lowest rung of the ladder washing out the paint buckets and doing all the flat painting and someone else would come in and do the more detailed stuff. At that point one of the directors who was running the Citizens, Philip Prowse, was a designer who had moved into directing, and I thought the two disciplines were the same thing. My aspiration was always to do what he was doing. Then later on I realized that for most of the world actually it was two separate disciplines.

AJM: Do you think when you're designing that even though you're not the director you're actually directing it in your head?

SL: Yes, I do, and one of the directors I work with – I do very little pure design now – but one of the directors I do still work with is the English director Richard Jones – and he says that in a true collaboration between director and designer that the designer needs to let the director design some of the show and the director needs to let the designer direct a little bit of the show. I think there's a lot of truth to that, actually that they are tied together.

AJM: Moving on to *The Salon Project* how did that come about?

SL: It came from several things. I have a real interest in period costume but a lot of the design work I was doing – a lot of operas – was in modern dress just because that felt like the right thing to do. I really wanted to find a way of exploring this thing that excited me, which was period costume. For me, there's a real pleasure in that. Then a friend of mine was designing a period movie – she's a set designer in the movies and she was designing the Joe Wright film of *Pride and Prejudice*. Her son who was about eleven years old at the time wanted to be an extra in it, but they wouldn't pay for a chaperone. Somebody had the idea that I should be an extra as well and go and look after him on set so I went off to go through this experience of being fitted for costume. It's the first time I've ever been on the other side of the fitting room; I'd always been the person who was going, 'Yes, you're wearing that, I don't care if you like it, I don't care if it makes you look fat, I don't care if the colour doesn't suit you, that's how I think you should look,' and then I found myself being in the position of this person who had absolutely no power with someone else saying, 'No, this is how I think you should look, I don't care if you don't like it. I think it's appropriate," and I found that a really interesting experience. And all the other extras who were there that day I thought were really interesting – this community of people who loved being part of that experience, getting dressed, being on the edge of things. I came out of that saying, 'Let's make a project where dressing is at the heart of it,' so all of our early conversations and thoughts about The Salon Project were about dressing people. It was almost like afterwards we thought, 'When we've got them all dressed what are we going to do with them?' So then we devised the actual activity inside the salon.

AJM: You said you got a real pleasure from it …

SL: Yes. In conventional theatre that is the hidden part of the process and I just thought it would be really interesting to let an audience into that.

AJM: Yes, because actually the audience probably spent as much time getting dressed as it did in the Salon …

SL: Yes, very much so. I think it's something that people really liked. It's that thing about giving up power. It was always very important for us that we would choose the costumes for somebody. It wasn't like a fancy dress party where we would ask people to come dressed up or that they would go into a room full of clothes and choose. The control over it was quite important for us so that people would have the experience of somebody else saying, 'Oh, I think this outfit is good for you …'

AJM: I wondered if you ever got people who didn't like what you had chosen and how they responded?

SL: Yeah, if people were vocal about it we would always try to do something about it.

AJM: Did it happen very often?

SL: I think there was always somebody every night. But it's part of being a costume designer negotiating that situation. There is something really interesting about costume design because it is such a personal thing. Dealing with people's bodies, that's what it comes down to, and I think we all have difficult relationships with our bodies. The way costume designers negotiate that is very interesting psychologically.

AJM: Was that what it was usually about, about the fact that they didn't like the way it made them look?

SL: Yes, all of the conventional stuff like 'This makes me look too big', or 'I thought I was going to look like that person over there', but we really wanted it to be a good experience for the audience. We had a conversation after we did it in London about being much more upfront in telling people that they might not like their costume, to slightly lower people's expectation that they were going to look amazing. Because actually my experience of doing the extra work is that I hated what they put me in, I hated it, but it was still a really interesting experience

AJM: Did it make you feel different to be wearing something you didn't like?

SL: Yeah, it just made me want to be in the background in a corner, rather than want to push to the front.

AJM: One of the things it says on your website is that the heart of *The Salon Project* is 'the visual spectacle of each audience member transformed' and it made me wonder how much it was about when you walk into the room and you see everybody else in costume and how much is it is it about each individual?

SL: I think it's a mix. We didn't have full-length mirrors in the dressing rooms; it was a deliberate choice that we wanted to try and hold that back until people were actually in the Salon. We had mirrors for the make-up and hair, but they were really at an angle so it was very difficult to see the whole thing.

AJM: I remember I was very conscious of what my costume felt like because I couldn't see it.

SL: I think there was quite a subtle transformation of people; it did give people license to behave in a different way.

AJM: How did you design the costumes? Did you draw them? Did you give the people who were picking out the costumes a brief? Did you pick them out yourself?

SL: The first time we did the show the costume designer was Theo Clinkard – who I had worked with before. We shared a lot of research: he had a tumblr blog where he was looking at things that interested him, and I had a tumblr blog where I was looking at what interested me …

AJM: Was it about a particular period?

SL: Yeah, originally it was to do with a particular period. We were doing research on Marcel Proust at the same time and his long novel *A la Recherche du Temps Perdu* and the period of the novel. It starts around 1885 and ends at the start of the First World War so that was very loosely the period we were looking at. Then just because of what was available Theo ended up using a lot of stuff that was earlier and quite a bit of stuff that was later. So it drifted at either end but that was the period we set out to look at.

AJM: How much did the accuracy matter?

SL: Not very much …

AJM: So if you weren't looking for period accuracy, what were you looking for?

SL: Well, as a costume designer I've never been a great stickler for period accuracy. I always like something with more of a feel and a flare for a period rather than checking that the seams are in exactly the right place and that the fabric is absolutely authentic. I think there is room for different approaches in the world but that one is not for me. One of the things that interests me is that filter you get of seeing an idea of the past that is filtered through the present. Like the Marilyn Monroe movie, Some Like it Hot, which is set in the 1920s but the defining look of it is entirely 1950s, which is when it was made. It's really corseted and exaggerated and actually that profile's got nothing to do with the 1920s, so when you're watching the movie it's actually quite confused because those are two really opposing silhouettes, but the point where they meet is quite interesting. Also you got the thing where people are deliberately pursuing that, like Anna Karenina, the recent Joe Wright movie. I think his brief to the costume designer, Jacqueline Durran, was that it should look like 1950s Christian Dior so you get that layering of periods. I think you need to be a real scholar to put your finger on what's authentic and what's not.

AJM: So if you're not a scholar, what does that do for you when you're watching?

SL: I always find it quite exciting as a visual spectacle. But then I find the visual spectacle of what Jenny Tiramani does at the Globe really exciting as well, where period authenticity is what governs her design choices. I saw *Richard III* last summer and my eyes were popping out of my head at the extremity of what she was able to do in that very, very rigid format that she gives herself, like the little princes wearing bright pink suits, really eye-popping.

AJM: The other thing I noticed was that the clothes were quite formal, particularly the men's clothes. What sort of reaction did you get?

SL: I think the men found it much easier, that formal dress, easier than the women. A lot of men still wear that when they go to weddings and so it was still within their comfort zone. It made them stand up straight, that was one of the things I really noticed that it really gives you good posture. But the range of options are so much more limited for men; if you look at Tissot's paintings, the men are all dressed the same and the women have some sort of diversity.

AJM: So just thinking about the audience in the space again. It was very much about people who were performing and people who were participants being together. What difference did that make? When I was there, people were quite shy …

SL: I think that by the time we got to London we were trying harder to involve them.

AJM: Is that what you wanted?

SL: If I was going to go to this, if I was an audience member, I would probably spend quite a lot of time in the corner just looking. I didn't want to do a piece of participatory theatre where the audience were being forced to do something all the time. I wanted to do something that was much gentler than that. There were those people who wanted to chat away and make an entrance across the room, and that was fine, but actually if somebody wanted to sit in a corner I thought it was their right to do that … and I don't see that as failure on my part as the person who made the piece of theatre.

One woman brought her Kindle along one night and I thought that was okay because first of all I really admire the fact that she booked to come and see the show alone and she had no idea what to expect. She thought 'I'll take my book in case I get bored' and she sat in the corner and she read her Kindle and I had a nice chat with her. She was really happy to be there and look up and around and then stick her nose back in her book. I'm sure in those period salons that had inspired us there was somebody who would be distancing themselves from the event as well as being in the event.

AJM: Did you have times when the audience contributed quite a lot?

SL: Yes, we did. It was completely different every night. One of the interesting things was seeing what the different energy from the audience was from one night to the next. I think this connected to the costumes as well because it's a bit like having a mask. It gives you licence to have a conversation with somebody that, if you were in a bar say, you might not have. And you don't have your usual signifiers. When I had a conversation with someone I hadn't seen get dressed I wouldn't know what they had looked like in their own clothes, so all the assumptions you make about someone's clothes, in terms of class and gender and occupation and sexual availability, all those signals, are just not there.

AJM: Your website said *The Salon Project* would 'allow the audience to take on the past whilst imagining the future'. Can you say a bit more about that?

SL: The brief to all our speakers was to talk about the future. At one point we talked about getting people to come in and talk about Victorian technology and science, and we just thought it would be more interesting to have real contemporary scientists and artists and other experts to talk about the future, so even though you're in a visual environment that is all about looking backwards there is part of you looking forwards. Something we really hoped was that people wouldn't have to pretend conversations and, although I never went through that process of getting dressed with the audience at any point, I understand that people were encouraged to have real conversation.

AJM: Did it achieve what you wanted?

SL: I get asked the question a lot … I think the way I make work is very intuitive, and I don't imagine a finished thing in my head and then work towards it. I think it's much more, 'Today we began to push it in that direction, the next day we shifted it a little bit there and the day after that, we added this into it.' I was really pleased with it. I liked being in it. I'm very proud of it. I don't particularly know what I set out to achieve.

AJM: I was going to finally ask you what costume means to you in general. You've spoken about that already but maybe you'd like to say a bit more?

SL: Well, that's a really difficult question, but one of the things I'm really glad about is that my education was about costume being part of the whole stage picture. You very rarely get a set and costume designer in a movie or in American theatre. So one of the things you get doing both is about popping people out of the environment just in terms of that stage picture. If the environment is one thing how do you define that person within the environment? Are they in contrast to it? Do they feel part of it? I think in terms of colour there's something very intuitive about it as well, but it is to do with making pictures. That's acknowledged a lot in opera and even in cinema, but I think in theatre making the picture doesn't get the attention that is due. I wish directors and designers thought more about actually composing a picture – a picture that moves.

AJM: Do you think that some people might worry that could be seen as a bit superficial?

SL: Is visual information superficial? I navigate the world through visual information and I'm very aware that's the way I navigate the world. I think so much British theatre comes out of the English Department at universities and is to do with the purity of the text and the way text is delivered. I think some directors may think, 'If I worry too much about costumes people won't take me seriously as a director.'... But I find the psychological thing about costume really profound and really exciting. How you define the individual through what they have got on, that's really exciting. If there are a lot of people on stage how do you design that society, show who that society is, and who the individual is within that society? That's not superficial to me at all, it's really worthy of long thought and consideration. It's really important.

Chapter

5

Artists and the 'Scenic Body'

Ali Maclaurin

'Character, character, character'.
(Thomson, 2013)

For Mark Thomson, artistic director of the Lyceum Theatre, Edinburgh, this is the biggest function of stage costume, and most people interested and involved in the practical business of making and watching theatre would probably agree. Yet, under close analysis (Monks, 2010, pp.1–8) costume can and does do much more or much other than this, even when located firmly within the world of recognizable clothing and visible bodies. In this chapter I will argue that, under certain conditions, the costumed body functions more as a scenic or environmental element than an individual signifier of character and would be more usefully analysed as such. As Butterworth and McKinney state,

> Regard for the performer within the scene underlines the essentially three dimensional nature of scenography and the way this evolves over the duration of the performance. ... Performers, too, may from time to time be implicated in the scenography. In performance terms it is sometimes hard to distinguish clearly between what is achieved through the performer's body and movement of the performer's costume. Does the performer animate the costume? Does the costume determine bodily gesture? ... Non-naturalistic costume can behave like an environment for the performer; it takes up space and receives light.
> (McKinney and Butterworth, 2009, pp. 6, 7)

I would argue that, under some circumstances, naturalistic costume may perform in a similar manner, particularly if the performers are working as an ensemble. This is not to say that the performers within these costumes may not speak or even function individually from time to time but that together they serve as a kind of living landscape. Costume may, in addition, hide the human body physically, assimilate performers' bodies to a physical stereotype, for example in blackface roles (see Chapter 4), or visually overpower the performer's 'person-ality' through its design. The latter type is usually to be found, I suggest, in a design style that is at least to some extent non-naturalistic and explicitly concerned with form and materials in a way which is more akin to the priorities and practices of visual art than text-led theatre. Because of this, I want to begin my exploration by considering a series of examples from the early twentieth century that push costuming not only beyond the idea of clothes but beyond the human body itself.

In 1907 Picasso painted 'Les Demoiselles d'Avignon' and in 1908 Edward Gordon Craig published an essay entitled, 'The Actor and the Uber-Marionette' in his book, *On the Art of Theatre*. Picasso, by rejecting objective reality and finding a new way to paint what philosopher Apollinaire, writing in 1913, termed 'the immensity of space prolonging itself indefinitely in all directions at any given moment' (Apollinaire, 2000), produced an image of three prostitutes in the fractured geometric Cubist style that is familiar to a twenty-first century eye but was utterly alien to most contemporary spectators for whom the painterly semi-abstraction of Post Impressionism was quite modern enough. Influenced in some part by pieces of costume, specifically the stylized forms of Iberian and African masks, Picasso distorted the human face and body in order to acknowledge, even celebrate, his own moving viewpoint and the flat surface of his canvas. A year later in 1908, Craig's essay decried the messy uncontrolled emotionalism of the actor and sought total authorial control of the stage space by transforming the performer's role into that of an 'ubermarionette', a controllable body that 'will not compete with life –rather will go beyond it' (Craig, 1912, p. 84).

Both seminal works encapsulate the idea of a regulated self-contained visual style that seeks to make use of the medium's particular features and both reject living bodies in their unpredictable visceral reality in favour of a constructed subjective reality over which the artist has ultimate control. In Britain, Harley Granville Barker's landmark 1912 Shakespeare season at the Savoy Theatre showed a similar tendency, for example, in the highly stylized geometric sets and costumes for *Twelfth Night*. Although neither Craig nor Picasso saw their ground-breaking artistic ideas as political, for some who followed in their wake, members of the Italian Futurists, the Russian Constructivists and the German Bauhaus, their work presaged the overturning of the old world order and the building of an explicitly modern world in which everything was new and 'purpose-built'. For these young artists, all life, including music, art and literature, needed to be turned on its head in order to embrace such modern prerequisites as speed, movement and new technology, and new forms of clothing and new forms of theatre were part of the New World they were building.

The Italian Futurists published their noisy demands for change in a series of manifestoes, and Giacomo Balla, fashion designer and scenographer, wrote with characteristic Futurist vim and vigour in *The Futurist Manifesto of Men's Clothing* (1913)

We must destroy all passéist clothes, and everything about them which is tight-fitting, colourless, funereal, decadent, boring and un-hygienic. As far as materials are concerned, we must abolish: wishy-washy, pretty-pretty, gloomy, and neutral colours, along with patterns composed of lines, checks and spots. In cut and design: the abolition of static lines, all uniformities such as ridiculous turn-ups, vents, etc. Let us finish with the humiliating and hypocritical custom of wearing mourning. Our crowded streets, our theatres and cafes are all imbued with a depressingly funereal tonality, because clothes are made only to reflect the gloomy and dismal moods of today's passéists. We must invent Futurist clothes, hap-hap-hap-hap-happy clothes, daring clothes with brilliant colours and dynamic lines. They must be simple, and above all they must be made to last for a short time only in order to encourage industrial activity and to provide constant and novel enjoyment for our bodies. Use materials with forceful muscular colours – the reddest of reds, the most purple of purples, the greenest of greens, intense yellows, orange, vermilion – and skeleton tones of white, grey and black. And we must invent dynamic designs to go with them and express them in equally dynamic shapes: triangles, cones, spirals, ellipses, circles, etc. The cut must incorporate dynamic and asymmetrical lines, with the left-hand sleeve and left side of a jacket in circles and the right in squares. And the same for waistcoats, stockings, topcoats, etc. The consequent merry dazzle produced by our clothes in the noisy streets, which we shall have transformed with our Futurist architecture, will mean that everything will begin to sparkle like the glorious prism of a jeweller's gigantic glass-front.

(Apollonio, 1973, pp. 132, 133)

Besides the demand to embrace colour, pattern and asymmetry, which reflect the opposite of what is conventional, emerges the novel and revolutionary idea of the 'throwaway' garment, reflecting the continual turnover of new ideas and the unashamed pursuit of novelty. Balla designed a series of highly coloured and patterned, although conventionally shaped, waistcoats, and it is easy to imagine him wearing one as he declaims his manifesto to a stream of weary commuters on a busy Italian street. Marinetti, the self-styled leader of the Futurists who later allied himself with the Fascist cause, found the tone of Balla's writing far too happily enthusiastic and rewrote, 'today we Futurists will brandish these anti-neutral clothes, cheerfully bellicose … the youth of Italy will recognise us, who wear these clothes, its Futurist living flags for our great, necessary, urgent war' (Taylor, 1975, pp. 77–78). To put this into practice, in one of a series of characteristically colourful and provocative 'spontaneous' events, Berghaus recounts (Berghaus, 1998, p. 76) how the writer Cangiullo wore a specially tailored suit in the colours of the Italian flag and tricolour beret to a lecture by a pacifist (in Marinetti's eyes) professor at a university in Rome. The Futurists were recognized by the students and a restless atmosphere began to build. Cangiullo recounts, 'in one big gesture I unbutton my coat. … From under the rind of my Loden [coat] appears a living flag in human shape. Pandemonium reigns … I don't know what happens to me, if I'm going to be burned at the stake or carried in triumph.' By the time he escapes the crowds the suit is ripped to shreds, but news of the event has carried around the town and the participants judge the performance, for so it was, a success (ibid., pp. 72, 73).

Balla and other Futurist scenographers, particularly Prampolini and Depero, were less interested in overtly political performance events and instead sought to stage their revolutionary ideas in more mainstream theatrical spaces through the use of cutting-edge technology. They went the furthest in taking Craig's ideas about the 'ubermarionette' literally, and the surviving writings of Prampolini and Depero (translated and reprinted in Kirby's 1971 *Futurist Performance*) reveal their ambitions. Prampolini in 1915 in *Futurist Scenography* wrote forcefully that 'human actors will not be tolerated', and sought to refigure costume's relationship with the human form. In his *Notes on a Theatre* written in 1916 he imagines

> Decompositions of the figure and deformation of it, even until its absolute transformation: e.g. a dancing ballerina who continually accelerates, transforming herself into a floral vortex ...
> Moustaches, beards, wigs; red, yellow, green, gold
> Masks of all shapes;
> Moveable and intensely coloured,
> Headlight-eyes
> Megaphone-mouths, funnel-ears
> In movement and transformation
> Mechanical clothes,
> (Prampolini, 1916, cited in Kirby, 1971, pp. 207 and 210)

Here emerges a Modernist vision of bright colours, continual movement and mechanization, ideas which were innovative enough in 1916 to lead Diaghilev, the Russian entrepreneur and producer of the well-documented Ballets Russes, to commission Futurist 'ballets' from both Balla and Depero. As a determined espouser of the 'new' in general rather that one particular artistic style, and as an entrepreneur needing to commission artists that would produce innovative, and crowd pleasing, work, Diaghilev wrote to Nijinsky in 1917, 'Futurism, Cubism, is the last word. I do not want to let the position of an artistic leader slip away from me' (Diaghilev, 1917, cited in Nijinsky, 1935, p. 360). Both these commissioned works took the Futurist ideal to remove any visible signs of the human body to the extreme whilst seeking to harness new technologies such as lighting and mechanics in an entirely new theatrical experience. Balla's *Feu d'Artifice* had originally contained a performance by dancer Lois Fuller but, in this incarnation, exchanged human performers for a series of mechanically dancing scenic shapes that would light up in time to Stravinsky's music. Tragically, there was a dispute with the technicians before the first performance in 1917 (Berghaus, 1998, p. 257), and they refused to operate the work. Hence it was deemed an artistic failure and never performed again. At about the same time, Depero was commissioned by Diaghilev to design sets and costumes for a version of Hans Anderson's *Le Chant Du Rossignol (The Emperor's Nightingale)*. In Depero's own words, the costumes were

> solid in style, mechanical in movement; grotesque enlargements of arms and large, flat legs; hands made of cans or discs or fans with long, pointed and rattling fingers; golden or green masks showing only one nose or set of eyes or a luminous smiling

mouth made out of a mirror; bell shaped coats and trousers and shirt sleeves; all of them polyhedral and asymmetric, all of them unscrewable and mobile.

(Depero, cited in Berghaus, 1998, p. 304)

The three designs that survive – an unnamed figure, a mandarin and a Chinese woman courtier (all reproduced in Belli, 1989, pp. 92–97) – are stunningly bold images composed of geometric shapes in orange, yellow, gold and brown which appear to have been made from flat collaged pieces of coloured paper. They show a semblance of human form but mainly demonstrate the accuracy of Depero's description – long cones for arms or legs, big circles which might be hats or parasols, large-scale pinked and fringed edgings and pyramidal hands. In an annotation to these designs, he made clear his aims, 'The human figure disappeared under the volume, the wings and the shield of fantastical plastic appearance. The person was nothing but a hidden mechanical means to guide these mechanical and abstract costumes and their lively and ever changing appearance' (Depero, 1916 cited in Berghaus 1998, p. 305). Despite the fact that no photographs or working drawings survive, the words of his friend, Martio Recchi, who saw them half-finished in January 1917, are revealing,

[The materials] seemed most unsuitable for something as soft and flowing as clothes ... but to a large degree he was successful in doing just that, creating costumes from an unthinkable material: the steel and cardboard he used for his sculptures. The resulting constructions maintain the rigidity and unbending quality of sculptures, despite their lightness and pliability, which are conditioned by their functional requirements. The manner of construction compels the dancer to create new types of movements, but also forces the clothing into a harmony with the movements of a person who wears them rather than deforms them in accordance with the intentions of the designer.

(Recchi cited in Berghaus, 1998, p. 305)

Massine, Diaghilev's choreographer and dancer, reiterates this, 'I do not know how people are going to move around in Futurist costumes but in any case the *quality* of their movements will change totally' (ibid. p. 305). What we do know is that finally Diaghilev chose to stage Picasso's 'Parade' instead, even though the three-dimensional reproductions of Cubist collage worn by the two Manager characters look like lumpy, unsophisticated cardboard boxes compared with Depero's designs. Tragically for Depero, there is evidence that he helped Picasso to realize his Cubist constructions (Berghaus, 1998, p. 322), and the dance-drama, staged in 1917, is probably one of the most well-known pieces of Modernist performance. Performers wearing the Manager costumes were 'incapable of motion except that of a mannequin' (Glover, 1980, p. 33), and inevitably such extreme costumes affected the choreography.

It does appear that for committed revolutionaries such as Depero, the creation of a new kind of movement that overcomes the limitations of the human body was part of the costume's function, not just to portray the new world that such artists were building, but to embody it. Several artists, such as Prampolini, went as far as abandoning the body altogether to work with puppets. Oscar Schlemmer, another artist revolutionary, joined the Bauhaus in Weimar, Germany, in 1921 to teach sculpture but gradually moved into theatre where the Bauhaus leader, Walter Gropius, described how he 'transform[ed] dancers and actors into moving architecture' (Gropius, 1961, p. 9). In the essay *Man and Art Figure* Schlemmer wrote,

> The endeavor to free man from his physical bondage and to heighten his freedom of movement beyond his native potential resulted in substituting for the organism the mechanical human figure … Possibilities are endless in the light of today's technological advancements: precision machinery, scientific apparatus of glass and metal, the artificial limbs developed by surgery, the fantastic costumes of the deep-sea diver and the modern soldier, and so forth
>
> (ibid., pp. 28, 29)

Schlemmer's costumes of padded canvas, wire, wood and metal extend and distort the body, transforming it into something akin to a doll or automaton. By comparing his words with the views of other artists presented in this book, we can observe how different styles of theatre seem to require different working relationships between human body and costume. For Alex Rigg (see interview), the performance is created by the dancer's struggle to make his or her body perform a set of movements within the confines of a costume made deliberately difficult to wear, and which has deliberately not been rehearsed with. This creates a relationship between performer and costume driven by choreographic instruction but unpredictable in its delivery. Rigg's acceptance of his limited control of the end product, indeed his desire and fascination for it, contrasts sharply with the frustration with and ultimate rejection of the limitations of the human body found in the writings of Modernist designers, and with Joanna McCallum's request recounted in Chapter 3 for tuition in how best to fall in her long skirt, which suggests a need to remove the unpredictability of relationship between body and costume by 'taming' the costume as well as modifying the body in order to repeat the fall identically night after night.

Perhaps the most complete examples of sculptural costuming aimed at hiding the human form took place in Russia between about 1913 and 1923 where groups of independent revolutionary artists designed, wrote and realized their modernistic visions. In the quest for a new theatrical language, Malevich's costume designs for the anti-opera *Victory over the Sun* stand out as the raw defiant antithesis of all that is subtle and naturalistic. The piece was conceived on a weekend in the country by three 'bad boys' of the Russian artistic avant-garde, the writer Kruchenykh, the composer Matyushin and the artist Malevich, and performed only twice in 1913 on a shoestring budget after two rehearsals. It was revived briefly in 1920 and the artist El Lizzitsky made a series of beautiful colour sketches for an unrealized marionette version in 1923. Its plot to capture the sun, conventionally a powerful symbol for good in Russian folklore but here representing a reactionary force unnecessary to modern urban life, was performed in an operatic but mainly spoken style, full of violence and aggression. Writes Glover, 'heroes … replaced the old world order with a new aesthetics in which dissonance replaced harmony, alogicality and absurdity replaced reason and language became a cacophony of nonsensical sound' (Glover, 1980, p. 15).

The costume designs which survive are gloriously bold watercolour sketches, comprising various large geometric shapes stacked one above the other in vivid slashes of fuchsia, yellow, purple, orange and green with black and white. The two performances sold out to an audience full of students and 'intelligentsia', and Liubov Gurevich writes in a contemporary review,

> Finally the safety curtain was raised and another revealed, white calico, with portraits of a few Futurists. A character dressed in a black and white costume with a similarly coloured triangle covering his entire face down to his chin, with slits for eyes, came out from behind the curtain and walked along the footlights and then read Khlebnikov's 'Prologue' … Explosions of laughter in the auditorium … often drowned the reader out … The reader withdrew … and two multicoloured people then peered out from behind the curtain and … tore it in half from top to bottom without any particular effect. Two large figures in costumes sewn from white and black squares and triangles appeared against the backdrop, with similar fabric covers or masks on their faces [These were the two Strong Men] … Multicoloured squares and other geometric shapes with the partial depiction of various objects, some realistic, some stylised, with fragments of words and numerical formulas, adhered to each other and teased the imagination with their incongruity. And against this background walked human figures with carelessly sewn costumes made of scraps of cloth of different colours, some in masks, some without, declaiming in an overblown theatrical manner and sometimes singing to the accompaniment of a piano.
> (Gurevich, 1913, cited in Bartlett and Dadswell, 2012, pp. 93 and 94)

Only two photos survive from the actual performances in 1913, but they show the scale of the performers' paper mâché head and body masks, with the heads measuring about half the height of the performer's bodies. The writer Kruchenyck wrote, 'The actors were like moving machines. The costumes … were Cubist in construction; made from cardboard and wire. This altered the anatomy of a person – the performers moved as if tied together and controlled by the rhythm of the artist and director' (Ratikin and Sarabianov, 1975, p. 67). Bright searchlight beams were used to pick out specific parts of the scene and the Futurist writer, Benedict Livshitz observed,

> The figures themselves were cut into shapes with the knives of the searchlights and robbed alternately of their arms, legs, or head, since for Malevich they were only geometrical bodies subject not merely to dissection into their component parts but also to complete extinction into the picture space.
> (Bowlt, 1977, p. 164)

In a playing space as shallow as an artist's canvas against a monochrome geometric backdrop and under strongly gelled, choreographed lighting, the sense of human bodies must have been almost completely lost, supplanted instead by a horizontal row of moving geometric shapes. The materials are significant, too, purposely exchanging the soft fabrics of traditional clothes that can be moulded to the body for the flat inflexible planes of timber and board that will conceal, enlarge or deform it. Nick Cave, a black American textile artist with a background in dance, has used similarly unconventional and unforgiving materials in his series of 'Soundsuits'. These startling full body suits 'camouflage the body, masking and creating a second skin that conceals race, gender and class, forcing the viewer to look without judgement' (Jack Shainman, 2013). Constructed from a moveable body frame onto which a range of castoff materials such as gloves, handbags, crocheted coasters, artificial flowers, fur fabric or twigs are fixed, the suits make noises as he moves in them and 'like a coat of armor, they embellish the body while protecting the wearer from outside culture' (Inspiration Green, 2013). Although Cave's Soundsuits enclose and transform the body like those of Malevich, the nature of Cave's authorship is radically different because of his personal relationship with the costumes and their meaning.

In contrast to Malevich's goal of hiding the human in a kind of sculptural armour, other designers in the early twentieth century saw both their task and the role of the costumes, in a materially different, though equally scenic, way. Popova and Stepanova were two revolutionary Russian designers working between 1917 and 1923 who were members of the Productivists, a group of the most hardline Communists. Active members of INKhUk, the Institute for Artistic Culture, they reflected and wrote constantly about their art and, in 1921, Stepanova wrote of artists 'our task is to find ourselves a place in real life' (Andrews and Kalinovska, eds, 1990, p. 78). Both artists sought to rethink both everyday dress and theatrical costume as part of a consistent and systematized world in which, according to art critic Fedorov-Davydov in 1931, the task of the Communist clothing designer was 'the organisation of the socialist environment, the organisation of the behaviour of collectivist man, and, through the organisation of behaviour, the transformation of man's character, psyche and emotions' (Noever, ed., 1991, p. 205).

In her work in the First Cotton-Printing State Factory, Stepanova wrote about three kinds of dress, the prozodezhda, or production clothing perfectly adapted to the requirements of its wearer's profession, the spetzodezhda or protective clothing, and the sportsodezhda, sports clothing. According to Rudnitsky (Rudnitsky, 1988) the first time these were used in performance was in Meyerhold's *Mystery-Bouffe* of 1918 (designed by Malevich) where they formed just one recognizable group, set against other visually differentiated costumes. Strictly though, as a consistent 'theatre workers' uniform', they were used first in 1922 by Stepanova and Popova, designing for Meyerhold, who both costumed all the play's performers almost identically in these 'actor's uniforms' (Rudnitsky, 1988, p. 43). Interviewed by the theatre magazine *Zrelischa* in 1922 Stepanova said 'Prozodezhda can be created for various spheres of labour, physical exercises, in the theatre for biomechanics – where there is a precise productional task and an operative system' (Stepanova, in Stern 2004, p. 52), and in *The Death of Tarelkin*, her versions were voluminous two tone boiler suits or tunic and trousers covered with striped or geometric designs which worked against body shape but in harmony with the continuous wooden panels of the abstracted set that held hints of prison, playground and circus. The shallow depth of field, a feature of this style of theatre, and the repeated geometric forms helped to 'lose' the human bodies in the pictorial whole. Glover suggests that the costumes were so baggy they obscured the actor's movements which, coupled with technical problems, meant the production was not well received (Glover, 1980, p. 64). What is significant is that 'the audience observed the prompter, dressed in the same prozodezhda as the actors, sitting in the first row of the stalls and from time to time very loudly "cueing" the performers' (Rudnitsky, 1988, p. 95). In other words, the costume as worker's uniform was worn by production staff as well as actors in a very different picture from that described at the Globe in Chapter 3.

Popova, whose adherence to materialism was so great that she almost rejected theatre because the audience could not see the back of the set (Rudnitsky, 1988, p. 92) was equally determined to systematize the artistic impulse and remove from it any possible individualism or aestheticism. When she designed *The Magnanimous Cuckold*, her justification to the Institute for Artistic Culture reveals her almost desperate attempt to work artistically according to Communist principles ...

> my desire [is] to translate the problem from the aesthetic to the production plane, to deal with the question differently from its usual aesthetic resolution, ... [which] may be formulated as follows: to equip the theatrical action with its material elements. ... In this, one criterion should be utilitarian adaptability and not the resolution of any formal-aesthetic problems such as the question of colour or volume, or the organisation of the theatrical space, and so on ...
>
> [On] the question of the work uniform ... The elements of analysis had to be sought intuitively; thus there were the modern elements of the acrobat, athlete, sailor, military worker, agitator, and so forth. In addition, the costume was intended for the actor's daily, ordinary life and work and therefore had to be utilitarian both for this purpose and to replace all other clothing, so that it was necessary to add, for example, an overcoat, and so forth. In all, the costume was intended for seven or eight sorts or types of work. There was a fundamental disinclination to making any distinction between the men's and women's costumes; it just came down to changing the pants to a skirt or culottes.
>
> (Popova (1922) in Sarabianov and Adaskina, 1990, p. 378)

The ensemble's baggy blue tops and trousers with reinforced external seams and exaggerated legs resembling wide-legged jodhpurs were utilitarian in design, very frontal in form and originally unadorned. On the shallow stage against a brick wall, the mechanical angular movements of the acting ensemble together with the sharp lighting were designed to locate the human bodies in the wooden multi-levelled set with its wheels, slides and doors as part of an integrated 'acting machine', paralleling Meyerhold's desire to reinstate an aesthetic of the 'theatre theatrical' and in total contrast to the realism of Stanislavsky (Glover, 1980, p. 39). Popova's uniform was so successful in erasing visual clues for the audience that she was forced later to add some minimal pointers such as pompoms or eyeglasses in order to differentiate the figures on stage.

Alexandra Exter, on the other hand, was not as politically hardline as her two colleagues, but she had very strong ideas about how costume should work on the stage and was not afraid to critique the work of others. In the passage below from *In Search of New Clothing* (1923) she seems to be implying that prozodezhda, the production clothing, had to be consistent and specific to an actor and could not reproduce those of other labourers or else they were not actually fulfilling their purpose. In doing this she appears to be questioning the work of the colleagues with whom she is so often allied, Popova and Stepanova. The theatrical form her costumes take are very different from theirs, and I wonder if the stage work of the three would be so often discussed as a trio if they had happened to be born male. In 1919 in an essay entitled 'The Artist of the Theatre' (having begun her work with Tairov), she writes,

> Free movement is the fundamental element of the theatrical act. The bland contemporary stage must be enriched above all with movement. As a consequence, the artist's mission is to give as much space on the stage to the dynamic powers of drama as possible while at the same time keeping them under control. For the costumes it is essential to employ the same principles as in stage construction: principles of dynamic action. The composition of the costume, its form and color, should conform strictly to the character of the bearer's movements. This is fully attainable, since the various combinations of form and color may either strengthen or weaken the effects of the movement by imparting this or that tone to them. When studying the stage and the actor as a plastic whole, moreover, it is difficult to agree with the use of costumes made of 'real' material alongside simplified, conventional three dimensional sets. Costumes should be painted by the artist: the folds may be suggested by the paintbrush, [and] ornaments may be presented as individual fragments and in greatly exaggerated proportions, so that accidental folds and intricate needlework will not disrupt the clarity and integrity of the overall impression.
>
> (Exter, 1919, in Bowlt and Drutt, 1999, p. 303)

Then in 1923 in *In Search of New Clothing,* she writes,

> Experiments for specific 'production clothing' have also been undertaken in the sphere of theatrical costume. Here, however, there is still a confusion of conceptions between the costume of the theatrical performer and the outfit of workers in other areas of production. The actor [could be] dressed in a worker's outfit, whether of a mason or of a carpenter, which had no real connection with the

performer. ... It has to be said that the contemporary specialized costume for stage performers has still not been discovered. However, this kind of production clothing has existed for centuries –, the 'tutu,' i.e., a costume constructed according to the movement of the body during a classical dance. Ballet shoes, leg tights, lightness of the skirt, flexibility of the torso – all these are logically connected with the dance and make the 'tutu' the production clothing of classical ballet. Right now, when the theatre is studying every possible kind of movement (physical, emotional, tightrope walking, etc.), the theatre should base its production clothing on the movement of the actor's body.

(Exter 1923, in Bowlt and Drutt, 1999, pp. 301–302)

Exter worked several times with the director Alexander Tairov who shared a similar political position to her and sought to find a theatrical style somewhere between the realism of Stanislavsky and the abstraction of Meyerhold. 'He sought ... to establish pictorial and internal harmony on his stage with the actors masked and moving in prescribed rhythms aft the fashion of Gordon Craig's Über-marionette. "Remember you are on the stage" he ever admonished his actors' (Oenslager, 1974, p. 192). To this end in 1916 in the poetic play, *Famira Kifared*, Exter designed costumes that revealed large parts of the body which were then painted and shaded for emphasis with make-up, including nipples painted onto bodices (Rudnitsky, 1988, p. 18). Exter's costumes in her work with Tairov were individual in their details but had a unity of style both with each other and with the sets that she also designed. Nakov writes,

Compared to [her contemporary paintings] the costumes reveal the same passion for movement and the same desire to articulate different planes, stratified and disposed in a spiral and centrifugal movement. Contrary to the then current practice of submitting a descriptive full face project for a costume, Exter's designs are 'in motion', describing the composite movement the actor would create on stage, and which movement would make possible the realisation of the full plastic amplitude of the costume.

Exter ... explored the use of various materials (wood and metal) to create true living sculptures. The performers' natural dynamic qualities were used to attain a new level of expression: the actor's legs were painted in order to emphasise the changing plasticity of musculature in action. Thus, the old Futurist practice of painting the body ('épatage' – to shock the bourgeoisie) ... became part of the formal requirements of a different order: ... demonstrating the dynamic structure of the image. In a similar way, the Constructivist principle of texture referring to the variety of materials, was extended to the use of the most unexpected materials, the actor's own physical musculature thrown into motion.

(Nakov in Oenslager, 1974, pp. 10, 11)

Exter also designed *Salome* for Tairov and finally *Romeo and Juliet* for which there survives a striking photograph of a scenic space composed of a number of multicoloured and faceted levels on which are posed a crowd of characters in stylized geometric shapes and strongly contrasting tones very reminiscent of her own paintings. Writes Kennedy, 'Exter's costumes, though eminently wearable, were dynamic exhibits of colour and form. Cubist designers tended to make actors into two-dimensional pictures ... Exter achieved something different and much more theatrical, an application of Cubist principles that assisted characterization and acting.' Although Exter undoubtedly found a uniquely theatrical Cubist design style, Kennedy's assertion as to the wearability of the costumes may be a little optimistic. The costumes in the photograph are starched, pinned and wired to look almost exactly like her powerful Cubist designs and appear both to distort the human form and to ignore the inherent qualities of her materials, for example, the softness of fabric. Her interest in the movement of forms in space, including the movement of actors on stage, whom she imagined as living non-objective structures in motion, meant that to show the costumes off best the actors were expected to execute complicated and inconvenient rotations about which they were less than happy (Oenslager, 1974, pp. 13, 14). Her strong vision of how the costumes needed to function must have pushed to the limit one of the key relationship in the theatrical process, that of director and designer; the scenic effect was visually overwhelming and Tairov did not work with her again. It is notable, however, that his work with designer, Alexander Vesnin, such as *Phaedra* (1922), continued in a similar if simpler style in which, 'the stage space contained the actor and the actor the space, so that actor and space were united in one homogenous pictorial landscape' (Glover, 1980, p. 86).

Perhaps the most obvious use of actors in this scenic way in more mainstream theatre is as a crowd, chorus or ensemble. 'A single organism made up of dozens of heads and arms, like a sort of giant squid', is how Silviu Purcarete, evocatively if exaggeratedly describes the group of about twelve performers who commented on the action in Greek tragedy (Interview, 1988). Jacques Lecoq describes it in a similar manner: 'As a collective body, it possesses a centre of gravity, extensions, breath. It is a sort of organism that can take different shapes according to the situation in which it finds itself' (Lecoq, 1997, p. 137). If the chorus functions more like a single entity than a series of individuals, then I would suggest that an audience does not read their costumes as signifying individual character but interprets the overall 'feel' of the group in relation to the space. Watching a video recording of Peter Hall's 1981 version of the Oresteia, I am struck by how the identical static masks and the similar but not identical clothing consisting of flowing robes which move like water around the chorus do indeed create one entity, made even more powerful by the fact that for an audience member, it is not always clear which individual is actually speaking which lines, rather that their words emerge from the crowd. Similarly, in the National Theatre of Scotland's 2007 version of *The Bacchae*, directed by artistic director John Tiffany, the chorus, who chanted and sang their commentary, consisted of ten black women wearing flowing red cocktail dresses who posed and occasionally emerged from the edges of the stage space. The costumes were mainly strapless with a fitted bodice and a long flowing textured skirt made of marabou, frilled, tiered, fringed or Fortuny pleated, beaded and sparkling, made to work best in movement. They related to Dionysus in his cabaret garb of lurex kilt and waistcoat, whilst remaining separate both spatially and sartorially from the king, Pentheus, in his conventional black suit. Their glamorous 'similar but not the same' costumes gave them an obviously collective body whilst allowing enough individuality to avoid the feeling of an army. It allowed the anarchy of 'dozens of heads and arms' without implying the conformity and subservience of sameness. In an interview with Alexis Soloski of The Village Voice (24 June 2008) John Tiffany said he was '"allergic to Greek choruses, when they chant together and wear masks" instead, for him, "it's about glamour and a kind of sexy worship" characterising the first half as the best party in the world and the second as the worst hangover. He [saw] the Bacchantes as gospel singers and the style as "informed by the Broadway musical". It wasn't until he came up with this idea that he could see how to do the play in a modern way. He didn't want to "update" its setting just update its theatrical style.' This 'Dreamgirl-ish Greek chorus' (Vanity Fair, July 2008) inhabit a scenic world where 'colours are carefully choreographed: Dionysus in his gold kilted skirt, the scarlet and sequin clad Maenads who lounge against the white curved walls and the brown fur coat and bloodied hands of Paola Dionisotti's Agave adding vivid contrast' (Walker, 2007). The choice of using a theatrical version of African Caribbean women's gospel choir as the followers of Dionysus may have been critically controversial but the costuming style which allowed an individual to stand out for a moment before merging back into the crowd to become a part of the moving musical mass was thematically successful as well as sensually glamorous in its swish and swirl.

Similarly Peter Brook, when discussing his production of *King Lear* in 1962, advocates that an audience can only recognize a few characters as individuals and that, for clarity, 'crowds' should be costumed simply and generically:

> So Lear is barbaric and Renaissance; it's those two contradictory periods … We've evolved costumes which carry the minimum necessary real statement that each character needs. For instance, King Lear has to wear a robe because I think you can't go round that point. There are certain necessities for an actor as Lear. Even if you take everything else away from him, he has to enter with something that covers his legs for a certain regality of the character to appear. He has a robe therefore which no-one else has. There's no one else in the play who needs one. At the very beginning of the play, then, he has robe which is very rich, and after that he goes into a very simple costume made of leather. All the other costumes we have simplified so that only the essential remains. When in a Shakespeare play you have thirty or forty equally elaborate costumes, the eye is blurred and the plot becomes hard to follow. Here, we only gave important costumes to eight or nine central characters – the number one can normally focus on in a modern

play. It is interesting to hear people saying 'how clear the play seems!' without realising that the secret was related to the clothes.

(Brook, 1989, pp. 88–91)

Anne Hollander thinks of crowds differently, suggesting

The costumes worn by extras automatically convey more than the principal actors or singers' costumes do, since they are performing a purely visual function. Audiences for naturalistic drama, classical or modern, will accept the most minimally conceived costumes on the chief actors, who can convey all the significant atmosphere by their speech and movement. Hamlet can wear anything, so can Gertrude; the only restrictions on their dress might be that no jarring elements be superadded. But extras in Hamlet, particularly if they are not expected to behave dramatically, must wear carefully conceived clothes, which may be a lot more elaborate than the ones on the chief actors. This difference can itself have a spectacular dramatic effect as long as the extras can dramatically act the part of people properly wearing those clothes. If they cannot and are insentient bodies, the fancy garments of extras will look ludicrous.

(Hollander, 1975, p. 238)

Whether simple or complicated, writers agree that the main characters need to stand out visually from the ensemble. Aston and Savona make the point strongly:

In twentieth-century traditions of Western theatre, the responsibility for organising the theatrical sign system has fallen to the director. Whilst the dramatist is the originator of the linguistic sign system, the director nowadays has control over the theatrical (as opposed to dramatic) shape and is faced with the task of organising the signifying systems of theatre at her/his disposal (lighting, scenery, props and so on) into a codified process appropriate to the production of a text. If the director fails in this task, then the performance will not make sense to the spectator. Trying to make sense of a badly organised sign system can be a frustrating and unrewarding experience and is generally the sign of a director's failure. Students who saw Shared Experience's production of Nana, adapted by Olwen Wymark, were initially unable to identify Nana, because the colour coding of the costumes gave prominence to a supporting character (Sabine, dressed in bright red finery) at the expense of the heroine (attired in the white undergarments which all the women in the cast used as a quick-changing base for multiple role-playing). Narrative confusion arose because the signification of the 'scarlet woman' was misplaced.

(Aston and Savona, 1991, p. 100)

Just because crowd or chorus needs to work as one entity, it does not have to sink into the background as Tiffany's 'The Bacchae' has demonstrated. The Stuart court masques showed a similar phenomenon. These lavish one-off events were primarily visual shows, and the sumptuous costumes in design 'favoured en-suite appearances for the aristocracy' (Ravelhoffer, 2009, p. 168). Such was their visual splendour that they became the subject of one of the first documented quarrels over the primacy of text or image on stage, analysed by Nicholas Till in the essay 'Oh, [to] Make the Boardes Speak!' (Collins and Nisbett, 2010, pp. 154–161). Having previously collaborated successfully with Inigo Jones, by 1616 in the folio edition of his masques Ben Jonson omitted all stage directions and staging descriptions, complaining about their over elaborateness. (Ravelhoffer, 2009, p 205) When, in 1631, Jonson declared himself 'inventor' of *Love's Triumph through Callipolis* and Jones finally complained, Jonson replied with a savage attack entitled, 'Expostulation: To Inigo Marquis Would be'. He begins,

> O Showes! Showes! Mighty Showes!
> The Eloquence of Masques! What need of Prose
> Or Verses, or Sence t'express Immortall you!
> You are the Spectacles of State!
>
> (Collins and Nisbett, 2010, p. 154)

However much Jonson disapproved and despite careful scripting by him and other early seventeenth century writers, masques were principally about spectacle. 'Purpose made for a specific performance, masque costume represented visual political currency, often with substantial material value. They were perhaps the most expensive items in masque productions, therefore important factors in stressing the exclusivity of the event' (Ravelhoffer, 2009, p. 125). When we realise that for *The Masque of Oberon*, staged in 1611, the costumes alone cost over £1000, we may get some idea of their lavishness. Hollander, siding squarely with Inigo Jones, writes, 'In ritual and emblematic rather than dramatic productions, such as masques and pageants, principals, whether they talk or sing, must wear appropriately significant garments, since the medium is visual and the theme ideal. *The costumes are the drama* (my italics). The characters are known by what they wear, and any accompanying words support the clothes instead of the other way round' (Hollander, 1975, p. 238). The strongest example in modern theatre of this approach, although very different in context and intent, is probably to be seen in Musical Theatre, for example in *Wicked*, where the pupil ensemble wear costumes that all incorporate elements of school uniform; blue blazer, stripes and badges, whilst each is individually designed in a highly structured and tailored style complete with asymmetric tail coats, corsets and bustles. The design style illustrated in *Wicked* and in comparable musicals, such as *We Will Rock You*, gives enough information to place the ensemble in an identifiable world but allows for a bravura design style that shouts its non-naturalism gleefully to an audience who revels in its visual detail.

In the Stuart masque the accepted male masquing 'uniform' was the garb of the traditional Hero comprising a tight garment with a small high waist and a full skirt, a headdress with lots of plumes to add height and leather buskins over muscular calves (not always real!) with high-heeled shoes. Women wore a full-skirted dress of typical Stuart shape, sometimes with classical drapery and possibly sometimes with shorter skirts or bared breasts. These highly stylized costumes were made from exquisitely detailed designs in colours of white with carnation (shades of red) or watchet (a greeny blue) trimmed with acres of silver and gold, with groups of male and female masquers identically apparelled and the 'leader', the king or queen, made recognizable by a small signifier such as a red wrist scarf or extra plumes. Despite Johnson's later condemnation of visual spectacle in 1611, he cannot resist describing, in a postscript to the published text, the magnificence of the costumes in the masque *Hymenai* in all their sparkling detail:

> Yet, that I may not utterly defraud the reader of his hope, I am drawn to give it those brief touches, which may leave behind some shadow of what it was: and first of the attires.
>
> That of the lords, had part of it, for the fashion, taken from the antique Greek statues, mixed with some modern additions: which made it both graceful and strange. On their heads they wore Persic crowns, that were with scrolls of gold plate turned outward, and wreathed about with a carnation and silver net-lawn; the one end of which hung carelessly on the left shoulder; the other was tricked up before, in several degrees of folds, between the plaits, and set with rich jewels and great pearl. Their bodies were of carnation cloth of silver, richly wrought, and cut to express the naked, in manner of the Greek thorax; girt under the breasts with a broad belt of cloth of gold, embroidered, and fastened before with jewels: their labels were of white cloth of silver, laced, and wrought curiously between, suitable to the upper half of their sleeves; whose nether parts with their bases, were of watchet cloth of silver, cheveroned all over with lace. Their mantles were of several-colored silks, distinguishing their qualities, as they were coupled in pairs; the first, sky-color; the second, pearl-color; the third, flame-color; the fourth, tawny; and these cut in leaves, which were subtly tacked up, and embroidered with O's, and between every rank of leaves a broad silver race. They were fastened on the right shoulder, and fell compass down the back in gracious folds, and were again tied with a round knot to the fastening of their swords. Upon their legs they wore silver greaves, answering in work to their labels. And these were their accoutrements.
>
> The ladies attire was, for the invention, and full of glory; as having in it the most true impression of a celestial figure: the upper part of white cloth of silver, wrought with Juno's birds and fruits; a loose under garment, full gathered, of carnation, striped with silver, and parted with a golden zone; Beneath that, another flowing garment, of watchet cloth of silver, laced with gold; through all which, though they were round, and swelling, there yet appeared some touch of their delicate lineaments, preserving the sweetness of proportion, and expressing itself beyond expression.
>
> (Luminarium, 2013)

These Grand Masquers, about fifteen regal and noble actors who performed the Masque itself, probably performed on a small raised stage before descending into the central dancing area later to mingle with the audience. The sight of such a crowd, dressed in sparkling finery, must indeed have been a scenic feast.

> Uniformity in colour produced a strong theatrical ensemble effect. Pragmatism turned into theatrical expediency as the theme of concord became one of the

underlying principles of Stuart masques. Jones was expected to create a vision of an orderly stage realm, which in its turn served as a wishful representation of the wider kingdom of Britain. … After the dramatic part of the masque, … nobles in courtly dress danced with other nobles in fancy dress … the two modes blended together because they were constructed and embellished according to the same high standards and from the same materials. The scale of trim and degree of detail were the same; they were intended to be seen from the same range of distances, under the same quality and intensity of artificial lighting.

(Ravelhoffer, 2009, p. 168)

So here again is the suggestion that a unified design style on the stage creates in an audience the feeling of a unified world, but this time the portrayal is an idealized vision of a world not just aspired to (as seen in Modernism) but already in existence.

When it comes to the scenic power of costumes, such a power is almost always strengthened by the use of clever lighting, and Stuart masques were no exception. According to Palmer in his book in this series on lighting, 'Inigo Jones … was central to the development of lighting techniques in Britain' (Palmer, 2013, p. 30). Masques, played in a darkened auditorium, were lit by candles skilfully moved around on pulleys and reflecting through water or against burnished metal onto walls hung with glittering metallic tapestries. In a section which vividly conjures the sparkle and splendour of a Stuart masque, Ravelhoffer concludes, 'A masque costume played by itself, softly caressed by flickering illumination. It already performed before the wearer started moving at all' (Ravelhoffer, 2009, p. 169).

The idea of the landscape created by costume is particularly evident when the performers and the audience mingle and merge as they did in court masques. Although there have consistently been theatrical events and traditions that involve the audience dressing up in the costumes of a specific era or style, for example the music hall television programme, *The Good Old Days* of the 1970s and 1980s, cult musicals such as the Rocky Horror Show and themed children's shows, such as the Scottish phenomenon, *The Singing Kettle* which gives reduced ticket prices to children who arrive in costume, usually in such productions performers and audience are kept largely apart. Recently, though, I participated in *The Salon Project,* a work by Stewart Laing's company, *Untitled Projects*, in which performers and audience were thrown together into the same space. An interview with Stewart Laing can be found between Chapters 4 and 5. According to the company's website, 'The heart of *The Salon Project* is the visual spectacle of each audience member transformed' (The Salon Project, 2013). To enable this to happen, when an audience member booked a ticket, he or she filled in a measurement form so that a costume could be chosen and provided by the wardrobe staff for the duration of the event. On arrival, each individual was personally dressed, coiffed and made up by a team of professionals before being released in groups into a stunningly re-created late nineteenth-century Salon. Once inside, participants were encouraged to experience a variety of appropriate events such as talks, live music, readings, videos and tableaux whilst chatting, mingling, admiring themselves and each other in full length mirrors, drinking champagne and having their photograph taken. They were instructed not to pretend anything; the presentations were modern, the technology was modern, the ideas were modern. The company website explains that *The Salon Project* offers audiences 'the opportunity to explore the past while imagining the future, to mirror the contrasts and paradoxes between the golden age of salon society and our own era of economic excess' (The Salon Project, 2013). Such an event turns on its head the whole argument about recreation and authenticity by creating an event which parallels the Paris salons in its insistence on the present and the future but costumes the bodies present in the past as an act of liberation from inhibition. This particular version of immersive theatre is very different from the type where the audience wander from place to place like unseen ghosts powerless to intervene. Instead the radical act of costuming everyone similarly and lighting the space fully creates a democratic complicity between audience and performer.

Once we start to consider the ways in which stage costume can be used scenically, it is possible to identify and distinguish different ways in which this can happen. Individual garments can be exaggerated, simplified, expanded, repeated or extended for theatrical reasons, both dramatic and comical, for example the pantomime dame wearing endless pairs of increasingly large and silly bloomers. Garments can also be seen to transform from the sartorial to the scenic and vice versa, and examining some examples reveals the breadth of expressive scenic possibilities that costume can offer. In the National Theatre of Scotland's very successful and highly theatrical show, *Black Watch*, most of the costume was naturalistic 'modern dress' comprising uniforms and some unobtrusive civilian clothing. However, there is one scene which proves a notable exception. In it, the history of the regiment is told through the costume by sending an actor down a rolled-out red carpet like a dummy, whilst his regimental colleagues twist and turn him as they dress him in the uniform of one era, undress and redress him in an act of storytelling through costume rarely bettered on stage. The scene is so striking that it is mentioned in probably eighty percent of the reviews in the National Theatre of Scotland archive box of the first fringe run and subsequent tour to the US. Dominic Cavendish likened the effect to a 'whirling human mannequin' (*Daily Telegraph*, 2006), and in an interview John Tiffany explains its inception, mentioning the Military Tattoo and the style of 7:84 Theatre with their use of music and movement, as influences.

TB: Perhaps that explains the famous red carpet sequence then?

JT: Exactly. Both Stephen Hoggatt, who was the movement director on Black Watch, and I were fascinated by the idea of the Royal Tournament where you see soldiers assembling and reassembling artillery in ten seconds flat. We went from that idea to combining it with a history of the Black Watch. But it was a very complicated sequence to get right and some of the cast were convinced we were going to cut it before we got to the first preview.

(Barr, T., 2010)

Jessica Brettle, the costume designer, confided to me in an email (Brettle, 2013), 'I thought it would be more visually interesting to have some historical costume in it. Between [John Tiffany] and Stephen Hoggatt, the movement director, they devised the movement sequence and my part was to histori-cally and accurately research, source and make costumes for it. I went to the Black Watch Museum in Perth and they were really helpful to me. Then I had to work out how they could be taken on and off easily! With the help of vari-ous colours of Velcro and false fastenings we worked out a way of getting the costumes on and off in sequence. Getting ten boys to dress someone properly was no easy task. We eventually started to give them scores out of ten which encouraged a bit of competition and dramatically improved their efforts!'

Recently, in the National Theatre's 2013 Christmas family show *Emil and the Detectives*, the adult ensemble is used not so much as a speaking chorus but to conjure the speedy world of 1930s Berlin in a play in which the large cast of children do most of the acting. Their tightly choreographed shapes shift in and out around the child protagonist and his friends on their search for his stolen money, their black clothes give the audience a flavour of the era without any real sense of individuality and their crisp movements in fast geometric formations suggest bodies as urban architecture whilst pushing around moving scenery such as lampposts almost as if they are umbrellas. In the reviews, though, these adults are noticeably absent: 'The children are the only human element in this expressionist cityscape' writes Caroline McGinn (Time Out 5 December 2013) and, according to Robert Shore, 'Street lamps skate around the cinematically framed stage' (The Metro Mon., 9 December) In Chapter 2, I suggested that there were times when modern dress is almost invisible as costume on stage as it becomes somehow projected by the audience onto the actors (or the audience) in their offstage lives. But in this instance, although the actors are naturalistically costumed and in full view on the broad Olivier stage, their dark unobtrusive garments and their role as scenery shifters render both them and their costumes invisible.

Having seen costume scenically foregrounded and backgrounded, it is also possible to see it, in particular instances, alternate and vacillate between a role as scenery and clothing which is sometimes comic and sometimes highly dramatic. The 'transposability' of some garments seems to make them particularly useful for scenic effects, and the voluminous skirt or cloak is one such example. In the eighteenth century, the hooped skirt was customary for women on stage whether they were playing Shakespeare's Cleopatra (Laver, 1964, p. 112) or a princess in an opera-ballet designed by Louis Boquet. By the early twentieth century a similar skirt is used as a comedic scenic device in a design by the Russian modernist artist and designer Michael

Larionov for the Ballets Russes' *Les Contes Russes*, in which a woman in an enormous hooped skirt, first seen from the back, turns to reveal from the front, multiple children hiding within and revealing themselves coyly to the audience. In pantomime too we see the comic device of a character hiding in the dame's voluminous skirt. Similarly, the puppeteer Shona Reppe, in her charming show, *Olga Volt, the Electric Fairy*, used the effect to open her show by introducing herself as a three-metre-high giant wearing, it seemed, a Victorian-style dress with a huge blue crinoline skirt. Then as she disappeared through her own waist, she emerged from below to draw aside her skirts and invite the audience into her home as the crinoline transformed to become a kind of igloo.

In summer 2013 the circus company NoFit State in their show, *Bianco*, used the effect in a less comedic and much more sensual way. They created a seemingly endless garment as they hoisted an aerialist high into the roof of their big top, her flowing white tent-like skirt extending endlessly from her tiny waist to the floor far below ... until suddenly she releases it, undresses in a moment, the audience gasps and the 'skirt' cascades and floats gracefully down, down to become, in a moment of pure sensation, a white pool of silken light. These examples all use clothing in some way as a scenic device but they also exploit the material qualities of the costume's fabric: the crisp shiny electric blue satin of the crinoline and the soft white drape of the silk.

So too does the scenic costume used in Gordon Craig's designs for his version of Hamlet. There is a beautiful drawing from about 1910 of scene II in which the king and queen and the whole court are on stage. In Craig's version, as described by Stanislavsky,

> The King and Queen sat on a high throne in golden and brocaded costumes, among the golden walls of the throne room, and from their shoulders there spread downwards a cloak of gold porphyry, widening until it occupied the entire width of the stage and fell into the trap. In this tremendous cloak there were cut holes through which appeared a great number of courtier's heads, looking upwards at the throne. The whole scene resembled a golden sea with golden waves.
>
> (Stanislavsky, 1924 [1987], p. 514)

Kennedy comments, 'the effect was accomplished not with a single piece of cloth but with capes on individual courtiers, and it was necessary for the actors to remain motionless for most of the scene; although this was physically demanding, it increased the nightmare mood' (Kennedy, 1993, p. 54). The visual effect must have been striking, but in this style of theatre the actors were treated like shop dummies and were expected to forget their aching limbs for the sake of the overall visual effect.

Robert Lepage, the Canadian director/theatre maker, reversed Craig's idea to devastating effect in *Elsinore* (1997/8), his one-man version of Hamlet. The set was a series of moving, sliding apparently solid panels which formed walls, floors and platforms in a seemingly infinitely fluid selection of possibilities. He was dressed both as 'Hamlet' and as a typical ham Shakespearean actor in a big floppy white shirt and tight black trousers tucked into boots. It is clear from my interview with Jenny Tiramani how clichéd this is considered now and I am sure Lepage knew this when he chose to costume himself thus. As the text unfolded (in a version heavily cut and manipulated by Lepage) towards Ophelia's speech about Hamlet coming to her closet, one of the huge, probably three metre square, moving platforms appeared to be descending horizontally towards Lepage in order to crush him. When it reached his head it became suddenly plastic, his head and arms emerging through it as the platform continued its descent to the ground around him, transforming him from Hamlet to Ophelia clad from the neck down in an enormous white lace lycra dress which had, seemingly seconds earlier, been a solid flat platform. Karen Fricker writes,

> As Innes reminds us, the ideas of an auteur figure with ultimate creative control over all aspects of a production and of theatre as a machine (recall Lepage's company is called Ex Machina) have their roots in theatrical modernism, particularly in the work of Edward Gordon Craig, who conceived of Hamlet as a mono drama, including a scene with the stage covered entirely with a gown.
>
> (Brown, 2008, p. 246)

So we end the chapter as we began it, with a visual artist and auteur who sought total control over both environment and actor and whose philosophy articulated so clearly the idea of the scenic body.

Bibliography

Addressing the Century (1998) Exhibition Catalogue (London: Haywood Gallery).

Andrews, R. and Kalinovska, M. (1990) *Art into Life: Russian Constructivism, 1914–1932*. (New York: Rizzoli International Publications).

Annand, S. (2008) *The Half: Photographs of Actors Preparing for the Stage* (London: Faber and Faber).

Apollinaire, G. trans. Roseberry, P. (2000) *The Cubist Painters* (Harrogate: Broadwater House).

Apollonio, U. (1973) *Futurist Manifestoes* (London: Thames and Hudson).

Aria, E. D. (1906) *Costume: Fanciful, Historical and Theatrical* (London: Macmillan and Co.).

Arnold, J. (1964) *Patterns of Fashion 1: Englishwomen's Dresses and Their Construction c.1660–1860* 1977 edn (London, Basingstoke and Oxford: Macmillan).

Arnold, J. (1966) *Patterns of Fashion 2: Englishwomen's Dresses and Their Construction 1860–1940* 1977 edn (London, Basingstoke and Oxford: Macmillan).

Arnold, J. (1973) *A Handbook of Costume* (London and Basingstoke: Macmillan).

Arnold, J. (1980) *Lost from Her Majesties Back* (London: Costume Society).

Arnold, J. (1985) *Patterns of Fashion 3 1560–1620* (London, Basingstoke and Oxford: Macmillan).

Arnold, J. (1988) *Queen Elizabeth's Wardrobe Unlock'd* (London: Maney).

Arnold, J. (2008) *Patterns of Fashion 4: The Cut and Construction of Linen Shirts, Smocks, Neckwear, Headwear and Accessories* (London, Basingstoke and Oxford: Macmillan).

Aston, E. and Savona G. (1991) *Theatre As Sign System* (London: Routledge).

Barr. T. (2010) 'Theatre Review: *Black Watch*', *News of the World*, 12 September.

Barthes, R. (1977) *Image, Music, Text* (London: Fontana).

Barthes, R., transl. Howard, R. (1972) *Critical Essays* (Evanston: Northwestern University Press), pp. 41–50.

Bartlett, R. and Dadswell, S. (2012) *Victory over the Sun: The World's First Futurist Opera* (Exeter: University of Exeter Press).

Barton, L. (1935) *Historic Costume for the Stage* (London: Adam and Charles Black).

Baugh, C. (1990) *Garrick and Loutherbourg* (Cambridge: Chadwyck-Healey in association with The Consortium for Drama and Media in Higher Education).

Belli, G., Boschiero, N. and Passamani, B.eds (1989) *Depero: Theatro magico* [catalogo di una mostra itinerante].

Benjamin, W. (1968) 'The Work of Art in the Age of Mechanical Reproduction', *in* Arendt, H. (ed.) *Illuminations* (London: Fontana).

Berghaus, G. (1998) *Italian Futurist Theatre 1909–1944* (Oxford: Clarendon Press).

Berman, M. (2010) *All That Is Solid Melts into Air* (London & New York: Verso).

Bernard, B. (1839) *His Last Legs* (New York: Samuel French).

Bernard, B. (1847) *The Irish Attorney: Or, Galway Practice in 1770* (New York: Berford and Co).

Bernstein, S. (1998) *Virtuosity of the Nineteenth Century: Performing Music and Language in Heine, Liszt, and Baudelaire* (Sanford: Stanford University Press).

Bhabha, H.K. (1994) The *Location of Culture* (London & New York: Routledge).

Bicât, T. (2001) *Making Stage Costumes: A Practical Guide* (Ramsbury, Crowood Press).

Bicât, T. (2006) *Handbook of Stage Costume* (Ramsbury: Crowood Press).

Bigsby, C.W.E. (1982) *A Critical Introduction to Twentieth Century American Drama 1900–1940* (Cambridge, London, New York, New Rochelle, Melbourne, Sydney: Cambridge University Press).

Blumenthal, E., Taymor, J., and Monda, A. (1995) *Julie Taymor: Playing with Fire* (San Francisco: Harry N. Abrams, Inc.).

Booth, M. (1981) *Victorian Spectacular Theatre 1850–1910* (London: Routledge and Kegan Paul).

Boucher, F. (1996) *A History of Costume in the West* (London: Thames and Hudson).

Boucicault, D. (1987) *Selected Plays* (Gerrards Cross: Colin Smythe).

Bowlt, J.E. and Drutt, M. (1999) *Amazons of the Avant-Garde* (New York: Harry N. Abrams, Inc.).

Boym, S. (2001) *The Future of Nostalgia* (New York: Basic Books).

Brandstetter, G. (2007) 'The Virtuoso's Stage: A Theatrical Topos', *Theatre Research International*, 32.2, 178–195.

Brantley, B. (1996) *The New York Times*, 4 April.

Brettle, J. (2013) personal email, 3 October.

Breward, C. (1995) *The Culture of Fashion* (Manchester: Manchester University Press).

Brook, I. (1939) *Western European Costume and Its Relation to Theatre* (London: Harrap).

Brook, P. (1970) *The Empty Space* (London: Penguin).

Brook, P. (1989) *The Shifting Point* (London: Methuen).

Brown, J.R. (2008) *The Routledge Companion to Directors' Shakespeare* (London: Routledge).

Bryant, D. (1864) *Bryant's Minstrels Souvenir Programmes*, Vol. VIII, No. 2 & Vol. VIII, No. 5 (New York: T.B Harrison).

Burnett, K. and Ruthven Hall, P. (2002) *2D>3D: Design for Theatre and Performance* (London: Society of British Theatre Designers).

Burnett, K., Allen, K. and Shaw, P. eds (2007) *Collaborators: UK Design for Performance 2003–2007* (London: Society of British Theatre Designers).

Butler, J. (1993) *Bodies that Matter: On the Discursive Limits of Sex* (London & New York: Routledge, 1993).

Butler, J. (1999) *Gender Trouble: Feminism and the Subversion of Identity*, 1990, 1999 10th Anniversary Edition (New York & London: Routledge).

Callens, J. (1999) 'Negotiating Class and Gender Differences in the Wooster Group's Production of *the Hairy Ape*', in Chantal Cornut-Gentille D'Arcy (ed.) *Culture and Power IV: Cultural Confrontations* (Zaragoza, Zaragoza Dpto: Filologia Inglesia [Universidad de Zaragoza])).

Carson, C., Cooper, F.K., eds (2008) *Shakespeare's Globe: A Theatrical Experiment* (Cambridge: Cambridge University Press).

Carter, M. (2003) *Fashion Classics from Carlisle to Barthes* (Oxford: Berg).

Case, S.E. (1996) *Split Britches: Lesbian Practice/Feminist Performance* (London & New York: Routledge).

Cave, R. (1991) 'Staging the Irishman', in Jacqueline S. Bratton (ed.) *Acts of Supremacy: The British Empire and the Stage, 1790–1930* (Manchester: Manchester University Press), pp. 62–129.

Cavendish, D. (2006) 'Theatre Review: *Black Watch*', *The Daily Telegraph*, 23 August.

Clapp, S. (2000) 'A Soldier to Cry On', *Observer*, 18 June.

Cochrane, C. (1993) *Shakespeare and the Birmingham Repertory Theatre 1913–1929* (London: Society for Theatre Research).

Collier, C. (1929) *Harlequinade* (London: John Lane: The Bodley Head).

Collins, J. and Nisbett, A. (2010) *Theatre and Performance Design: A Reader in Scenography* (Abingdon: Routledge).

Cottis, E. (2000) 'Costumes at the Globe', in Eynat-Confino, I. and Sormova, E. (eds) *Space and the Postmodern Stage* (Prague: Ekon), pp. 100–105.

Craig, E. G. (1912) *On the Art of Theatre* (Chicago: Browne's Bookstore).

Crawley, G. (2011) *Transformation and Revelation: UK Design for Performance 2007–2011* (London: Society of British Theatre Designers).

Cumming, V. (2004) *Understanding Fashion History* (London: Batsford).

Curtis Jr., P. (1997) *Apes and Angels: The Irishman in Victorian Caricature* (Washington & London: Smithsonian Institution Press).

Daily Mail Reporter, 2012. 'The lady is a vamp! Anna Friel emerges from the stage door looking every inch the theatre princess in a fur wrap', http://www.daily mail.co.uk/tvshowbiz/article-2247957/Anna-Friel-emerges-stage-door-looking-inch-theatre-princess-fur-wrap.html, date accessed 16 December 2013.

Daly, N. (2009) *Sensation and Modernity in the 1860s* (Cambridge: Cambridge University Press).

De Jongh, N. (2000) 'Grown Up Boy Truly Lost' *Evening Standard*, 12 June.

De Marly, D. (1982) *Costume on the Stage 1600–1940* (London: Batsford).

Dorney, K. (2011) 'Review: *The Actor in Costume* by Aoife Monks' in *V and A Online Journal* Issue No. 3 Spring 2011.

Dryden, J. (1667) *The Indian Emperor or the Conquest of the Americas by the Spaniards* (London: Herringman).

Dumont, F. (1914) 'The Golden Days of Minstrelsy,' *New* York *Clipper*, 19 December.

Elizabethan.org, 2013. http://www.elizabethan.org/sumptuary/who-wears-what. html, date accessed 23 September 2013.

Escolme, B. (2005) *Talking to the Audience: Shakespeare, Performance, Self* (London & New York: Routledge).

Evans, L. (2003) 'Facile Histrionics', *The Spectator*, 17 May.

Fairholt, F. (1846) *Costume in England: The History of Dress from the Earliest Period Till the Close of the Eighteenth Century* (London: Chapman and Hall).

Fawkes, R. (1979) *Dion Boucicault: A Biography* (London, Melbourne, New York: Quartet Books).

Fay, S. (2000) 'Beautiful but Underpowered', *Independent on Sunday*, 18 June.

Fernald, M. and Shelton, E. (1937) *Costume Design and Making: A Practical Handbook* (London: A. and C. Black).

Freud, S. (2003) *The Uncanny* (London, New York, Victoria, Toronto, New Delhi, Auckland, Rosebank: Penguin).

Gerrard, C. (2003) *Aaron Hill: The Muse's Projector: 1685–1750* (Oxford: Oxford University Press).

Gibbs-Smith, C. (1976) Edition 10. *Costume (Journal of the Costume Society)*. Leeds: Maney.

Globe Correspondence, *Hamlet* Costume Bible, Globe Archive, 2000.

Globe Correspondence, *Richard II* Costume Bible, Globe Archive, 2003.

Globe Costume Notes, *Hamlet* Costume Bible, Globe Archive, 2000.

Globe Costume Notes, *Richard II* Costume Bible, Globe Archive, 2003.

Globe *Hamlet* DVD, 2000.

Globe Production Meeting Minutes, 2000. *Hamlet* Costume Bible, Globe Archive, Tues 2 May 2000.

Globe Stage Management Notes, 2000. *Hamlet* Costume Bible, Globe Archive.

Glover, J. (1980) *The Cubist Theatre* (Epping: Bowker).

Goethe, J. and Eckermann, J. (1998) *Conversations of Goethe with Johann Peter Eckermann* (Cambridge, MA: Da Capo Press).

Gore-Langton, R. (2000) 'The Crane of Cawdor', *Daily Express*, 16 June 2000.

Grazia Magazine, 2013. 'Katie Holmes, Jessica Chastain and Anna Friel's Dos and Don'ts of Stage Door Chic', http://www.graziadaily.co.uk/fashion/news/katie-holmes--jessica-chastain-and-anna-friels-dos---donts-of-stage-door-chic, date accessed 16 December 2013, 8 January.

Gropius, W. (1961) *Theatre of the Bauhaus* (Middletown: Wesleyan University Press).

Gurr, A. (2000) *Staging in Shakespeare's Theatres* (Oxford: Oxford University Press).

Hamera, J. (2011) *Dancing Communities: Performance, Difference and Connection in the Global City* (Basingstoke & New York: Palgrave Macmillan).

Hampton-Reeves, T. and Escolme, B. (2012) *Shakespeare and the Making of Theatre* (Basingstoke and New York: Palgrave Macmillan).

Hill, A. (1760) *The Works of the Late Aaron Hill, Esq Vol. 1* (London: Printed for the Benefit of the Family).

Hodgdon, B. (2012) 'Material Remains at Play', *Theatre Journal: Special Issue – Theatre and Material Culture*, ed. Knowles, R. Vol. 64, No. 3 (October), 373–388.

Hollander, A. (1975) *Seeing Through Clothes*. 1993 edn (Berkeley and Los Angeles: University of California Press).

Holt, A. (1880–1896) *Fancy Dresses Described, or What to Wear at Fancy Balls* (London: Debenham and Freebody).

Hughes, T. (1913) *Dress Design: An Account of Costume for Artists and Dressmakers* (London: J. Hogg).

Hunnisett, J. (1991) *Period Costumes for Stage and Screen: 1800–1909: Patterns for Women's Dress* (Studio City, CA: Players Press).

Hunnisett, J. (1991) *Period Costumes for Stage and Screen: Patterns for Women's Dress 1500–1800* (Studio City, CA: Players Press).

Hunnisett, J. (1996) *Period Costumes for Stage and Screen: Mediaeval-1500: Patterns for Women's Dress* (Studio City, CA: Players Press).

Hunnisett, J. (2003) *Period Costumes for Stage and Screen: Outer Garments I:.Cloaks, Capes, Stoles and Wadded Mantles* (Studio City, CA: Players Press).

Hunnisett, J. (2003) *Period Costumes for Stage and Screen: Outer Garments II:Dominos, Dolmans, Coats, Pelisses, Spencers, Calashes, Hoods and Bonnets* (Studio City, CA: Players Press).

Ingham, R. and Covey, L. (1983) *The Costume Designer's Handbook: A Complete Guide for Amateur and Professional Costume Designers* (London: Prentice-Hall).

Ingham, R. and Covey, L. (2003) *The Costume Technician's Handbook* (Portsmouth: Heinemann).

Inspiration Green, 2013. http://www.inspirationgreen.com/nick-cave-sound-suits.html, date accessed 13 December.

Jack Shaiman, 2013. http://jackshainmangallery.com/artists/nick-cave/, date accessed 13 December.

Jackson, S. (1978) *Costumes for the Stage* (London: Herbert).

Jeffery, T. (1757–1772) *A Collection of Dresses of Different Nations, Ancient and Modern, also of the Principal Characters of the English Stage*, vols. 1–4 (Madrid: The Complutense University of Madrid).

Johnson, K.K.P., Torntore, S.J. and Eicher, J.B. (2003) *Fashion Foundations: Early Writings on Fashion and Dress* (Oxford: Berg).

Jones, A. R. and Stallybrass, P. (2000) *Renaissance Clothing and the Materials of Memory* (Cambridge: Cambridge University Press).

Jones, R. (1941) *The Dramatic Imagination* 1969 edn. (New York: Theatre Arts Books).

Kaplan, J. H. and Stowell, S. (1995) *Theatre and Fashion: Oscar Wilde to the Suffragettes* (Cambridge: Cambridge University Press).

Kennedy, D. (1993) *Looking at Shakespeare* (Cambridge: Cambridge University Press).

Kewes, P., Archer, I.W. and Heal, F. (2012) *The Oxford Handbook of Holinshead's Chronicles* (Oxford: Oxford University Press).

Kirby, M. (1971) *Futurist Performance* (Baltimore: John Hopkins University Press).

Komisarjevsky, T. (1931) *The Costume of the Theatre* (New York: Henry Holt).

Kustow, M. (2008) 'Introduction', in Annand, S. (ed.) *The Half: Photographs of Actors Preparing for the Stage* (London: Faber and Faber).

Langer, R. (1984) 'Compulsion and Restraint, Love and Angst', *Dance Magazine* 58, No. 6.

Laver, J. (1937) *Taste and Fashion* 1945 edn. (London: George G. Harrap).

Laver, J. (1964) *Costume in the Theatre* (London: Harrap).

Laver, J. (1969) *A Concise History of Costume* (London: Thames and Hudson).

Lecoq, J. (1997) *Le Corps Poetique*, Acts Sud-Papiers 10 (Arles: Anrat).

Livshitz, B. translated as *The One and a Half Eyed Archer* (1977) translated by Bowlt, J.E. (Newtonville MA: Oriental Research Partners).

Lott, E. (1993) *Love and Theft, Blackface Minstrelsy and the American Working Class* (London & New York: Routledge).

Lover, S. (1839) *The Happy Man* (London: Webster and Co), first performed Theatre Royal Haymarket, London: 20 May 1839.

Lublin, R. (2011) *Costuming the Shakespearean Stage* (Farnham: Ashgate).

Luminarium, 2003. http://www.luminarium.org/editions/hymen/htm, date accessed 13 October 2013.

Macaulay, A. (2000) 'An Uncomfortable "Hamlet"', *Financial Times*, 13 June.

Mackintyre, J. (1992) *Costumes and Scripts in the Elizabethan Theatre* (Alberta: University of Alberta Press).

Margolies, E. (2000) 'Though it Make the Unskilful Laugh', *Times Literary Supplement*, 7 July.

McClintock, A. (1995) *Imperial Leather, Race, Gender and Sexuality in Colonial Contest* (New York & London: Routledge).

McFeely, D. (2012) *Dion Boucicault: Irish Identity Onstage* (Cambridge: Cambridge University Press).

McGinn, C. (2013) 'Theatre Review: *Emil and the Detectives*', *Time Out*, 5 December.

McKinnon, P. and Fielding, E. (2012) *World Scenography* (Taipei: Oistat).

McKinney, J. and Butterworth, P. (2009) *Cambridge Introduction to Scenography* (Cambridge: Cambridge University Press).

Metro London (2000) 'Theatre Review: *Hamlet*', *Metro*, 9 June.

Metro London (2013) 'Theatre Review: *Emil and the Detectives*', *Metro*, 9 December.

Monks, A. (2010) *The Actor in Costume* (Basingstoke & New York: Palgrave Macmillan).

Mullin, M. (1996) *Design by Motley* (Newark: University of Delaware Press).

Newton, S.M. (1975) *Renaissance Theatre Costume and the Sense of the Historic Past* (London: Rapp and Whiting).

Nicoll, A. (1930) *A History of Early Nineteenth Century Drama 1800–1850 Vol. 1* (Cambridge: Cambridge University Press).

Nightingale, B. (2000).'Rylance's Mad-for-It Prince', *The Times*, 12 June.

Nijinsky, R. (1935) *Nijinsky* (London: Gollancz).

Noever, P., ed. (1991) *The Future Is Our Only Goal: Aleksandr M. Rodchenko, Varvara F. Stepanova* (Munich: Prestel).

O'Neill, E. (1998) The *Emperor Jones, Four Plays by Eugene O'Neill* (New York, Canada, U.K., New Zealand, Australia: A Signet Classic).

Oenslager, D. (1974) *Alexandra Exter: Artist of the Theatre.* (New York: NY Public Library, Aster, Lennox and Tilden Foundations).

Orgel S. and Strong, R. (1973) *Inigo Jones: The Theatre of the Stuart Court* (London: Sotherby Parke Bernet).

Palmer, S. (2013) *Light: Readings in Theatre Practice* (Basingstoke: Palgrave Macmillan).

Payne, D.R. (1974) *The Scenographic Imagination,* 3rd edition 1993 (Carbondale and Edwardsville: Southern Illinois University Press).

Planché, J.R. (1823) *Costume of Shakespeare's Historical Tragedy of King John* (London: John Miller).

Pecktal, L. (1999) *Costume Design: Techniques of Modern Masters* (New York: Backstage Books).

Pepys, S. (1665) *The Project Gutenberg EBook of Diary of Samuel Pepys, 1666*, http://www.gutenberg.org/files/4171/417h/4171h.htm#2H_4_007, date accessed 16 December 2013.

Punchdrunk Website, http://punchdrunk.com/company/article/about, date accessed 16 December 2013.

Ratikin, V. and Sarabianov, A, eds (1975) *Our Arrival: From the History of Russian Futurism* (Moscow: RA Archives of the Avant-Garde).

Ravelhoffer, B. (2009) *The Early Stuart Masque: Dance, Costume and Music* (Oxford: Oxford University Press).

Rayner, A. (2002) 'Rude Mechanicals and the Specters of Marx', *Theater Journal*, Vol. 54, No. 4 (December), 535–554.

Ridout, N. (2006) *Stage Fright, Animals and Other Theatrical Problems* (Cambridge: Cambridge University Press).

Roediger, D. (1991) *The Wages of Whiteness, Race and the Making of the American Working Class* (London & New York: Verso).

Roediger, D. (1997) 'White Looks: Hairy Apes, True Stories and Limbaugh's Laugh', in Hill Mike (ed.) *Whiteness, A Critical Reader* (New York: New York University Press).

Rudnitsky, K. (1988) *Russian and Soviet Theatre: Tradition and the Avant-Garde* (London: Thames and Hudson).

Ruthven Hall, P., Burnett, K., Allen, K. and Shaw, P. eds (1999) *Time and Space: Design for Performance 1995–1999* (London: Society of British Theatre Designers).

Sarabianov, D. and Adaskina, L. (1990) *Popova* (London: Thames and Hudson).

Savran, D. (1988) *Breaking the Rules: The Wooster Group* (New York: Theatre Communications Group).

Schneider, R. (2011) *Performing Remains: Art and War in Times of Theatrical Reenactment* (London & New York: Routledge).

Schoch (1998) *Shakespeare's Victorian Stage: Performing History in the Theatre of Charles Kean* (Cambridge: Cambridge University Press).

Schweitzer, M. (2009) *When Broadway Was the Runway: Theatre, Fashion and American Culture* (Philadelphia: University of Pennsylvania Press).

Senelick, L. (2000) *The Changing Room: Sex, Drag & Theatre* (London & New York: Routledge).

Sennett, R. (1976) *The Fall of Public Man* (London, New York, Victoria, Toronto, New Delhi, Auckland, Rosebank: Penguin).

Sennett, R. (2009) *The Craftsman* (London, New York, Victoria, Toronto, New Delhi, Auckland, Rosebank: Penguin).

Soloski, A. (2008) 'Theatre Review: *Black Watch*', *The Village Voice*, 24 June.

Spencer, C. (2000) 'Rasping Rylance Soars Far Above Most of His Cast', *Daily Telegraph*, 10 June.

Split B. Website, http://splitbritches.wordpress.com/, date accessed 16 December 2013.

Stanislavsky (1924) *My Life in Art*, 1987 edn. (London: Routledge).

States, B.O. (1984) *Great Reckonings in Little Rooms: On the Phenomenology of Theatre* (Berkeley & Los Angeles: University of California Press).

Steele, V. ed. (1997) *Fashion Theory: The Journal of Dress, Body and Culture* (Oxford: Berg).

Stern, R. (2004) *Against Fashion: Clothing as Art 1850–1930* (Massachusetts: MIT).

Strong, R. (1981) *Designing for the Dancer* (London: Elron).

Strutt, J. (1792) *Complete View of the Dress and Habits of the People of England from the Establishment of the Saxons in Britain to the Present Time* (London: J.Nicholls for J. Edwards, R. Edwards, B. and J.White, G.G. and J. Robinson and J.Thane).

Styan, J. (1996) *The English Stage: A History of Drama and Performance* (Cambridge: Cambridge University Press).

Tan, H. (2004) *Costume Character Figure Drawing* (Harlington, MA: Focal Press).

Tarrant, N. (1994) *The Development of Costume* (London: Routledge).

Taylor, C.J. (1975) *Futurism: Politics, Performance, Painting* (Michigan: Ann Arbor).

Taylor, L. (2002) *The Study of Dress History* (Manchester: Manchester University Press).

Taylor, L. (2004) *Establishing Dress History* (Manchester: Manchester University Press).

Taylor, P. (2000) 'Fresh and Daring, Rylance's Prince Creates a Rapport That Nears Genius', *Independent*, Saturday 10 June.

Taymor, J. and Blumenthal, E. (1995) *Playing with Fire: Theatre, Opera, Film* (New York: Harry H. Abrams).

Taymor, J. (1998) *Pride Rock on Broadway* (New York: Hyperion).

Thorne, G. (2001) *Designing Stage Costumes: A Practical Guide* (Ramsbury: Crowood Press).

Tomkis, T. (1607) *Lingua: Or the Combat of the Tongue, and the Five Senses for Superiority* (London: Simon Waterson).

Thomson, M. (2013) 'Interview', 7 August.

Tirimani, J. (2003) 'Programme Note 23: Clothing, Properties and Hangings', Globe *Richard II Programme.*

Tiramani, J., Coostigliolo, L., and Mollgaard, L. (2008) 'Exploring Early Modern Stage and Costume Design', in Carson, C., Cooper, F.K. (eds), 2008. *Shakespeare's Globe: A Theatrical Experiment* (Cambridge: Cambridge University Press), pp. 57–66.

Truman, N. (1936) *Historic Costuming* (London: Pitman).

The Salon Project, 2011. http://www.untitledprojects.co.uk/projects/The-Salon-Project, date accessed 13 December 2013.

Vanity Fair New York (2008) 'Theatre Review: *Black Watch'*, *Vanity Fair,* July issue.

Vecellio, C. (1590) *Renaissance Costume (De Gli Habiti antichi et moderni do Diverse Parti del Mondo)* 1977 edn (New York: Dover).

Waugh, N. (1954) *Corsets and Crinolines* (New York: Theatre Arts Books).

Waugh, N. (1964) *The Cut of Men's Clothes* (New York: Theatre Arts Books).

Waugh, N. (1968) *The Cut of Women's Clothes* (New York: Theatre Arts Books).

Walker, L. (2007) 'Theatre Review: *The Bacchae,' The Independent*, 13 August.

Weltman, S.A. (2007) *Performing the Victorian: John Ruskin and Identity in Theater, Science, and Education* (Columbus: Ohio State University Press).

Wiles, D. (2000) *Greek Theatre Performance: An Introduction* (Cambridge: Cambridge University Press).

Williams, C. (1937) *Thomas Platters's Travels in England 1599* (London: Jonathan Cape).

Wilson, E. (1985) *Adorned in Dreams: Fashion and Modernity* (London, Virago).

Woddis, C. (2000) 'Theatre, Hamlet', *The Herald Glasgow*, 13 June.

Worthen, W.B. (1997) *Shakespeare and the Authority of Performance* (Cambridge: Cambridge University Press).

Zapf, H. (1988) 'O'Neill's Hairy Ape and the Reversal of Hegelian Dialectics', *Modern Drama*, Vol. XXI, No. 1 (March), 35–40.

Index

ALINA BELLCHAMBERS

The ORDER of MASKS

HODDERSCAPE

First published in Great Britain in 2024 by Hodderscape
An imprint of Hodder & Stoughton Limited
An Hachette UK company

1

Map by Barking Dog Art

A CIP catalogue record for this title is available from the British Library

Hardback ISBN 978 1 399 73077 8
Trade Paperback ISBN 978 1 399 73078 5
ebook ISBN 978 1 399 73079 2

Typeset in Baskerville MT by Hewer Text UK Ltd, Edinburgh
Printed and bound in Great Britain by Clays Ltd, Elcograf S.p.A.

Hodder & Stoughton policy is to use papers that are natural, renewable
and recyclable products and made from wood grown in sustainable
forests. The logging and manufacturing processes are expected to conform
to the environmental regulations of the country of origin.

Hodder & Stoughton Limited
Carmelite House
50 Victoria Embankment
London EC4Y 0DZ

The authorised representative in the EEA is Hachette Ireland,
8 Castlecourt Centre, Castleknock Road, Castleknock,
Dublin 15, D15 YF6A, Ireland

www.hodderscape.co.uk

To everyone fighting to shape their own destiny,
this is for you.

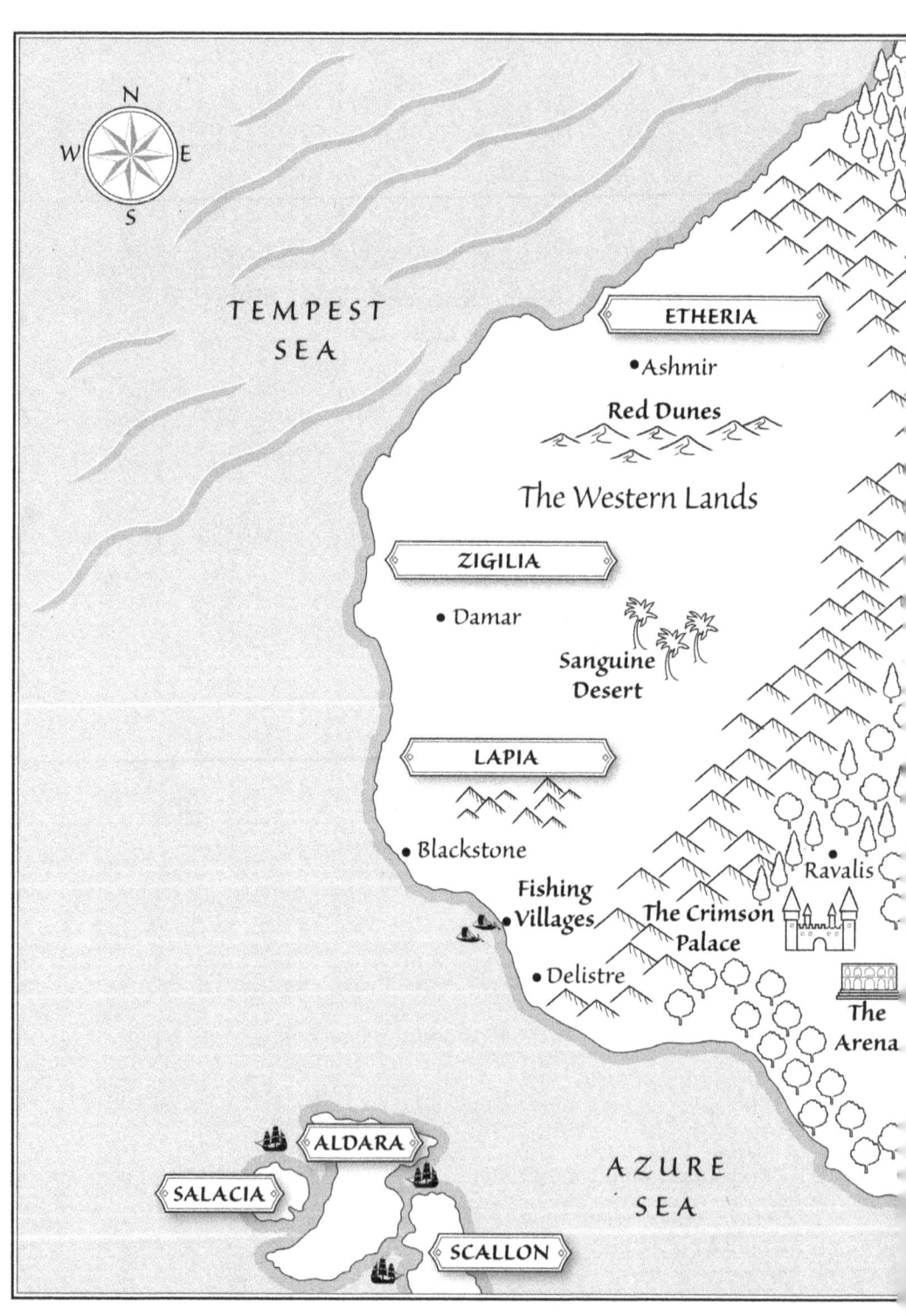

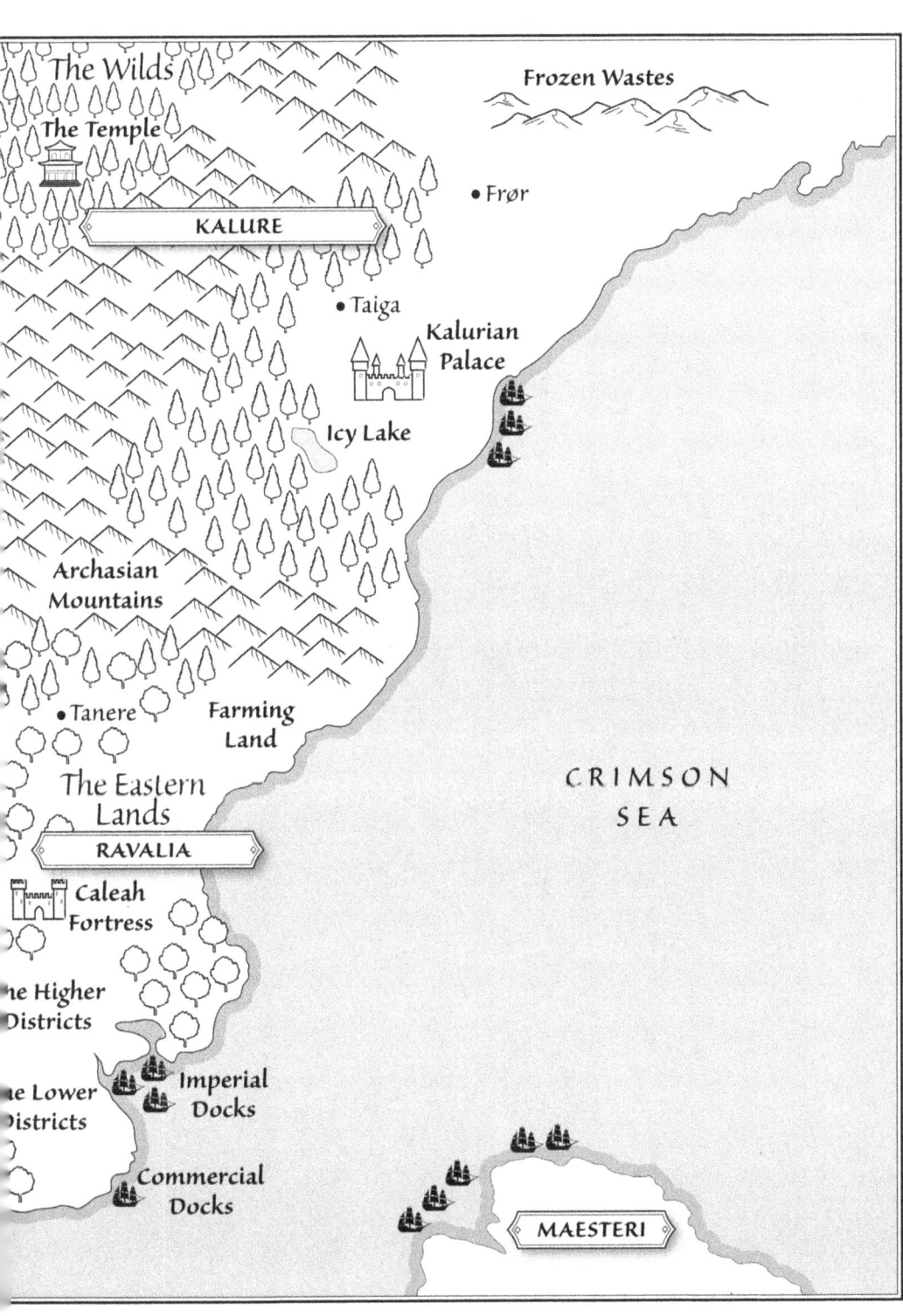

The Wilds

The Temple

KALURE

Frozen Wastes

• Frør

• Taiga

Kalurian
Palace

Icy Lake

Archasian
Mountains

• Tanere

Farming
Land

The Eastern
Lands

RAVALIA

Caleah
Fortress

CRIMSON
SEA

The Higher
Districts

The Lower
Districts

Imperial
Docks

Commercial
Docks

MAESTERI

CHAPTER ONE

Mira

By the time I turned sixteen, I'd lived many lives.

I was too young to be what I was – a pickpocket, a noblewoman's daughter, a circus performer. I'd played so many roles that they all blurred together. Sometimes when I looked into my reflection, even I didn't know which Mira was staring back.

To my mother, our lives were an endless adventure. A dangerous, exhilarating game that she played with daring smiles and boundless confidence.

'Who do you want to be, Mira?' she would ask, her eyes glinting with anticipation.

It didn't matter what answer I gave. The ending was always the same. *Look forward, don't dwell, move on.*

Those were the rules we'd lived by, for as long as I could remember. The rules that kept us alive.

The roar of the audience thundered through the circus, pulling my attention towards the distant stage. It was encircled by fire, as was tradition in Zigilia. Despite the sweltering heat, I appreciated the effect: in the night-time, with nothing but the fire braziers for light, the performers were cast in shadow. They looked like they really were magical, like they belonged to one of the three royal Orders.

From where I sat by the fortune-teller's tent, the smell of rich spices and sizzling meat wafted from the food carts lining the narrow walkways. Eager patrons made their purchases, most dressed in typical Western fashion: the men in brightly coloured vests and airy, billowing pants, the women draped in richly dyed silks. Some of the vendors were familiar, but I didn't recognise any of the people they were serving. Damar was a large city, and one person easily blurred into another.

Which was precisely the point.

One of the vendors handed a kebab to a female customer, and as the woman turned, I glimpsed my mother's vibrant face. She sashayed towards me, still in her dancer's outfit: a purple beaded top cut just above her navel and a matching full-length skirt. Even nibbling on a kebab, she managed to turn heads, yet she seemed oblivious to the eyes on her.

Only I knew that naivety was a charade, executed so skilfully that no one else would sense the lie. My mother was a born performer. And she never stopped performing. Not even with me.

'Choose a card.' Celeste slid into the seat opposite, brandishing a crimson deck.

I hesitated. Deira would be furious if she returned from her break to find her assistant playing cards. I should be waiting for customers who wanted their fortunes read – not literally, of course, but I'd developed an instinct for reading people and telling them what they wanted to hear.

Then again, the night had been slow; I hadn't had a single customer since Deira left.

I glanced at Celeste, who was wearing an impish smile. This was for practice, but it was also for fun. She liked showing off her abilities, her little parlour tricks.

But tonight, I had something different in mind.

'No,' I said, keeping my expression neutral. 'It's your turn to choose.'

Celeste arched an eyebrow, and I knew what she was thinking. Card games had never been one of my strengths. Even if they had been, no one could replicate my mother's quick, effortless manipulations.

Leaning back in her chair, she confidently handed over the pack of cards. I fanned them out across the stall table, arranging them face down.

'This one,' Celeste said, picking up a card with her manicured fingers.

Gathering it up with the others, I methodically shuffled the deck. But my mother's stare lingered on me, filled with silent challenge, and it wasn't long before my fingers were turning the cards into flickers of colour.

'What do I get if I choose correctly?' I asked.

My mother tilted her head. Her auburn hair was swept back from her face, displaying her sudden wariness to full advantage. 'What do you want?'

'Nothing much. Just a question.'

'A question,' she repeated.

I met her gaze steadily, not blinking. 'Yes. Just one.'

Applause cut through the tension between us. I wasn't sure who was on stage, but they must have been good. Maybe the twins. Or it could have been Reverie, the hypnotist.

'Alright,' my mother said, as I set the cards down. 'Guess correctly, and I'll answer one question.'

I knew she thought it was a safe bet. From the back, the cards looked identical. But I let their red and gold outlines blur before my eyes, waiting for the pull. The insistent, sharp *tug* that would tell me which to choose.

Almost involuntarily, my hand reached out to touch one of the cards. I felt a sudden chill as I picked it up.

Celeste looked on in stunned silence as I flashed the title at her, displayed in elegant, golden letters: *The Sorceress*.

'You're getting better at this,' she said, but her tone was accusatory.

Did she think I'd cheated somehow? *Was* relying on intuition a cheat?

'I had a good teacher,' I said absently, distracted by the woman on the card: dark-haired and dark-eyed, with the beguiling smile of a trickster.

She was beautiful, but it wasn't her beauty that drew me in. It was the power emanating from her. I wasn't sure if it was a good kind of power, like in my mother's stories – or a darker sort, like the tales told over campfires in the icy North. Whatever it was, it intrigued me.

As I angled the card towards the firelight, it seemed to come alive, taking on a reddish glow. The woman closed one cat-like eye in a wink—

And then she was gone.

I dropped the card as if it had burned me. It fell to the table, deceptively ordinary amongst the others – but still blank.

I glanced up, wondering whether my mother saw it too. But she was focused on me. 'I suppose you've won your question.'

I blinked, feeling like I'd resurfaced from a dream. That would make more sense. Cards, even *Eastern* cards, didn't just change. In the Ravalian Empire, magic was restricted to the three Orders: Warriors, Artisans and Masks.

'I've been thinking,' I began, 'that other daughters know a great deal about their mothers. But I don't know even the most basic facts about you.'

Celeste's shoulders tensed. 'Mira, you know it isn't so simple.' There was a warning in her voice, one I ignored.

'I obey all your rules,' I retorted, bracing my arms against the table. 'I've spent my life running, never asking any questions. But now I'm asking.' I paused. 'What's your name?'

'Celeste,' she whispered, barely an exhale of breath.

'Your *real* name.'

'No, Mira.' Her voice turned hard. 'Not that.'

And I knew that the contest didn't matter. My mother's true identity would always be kept from me, a secret buried so deep it would never surface.

Celeste collected the cards and tucked them into a small pouch. She stood abruptly and strode into the crowd without a backward glance, leaving me feeling like I'd disappointed her. Like I was the one who had hurt her, and not the other way around.

As I glanced back at the table, I realised she had forgotten a card – the one with the dark-haired woman who had winked at me. The woman who had, inexplicably, reappeared.

A shiver crawled down my spine. In our histories, there was the story of an immortal sorceress. A sorceress who had travelled the world for centuries, watching kingdoms rise and fall. I stared down at the card, taking in the woman's striking features. And as I did, I wondered.

I wondered if immortality had begun to weigh on her, until it was a curse rather than a gift. I wondered if living so many lives had felt somehow empty, like it did with me. Because no matter how many roles I played, it was like trying to quench an endless thirst. I had a sip each time, a fleeting taste, but it was only ever that – fleeting. That was the overarching rule in our lives, the rule that followed us wherever we went: nothing ever lasted.

It was so subtle that I almost missed it. The pull.

It drew my gaze across the bustling crowd. At first all I saw were the usual sights: street vendors selling their wares, people haggling over prices, and a crowd grouped around the raised stage at the far end, where the performers were still entertaining. But then my eyes fell on him.

The stranger was watching me from a few tents away, his arms folded as he surveyed the spectacle. Now that I'd seen him, it seemed odd I hadn't noticed him before. He was older than I was – at least Choosing age – and he was arresting even from a distance, with ebony hair and cut-glass cheekbones. Something about his hawk-like stare made me uneasy, a feeling that only intensified as he came closer.

Black whorls of ink covered his face, obscuring even his dark skin from view. The details of the tattoos were impossible to make sense of: every time I tried to focus on an image, it started to transform.

'Are you doing my job for me?' he asked, his voice pitched low.

A fortune-teller. A real one.

Sweat beaded across my forehead, but I met his eyes steadily. His eyes were the only features truly visible on his face, unobscured by the tattoos. One was so dark it was nearly black. The other was an eerie, colour-leached grey.

'You're from the Order of Artisans,' I said, standing and facing him.

He smiled. His lips were covered in ink – the upper wholly black, the lower dusted in gold. The effect was beautiful and disturbing all at once.

Run. I should run.

I didn't move. I wasn't sure I could.

His gaze lowered to the card resting on the top of my stall's table. The red was very bright against the black sheeting. It gleamed like a drop of blood.

'I wasn't predicting anything,' I said quickly. 'I was just—'

'I know what you were doing.' He picked up the card in his hands, turning it over. I noticed that he held it very gently, like it was something precious. 'The Sorceress,' he murmured, his disconcerting eyes flicking to me.

I tensed, uncomfortable with the scrutiny.

'So much fear,' he said in a low voice. 'What do you know of fear?'

I knew a great deal. But I didn't answer. I didn't want him to know anything about me.

His mouth twitched, as if my reaction amused him. 'Relax,' he said. 'I'm not going to hurt you.' His teeth were startlingly white against the black of the ink. 'In fact, I might even tell you a secret. Would you like that?'

If I could, I would have declined. But there was no way to politely decline anything freely offered by an Artisan. 'What would you tell me?'

He considered me for a long moment. 'First,' he said finally, 'look down – and tell me what you see.'

I followed his gaze down to his hands. Down to the ink that seemed to lighten and shift underneath my gaze, forming into the charcoal likeness of a person.

'My mother,' I breathed.

Apprehension crept over me as I took in the details of her face: the hollows of her cheeks, the harsh line between her brows, the pinch to her full lips. She looked scared. No – she looked *terrified*.

Even as I watched, a tear fell from her inky eyes, so dark that they could have been empty sockets. Her mouth opened, as if to form a name. *My* name.

And I knew, with shocking certainty—

I was watching my mother die.

'I know what she is,' the Artisan said, a million miles away. 'She can run from the past all she likes, but the past always leaves traces. It leaves a trail.'

He leant in, his lips brushing my ear.

'And if I can see the trail,' he whispered, 'then so can *they*.'

CHAPTER TWO

Scarlett

I only remembered flickers.

Russet hair and a cruel smile. The sound of ice cracking. Terrified realisation that came a second too late.

After that, everything happened in a rush: a haze of panic and confusion as hands reached out, not to help me, but to *push* me—

I tried to scream, but water flooded my mouth instead. And there was nothing I could do as I dropped like a stone, my heavy clothes dragging me under.

Desperation gave me strength as I tore off the furs and kicked towards the distant surface. Only when I reached it—

It wasn't there.

I could have cried then. Could have wept and raged at the thick, translucent barrier above me, at the unbearable closeness of the sky.

Footsteps thudded overhead; my brother was moving, but I couldn't see him. I slapped my palms frantically against the ice, trying to break through even though I knew it was useless. Roran clearly knew it too, because the echo of his boots grew fainter.

My only hope was for someone to rescue me. For one of my guards to dive in and pull me from a watery grave.

But there were no guards. My brother had sent them all away.

I swam frantically, searching for the hole I'd fallen through. I didn't even know if I was going in the right direction, but I tried anyway, propelling myself forward with increasingly numb arms. My lungs were burning now, begging for air.

But there was no air. There was no escape.

There was only cold and silence.

Strangely enough, I no longer felt afraid. It was almost peaceful, the panic and fear dissolving as I sank slowly beneath their reach.

How nice it would be, I thought dimly, *to close my eyes and drift.*

But just as I prepared to stop fighting, I saw *her.*

The girl was directly above me, kneeling on the other side of the eerie blue ice. She was as cold and infinite as the frozen lake that would become my tomb, and it was impossible to tell whether she was flesh and blood at all. If it hadn't been for her halo of long red hair, she would have been indistinguishable from the snow around her.

Even in my delirium, I knew that what I was seeing wasn't real. In the throes of death, my mind had summoned the only comfort it could: myself.

Except I had never looked so beautiful or terrible in life. It was like staring into a distorted mirror image: wrong in every way, yet achingly right. Was that what my drowning self looked like, lips tinged with blue and all warmth leached from my veins?

My doppelgänger placed a corpse-white hand against the ice. As if in a dream, I raised my palm to meet hers—

A thunderous boom sounded as the surface split apart. Ice cracked and rained down around me like a million shards of glass.

And I *breathed.*

It was night by the time someone reached the frozen lake. When they rushed over to where I lay, motionless on the ice.

I was only vaguely aware of the man's presence, his words muffled, as if coming from a vast distance. But I did notice when I was wrapped in fur and lifted, gently and firmly, into a pair of strong arms.

Those arms held me close as I was carried across the icy plateau and into the grey stone palace of Kalure. Surely the court had discovered I was missing by now – and yet when we reached the doors of the great hall, I heard the unmistakable sounds of laughter and music. No one inside had bothered to cancel the revelry, to feign even the appearance of concern.

If it had been one of my half-brothers, the nobles would have offered their assistance as a way of currying favour with the emperor, and no expense would have been spared in the search. For *me*, though . . .

'Put me down.' My voice was hoarse and barely audible, but the order was clear.

'Are you sure that's wise?'

'Put me down,' I repeated, and this time, he obeyed.

Clutching his tattooed arm for support, I waited for my surroundings to right themselves. It took a moment, but slowly everything came back into focus – including the Artisan, his mismatched eyes piercing right through me.

If I could have flushed, I would have. I had seen Severin around the Ravalian Court, but always from a distance. And he had never looked at me like this before – *really* looked at me, as if I wasn't Zandri's daughter or a princess, but simply a young woman. A young woman he was still standing awfully close to.

'Did my mother send you?'

He nodded. For a second, I thought his face held a glimmer of concern – concern that went beyond whatever orders my mother had given him. But that softness quickly disappeared, leaving smooth perfection in its wake.

'Let me escort you to your chambers, Your Highness,' he said, his voice rich and melodic. 'I can summon a healer—'

'I don't need a healer.'

A dark eyebrow rose.

'I'm perfectly fine,' I said, which couldn't have been further from the truth. 'And I have no intention of going anywhere. I intend to face my family – on my own.'

Severin's gaze swept over me once more. There was something strange about his stare – something assessing I wasn't sure I liked. But he inclined his head and said smoothly, 'As you wish, Princess. I'll be nearby if you need me.'

'I won't,' I said immediately.

His lips curved. 'We'll see.'

Without waiting to be dismissed, he turned on his heel. I watched him for a moment, wondering if Severin was right – if I *should* retreat to my chambers. But I shook off the thought. I'd be damned if I let Roran believe I was afraid of him.

Setting my jaw, I pushed open the carved doors.

The great hall spanned before me, its wooden tables piled high with meats from the ceremonial hunt. Courtiers gathered around those tables, men and women who I had known for years, but out here, dressed in heavy clothes and adorned with weapons, their veneer of civility had been stripped away.

As I stepped into view, the music abruptly stopped. Murmurs spread through the hall as everyone turned to stare. I must have been an unusual sight: barefoot and waterlogged, my hair framing my face in snake-like tendrils.

I kept my head high as I walked between life-sized sculptures of our ancestral kings, all poised to cut down their enemies. Emperor Kalias had commissioned them himself: he was fiercely proud of reclaiming the North and dragged the court back to Kalure once a year to live a simpler, harder existence. He believed his people had become soft since relocating to Ravalia, reaping the benefits of the fertile soil and forgetting what it was to struggle against the elements.

I like the harshness of Kalure, he once told me. *It separates the strong from the weak. Here, survival isn't a right. Survival is* won.

Not that we were supposed to hunt and kill *each other*, but with my body drifting beneath the ice, no one could have linked my death to Roran – and there would have been one less sibling to threaten his position as heir to the Ravalian throne.

'What is the meaning of this?'

The demanding voice was instantly familiar and entirely unwel-come. It was a monumental effort to keep my expression unreadable as I faced my stepmother, who was reclining on an austere throne, warm and rosy-cheeked in her furs.

'It looks like she fell into the lake, Mother,' Roran cut in. The sound of his voice was enough to make me feel sick; my fury was almost overpowering. 'Didn't I tell you it was too dangerous to let her roam the grounds?'

The empress regarded me disdainfully. 'Is that what happened?'

Roran's handsome face was impassive, but his jade green eyes were so sharp they could have cut stone. He was *daring* me to contradict him.

'Yes,' I said, forcing the word past my numb lips. 'That's what happened.'

Empress Ivalene smiled thinly. I had no doubt she knew the truth – perhaps she had even encouraged Roran to attack me. My father's decision to include his bastard daughter in the line of succession hadn't made me popular.

'Foolish girl. Take her to the infirmary,' Ivalene instructed the guards, 'and don't let her out of your sight. We don't want a repeat of this idiocy.'

I turned away from the dais – but not before I saw the satisfied gleam in Roran's eyes. He might not have succeeded in killing me today, but he would try again.

The thought didn't bother me like it should have. If anything, I welcomed the challenge – and the opportunity to outwit him. How satisfying it would be, to watch his head cleaved from his shoulders. Even more satisfying, if I was swinging the sword myself.

I smiled as I passed the nobles, who parted respectfully but whispered behind their hands. I assumed they were muttering about my dishevelled appearance or my interaction with the empress. It was only when I reached the mirror-lined corridor that I understood.

In the glass, a drowned girl was reflected back at me. The girl I thought I'd imagined in the ice.

She was no illusion now. She was real, and she was staring at me with knowing blue eyes—

Except mine had been green.

With a rush of horror, I raised a hand to my cold cheek. There had been a moment under the ice, just a moment, when I'd thought . . . I'd thought I'd stopped breathing.

What had my mother said once? Death *lingered*.

The proof was there in the whiteness of my once-olive complexion. The unnatural chill to my skin. The strange colour of my eyes – the same colour as the water that had filled my lungs and stilled my heart.

Because I had died in that lake.

Only for me, death wasn't the end. It was just the beginning.

CHAPTER THREE

Mira

Two Years Later

The sound of tolling bells made the crowd thicken, islanders lining the craggy cliffs to watch the three Ravalian ships approach. They were beautiful vessels, large and sleek, with crimson and gold sails that glittered brilliantly in the sunlight.

Children jostled for better positions as they fought to catch a glimpse of the royal representatives. The adults were more restrained, used to the yearly visits. But anticipation was heavy in the briny air, so thick it was nearly tangible.

And this year, that same anticipation raced through my veins. Because this year, the royal representatives were here for *me*.

Waves lapped against the harbour breakwater, muffling the sound of footsteps, but I heard them anyway. Even if I hadn't, it would have been impossible to miss the path clearing in front of me.

Nikolas Atwood strode to the front of the crowd, his narrow face hard with disdain. His eyes, chips of grey ice, weren't fixed on the spectacle in the harbour or the glamorous blonde on his arm – but on me and Lillian.

Not today, I pleaded silently. *Don't cause a scene today.*

Even as I thought it, I knew it was useless. Nikolas was the entitled son of Lord Atwood, Governor of Aldara. There was nothing he couldn't get away with.

And he had a score to settle.

Lillian looked up, noticing my sudden preoccupation. Her eyes darted to the young noble and his fiancée, studying them with something like awe – a reaction that bothered me until I realised she wasn't admiring *them*. Only their fine clothing.

'This is unexpected.' A contemptuous smile bloomed on Stacia's perfectly made-up face. 'Business a bit slow this morning? No one to entertain with your cheap tricks?'

I locked eyes with her. 'We can't all be born pampered nobles, waited on hand and foot.'

Stacia exchanged an unpleasant glance with Nikolas, sending her ringlets fluttering in the breeze. 'You're a *performer*,' she said, making the word *performer* synonymous with *scum*. 'Show your betters some respect.'

'Respect should be earned,' I retorted. 'And you haven't earned mine.'

'What about me?' Nikolas asked mildly.

There was only one acceptable answer, and we all knew it. With his father's influence, he could make my life very difficult if he chose. Then again, he often singled me out – talking down about me to his influential friends, interrupting me at work and smiling when his interference cost me patrons.

'Mira didn't mean anything by it,' Lillian cut in. I shot her an irritated look, but she continued: 'Can we please forget it and enjoy the show?'

Nikolas studied Lillian, taking in her demure lilac dress and halo of buttery curls. Unlike me, she was everything he believed a common girl should be: respectful, mild-mannered, and beautiful in a soft sort of way. The kind of girl who inspired feelings of protectiveness in everyone, even snobs like the Atwoods.

'Alright,' he agreed. 'So long as you remember it's only a show.'

I knew what he meant – that the Trials weren't for people like us. I bit my lip to stop myself from saying something unwise, but my expression gave me away.

'You disagree?' Nikolas said, as if the mere idea was ludicrous. 'Someone like you wouldn't last a minute in the Trials.'

'I suppose we'll find out. *In* the Trials.'

A flicker of anger sparked in Nikolas's eyes. 'If you do compete,' he warned, his hand brushing the sword strapped to his side, 'you're going to regret that arrogance. I'll make sure of it.'

Without waiting for a response, he brushed past, knocking his shoulder into mine. I stumbled back, watching as he and Stacia faded from view. Even as they disappeared, Nikolas's threat remained. It hung in the salty air, heavy and ominous.

'What were you thinking?' Lillian demanded, grabbing my arm. 'You know better than to antagonise them. And the very *idea* of entering the Trials . . . it's . . .' Her voice trailed off at whatever expression she saw on my face. 'That wasn't something you said just to provoke them. You were serious.'

I glanced away from my friend – from the hurt in her clear blue eyes. 'Not now, Lil.'

Lillian dropped my hand. 'I can't believe this,' she said. 'I can't believe *you*. The Trials are dangerous, Mira.'

'I know,' I replied, but I wasn't looking at Lillian. I was looking at the royal representatives in the distance.

What Lillian didn't understand was that some things were more important than safety. Some things were worth the risk.

Because Nikolas and the others had underestimated me. They had underestimated the strength of my resolve.

The Trials didn't scare me. *They* didn't scare me. And one day soon, I was going to prove that to everyone.

One day soon, I was going to make Nikolas regret *his* arrogance.

The field where the circus pitched its tents was quiet and still, the performers getting ready for the evening or enjoying the markets in the town square. Soon, this entire place would transform: filling with the clamour of patrons, the deep pounding of drums, and dramatic bursts of fire.

Thankfully, I wouldn't have to worry about dancing or telling fortunes tonight. Only the most impressive acts were reserved for the arrival of the royal representatives: acts like Verex's knife-throwing and Celeste's fire-dancing. I might have stayed to watch, if I didn't have somewhere else I needed to be.

When I stepped into the faded tent I shared with my mother, my eyes went straight to the dress. It was draped over the chair, a gown of deepest, darkest blue. Even in the dim light, it glittered like a thousand stars.

'I thought you'd like it.' My mother was standing across the tent, a smile on her full lips. 'You should try it on.'

'It's incredible,' I breathed, lifting it into my arms. It was so soft it felt like gossamer against my skin. 'But how did you . . . ?'

'Think of it as an apology,' Celeste said, her cobalt skirt swishing elegantly as she moved closer. She put a hand on my shoulder and squeezed. 'I know you're settled here, Mira, but it was only supposed to be temporary. It's best we move on soon.'

I set the dress back down. *First Nikolas and Lillian, and now this. Can't* one thing *go right today?*

'This is the longest we've stayed in the same place—'

'Exactly,' Celeste replied, twisting to examine her outfit in the tarnished mirror. 'We've lingered too long here already. This shouldn't come as a surprise.'

It didn't. I'd seen the signs for weeks now, but I'd ignored them. Since joining the island circus, Aldara had become home – the first and final stop on the circus's annual tour around the Elusive Isles, where the performers returned to repair equipment and spend time with their families.

And now my mother was asking me to give that up. To leave everything behind yet again.

Well, not this time.

'It's been two years since we left the Western Lands,' I reminded her. '*Two years* since the Artisan's warning, and nothing's happened. Maybe we're safe here. Did you ever consider that?'

Celeste shook her head. 'It's not that easy, Mira.'

'Maybe it is,' I countered. 'Maybe it should be.'

Silence fell between us. I'd never been this assertive with her before, and I knew she noticed the difference.

If we'd been a normal mother and daughter, with normal mother-daughter problems, we might have talked it out. Tried to compromise. But she had already decided. In the same way she decided everything.

I paced across the tent – past the tiny, shabby dining table, the handful of pillows that made up our living room, and the pallets that acted as our beds. It wasn't much, but I didn't want to give it up.

I would have to, of course, if I announced my candidacy for the Trials. But at least it would be my choice to make.

'I knew we should have left sooner.' Celeste sighed as she sank into a wicker chair. 'I just wanted you to have a taste of normalcy – for a little while, anyway.'

She hadn't put on her stage makeup yet, and even in the candle-light, I could see the faint lines that were usually concealed – worried creases between her arched brows and in the corners of her eyes.

My frustration softened into tenderness. No matter how much Celeste tried to pretend otherwise, our lives weren't a game – and she had spent far too long trying to protect me. Now it was my turn to protect *her*.

For a moment, I debated telling her everything. It was possible she would understand – that she would even be proud of me. I knew my mother loved me. That wasn't the problem. The problem was over-coming decades of entrenched fear.

My lips parted to confess everything – but I hesitated. If I told her my plans, she might convince me to run again.

And if we did, when would we ever stop?

'I can't live like this.' The words settled between us, tense and charged. 'It was one thing, when I was younger. But now . . . I want my own life.'

Celeste closed her eyes. 'You won't have a life, Mira, if these crimi-nals catch us.'

I thought back to the only time we'd been discovered. I didn't remember much more than a shadowy figure standing over me and then the spray of blood as a circus performer slit their throat. But that experience had made the threat against our lives far more real – and terrifying.

It was the reason I'd decided to compete for a place in the Order of Warriors. I wanted to fight for a better life for myself and my mother, but also for the chance to defend the empire. To keep the peace and protect people who couldn't protect themselves.

I slid into the chair opposite my mother, watching as she applied her makeup with practised hands. 'If you want me to understand,' I said, softly but firmly, 'if you want me to trust you, then you need to start sharing things with me. I'm not a child anymore.'

'No,' Celeste said. 'You're not.'

It wasn't exactly an agreement, but I decided to take it as one.

'Let's start with something simple,' I said, my gaze intent on hers. 'What was my father like? Where did you meet him?'

She didn't answer. Her silence wasn't a surprise, but it still hurt. It cut, like the sharp edge of a blade.

I had my suspicions, of course. There were certain things even my mother couldn't hide. She held herself with the bearing of a noble, and was striking in the most vivid sort of way, with light, pearlescent skin, and auburn hair that burned like a flame in the sun.

Though she'd never spoken about my father, I used to fantasise that he was a fierce warrior from the Red Dunes, or a visiting diplomat from beyond the empire. When I was younger, I would gaze intently into mirrors, imagining the man who had given me my darker skin and midnight hair.

But that was a long time ago. Now, every time I looked into a mirror, the sight of my reflection stung – a constant reminder of how little I knew. Of the secrets my mother was determined to keep.

'Just tell me *something*.' I'd intended my words to sound forceful, but they came out more like a plea. 'I don't care about bloodlines. You know I don't. It doesn't matter to me where he came from.'

'I never thought it would,' Celeste replied. She considered me for a long moment, as if she was debating whether to answer. 'Your father,' she said finally, 'was someone I greatly admired. You resemble him in more than just appearance. You have his strength of character, too.'

It wasn't much, but it was more than she'd ever said. I gazed across the tent, letting her words settle over me.

'I'd never met anyone like him, Mira. He made me feel . . .' Celeste paused, and I wondered if it was too painful for her to continue. Then she said, 'I gave up everything to be with him. If circumstances had been different, I never would have left his side.'

'You must have loved him very much,' I murmured.

Celeste smiled, but it was bittersweet. 'That kind of love . . . I hope you experience it one day, Mira. But perhaps it's better if you don't. It can be a curse.'

A shiver of foreboding went down my spine. Even after all these years, I caught glimpses of the pain my mother tried to hide. She had given up a piece of her heart, and now that piece was lost forever.

'What happened to him?' I pressed.

Sadness glinted in my mother's hazel eyes. 'He died,' she said, standing abruptly. 'No more questions, Mira.'

I watched her leave, swallowing a lump in my throat. In three days' time, she would lose me too.

The dress glittered accusingly at me from the chair.

Ignoring it, I grabbed my well-worn brown leather boots and did up the laces. I braided back my hair, then reached under the bed for the wooden practice sword I kept hidden there.

Its weight should have felt steadying in my hand, but instead it reminded me of previous Choosing Ceremonies. I found myself thinking of the candidates who announced their decision right before the boats left, the ones who hadn't told their parents. It was awful to watch. It was even harder to listen to: sometimes the mothers would cry or beg them to reconsider.

But once the choice was made, it couldn't be unmade.

CHAPTER FOUR

Mira

'Easy,' Aric cautioned as I slashed towards his ribs, our practice swords grating together. 'We're not in the Trials yet.'

I didn't answer. I'd barely spoken since meeting Aric at our training spot – a secluded mountain meadow above the circus, where there was little danger of being observed. Not that secrecy would matter much longer.

Soon enough, all my plans would be out in the open. It should have been a relief, not having to hide my intentions – but a small, uncertain part of me wondered whether Nikolas was right. What chance did I really have against people like him? Nobles who had been training as Warriors most of their lives?

Shoving the thought aside, I twisted to the left and lunged at Aric – who barely blocked the strike in time. He was panting as we locked swords once more, and there was razor-sharp concentration in his face.

I pulled away, circling. Aric mirrored the action, and I knew we were both sizing each other up, waiting for an opening.

Patience had never been my strong suit. I charged, hoping to take Aric by surprise. But he parried my blows with practised ease. When my arms were starting to tire, he went on the offensive. His eyes held an eager glimmer, one that was instantly recognisable.

He was going in for the kill.

I backed away, trying to avoid the attack. His sword curved through the air, but while I was distracted by his blade, Aric knocked me off-balance—

Into the stream.

It wasn't deep, but it was cool. I surfaced, spluttering as I wrung out my wet hair.

Aric waded in after me, infuriatingly smug. My stomach gave a traitorous flutter as I noticed the way his wet linen shirt clung to him, emphasising his muscular chest and broad shoulders. He had filled out even more since my last circus tour, and the result was entirely too distracting.

His familiar brown eyes, the brown of freshly tilled soil, held mine intimately. But there was nothing intimate about the smirk in his voice.

'You're still too impulsive,' he said, raking a hand through his dishevelled hair. 'I can predict your every move before you make it.'

'If I'm so easy to beat, why are you sweating so much?'

Aric flashed me a smile I could only describe as wolfish. 'Touché.'

Laughing a little, I splashed some water in his direction. I expected him to return the favour, but Aric looked at me with an intensity that made me shiver, raising goosebumps on my bare arms.

I stared up at him in the fading light, my heart racing at his closeness. The olive trees cast spiky shadows, partially obscuring Aric's expression – but for a brief, delirious second, I thought he might kiss me.

Instead, he offered me his arm. 'Come on,' he said, shattering the moment. 'You must be freezing.'

I tried not to let my disappointment show as we crossed the stream together. Aric had been the first friend I made in Aldara, an unlikely friendship formed when the governor's son accosted me on my way back to my tent. I'd never told anyone how Nikolas put his hands on me, or how helpless the strength of his touch made me feel. But Aric saw it all – including how it ended, with me kneeing Nikolas in the groin.

Nikolas had never forgiven me for humiliating him, or Aric for witnessing his humiliation, but afterwards Aric had invited me to practise swordsmanship. We'd been sparring partners ever since.

Maybe it was foolish for me to want more. I knew Aric received plenty of offers, from girls prettier and more experienced than I was. But aside from the occasional fling, he'd never shown much interest in them. I'd heard them grumble about how he spent all his time training. Training – with *me*.

And lately, I could have sworn he felt the same attraction I did. The signs were subtle but unmistakable: the heated stares, the way his touches would linger, how he found any excuse to be close to me. Add to that the fact that we saw each other every day, sharing our hopes and dreams, planning a life in the Ravalian Court . . . what else was I supposed to think?

I flopped back on the slope with a soft sigh. Aric lowered himself onto the grass far more gracefully, keeping his sword within easy reach.

The town of Aldara stretched out below us, fringed with open fields, rich grazing land and orchards brimming with colourful fruits. As the sky darkened, my attention was drawn to the largest field, dotted with conical circus tents and illuminated by flashes of fire. Distant strains of music reached my ears, but in the stillness of dusk, all that light and noise felt very far away. Leaning back, I thought how peaceful it was.

'A blacksmith came into town today,' Aric said, breaking the silence. 'My mother offered him coin to take me on as an apprentice. She thinks it's my best chance at a safe future.'

A safe future, perhaps, but not the one we'd always dreamt of.

No risk, no reward. That was the unofficial motto of the islanders who entered the Trials. And they weren't alone.

The promise of a glittering future was the reason parents across the empire took their children to fortune-tellers, hoping they had potential to be selected by the Order of Artisans. It was why so many young boys – and sometimes girls – trained from sunup to sundown, strengthening their bodies to catch the attention of the Order of Warriors. Only the Order of Masks stood apart – mysterious and out of reach, to all except an invited few.

I shook my head at Aric, angry with him for making me question a decision we'd made long ago. While competition was fierce and sometimes deadly, those who made it into an Order were elevated beyond ordinary citizens, afforded status, wealth, and protection – benefits that extended to their immediate family as well. Benefits that would extend to my mother.

'I thought you wanted to be a Warrior. It's all you've ever talked about.'

Aric didn't quite meet my eyes. 'I did. I *do.*' He paused. 'It's just . . . after Kain—' He broke off, and I felt like a monster for pushing him. In a quieter tone, he said, 'I can't blame my mother for being afraid. I don't want her to lose another son.'

I studied Aric's profile, thinking that he looked determined and strong – the kind of person the Order of Warriors were sure to select in the Trials.

Then again, Kain had looked equally capable.

I remembered how proud his mother had been, the day Kain was taken to Ravalia. Eliana had tearily hugged him goodbye, but I didn't think it had really occurred to her that her son might die. The irony was terrible; they'd celebrated his success in the Trials, only to mourn his death three months later. He hadn't lasted past his first battle campaign.

Aric was so like his brother that it was disconcerting; they had inherited their father's strong build, dark hair and golden-brown skin. The similarities were striking enough that I sometimes caught Eliana looking away from Aric, as if he was a walking reminder of the people she'd lost.

I'd never raised it, and Aric hadn't spoken about his brother since the death letter arrived, but I'd seen the toll it had taken. It had been weeks before he picked up the wooden sword again, and when he went through the exercises his brother had shown him, he no longer treated them like a game.

'So are you going to take it? The apprenticeship, I mean?'

Aric didn't answer at first. Finally, he said, 'Last year, I spoke with a soldier who fought in the Western Lands. He told me that Kain and several other Warriors were sacrificed by the crown prince, used as bait to draw out the enemy.'

It was such a ludicrous claim that it might have been comical. Might have been, if Aric's expression wasn't deadly serious.

'And where did you speak with this soldier?' I demanded. 'In the tavern, after a few drinks?'

His silence was enough of an answer.

'You know full well Warriors aren't ordinary foot soldiers,' I said. 'There's no way Kain would have been sacrificed in battle. As the death letter explained—'

'The death letter explained *nothing*.' Aric's voice was rough. 'I'm not going to rely on a piece of parchment to tell me what happened to my brother. I'm going to find out for myself – and if the prince *was* responsible, his title won't protect him from me.'

Terror constricted my chest. Even questioning the actions of the crown prince was a death sentence, and what Aric was talking about . . . what his hard tone *implied* . . .

'He'd kill you,' I breathed. 'Aric, he'd *kill* you.'

'Maybe.' The smile that upturned his lips held no emotion. No fear. 'But maybe I'd take him with me.'

I drew back from the fierceness of his voice. All this time, I'd pictured a successful, privileged life in the Order of Warriors. I'd imagined us travelling the continent and safeguarding the empire together. I'd imagined a *future*.

And now he was going to destroy that future. All based on a rumour.

'Then why go at all?' It sounded like I was pleading with him, and the irony wasn't lost on me. All I'd ever wanted was for us to face the Trials together, as a team. Now, I wished for the opposite. 'You have an alternative. Lots of people want an apprenticeship – do you know what most young men would give for this chance?'

'A good number of things, I would imagine,' he said. 'One of them can have the position. It doesn't mean anything to me.'

I stood abruptly, my entire body trembling – and though the night air was cool, I knew it wasn't from the cold. I didn't feel cold at all; I felt hot, burning with the knowledge that Aric would rather die than be with me. As though everything we had shared, all our plans and hopes, meant nothing.

As though *I* meant nothing.

'I'm leaving,' I said harshly.

Aric rose to his feet. 'What do you want from me, Mira?'

In that moment, if I'd had a sword in my hand, I could have won. I could have delivered a blow so hard that it knocked him over.

'I *want* you to care about your own life,' I said, my voice all venom. 'I want you to consider the people who love you, and how they would feel if you died. I want you to make decisions not just for yourself.'

When Aric spoke, his voice was soft but firm. 'It's my life.'

'It might be your life,' I retorted, 'but I won't be a part of it. Not if you're going to destroy yourself.'

CHAPTER FIVE

Scarlett

Most princesses were given clothes or jewels for their birthday. I was given a country.

I traced the map of Kalure with curious fingers. It was an imposing mass of land that extended across the top of the continent, split in two by the Archasian mountains. I was familiar with the eastern side, its snow-covered forests fringing the Kalurian palace and capital city of Taiga. My eyes drifted up to the smaller city of Frør, just below the Frozen Wastes – but I was far more interested in the mysterious region to the west, where my father had lost an entire regiment last month. On that half of the map, there was nothing except two words: *The Wilds.*

'Why isn't it properly labelled?' I asked.

Governor Halvor looked over from the window, where he was surveying the palace grounds. The afternoon sunlight played across his structured velvet tunic, emphasising his strong shoulders and trim waist. 'Before the invasion,' he replied, crossing to the long wooden table in the centre of the room, 'our borders were closed to outsiders. Your people must not have updated it since then.'

His word choice grated, as it was no doubt supposed to. My great-great-grandfather had once *ruled* Kalure – until King Ravalis had been slaughtered by his own people, who had pledged their allegiance to the Sorceress and her descendants. It was the reason we had ended up here, in the prosperous Eastern Lands of Aqualis, which King Ravalis's son had renamed Ravalia in honour of his murdered father. Ravalia – the perfect name for a new country, a new *empire*, but one that would never forget it was forged from blood and betrayal.

'Perhaps you can help us fill in the map,' I couldn't resist saying, 'as a demonstration of good faith. After all, we're hardly outsiders now.'

If Governor Halvor took offence at that remark, he covered it well. Only the slightest trace of tension in his face betrayed any sort of reaction.

'What exactly is in the Wilds, anyway?' I asked, rolling up the map and striding out of the receiving room. 'Those forests must conceal something important, or my father wouldn't be so intent on conquering them.'

'They're ancient lands,' Halvor replied tersely, hurrying to keep up with me. 'Ones we rarely venture into.'

An evasive response, but I didn't push further. I couldn't afford to upset my father by starting a diplomatic incident, and it wouldn't look good if my first order of business was to dismiss the governor.

'It's quite different to the Kalurian palace, isn't it?' I said, as Governor Halvor slowed to admire the polished marble floors and soaring ceilings, inlaid with vibrant tessellated tiles.

'It didn't used to be,' Halvor murmured, his voice so quiet I had to strain to hear the words.

I frowned as I took in the white-and-gold expanse around me. The Ravalian palace was light and airy, built around a series of open water gardens. It was nothing like the austere grey fortress in Kalure – but I supposed I'd never seen the original palace, before my father had ordered it rebuilt. Either way, I couldn't imagine it being as spectacular as this: four imposing storeys filled with hundreds of rooms and a subterranean level for the servants.

'And your people?' I asked as we made our way through the grounds. 'What are they like?'

'Fierce,' the governor said, with no small amount of pride. 'Fierce and loyal.'

I cast him a sideways glance, wondering whether his comment was a subtle threat.

'I trust the Kalurians will demonstrate that loyalty in service to the empire,' I said pointedly.

The words tasted bitter in my mouth; they were my father's, not mine. But it was important to remind the governor exactly who controlled Kalure – and who didn't.

We entered the greenhouse and I closed my eyes, basking in the humidity. Since Roran's attempt to drown me, it was rare for me to feel warm. Sometimes I wondered if I was as cold-blooded as the reptiles that lived here.

My companion walked beneath a dangling tree snake, its yellow eyes fixed on his head. I brushed it aside as I followed, watching him reach towards a luminous flower with a red mouth.

'Careful,' I called. 'She bites.'

The governor retreated to a safer distance, but his eyes remained on the carnivorous plants, taking in their bright colours and striking patterns. 'What a fascinating place.'

Most visitors found the greenhouse intimidating; that was precisely the reason I'd taken him here. If I'd known he would react like this, I might have opted to bore him with afternoon tea in the royal parlour.

But I merely said, 'I'm glad you think so.'

Perching on the edge of the bubbling stone fountain, I studied Governor Halvor. He wasn't unattractive, with a chiselled jawline and discerning grey eyes. Even the faint streaks of silver in his dark blond hair gave him a distinguished appeal. But he was no match for Severin, and his conversational skills were barely adequate. Which meant that spending an entire afternoon with him – country or no country – was beginning to irritate me.

'You've seen most of the palace by now,' I said, trying to keep the boredom from my voice. 'Shall we retire after this? Or is there another reason you specifically requested my presence?'

'My, you're blunt,' he said. 'I had hoped the rumours were exaggerated.'

'Well, they're not,' I said, with a cool smile. 'What else do people say?'

'They speak of your intelligence. And your rare beauty.' His eyes softened as they lingered on my face, but his tone was begrudging. I wondered if he thought of me like one of these plants – alluring on the outside and deadly within.

My smile widened, and this time, it was sincere. 'You really don't like me, do you?' He started to reply, but I spoke before he could. 'Don't bother trying to deny it. If our circumstances were reversed, I wouldn't like you either.'

Though I doubted I would have been sitting here in his place, politely interacting with my enemy. That was the difference between us; he was willing to do whatever it took to survive, even if it meant losing his standing in the process. I wasn't.

'What are you thinking about?' His voice held a thin note of anxiety; most likely, he was worried he had offended me and hoped to steer the conversation towards safer topics.

Perhaps it was cruel of me, but—

'I'm wondering why you haven't mentioned her yet. My mother.'

He predictably stiffened. In retaliation for her exile from Kalure, my mother had created the Ravalian Orders: the Warriors to physically overpower Emperor Kalias's enemies, the Artisans to assist with strategy, and the Masks, a group of women trained to infiltrate and destroy kingdoms. It was thanks to Zandri's operatives that the Kalurian king had been assassinated – and my father had retaken Kalure.

'Most people tend to avoid uncomfortable topics,' the governor said. 'Yet you seem to delight in bringing them up.'

'I don't shy away from anything – unpleasant or otherwise.' When he didn't respond, I asked, 'Why did your king banish Zandri, anyway?'

'Perhaps you should ask your mother that question.'

I gave him a long, displeased look. Zandri had a notoriously short temper, particularly where Kalure was concerned. She had discarded her birth name when she arrived in the Ravalian Court – and her past had been discarded along with it.

'Perhaps *you* can tell me instead,' I said, the order clear.

Governor Halvor's jaw tightened, and I could have sworn his eyes flashed as they met mine.

I held his stare with renewed interest. Defiance was something I could understand – respect, even. But like my father, I intended to rule with an expectation of absolute obedience. Which meant the governor would have to get used to obeying my commands.

'It had something to do with Queen Rúna's death, didn't it?'

I knew I was right when the governor's expression twisted. Loathing was an emotion I recognised well. I'd seen it on my mother's face enough times.

But Governor Halvor's voice was measured as he replied, 'After ascending to the throne, Queen Rúna made it illegal to practise or worship blood magic. She considered it perverted and evil, a sickness infecting her court and her daughter, Vanora – as Zandri was known back then.' He paused for a moment, then continued, 'The high priestess educated Zandri in secret, and Zandri grew older and more powerful studying the Sorceress's grimoires. When the queen found out, she discounted a century of matriarchal tradition, promising Zandri's brother the crown that would have been hers.'

'And further straining her relationship with the Temple,' I finished, recalling how reverently Zandri always spoke about blood magic. Even a century after the Sorceress's disappearance, the Temple still considered it as such: sacred magic passed down to the Sorceress's female descendants.

'Exactly,' Governor Halvor said, his fingers curling around the lip of the stone fountain. 'The Temple's retaliation was swift and brutal. They murdered Queen Rúna and her consort in their beds, with the intention of installing Zandri as queen in their place. The second part of their plan was unsuccessful. Once King Arioch was crowned, he banished Zandri from Kalure, forbidding her to return on pain of death.'

I gazed unseeingly across the greenhouse, letting the new information settle over me. I knew my mother was capable of cold decisions. She had come to Ravalia to take revenge against her brother, allying herself with Kalure's greatest enemy. Even her brief affair with Emperor Kalias had been calculated: she had wanted an heir, a daughter whose blood ran thick with the Sorceress's power. A daughter who had a claim to both the Ravalian and Kalurian thrones.

But matricide . . . It was one thing knowing that my mother was capable of murder, and quite another to realise she was responsible for the deaths of her entire family – the very public, bloody deaths that had set the Kalurian people against her. And possibly against me, too.

No matter. If the Kalurians couldn't be won over by diplomacy, they would bend to force.

I would make sure of that.

'Tell me, Governor,' I said, brushing off my skirts and standing, 'what did you think of your king?'

The governor rose to his feet as well, his grey eyes level with mine. 'King Arioch was a great man,' he answered unhesitatingly, 'and an even better ruler. I was honoured to serve him.'

A loyal man, then. He seemed an odd choice for governor, but perhaps my father had believed his appointment would placate the loyalists.

'And what of me? Will you serve me as loyally as you did him?'

There was something peculiar about the way he looked at me then – as if I had missed a crucial point.

'Is that what you think?' Governor Halvor appeared genuinely surprised, and perhaps even amused. 'That you're going to rule Kalure in your father's name?'

I blinked at him. That was *exactly* what I thought. 'The emperor promised me Kalure—'

'He promised you to *me*,' the governor interrupted.

And then he said something I could barely understand, his words almost drowned out by the sudden roaring in my ears—

'You're to be my wife.'

CHAPTER SIX

Scarlett

I found the blades lying on my vanity table. They were thin and deathly sharp, sleek enough to be disguised as hair sticks.

My mother's handiwork, no doubt – intended as a last line of defence. A timely one, considering Roran was returning tonight. But right now, I felt vengeful enough to use them without provocation.

'Aella,' I called, 'come and help me get ready.'

The servant rushed across the tiled floor, her copper plait bouncing against her starched white uniform. Aella was the third attendant I'd had in as many months, but I had a good feeling about her. So far, she'd lasted two weeks without entering either of my siblings' employ, which was a new record.

I still made sure to touch her hand before she reached for the knives. It was the work of a second to brush her skin and ensure she saw only generic hair sticks; the illusion was so subtle that even my mother would have admired my finesse.

But my satisfaction faded when Aella shuddered at my touch.

'Are you cold, Your Highness?' she asked, clasping her hands protectively in front of her.

'Not at all,' I said sharply. 'Who could possibly be cold *here*?'

As if to highlight my point, a balmy breeze drifted through my bedchamber, parting the gauzy curtains that hung over the balcony entrance. It did nothing to banish the chill in my bones.

Aella said nothing else as she arranged my hair into my preferred style: half-up and half-down, my dark red waves framing my face like a circlet of fire. I glanced in the vanity mirror, admiring the way the silver knives pierced my bun like skewers.

'The crimson one,' I ordered as Aella reached for the cluster of hanging gowns. 'Has it been examined?'

It was probably lax of me to rely on Aella's word, but I was tired of precautions and common sense. Besides, it was unlikely that my would-be poisoner would try to assassinate me the same way twice.

'Yes, Your Highness. Each has been thoroughly inspected.'

That was all I needed to hear. I stepped into the gown, silk rustling softly against my skin. I'd once luxuriated in the feeling; it was a shame even that simple pleasure had been stripped from me. Now when I dressed, I was forever reminded of Aella's dead predecessor, and her last moments spent writhing on the floor.

It took less than five minutes to add the finishing touches and step out of my chambers into the hallway beyond. Black-garbed Warriors were already waiting – two, as was customary – and they bowed their heads in respect.

I ignored them, lengthening my stride so they had to hurry to catch up.

Most visitors found the palace disorientating – a gilded maze, filled with soaring ceilings and a labyrinth of interconnecting hallways. As a child, I'd regarded it as a puzzle to be solved – exploring every inch of the place, including the secret passageways and underground tunnels.

Winding my way through the halls, I paused on the first level. My gaze went to the arched windows, where the distant glow of hundreds of fire braziers stood out against the black sky.

What fun would a simple dinner or dance be, to welcome home my brother, the conquering general? No. Only the very best for Roran, which meant the arena.

'Leave me,' I ordered.

The Warriors hesitated, but obeyed. I waited until the rattling of their armour faded before crossing over to a nearby balcony. Severin was waiting for me, his hair windswept – as if he had come straight from the harbour to the palace.

Light from the wall sconces bathed him in a reddish glow, reminding me of the first time I'd seen him. It had been in the gardens during a revel like the one unfolding below, and many ladies had been looking in his direction. But I hadn't been admiring the way the torchlight played across his tattooed skin, illuminating his striking eyes and the sharp angles of his face. No – I had been drawn to the strength of his presence, to the confident way he held himself.

I'd never seen someone who kept themselves so separate from the court and appeared glad of it.

'Radiant,' Severin murmured, drinking me in. 'You look radiant.'

'I'm glad you like the dress,' I replied.

'I like more than that,' he told me, striding closer. His inked lips brushed my cheek. 'Are you alright?'

Without answering, I reached up and threaded my fingers through his ebony hair. I kissed him with a passion that he returned, walking backwards until my lower back hit the balustrade. It was deceptively easy to lose myself in the moment: in the unique, sandalwood scent of him, the way his tongue danced with mine.

Gods, even a single touch could ignite my frozen body, could make me feel—

Alive.

The thought was like a touch of ice, unpleasant and unwelcome. But I didn't allow my mind to drift back to that horrible day, to remember what it had felt like to die.

Anchoring myself firmly in the present, I allowed my hands to roam Severin's shoulders, his back, wanting to explore his bare chest. Wanting more of him. Always more.

Severin was more restrained, his skilled hands lightly brushing my neck, wary of upsetting my hair or makeup. All too soon, he was pulling away, and I moaned in frustration. I was tired of these stolen, secret moments; I wanted all of him.

Of course, it was entirely selfish of me. If we were caught, he would be the one who was punished, for daring to step above his station. Every time we met, we courted disaster. But—

'I missed you,' I admitted, and was surprised to realise just how much I meant it. Severin brought out a gentler side in me, one I barely recognised.

'It was hard being away from you,' Severin replied. 'It always is.'

'Well, it was certainly harder this time,' I said, hating how petulant I sounded. 'You shouldn't have to go on those battle campaigns. You're the head of an Order; my brother has plenty of other Artisans to inform his strategies. And Roran is . . .'

'I know,' Severin said. 'I was careful.'

I rested my head against his shoulder, suppressing a sigh. How long would being careful matter?

Severin was the most powerful Artisan in existence, and the youngest person to head an Order. But rather than affording him protection, his power had turned him into a coveted resource. Emperor Kalias relied on Severin's predictions to inform his political and battle strategies, while Zandri sent Severin on clandestine missions he was forbidden to speak about afterwards. My parents fought over him in a way they had never fought over me, and their tug-of-war would only end when they inevitably broke him.

'Do you ever think about leaving all this behind?' I asked abruptly. 'You have reason to. You more than most.'

My comment veered dangerously close to uncomfortable territory. I'd never broached the subject before this, of what it had been like for Severin to grow up in Zigilia – only to end up serving the very people who had conquered his home. I'd never dared.

'Emperor Kalias made it clear that if I betray him in any way, he will raze the Western Lands to the ground – and then there's your mother. As you know, she has her ways of ensuring obedience within the Orders.' Severin's voice was carefully matter-of-fact, but I could hear the pain he kept hidden. 'Is that what you would want? To leave this behind?'

It seemed heartless to tell him the truth: that I would never willingly leave the Ravalian Court. That what I wanted, more than anything, was to be a part of something he hated. To prove to my family and the court that I had what it took – not just to survive here, but to *thrive*.

'It doesn't matter what I want,' I said at last. 'Not really.'

'It matters to me.' The sincerity in his face was impossible to doubt. 'I want you to be happy. I want to *make* you happy.'

I needed to mention my engagement to the governor. To explain the impossibility of my situation. But looking into his shining eyes, I couldn't do it. 'You already have.'

'Then why do you look so sad?'

I leant into the warmth of his chest without answering. Even though it was a lie, when I was with Severin, I felt safe. Protected. The irony was unmistakable; I felt safe with him, yet he was the farthest thing from safe with me.

Changing the subject, I said, 'Tonight was supposed to be for me, you know. I turned nineteen today.'

'I hadn't forgotten.' Severin looked as though he was fighting back a smile. He probably thought me spoilt, but he'd never come right out and said so. 'I bought you a present. It's not much,' he added quickly. 'Nothing like the riches you're used to, but I hope you'll like it.'

'I will love it,' I corrected, 'because it's from you.'

Immediately, I regretted my choice of words. It was cruel of me to give him false hope, to pretend that this was anything more than a temporary arrangement.

We subsided into silence, and I avoided meeting Severin's probing stare. This was one of the times when I was sorely tempted to discover what the future held for us. But he'd made me promise not to ask, and part of me always wondered if I'd like the answer.

So instead, I focused my attention over the balcony – towards the glowing circular arena beyond the palace. Just the sight of it helped to chase away my melancholy thoughts, making my blood quicken with anticipation.

'Will you stay?' I asked, hoping he would say yes. As exciting as the fighting matches were, they would be far more invigorating with Severin by my side.

'I'll escort you inside, but I won't watch.' His melodious voice was firm, decisive. 'I don't take much enjoyment in it.'

I blinked up at him. 'Everyone enjoys the arena; that's the point.'

'I just think,' he said quietly, 'that life and death shouldn't be a game.' Before I could reply, he tucked a strand of hair behind my ear, making me shiver. 'I'm leaving on a sea voyage tonight anyway – your mother has a mission for me to complete. But I couldn't leave without giving you this.'

My gaze dropped to the teardrop necklace in his palm. It was beautiful, delicate, *perfect.*

'It's aquamarine,' Severin said, holding up the stone. It winked at me even in the dim light. 'When I looked at it . . . I was reminded of your eyes.'

'I adore it,' I breathed, unexpectedly touched. Most of the court had become accustomed to my changed appearance over time, but in the beginning, whispers had followed me everywhere. Even now, I sometimes noticed courtiers tracking my movements, or husbands steering their wives away from me – as if they somehow sensed I was unnatural. Severin was the only person who had never treated me any differently. Who had embraced me completely.

'It's not a ring,' he continued, 'but perhaps you can think of it as a promise. Because I want to be with you, Scar. There's nothing I want more.'

I stared at him, wondering if he understood exactly what he was promising. He had to know marriage was out of the question; even without the Kalurian governor, Severin was too low-born for the emperor to consider. But would he really be content with *this* – stolen moments in the shadows, while in public I was another man's wife?

As I pressed my face into his neck, breathing in the familiar sandalwood scent of him, I knew the answer. Whether it was in a day, a week, even a month from now, I would lose him.

I waited for the pain to hit, because surely I loved Severin. If there was anyone I loved, it would be him.

And yet, even at my most hopeless, I wasn't human enough to cry. To shed even a single tear.

CHAPTER SEVEN

Scarlett

The arena was the beating heart of Ravalia, and it felt like it. As I approached the royal box, the atmosphere built into something pulsing and electric.

I couldn't see much of the fighting below, but if the audience's shouting was any indication, it must have been exciting. Were two favourites competing, or were the contenders closely matched?

I was eager to find out as I took a seat next to Odessa Tiran, who flicked her white-blonde hair and gave me a haughty glance. The dislike was entirely mutual, but I didn't allow my impassive expression to falter.

Never let them see your true face, my mother had always instructed. *Only show them what you want them to see.*

'Where's your fiancé tonight?' I asked sweetly, just to irritate the other girl.

Odessa didn't reply. Most likely, she didn't know. My younger brother was notoriously unpredictable; Cassius was probably off scheming somewhere, and he wasn't in the habit of sharing his plans.

Trumpets rang through the stands, diverting my attention. The crowd turned at the sound, the fighting match below temporarily suspended.

Emperor Kalias strode through the stands with purpose, his ceremonial robes embroidered with the imperial symbol of a lion. He was every bit as imposing as he was cold, the sharp spikes of his gold-tipped bone crown glinting in the firelight.

I watched him intently, my fingers inching towards the blades in my hair. After Roran's attempt to drown me, I had realised two things: first, that for all my mother's magical power, she still hadn't been able to stop him in time. And second, that I had kept myself separate from the court for too long.

So I had made my choice: to ingratiate myself with my father. To do whatever it took to obtain status and protection that way.

But he didn't care how hard I worked, or how skilled I was. None of it mattered to him. Not my years of weapons training; not my daily lessons on culture, history and battle strategy; not even the months I had spent shadowing him on military campaigns.

He had been *humouring* me, never intending to give me any real power. I was to be a token bride, sold to man who had a weaker claim to the Kalurian throne than I did. A husband who wasn't royal, wasn't even a prince, but a useless *bureaucrat*.

Before I could think better of it, I was on my feet. I had never confronted my father before – and certainly not in public. But I was no longer thinking rationally. No longer considering the consequences.

'When were you going to tell me?' I demanded, keeping my voice low – too low, I hoped, for Roran to overhear. Or the Kalurian governor, who stood a few steps behind my brother, looking like he would have preferred to be anywhere but here.

My father stared down at me, shadows darkening his features. The torchlight reddened his grey eyes to a more fitting colour. 'You do not have the right to address me without permission,' he said, his face tight with disapproval. 'And you certainly do not have the right to question my decisions.'

I drew back, my cheeks flushed. 'I wasn't—'

'I have indulged you far too long,' Kalias interrupted, 'giving you freedoms that should have been reserved for my sons. It is clear to me now that was a mistake. As of this moment, all your lessons are cancelled – except etiquette. It is time that you learnt to behave like a proper princess, and to accept this marriage with grace.'

He said nothing else as he claimed the throne next to his wife. Roran took the seat to his right, and just like that, I was ignored and forgotten. When I saw Odessa's satisfied smile, my nails sunk into my palms.

In my anger, I'd almost forgotten my future husband. He slid into the chair on my other side, his face set in serious lines. I wondered if he realised how much I despised him.

'Your Highness,' he said, his voice a deep baritone.

'Governor.' Sensing his distaste as he surveyed the fighting below, I asked pointedly, 'How are you enjoying the spectacle?'

He didn't reply for a while, and when he did, his tone was guarded. 'I confess, I am unused to such practices. Do they happen often?'

'Usually only on special occasions,' I answered stiffly.

Technically, these games were supposed to be in *my* honour. In the lead-up to Cassius's birthday, there had been three days of arena fights – and he didn't even care for them, dismissing the matches as boring and predictable. He had clearly felt the same about the long line of courtiers who approached, eager to bestow him with trinkets and well wishes. And yet they had flocked to him all the same.

Just like they flocked to Roran now, filing past me without a single glance or nod of acknowledgement. All anyone could talk about was Roran's campaign in Etheria, and how the walled city of Ashmir had finally fallen. Thanks to my brother, the Ravalian Empire now spanned the entire continent, and no one wanted to anger Roran by showing a shred of interest in his half-sister.

'Even so,' the governor continued, his jaw tightening, 'you must run out of citizens to compete.'

I resisted the urge to roll my eyes as, down below, the victor cleanly beheaded his opponent. *Diplomats and their delicate sensibilities.*

'These men are criminals, given the opportunity to fight for their lives in the arena. We're not barbarians.'

The governor raised an eyebrow, but said nothing.

Turning away from him, I tried to focus on the next match. Normally I enjoyed the sport of the arena, but tonight all I could think about were my father's harsh words. It was infuriating to sit quietly, forced to hear Roran entertain our father with stories of his latest military victory. Infuriating to understand exactly how little I meant to either of them.

Even Roran thought of me as a temporary inconvenience rather than a threat. He had expended far more effort trying to get Cassius out of the way – but Cassius was as cunning as a Mask, and had created a court of his own, which was fiercely loyal to him and difficult to infiltrate.

Maybe I should have done the same. But I wasn't as charming as Cassius, and I didn't have his connections. I only had Zandri. Zandri, whose schemes were every bit as ruthless and *final* as the blades she had left in my chambers.

But perhaps that ruthlessness was exactly what I needed right now.

My father had made his position perfectly clear: no matter how capable I was, I would always be a princess – and what power would a princess ever have, when there were two princes to take the throne?

But if Roran were dead . . . if Cassius were outmanoeuvred . . .

I narrowed my eyes, watching the people laugh and cheer as another fight ended – and with it, another life. Watching my father and brother already planning another invasion.

Severin was right, I realised. In the Ravalian Court, life and death was a game. It was a game that had no beginning and no end, because there was nothing more sacred or changeable than power. In my world, there was only the shifting sands of political influence, the ebb and flow of sovereignty.

Roran's military campaigns tipped that balance in his favour. He was the crown prince for a reason; his plans were calculated and brutal. To him, death was nothing more than a strategic move – the discarding of rivals on a chessboard.

Except our tutors had taught *me* chess, too.

As I listened to my brother's plans for war, I realised that, yes, the game would continue.

Only this time, it had a new player.

And I intended to play to win.

CHAPTER EIGHT

Mira

When I first arrived in Aldara, I thought the buildings on top of the cliffs were snow. The reality of them was less romantic: utilitarian slabs of white-washed stone, each blurring into the next.

Weaving my way downward, I relied on instinct rather than defining landmarks. Aldara was known for its jumble of passageways, originally designed to hinder enemy invaders. Now, those passageways served as a reminder of a harder time, back before the islanders had reaped the benefits of Emperor Kalias's protection. Back when pirate attacks had been common, and these same streets had run red with blood.

The path I was following suddenly emerged into the bustling main square, the air rich with the sounds of hawkers and the smells of sandalwood and spice. It was always like this when the royal representatives visited: packed with market stalls displaying the best Aldara had to offer, in the hopes of harvesting Ravalian coin. It had been over a decade since Aldara was absorbed into the empire, and while some of the islanders still grumbled – mainly about the appointment of a provincial governor – most welcomed the increased opportunity for trade and commerce.

I passed a stall laden with mangoes and inhaled deeply as I approached tray after tray of aromatic herbs. There was even a wide selection of succulent meats and gourmet breads, far more than I usually saw displayed at markets.

'Mira!'

My head turned at the sound of the clear, sweet voice, and a smile broke over my face.

Lillian was waving at me from a nearby stall, bolts of fabric draped over her arms and a coronet of wildflowers in her hair. Judging by the lightness in her expression, it seemed like our argument from the other day was forgotten.

As I came closer, I noticed that the stall was surrounded by noble ladies, young and old, inspecting the material with acquisitive eyes. And not just ladies. A handful of boys stood off to one side, looking put out as they lost Lillian's attention.

'I knew that dress would be perfect for you,' Lillian said, her voice thick with satisfaction. Her bright eyes canvassed me from head to toe, and I gave her a twirl, my skirts flaring. 'You look stunning.'

Lillian was the stunning one, wearing a pastel pink dress that complemented her fair complexion perfectly. The very image of a Ravalian lady.

'It's beautiful,' I replied, hugging her close. 'You're a genius.'

Lillian ducked her head bashfully, but we both knew how talented she was. Once she was done with her apprenticeship, she intended to move to Ravalia and open her own dress shop. I'd spent many afternoons imagining our lives together: Aric and I training during the day and visiting Lillian in the evening.

'Am I interrupting something?' I asked, glancing over my shoulder. The boys were still watching Lillian, their gazes wistful.

'I wasn't actually *interested* in them,' Lillian said, lowering her voice conspiratorially. 'I was just passing the time.'

I laughed. 'What about Felix?'

'That's my mother's idea, not mine. With Aric leaving, she seems to think marriage is the best way of keeping me here. But Felix is so dull! Did you see him earlier? He didn't come up to speak to me, not even to say hello. And he had the most unattractive frown on his face.'

'Well,' I said, suppressing a smile, 'you do get a lot of male attention. He might find that intimidating.'

Before I could say anything else, a rail-thin woman with a pinched face and snow-white hair interrupted us. 'I didn't leave you in charge so you could gossip with your friend. Well?' the weaver prompted, when Lillian remained silent. 'What do you have to say for yourself?'

Lillian smiled innocently. 'We were just discussing the dress I made for Mira. She's thinking of commissioning another. I thought we could take a turn around the market and discuss it further.'

The weaver's gaze raked over me, none too impressed, but she nodded. 'Go on, then. But don't take too long – Lord Nevin is planning to come past with his wife, and we both know how much she likes to spend his coin.'

'Thank you,' Lillian called, already taking my hand and backing away. She whispered, 'Quickly, before she changes her mind!'

We raced through the square, filled with a sense of freedom I rarely experienced. But Lillian was like that. She found joy everywhere – even in the small moments. It was one of the things I most admired about her.

When we were out of view of the weaver's tent, we slowed to a walk. I smoothed down my long dark hair, which was a windswept mess.

'Worried about someone seeing you, Mira?' Lillian paused at a stall, tracing a blue ribbon with her fingertips. 'My brother, perhaps?'

I avoided her devious glance. I *had* been wondering whether Aric would be at the market, but he was the last person I wanted to discuss. *And I shouldn't be thinking about him at all.*

'I really need to find a less perceptive friend,' I retorted.

Lillian grinned. 'What *is* happening with you two, anyway?'

I shrugged, pretending to focus on a pair of richly dressed traders. They must have come with the royal representatives; they flaunted the red and gold colours of the Ravalian Court. 'You'd have to ask him.'

'Aric is far too talented at keeping his feelings to himself,' Lillian said, rolling her eyes. 'But I know he cares about you. He always has.'

She paused, so suddenly that a street vendor barely avoided knocking into her. 'Actually, there is something you can do for me. Can you talk to him about the apprenticeship?'

I paused, too, staring at my friend. Lillian's pale blue eyes were locked on mine, curiously beseeching.

'By talk to him, you mean . . .'

'Convince him to take it.' Lillian grasped my hands. 'Please, Mira,' she said. 'I know Aric would listen to you.'

'I already talked to him about it,' I said gently, trying to soften the blow. 'It didn't make any difference.'

I expected Lillian to nod, her face filled with resignation. I didn't expect her to drop my hand and step away from me.

'I'm sure you tried very hard,' she muttered.

'What's *that* supposed to mean?' I asked, following her over to a less busy corner of the market, where fishmongers were haggling over prices.

'My brother died fighting for the empire,' Lillian said flatly. 'Do you really think I'd want that for you? For Aric?'

'I understand, I really do. But—'

'You're not thinking clearly.' Lillian's hands went to her curvy hips. The pose was a strong one, but her mouth was downturned with worry. 'Why risk your life? Why risk *everything*, Mira, when you have—'

'What?' I interrupted. 'What do I have, Lil? I bow and scrape to nobles every day, all so they'll toss me a few coins. I barely get by on their supposed *generosity*.' The bitterness in my voice startled me, but I kept going. 'You saw what Nikolas and the others think of performers. They don't respect us, and I don't want to spend my life pretending I'm less than they are.' My hands balled into fists at my sides. 'This is the only way.'

Lillian's eyes were filled with uncharacteristic gravity. 'Do you really believe that?'

The seriousness in her face made me think of the years I'd spent on the run. The past that my mother refused to discuss, yet that continued to haunt her. To haunt us both.

But if I became a Warrior, I would no longer have to hide. And neither would my mother.

'Yes,' I said decisively. 'I do.'

Lillian said nothing else as we left the square, following the sloping path up to the governor's manor house. The crowds grew denser as we approached – no longer just Aldarians hawking their wares, but traders from across the empire, including the neighbouring islands of Salacia and Scallon. I went first, clearing a path for Lillian to follow. But when I turned to check on her, she wasn't behind me.

Retracing my steps, I found Lillian lingering outside a curious-looking tent. It was inky black, a shock of darkness amongst the bright stalls. The vendor leant against the entrance, his dark skin and crimson vest marking him as a Westerner from across the Azure Sea. He reminded me uncomfortably of the fortune-teller I'd met in Damar, but this young man's skin was clear of tattoos, and his eyes were the same colour.

'Do you have a question?' His voice was low and smooth, cultured.

'No,' I said quickly. 'I was searching for a different stall.'

The vendor seemed amused by my obvious lie. 'What about you, young mistress?' His attention shifted to Lillian, who didn't seem unnerved in the slightest.

'What are you selling?' Lillian asked, trying to peek inside the tent. 'Fabrics? Spices?'

He blocked her gaze, his smile turning lupine. 'Nothing so common as that. I deal in knowledge and secrets.'

With a prickle of unease, I understood. 'You're an Artisan.'

'Yes.' He looked at me too shrewdly, like he could uncover my secrets with a single glance.

A chill darted down my spine as I remembered my last, strange interaction with an Artisan. To this day, his words still scared me. The tattooed image I'd seen – the one with my mother's face, her lips straining to form my name – haunted my nightmares. I inched away from the vendor, unwilling to deal with him.

But his announcement had the opposite effect on Lillian, who regarded him hungrily. Artisans were rare, their gifts renowned. Once they made a prediction, it almost always came true.

'You mean ...' Lillian lowered her voice, 'you can tell us the future?'

He considered her. 'Perhaps. The future is not always so clear. But I can answer your questions – for a price.'

'Lillian,' I warned, tugging on her arm, '*don't.*'

But Lillian didn't move, her eyes riveted on the fortune-teller. 'Who will I marry?'

'No one,' he said. 'You will marry no one.'

Lillian stared at him, her vibrant face suddenly pale. 'But how can that be? Surely I will have suitors?'

The Artisan watched her steadily, but a flicker of something – some emotion I couldn't read – unsteadied his cool countenance. Then I blinked, and he was perfectly composed once more.

He bent down to murmur in Lillian's ear, too low for me to hear. When he drew back, there were tears in her eyes. Her face was bone-white.

Lillian's shaking hand formed a fist, like she might strike him. But she only straightened, turned, and strode away. She didn't wait for me, and I knew better than to rush after her and try to discover what the fortune-teller had said.

Instead, I asked him, 'What of her payment?'

'She can keep her secrets,' the Artisan said, his piercing eyes following Lillian's silhouette as she walked too quickly through the market stalls. 'She will have no need for them much longer.'

CHAPTER NINE

Mira

The sun was truly gone now, smoke from the torches thick in the air. I pushed my way through the mass of people, but Lillian had already disappeared. Swallowed up by the thick crowd.

Whatever the Artisan had said, it must have been bad. Lillian wasn't the sort of person to jump at shadows, and the terror in her eyes scared me more than I wanted to admit.

'Are you alright?'

I whirled around, my heart pounding. A strong hand steadied me as I stumbled.

'I'm fine,' I said, staring up into Aric's face. I felt my skin flush at our closeness and hoped the darkness hid the redness of my cheeks. 'I'm just worried about Lillian. We bumped into a fortune-teller, and he told her . . . I don't know what he said. Now she's disappeared.'

'If I know my sister,' Aric replied, 'she just needs to be alone. She'll come back when she's ready – she's never been one to brood for long.'

'I guess,' I said, full of dread I couldn't shake.

A pair of pretty traders brushed past me, only to do a double take when they spotted Aric. My teeth ground together, though he seemed oblivious to their coy glances and inviting smiles. His gaze was on me, and I was suddenly conscious of the way my dress hugged my body.

The heat in his stare made my throat go dry, and I found my eyes lingering on his rugged features and tanned, muscular forearms. He was particularly handsome tonight, in the fine linen top and leather breeches Lillian had made for him.

'Come on.' Aric's smile lit up the markets, brighter than the lanterns above us. 'Let's have some fun.'

Just like that, I felt myself soften. It was difficult to stay angry with Aric – especially on a night like this.

Taking his hand, I let him lead me through the iron gates of the Atwoods' manor – tonight, flung open for all – and into the mani-cured gardens beyond, where musicians were playing with abandon. A few people were dancing, but most milled around the grounds, sipping spiced wine.

The royal representatives kept to themselves, waited on by servants as Governor Atwood spoke with General Tiran, the Warrior in charge of the Choosing Ceremony. The thought of him assessing me in the town square was panic-inducing, and my stomach coiled into knots. My nerves weren't helped by the sight of Nikolas and Stacia, but thankfully Aric steered us in the oppo-site direction – to a far corner of the gardens, where we had a bubble of privacy.

'May I have this dance?' he asked, bowing in a courtly fashion that made me laugh.

'You may,' I allowed, turning my voice haughty and cool – like a noble Ravalian lady, bestowing him with a great honour.

His arms encircled my waist, holding me close as we swayed to the rhythm of the string band. It was clear Aric didn't know any of the dances favoured by the Ravalian Court, but that didn't matter. I wouldn't have traded this moment for the most talented dancer in the empire. I wouldn't have traded this moment for anything.

He leant back slightly, his gaze capturing mine. 'I'm sorry that I told you so abruptly, Mira. I never wanted to hurt you.'

'You didn't hurt me,' I said, but I didn't think either of us believed it. 'I just – I wish—'

I wish I was enough.

'I know,' Aric said softly, and the sympathy in his voice was cutting.

I pulled out of his embrace. Was it possible that even if he *hadn't* decided to avenge Kain, he might not have wanted a future with me? Was his sympathy because he couldn't return my feelings?

'I care about you, Mira. I just . . . I can't be what you need.'

His face was suddenly inches from mine, and the intensity in his eyes told a very different story. There was a part of him that felt *something* for me. Maybe it was an instinctual reaction to the dress, the dance, the romance of the moment – but he wanted me too.

All of a sudden, I saw everything in a new light. All those times he'd pulled away from me, the attraction he'd never acted on . . .

'You told me you spoke with that soldier a year ago,' I said in a choked voice. 'How long have you been planning this, Aric? *How long?*'

He didn't quite meet my eyes. All this *time—*

'I know I should have said something sooner. But I couldn't let you go, Mira. I *couldn't.*' His voice turned pleading. 'I wanted a future with you. I still do. If circumstances were different—'

'But they aren't.' I took a deep breath. 'What if I told you that I wanted that too? To be with you?'

Aric pressed closer, and I knew I needed to back away. To put as much distance between us as possible, before he hurt me more than he already had. But I'd never been able to refuse Aric anything, and I couldn't refuse him now.

Instead, I closed my eyes as his lips brushed mine. It was tentative at first, like he was giving me the chance to pull away. When I didn't, he deepened the kiss.

It was nothing like my unpleasant encounter with Nikolas two years ago, or the fumbling kisses I'd shared with other boys. My surroundings disappeared, until I was only aware of Aric – the feeling of his body and mouth pressing against mine, the unfamiliar, exhilarating warmth spreading through my veins.

It was only afterwards, when he pushed me away from him with gentle, firm hands and whispered, 'I'm sorry,' that I understood.

Aric's kiss wasn't a beginning. It was an ending.

It was goodbye.

I wasn't sure how long I sat there, in a darkened corner of the gardens. From here, the laughing, twirling forms of the dancers were like something out of another world.

I raised a hand to my face, where I could still feel a flush on my cheeks. But whatever emotion Aric had stirred in me had dissipated. Eventually it would hurt, but right now, it seemed I was beyond even that.

'I hoped I would come across you again.'

I stood abruptly, shocked out of my thoughts. The Artisan's foot-steps had been so quiet I hadn't heard his approach at all.

'I think you like scaring people,' I said harshly. 'Whatever you said to Lillian was terrible.'

'Terrible . . .' He stretched the word out in his melodic voice, as if examining the syllables. Then he nodded. 'I suppose it was terrible. Though not for the reason you think.'

'What did you say to her?'

The Artisan smiled faintly, and I noticed that his skin was covered in tattoos. They crawled across his features, obscuring them like shadows. As I stared at him, realisation came in a rush. My eyes dropped to his lips: the upper tattooed black, the lower gleaming gold in the moonlight.

'It's you,' I breathed. 'You're the same fortune-teller I met in Damar.'

His smile curved wider. 'I wondered when you would realise.'

'But your skin was clear of tattoos a few moments ago,' I protested. 'You didn't look . . . like you do now.'

He waved a dismissive hand. 'Parlour tricks.'

It was such a casual answer for something so unbelievable. I took a wary step back.

The Artisan watched me, his mismatched eyes filled with amuse-ment. 'I don't mean you or your mother any harm.' Then he turned serious, folding his muscular arms as he said, 'You didn't heed my warning.'

And if I can see the trail, then so can they.

'We left,' I said tightly. 'We came here.'

He didn't contradict me, but I had the sense I'd missed an important point. My eyes shifted to his cheeks, where the ink of his tattoos seemed to waver. On the left side of his face, I saw a toothy smile. The right depicted a snarl.

'The dualities of nature,' he said, catching me looking. 'A reminder that everyone has the capacity for both light and dark. The future is no different.' He paused. 'What I told your friend was for her alone. But I can discuss your future.'

I hesitated, but couldn't help myself. 'I want to know why you warned me. And why you're here now.'

'Two interesting questions.' He rested a finger on his bottom lip. 'The answer to your first question is simple: I wanted to help you. As for the second . . . I was sent here.' He tilted his head. 'You're really not going to ask about the future?'

Why are you so interested? I almost asked him. *What do you know about me and my mother?*

But those questions seemed too dangerous, somehow. Too personal.

'Does Aric survive?' I asked instead. 'Does he become one of the emperor's Warriors?'

I had the sense that the Artisan was surprised by my choice of question, but his unreadable expression didn't alter. 'The boy will become a Warrior, but he will never fight for the emperor.'

'But that doesn't make sense!'

He ignored me. 'As to his survival,' he continued, 'that very much depends.'

'On . . . ?'

The Artisan studied me for so long that I wondered if he saw something I couldn't, if my future was inked across my skin like his tattoos. 'You, Miss Tundra. And the princess.'

I blinked at him, wondering if I'd misheard. Even with our plans to enter an Order, it seemed unlikely that Aric's future would be linked to the princess in any way.

Without waiting for a reply, he asked, 'What do you know of your mother's enemies?'

'Nothing,' I said. 'Only that we're running from someone.'

He nodded slowly, as if weighing my response. Then he said, 'Running won't save you. Your mother's time is drawing to a close.'

The words hit me like hammer blows. 'What are you saying?' I whispered, thinking of my mother's face as he'd shown it to me: trembling and afraid.

'Your mother made a choice, a long time ago,' he replied. 'That choice has haunted her ever since. It haunts you now, too. But her death will set you free.'

Her death.

'No.' My voice broke on the word. 'No, that can't be possible. There must be some mistake—'

'There is no mistake,' the Artisan interrupted. 'She will die, one way or another. But before she does, you need to find the locket. Always keep it with you and tell no one you have it.'

'What?' I stared at him uncomprehendingly. 'What locket?'

He closed his eyes. When he opened them, they were unnaturally bright. 'Search behind your tent. Something of yours is buried there.'

'My mother wouldn't take something from me,' I protested. 'Even if she did, I have nothing of value.'

'Ah,' he replied, 'but your mother has already stolen something once.' He turned away, towards the distant lights.

'But I don't understand,' I called after him.

The Artisan glanced over his shoulder, a pillar of shadow and ink. The tattoo on his left cheek winked at me in the moonlight: a ghoulish grin.

'You will.'

CHAPTER TEN

Mira

I frowned at the shovel in my hand. If anyone saw me right now, they'd think that I'd lost my mind. Maybe I had.

But I started digging all the same.

It wasn't long before the shovel hit something hard in the dirt. Kneeling, I reached into the small hole, my fingers brushing cool metal.

Recognition, when it came, was fast and sudden.

I had found this box once, wrapped in cloth and stashed at the bottom of my mother's trunk. Celeste had caught my hand before I could touch it. *No, Mira,* she'd warned. *It's magic.*

But I want to see magic, I'd said, my excitement impossible to contain. *Magic is good, isn't it?*

It's not that kind of magic, my mother had answered.

Perhaps that memory should have given me pause. Magic was carefully policed in the empire, and most people felt safer knowing those with special abilities were sworn into the emperor's service. But free magic had never been an evil thing to me. I'd grown up listening to my mother's tales – tales of incredible, impossible feats. Women like the Sorceress, who could enchant with a single word. Fierce Warriors of the Western dunes, who could shoot arrows from their hands. I had grown up imagining shamans and seers, glittering power and endless possibilities. None of it had seemed dangerous. Just fantastical.

With reverent fingers, I lifted the lid, revealing a mask, exquisitely detailed. Intricate spiderwebs were crafted in lace over delicate flowers with sharp, blood-coated thorns. The instant I touched the mask, the images changed. I saw beasts prowling, barbed vines snaking around the outline of dark eyes.

Then I blinked. Though I'd been sure there was nothing else inside, a gleam of red caught my eye. A ruby.

A *blood* ruby.

How on earth had my mother acquired something like *this*? More importantly, why go to the trouble of concealing it? It was small, but surely it would fetch a considerable price. It made no sense to bury it. *None* of this made any sense.

I reached towards the gemstone, but before I could touch it, the ruby re-formed into something else.

Eyes wide with wonder, I stared at the necklace in the box. *The locket.*

It was gold, the chain thin and delicate, the locket itself round and solid. There was an engraving on the gold: a crown. A wreathed crown.

I clutched the locket in my hand, almost afraid to open it. But when I tried, it remained firmly shut.

After a long hesitation, I reburied the silver box and the mask. But I fastened the locket around my neck, hiding it beneath the bodice of my dress. It felt warm and familiar against my skin, almost like a living thing.

And for a moment, I could have sworn I felt it thump rhythmically in time with my pulse—

Like a second heartbeat.

That night, my dreams were filled with horrors.

I saw Lillian's terrified face, her skin leached of warmth and colour. I reached for her, but her hands were wet and slippery, difficult to grasp. And when I pulled away, I realised that my palms were stained red with her blood.

Then I was looking at my mother, who was dancing in a beautiful ballroom. She resembled a queen, with a diadem in her hair and a shimmering gown that transitioned from white to blue, like rippling ice. But when she smiled, my eyes went to the necklace around her throat. The one with the wreathed crown.

Other images assaulted my senses. I dreamt of masks, of blood rubies, of ancient beasts and serpentine sea monsters. I saw so many things, but the moment I glimpsed them, they slipped from my memory like water slipping through my fingers.

Even now, hours later, the dreams bothered me. They felt ominous, like a warning. But a warning of what?

Striding through the cavernous red and white expanse of the main circus tent, I searched for my mother. She was usually entertaining on the raised platform, but tonight Verex had captured the crowd's attention. His vivacious assistant Yasmine was tied to a spinning target, a succession of knives already outlining her body – with one noticeable exception. People gasped as Verex lined up his final throw, the blade missing her left ear by an inch.

Though impressive, it was an act I'd seen dozens of times before. But as I started to turn, I saw my mother.

She glided onto centre stage, impossible to miss in her bejewelled dancer's costume. The audience clapped as musicians struck up a lively tune, Verex and Yasmine taking their final bows before disappearing down the side steps.

My mother twirled around the platform, so quickly and fluidly that for a few delirious seconds, she transformed into colour and shadow. She spun, effortlessly in time with the wild beat, throwing the audience a smile that they ate up. It was a smile I recognised: beautiful, entrancing, with nothing real behind it. It was the smile she wore when she was pretending.

My hand dropped to the locket I wore. I'd always assumed the criminals we were running from were the enemy, that my mother was the innocent one in all of this. Now, I was forced to reconsider. What else was Celeste hiding? And what had she done that was terrible enough to result in a lifetime of running, for the both of us?

Turning resolutely away from the stage, I strode through the ring of circus tents without looking back. The Choosing Ceremony was tomorrow, and if I'd had any lingering doubts, they were gone now.

Dangerous or not, the Trials were my ticket to freedom – to a life that no one, not even my mother, could control.

CHAPTER ELEVEN

Scarlett

My hand hovered above the golden handle.

Every time I came here, I found myself frozen with indecision. Battling the urge to walk away – while I still could.

But it was too late for that. To claim real power, I would have to take it. By any means necessary.

I turned the handle.

The workroom beyond was a mess. Jars and vials were spread across the benches, filled with murky liquids, lumps of human flesh and misshapen organs. I shuddered as I passed a string of human teeth suspended inside a wine decanter. Probably a potion of some kind.

Zandri turned at my approach, fixing me with her tar-black eyes. 'You've been neglecting your studies.'

There was no good answer to that, so I said nothing. My mother enjoyed experimenting with the limits of her power; it was the reason she spent so much of her time in this austere tower, where she wouldn't be interrupted by visitors or servants. To her great displeasure, I didn't share the same fascination.

'What are you working on?' I asked, peering over her shoulder.

Almost immediately, I wished I hadn't. A raven was laid out on the table, and it wasn't moving.

I must not have concealed my distaste fast enough, because Zandri's thin red lips pursed in displeasure.

'Come here,' she instructed, beckoning with a slender, impatient hand.

I hesitated when I saw the ceremonial dagger, silver and sharp, dangling from her fingers. 'I didn't come here for magic lessons.'

'No,' Zandri agreed. 'You came here because you ran out of options.'

'Well, I'm here now,' I said, refusing to grovel. 'I need your help to deal with Roran – and Governor Halvor.'

Zandri's eyes flicked towards the ceiling, as if she were praying for patience. 'Roran is hardly your most pressing concern.'

'Roran is the crown prince. With him gone and Cassius sidelined, I would become my father's heir—'

'After all this time, you don't know your father at all. Even if you weren't engaged to the governor, Kalias would shackle you to another man of his choosing, and that man would be his successor. You would find yourself as trapped as you are now – and *I* would find myself with yet another mess to deal with.'

The harshness of her words hit me like a slap. As did the truth of them.

I felt the weight of my mother's stare on me, but I didn't meet it. There were two things Zandri couldn't tolerate: stupidity and naivety, and I had been guilty of both.

'The only way you will ever have true power, Scarlett,' she continued, 'is if your father dies. Then, during the mourning period, we can turn our attention to Roran and Cassius. Not to mention all the tedious political manoeuvring it will take to win over the court.'

I swallowed. Zandri had never stated her intentions quite so baldly before, and they gave me pause. But wasn't that the reason I had come to her, knowing what Zandri had done to her own family? So that she would give me permission to make an equally monstrous choice?

I allowed myself one final hesitation. If I agreed to this, there would be no turning back. Either the emperor would die – or we would.

But the guilt I was expecting didn't come.

'What's your plan?'

Zandri smiled – the thin-lipped smile that had terrified me as a child. 'The blood oath Kalias forced me to swear prevents me from killing him, or forcing someone to do it on my behalf. But now that Severin has ingratiated himself with your father, Kalias is vulnerable.'

Only years of practice kept my expression unreadable. If he even *suspected* Severin was plotting against him . . .

'My father has ways of ensuring Severin's loyalty—'

'—and I have mine,' Zandri finished. 'Regardless, we can't act until he Sees a future in which Kalias will fall. But when he does . . . there will be someone who can commit the murder in my stead. Perhaps even you.' Her dark eyes glittered as she studied me, then the lifeless bird lying on the table.

Before I could protest, the tip of Zandri's dagger pierced my palm. I winced as a drop of blood fell onto the bird's plumage.

My pulse faltered as the raven's heart began to beat once more, its wings flapping against the bench. Though I'd seen this done previously – mostly on rats and mice – there was something mesmerising about the way the bird fixed me with its intelligent black eyes.

'It's beautiful,' I whispered.

'It is,' Zandri agreed, but she wasn't looking at the raven. She was looking at my hand, where blood welled against my pale skin.

I followed her gaze down to the droplets of red. Blood magic was powerful – powerful enough to have allowed Zandri to create the Ravalian Orders. But I preferred the illusion magic I'd been born with – which wasn't associated with unpleasant memories.

As if she was thinking along similar lines, Zandri murmured, 'Blood magic requires sacrifice.'

I smiled mirthlessly at the thought. Deep in my bones, I knew what I had sacrificed to access this power. I had sacrificed the most precious thing of all: my life.

What are we? I wanted to ask the bird. *Are we real, or are we artifice?*

But, of course, it didn't have the answer. Neither of us did.

'Severin brought some useful information back from his travels,' Zandri said suddenly, and I looked up, the raven momentarily forgotten. 'I will be leaving tonight for the Elusive Isles.'

'What's so important that you have to go in person?'

'Let me worry about that.' Zandri's eyes gleamed. 'You just focus on the governor. In my absence, I'm trusting you to deal with him.'

I didn't like the idea of murdering Governor Halvor, but I knew better than to say so. Zandri would see it as a weakness – and, in the Ravalian Court, any weakness was quickly exploited.

Thankfully, Zandri seemed to take my silence as assent. 'Would you like me to summon an attendant?'

Ravalian attendants were talented in all manner of skills. Their abilities in beautifying were close to magical, but I had no desire to be around strangers right now.

'No. You can do it.'

My mother smiled, a self-satisfied smile that I ignored. Climbing the stairs to her personal chambers, I took a seat in front of the vanity mirror. With her reflection so close to mine, the similarities between us were obvious – we had the same angular features, high cheekbones and proud faces. But while she had inherited the Sorceress's dark hair and eyes, the emperor was present in my red hair and lighter skin. However slight, I knew those differences were just another disappointment to Zandri.

But tonight, she seemed determined to play the supportive mother. I was surprised at how comforting it felt for her to take over Aella's usual role, sweeping bronze powder over my skin and rubbing rouge into my cheeks.

'The perfect consort,' Zandri pronounced with an ironic smile, her clever fingers arranging my hair around a silver diadem. 'I'm sure the governor will agree.' Dark, assessing eyes met mine in the mirror.

And I realised that my earlier hesitation hadn't gone unnoticed at all.

'He won't be a problem,' I said stiffly.

Zandri reached up, pinning the last of my hair. As she did, her sharp nails bit into my skin, just hard enough to be uncomfortable.

'I'm sure he won't.'

CHAPTER TWELVE

Scarlett

Applause echoed through the banquet hall like a rumble of thunder.

Hundreds of eyes shifted to me in the wake of Emperor Kalias's announcement – and I tensed as the court raised their goblets, toasting my betrothal to Governor Halvor.

I wrenched my hand from the governor's, but the damage was done. Down the long table, Severin's face was resolutely averted from mine, and I could only imagine what he was thinking. In contrast, the empress looked positively delighted. No doubt she would be counting the hours until I was shipped off to Kalure.

The emperor sat and I followed suit along with everyone else, sweeping the silken train of my blush-coloured gown to one side.

Blood red would be more appropriate, I thought. *Or mourning black.*

But black would come later, once the governor was dead. Tonight, I wanted him to underestimate me – and what better way than by playing up my femininity? It was all the people in this hall seemed to notice.

Ignoring their furtive glances, I tried to focus on the meal. The succulent smell of roast boar – freshly caught on my father's hunt – made my mouth water. It was displayed proudly in the centre of the main table, servants slicing portions and delivering them on silver platters. I piled my plate with roast vegetables and thick bread dripping with gravy, but it was difficult to savour the food; I was seated next to Roran, and his amused expression was seriously testing my patience.

'I know you're involved in this somehow,' I murmured between bites. 'What, didn't have the balls to try to kill me a second time?'

'Why would I bother?' Roran asked idly, swirling his wine glass. 'I have all the power here. You're nothing to me – hardly worth exterminating.'

'Yet you tried in Kalure.'

'That was just entertainment.' A condescending smile curved his lips. 'But I'm pleased you survived. It was worth it just for this – to watch you sold like a prize sow to advance Father's interests. The only surprise is how long it took to marry you off. He must not have had many offers.'

Roran turned his back on me like it was nothing. Like *I* was nothing.

I stared at the back of his head, wishing I could shatter his skull. Wishing I had an outlet for the wrath building inside me.

Instead, I took a sip from a heavy golden goblet. The cider left a bitter taste in my mouth as Severin avoided my gaze.

Did he blame me for not saying something sooner? For allowing him to find out like this?

He probably did, but there was no way for me to fix it. Not now, with so many people watching.

And it won't matter, I told myself firmly. *I'll deal with the governor, and things can go back to the way they were.*

'You've barely touched your food.' Governor Halvor's deep voice interrupted my thoughts.

'I don't have much of an appetite,' I retorted, and his shoulders stiffened. Not for the first time, I wondered what he thought about our impending marriage. Was the prospect as distasteful to him as it was to me?

'I need some air,' I said, standing.

'I'll accompany you,' he replied smoothly.

'It's really not necessary—'

'I insist.'

Any more protests would cause a scene, so I reluctantly took his arm. Together, we descended the dais and made our way towards the external doors.

The paved courtyard beyond appeared deserted. I took no enjoyment in being alone with the governor, but the silence and cool air were a relief. Above us, the stars were out, bright pinpricks of lights dotting the sky.

'I didn't need a chaperone,' I said, slipping my arm from his.

'And how would it have looked, if you had left without me?' he asked. 'I know you're not pleased with this arrangement, but that doesn't mean we need to be at odds.'

I walked away without answering. When he followed, my hand went to the silver dagger concealed in my gown. Could I do it now? Stab him through the throat and scream for the guards?

It wasn't the way I'd intended to do it, but with a single brush of my skin, I could make the guards believe they saw the killer fleeing the scene. Any suspicion would be removed from me, and the governor would be unable to bother me again.

Such a tidy thing, plotting murder. Except there was nothing tidy about the actual *act*.

'As my wife,' the governor continued gently, 'you will be protected. I will keep you safe, and I won't be cruel to you. Does that sound so terrible?'

Yes.

'No,' I murmured, my hold tightening on the dagger. 'No, it doesn't sound so terrible.'

His voice softened further. 'Perhaps it's too much to wish for your happiness, but I believe you could grow to like Kalure. You would be free to do as you wish there, without needing to worry about your father or brothers.'

He was insightful enough to grasp the dangers of court politics, then. But how little he understood *me*. I didn't want a peaceful life as a kept woman. I was too much of my father to be satisfied with anything less than a full victory, and what he proposed would take me right out of the game.

Do it now, I ordered myself. *Do it!*

But the way he looked at me . . . the kindness in his eyes—

'I don't need you to protect me,' I told him. 'I don't need *anyone* to protect me.'

'Then what do you need?' the governor asked softly, still so close. *Too* close.

How easy it would be. His face was inches from mine; if I kissed him, would he even feel the sting of my blade? It would be quick, so very quick, and he would be gone. It wouldn't be painful. It wouldn't be painful at all . . .

'Right now, all I need from you *is to be left alone.*' My tone was filled with enough warning to make him step back. The governor studied me for a moment, nodded sharply, and then left.

'That was harsh,' a familiar voice drawled. 'Even for you.'

I stiffened, slipping the weapon back into the folds of my dress. My eyes searched the gloom before settling on the speaker: a golden-haired figure leaning against the far wall, his high-collared silver tunic reflecting the distant torchlight.

'You've been spying on me,' I accused as my younger brother sauntered closer.

'*Spying* is a strong word. I've merely been observing.' Cassius's dark blue eyes lingered on my throat, and I realised I was still wearing Severin's gift. 'Nice necklace.'

My heart stuttered. Cassius couldn't know that Severin had given it to me – could he?

'There's no need to be so tense,' he commented, watching me with amusement. 'We have something in common, after all.'

'And what's that?'

'We both came here to escape our fiancés.'

Cassius sounded sincere, but that meant nothing: he wore emotions like masks, discarding one and easily replacing it with another. Everything about him was calculated, and he was never more dangerous than when he was being pleasant.

Not that he had ever tried to physically harm me. Cassius wasn't Roran, and though our relationship had grown tense in recent years, a part of me would always care about him. Even when I'd realised I would need to deal with Roran – in a very permanent way – I'd known I wasn't willing to do the same with Cassius. For Cassius, I was willing to negotiate. To come up with a deal that suited us both.

Which didn't mean that I could trust him.

'I should get back to the party,' I said, unwilling to become caught up in his games. 'I've stayed away too long as it is.'

Cassius's lips quirked upwards. 'Do you always do what people expect of you, Sister?'

'If you saw me with the governor,' I retorted, 'then you know I don't.'

'Shall I tell you what I saw?' His carefree facade disappeared, replaced by a charged intensity. 'I saw a girl following her mother's instructions blindly. I saw someone so desperate to be free that she was contemplating murder.'

'You don't know what you're talking about.'

'I know how Zandri thinks. And I know how *you* think.' Cassius tilted his head, a lock of blond hair falling across his angular face. 'But you couldn't do it. In the end, you hesitated. Why is that?'

I said nothing, but he was undeterred by my silence.

'A dagger is such a close-range weapon,' he continued contemplatively. 'You have to really *mean* it. Your problem, Scarlett, is that you don't hate the governor. You need him out of the way, but there's a world of difference between wanting someone gone and actually stabbing them.'

'And your point is . . . ?'

'Your mother overestimated you. If you want your fiancé dead, you need distance.' Cassius considered me for another long moment. 'Try Madam Mandrakes in the Lower Districts. It'll have what you need.'

I stared at him. 'Why would you tell me that?'

His laugh was low and deep. 'Let's just say, I'm curious to discover exactly what you're capable of.'

CHAPTER THIRTEEN

Mira

The town square was packed with people, but they were unnaturally still. Even the children who looked on with eager eyes – too young to Choose – were respectful and quiet. There was no trading or jostling today.

Celeste wasn't in the crowd. She was back at the circus, packing up our things. 'Say your goodbyes quickly,' she'd told me. 'We leave tonight.'

I felt shaky with nerves, my palms sweaty. Now that I was here, I wasn't sure whether I was making the right decision. If I went through with this, would my mother ever forgive me? But if I backed down, I wouldn't get another chance. The whole point of the Trials was to choose candidates worthy of being gifted magic – and only eighteen-year-olds were deemed malleable and strong enough to receive powers during Initiation.

'Have you seen Aric?' Lillian called, pushing her way through the mass of people.

I shook my head. 'I haven't seen him since the royal reception.'

She nodded distractedly, her eyes on the stage in front of us. Then her gaze fixed on me. 'Are you going to do it?'

I was saved from answering by the sound of hoofbeats. The royal representatives were impossible to miss as they rode into view, their fair hair streaming behind them. Three wore black armour, marking them as members of the Order of Warriors. They sat astride jet-black stallions – beautiful beasts, trotting in uniform, precise lines. Legend had it they were originally racing horses from the Western Lands. When the Zigilian queen had visited Ravalia, long ago, she had given the royal family one of her prized breeding stallions as a gift.

A large crimson coach glided behind the Zigilian stallions, and I caught a glimpse of two guards sitting beside the driver. Whoever was inside must be important. They were definitely from one of the Orders – but which?

When the horses reached the stage in the centre of the square, a heavyset man at the front of the procession dismounted. He removed his helmet, displaying a strong face with a square jaw and a battle scar through his right eyebrow, giving the impression of a permanent frown.

'Islanders,' General Tiran called, his voice projecting effortlessly over the hushed crowd, 'today is a day of celebration. Today, your children will choose to compete in the Trials. For the lucky few accepted into an Order, a life of privilege and glory awaits.'

His words might have been inspirational, if it wasn't for the flat, bored tone he delivered them in – and their similarity to his speech the year before. I wondered if General Tiran resented this assignment. Perhaps he felt his time would be better spent elsewhere.

The coach rolled to a stop next to the stage, and a woman stepped out. Even from a distance, she was intimidating. Her ebony hair was cut short, accentuating her olive skin and cool dark eyes. Everything about her was sharp and precise, from the form-fitting leather she wore to the red torque glinting at her throat. But what captured my attention was the mask covering the top half of her face, glittering like obsidian.

'What's someone from the Order of Masks doing here?' I whispered to Lillian. In all the Choosing Ceremonies I had attended, no one had ever announced their candidacy for the Masks.

Lillian didn't reply; I wasn't sure if she even heard. She was scanning the crowd for Aric, her entire body tense.

Behind the mask, the woman's black eyes locked with mine – as if she somehow knew I was focused on her.

I immediately dropped my gaze, glancing back at General Tiran, who was inviting the male candidates forward.

Unsurprisingly, Nikolas was first in line. He walked with confidence, the kind of confidence that came from having everything handed to you your whole life, and even I had to admit he looked the part. The Warriors took note as he passed, giving him considering glances.

But their reaction was nothing compared to the awed murmur for Nikolas's friend Brutus. In a show of favouritism, his father was even in attendance today – the senior Warrior standing at General Tiran's right-hand side. He clapped his son proudly on the back as he passed.

I felt sick as I took in Brutus's height and powerful build. As the child of an Order member, he was guaranteed admittance into the Trials, and was almost certain to join the Order of Warriors. I had no such guarantee: if General Tiran deemed me unsuitable, he could deny me the opportunity to compete. It would be the ultimate humiliation – to fail before I even had the chance to *try*.

Lillian squeezed my hand tightly as Aric strode towards the stage. With his focused expression and set shoulders corded with muscle, he resembled a Warrior already. The general studied him appraisingly, as if he thought the same.

But I didn't think General Tiran caught the hard glint in Aric's eyes as his gaze locked, just for a second, with mine. If he had, it might have unsettled him as much as it did me. It might have been enough to give him pause.

Because there was nothing more dangerous than a young man – a *Warrior* – who believed he had nothing left to lose.

'And now, for the female candidates.'

No one came forward. No one spoke.

Lillian's nails dug into my arm, hard enough to draw blood. For a moment, it felt like everyone was holding their breath.

'If that's it,' General Tiran said impatiently, 'then we will progress to—'

'Wait.'

A second after the word left my lips, I realised I was the one who had spoken.

The people nearest to me backed away, others craning their necks to peer in my direction. I left Lillian and climbed the steps to the raised platform, keeping my head held high. I wanted the general to think of me as someone like Aric: confident and capable. But I couldn't have felt more terrified.

General Tiran's pewter eyes were impassive, but I could see the surprise on his face. 'And you are . . . ?'

'Mira Tundra, sir,' I answered, swallowing.

Everyone was staring. All the candidates, the Warriors, the crowd. Even the masked woman from the coach, whose bottomless eyes bored into mine like she was searching for something.

'Mira Tundra,' the general repeated slowly. 'I assume you're competing for a position within the Order of Artisans?'

I shook my head. My gaze found Aric's, who was watching me steadily. He nodded encouragement.

'No,' I said, but my voice was too soft. The general leant in, trying to hear me. 'No,' I said more loudly. 'I'm competing for the Order of Warriors.'

The general's heavy gaze turned calculating. I knew what he saw — what they all saw. A young woman, slight for her age, blessed with a handful of pretty features and wearing a homespun dress. Even if I'd announced I wanted to be an Artisan, they might have been sceptical. But one of the empire's legendary five hundred Warriors? That just seemed absurd.

General Tiran hesitated. 'The Order of Warriors,' he repeated.

A smattering of laughter rang out in the audience. On the other side of the stage, Nikolas was openly smirking.

'That's right,' I said firmly. 'I want to be a Warrior.'

The general considered me for another moment before jerking his hand towards the others. 'Go on, then,' he said, and in a lower voice: 'I hope you know what you're doing, girl.'

As I crossed the stage to stand with my competition – all bigger and stronger than I was – I hoped so too.

General Tiran gave us the night, to say our goodbyes. Tomorrow morning, we would leave for Ravalia.

Aric was hugging his sister tightly, his eyes closed as he leant into the embrace. His mother was crying, tears streaming down her face.

I wanted to join them, but it wasn't the time. As much as they cared about me, their attention was on Aric now. As it should be.

I wove through the square, my sense of dread increasing with every step. I didn't regret keeping my plans from my mother – not really. She wouldn't have let me announce my candidacy if I'd told her what I was going to do. But I knew this was going to hurt her, and I wasn't sure if our relationship would ever be the same.

'That was a brave thing you did.'

I turned to see the masked woman from earlier, observing me with those unnatural black eyes. I'd never seen eyes that dark, and they gave me a chill. *Like they suck in all the light.*

'I didn't do it to be brave. I did it because I know I can become a Warrior.'

'I don't doubt it,' she said after a pause, considering me intently. It was the same expression she'd worn when our eyes had locked in the crowd, and it was no less disconcerting for the second time.

'Well,' I said, suddenly uneasy, 'I'd better get back. My mother will be wondering where I am.'

'I'll walk with you,' the woman replied, motioning two Warriors forward with a careless hand.

Unable to think of a polite way to decline the offer, I said nothing. We started walking, her guards flanking us at a polite distance.

'You remind me of someone,' she commented, 'but I can't place who it is. I don't usually have much cause to come to the Elusive Isles. Is your mother from Ravalia?'

'No.' I was careful to keep my expression bland, but my pulse sped up, the question sending warning bells ringing in my mind.

You're being paranoid, I told myself. *What are the chances she's ever met my mother? And even if she has, she's clearly no criminal.*

I studied the woman carefully as we made our way through the cobblestone streets. Her fitted black combat clothes drew my interest: they were made of a strange material that gleamed like scales. Feathers extended from her shoulders, giving her an avian appearance.

'Are you a Warrior, too?'

The woman smiled, just the thinnest tilt of her red lips. 'Not in the way you mean.'

She seemed content to let the silence linger. I tried to do the same, but my curiosity was overpowering.

'What's your name?'

'Names are powerful things,' she said. Her stare lingered so long that I began to think she wasn't going to answer at all. Then she told me carefully, 'Zandri is the name I use.'

I puzzled over the strangeness of her words. *Zandri is the name I use.* Not *Zandri is my name.* The distinction suggested that those two things were different, and I couldn't understand why they would be. But she didn't explain further.

Her sharp eyes remained on me as we walked through the ring of tents, and I cursed my bad luck. No one had ever shown much interest in me before, especially not someone so obviously important, and far from being flattered, I was starting to feel panicked. Where could I take her? Should I try to lose her amongst the tents?

But no – that would be foolish. There was no point drawing unnecessary attention and damaging my chances in the Trials. Not when I didn't know if there was any danger.

'I'm good from here,' I said when we reached the main tent, hoping Zandri would take the hint and leave.

Instead, she addressed her guards. 'Stay here,' she instructed, and followed me inside.

Celeste was sitting at one of the far stalls, closest to the raised stage. She set down a stack of cards and smiled at my arrival. That smile disappeared the moment she noticed Zandri, who studied my mother with a sharp sort of intensity that put me on edge. My mother, whose face was suddenly bloodless and afraid.

'Adalyn.' Zandri's lips curved into a slow smile, but it wasn't a kind smile. 'How unexpected, seeing you again.'

She stepped closer, her next words stopping my heart—

'Seeing you *alive.*'

CHAPTER FOURTEEN

Mira

'I barely believed it,' Zandri continued, her attention fixed on my mother, 'when my Artisan reported a sighting of you. After you set the palace ablaze, no one could be certain whether you were dead or alive.'

It was the casual tone of her voice that really shocked me, as if arson was the least of Celeste's – *Adalyn's* – offences. It was the way my mother's expression suddenly transformed, turning cool and resolute.

'I did what I had to,' she replied evenly.

'And the bodies left behind in the ruins? Were those necessary, too?'

'I thought you'd approve,' Celeste said harshly. 'Since when do *you* care about collateral damage?'

Zandri opened her mouth to reply, but I broke in before she could. 'You killed someone?'

Even as I said it, I realised that wasn't quite right. Zandri had said *bodies*. My mother had killed more than one person. But I didn't correct myself. I couldn't.

Celeste's face shuttered so fully that I couldn't read her feelings at all. She looked away and didn't reply.

Zandri tilted her head as she observed me, her dark eyes filled with punishing intensity. 'What about the girl? How much does she know?'

'Nothing,' Celeste said quickly. 'I told her nothing.'

'That makes this easier, I suppose.' Zandri's hand drifted down to the ornate silver dagger resting on her hip. 'I think you know what happens next.'

My mother nodded, but she clutched one of Verex's throwing knives in a white-knuckled hand – like she was planning to use it as a weapon. Zandri must have thought so too, because her expression darkened.

'You've never struck me as a fool,' Zandri said with lethal softness. 'It would be a shame if you forced me to reconsider that assumption now. There's only one way this ends.'

My mother's eyes darted from Zandri to me and back again. I stepped forward, preparing to stand and fight at her side. But at my movement, she relaxed her grip on the weapon and sagged in defeat.

'Good.' Zandri relaxed too. 'Now, I think it best—'

Something streaked through the air from behind me. Zandri threw up an arm and a knife sliced into her skin, blood welling in its wake. She blinked at the wound, like she'd forgotten she could bleed. Then she turned slowly, her bearing filled with menace. The red torque at her throat gleamed with bloody inner fire.

'Attack me again,' she said slowly, 'and it will be the last thing you ever do.'

Fear surged through me. Not just for myself or my mother – but for Verex, who had come to our defence. The large, imposing man was armed with a handful of his throwing knives. I knew he was lethal; I'd seen his unnerving accuracy during performances. But this time, I wasn't sure accuracy would be enough.

'You won't be taking them,' Verex said in his low, rumbling voice. He twirled another a knife against his palm – a threat and a promise.

'Last chance,' Zandri warned.

Verex's gaze took in my mother, her hand curled tightly around the weapon. Then he looked at me. The fear in my face only seemed to feed his conviction.

He aimed the knife, sending it careening through the air. I watched in desperate, breathless hope, waiting for it to slam into the raven-haired woman.

But Zandri moved with inhuman speed, dodging the knife and catching it in a single, lithe movement. She glanced at the weapon, then at Verex. He paused, whatever he saw in her expression rooting him to the spot. Then he took a step back—

His own blade struck him in the throat, sending a spray of blood through the air. Verex crumbled to the ground and Zandri strode over, calmly retrieving the knife from his neck. Arterial blood spurted over her black leather, but she didn't seem to notice. She raised her head, the dagger dripping red onto the grass.

'I can do this all day,' she announced – and, as if to prove her point, flung the knife in the direction of the stage.

I flinched as it thudded into the centre of the target. The cruelty of the gesture was what struck me, because that target had been Verex's. Just like that knife had been Verex's, the one she had used to—

'You murdered him.' Just like that, I was propelled into action. I didn't have a weapon in my hand, but in that moment, it didn't even matter.

'Mira,' Celeste said sharply.

I ignored my mother, focused on Zandri. I wasn't sure what I expected her to say. Maybe that she'd tried to warn Verex and he hadn't listened. Maybe that he'd thrown the first knife. But all she said was, 'He was in the way.'

The coldness in her voice, the apathy, enraged me. Without thinking, I dived for Verex's body and picked up his discarded knife.

'You're not taking us anywhere,' I told Zandri with false confidence, ignoring the tremble of my hands.

'Mira—'

Whatever my mother was going to say dissolved into choked silence. Zandri hadn't spoken, hadn't so much as moved, but suddenly Celeste was on her knees.

I raced to my mother's side. My mother, who was struggling to form words, blood dribbling from her lips instead—

Like in the Artisan's vision.

Panic constricted my chest as I turned on Zandri, as I shouted, 'Stop it! You're killing her!'

Zandri's inscrutable expression didn't alter. Silhouetted against the red tent, she was a pillar of darkness.

My mother was gasping for breath now, and I had never felt more helpless. Somehow, I managed to climb to my feet. Fury raced through my veins as I faced Zandri, turning my blood molten. Like fire.

Like fire—

And just like that, the tent was alight.

Zandri stumbled back, staring at the flames in astonishment. Black flames.

They were running along my arms, too. I could feel them, but they didn't burn.

All I'd wanted was to stop Zandri. To protect my mother. But now—

'Mira.' Celeste's eyes were riveted on my neck. It took me a second to make sense of her hoarse words, to understand what she was saying: 'The locket. Use the locket.'

I grasped for the locket, expecting it to feel cold beneath my fingers. A pained hiss left my lips; it was as hot as the flames surrounding us.

'Breathe, Mira. Focus.'

Screwing my eyes shut, I sucked in a deep, steadying breath. As I did, the locket began to cool. When I reopened my eyes, the black flames had disappeared – as if they'd never existed.

But as I took in my surroundings, whatever relief I'd felt was extinguished. Because the circus . . . the circus was burning.

'Mira,' Celeste shouted, slashing through the tent with Verex's knife. 'We have to go!'

I didn't hesitate. I climbed out after my mother, and we ran.

Magic. I had just used *magic*.

It seemed impossible. Unbelievable. But there wasn't time to dwell on it now.

My jaw gritted with effort as I fought to keep moving, racing towards the white-washed buildings. Shouts and screams carried to me on a smoke-drenched breeze, and tears welled in my eyes as I thought of the performers. If anything had happened to them—

I risked a glance back over my shoulder, but all I could see was chaos. Destruction.

And something else.

Across the field, Zandri's distant figure was visible. She was standing on the other side of the wall of flame, and I should have felt safe, because surely there was no way Zandri could get to us now.

Instead, I was filled with trepidation. A normal person didn't stand so still, facing the flames without moving. And yet Zandri remained in place, making no attempt to flee. What was she *doing*?

A second later, I had my answer. It came in the form of a huge burst of energy that surged through the field, sweeping aside tents and extinguishing the flames.

Even racing down through the streets, the force was enough to make me stumble. I cried out but managed to keep my footing. Celeste pulled me along, panting with effort. If she was aware of what just happened, she didn't show it. She just picked up her pace, sprinting in the direction of the harbour.

Thankfully, no one seemed to have raised the alarm. My first impression was one of stillness and calm: only a few sailors were present, lingering near the wharf or next to their vessels. I counted a handful of merchant ships and half a dozen fishing boats, bobbing gently on dark water.

'Let me do the talking,' Celeste instructed, already striding forward.

I watched as she spoke to one of the captains. He looked in my direction a few times and finally my mother motioned me over with an impatient hand.

'This is my daughter, Lillian. She's been offered an apprenticeship in the capital.'

The captain ran a sceptical eye over me. 'What kind of apprenticeship is it?'

'Dressmaking,' I replied, playing along. 'The weaver – my

mistress – has a connection in Ravalia. But she wants me to start right away.'

He nodded slowly, the suspicion beginning to clear from his eyes. 'You're leaving it mighty late,' he remarked, looking over at the rapidly darkening horizon. 'It makes more sense to come back tomorrow.'

Celeste shook her head firmly. 'We're in a hurry,' she said, passing him a coin – no, a gold *piece*. I stared at it in shock, wondering where it had come from.

The captain considered the gold, then us. With an ironic smile, he said, 'Far be it for me to turn down paying customers.'

He escorted us down the gangplank and onto one of the merchant ships, its small crew springing into action. It didn't take long for the sailors to unmoor the ship and unfurl its ghostly white sails.

Soon enough, we were sailing out of the sheltered harbour and across the churning sea. I waited, heart in my mouth, for other vessels to try and pursue us. But, somehow, our luck held.

I crossed the deck to where my mother was standing, her expression remote as she gazed over the black water. In the distance, Aldara was little more than a speck of land, and I swallowed past a sudden lump in my throat.

In the morning, Aric and Lillian would wake to find me gone. No goodbye. No explanation. Nothing.

Would they discover the truth – that my mother and I were fugitives? Or would Zandri keep that knowledge to herself?

I hoped she did. I didn't want Aric and Lillian to believe I hadn't trusted them. I knew how deeply that pain could wound.

'I'm sorry for involving you in all of this,' my mother said, and I realised that she'd been watching me closely.

I glanced at the sharp, unsmiling lines of her face. The pleasant-faced performer was gone, if she'd ever really existed.

'I don't even know what to call you,' I said softly, my words almost lost over the groan of the rigging. *I don't even know who you* are.

'Call me Celeste,' she murmured. 'Adalyn is my past. That's all.'

I wished it were that simple. I wished it were *true*. But whatever she'd done, whoever she'd been, today had brought that past to the surface. And I didn't like what it had revealed.

'What exactly are you involved in? Why did Zandri want you so badly?'

My mother didn't respond. I was so angry that I was trembling, but I forced my voice to remain calm. Steady.

'Back at the circus . . . I used magic, didn't I? How?'

'Your emotions summoned the magic inside the blood ruby. There's a reason I kept it hidden from you, Mira; if anyone discovered you had this, you would forfeit your life.' Celeste hesitated. Though she was usually filled with energy, she suddenly seemed exhausted. Drained. 'How did you find it?'

'An Artisan told me something of mine was buried behind our tent.' My voice turned challenging. 'What did he mean? Is the blood ruby mine?'

'No. It belongs to me.' Celeste rubbed her temple, as if fighting back a headache. 'The locket I concealed it in . . . that was always meant to be yours. Your father gave it to me for safekeeping.'

My hand enclosed reverently around the necklace, nestled inside the bodice of my dress.

My father's *necklace.*

'You can have it back one day,' she said, stepping closer. 'But for now, it needs to stay with me.'

Before I could react, her nimble fingers quickly undid the clasp. As she took it, I felt a sense of loss. A lightness and heaviness all at the same time.

'It seems I wasn't the only one keeping secrets,' Celeste said after a marked pause. 'I don't recall you telling me you intended to enter the Trials.'

'And I seem to recall *you* telling me we were running from criminals.'

Her silence was confirmation of the lie. One more to add to a mounting list.

'Once we're safe,' she said, 'I'll tell you everything. But until then, we need to focus on staying alive.'

I inhaled deeply, clinging to patience. 'And where *is* safe? Ravalia?'

'No,' Celeste replied. 'We need to pass through Ravalia to source a larger ship and crew, but I don't intend to remain longer than necessary. Once we're prepared for a long journey, we'll sail around the bottom of the continent and up to the North. To the Wilds of Kalure.'

'*That's* your plan?' I turned to gape at my mother – what little I could see of her face in the darkness. I didn't know which part was more shocking – that she wanted to flee to the Wilds, or the route she intended to take to get there. 'Even if we make it across the Tempest Sea alive, Kalure is occupied by Ravalia. The entire country is a powder keg waiting to explode.'

'That's why we're going to the Wilds.' Celeste smiled faintly. 'You should be excited. I know how much you loved my stories about free magic. If we make it there, you won't need to listen to those stories anymore. You'll be living them.'

'Don't try to make this sound like an adventure,' I said sharply. 'Kalure is dangerous, and I've heard the Warriors talk. Last month, Emperor Kalias sent an entire regiment into those forests.'

'I heard that too,' Celeste replied, irritatingly calm. 'I didn't hear anything about those soldiers returning.'

I stared at her. Just stared. 'You want to risk our lives based on – what? A *hunch?*'

'All rulers love to publicise their victories, Mira, but not their failures.' Celeste's fingers tightened around my father's locket. 'Even with Emperor Kalias's command over the Orders, some places – and magic – are too powerful to be conquered or controlled.'

I wasn't convinced. Surely no one – no *place*, even – could stand against the full might of the Ravalian Empire. And if it could, then it was dangerous in a whole other way.

My doubts must have been obvious, because my mother said, 'We'll be safe in the Wilds, for a little while at least. And if a time comes when we're not . . . well, there are worse places to take a stand. I promise you that.'

The hard note in her voice gave me pause. It scared me in a way that not even Zandri had scared me.

I didn't want to believe that I was on the wrong side of this. I loathed Zandri for what she had done to Verex, but I couldn't forget the accusations she had levelled at my mother.

'She said you burned down a palace,' I muttered, and the unease was clear in my voice. 'She said you killed people.'

Celeste's eyes locked with mine. They were the same eyes I'd stared into all my life, usually filled with compassion and a hint of mischief. Tonight, though, they were hard and cold.

I was looking at a stranger who wore my mother's face.

CHAPTER FIFTEEN

Scarlett

After nightfall, the city was spectacular. Perfumes and spices filled the spring air, while fire braziers illuminated the colourful shops. Everything was chaotic and yet filled with life, in a way the perfect halls of the palace never would be.

But I wasn't interested in the luxuries of the Higher Districts. I was looking for a specific place, the kind that dealt in gold and secrets.

The streets sloped downwards, drawing me closer to the docks. Winding my way through the twisting alleyways, I kept a careful eye on my surroundings. The Lower Districts were filled with brothels, unscrupulous traders and fighting pits. It wasn't the kind of place I could let my guard down.

Passing a collection of dim shopfronts, I paused in front of Madam Mandrakes. The apothecary appeared dark and unwelcoming, sinister even from the outside.

I couldn't believe I was doing this. Was I really going to take *Cassius's* advice?

Then again, I was running out of time and options. If I didn't act soon, I might not get another chance.

And I was curious. Curious enough to allow this to play out – for the moment.

'In the market for something untraceable, dearie?'

I turned quickly, expecting to find a sinister-looking poisoner. Instead, I found a young woman with silvery hair and pale eyes framed by long lashes. Her appearance was disarming, but I knew better than to trust appearances.

'And if I was?' I challenged, rankled by her use of the word *dearie*. 'Would you be open then?'

The vendor followed my gaze to the sign hanging from the door: CLOSED. Her slow smile displayed even white teeth.

'For you, Your Highness,' she said with a slight bow, 'I am always open.'

The title sent a shiver down my spine. I hadn't expected to be recognised, and I couldn't afford for anyone to know about this visit. 'I don't know who you think I am, but—'

'Oh, I think you do. But if you prefer to remain anonymous, that's understandable.' The vendor reached for the door, extending a silver key. 'Most people who visit my shop require discretion.'

I didn't like the idea of relying on anyone's discretion, least of all in a place like this. But I followed the vendor inside.

'So,' she continued, lighting a handful of candles, 'what can I help you with?'

I hesitated, watching her walk over to the selection of plants displayed on the far wall. In the candlelight, her appearance flickered – shifting between a young woman and a crone, her back bowed like an ancient, gnarled tree.

My fingers rose to the blades embedded in my hair, but I didn't draw them.

'I assume you stock poisons?'

'Of course.' Her smile was devious. After slipping on a pair of gloves, she reached for her shears. 'Perhaps you might recognise some.'

The candles barely illuminated the plants in the darkness, but I identified the purple, bell-shaped flowers of deadly nightshade, and the white clusters characteristic of hemlock. There were others that I'd never seen before: exotic plants and strange-coloured liquids whose origins, no matter how intently I studied them, remained a mystery.

'Poisoning is an art,' the vendor continued, 'and one that is often undervalued. But I see that you value it.'

I wouldn't go that far. After surviving multiple attempts on my life, I'd learnt about poisons out of necessity. Zandri had worked with me to develop a tolerance to some of the more common toxins, but that had been the extent of my interest – until now.

'I can certainly appreciate your skill,' I agreed, not wanting to offend the vendor, who was clearly more than she seemed. 'I don't know how I'd fare, working amongst poisons all day. I imagine even the slightest mistake could prove fatal.'

'Rather like surviving the nest of vipers at court,' the vendor returned, wearing a strange smile.

'Yes,' I said slowly. 'I suppose it is.'

Still smiling, the vendor removed her gloves and turned away from me. She rummaged around for a few moments before finding what she was looking for.

'A single drop of this is enough to cause a slow and untraceable death,' she said, passing over a porcelain vial. When I hesitated, she looked amused. 'You're perfectly safe – see, I don't even need my gloves.' I took it warily, allowing our skin to brush as I did. 'And this,' she added, selecting a glass vial that contained amber-coloured liquid, 'is distilled cobra venom. The onset is sudden; the victim will be dead within minutes.'

'How much for both?' I asked, considering the vials.

'Two silver pieces,' she announced. It was a large sum for most vendors in the Lower Districts, but not as much as I'd been expecting her to ask for. Not from a princess.

My body flooded with adrenaline. 'So cheaply priced,' I said, thinking quickly. 'In that case, perhaps I should look around further. Your plants are intriguing – which is the deadliest?'

The vendor looked down at her hands and saw that she was wearing her gloves again. Satisfied her hands were protected, she reached towards a red and white flower. Its green stems crawled along the far wall like vines.

'This one can kill with a single touch,' she told me, her face filled with admiration. 'It's not as quick as the cobra venom; it must enter the bloodstream first, but when it does, it leads to paralysis and then death.'

'Impressive,' I replied, but it was becoming harder to keep the tension from my voice. I reached into my pocket with my gloved hands, selecting two silver pieces. 'Thank you for your assistance. I'll have to come back again soon.'

'Any time,' the vendor said, but her eyes weren't on the silver. They were on my neck – on my pulse.

I took a few shallow breaths, steadying myself against the counter. When I looked up, the vendor only smiled.

'Don't worry,' she said gently. 'I placed a few drops of a fast-acting toxin on the vials of poison; it's virtually painless. He insisted on that.'

'Who did?' I forced out.

'I never asked his name. But I remember him well; he had such vivid, golden hair, the colour of the expensive coins he paid me.'

I bit through my lip, the taste of blood flooding my mouth. Cassius and his schemes. Always one step ahead, wasn't he?

Well, not this time.

I straightened from my position against the counter, and the vendor's eyes widened. I smiled faintly at her shock. I had known this was a possibility ever since Cassius had suggested Madam Mandrakes, and I had come prepared.

I held up my hands: my *gloved* hands. 'I put these on when you turned around, searching for those vials.' I nodded at her hands, which were unprotected and covered with angry-looking blisters.

She cried out and stumbled back, jars and beakers crashing onto the floor. In the glow of the candlelight, her skin had a sickly pallor, her forehead coated with perspiration.

'I imagine you're not feeling so well,' I said conversationally, perching on the edge of the bench.

Terrified realisation lit her eyes. 'But – I was wearing gloves! And when I passed you those vials, your hands were bare—'

'An illusion,' I replied evenly. 'Unfortunately for you, even my brothers don't know the extent of my powers. All it takes is the slightest brush of my skin against another's, and I can make them see whatever I wish.'

She slumped against the counter, her image returning to its true form – the crone I had glimpsed earlier, with a bowed back and thinning silver hair.

I felt no satisfaction at the sight of her contorted face. The vendor had tried to kill me, but I didn't blame her for it: I blamed my brother. Even if Cassius hadn't offered her a substantial bribe, no commoner would dare refuse a royal. Not unless they had a death wish.

'I'm sorry for the choice of poison,' I said, and meant every word. Kneeling at her side, I picked up the vial of distilled snake venom.

Paralysis must have set in; she was immobile, but her rheumy eyes held keen intelligence. If what she'd said was accurate, the plant poison was slower-acting. It was impossible to tell whether she was in pain, but given the choice between a quick death and a slow one, I knew which I'd choose.

I placed the vial of snake venom against her stiff lips. They parted, ever so slightly, her final choice.

A single drop was all it took.

As I watched the vendor's chest go still, I was reminded of what she'd said earlier: *Rather like surviving the nest of vipers at court.*

I collected the two vials and turned to leave, thinking that it was so fitting it was almost poetic.

Snake venom – for a nest of vipers.

My nest of vipers.

CHAPTER SIXTEEN

Scarlett

My first impression of Cassius remained clear to this day – a golden-haired, slender boy, with delicate features and a nervous face.

I had loved Cassius once. Growing up, it had been instinctual to want to protect him, to shield him from the court and its machinations. The emperor had never intended for us to be close, but it was hard not to care about someone you'd shared all your remembered life with. Half-siblings or not, children didn't discriminate with their affections like adults did.

Of course, we were no longer children.

The cracks had been there for a while, but everything had changed a year ago, when I was invited to my first war council. I had expected to have a small role or none at all; it was an honour to be seated next to my father, facing his top generals and advisers. An honour Cassius clearly didn't believe I deserved, his eyes glittering dangerously as he approached the imposing circular table.

'Bring another chair,' he ordered, addressing the servant who was laying out refreshments.

'That won't be necessary.' Emperor Kalias fixed cool grey eyes on his son. 'You were informed that your presence was no longer required.'

'And yet here I am,' Cassius replied, 'willing to take my place at your side. Fulfilling your public promise to give me more responsibility.'

Though his tone was polite, the barb was obvious. I tensed, trying to catch Cassius's eye. He knew the consequences of antagonising our father in public, but perhaps frustration had momentarily over-ridden his good sense.

The emperor's voice was quiet but powerful. 'Responsibility must be earned. All this childish display proves is that you are not worthy of my tutelage, let alone taking over Roran's duties while he's in the Western Lands.' At a gesture from the emperor, two guards hurried over. 'Remove my son and teach him some respect. Just as you would any Warrior in your ranks.'

Cassius was escorted from the room. He walked with his chin held high, refusing to acknowledge our father or the guards' iron grip on his arms. But I knew the humiliation had to sting.

When the meeting ended, Kalias swept out of the room, already in conversation with General Tiran about collecting tithes from the neighbouring farmland around Tanere. His other generals and councillors followed closely, ignoring me as usual.

But nothing could tarnish my good mood. Not as I recalled the way my father had leant in – too low for the rest of the room to hear – and informed me that Kalure would soon be mine.

I was still smiling as I entered my chambers. But the smile fell from my lips as I noticed Cassius standing in the parlour, his back to me. The setting sun filtered in through the windows, gilding his golden hair.

'Are you alright?' I asked, ashamed to realise that I hadn't thought about him at all.

'Today was supposed to be *my* victory; the first step in Father preparing me for a campaign of my own. Except there you were, already clawing your way into his favour. Sitting at his right-hand side.' Cassius's words were sharp – like anger that had hardened into cold steel. 'You must have done something to change his mind. Shall I guess what that was, or would you like to tell me?'

I paused, unsure what to say. How to clear the bitterness from my brother's voice.

I hadn't done anything, but Cassius wouldn't believe that. I knew he was wondering if he had underestimated me, if all along, this had been my plan – to bait him into angering our father and disgracing himself in the process.

'The war council was about Kalure,' I reminded him. 'That's probably why I was chosen to attend. I have a personal connection to the country, and Father needs a new leader to keep the people in line. He promised me as much after the meeting.'

'Your snake of a mother must be thrilled,' Cassius said mirthlessly. 'But I'd be careful, if I were you. Father makes promises all the time, and he doesn't always keep them. At least not in the way people expect him to.'

My teeth ground together, but my irritation was replaced by concern as Cassius turned, affording me a full glimpse of his bloodied face. His right eye was dark with bruising.

'Here,' I said, hurrying to fetch a cloth and wetting it with a pitcher of water. 'Let me—'

Cassius stilled me with a glance. 'I don't need your help. Or your pity.'

'I'm not implying that you do,' I retorted. 'It was an offer to a friend. Nothing more.'

'A friend,' he repeated, his face unreadable.

'That's what we were once,' I said, testing out a tentative smile. 'It's what we can be again. You're my brother, Cassius. I love you.'

'Why should I believe you?' he asked, backing away from me – and the cloth in my hand. As if it was something obscene. Something dangerous. 'You steal our father's attention. You threaten my inheritance. You take everything from me, whether you mean to or not.' He shook his head. 'Even if I did believe you, what does your love matter? What does it get me? *Nothing.*'

I stared at him in disbelief, unable to fully comprehend what I was hearing. 'You can't really think like that.'

'But I do.' His smile was as cold as his eyes. 'So go ahead, Sister. Attend the strategy meetings and prove yourself to our father. Hope for me to continue angering him, to make a fool of myself in front of the court. That's what you want, isn't it? For me to fail? It should be.' Cassius braced his arms against the wall behind me, either side of my shoulders. Caging me in. *'Because my success means your demise.'*

'You're not thinking clearly right now,' I said, trying not to react. That was what he wanted; he was saying those things to get a rise out of me, to hurt me like I had clearly hurt him. He couldn't possibly be *serious*. 'We've spent years looking out for each other. You can't throw away love so easily.'

Cassius's midnight-blue eyes held no trace of softness. Slowly and deliberately, he said, 'I threw it away long ago.'

I shoved him so hard that he tripped on the rug and fell to the floor. Shock tightened his face as my hand dropped to the hilt of my dagger. I could draw it, right now. I could cut him, just like he had cut me.

But I didn't.

I didn't, because I still remembered the little boy who had been afraid of the dark. Who had been scared of his elder brother, just as I was. Who I had held in my arms and promised never to let go.

Abruptly, I stepped back. 'We don't have to be enemies, Cassius. I am not your competition.'

His expression was cold and unyielding as he looked up at me from the floor, his blood dripping steadily to the tiles.

'You will *always* be my competition.'

I thought of that memory now, letting it harden me. Letting it ground me as I approached the grand ballroom.

'Her Imperial Highness, Princess Scarlett Valerian—'

I strode past the herald, drawing the gaze of every noble inside. The ball had already begun; I had deliberately arrived late, just for this moment, for the flicker of surprise in Cassius's eyes as he looked up and saw me.

Cutting across the timber dance floor, I ignored the disapproving stares of the twirling court ladies and their partners. It was harder to ignore the displeasure on my father's face, but tonight, I was more concerned with my brother.

Despite our argument a year ago, and my precautions with the vendor, I hadn't expected Cassius to threaten my life. Perhaps because I had never considered harming *him*.

What a fool I had been.

I approached the refreshment table at the far end of the room and flashed Cassius a barbed smile. 'What, no greeting for your sister?'

He regarded me steadily, and I could almost *see* his calculating mind at work. Sometimes, I thought that was why our father had chosen Roran as his heir: not just because he was the eldest son and the favourite, but because he was easy to understand. Predictable. Cassius was the opposite; his mind didn't work in one way, but dozens.

'Care to dance?' he asked, offering his hand in a gentlemanly fashion.

The boredom on his face would undoubtedly convince the onlookers, but it didn't convince me. I slid my arm through his anyway, letting him lead me beneath the twinkling chandeliers.

'I almost thought you weren't coming,' he said, a probing statement.

'I'm sure,' I replied as we moved onto the dance floor. At Cassius's nod, the musicians shifted to a slow, lilting tune. 'I trust my arrival was a pleasant surprise?'

He spun me expertly, before catching my lower back with his hand. 'Of course.'

How *convincing* he was. If I hadn't known better, I might even have believed him.

We matched each other's steps perfectly; we had practised together endlessly as children, and I knew the way his body moved as intimately as my own. Bitterness rose up inside me at the memories – bitterness and sadness and anger all at once.

'I suppose,' I said finally, 'that I should be thanking you.'

'Thanking me?' Cassius's eyes were wary. 'For what, exactly?'

'For suggesting Madam Mandrakes, of course. It had exactly what I needed – though I wouldn't recommend going there again. I doubt it's operating anymore.'

I had the satisfaction of seeing his unease. *Good.* Let him wonder exactly what I was going to do with those poisons. And what I'd done to the vendor.

But it wasn't enough to watch my brother squirm. I wanted answers, not polite conversation.

'Did you really believe it would be so easy?' I asked, lowering my voice. 'That you could get rid of me by bribing a *merchant?*' When he didn't answer, I let my nails sink into his arm; not enough to leave marks, but enough to make my message perfectly clear. 'If you want me dead, at least have the courage to do it yourself. *Roran* would have.'

Cassius's jaw tightened. 'I'm not Roran.'

'No,' I agreed. 'You're worse.'

As the song drew to a close, I imagined how we must look to our audience. Two loving, elegant siblings, taking a turn across the floor.

But Cassius wasn't an honourable, dashing prince. I wasn't a sweet, toothless princess.

And this was no fairy tale.

It was war.

CHAPTER SEVENTEEN

Mira

We arrived in Blackstone at dawn, a small port used to ship obsidian to the rest of the empire. It was located on the south-western side of the continent, but rather than looking east towards Ravalia, I faced the hot, stinging wind from the Western Lands, imagining the rolling dunes of the Sanguine Desert.

I had liked Zigilia – the dry heat, the colourful people, the vibrancy of the culture. Surely it made more sense to hide there, where we could blend in amongst the crowds. Or, if not Zigilia, somewhere more remote. I had always wanted to meet the shamanic tribes of Etheria, or the seafaring men and women who hailed from the island kingdom of Maesteri.

I glanced back at my mother, intending to say as much, when I noticed her hand resting on her dagger.

'Are they dangerous?' I asked, searching the dark expanse for signs of life. 'The stone people, I mean?'

'Don't call them that,' Celeste said sharply. 'They don't like it. It's a Ravalian term.'

The chastisement stung. *Everyone* called them that; most people, including me, had forgotten they were ever known as Lapians.

As the sky finally began to lighten, I was able to make out more detail. The buildings were crafted from obsidian; they extended into the distance, continuing towards the shadowed shapes of slumbering volcanoes.

'I thought the stone people – I mean, the Lapians,' I corrected, 'lived underground.'

'They did,' Celeste replied without looking at me. She was walking quickly, like she wanted to put as much distance between us and Blackstone as possible. 'Before the invasion, they lived in volcanic caves as part of their culture. Then the emperor instructed them to create Blackstone, and now they spend their lives breaking those same caves apart.'

I felt an uncomfortable pang at her words. I'd known, of course, that the empire was expanding – but that had never seemed like a bad thing to me. Even when I'd seen temples dedicated to the Sorceress torn down in the Western Lands, huge, pillared buildings with windows of coloured glass, I had dismissed it as the price of progress.

But I found myself frowning as I studied the mining settlement around me. The Lapians were undeniably skilled, and Ravalia needed the resources they provided. Still, it was their sacrifice that made all this possible. It should be their choice to make.

For hours, we trudged along the quiet road that followed the coast. It was evenly paved and well-maintained, built by conquering Ravalian soldiers to allow easier access to the West – and avoid the Archasian mountains, which ran like a spine down the middle of the continent, from the frigid North to the hot South.

'Are we close?' I asked, raising a hand to shield my face from the fierce sun. Our surroundings had changed into lush farmland, interspersed with small fishing villages.

'We're nearly at Delistre.' Though Celeste held herself tall, fatigue was obvious in her voice. 'From there, we can take a coach straight to the capital.'

Her words filled me with sudden fear. The closer we came to Ravalia, the closer we came to disaster. To a mad, insane flight to Kalure—

To a desperate gamble that might cost us our lives.

Delistre was a bustling city, filled with life and noise. But it was nothing – absolutely *nothing* – compared to the Ravalian capital of Ravalis.

When the coach cleared the hill between the mountains and ocean, it came into view: an immense, sloping city continuing all the way to the Azure Sea. The Ravalian palace perched over it like a bone-white spectre, its turrets gleaming blood-red in the morning light. It was encircled by acres of manicured gardens and dense forest, where the emperor and his nobles were known to hunt. Reflective white walls barred the palace from the rest of the city, decorated with lion motifs. In the middle of those walls, I caught a glimpse of imposing iron gates.

Outside those gates were the Higher Districts, famed for their markets, open-air gymnasia, communal baths and theatres. The buildings were all remnants of the conquered city of Aqualia and well-maintained, except for the temple, which was little more than a ruin. I wondered what kinds of gods the Aqualians had worshipped, and if anyone still remembered their names.

The Imperial Road travelled from the Crimson Palace down to the docks, cleaving the city into two halves. The arena loomed in the middle, a huge, dark structure made entirely of obsidian. My blood quickened just looking at it, though there was no chance of me competing in the Trials now.

Soon enough, Aric would be seeing the same view. It hurt to think of him competing without me, our lives wrenched unceremoniously apart.

Stepping out of the coach, I stared at everything: the ornate build-ings and bustling streets, the ivory-coloured procession of carriages. Then I noticed the soldiers. They were everywhere, dressed in the same golden armour as the retinue that had visited Aldara, their cloaks matching the turrets of the palace.

Above me, crimson Ravalian banners hung from balconies. A roaring golden lion dominated the top of each banner, with the three Order symbols arranged in a triangular pattern below: a gleaming sword, an ornate black mask and a palm with an eye gazing out of its centre.

No one took any notice of us as we walked; the crowds were thick, filled with people from all corners of the empire, and I started to relax. Surely the heart of Ravalia was the last place Zandri would look for us.

But Celeste's strained face held none of my confidence. Her gaze was focused ahead, to where a handful of soldiers were blocking the route to the docks and checking identification.

We doubled back before they could see us, and I shot my mother a worried glance. What were we going to do *now*?

'I need to find a friend of mine,' Celeste said quietly. 'He may have a way of getting across the Tempest Sea.'

I started forward, eager to discover one more piece of her past. 'Let's go.'

'No.' Celeste grasped my arm. 'If the soldiers have been warned, they will be looking for two people – a mother and daughter. Stay here, and get us a room if I'm not back before sunset.' She motioned toward an inn with a carving of antlers above the door. 'I'll meet you when I can.'

I opened my mouth to protest, but my mother was already gone.

I threw myself into the crowd after her, dodging stalls and people. The mass of bodies blocked my view, and when I next caught sight of my mother, she had reached one of the ivory-lacquered carriages.

Waving down another, I ignored the driver's strange expression when I asked him to follow. I overpaid by at least two coppers, hoping to buy his silence as well. Even with the additional fee, he seemed glad to be rid of me when I disembarked behind Celeste's empty carriage.

It was much quieter here, at the lower end of the Imperial Road. There was no sign of the colourful crowds from earlier, and if there were soldiers, I had yet to spot them. The few people I saw were grimmer, harder, their stares menacing.

When I reached a small square, I knew I was in trouble. Celeste was nowhere in sight, and the last thing I wanted was to look unsure in a place like this. Already, I'd attracted the attention of two people loitering nearby, and neither looked friendly.

One of them, a girl wearing a threadbare dark cloak and a disdainful smile, approached. 'Are you lost? Maybe we can help.'

A boy, probably her brother, sidled up to me until I was pinned in at both sides. He brushed against me, and I grabbed his arm – a second before he could snatch my purse.

'Not so fast,' I said, my grip tightening until he winced. He looked even younger up close, and I abruptly released him. He stumbled back a few steps, rubbing his wrist.

The girl was no longer smiling.

'Go and bother someone else,' I told her, my hand dropping threateningly to the blade on my hip.

But as she glared at me, I tossed a copper to the boy. He caught it reflexively and darted off without a word of thanks, perhaps afraid I'd change my mind.

I followed the only alleyway out of the square, pausing when I noticed a tavern up ahead. I stole a glance inside; it was busy, packed with customers. The kind of place I could find answers, if I dared.

The door opened silently, on well-oiled hinges. I squinted through the smoky air; no one was looking in my direction. They were more interested in drinking their ale, making outrageous jokes, or throwing—

Knives?

For an instant, it was like being back at the circus. I watched as a handsome, one-armed man pulled a long blade from his belt. A woman nearby gasped, but he merely flashed her a smirk and released the knife. It hurtled through the air with impressive speed, hitting the board with a heavy *thunk*. His accuracy was uncanny; he couldn't have glanced at the target for more than a second, and yet it had still sunk into the smallest circle.

'Show-off,' one of his companions shouted good-naturedly, before returning to guzzling his ale.

The dark-haired man merely grinned, and someone else moved up to take his place.

'A little young for this place, aren't you?' I turned to see a brunette woman looking me over curiously.

'I'm trying to find someone. About my height, long auburn hair—'

The brunette held up a hand. 'Honey, the Lower Districts are a big place.' When I opened my mouth to plead my case, the woman sighed. 'Let me give you some advice. The people here aren't exactly the helping sort, and someone like you . . .' her eyes raked over me once more, 'stands out in a crowd. You'd best get going, before you catch the attention of someone you shouldn't.'

'I'm not leaving without answers.'

The woman laughed, but it sounded unkind. 'Have it your way.' She pointed towards the crowded bar. 'Ask for Wyatt. He's the one you're after.' Before I could thank her, she was gone.

I almost lost my nerve when I reached the bar. It reminded me of the small, dingy places the male islanders used to frequent back on Aldara. Places I'd never been welcome.

It was even worse when I claimed an empty bar stool and asked, 'Which of you is Wyatt?'

The chatter died instantly. A large, heavily built bartender turned in my direction.

'I need some information,' I said cautiously, 'and was told you could help.'

'That depends.' When I didn't say anything, he fixed me with a scowl. 'I assume you didn't come here empty-handed.'

I hesitated, then held out the few coins I had left. They rolled invitingly in my open palm.

He drank them in greedily as I continued, 'I'm trying to find someone. My mother. She came this way about half an hour ago; she said she was looking for a friend of hers. Someone who had connections down at the docks.'

The bartender displayed yellowed teeth as he smiled and snatched the coins. 'No one goes lookin' for our sort, sweetness. And the emperor's Warriors pay very well to capture fugitives.' His bloodshot eyes fixed on mine. 'Very well indeed.'

I nodded to the coins, refusing to be cowed. 'That's all I have.'

He didn't look impressed. 'If that's all you've got, then that's all I'm sayin'.'

'But—'

Wyatt nodded at a burly man to my right, who seized my arm in an iron grip.

'Never had much patience for whiny kids,' the bartender said. 'I think I'll give you over to the soldiers myself.'

I struggled, but my captor held firm. All I could think about was my mother, and how she was going to feel when she returned to that inn only to discover I was missing. Was what I'd said to Wyatt enough to get Celeste caught and imprisoned – or worse?

Almost by accident, my eyes locked with the man I'd been watching earlier: the one-armed man who had thrown the knife. He was watching me, too. After a moment, he took a step forward.

'Not so fast,' he said, holding up his hand. There was power even in that simple gesture, as if he was used to being obeyed.

'This isn't your concern, Darius,' the bartender growled.

'Maybe I'm *making* it my concern,' Darius replied with an amused flash of white teeth.

'Think of the profits! The girl—'

'I thought I was clear,' Darius interrupted. 'No turning anyone over to the emperor's justice, regardless of the reward.'

'She's not one of us,' Wyatt continued angrily. 'I'm not about to risk my life by sheltering her here. Are you?'

'I haven't decided that yet. But I'd like to speak to her before I make any permanent decisions.' Darius eyed the bartender. 'Unless you'd rather challenge me for that right?'

Wyatt looked as if that was exactly what he wanted to do, but he said nothing. The man holding me reluctantly released my arm.

Darius didn't seem bothered by the hostile stares levelled in his direction. 'Come on, darlin',' he told me. 'I know somewhere we can talk safely.'

I didn't move. He might have helped me, but if he thought I was naive enough to trust him—

Darius glanced back over his shoulder. A taunting smile curved his mouth. 'Unless you'd rather stay, of course. They did agree to behave, but . . .' He shrugged. 'How much is a promise from a criminal really worth?'

CHAPTER EIGHTEEN

Scarlett

The Ravalian Court was progressive in some ways and utterly stifling in others.

Gazing out over the gardens, I noted the conspicuous absence of noblemen. Instead, court ladies strolled the paths in their gauzy finery, accompanied by liveried servants. Despite my mother's insistence that the Orders be open to men and women alike, ladies of nobility were still forced into traditional roles – while their husbands were free to exercise in the gymnasia, conduct deals in the marketplace, and meet for endless discussions on imperial matters.

No doubt my brothers were amongst them now, honing their bodies and making useful political connections. While *I—*

I was stuck *here.*

'Are you paying attention, Your Highness?'

I glanced at the speaker, a slender older woman with a razor-sharp smile. 'Of course.'

'Then perhaps you can demonstrate for us.'

Hostility seeped from the other ladies as they watched me walk to the front of the room, taking in the outfit I wore – a fitted blouse and split skirt, showcasing my leather pants and knee-high boots. It was my own design, and far more practical than the elaborate Aqualian fashions preferred by the court.

'Straighter, straighter,' Lady Verne instructed as I sank down, swatting the back of my neck with her fan. 'A proper curtsy should be maintained until a person of greater rank gives you leave to stand.'

A few titters came from Odessa and her group of friends, who were watching me disdainfully from behind their fans. Curtsying was straightforward, something they could do perfectly. But they were minor nobles.

I was royal. My body wasn't made for subservience.

I held the pose until I couldn't stand it anymore.

'This is ridiculous,' I said. 'I'm the princess; people bow and curtsy to *me*. This is a waste of my time.'

'It most certainly is not!' Lady Verne sounded personally affronted. 'Everything that you do reflects on this great empire, and His Imperial Majesty personally tasked me with readying you for your upcoming marriage.'

Which wouldn't happen, not if I had anything to do with it. But as tempted as I was to retort, Lady Verne's face was already an alarming shade of red.

'I'll practise more often,' I lied.

'Very well,' she said, decidedly unconvinced. 'Perhaps observing Lady Tiran will help.'

Odessa Tiran was the reason for the dislike emanating from the other girls; her mother was one of Empress Ivalene's ladies and considered my presence at court an insult to her mistress. The legitimisation of a bastard child wasn't unheard of, but it was unusual when the father already had true-born sons. I found it amusing that she disliked me so much, when my mother had gone to great pains to conceal her Kalurian heritage – and mine – from the court. I could only imagine what Ivalene and her ladies would make of that. They seemed to consider Kalure's matriarchal culture a perversion.

While Lady Verne was watching, Odessa's expression was pleasant as she curtsied flawlessly. But the moment the instructor looked elsewhere, Odessa shot me a venomous glare.

'That's enough for today,' Lady Verne said at last, clapping her hands. 'Until next week, ladies.'

We filed out, Odessa and her circle of friends leading the way. None of them so much as glanced at me, but they did stare at the governor, who was already striding towards the ladies' parlour.

'Your Highness,' he said, with a slight dip of his head. 'I was told you might be here.'

'Governor,' I replied. 'I'm afraid I can't stay. I have sparring practice after this.'

'I know. I came to join you.'

'To join me?' I repeated, arching a brow. 'I hadn't expected you to enjoy sword fighting.'

'Because you think me unskilled?'

'Because I remember your distaste of the arena,' I corrected diplomatically, though that wasn't true.

'I dislike unnecessary death,' the governor said as we emerged outside, protected from the sun by an elegant colonnade, 'but that doesn't mean I don't know how to fight. Perhaps we can cross swords together some time.'

'Perhaps we can,' I agreed with a faint smile.

We passed a group of ladies escaping the heat of the afternoon by an ornamental pond. One was reading to the others while a liveried servant fanned her; Governor Halvor smiled in acknowledgement, and she shut the book with a snap, her attention shifting to us. Her friend murmured something, the soft sound of their laughter following us from the courtyard.

'You shouldn't acknowledge them,' I said. 'It lowers you in their eyes.'

The governor glanced at me in surprise. 'I was merely being courteous.'

No – he was being kind. He *was* kind, which made this so much harder.

'They mistake your kindness for weakness,' I told him. 'It's better to keep your distance.'

Governor Halvor considered me thoughtfully. I didn't like the expression on his face – the hint of understanding. As if he believed that comment applied to me, and I had simply learnt to keep my softer side hidden.

Sunlight reflected off the columned facades of the Order residences, the white marble decorated with carvings of their respective symbols. They were grouped closely together, but the largest

structure sprawled in front of the other two: the rectangular residence of the Order of Warriors, its open training courtyard adjacent
to the palace. A few faces watched from the palace windows high
above, but I doubted it was because the ladies had much interest in
sparring or weapons. Their gazes were fixed on the Warriors – many
of whom had discarded the tops of their uniforms under the heat of
the midday sun.

The captain of the royal guard looked up at my arrival. 'Your
Highness,' he said as I crossed the courtyard. 'You're late.'

'Lady Verne kept me longer than expected. And then I came
across the governor.'

His impatience lessened as he took in Governor Halvor, assessing
his solid build and the sword strapped to his hip. When they moved
on to an in-depth discussion of weapons, I unsheathed my own
blade.

The captain didn't expect much from me, so he usually left me
alone to complete various drills. I never minded. Having time to
myself was a welcome reprieve.

Ducking and weaving, I practised a few slashes and parries. The
physical exertion helped clear my head; there was something refresh-
ing about the simplicity of sword fighting, the ease and familiarity of
the motions.

Then I turned – and nearly overbalanced.

Severin was observing me from the shade of a nearby arch, drinking from a waterskin. His bare chest was covered in a thin sheen of
sweat; he'd clearly been working out before I arrived, and I was
disappointed to have missed seeing him in action. But I forced the
thought aside.

'You've been avoiding me.'

'I thought it best,' Severin said, lowering the waterskin.

My hand tightened around the leather hilt of my sword. 'How
easily your feelings change. What happened to your grand proclama-
tions on my birthday?'

'That was before—' Severin broke off, shaking his head. 'You
know it can't be the same. You're to be *married*.'

'I'm not married yet.'

'I'm not sure that makes any difference.'

'Maybe it does.' I cast a wary glance around me, but no one was looking in our direction. 'Meet me tonight. On the southern balcony, the one where—'

The governor strode towards us, his boots kicking up plumes of sand. He took in Severin curiously, but didn't acknowledge the Artisan. 'Shall we?' he asked.

I wordlessly threaded my arm through his. It was difficult not to look back at Severin, but nothing good would come of it if I did. I had already paid him too much attention, and I couldn't afford for the governor to become suspicious.

'I already have a sword,' I said as we approached a rack of weapons mounted on a wooden stand.

'I can see that,' the governor responded mildly, selecting two bows. 'The captain told me of your love of archery; I thought you might prefer to do that instead. Or was he wrong?'

I eyed the bows, itching to hold one. 'He wasn't wrong,' I admitted.

Growing up, I had been on many royal hunts. Determined not to be outdone by my brothers, I'd mastered the skill of archery.

The technique was so familiar to me now that it was instinctual. I shifted to face a target at the far end of the courtyard, nocking and releasing four arrows in rapid succession.

'Expertly done, Princess.' Governor Halvor fired his own arrows confidently, though they hit the target slightly off-centre.

'I could say the same of you,' I replied, feeling inclined to be generous.

The governor studied the ring of arrows within the bullseye. 'It seems you've won.'

'It seems I have,' I said, but I felt no delight at my victory.

Looking across the courtyard, I searched for Severin amongst the Warriors. I'd hoped he might be watching, but his back was turned decisively away from me, his shoulders stiff.

'Shall we retire for afternoon tea?' I asked.

'That sounds delightful,' the governor said, and his tone was so sincere that I believed he meant it.

It really was a pity he had to die.

Alone in Governor Halvor's parlour, I reached for the vial concealed in my skirt and emptied it into his tea.

I twisted my trembling hands in my lap, waiting for the governor to reappear. It wasn't his fault the emperor had decided to make him my husband. He had done nothing except be kind to me, and it was a kindness I would repay with murder.

Filled with restless energy, I stood and started pacing the parlour. He had been given one of the chambers reserved for diplomats, and I supposed it might have been impressive – if I hadn't grown up in the royal suites.

I risked a glance out of the window, where the governor was still speaking with his page. He asked a question and, although I couldn't hear what was being said, it was clear he was agitated. When the page answered, Governor Halvor abruptly turned on his heel and strode away, too quickly to be casual.

I acted immediately, pouring my tea – and the governor's poisoned one – into a nearby flowerpot. Rushing out of the parlour, I almost collided with the page on the stairs.

'Your Highness,' he said with a hasty bow. 'The governor has been called away on urgent business. He asked that I relay his apologies, and his promise to—'

'Of course,' I said distractedly, already brushing past.

As I'd hoped, the governor was still visible. He was walking at a fast pace, casting furtive glances over his shoulder. It was clear that he didn't want to be followed, and that realisation was intriguing enough to propel me through the palace grounds and out the main gates.

Trailing him through the congested streets of the Higher Districts, I used the street vendors and lines of eager customers to mask my presence. I wasn't sure what to expect from the governor, but my interest increased as he drew closer to the harbour.

While there was no rule against visiting the Lower Districts, I had only been there a few times – and never during daylight hours. In the bright light of the afternoon, it seemed shrunken and neglected. Many doors and windows were boarded shut, and scraps of rubbish blew across the cobblestones.

'Lonely, honey?' a woman cooed to the governor, who didn't pause.

I kept my head down, hoping to avoid her notice. The perfumed scent of a brothel wafted to me as I passed.

When I looked up again, the governor had stopped in front of a solid wall. Wondering what on earth he was doing, I took shelter in an alcove and peered around the corner – just as a wooden door materialised.

Magic.

It was rare to see it outside of the three Orders. Even rarer to see it here, in the heart of the empire.

I was tempted to find out what would happen if I approached the wall. Did the enchantment only respond to certain individuals, or was the door simply concealed?

But even if it did work, I knew better than to follow the governor inside. Never was I more aware of my own limitations than at times such as these. If only my illusions weren't limited to touch.

The faint sound of conversation warned me I was no longer alone. I slipped into the shadows of a nearby doorway as two figures stepped into view.

'What is this place, Darius?' It was a girl who spoke, her clear voice filled with curiosity. 'Who were those people?'

'This is what we call the Lower Districts. No city – no matter how beautiful – can exist without its darker underbelly.'

I didn't recognise the man, but it was the girl who caught my attention: her dark hair hanging in loose curls down her back, her olive skin bright and warm. She had dressed to blend in, but she still didn't quite fit – she walked like a fighter, not a lady, and the steely set of her shoulders spoke of determination. Though I was sure I had never seen her before, there was something so *familiar* about her.

Darius raised his fist to knock, and once again the wall transformed into a door. This time a symbol blazed to life, as if burned into the wood: two swords intersecting in an X.

A knock, and it swung open – as if opened by an invisible presence.

'You look like you've never seen magic before,' Darius drawled to the girl, disappearing inside. His voice became distant as he moved further away. 'Keep up, darlin',' he called.

As if she sensed my presence, the girl glanced back over her shoulder. Her gaze swept over the doorway where I watched, still and silent from the shadows. Then, shrugging a little, she followed her companion inside, the door closing behind her.

My curiosity was almost overpowering as I climbed onto the roof of the building opposite, wondering who this mysterious girl could be. And what her connection was to the Governor of Kalure.

CHAPTER NINETEEN

Mira

I paused at the top of the stairs. Battered wooden tables were scattered around the room, hosting a variety of unsavoury-looking people. But it was the sight of my mother that stole the breath from my lungs: laughing with these people, a dagger twirling casually in her fingers.

I pressed closer to the doorway, not ready to be seen. I barely made out her words as she murmured, 'I need to get across the Tempest Sea, today. Do you have access to a ship?'

The man she was speaking to was older – perhaps mid-forties – with dark-blond hair and shrewd grey eyes. Though he was dressed simply, the quality of his clothes hinted at wealth. 'As it happens,' he said, 'my ship is in port. It has enough provisions for a long journey, but I can't risk recalling my crew and making the emperor suspicious. I'll need more men.'

'That can be arranged,' Darius said, entering the room and smiling at my mother. 'Hello, Adalyn.'

'Darius,' she breathed. She threw herself into his embrace, a choked sound leaving her lips.

With shock, I realised that my mother – my unflappable, composed mother – was crying.

'I thought you were dead,' Darius said, and though his voice was muffled, it was thick with emotion. 'For years, I thought—'

'I know what you thought.' Celeste pulled back from him, her eyes bright with tears. 'It's a long story, and one that I want to share with you. But first, I need to save my daughter.'

Darius glanced over to where I was still standing, shock-still, in the doorway. The sudden realisation on his face was somehow worse than amusement or threats. In that moment, he stared at me like I was something unexpected. Something valuable.

Celeste twisted guiltily to face me. 'Mira,' she started, 'I can explain—'

'I understand perfectly,' I said, casting my gaze over the room – and its rough-looking occupants. *Her accomplices.*

Maybe Celeste saw the accusation on my face, because hers twisted in pain.

'I'm not going anywhere with you,' I told her firmly, taking a step back just as she took one towards me.

'You have to,' Celeste said urgently. 'Mira, we need to leave for the docks. We need to leave *now*, before the emperor's Warriors discover we're here. I promise I'll explain everything once we reach open ocean. But please, stay with me until then. Hear me out.'

Some of my anger faded at the pleading tone of her voice. The desperation in her words.

At my hesitant nod, she quickly turned back to Darius. 'Can I count on you?'

Darius didn't hesitate. 'Always.'

My mother smiled, like that was all she needed to hear. Like she trusted this man implicitly.

But I was less convinced. And as I listened to them plan, I was reminded of Darius's earlier words:

How much is a promise from a criminal really worth?

The ship we were going to use was moored at the commercial dock. According to Darius, it was heavily guarded, though nothing like the central harbour that sheltered the Imperial Fleet.

I still thought our chances of success seemed unlikely, but I didn't say so. Instead, I studied my mother as we moved through the Lower Districts, noting how even her walk had changed. She didn't glide along anymore; she strode with purpose, matching the rest of Darius's small entourage.

'I don't believe we've been properly introduced,' said the man who had offered us his ship. 'I'm Governor Halvor, and you must be Kasmira.'

'It's Mira,' I corrected, wondering where he'd gotten Kasmira from. '*Just* Mira.'

'Mira, then,' he agreed, his pleasant smile belying the intensity in his gaze. He studied my face, as if he was examining the shade of my skin, the slope of my eyes, the colour of my lips.

He looked away before I could become too uncomfortable, and suddenly I was the one staring unabashedly at him. Sizing him up.

'Why did you volunteer your ship?' I asked. 'If you're found out—'

'I've worked with the Ravalian resistance before,' Governor Halvor interrupted. 'Not quite as directly as this, but I understand the risk. Like the loyalists in the Wilds, I believe Kalure should be ruled by the Sorceress's descendants – not a tyrant like Emperor Kalias, but someone in tune with nature and magic, who can unite Kalure. Part of that belief involves helping Darius's people survive – smuggling the bravest rebels to the Wilds, where my contacts can shelter them.'

The governor said it as though I should be pleased. As though breaking the law should meet with my approval.

I wondered how he would react if I told him that, up until a day ago, I had wanted to become a Warrior. To protect the empire and safeguard it from exactly the kind of people I now found myself with.

At that moment, a flash of colour caught my eye. It drew my attention up to the rooftops, and I had a glimpse of red – a girl from above, watching me.

'What is it?' The voice belonged to a lithe, dark-haired woman who had introduced herself as Jadis.

I was only distracted for a second, but when I glanced back at the rooftop, the girl was gone.

'I thought I saw . . .' I shook my head, feeling foolish. 'Never mind. It's nothing.'

Jadis didn't look convinced, but she didn't question it. She was one of two guards Darius had assigned to escort us to the docks, while he prepared the ship. Her brother Elian guarded the front of our small group, silent and grim.

Jadis caught me looking. 'He doesn't speak,' she said. 'Not since the Masks got to him a few years back.'

I stared at Elian, wondering what had been done to him. I wanted to say something conciliatory, but he seemed the type to despise sympathy in any form.

We covered a few more blocks without incident. Then we rounded the corner, and I stopped dead in my tracks.

'Wait,' I said urgently. 'That's—'

Wyatt looked up from where he was speaking to some soldiers up ahead, and for an instant, I thought distance might be enough to disguise me. But then the bartender's expression hardened in recognition, and I knew we were out of luck.

Jadis didn't ask questions. 'This way,' she directed, turning down a nearby alleyway.

I ran after her, straining to match her pace. Even as we tore through the streets, I heard the unmistakable sound of pursuit – heavy boots pounding against cobblestones.

Elian must have heard it too. He slowed, nocking an arrow and aiming for the soldiers, while Celeste grasped my hand and pulled me on. People shouted as we pushed roughly past, but we ignored them.

Somehow, we made it to the docks – which were much larger than in Aldara, and heavily patrolled. Warriors and soldiers were everywhere, a glittering sea of black and gold.

My pulse was racing by the time I slowed to a brisk walk. Next to me, my mother's breath was coming in pants.

'Follow me,' Governor Halvor instructed.

As we approached the wharf, I had my first glimpse of his ship: an imposing vessel with *Drakkar* painted on its side and the carved head of a dragon adorning its high prow.

Nearly there. Nearly—

'Stop!' someone shouted. 'Halt in the name of the emperor!'

The sails were already unfurled, Darius and his men working quickly to stow supplies and provisions. We stepped onto the gangplank, single file. The ship loomed just ahead when the first arrow sliced through the air.

I flinched but didn't stop moving. The warning shot soared harmlessly over our heads.

Just a few more minutes—

Another arrow. This one closer.

'Take another step,' the archer warned, 'and my next shot won't miss.'

I glanced back at the docks. We were in the worst position possible: halfway from the soldiers, halfway from safety, and unable to move without risking death.

'On the count of three, you run.' Jadis's voice was soft and certain. She didn't look afraid of those arrows, or the men on the shore. 'There's only one archer. Keep your head down, run as hard as you can, and *get to that boat*. Do you understand?'

'I don't—'

But Jadis wasn't listening. She was murmuring something to two sailors.

'One . . .'

There was only one archer, but he wasn't likely to miss from this distance. If we ran for the ship, how many of us would make it?

'. . . two . . .'

I exchanged a terrified glance with my mother. But Celeste nodded grimly, her lips forming the word: *Run*.

'. . . *three*.'

I ran, keeping my head down. A rebel sailor let out a terrible, gurgling sound as an arrow pierced his throat. Celeste's hand was ripped from mine as a second sailor tried to push past us, only to receive an arrow to the back.

My mother screamed my name, but I couldn't move. I was trapped, the sailors' bodies blocking my only route forward. Twisting towards the docks, I saw the archer take aim, his attention fixed on me.

Just as his arm drew back, preparing to release that final, fatal shot, an authoritative voice cut across the chaos.

'Hold your fire!'

The archer didn't lower his bow. And then the voice shouted something that made no sense, that my shock-numbed mind couldn't process—

'That's the princess!'

CHAPTER TWENTY

Scarlett

I hadn't intended to save Mira's life.

I had a complicated relationship with family, and there was no reason to believe Mira would be any different than Roran or Cassius. But the moment I realised who she was, the moment I understood what we were to each other . . . I hadn't been able to watch her die.

Studying her slack face, I searched for the similarities I knew would be there. They were subtle, since I no longer shared her olive skin – but our pointed chins and almond-shaped eyes were the same. My gaze snagged on a constellation of freckles across her forehead. Such a small thing, but I found it endearing.

The coach went over a bump, and Mira's eyes flew open.

I flinched back in surprise – I had leant further forward than I'd realised – and folded my hands in my lap.

'It's alright,' I said, more gently than I'd intended. 'My name is Scarlett. You have nothing to fear from me.'

Mira jerked upright from a set of plush cushions. Her hazel eyes took in the coach, pausing on the armoured men sitting opposite us.

'What happened?' she choked out, her gaze warily returning to me.

'One of the Warriors used magic to knock you out. I told him it was unnecessary, but . . .' I shrugged. 'Sometimes, they can be a little overzealous. I had him reverse the effects once you were in the coach.'

Mira frowned, tilting her head like she was trying to work

something out. I wondered whether she recognised me from the rooftop, or whether she was simply taking in my unnaturally pale skin. Most people stared at that first.

'Why did you save me?'

'I didn't do it to be kind,' I said, a hint of apology lacing my voice. I paused, irritated by the softness. More firmly, I added, 'I knew the emperor would want to deal with you himself.'

There. A perfectly reasonable explanation, and one I could use on my mother, too – though she might still be furious.

But that was a problem for another time.

'I remember,' Mira said quietly, 'but I don't understand. What you called me . . .'

Hold your fire, I had shouted. *That's the princess!*

I glanced at the Warriors, who could hear every word. This wasn't the time for warmth, misguided or otherwise. And it definitely wasn't the time to discuss our familial connection.

When I turned back to Mira, she was gazing at the circlet I wore – the one marking me as a member of the royal family. I knew she was wondering if we were related, trying to determine if she could be a *Ravalian* princess.

No such luck, I wanted to tell her, but I held my tongue. Mira would learn the truth soon enough.

'When we arrive,' I told her, 'you'll have your answers.'

Since I knew how intimidating I could appear when I wanted to be, I expected Mira to accept this in silence.

Instead, she lifted her chin. 'At least tell me what happened to my mother,' she said – more of a demand than a request. 'I deserve that much.'

That was debatable, but I couldn't see the harm in indulging her.

'She's still alive. You'll have the chance to see her.'

Across from me, the two Warriors exchanged a heavy glance. Mira's sharp eyes caught the movement, her hands balling into fists.

It was suddenly too difficult to look at Mira, so I looked outside instead. People stopped to point as the royal coach passed – emblazoned with an imperial lion, as befitted my station. The crowds thickened as we travelled further into the city, eager to catch a glimpse of the coach and its occupants.

As we continued down the Imperial Road, I noticed Mira's face reflected in the glass. Her eyes were screwed shut, as if she was imagining herself somewhere else. It occurred to me that she must have had a home before this. A home she probably missed.

That brief moment of weakness warmed me to her. The more glimpses of vulnerability I saw, the harder it was to think of Mira as a potential threat. And the harder it would be to watch what came next.

The timing seemed especially cruel when the massive obsidian dome came into view. Though the paved road continued around the arena, the coach slowed to a graceful stop.

I wanted to ask Mira so many things. I was curious about her life, and the freedom she must have experienced before her mother's past caught up with them. But then I thought of the woman beside her on that gangplank. The love and fear and desperation on her face.

At least Mira has a mother who loves her, I thought bitterly, and I had the sudden urge to drag her from the coach myself.

'Time to go,' I announced, turning to one of the Warriors inside the coach. 'You know what to do.'

'Yes, Your Highness.' He picked up a set of manacles beneath the seat.

Mira didn't try to fight him, even as realisation dawned on her paling face. She understood now, why we had stopped at the arena. Why the manacles were necessary. Why she hadn't died in the harbour.

I hadn't saved her at all. I'd only delayed her death—

So she could die alongside her mother.

I turned away from Mira, but not before I saw the condemnation burning in her eyes.

CHAPTER TWENTY-ONE

Mira

For hours, I stared at the door to my cell.

The darkness was so complete that it had started to feel like a living, breathing thing. Aside from Darius, who was in the cell next to mine, I couldn't see the other prisoners clearly. But I could *hear* them: sometimes they screamed, clawing against the walls. Other times, they only groaned.

I closed my eyes, trying to block it out. For a short, wonderful moment – when I'd first woken up in the coach and felt its faint rocking motion – I'd believed that I had made it onto the *Drakkar* after all.

At least until Scarlett had brought me back to reality.

'They're going to execute my mother,' I said, thinking of everything the princess had told me – and everything she hadn't. 'They're going to execute us both, in front of a crowd of witnesses.'

'Yes.' Darius's voice was carefully even. 'I'm sorry.'

I laughed humourlessly. I'd trusted Celeste so much I had almost believed that together, we could do the impossible. But no one escaped the empire's justice. How ironic that it had once been a source of pride to me – even hope. Hope for a better life, free of our pursuers.

Darius stood, facing the bars of his cell. I wondered if he'd been in the emperor's dungeons before. He'd told me that Jadis and Elian had escaped; maybe they could orchestrate a rescue.

But Darius didn't look like he was thinking about plans for escape. His sea-green eyes were fixed on me. 'I loved her. Your mother,' he added. 'Despite everything, I love her still.'

I didn't know what to say to that, so I said nothing. I leant against the bars instead, bowing my head as moisture welled in my eyes. But I didn't feel sad. I felt numb, separate from my body except for the gnawing ache of hunger.

'I met Adalyn when she was a pickpocket in the Lower Districts,' Darius continued. 'She took me under her wing – saved me from starvation, like she'd done for others in her crew. We lived hand to mouth for years, eking out a living through petty crime. It was the closest thing to a family I'd ever experienced.'

Somehow, his words – and the sincerity in them – reached me. This description of my mother made more sense than the callous murderer Zandri had described. 'Do you know why she was on the streets?'

He shrugged. 'Adalyn liked to live in the moment; the past was never her favourite subject.'

Look forward, don't dwell, move on.

'That sounds like her,' I said, overcome by a crippling wave of guilt. If I had continued living by those rules, Zandri never would have followed me to the circus. And maybe . . .

I stopped the thought before it could form. There was no point wishing I had made a different choice. It wouldn't change anything.

'That group my mother started – that became the Ravalian resistance, didn't it?'

Darius smiled a little. A smile that quickly faded. 'Years later, that's what I turned it into.'

There it was again. Pride at standing up to the regime – at spitting in the face of the emperor.

It rankled me. Even now, trapped in a Ravalian dungeon.

'We lived in the Western Lands for a while,' I said suddenly, unable to help myself. 'It was a prosperous place back then, its people mostly peaceful. Then a faction of insurgents gained hold in the countryside and incited the people into violence. A few Warriors told me what the regional towns look like now – thousands of mud-brick buildings reduced to rubble.'

Darius stiffened. 'It's not about inciting violence for us. It's about protecting people – ordinary people – who have no one else to turn to. You've seen the state of the Lower Districts.'

'Surely the emperor—'

'The emperor doesn't care.' The words were flat and cold. 'He knows, but he doesn't care. As for Zigilia – it might have been prosperous on the surface, but many of its people are born with magic. They're stolen from their families, forcibly inducted into the Orders—'

'Where they're given every luxury—'

'Except choice,' Darius finished. 'You don't see it yet, but the empire is corrupt and brutal – a tarnished husk of what it used to be, with the court as its rotten centre. I should know. I have recruits in the Orders – or I did.' Even in the darkness, I saw the way his jaw clenched. 'They only lasted a few months before the crown prince discovered them. They were—'

'Sacrificed,' I said through numb lips, thinking of Kain. 'In battle.'

'Yes.' Darius glanced at me curiously, but I didn't elaborate. Everything I believed was reframing itself into something twisted and awful. 'And now, with me locked up . . . I'm not sure the resistance will survive. Jadis and Elian are tough, but the others are scared. There's been too many defeats recently, and I was hanging on to my leadership by a thread before – well, before all this.' His grip tightened around the bars.

I reached out, offering Darius my hand. He only hesitated for a second before grasping it, his skin warm and calloused around mine.

'What happened?' I asked softly. 'What did my mother do that was so terrible?'

His smile didn't reach his eyes. 'She fell in love.'

I wasn't sure what I'd been expecting, but it wasn't that. I thought of the father I'd never had the chance to know, whose identity had always been kept secret.

Then I thought of my mother's insistence on fleeing to Kalure. The presence of the Kalurian governor.

'He was Kalurian, wasn't he?'

'Yes,' Darius answered. 'His name was Arioch. Adalyn met him when she travelled to Kalure.'

Arioch.

I inhaled sharply. It was a name I'd heard only once before: during my history classes back on Aldara.

It was the name of the Kalurian king.

'The Ravalians assassinated the royal family first,' Darius continued, 'and then sent their ships. Your mother fled with you just before the invasion; she always was remarkably resourceful. Most people believed she was killed in the fire that destroyed the Kalurian palace.'

The roaring in my ears drowned out Darius's words. Of course Zandri had wanted to capture me and my mother. Of course the emperor wanted to make a spectacle of our execution.

I was the princess and rightful heir to the Kalurian throne.

I turned to Darius, intending to question him further, when booted footsteps rang down the hall. I straightened, my muscles protesting after remaining in one position for so long.

'The emperor likes to make an example of anyone who is different,' Darius said quickly, 'and I've been different from birth.' He gestured to his missing arm. 'But this doesn't make me weak; it makes me strong. Just like your Kalurian blood makes you strong.'

I felt the strength of his conviction seep into me. The worst had come to pass, but I wasn't crumbling. And I refused to give them the satisfaction of watching me break.

'Remember, darlin',' Darius said, low and fierce, 'they want a spectacle. So don't give them one.'

I nodded and turned to face the guards. My composure didn't falter as they undid my manacles, the restraints clattering heavily to the floor. It didn't falter as I followed them through the dark corridors, past the endless rows of cells.

Because Darius had given me exactly what I needed – an enemy to fight. He'd reminded me of the girl I had been, the one so determined to survive the Trials. To succeed, even in the face of overwhelming odds.

And as the guards led me up into the searing light, I clung to that conviction like a lifeline.

Whatever happened, I would face my death like a Warrior – like the Warrior I would never have the chance to become.

The roar from the stands was deafening. The Trials hadn't officially begun, but this was the opening show. And the crowd wanted blood.

My mother was already in the staging area, her face pale but calm. She met my eyes steadily, holding her head high. But I could see the faint tremble of fear in her hands.

'Mira, I—'

'I know,' I said softly, giving her the bravest smile I could manage. 'Darius told me about my father. It doesn't matter now. None of it matters.'

We were about to enter Ravalia's famous arena, and the irony wasn't lost on me. I'd spent so long hoping to stand, victorious, on the onyx podium in the centre of that arena. Instead, I was preparing to face my own death.

Would Aric be somewhere nearby, preparing for the Trials? I hoped with all my heart that he wasn't in the stands. That he wouldn't be forced to sit and watch while—

'I've made so many mistakes,' my mother murmured. 'I should have told you everything, but I wanted to protect you – to shield you from my past. And I . . . I didn't want you to hate me.'

Those last words were little more than a whisper, but they were heartfelt and precious. Filled with truth.

'I could never hate you,' I breathed. *'Never.'*

My mother entwined her fingers with mine. Her lips were pale, bloodless, as she whispered, 'They still might spare you.'

It would take nothing short of a miracle to save either of us. But I held her hand tightly, trying to communicate everything I couldn't say – all the love and fear I was keeping locked in my chest, hidden from the callous eyes of our audience.

'At least we'll be together,' I said quietly, my eyes darting to my mother's and then away. It was an effort of will to keep my expression steady, to force myself to remain strong.

'Together,' she agreed, tears spilling down her cheeks.

'It'll be quick,' I reassured her. 'So quick we barely notice.'

There was a flicker of something in my mother's eyes, something close to approval.

'You would have made a brilliant Warrior, Mira.' Her lips curved into a soft, sad smile. 'You would have made an even better ruler.'

It looked like she might say more, but she never had the chance. Black-garbed Warriors filed in, one on each side of us.

The message was clear. Time to go.

Time to die.

As my hand was ripped from my mother's, her hazel eyes met mine unflinchingly. Her last words to me were:

'Your father would have been proud.'

CHAPTER TWENTY-TWO

Mira

The arena was more magnificent and more terrible than I ever could have imagined.

Striding onto the volcanic sand floor, we were engulfed by the towering, circular stands – a crushing wave of colour and noise. The roar swelled to a crescendo, filling my ears and drowning out everything else. Then I heard the clapping, the audience turning towards what could only be the royal box. The guards had placed us just below, and as I looked up, I had my first glimpse of the emperor and his family.

Emperor Kalias was a striking, muscled figure. His crimson robes were pinned with military medals that glittered brilliantly in the sun. He didn't acknowledge the crowd as he lowered himself into a throne-like chair, the sharp points of his bone crown jutting upwards like spires. An uncaring, willowy woman followed just behind him, flanked by two royal heirs – a red-headed prince and his female counterpart. The girl from the coach.

'We are gathered here,' the emperor announced, 'to witness a criminal brought to justice. This woman—' hundreds of eyes turned back to us, fixing on Celeste with hungry anticipation — 'was one of our own. She belonged to an Order, and she betrayed us.'

I'd known that my mother was someone important. I'd suspected that she had come from a noble family, from somewhere in Ravalia. But from an *Order*?

No one left the Orders. No one.

'On a critical assignment in Kalure, this woman turned traitor, failing in her mission to assassinate the Kalurian king.' Rapt silence fell over the stands. 'For years, she has been on the run – but the empire always prevails.'

I could barely take in the words, the implications. Celeste had been sent to kill my father, but she hadn't gone through with it. I glanced sideways at her, and the tenderness and pain on her face took my breath away.

I remembered asking Darius what she'd done that was so terrible. His answer: she fell in love.

It would take longer than this moment to puzzle through her secrets, the motivations behind her decisions. But as I looked at my mother, I felt myself soften – because she'd done it for love. And I refused to believe that anything done out of love could be too terrible.

But, high above us, the crowd clearly disagreed. The audience was animated in their hatred, cheering for Celeste's death. Cheering for the execution of a woman they didn't even know.

I felt sick as I stared into the sea of unfeeling faces. Would they be so unfeeling if they were down here, looking up? Would they be as confident in their cruelty *then*?

'Traitor of the Third Order,' Emperor Kalias announced, 'I pronounce you guilty of treason. For crimes against the Ravalian Empire, I sentence you to death.'

The words fell like hammer blows. I turned to face my mother, and I knew the terror was obvious on my face.

'No!' I cried, a broken rasp of a sound.

It's okay, Mira, she mouthed.

I knew better. I knew that nothing was going to be okay, ever again.

'As for her daughter . . .' The emperor paused, waiting for the crowd to grow silent once more. 'It might seem harsh, to punish a girl for her mother's mistakes. But this is no ordinary girl. She is a threat to our empire – a descendant of the traitorous line that usurped Kalure from our ancestors.' There was no remorse in his face as he continued, 'Princess Kasmira Volaris will join her mother in death. Prince Roran, if you would?'

I didn't know what shocked me more. The pronouncement of my execution, or my name.

Kasmira Volaris.

Even my *name* was unfamiliar to me.

The prince, sitting to the right of the emperor's throne, stood. As he left the royal box, my eyes locked with Scarlett's. I could have sworn there was pity on her face.

I tore my gaze away, watching Roran descend through the stands. The audience cheered, but not as loudly as before. Did they see a rival royal, an enemy of the Ravalian Empire? Or did they see a girl – a girl barely older than eighteen, filled with fear and despair as she prepared to die?

Celeste didn't react to the emperor's pronouncement. Her expression was very calm, and I wondered how such a thing was possible. She smiled at me, the same gentle smile that had greeted me every morning over breakfast.

'Mira,' she said, 'the emperor just publicly declared me an Order member. That means there's a way out for you, if you decide to take it. And if you do, return to the docks and enter the water. The locket will find you.'

'I don't under—'

'No talking,' one of the Warriors interjected, his arm enclosing threateningly over mine.

For a moment, all I felt was confusion. Then realisation came in a sudden rush. I might have been part Kalurian, but the emperor himself had announced that my mother was one of his own, that she belonged to the Order of Masks.

Even Emperor Kalias wasn't above the sacred laws of the Ravalian Empire. And my mother was right. There was one loophole, one desperate way out. But did I want to take it?

The prince strode into the arena and paused, waiting for the emperor's next order. His flinty eyes were fixed on the royal box, and not once did they land on me or my mother.

'Please,' I begged. 'Please don't do this.'

He kept his attention fixed resolutely ahead, as if I was nothing to him. Less than nothing.

The emperor might as well have been carved from stone, like one of his many self-styled statues. Even as I stared up at him, he said nothing. Did nothing. I realised that he was drawing this out for maximum effect. If I hadn't hated him before, then I hated him now. I hated him with all of my desperate, breaking heart.

One nod. That was all it took.

Roran turned from the emperor, focusing his attention on Celeste, who was forced to her knees by two guards. His sword was the most horrible thing I'd seen in my life. My breath came in sharp pants, my heart racing frantically in my chest – as if it knew its beats were numbered. All I could think was: *that sword is going to kill her. That sword is going to kill my mother.*

And then it's going to kill me.

Desperately, I wrenched my arm from my guard's bruising grip. His surprise gave me the seconds I needed to rush to my mother—

'Restrain her,' Roran ordered.

I was jerked back before I could make contact, and I realised that I was crying.

Above me, the sky was a brilliant, bright blue, but it should have been grey and cold. It should have been bleak and lifeless, because surely the world was ending. Surely nothing could continue after this.

'All my life,' Celeste said resolutely, 'I've tried to keep you safe and hidden. But you were never meant to hide your light. You were born to *shine.*'

There was power in the gaze she levelled at me, filled with love. With the kind of strength no one could take away, even as the guards pushed her head down.

'Look away, Mira,' she instructed. 'Close your eyes and look away.'

I kept my eyes open – even as the prince raised his sword and aimed it at the back of her neck.

My lips parted, like I might try to speak. Like I might tell my mother that I loved her—

The sword cleaved through the air.

My mother's gasp might as well have been a scream. Her head hit the ground with a thud, the loudest sound I'd ever heard. And though her eyes were still open, staring up at the sky, she was no longer seeing it. She was no longer seeing anything.

I dropped to my knees beside my mother's body. Her blood stained my hands, my clothes, my skin. I didn't care. My heart was breaking, shattering into a thousand tiny pieces.

At that moment, I welcomed the prince's sword. Death was the easy, peaceful way out. Death would be a relief.

It was life that was unbearable.

Behind me, I heard the approach of heavy footsteps. Roran would do it quick and clean; he would slice through the back of my neck, and it would be done. I would be gone, like my mother was gone.

But as I closed my eyes, preparing to surrender to my fate, I realised—

I wasn't ready to die.

I twisted at the last second, rolling out of the way as the sword flashed in a downward arc. The blade embedded into the arena floor, but I was already up and moving, meeting Roran's stare with searing hatred.

If I could have, I would have damned everything to hell and run at him. But I had a matter of seconds before the soldiers descended, and I needed every one of them.

The audience murmured their confusion as I took a step forward, away from my mother's body, away from the prince. Every eye in the arena was fixed on me now, the girl marked for death. The girl suddenly refusing to die.

'I choose to compete,' I shouted. 'As the daughter of an Order member, I invoke my right to compete in the Trials!'

If the emperor was surprised, he didn't show it. He ignored the crowd's cries, regarding me with an assessing gaze. His pause lingered for what seemed like an eternity, and my heart sank.

Then, slowly and deliberately, he raised a palm. There was power in that single gesture—

The power of life.

My eyes locked with the emperor's, and I wondered what he saw. I wondered if he realised that it would be a mistake, keeping me alive.

Because I didn't care what he did to me, or what obstacles he put in my way. I didn't care about anything except one singular, all-consuming goal—

Making him pay.

CHAPTER TWENTY-THREE

Mira

The trembling started when I was out of Emperor Kalias's view, growing worse as a Warrior escorted me through the massing crowds.

I had the impression of steps, of people, of bright colours flashing in the afternoon sun. All of it was wrong. Too loud, too vivid, too jarring. It pressed in on me – threatening to suffocate me.

My mother is dead. The words encircled my mind, a constant loop. They still didn't feel entirely real.

But they were real. Celeste would never smile at me again. Never wrap her arms around me and hold me close. The sound of her laughter would become just another memory – until that, too, was forgotten.

'Keep moving.' Rough hands pushed me forward.

I followed the directive on unsteady legs. My eyes were blurry – probably with tears – but I kept my gaze fixed on the entrance to the arena. Everything would be better when I reached that obsidian arch. When I left the crowds and the memories behind.

But Ravalians swarmed against me, their bodies caging me in. A prison of heat and muscle and sneering faces.

And amongst them—

My heart seized as I recognised Nikolas speaking to a girl with white-blonde hair. Blood rushed in my ears, blocking out the sound of her purring laughter.

Laughter – after my mother had been murdered. And the others, all my age, all dressed in fitted black leather . . . the rest of the candidates. My competition.

They had been watching, I realised. They had *seen*—

I lurched to the side and hurled my guts up.

There was a disgusted sound – some noblewoman, probably, worried about sullying her expensive shoes – but I was shaking too hard to care. I felt like I was about to shake apart, and even the new bubble of space around me gave me no relief.

Calloused hands took hold of my shoulders. The Warrior's breath was hot on my face as he issued instructions. His words meant nothing to me. My eyes were on his sword, glinting faintly in the sunlight.

Maybe I should have let Roran end it. I didn't know if I could endure this.

'Get up.' The Warrior's order was hard, uncompromising. 'Get up now, or—'

'Don't touch her.'

A familiar figure pushed his way through the crowd, his brown eyes burning.

A Warrior moved to intercept him, and I tried to force my unco-operative body to stand. My breath came in shallow gasps as I imag-ined Aric being clapped in irons and dragged away, perhaps to the cell I had just vacated—

'Let him through.' The cool voice spoke with unmistakable authority, a perfect match to his slow, strolling footsteps. 'Give them a moment, and then take the girl to the palace. Emperor Kalias has organised accommodations for her there.'

I wanted to see who was speaking, but another wave of nausea swept through me. This time, the hands on my shoulders were warm and comforting. And then there was a familiar voice at my ear, murmuring my name. Telling me to *breathe.*

I can't. I wasn't sure if I thought it or said it out loud, but Aric's grip tightened in understanding.

'You can, Mira,' he said. He squeezed my palm and held it against his chest, allowing his heartbeat to reverberate through us both.

I kept my eyes shut, focusing on the rhythm until I felt steadier, too. Still shaky, but no longer in danger of falling apart.

'Listen to me.' Aric's voice was low and urgent. 'When the Warriors escort you from the arena, you need to seem cool and unaffected. The candidates will be watching, and that's the image they need to see. No trace of weakness, do you understand? You can't afford it. Not here. Not *now*.'

A different kind of hopelessness engulfed me. 'They've *already* seen—'

'They've seen *nothing*.' His words were fierce. 'Now stand up. Shoulders thrown back, chin high.'

As my trainer, Aric had given me plenty of guidance over the years – lessons on how to hold a blade, exercises to build muscle, advice on strategy. Years of following those instructions allowed me to follow them now.

'Good,' Aric said, but the way he looked at me – the tenderness in his gaze—

I leant into him as he took my face in his hands, and for a moment it was just us in the near-empty arena, breathing the same air.

I braced myself for what came next – his questions and condolences, the pain of reliving my mother's execution, but instead Aric rested his forehead against mine. In that gesture, I felt all the fear and sadness and affection he was battling down even now. Knowing that now wasn't the moment to give voice to them.

When he pulled back to look at me, his eyes were brighter than before – filled with a smouldering intensity that made my heart stutter. Aric's lips crashed down on mine a second before the Warriors took hold of my arms.

'You can survive whatever they throw at you, Mira,' he shouted as we were prised apart. 'We both can. *Together*.'

Despite his assurances, there was something frantic about the way he strained against my guards, his eyes drinking me in—

As if he might not get another chance.

A cell would have been better.

Anything would have been better than this – this mockery of luxury. I could feel the emperor's hand in these chambers: every tessellated tile, every glint of marble and gleam of gold laughing at me.

When I didn't move, the Warriors pushed me forward – through a set of bronze doors and into a receiving room dominated by paintings of Ravalian domestic life. The doors shut behind me with a ringing thud.

Trapped. As easily as that.

I took in my new prison with wary eyes. Blinding – it was absolutely blinding, everything decorated with gold and upholstered in rich shades of crimson. Despite the high ceiling and ridiculous amount of space, I had never felt more penned in.

Look, the opulence screamed. *Look at the life you might have had. The life I took from you.*

Three attendants rushed to meet me, unnaturally pristine in their white uniforms.

One of them raised a hand to her mouth – then turned and dashed for the bronze doors, unable to face the task ahead of her. Or maybe just unable to face *me*.

I knew what I must look like, splattered with red – like a monster rather than a girl. But that was fine with me. Mira Tundra had died with her mother, and when I'd walked out of that arena, I'd made the choice to leave her behind for good. All that was left was numbness. A void that could only be filled by vengeance – vengeance that would drive me forward.

And I was glad of it.

The Trials were supposed to begin tomorrow, but for me, they'd already started. Which meant I needed to cling to that numbness with everything I had. If it faltered, I would too.

'Come,' the senior of the two attendants said, her voice clipped. The other girl didn't so much as meet my eyes.

They led me underneath imposing arches that reminded me of the arena, and as they did, I caught glimpses of other rooms: a dining space complete with over a dozen chairs, a study with a mahogany desk, and a bedchamber dominated by a canopied bed, which extended into an adjoining bathing room.

The doors to the balcony were flung open, sunlight streaming in along with the floral scent of the gardens. It was painfully beautiful. Idyllic.

It hurt my eyes just to look at it.

I'd passed the other Trial candidates on my way here, gathered outside the three buildings reserved for the Orders. They had gone quiet at the sight of me, and I had understood then. Why the Warriors had taken that route through the grounds – and why the emperor had given me rooms in the palace.

This was just another opportunity for him to alienate me from the other candidates. Another way of making the citizens of Ravalia resent me.

My attendants were no exception.

They bathed me efficiently, not speaking a word. Their eyes didn't stray towards mine, and their hands didn't brush my skin for a second longer than necessary. They might as well have been preparing a corpse for burial.

It took them over an hour to make me presentable enough to meet the emperor – to remove every trace of my mother's blood, to apply cosmetics to my face and rub oils into my skin. I shut off my mind and let my body go limp, allowing them to do whatever they wished. Instead of being grateful for my compliance, they seemed increasingly unnerved. Their relief was almost palpable as they shifted me to the bedchamber and reached for—

'Not the dress.' It was the first I'd spoken since leaving the arena, and the words came out harsh and clipped.

The attendants exchanged a glance. 'Emperor Kalias chose it for you. It would be an insult to refuse.'

'I'm not wearing that,' I said when one of them brought the gown forward. It was soft and light, virginal – a perfect match to my chambers, with their pale walls, gauzy curtains and woven floor rugs. A dress and chambers selected for a delicate, ornamental princess.

A princess who would die quickly.

'But it's an honour,' one of the attendants protested. 'You will look beautiful.'

'I will look *weak*,' I corrected.

The two attendants hesitated, exchanging another nervous glance. But at least they were paying attention to me now.

'This is how it's going to be.' It was an effort to force cool command into my voice, to try and pretend to be something other than the empty shell I was inside. 'Get rid of that dress and find me something else. I'm competing in the Trials, and I want to look like it.'

The attendants hesitated but conceded, their white-and-gold uniforms winking at me as they rushed back through the suite of rooms. When they returned, they brought exactly what I'd asked for.

I dismissed them curtly and dressed myself.

When I was done, even I was intimidated by the young woman in the mirror. The form-fitting leather hardened me, making me look like I was about to charge into battle.

'Black suits you.'

I spun around to see a young man standing in my bedchamber, as if he had every right to be there. His eyes were a deep, hypnotic blue – the same relentless, all-consuming blue as the Tempest Sea – and utterly ruthless.

I folded my arms. 'Who exactly are you?'

'Call me Cassius,' he said, running a hand casually through his golden-blond hair.

It didn't escape my notice that he'd only told me his name, and not his title. I cast an eye over his pristine ebony tunic, with its silver trim and distinctive high collar. He must have been a noble, for he was too finely dressed to be anything else. And yet, despite his refined appearance, there was something nonchalant about him – a kind of irreverent charm I didn't trust.

'You burn with it,' he continued idly.

'Pardon?'

'The anger,' he said, moving closer. 'I was watching you, in the arena. It smouldered in your eyes, just like it does now.'

The arena. He mentioned it so casually, like it was nothing. I stared up into his perfect face, wanting to claw at it with my nails.

'*There* it is,' he said, sounding satisfied. 'Let me give you some advice – if you want to survive in this court, you're going to have to hide your emotions.'

I said nothing. If I tried to speak, I might lose control. I might do something very unwise.

Cassius's lips quirked into something not quite a smile. 'Try not to be too obvious in your hatred when you're introduced to the emperor,' he said, extending his arm.

I hesitated but begrudgingly took it. Two Warriors followed as we walked along the hallway, though neither of us acknowledged them. Whether they were there for Cassius's protection or to keep me in line, I didn't know and didn't care.

We continued down the grand staircase, passing beneath candlelit chandeliers as we descended three opulent levels. Just like in my chambers, the mosaic floors and painted walls depicted scenes of Ravalian life, only these scenes were far from domestic: black-garbed Warriors charged into battle astride hulking stallions, while red and gold soldiers cut down their opponents on the battlefield.

Cassius must have noticed my interest because he murmured, 'Impressive, aren't they?'

If circumstances had been different, I might have found the paintings impressive. Instead, I found them monstrous. Sickening.

'You're welcome, by the way,' he said offhandedly. 'For intervening with those Warriors.'

It took me a second to put it together. To remember that cool, cultured voice, instructing the Warriors to stand down.

'Why did you?'

Cassius paused on the ground floor, and I realised that I had stopped walking. The candlelight played across his golden hair and fine-boned face and, for the first time, I allowed myself to notice how handsome he was. The kind of handsome that had the power to rob you of breath or thought.

'Few people stand up to the emperor the way you did,' he said at last, his voice soft. 'Perhaps I felt that such bravery should be rewarded.'

I dropped my hand from his arm, stepping back from that penetrating blue stare. 'Somehow, I don't think that's it.'

'Fine,' Cassius said, amusement thick in his voice. 'You want the truth? I liked the stir you caused amongst the court. It was about time someone shook them up. But then, when I sought you out, you were about to ruin it all.'

My brows drew together.

'You were seconds away from breaking – in a very public setting.' His sensuous lips twitched into another half-smile. 'I thought it would be a shame to destroy such a wonderfully intimidating first impression.'

He continued down the entrance hallway, forcing me to hurry to keep up with his longer stride. Before I could say anything else, the Warriors opened a set of towering doors. The throne room was so large that I had to pause to take it in: a cathedral-like space, with a high, vaulted ceiling and imposing black marble pillars. Crimson tapestries formed a backdrop to the raised dais, where an enormous stone throne loomed over the gathered courtiers. Though the throne was clearly intended to be intimidating, it was nothing compared to its occupant.

Emperor Kalias, ruler of the Ravalian Empire.

And my mother's murderer.

'You go alone from here,' Cassius told me with disconcerting casualness. 'I don't have much patience for these sorts of things.' His striking eyes slid to mine. 'I daresay the feeling is mutual.'

I turned to face him. I didn't trust Cassius, but suddenly I didn't want him to leave.

'What's going to happen when I go in there?'

Cassius considered me for a moment. 'It won't be needlessly dramatic,' he replied. 'The emperor can hardly execute you now. He'll meet you and introduce you to the posturing fools inside.'

I stared at him in surprise. 'That's . . .'

'Treasonous?' Cassius flashed me a smile. His teeth were very white against his black clothes. 'Feel free to report me.'

'And who, exactly, would I be reporting?'

'You'll find out soon enough,' he said, walking away. His smooth voice carried over his shoulder: 'I do hope you survive, Kasmira Volaris.'

I opened my mouth to respond, but I was already being announced. Every face turned towards the entrance in unison, like puppets connected to the same string.

Almost automatically, I took a step forward. Each step was slow and deliberate, in time with the beat of my heart. Blood roared in my ears, drowning out everything else. Everything but him.

Emperor Kalias watched me as I approached, walking between the row of giant gold candelabras. The closer I came, the more imposing he was. He had handsome features, but they were outweighed by the cruel twist to his lips, the apathy in his sculptured face. There was no humanity about him.

This was the emperor I'd spent so long wanting to serve? This was the ruler I'd learnt about in school, who was revered across the Ravalian Empire?

His hard grey eyes bored into mine – as if he was daring me to look away.

I didn't. As I moved closer, I didn't back down an inch.

I remembered the callous dip of his head in the arena, the gesture that had cost my mother her life. This man didn't deserve my respect. And I wouldn't give him the satisfaction of seeing me cowed.

'Princess,' he said. It sounded less like a title and more like an insult. This man wanted me gone. And Emperor Kalias was used to getting his way.

I don't care what you want, I thought back at him. *You can try to kill me all you like, but I'll find a way to survive. And one day – in a month, a year, even a decade from now – I will make you pay for what you did.*

I will make you bleed, like you made her *bleed.*

I smiled. 'Your Majesty.'

Emperor Kalias leant back on his throne, his expression calculating. 'I chose to spare you,' he said, 'but that doesn't make you one of us. Which country are you loyal to, Princess? Ravalia or Kalure? Because you can't be loyal to both.'

Silence fell over the gathering. Everyone was watching me, waiting eagerly for my answer.

An answer I didn't have.

I couldn't have felt more removed from the girl I had been. As for the girl I was *supposed* to be – the hidden identity that had nearly gotten me killed – she was a stranger.

Kasmira Volaris. It was entirely alien to me. And so was Kalure.

How was I supposed to feel a sense of loyalty towards a people I'd never met? To love a place that I'd never seen?

As my pause grew longer, so did the emperor's satisfaction. I realised that he had asked me this question deliberately, to weaken me in the eyes of his court. To allow my hesitation to damn me.

I forced myself to meet the emperor's stare. In a carefully neutral tone I said, 'I've lived my whole life in the Ravalian Empire. It's my home.'

Emperor Kalias searched my face for a lie. He wouldn't find one.

'Yes.' The emperor was smiling. 'I suppose it is.' He watched me for a moment longer before clapping his hands together and addressing the crowd. 'Either way, we'll find out soon enough what you are. For the final stage of the Choosing is already underway.'

He sounded far too pleased by this, and I was filled with trepidation. What did he mean? I'd already been accepted into the Trials.

The emperor must have noticed my confusion, because his smile widened. 'You may think you have an automatic right to compete for a place in my Orders,' he told me, 'but you don't. The heads of my Orders will decide if they want *you.*'

And with a callous wave of his hand, I was dismissed.

CHAPTER TWENTY-FOUR

Mira

The arena was lit on all sides by flaming torches, intensely bright in the blackness. I felt a distant rush of familiarity: in the evening, surrounded by fire, it reminded me of the circus's stage. The thought gave me some confidence. If I could pretend this was just another performance, maybe I could come out of it alive.

The other candidates were already present, organised into three lines. I kept my gaze fixed resolutely ahead, resisting the urge to search for Aric. There were close to thirty contenders in total, and every pair of eyes was riveted on me.

While their stares were unnerving, they were nothing compared to the three figures standing in front of them. They turned at my arrival, their faces cast in the eerie reddish glow of the torches. The heads of the Orders, who would decide whether I lived past morning.

I noticed the head of the Order of Warriors first: General Tiran, his shining armour emblazoned with a lion. Behind him was Zandri, her masked face saying enough about which Order she was representing. The final Order head stood apart from the others, his muscular arms crossed. He was tall and dark-skinned, and for a moment shock overpowered my fear. I was looking at the Artisan from the Elusive Isles. *Her death will set you free.*

My nails bit into my palms as I noticed the three royal patrons watching from their thrones, arranged in the same sequence as the Order heads: Warriors, Masks and Artisans. Roran eyed me with a cruel smile; clearly, he hadn't forgotten how I'd shown him up in the arena. At his side was Scarlett, her red waves swept off her face by two solid gold scorpion hair pieces. The youngest prince appeared bored, half reclining in his throne. I had a glimpse of a gleaming crown, the flash of a razor-sharp smile. And then I saw his eyes. Those ruthless, dark blue eyes.

No wonder Cassius had been amused when I'd asked who he was. *You'll find out soon enough,* he had said. Well, this was sooner than expected.

I clenched my fists and looked away, my eyes darting to the spot where I'd watched my mother die. That section of sand was as smooth and unblemished as the rest, but to me it would always be stained with blood.

'Tell me, girl,' Roran demanded, 'does being royalty make you feel as if you have certain privileges? Does it make you feel somehow *powerful?*'

'No,' I gritted out. 'Of course not.'

'Then why have you kept us waiting?'

I knew nothing I said would be good enough, but I tried anyway. 'The emperor wanted to see me. He—'

'So it's the emperor's fault, is it?' The prince's jade eyes glittered, menacing even in the partial darkness.

'Let it go, Roran.' It was Scarlett who spoke, and though her tone was dismissive, I couldn't understand why the princess would speak on my behalf. 'She can redeem herself during the demonstration.'

Ignoring his sister, Roran continued, 'General Tiran told me that you attended the ceremony in the Elusive Isles. According to him, you wanted to join the Order of Warriors.' He paused significantly. 'Is that still true?'

Movement drew my attention to the other candidates. As if by instinct, I found Aric's clear brown eyes. In them, I saw tenderness and concern. And fear.

He shook his head at me, a tiny gesture. A warning.

But Roran was smiling, an infuriatingly smug smile that I wanted to slap off his face. And even though I knew that I shouldn't, that it couldn't possibly end well—

'I'm competing for the Order of Warriors.'

Cassius didn't bother to hide his surprise as he raised a blond brow, his gaze lingering on Roran.

'In that case,' Scarlett said, her face unreadable, 'General Tiran will pair you with another candidate from the Order of Warriors, so you can demonstrate—'

'Since the girl wants to be accepted into *my* Order,' Roran interrupted, 'I will be the one to test her.'

'That isn't how the Choosing is done,' his sister protested, but the prince was already moving.

'Give the girl your sword and shield,' he instructed General Tiran, who handed them over and retreated to a respectful distance.

The sword was heavier than anything I'd practised with before, and the shield weighed me down even more. Roran clearly knew it too. There was a satisfied gleam in his eyes as he stalked closer, unsheathing his own blade. His polished black armour shone, a chilling reminder of his position. He was no Trial candidate: he was a full-fledged Warrior, with plenty of experience slaughtering soldiers on the battlefield.

A servant ran up to slide a golden shield onto Roran's arm. As he did, the prince tossed me his dagger. I fumbled, the blade clattering to the ground. I quickly bent to retrieve it, ignoring the laughter of the onlookers.

Roran didn't give me the chance to regain my composure. He moved first, and for someone so large he was unnaturally fast, unleashing a series of brutal overhead blows that dented my shield and threatened to make it buckle. I deflected as best I could, my teeth gritted with the effort. If any of those blows landed, they would cleave my skull apart.

Step after step, he forced me back towards the arena wall. My ears ached at the noise. My arm muscles were screaming.

And then he broke through my shield.

I hurled the useless thing at him. Roran laughed and sidestepped, his breathing slow and even.

Our swords met in a shower of sparks, and I felt an icy stab of fear. His strikes and parries were so fluid that I could barely see his blade. Whether it was a result of his own talent or magical intervention, it was obvious that I was hopelessly outmatched.

Roran smiled lazily as he flourished his sword in an elegant movement, forcing me to counter with my own blade. When I did, he smashed his shield into my right shoulder – spinning me around and slamming me face first into the arena wall.

A sickening crack sounded as my forehead collided with stone. The pain was dizzying. Disorientating.

My sword slipped from my fingers. I heard its heavy clatter as Roran kicked it aside.

'Pathetic,' he spat, his voice hot in my ear. 'You don't deserve a place in the Order of Warriors. You don't deserve to survive.'

The dagger was my only chance. Left-handed, I slashed at his side, aiming for a thin gap in his armour—

Roran wrenched the blade from my hand. I stumbled back from him, blood pouring from my forehead and into my eyes. Through a red, blurry haze, I fell to the ground and frantically felt for my discarded sword. My hand enclosed around the leather hilt just as Roran's footsteps crunched across the sand.

Desperately rubbing the blood from my eyes, I twisted to see a flash of silver descending towards me. Roran's sword, preparing to sever my head from my shoulders—

A dark blur slammed into the prince from the side.

I looked on in disbelief as Aric and Roran went tumbling in the sand, a jumble of bodies and fists. When the prince tried to stand, Aric dragged him back down and punched him square in the face. It was almost comical: one of the best swordsmen in the empire, and Aric had reduced him to fighting like a street thug.

Warriors swarmed into the arena, a mass of black. Roran barked at them to stay back as he hurled Aric to the arena floor and struck him repeatedly across the face.

'Restrain him,' Roran ordered, spitting blood onto the sand.

Two Warriors pinned Aric's arms and pushed him to his knees. An easy target for the prince.

'*No!*' I shouted, my grip tightening on the sword as I rushed forward.

I was less than five metres away when the Warriors restrained me. So close that I could almost brush Aric's fingertips with mine—

Aric looked up at me, his expression resigned. There was fear in his eyes, but I knew that fear wasn't for himself. It was for *me.*

Roran stepped forward, obscuring my view of Aric's face. Kain's murderer, and Aric would die not knowing it, unable to avenge his brother—

'No,' I said again, brokenly this time.

I could barely breathe as I watched the prince raise his sword. *Not Aric. Not him too.*

'Wait,' a smooth, confident voice rang out.

The prince hesitated, the sword pausing in mid-air.

I twisted to look back at the heads of the Orders, to where a shadowy figure had stepped forward. She crossed the arena with authority, her onyx mask glittering in the firelight. And then she said the words I would never have expected.

'I will take them.'

I found myself staring into a pair of dark eyes. Into the impassive face of the woman who had, inexplicably, saved both our lives.

Zandri.

'What's going to happen to Aric?' I asked as I followed Zandri below the arena.

Zandri didn't look at me. She hadn't since she'd made her announcement, and I wondered if she regretted her decision to intervene. I wondered why she would make such a decision at all.

'You should be more concerned with yourself,' Zandri replied evenly, the sharp angles of her face even more pronounced up close. 'The boy will be fine. Roran overstepped his bounds; the heads of the Orders decide what happens in the Choosing, not the royal patrons. I will have a word with General Tiran on your friend's behalf. If he makes it through the Trials, he can become a member of my daughter's personal guard.'

It was the best outcome I could have hoped for: a safe position for Aric, and some distance from Roran. But I wondered what the price would be. Here, no one did anything without getting *something* in return – and I didn't like the idea of being indebted to Zandri.

Of course, it was too late for that.

The stairwell we were following came to a dead end, but instead of stopping, Zandri strode through what appeared to be a solid wall. The enchantment reminded me uncomfortably of entering the resistance's headquarters.

Though I couldn't see Zandri – or whatever was waiting for me on the other side – I could still hear her.

'Keep up,' she called.

I passed through the barrier, emerging into a roughly hewn tunnel lit with wall sconces. Zandri was little more than a distant shadow, moving with an ease that suggested she was retracing a familiar path.

I hurried after her, straining to hear the sound of her booted footsteps. The last thing I wanted was to follow Zandri anywhere – let alone further underground. But the alternative was losing my way in a maze of dank tunnels.

I caught up with her just as the tunnel opened into an obsidian hall encircled by full-length mirrors. The reddish glow of fire braziers were reflected in the metal gleam of weapons and the central staircase, which curved up to the ceiling like a snaking flame.

'We're deep under the palace grounds,' Zandri said, her voice lethally soft. 'No one but myself and my Masks frequent these tunnels.'

At her words, I backed up a few steps – positioning myself in front of a cache of daggers mounted to the wall. But Zandri wouldn't have saved my life to kill me now.

It was almost a pity. I would have liked an excuse to bury a blade in her heart.

'Why did you help me?' I asked tightly, my voice echoing around the cavernous expanse.

'You're raw, girl, but you have talent. It just isn't the kind of talent that the Order of Warriors look for.' Zandri paused. 'What do you know about the Order of Masks?'

As if from a lifetime ago, I remembered Elian. I remembered Jadis's words: *He doesn't speak. Not since the Masks got to him.*

'I've only heard it mentioned in passing,' I said cautiously.

'That's to be expected, I suppose. It's not often discussed.' Zandri's figure was nothing more than a column of shadow as she crossed the hall. 'As you know, your mother was a member. Perhaps that gives you a hint as to what the Order involves.'

I thought of what little I knew about my parents and how they'd met. My mother had been sent on a mission to kill the Kalurian king—

My mouth went dry. 'Assassination.'

'Not quite. They're individuals with unique abilities – ones allowing them to infiltrate rival courts, rival kingdoms, and exploit those positions to the empire's advantage.'

'So they're spies?'

Zandri shrugged. 'Every mission is different. Your mother was sent to seduce the Kalurian king and use his affection to advance our interests. But yes, she was eventually tasked with killing him. A task that she failed.'

The hard edge in her voice made it clear that Zandri hadn't forgiven my mother's failure – so why was I here? Why save me from execution? None of it made any sense.

'What's your role in all of this, exactly?'

'I oversee all the Orders, but I'm the head of the Order of Masks.' A thin smile. 'Fortunately for you, I don't like to watch talent go to waste.'

Yes, I thought bitterly. *How fortunate I am that you saved me. What a pity you didn't extend that same mercy to my mother.*

'If you expect me to be grateful, you'll be waiting a long time,' I said, when the silence lingered. 'If it wasn't for you, my mother would still be alive.'

'If it hadn't been me, it would have been someone else.' Zandri's tone was dismissive. 'The moment you announced your candidacy for the Trials, you were both living on borrowed time. I merely sped up the inevitable.'

Before I even realised what I was doing, I reached behind me. My fingers enclosed around something cold and sharp.

'Careful,' Zandri warned.

I didn't ask how she'd known. Nor did I try to hide the dagger. As I brought it in front of me, I saw there were runes running down both sides of the blade – the same runes I had seen on the twin blades my mother had buried near our tent. I wondered if she'd been given them when she was initiated as a Mask.

'I know what it is,' Zandri said, 'to desire vengeance, and to mete it out. But revenge is a dangerous game. Your instincts will tell you to act quickly, in a flash of hot-blooded passion. Those instincts will get you killed. Some games are only meant to be played slowly. Carefully.'

'Is that your way of asking me to put the blade back?'

'Not at all.' Zandri stalked closer, twirling a silver dagger that seemed to have appeared out of mid-air. The trick reminded me of Verex's circus act, and for a second, I could see his blood in my mind's eye: dripping steadily onto the grass.

'What are you doing?' I asked warily.

'Giving us both what we want,' came the smooth, unruffled reply. 'The Choosing Ceremony involves demonstrations of skill. Your fight with Prince Roran was a test for the Order of Warriors; now, I'm interested in testing you myself.'

She was so fast that she was little more than a blur. I watched her closely, trying to anticipate where she was going to strike, but it was impossible. Zandri moved with inhuman speed, like the feathers on her shoulders really were wings.

When she materialised in front of me, she had blades in both hands. I barely stumbled back in time, her dagger missing my skin by inches. But I rallied, raising my own blade and stabbing at her sternum—

Only to meet empty air.

'You can do better than that,' Zandri said as she circled, reflected in the ring of mirrors.

I kept pace with her, ready to take advantage of any opportunity. But even as my blood pounded a fierce drumbeat in my chest, I knew that the likelihood of cutting Zandri – let alone *beating* her – was slim.

'Stop thinking,' Zandri said, her booted foot kicking my legs out from underneath me. I fell heavily, my shoulder aching at the impact. 'Fighting should be instinctual. It's a dance – a deadly, beautiful dance.'

Her words reminded me of Aric. He looked like he was dancing when he fought, moving seamlessly from one move to the next. I'd felt that kind of ease maybe twice in my life, and both times had been when I was fighting with him.

I tried again, feinting and slicing at her exposed side. But Zandri whirled away, her dagger slashing my right arm. It wasn't a painful cut, but it unsettled me that she was able to wound me so easily. This was a test, and I was suddenly very afraid what the price of failure might be.

'Too slow,' Zandri pronounced, not even bothering to block my attack. 'Perhaps this was a waste of time.'

Zandri turned on her heel, and it felt like a defining moment. If she walked out of the hall, that was it. This was my last chance to prove myself a worthy contender for the Trials.

Closing my eyes, I weighed the knife in my palm. My focus tunnelled until all I was aware of was the blade, the silver cool against my skin. All I could hear was the sound of Zandri's distant footsteps.

And I felt it again. The pull.

I drew my wrist back—

The knife careened through the air in a circular motion, blade over hilt, blade over hilt. My eyes snapped open just as Zandri twisted, raising her palms. The knife stopped, inches from her face, caught between her hands. Over the silver of the blade, she regarded me in silence for a moment.

'Better,' she said, tossing the blade back at me.

I closed my eyes again, and when I reopened them, I had caught the blade hilt first.

'I can do this,' I told her, low and fierce. 'If you give me another chance, I'll prove it to you.' My voice was raw with a mixture of desperation and conviction. 'I can survive the Trials. I *will* survive the Trials.'

We stared at each other, and it was impossible to tell what Zandri was thinking. Her eyes were calculating as she regarded me, like she was assessing my worth. It was the same look the Artisan had worn when he'd predicted my future: as if she were staring past my face and into *me* – seeing everything that made me who I was, all my strengths and weaknesses, even those things I didn't want seen.

Finally Zandri nodded. 'Follow me.'

I kept pace with her as she crossed the hall, climbing the central staircase that pierced the stone ceiling. A shaft of light drew me upwards, into an imposing atrium filled with fire. Though I had never been inside, I recognised the distinctive pillars from earlier this afternoon.

The Order of Masks residence.

'Kasmira.'

I glanced at Zandri, startled by her use of my name. My *real* name.

'We both know I'm not really the person you want to kill. At the very least, I'm not at the top of your list.' Her lips upturned in a strange half-smile. 'But if you use a weapon against me again, outside of a training exercise, you had better finish what you started. Or I will.'

Zandri said nothing else as she stepped into the crisp night. But then her gaze went back to the fire braziers, which flared hotter and brighter as I passed. A strange expression crossed her face, there and gone before I could interpret it.

I wondered whether Zandri was remembering our altercation on Aldara. Did she know about the blood ruby? And if she did, why hadn't she mentioned it?

'Get some sleep,' Zandri said suddenly, turning her back on me. 'The first Trial begins tomorrow.'

CHAPTER TWENTY-FIVE

Scarlett

Resplendent in red and gold, Emperor Kalias resembled the sun. Walking a few paces behind him, Zandri was his shadow. A murderous, unsmiling shadow.

All activity on the royal balcony immediately ceased. Nobles bowed their heads, and white-garbed servants prostrated themselves on the marble tiles.

'As you were.' The emperor waved a dismissive hand. The golden rings he wore glinted like stars.

Conversation resumed as he strode between courtiers reclining on divans and servants circulating with golden trays. My mother followed, her suppressed rage almost palpable.

'Father,' I said, bowing my head.

Emperor Kalias tilted my chin upwards and I tensed, conscious of the strength in his fingers. The firmness of his grip.

Had he somehow discovered what we were planning? Or was he preparing to punish me in Zandri's place – to discipline her for accepting Mira into the Trials?

Then he spoke, and a whole new set of fears arose.

'Since your engagement fell through, I've been giving thought to future suitors.' He turned my head, studying me with the same intensity an artist might study a sculpture. With a satisfied nod, he released me – though I noticed he flexed his fingers, as if touching my face had chilled them. 'You have turned into a truly beautiful woman, even if that beauty is somewhat . . . unusual. This time, I don't intend to waste your potential on someone undeserving. I will see to it that you wed a prince, or perhaps even a king.'

'Scarlett can do more than that,' Zandri said. 'She possesses magic, and she has a mind for strategy. Once her skills are properly harnessed, she could become formidable—'

'I don't need her to be formidable, Zandri. I am formidable enough, and so are my sons.' He smiled at me, but I had the sense he wasn't really seeing me. Just what I could buy him.

'You mentioned suitors,' I cut in, before Zandri could argue further. I already knew that trying to change my father's mind was hopeless. The better strategy was to let him believe he'd won – and then negotiate terms. 'Will I at least have the opportunity to choose my betrothed?'

'You will have the opportunity to meet them, but the courtship will be short, and the choice will be mine to make. This is a political decision, not a personal one.'

The patronising edge to his voice was like salt to an open wound. It was all I could do to stop my fingers from inching towards the blades in my hair.

'How much time do I have?'

'No suitors will visit until after the Trials,' he replied. 'Perhaps another month—'

'I want six months.'

A smile pulled at his cruel lips. 'Three months.'

'Four.'

Emperor Kalias considered me for a long moment. A lesser person might have quailed under his scrutiny, but I didn't so much as blink. I had inherited more from my father than just his looks.

I had inherited his fortitude, too. And his pride.

'Four months,' he agreed, his tone indulgent. 'But I won't stand for any more complications,' he added, a chill entering his voice as he looked at Zandri. 'There have been enough of those already.'

She inclined her head. Tension arced between them, like lightning waiting to strike. But Kalias needed Zandri's magic to control the Orders, and she was trapped by the deal they had made in blood.

A deal that wouldn't protect him for much longer.

I retreated to the far end of the balcony without waiting for my mother. *Four months*, I thought. *I have four months to kill an* emperor.

Bracing my arms against the cool marble balustrade, I surveyed the Order of Warriors residence below, where the candidates were visible in the open training courtyard. Ever since Zandri had intervened on Mira's behalf, I'd known this year would be something special. My mother didn't forgive easily, and she wouldn't have spared Adalyn's daughter unless she had good reason.

I'd had my suspicions, but they had centred around Mira's importance to Kalure. I hadn't considered that *Mira* might be the missing piece my mother needed to act against Kalias. But I supposed it made sense; if my mother couldn't force someone to act against my father, then who better to use than someone who had every reason to want him dead?

A shout drew my attention to the centre of the courtyard. While most of the candidates were waiting for Empress Ivalene to arrive and explain the rules of the first Trial, some had decided to pass the time by sparring.

Zandri certainly has an eye for talent, I thought, watching Mira. Her opponent – presumably a female Warrior candidate – was inching out of reach, her feet on the chalk mark that made up their sparring circle.

Mira waited, her body taut with readiness. When the girl stepped back inside the circle, she was met with a series of expert jabs, backed up by strength and speed she couldn't hope to match. Mira had her opponent defeated and pinned in less than five minutes.

'She's perfect,' I murmured.

'*If* she survives long enough to be of any use to us,' Zandri corrected, joining me at the balustrade. 'Which remains to be seen.'

My mother's tone was sharp. She hadn't been pleased to learn that Governor Halvor was still alive, but that didn't matter. He was rotting in the cells, along with the leader of the resistance. Such a neat solution, and far more convenient than bloodying my own hands.

And now I had Mira, who was perfectly placed to solve all our problems. Or so I hoped, since Zandri hadn't been entirely clear on the details. But she had been clear about the first steps: keep Mira alive and induct her into the Order of Masks.

'You have such little faith in her,' I commented. 'Perhaps she'll surprise you. She is family, after all.'

Zandri's red lips twisted at the reminder. She rarely mentioned her old life or her birth name. She certainly never mentioned her brother, the King of Kalure, or his Ravalian wife and daughter.

'Regardless,' she said, 'the first Trial is only hours away. You need to stay focused.'

I gave my mother a questioning glance. 'I'm not a candidate,' I reminded her, 'and the emperor made it clear that neither myself nor my brothers are to have direct involvement in the Trials. He was displeased enough that you chose Mira in the first place.'

Zandri waved a dismissive hand. 'If Kalias wanted Mira dead, then she would be. He couldn't care less about the law, which means he must have another use for her. I think he's waiting to see how this plays out.'

'So either she dies in the Trials – or what? What would he do with her?'

'If I were him, I'd try to discredit her politically. Use her to get to Kalure.' Zandri shrugged. 'I'm sure he'll find something.'

'Even more reason not to get in his way,' I muttered. '*You* might be able to do what you like, but he made it clear what he expects from me.'

Zandri tapped a long, red-tipped nail against the stone. It must have been a signal, because a raven came to perch on the ledge, ruffling its feathers. I didn't need to ask to know it was the same one I had brought back to life. Its nearness made my skin prickle.

Then she said, 'Some things are worth the risk. The first Trial is team based; in order to succeed at their set tasks, the candidates in each group will need to work closely together.'

I stared at my mother, understanding all too well. Zandri didn't want me to observe the first Trial. No – she wanted me to *compete*.

'You set this up somehow, didn't you?'

'You have to get closer,' my mother said, 'to ensure that Mira doesn't fail. This gives you the opportunity.'

Plans shifted in my mind. I had thought I would be waiting, watching, advising . . . excitement pulsed through my veins.

No more waiting.

'Be careful with the girl,' Zandri warned. 'She's untrained, but her raw potential is enormous. Not to mention, her mother's blood ruby is still missing. None of my people found it when they searched them in the cells.'

That made me glance up in interest. 'I thought you said that was impossible. Isn't the vault supposed to be secure?'

'Clearly,' my mother replied, 'I underestimated Adalyn's daring. She must have stolen hers before she left for Kalure; she always was too smart for her own good. And if her daughter finds it . . .' Zandri unclasped the red torque from her throat. 'You'll need this.'

She removed the ruby – the *blood* ruby – from her necklace and handed it over.

I stared down at the jewel in my palm and breathed out in a soft, contented sigh.

Let the Trials begin.

CHAPTER TWENTY-SIX

Mira

'There will be three tasks,' General Tiran told us when he entered the Order of Warriors barracks. 'Each is designed to test traits valued by the empire. Regardless of which Order you are competing for, you must prove you have these capabilities in order to be initiated. Specific abilities can be developed later, if Emperor Kalias decides you're worthy.'

Including magic.

A thrill went through me at the thought. After Initiation, Warriors were granted enhanced speed and reflexes, while Artisans were trained to glimpse the future. I wasn't sure what magical abilities Masks developed, but if I learnt to harness that magic, I would be one step closer to achieving my revenge.

'The first Trial,' General Tiran continued, 'will test your cunning, intelligence and ability to think under pressure. The second will involve modified hand-to-hand combat, and out of fairness to the Mask candidates, some training will be provided beforehand. Due to the mental nature of Artisan abilities, they will be exempt from this task. Now, before anyone tries to tell me this is unfair—' the general shot a quelling look at a group of mutinous-looking Warrior candidates— 'the Artisan candidates will have to prove their intuitive abilities to Emperor Kalias before the third Trial. This test will be a private one, and by all accounts, the emperor is quite exacting.'

A dark-haired girl shifted next to me, but I didn't have it in me to feel sorry for her or the other Artisan candidates. I doubted Emperor Kalias would kill any of them for failing the Trials.

But he would certainly kill *me*.

'As for the final Trial . . .' The general paused, and I had the sense he was pleased that we were hanging on his every word. 'The third Trial is the simplest and the hardest – a test of loyalty, with fatal consequences for speaking even a single mistruth.'

A few whispers broke out amongst the assembled candidates, but no one seemed too concerned – though the third Trial was the one that worried me the most. I exchanged a glance with Aric, and I knew he was thinking the same. If Emperor Kalias had a way of ensuring we spoke the truth, then I was done for. And so was Aric, if the emperor asked him a question that exposed his hatred for Roran.

When the general dismissed the group, I squeezed Aric's arm in farewell and crossed the training courtyard to stand with the five other Mask contenders. There were far more Warrior candidates, reflecting the larger number of inducted Warriors – famously kept at a constant five hundred. Masks and Artisans were rarer, and from what I'd overheard this afternoon, their numbers never exceeded fifty each.

I had been introduced to the Mask candidates a few hours earlier. None of them had spoken to me – taking their cues from Odessa Tiran, who seemed to despise me on principle. I didn't understand why she was competing at all. As General Tiran's daughter and fiancée to the youngest prince, she already had a privileged life. What could she possibly gain by becoming a Mask?

Odessa's voice was a mocking purr as she murmured something to the girl standing next to her. Danica, a noble with honey-blonde hair and a permanent sneer, turned away from me.

Fine. I didn't want to interact with Danica, either. These girls were my competition – and any one of them would stab me in the back without hesitation. Besides, I was far more interested in the Warrior candidates, who had taken General Tiran's comment about hand-to-hand combat seriously.

In the ring, Brutus circled his opponent like a wolf around its prey. The comparison was unnervingly accurate, because there was hunger in his eyes as he studied the smaller boy – like he'd scented blood.

'Stop playing around, Brutus!' Nikolas shouted from the sidelines. *'Finish it!'*

The other candidate didn't have a chance as Brutus descended on him, throwing him effortlessly to the ground. He ignored the arms the other boy put up to defend himself, kicking him heavily in the ribs.

Even I winced.

'Exactly what I'm after,' General Tiran said with an approving smile. 'You have your father's killer instinct.'

In comparison, the look General Tiran gave Aric was downright hostile. But he nodded in acknowledgement when Aric pinned his larger, burlier opponent to the sand.

At the general's nod, Aric released the other boy and stood, his bare chest glistening with a faint sheen of sweat. Another candidate threw him a towel, which Aric caught with an easy smile. He strode past Nikolas and Brutus without a word, but I frowned as I noticed the way Brutus's gaze sharpened.

'Impressive,' a low, sultry voice said. I turned to see Odessa watching Aric, her stare far more disconcerting than Brutus's. Like Brutus, she was looking at Aric like he was a meal – but a very different kind. 'I don't suppose you can introduce me?'

My jaw clenched. Every time I looked at Odessa, I was reminded of her mocking laughter at my mother's execution. It was a pity we weren't Warrior candidates. If we were, I could pummel her in the ring.

'I'm surprised you have time for boys,' I replied, saccharine-sweet. 'Or are you that confident about succeeding in the first Trial?'

Odessa's amber eyes fixed on me. With her white-blonde hair and delicate features, she was easy to underestimate – at least until she opened her mouth. 'I always have time for boys,' she drawled. 'That's what we're here for, isn't it? To learn how to trap, entice, *infiltrate*.' She tilted her head, flashing me a hateful little smirk. 'Then again, some of us are better at that than others.'

'Maybe I'll surprise you,' I retorted, but I was no longer looking at Odessa. I was looking past her, at Empress Ivalene.

She entered the courtyard flanked by her personal guard, gliding forward as though she didn't realise – or didn't care – that she had kept everyone waiting. Her presence instantly halted the sparring matches, candidates bowing their heads and stiffening at her approach. Since the royal heirs weren't supposed to have direct influence over the Trials, it fell to the empress to decide the form they took. And I doubted she would play fair.

'As General Tiran has no doubt explained,' Ivalene said in a cut-glass voice, 'the first Trial will test your cunning, intelligence, and ability to think under pressure. But it will also test your ability to work within a team.'

No one looked particularly pleased by this, and I understood why. My gaze flicked towards Nikolas and then Odessa. I didn't like my chances if I was partnered with one of them.

'I will leave you to sort yourselves into groups of three.' At a flick of the empress's hand, a servant hurried to her side, raising a parasol to shade her pale skin from the sun. I noticed that a few stray strands of her blonde hair were already sticking to her shiny forehead. 'Select your teammates carefully. Each group will be given a specific object to steal, and you must work together in order to succeed.'

Odessa, Danica and Rae immediately formed a group, leaving myself and Elodie. The other Mask candidate didn't even glance at me before making a beeline for the Warriors. I almost followed, but I stopped myself at the last moment. Somewhere amongst them, I knew Aric would be making his way to me. But even as he did, his fellow candidates were forming into groups. I needed to find our third teammate.

And there were four Artisans.

I cast my mind back, but I could only remember seeing three of them this morning. Had the fourth been missing for a while?

But she was here now. I locked eyes with her, bracing myself for her to drop my gaze and turn away like everyone else.

Instead, she strode up to me, wearing an impish smile. Her waist-length brown hair bounced with every step, and there was an infectious energy about her.

'I'm Sabine,' she introduced. 'Of course, there's no need to ask who *you* are.'

Her friendliness was a little unnerving, though not unwelcome. But before I could reply, a warm voice remarked, 'It seems we have our team.'

Relief surged through me as I looked at Aric – though it quickly darkened into something else. My hand rose, hovering above his bruised cheekbone and split lip.

'It looks worse than it is,' Aric said, catching my hand with his and entwining our fingers together. 'A healer fixed my black eye after my fight with Roran. Didn't want me to be at a disadvantage for the first Trial.'

He smiled dryly, but I couldn't bring myself to smile back. Not as I inhaled the scent of lilies and rose oil.

Empress Ivalene drifted away from the Warriors she'd been speaking to and returned to General Tiran's side, flanked by half a dozen servants and a page. Her gaze swept over Aric and Sabine before settling on me. She motioned her page forward, whispering instructions as he scrawled three notes that were quickly folded and handed to a servant.

My chest tightened as the servant slipped them inside the folds of her dress. Beside me, I felt Aric stiffen. He knew what those notes were, too.

'I have dispatched instructions to each of your chambers,' the empress announced. 'They contain the name and location of the object I want each group to steal. I suggest that you return to your chambers and prepare as best you can. The first Trial will begin at dusk and conclude at midnight. Each group has until then to complete their task and return to the throne room.' She paused. 'If you do not arrive before midnight, or if your group fails to steal the object I assigned you, then you will be cut from the Trials.'

Aric's eyes found mine, and he smiled reassuringly. In that smile, I saw my nerves reflected back at me – but also the same thirst to prove ourselves. Unfortunately, in our case, I doubted it would be so simple. And as Ivalene's cold stare lingered on me, I knew my suspicions were correct.

This task wasn't one that I was supposed to pass. It was one designed to make me fail.

'Did you have to hit her so hard?' I whispered to Aric as we dragged the unconscious dancer into an alcove and out of sight. I couldn't see much in the darkness, but I knew she was going to have one hell of a bruise tomorrow.

'My main concern was stopping her from screaming,' Aric retorted, looking away while I stripped off my plain clothes.

Thankfully, the girl – Cassandra – was close to my height and build, and her dancer's outfit marked her as one of the hired performers. It was an opportunity too good to pass up.

I draped my cloak over her before leaving the alcove. The slitted skirt I'd stolen swished as I moved, reminding me of my mother.

'Do you know who lives here?' I asked Aric, peering up at the austere castle perched high on the hill. In the moonlight, its alabaster walls shone with an unearthly glow. 'Who we're supposed to steal the crown from?'

'No idea.' The frown on his face said that he didn't like going in blind. I didn't either, but we didn't have time to waste. Empress Ivalene's note had specified the location and time – *Caleah Fortress, ten p.m.* – which only gave us two hours to infiltrate this party, steal the crown and make it back to the throne room.

And there was still no sign of Sabine. Gods, where *was* she?

I studied the line of beautifully dressed men and women ahead of us. They progressed slowly, trickling into the castle as Warriors checked the list and let them through. Each wore a mask with an ornate design that complimented their elaborate gowns or tunics, and a spasm of panic went through me as I realised we didn't have one. Would that give us away?

'Relax,' Aric murmured from my side. 'It'll be fine.'

Some of the tension melted from my shoulders. Selfishly, I was glad that Aric was doing this with me – but I suspected the empress had set us up to fail. And I couldn't bear to see Aric punished because of me.

Then again, he already had a target on his back.

'You shouldn't have tried to protect me in the arena.' I'd wanted to say something all day, but I hadn't found the right time. Or the right words. 'You should have—'

'What? Stood by and watched Roran kill you?' Aric raised a brow. 'Mira, I thought you understood by now. I'll *always* try to protect you.'

At his words, I felt a faint spark of hope.

'Does that mean you've decided not to investigate Kain's death?'

'Of course not,' he said, and the hope guttered out. 'I have a much better approach in mind, from inside the royal court.'

I glanced at him warily. 'What approach?'

'Let's not worry about that now. First, we need to make it through this Trial.' His expression was determined, but his gaze lingered a moment too long as he took in the beaded top and skirt I wore, cut to expose a daring amount of my midriff. 'You certainly look the part,' he said, and I thought he sounded a little breathless.

My heart beat faster, remembering our kiss in the arena. It had been brief – a desperate crashing of his mouth against mine – but the emotion in it had been heady. Powerful.

I felt that same emotion surging between us now. I saw it reflected in his eyes, and I knew he saw it in mine.

'I wanted to tell you.' The words slipped out, soft and heartfelt. 'Every day on Aldara, I thought about telling you and Lillian the truth – that my mother and I were on the run.'

'Why didn't you?' Aric's voice wasn't accusatory. It was gentle, inviting.

'It wasn't my secret to tell.'

Aric studied me, and I wondered if he was thinking of my *other* secret – the one even I hadn't known. We hadn't discussed it except in passing – my new identity as a princess. A *Kalurian* princess.

I wondered if he saw me differently now. Everyone else seemed to.

But no – Aric looked at me the same way he always had. I would always be Mira to him. *Just* Mira.

'I wish you'd told me, but I understand why you didn't.' The flickering torchlight played across his features, illuminating the strong lines of his face and the dusting of stubble on his jaw. 'Just . . . no more secrets, okay? From here on out, we need to trust each other.'

I swallowed. I had told Aric everything that had happened since leaving Aldara, including my mother's links to the fractured resistance. Everything except what I'd discovered about Roran sacrificing Darius's Warrior recruits. It was too close to what Aric suspected about his brother's death, and I didn't want to add fuel to that fire.

'No more secrets,' I echoed. Kain's name was like a lodestone around my neck.

I threaded my arm through Aric's as we joined the line of nobles progressing quickly towards the castle entrance. All too soon, we were facing the four black-garbed Warriors blocking the route inside. Whoever lived here must be important to merit having Warriors as guards, rather than regular soldiers.

'Names,' one said, sounding bored.

'Nikolas Atwood,' Aric said. It was a gamble; we didn't know if Nikolas had been invited, but as the son of the Aldarian governor, it seemed likely his name would be on the list. And Nikolas and his group had their own mission, hopefully taking them far from here.

The Warrior waved Aric through. I started to follow, but he blocked my way. 'And *you* are?'

'Cassandra, sir,' I replied. 'I'm one of the dancers.'

The Warrior scanned the list and shook his head. 'You're not on here.'

'That can't be right,' I protested, and I didn't have to fake my surprise. 'Could you please check again?'

This time when he shook his head, it was more forceful. 'I'm sorry, but I can't let you in. I'll have to ask you step back—'

'I wouldn't do that, if I were you.'

Sabine's timing was so perfect that I suspected she had foreseen this moment and arrived late for dramatic effect. She glided towards us from inside the castle grounds, dressed in a cropped top and billowing pants that matched her moss-green eyes. A dancer's outfit very similar to mine.

The Warrior paused to take her in. Confidence radiated from her like an aura, and she rattled off her name with practised ease.

'Lenore Wayland,' she told the Warrior, who checked his list. 'I must apologise for my friend; she's filling in for Thalia, who was taken ill.' Her eyes met mine, narrowing in convincing annoyance. 'And she's late.'

After a pause, the Warrior nodded. 'Very well,' he said to me. 'You'd best hurry. It's not wise to keep important people waiting.'

I hardly dared to breathe as I followed Sabine through the arched stone entrance and into the fire-lit garden beyond, filled with the soft buzz of cicadas and conversation.

'I thought you lot were supposed to be good at this sort of thing.' Sabine was staring at me, an eyebrow raised. 'That was so easy, too! I could have gotten past those guards in my sleep.'

'"You lot"?' I repeated.

'Mask candidates,' she said, with a pointed glance at me. 'This Trial is practically designed for you, don't you think? It's all about trickery and deception. *Infiltration.*'

'Maybe you should be competing for the Order of Masks, then,' I replied. 'It seems like you have those traits down to an art form.'

Sabine laughed. 'Maybe I should.'

Eyes lingered on us as we walked through the gathering, and Sabine slipped her arm casually through mine.

Without looking at Aric, she said, 'Two dancers don't attract much attention, but it's unusual for dancers to be accompanied by a Warrior. It might be best if you wait here. When Mira and I are done, we're going to need a quick escape – perhaps you can deal with the guards before then.'

'No.' Aric's voice was so firm that I shot him a surprised glance. 'I stay with Mira.'

Sabine rolled her eyes at me, as if to say, *Is he always this protective?*

'Try to keep your distance, then,' she said with a sigh. And then: 'Here.'

I took the glittering black mask that she offered me and tied it in place. I had to give Sabine credit: she certainly came prepared. Perhaps it was an Artisan trait.

'I'll enter the ballroom first,' Aric murmured to me, 'but I'll be watching. If you need my help—'

'I'll find you,' I promised. 'Don't worry about me.'

Aric gave me a look that made it clear that was easier said than done. But he strode inside, smoothly timing his entrance to coincide with another group of nobles. It looked as if they had come together; none of the Warriors gave him a second glance.

'Do you know where it'll be?' I asked Sabine. 'What we've been sent to steal?'

'Oh yes.' Sabine's voice was low. 'It'll be in the most dangerous place possible. It'll be with *him.*'

I followed her gaze across the ballroom, to where a young man lounged on a throne, dressed entirely in black: glossy knee-high boots, leather breeches, and a tailored jacket with glistening silver accents. He was at the centre of the celebration, but he appeared disinterested – almost apathetic, his fingers toying with his high collar. Then he shifted slightly, uncrossing his lean legs, and I saw his face properly for the first time.

'You know the prince, do you?'

'I suppose you could say that,' I said, watching Cassius holding court in this strange castle. Then I glanced back at Sabine. 'No other candidate would be tasked with stealing from a royal, would they?'

Sabine's smile sharpened into something far more real.

'I like you, Mira, so I'll give you some advice.' She leant in, her lips almost at my ear. 'If you go through with this, then it's not the emperor you should fear. The prince plays games with people, and they rarely end well.'

'I think it's too late to turn back now,' I said with false bravado.

Sabine chuckled. 'You're right about that. Find a way to get him alone and take his crown – I'll make sure he can't come after us.'

Without further explanation, she turned and melted into the crowd. Though I'd watched her leave, it was impossible to pick out Sabine's lithe form amongst the sea of colourful dancers.

The message was clear enough: she'd gotten me in. Now I was on my own.

CHAPTER TWENTY-SEVEN

Mira

The golden crown winked at me tauntingly. It was the object of this task, but I couldn't simply reach out and take it. This was a riddle, one that I had to solve.

I crossed the parquetry dance floor, slipping between nobles and servants alike, observing Cassius. As I did, I ran through everything I knew about the youngest prince. Palace life bored him; that was why he had sought me out that night. I was an oddity, a newcomer to this game – which made me unique. It made me intriguing.

And the prince craved adventure, challenge, novelty, anything to break up the monotony of dealing with his father's court. *Posturing fools,* he had called them.

What had Sabine said? Cassius liked to play games. Well, maybe he could be tempted into playing one with me.

I remembered how easily my mother could slip into a new character, like donning a new cloak. Her words echoed in my mind: *Who do you want to be, Mira?*

Noblemen parted for me as I strode into the centre of the gathering. Cassius was surrounded by a few dozen other young men, all drinking and talking. As I looked on, one of them murmured something in his ear. He smiled back indolently, but then he looked up, his piercing eyes meeting mine. 'And who might you be?'

'Tonight's entertainment, Your Highness,' I said.

Cassius considered me a fraction too attentively. But then he waved a hand. 'By all means,' he said, his voice a low purr. '*Entertain* us.'

The other noblemen were watching me now, and the colourful crowd backed away to give me space. I recognised Sabine in the distance, saying something to the musicians. A handful of Warriors brought out full-length mirrors, which they set up in a semicircle before extinguishing all but three fire braziers.

Cassius's gaze raked me up and down, and I smiled. I knew what I looked like, silhouetted by fire. Thanks to my time at the circus, I knew exactly how to enthral an audience.

At Sabine's command, the musicians struck up a deep, resonating beat. I moved slowly at first, remembering all the times I'd watched my mother. *When I dance, Mira,* she had said, *I am a conduit for the music.*

And that was what I was now. A conduit.

The mirrors reflected multiple images of me: illusions that glimmered as brightly as flame, turning me into something beyond what I was. The drums increased in tempo until I matched every beat perfectly, the red of my slitted skirt like a slash of blood in the darkness.

I had never surrendered to the music like this before, and I understood now why mother had loved it so much. Something reckless drove me to accept a fire torch from Sabine. A gasp went through the audience as I increased my pace, the heat of the flames licking against my skin.

The dance was unpredictable, just as the beat was unpredictable – sometimes it was slow and sinuous, while other times it was filled with fast turns and heavy drumbeats. The fire turned me into a pillar of whirling crimson, sparks spilling out over the crowd.

And it was in that moment, as I twirled across the stage like a living flame, that my eyes locked with the prince's.

The expression on his face was hard to interpret, but there was something covetous about the way he looked at me. I held his gaze as I allowed my movements to slow, matching the fading song.

Cassius clapped his hands together, his emerald cufflinks catching the light and gleaming like dark scales. 'Very impressive,' he announced. 'A performance worthy of court dancers.'

I ducked my head, letting long dark hair shield my face. 'Thank you, Your Highness. You're too kind.'

'Trust me,' Cassius said, standing, 'kind is something I'm not.' He extended his arm.

I hesitated before taking it. His eyes narrowed, noting my reluctance.

'Is this all yours?' I asked, hoping to distract him.

Cassius followed my awed glance around the ballroom. 'This is nothing,' he said, leading me to a raised terrace.

Looking out over the lush grounds, I realised he was right. While the inside of the castle was impressive, it was nothing compared to the views from its hilltop vantage point. The entire garden was lit up to magnificence, continuing all the way to the sprawling city below.

'What is this place?'

'It's known as Caleah Fortress,' he told me as a servant approached with a tray of drinks. I had a glimpse of familiar brunette curls: Sabine. A glass vial gleamed as she slipped something into the prince's drink before handing it over. *Ten minutes,* she mouthed.

Anxiety constricted my chest. Sabine had said she'd find a way to stop Cassius from coming after us after I stole his crown. Whatever she'd given him, I needed to get the prince alone before the effects took hold.

'Apparently,' Cassius continued, and I remembered we'd been discussing the fortress, 'it was named after one of the old Aqualian rulers.' He waved a hand. 'Some queen or another.'

I hated the uncaring way he said it: as if the history of this castle meant nothing to him. I had been taught that Ravalia cherished other cultures, embracing their customs as our own. But I was swiftly coming to realise how naive I had been.

Cassius waited for me to take a sip before doing the same. 'As much as I like a good mystery,' he murmured, reaching for the ribbon of my mask, 'you're too intriguing to remain one for long.'

I stepped back before he could make contact, ignoring the way his eyes flashed as I did. This was a dangerous game I was playing, but part of me came alive with the thrill of it.

'Your castle is incredible,' I told Cassius, looking at him from beneath my lashes. 'There's so much more I would like to see. Perhaps you could give me a more . . . private tour?'

Cassius's smile was slow and deliberate. He offered me his arm and we crossed back through the party. A Warrior came up and murmured something in his ear. Cassius said something back – too low for me to overhear.

The Warrior strode through the ballroom—

And took hold of Aric's shoulders, dragging him forcibly towards the entrance. Aric didn't try to struggle. Desperately, I searched the crowd for Sabine, but Cassius's grip tightened on my arm, drawing my attention back to him.

'Don't be distressed,' he said. 'Any party I throw inevitably has a few trespassers.'

'And what happens to them?' I asked, my heart pounding at twice its usual speed as we climbed the central staircase.

'Usually nothing final.' I had the sense that Cassius was amused by the question. 'Unless they do something to *really* annoy me.'

He guided me through a long hallway and towards a set of heavy wooden doors at the far end. The rooms beyond possessed the same contradictions as the rest of the castle: they were austere from the outside but sumptuous inside, with elaborately carved divans, lacquered furniture and floor-to-ceiling tapestries depicting Ravalian hunts. The rich shades of green gave the impression that I had stepped into a dense forest. Perhaps the effect should have been soothing, but there was something unnervingly reptilian about the colour.

Cassius strode into the bedchamber, placing his crown on the bedside table. My eyes darted nervously towards the four-poster bed, with its green-and-gold duvet and mountain of satin pillows. No one denied a royal, and if I'd miscalculated, I could be in serious trouble.

'I'm surprised by your boldness,' Cassius drawled. 'I wasn't expecting you to infiltrate my party, and certainly not to stage such a delicious performance.'

We were suddenly very close, so close that I could make out flecks of silver in his dark blue eyes. I tried to pull away, but he caught hold of my wrist.

'Consider me flattered,' Cassius continued, his lips curving into a sharp smile. 'Not everyone goes to such elaborate lengths to get my attention.'

'That wasn't . . .' I trailed off, trying to collect my thoughts. 'I wasn't trying to get your attention.'

'Weren't you?' The smile was still on his lips as he said, 'If you wanted to meet with me privately, Kasmira, all you had to do was ask.'

He released me and I stumbled backwards, my pulse racing. Cassius followed smoothly, stalking me like I was one of the doomed creatures on the tapestries around us.

'You didn't think I'd be able to tell?' he murmured. 'I knew who you were from the moment you first spoke to me. I was curious to see how it would play out.' His gaze swept over me appraisingly. 'I can't say I'm disappointed with the result.'

I took another hurried step back, my hips connecting with the low stone wall of the balcony. As I risked a glance down, I realised exactly how high up we were. A gust of wind tore through my hair and buffeted my skirt.

'Considering jumping?' Cassius asked. 'I wouldn't recommend it.'

My eyes reluctantly returned to the prince. 'I have to go,' I said, too quickly. 'I have to get back to the party.'

'I doubt anyone will miss you,' he said, inching closer. 'As you saw, the man you came here with – the one who clearly *isn't* Nikolas Atwood – is otherwise occupied.'

A shiver darted down my spine. 'If you've hurt him—'

'And why would I do that?' Cassius asked, tilting his head so that his golden hair fell into his eyes. 'I have no reason to hurt you or your companion. Not unless you give me one.'

It was a silken threat, and it rooted me in place.

'Why did you really come here, Kasmira?'

So he didn't know the details of the first Trial. That was something, at least – though it was far from reassuring. I met Cassius's stare boldly, but I felt shaky with adrenaline.

'You know,' he mused, 'I've never had much patience for enigmas.'

'Maybe I like being an enigma,' I breathed back. 'Maybe I don't want to be another of your family's pawns.'

Cassius smiled, but there was something dangerous about the curve of his mouth. His body was inches from mine, all hard, sinewy muscle, and with a thrill of fear, I realised that I barely came up to his chin. It would be so easy for him to throw me to my death – to watch me break apart on the cobblestones below. His father might even reward him for it.

Cool fingers traced the line of my jaw, explorative and yet somehow challenging. Achingly slowly, Cassius brushed his thumb across my bottom lip.

Daring me to lean in, to close the gap between us—

And I did.

Threading my hand through his silky hair, I brought his face down to mine. He hesitated for only a second before wrapping his arm around my waist, pulling me to him and claiming my mouth. Before I knew it, he was moving us backwards, steering me towards the large bed.

Cassius laid me back on it, oddly gentle. But as he looked down at me, he no longer appeared hungry or threatening or even nonchalant. If anything, he seemed curious.

'Why are you really here, Kasmira?' he asked again, making no move to come closer.

I smiled up at him without answering, shifting onto my knees. Like this, my face was level with his chest; I had to crane my neck to meet his intent stare. Seductress was a role I'd never played before, but judging by the look in his eyes, I was doing something right.

Without releasing his gaze, I untied the ribbon of my mask, my movements slow and inviting. Cassius watched it fall to the sheets. When he glanced back at me, it was with the same covetous expression he had worn during my dance.

'No more talking,' I instructed, placing a finger against his lips.

Heat sparked between us as Cassius kissed my finger and then my mouth, allowing himself to be tugged down next to me on the feather-soft duvet. I undid his jacket while he kissed a sensuous trail down my throat, coaxing a sigh from me.

It was tempting to lose myself in the agonising pleasure of his caresses. My head fell back against the pillows as his mouth inched lower, his fingers lower still. But I kept my eyes open, studying his reactions.

Just as I was beginning to wonder if Cassius was immune to whatever drug Sabine had given him, the first signs became apparent. Sweat beaded on his forehead. His magnetic gaze lost some of its sharp, cunning clarity. Then it widened. His hands dropped from my waist as realisation crossed his monstrously handsome face.

'You don't know what you've done, Kasmira,' he said, his voice silk on steel. 'You don't want to play games with me.'

I tilted my head teasingly to one side as I moved above him, my inky hair brushing his neck. Right now, I had the upper hand – and we both knew it. Power was a heady, electrifying sensation in my veins. 'Why not?'

Cassius's golden head fell back against the pillows, and while his muscles might have been weak, the warning in his voice was unmistakable. He gritted out the words: 'They usually have deadly endings.'

I knew it was unwise to antagonise the prince, but I couldn't help myself. So I flashed him a devious grin – victorious and challenging and a hundred other things – and took the crown from his bedside table. It was heavy and cold against my fingers, the points as sharp as blades.

Cassius's eyes flared with impotent anger at the final insult. I only winked at him.

'Ah, but those are the best kind.'

CHAPTER TWENTY-EIGHT

Mira

I was still smiling as I descended the steps to the party, raising the mask to my face. There had been no easy way to disguise the crown, so I hadn't bothered to try. It rested on my head, and somehow, its weight didn't feel overwhelming. It felt just right.

Sabine was waiting at the base of the staircase. When she looked up, she laughed. 'Your Highness,' she said, dropping into a sweeping curtsy. 'You're going to be in *so* much trouble.'

'Not as much trouble as we're going to be in if we don't make it back soon.' My eyes canvassed the ballroom, pausing on one of the Warriors. He noticed me, too, and said something to his companion – who hurried up the spiral staircase. 'We're about to have company.'

Sabine nodded. 'Let's get going, then.'

But the Warrior moved quickly, blocking our way. 'Halt,' he ordered, his attention on the crown. 'That belongs to the prince.'

'Does it?' Sabine asked, running a finger along the back of the Warrior's hand. 'Perhaps you should look again.'

The Warrior studied Sabine, then the crown. He shook his head. 'But I could have sworn . . . my apologies, ladies. I must have been mistaken.'

'Think nothing of it, sir,' Sabine told him sweetly, dropping her hand. The ruby in her bracelet gleamed, like it was lit from within. 'Enjoy the party.'

The crowd paid us little attention as we strode through the cluster of chattering nobles. Dressed as dancers, no one questioned us, and on my head, the crown looked as though it could be for a performance.

'How did you *do* that?' I asked Sabine, careful to keep a smile on my face for our audience. I walked slowly, too, as if I had all the time in the world – even though instinct was screaming at me to hurry, to find Aric and leave before we were discovered.

'I'm going to be an Artisan, remember?' Sabine replied, as if it should be obvious. 'I can do all sorts of fun things.'

Something about that didn't ring true. I was sure Zandri had said we wouldn't be granted powers until *after* Initiation. Sabine might have a certain amount of intuition or foresight, but what she'd just done went far beyond that. But perhaps she had been born with natural magic.

That would explain her warmth towards me. If she was magical, then Sabine could have been forcibly brought to the palace like I was. She might have no other choice but to compete in the Trials.

Either way, I studied Sabine with newfound respect – and wariness. Artisans' gifts weren't to be taken lightly. Sabine might seem young and harmless, but appearances could be deceiving. I knew that better than anyone. 'Somehow, I suspect that's the least of what you can do.'

Sabine winked, and quickened her pace without replying.

'We need to find Aric,' I said to her retreating back. 'Cassius told me that he's being detained somewhere, but I don't know—'

'Way ahead of you,' Sabine said. 'What do you think I was doing, while you were alone with the prince?'

Relief surged through me. 'You mean you freed him?'

'Not exactly.' Sabine shrugged. 'I compelled one of the Warriors to accidentally drop the key he was holding. The rest is up to Aric.'

'You didn't think to maybe do a bit more?' I asked. 'How many Warriors were detaining him, anyway?'

Sabine's expression didn't change, but her tone cooled. 'I'm no Warrior. That's *his* role, and so far, he hasn't been particularly good at it.'

I opened my mouth to defend Aric when a shout cut through the gathering.

'Stop!' It was a Warrior – and his eyes were on us. 'Stop, in the name of the emperor!'

'And that's our cue to run,' Sabine said, grabbing my hand and tearing through the gardens.

More shouts sounded from behind us. I didn't turn, but I knew the Warriors were pursuing us, pushing past the revellers.

'I don't suppose you can cast some sort of illusion to make us invisible?' I shouted, my breath coming faster now. 'Or something to deal with the Warriors up ahead?'

Sabine's brunette curls trailed behind her as she ran. She didn't look back at me, but she called over her shoulder, 'I need to touch them to do that. My abilities aren't limitless, you know.'

Great. That was just great.

My hand tightened on hers as we kept running. We were close to the security checkpoint now, so close that I could see the Warriors guarding it beginning to turn – searching for the source of the commotion.

I wondered whether they would try to take us alive – or if they would cut us down instead. None of the Ravalian royals were renowned for their mercy, and if these men realised the crown I was wearing belonged to *Cassius*—

Just as I was readying myself to charge right into their onslaught, the lead Warrior suddenly looked over his shoulder. I saw the flash of a sword before he fell, unconscious, to the ground.

'Go,' Aric said, sizing up the remaining two Warriors. 'I'll be right behind you.'

I started to slow, intending to help Aric, but Sabine's grip on my hand tightened.

'You'd only be a distraction,' she said. 'He's the Warrior. Let him prove it.'

Though I knew she was right, it went against everything in me to leave Aric behind. But I kept my head down as we hurtled down the hill and into the narrow streets beyond.

'How much time do you think we have left?' I asked as we turned a corner and slowed to a brisk walk.

'Not much,' Sabine replied, frowning. 'We're cutting it close.'

I'd suspected as much, but it was worse to have my suspicions confirmed. What if we didn't make it back in time?

'We can't go in without Aric,' I said as we reached the imposing palace gates.

'If you want to wait, that's your choice,' Sabine said. 'But which of us do you think the emperor would be more pleased to fail? Right now, Aric is in less danger than you are.'

I hesitated, glancing back in the direction of the dark, sprawling city. Then I turned and hurried after Sabine, into the glittering, gilded cage of the Ravalian palace—

Where the outcome of the first Trial would be decided.

CHAPTER TWENTY-NINE

Scarlett

If I had known that wearing someone else's face would be so liberating, I would have done it years ago. Then again, Zandri wouldn't have given up the blood ruby before now. Not without a very compelling reason.

Standing in the entrance to the throne room, my eyes went to my father, who sat regally above the assembled candidates. Ivalene stood at his side, and just below her was Zandri, her shoulders decorated with dark feathers that gave the impression of wings.

No one had noticed us yet, but that could change at any moment. I glanced at Mira and frowned. 'You're not going to wear that in, surely.' Sabine's voice – a higher, more musical pitch than mine – was incredulous. 'Even I wouldn't antagonise the court so openly.'

'The emperor already wants me dead,' Mira said, reaching up to straighten the crown. 'He can't kill me twice.'

I raised a brow, torn between admiration and disbelief. The longer I spent with Mira, the more I liked her – and the more I worried that she wouldn't make it through the Trials.

But I only shook my head. 'It's your funeral.'

A hush fell as we stepped into view. All eyes turned to us, lingering longest on Mira. As we came closer, the emperor's gaze went straight to the golden crown she wore.

'What is the meaning of this?' he asked, addressing his wife. 'Why is that *girl*—' he stabbed a finger at Mira— 'wearing my son's crown?'

Ivalene flinched back from the emperor's disapproval. Her face was tight with shock, and I knew this wasn't the outcome she'd intended. She'd probably given Mira this task hoping that Cassius would kill her himself.

'It was her trial, Your Majesty. As you know, each of the candidates was instructed to steal a specific object. This was hers.'

Emperor Kalias considered Ivalene for an uncomfortably long time. 'Well, then.' His voice was low and cold. 'I suppose congratulations are in order.'

'Not quite,' the empress said quickly. 'The task is only considered complete if *all* group members are present. I can see only the candidates from the Order of Masks and Artisans – but where is the third?' She paused, her expression turning triumphant. 'Where is your Warrior?'

'I'm here,' a voice called.

I turned to see Aric striding between the giant candelabras. There was a shallow cut across his forehead, but other than that, he appeared unharmed.

'You're late,' Ivalene said harshly. 'According to the rules—'

'The Trial officially ends at midnight,' Aric interrupted. 'It's not midnight yet, Your Majesty.'

Though he phrased the words respectfully, the royal guards visibly bristled. Candidates weren't supposed to speak without being asked a direct question first. Aric had broken those rules. He'd done so politely, but the indication of rebellion was clear.

The emperor allowed the silence to linger, probably hoping Ivalene would protest further. When she didn't, he spoke. 'As I said, it would seem congratulations are in order. Approach the dais and receive your reward.'

I led the way, keeping my head down. My pulse raced as I walked up the steps to the black marble dais, but Sabine's features shielded me from the scrutiny of the audience.

I curtsied deeply when I reached the stone throne, and my father showed no ill will as he pinned a small gold token to my dancer's outfit. Our eyes met and for an instant, I feared he might recognise me. That he might order his guards to drag me away.

But, of course, he didn't. The illusion held.

'Thank you, Your Majesty,' I said softly, sweet and demure – the exact opposite of the girl I'd been pretending to be.

Then it was Mira's turn. If she was nervous, she didn't show it; she climbed the steps confidently, ignoring the hostile glances in her direction. Her gaze didn't shift from the emperor as she lifted Cassius's golden crown from her head.

'I believe this belongs to you,' she said, extending it to him.

He took the crown wordlessly, his eyes boring into her face. Even from a distance, I could see the promise of retribution in their depths.

Zandri was right. Keeping Mira alive was going to take a miracle.

I slipped away from the palace and into the fire-lit gardens beyond, inhaling the cool night air.

Holding the illusion – even with the blood ruby's assistance – was taxing. I pressed my fingers to my temple, feeling a headache coming on.

I only closed my eyes for a moment, but when I reopened them, I had the sense that I was no longer alone. It was an innate awareness, one that made me turn—

Severin was standing behind me. Even in the blackness, his beauty was devastating; that was the right word for it, I knew, because it ripped into me and left me breathless. He was cutting edges and creeping tattoos, intriguing and unfathomable all at once. *Devastating* was the perfect description.

'I've been watching you.'

His words sent a thrill through me, but I feigned nonchalance. 'Have you?' I asked, tilting my head in Sabine's playful manner. 'And why is that, I wonder?'

'Walk with me,' Severin said, 'and I'll tell you.'

My pulse quickened. I looked down at his outstretched hand for a moment before taking it.

We walked without speaking, our shoes crunching against the gravel. This was a path we'd retraced many times before, and that said enough. When it came to Severin, there was no such thing as coincidence.

'How did you know?'

Severin cast me a sideways glance. The moonlight played over the sharp lines of his face. 'I'll always recognise you, Scarlett. No matter whose face you wear.'

As if to solidify his comment, he turned towards the greenhouse. It was an expansive building with a curved glass roof, and unlike the rest of the palace grounds, it was somewhere that guaranteed privacy at night. As we knew from experience.

'What happened to the real Sabine?'

It sounded like an idle question, but I knew it wasn't. Severin was fiercely protective of the members of his Order, and candidates were no exception.

'She's fine,' I said quickly, thinking of the girl currently tied up in Zandri's tower. 'My mother will make sure she remembers none of this. She'll wake up tomorrow, relieved that she passed the first Trial.'

It was a testament to how well Severin knew Zandri that this didn't surprise him. He only nodded and said nothing more on the subject. I had no doubt he disapproved, but with my mother involved, there was nothing he could do.

While there were no braziers inside the humid greenhouse, there was little need for them. Moonlight filtered in through the glass, faintly illuminating the plants in their glorious wildness.

Severin and I strolled amongst the greenery until we were enveloped by the scent of night-blooming plants. I paused to admire a moonflower, its round petals glistening with a silvery sheen. Beside me, Severin was studying a tall flower with vivid red spots.

'This one is a blister lily,' he said when he caught me looking. 'It's native to Etheria – your brother's latest conquest,' he added, at my blank expression.

It seemed strange to associate Roran with a flower, even one so obviously poisonous. But no stranger than having Severin tell me its name, as if nothing had changed between us.

Perhaps he read that thought on my face.

'I'm sorry for avoiding you.' His eyes were earnest even in the semi-darkness. 'I couldn't stand to watch you with the governor, and I was afraid.'

'Afraid?' I asked, feeling myself soften.

'I was afraid you'd ask me to stay, even when you became another man's wife. And I was afraid that if you did, I wouldn't be able to refuse you.'

I was silent for a moment. Would I have asked that of him? If I hadn't had a plan for the governor, would I have convinced Severin to remain at my side – even if it broke his heart?

'You think me selfish,' I whispered, and the realisation wasn't a comfortable one.

'I think,' Severin said, slowly and cautiously, 'that you can be relentless when it comes to what you want.'

Which was another way of saying yes.

'But there's something else, isn't there?' I guessed, sinking into a nearby chaise. 'Something you're not saying.'

Severin took a seat next to me. 'I saw something in the Elusive Isles,' he admitted softly. 'An ending that I didn't understand, involving you. But I'm beginning to.'

He cast me a heavy glance that I couldn't quite decipher. As warm as the greenhouse was, I had to suppress a sudden shiver.

It was dangerous, asking Severin certain questions. Sometimes, the future was best left alone.

Still, I couldn't help myself. I had to know.

'What kind of ending?'

'I can't tell you that, I'm afraid.' He sounded apologetic, but it stung nevertheless.

'Fine,' I said coolly. 'Keep your secrets.'

I started to stand, but he caught my arm. His skin was deliciously warm against mine, thawing some of the ice within me.

'What I *can* tell you,' he said quietly, 'is that you're about to become a contender.'

I didn't have to ask for what. In the Ravalian Court, there was only one thing that mattered: power. And in my case, that meant the throne.

I should have been focused on the future he described, on that glorious, golden word – *contender*. And yet there was something about the way he said it that bothered me. His face was almost too expressionless, as if he was concealing a larger truth.

That was the problem with Severin; he read me so well, so *easily*, and yet he always managed to remain a mystery.

'What do I need to do? To succeed?'

Though my words were mild, adrenaline pumped through my blood, setting my nerves alight. Was he saying that he'd *Seen* me win against my brothers? That my mother's plan really would clear the path to the throne?

Severin fixed me with those piercing, mismatched eyes. 'I think you already know. I think you've known for weeks.'

I bristled at the accusation in his voice. 'You can't blame me for working with Zandri. Not when you're doing the same.'

'Not by choice,' Severin corrected. 'Zandri has my blood ruby. I have no option but to obey her.'

My irritation quickly faded. Blood rubies were Zandri's invention, her way of distilling the essence of a person – and their magical potential – into a form she could control. She had blood rubies for everyone she inducted into the Orders, but I hadn't known she was actively using Severin's.

'That will change,' I promised him, my hand tightening around the blood ruby Zandri had given to me – *my* blood ruby, resting reassuringly against my skin. 'Once Kalias is gone and the throne is mine, I'll be able to do things differently – *rule* differently. You'll be free. We both will.'

Severin regarded me steadily, in that irritatingly unreadable way of his. 'Scar, what Zandri is planning . . . it's—'

'I don't want to talk about Zandri right now,' I said sharply, brushing back the fabric of my clothes to bare my shoulders. Without releasing his gaze, I stood from the chaise and let the silk fall to the floor.

Answering heat burned in his eyes, the unbridled passion that always simmered just below the surface. I felt the stirrings of my own desire as I leant in and undressed him with slow, sensuous movements.

I shifted to straddle him, my long hair caging us both in a curtain of fire. With a light, reverent finger, I traced along his strong jawline. 'Did you mean what you said, the night of my birthday?'

Severin's naked body was vibrant in the moonlight, his eyes riveted on mine. 'You know I did.'

'Good,' I murmured, and claimed his lips.

My kiss wasn't gentle. It was searing and passionate, and I realised I preferred it like this. I preferred the fierce heat between us, like the harsh burn of a fever, chasing the memory of ice away. The knowledge that, for now at least, I was perfectly in control.

And if there was no more room for questions or conversation—
Even better.

CHAPTER THIRTY

Scarlett

It was late when I returned to my mother's tower, the candles having burned low. There was enough light to illuminate the strange jars and substances that crowded the benches, and I could only imagine how frightening it must have been to wake in such a place.

The real Sabine was slumped in the far corner, brunette hair spilling over her face in untamed waves. Moonlight poured in from the oval windows, illuminating her youthful profile. Even though we had shared the same features, I doubted I'd ever looked *that* young.

I approached slowly, not wanting to scare her further. But she didn't stir.

Only when I passed the benches in the centre of the room did I start to feel concerned.

The drug should have worn off hours ago. Sabine might have felt drowsy afterwards, but it seemed unlikely that she would sleep this deeply – not here, tied up in a tower and surrounded by vials of strange liquids and jars filled with lumps of flesh.

And glass.

'No—' The word left my lips as a gasp.

I crouched at her side, my hands shaking as I reached for her – only to touch cold skin. Sabine slumped forward, weak as a rag doll.

'What have you done,' I breathed, reaching for the glass beaker.

Sabine had smashed it – using the shards to try and free her bound hands. They were still tied behind her, and when I shifted to look, my stomach heaved at the sight of so much blood.

The shard had slipped. It had slipped, and—

I moved quickly away, unable to bring myself to feel for a pulse. The blood was dark – dried. I knew what that meant.

How could I have been so careless, so *stupid* to leave the beaker within reach?

But I knew why. I had been preoccupied, eager to get to the Trial and complete the first part of Zandri's plan.

To become a *contender*.

Severin had been right to look at me the way he had in the green-house, to question my motives—

Severin.

'Oh no, no, no . . .' I stood, pacing from the window to the bench and back again.

I had promised Severin that no harm would come to Sabine. I had *promised* I would return her to him unharmed, with no memory of being detained. And now . . .

The door creaked open.

At the sight of my mother, I felt relieved. If anyone could fix this, it was her.

But Zandri was frowning with disappointment.

'What a pity,' she said, stepping into the room. 'I thought you would attempt to resurrect the girl. Perhaps it was too much to hope your abilities would work on a person. Or perhaps . . .' She looked at me appraisingly, and I had the unsettling feeling that I knew exactly what my mother was thinking.

Perhaps that never even occurred to you.

Rather than rage at Zandri, I knelt at Sabine's side. If there was a chance of doing as my mother suggested, I had to at least *try*.

Clutching one of the discarded glass shards, I allowed it to bite into my palm. Just enough to cause a droplet of blood to well.

It had only taken a droplet to revive the raven, but when the blood hit Sabine's face, I felt nothing. My pulse didn't stutter, I didn't feel faint, and there was no awareness of anything other than my own beating heart.

A long-suffering sigh came from behind me.

'If you spent more time experimenting with your power,' Zandri remarked, 'your blood would be far stronger. Then again, the girl's been dead for hours. Even the Sorceress couldn't resurrect a person who was too far gone.'

'This is on you,' I said coldly, standing and facing my mother. 'Not me. You barely gave me an hour to kidnap Sabine before the first Trial. That's not enough time – not to do it properly. Not to do it *safely*.' To my embarrassment, my voice broke on the last word.

'If you want to rule, Scarlett, you'll have to learn to think on your feet.'

I shook my head. My hair fell across my face, tinting my vision red. 'There won't be any chance of me ruling now.'

'Don't be melodramatic.' Zandri crouched to gather up the broken shards of the beaker. 'The girl's death is unfortunate, but it's easily concealed.'

'Not from Severin.'

'Severin.' A raspy chuckle. '*Severin* does what I tell him. Besides, he can't See the fates of his fellow Artisans. When it comes to her—' Zandri jerked her head towards Sabine's lifeless form— 'he's as blind as the rest of us.'

'He's no fool,' I snapped. 'When Sabine doesn't return, he'll know something happened to her. And he'll blame you.'

'Perhaps.' Zandri smile was as thin as a knife's gash. 'Perhaps he'll blame us both.'

I went very still. The way she said it . . . it was as though she *knew* about my relationship with Severin. But how could she? We had been so careful, so discreet—

'Oh, don't look so stricken.' Zandri placed a cool hand on my shoulder. 'Mistakes happen. In fact, this might prove to be a useful lesson.'

I knew that I should be repulsed by Zandri's nonchalance. That I should flinch away from her touch.

But it felt nice to be comforted. Even by a monster.

'Now,' Zandri said abruptly, 'help me with her. We need to move the body.'

*

I knelt on the cobblestones beside Sabine's mangled body. The fall had not been kind to her – we had rolled her out of the fifth-storey window – and after wearing her face for so long, the damage felt intensely personal to me. As if I was staring at my own ravaged features.

Sabine's unruly curls fluttered in the breeze. I brushed them back, thinking that there was something unnervingly *alive* about the movement. And yet, her chest remained still, half her pretty face caved in. Her skin, once vibrant and sun-kissed, was corpse-white.

A perfect match to mine.

I pressed my palm against hers, noticing our hands were almost the same size. If it wasn't for the blood coursing through my veins, it would have been impossible to tell the difference.

I didn't need to touch Sabine for the illusion to take effect, but I didn't shift my hand from hers, as though holding her hand could make up for what I was about to do. It still felt cruel as I willed her appearance to change, turning Sabine into a nameless servant – all so I could continue impersonating her in the Trials.

A scream shattered the stillness.

I twisted to see a crowd of ladies further down the path. A few were frozen in place, hands comically placed over their mouths. The braver ladies started forward, only to stop when they recognised me.

In court, hierarchy meant everything. None of these ladies liked me, and they certainly didn't respect me, but they wouldn't risk over-stepping their bounds so publicly.

I was preparing to address my audience when someone pushed through the throng. It was Aric, his expressive ochre eyes darting from me to Sabine's disguised body and back again. A flurry of emotions crossed his face, and I knew that he mourned the death of this girl, regardless of her station in life. But his surprise and sadness were quickly contained, replaced by stoic professionalism.

'Your Highness,' he said, offering me his hand.

I allowed him to pull me to my feet, swaying a little. Aric's arm wound around my waist, steadying and protective. Exactly as I'd hoped.

'I'm so sorry,' I said, blinking up at him. 'I think it's the shock of finding her like—' I broke off.

'It's completely understandable, Your Highness. Perhaps I should escort you back to your chambers.'

The concern in Aric's voice matched his expression. He regarded me with unexpected warmth – and a furrowed brow as he took in the blood and dirt caking my skirts. I probably looked a mess, but for once, that worked in my favour.

'I don't want to leave her,' I murmured, so low that he had to lean in. 'She was one of my mother's servants. Someone should ask Zandri if she had a family that can be contacted.'

Aric's jaw tightened as he looked back at Sabine. 'Stay here for a moment – I'll send for the court Warriors and pass that on. Then I'll take you out of here.'

The moment he left, the court ladies converged on me. I could have ordered them away, but I knew what Zandri expected of me, and I intended to play my part convincingly.

So I told them what they wanted to hear, and I even allowed a trace of vulnerability to show as I explained how the girl had jumped from the ledge. No doubt the ladies believed they had glimpsed my soft underbelly, and plotted to use my weakness to their advantage. But I didn't mind. They would see every facet of me soon enough.

And when they did, they would never underestimate me again.

Still, it was a relief when Aric returned and steered me away from the grisly scene.

'Are you alright?' he asked, his eyes flicking down to my bloodied hem.

'Perfectly.' I forced a smile, but Sabine's death was too fresh for it to appear convincing.

Aric was diplomatic enough to let the lie slide.

We followed the twisting halls of the palace towards the main staircase, walking in companionable silence. I hadn't expected to take comfort in the presence of another, but there was some relief in not having to weather my guilt alone.

'I lost someone dear to me,' he said at last. 'My brother. Kain.'

In that instant, it all clicked into place. People weren't particularly complicated – the key was understanding enough about them to put the puzzle pieces together.

Aric loved his brother; that much was obvious. I could see that love – and grief – written in the pronounced lines of his face, the sudden heaviness of his steps. No wonder he had attacked Roran so passionately in the arena. Oh, he had done it for Mira as well – I had no doubt he had been willing to die for her – but he had another, more intriguing reason to wish the prince dead.

I could understand vengeance. I could respect it.

More than that, I could *use* it.

Before we reached the bronze doors of my chambers, I seized my chance. 'I knew your brother.'

Aric stopped abruptly, his arm falling from mine. 'You knew Kain?'

The shock in his voice, the sudden vulnerability – it was well worth the half-truth.

I had known *of* Kain, mostly because the other court ladies had considered him attractive. But I had only paid attention to him when I overheard Roran and my father discussing Kain's links to the resistance. His name had stuck in my mind ever since, because of how he had died, and the person responsible for that death.

I always knew Roran's brutality would be his undoing.

'I was . . . I became quite fond of him.' I hesitated, like there was a larger truth I was unwilling to share or discuss. 'I recognised you the moment you stepped foot in the castle. You're his spitting image.'

Aric's shoulders went rigid – no doubt that resemblance was a source of pain for him and his family. He relaxed with what seemed like an effort, and when he met my eyes again, there was a new openness there.

Sometimes, softness could be as effective as force.

We lingered in the hallway to my chambers, neither of us willing to approach the Warriors at the far end. I had the sense that Aric was waiting for me to speak, his entire being hanging on my next words.

Haltingly, I said, 'It would be nice to discuss Kain sometime.'

Aric smiled. Not a polite, careful smile, but the real thing – a crooked smile that lit up his golden-brown eyes and set them sparkling. 'I'd like that.'

I smiled back at him, aware that without Sabine's death, this moment would never have happened.

Zandri had been right. Tonight *had* proved to be a useful lesson.

One I wouldn't forget.

CHAPTER THIRTY-ONE

Mira

I closed my eyes, centring myself. Then I flicked my wrist and let the knife fly.

It smacked into the bullseye, though I'd envisioned a very different target. I had imagined a knife slicing through the emperor's throat, downing him instantly. I had imagined my blade cutting into Nikolas Atwood, into the crown prince.

'Good,' Scarlett said with approval. 'My mother will be pleased with your progress.'

But when I turned to nod at her, I noticed the watchful eyes of the other candidates. My competition.

Even Nikolas was sizing me up, like he was itching to face me in the arena. Worse than Nikolas was Odessa, whose amber eyes were narrowed into slits. She hadn't been pleased to discover I'd stolen her fiancé's crown during the first Trial.

'Let's go, Mira,' Scarlett instructed.

I ignored her. Without looking at the target, I hurled my last three knives – lethally fast and unerringly accurate.

A few weeks ago my competitors would have smiled. There were no smiles now.

'Take some time for yourself,' Scarlett said, not commenting on my theatrics. 'You'll want to be at your best tomorrow.' Her icy hand brushed my arm, and I felt a strange kinship that I couldn't explain.

The princess didn't seem to notice my reaction. She was distracted by Aric's approach, an uncharacteristic lightness entering her expression.

Even her uniquely pale skin seemed to warm, a hint of colour softening her features.

'Princess,' Aric said, bowing his head. Despite the formality of the gesture, he didn't shift his gaze from Scarlett's.

'Protocol is entirely wasted on you,' she commented, but she was smiling.

Aric returned her smile with a little too much familiarity. 'I'm sure there will be plenty of time to teach me after the Trials.'

His playful tone set me on edge, and when Scarlett said something flirtatious in return, I strode out of the training courtyard. Aric hurried after me, catching my arm to slow me down.

'I wasn't aware that you knew each other,' I said, sharper than I'd intended.

Aric seemed surprised by my attitude. 'Scarlett came to check on me after the Choosing. She wanted to make sure that being a member of her personal guard was something I wanted. And ...' He hesitated.

I struggled to keep my voice level. '*And . . . ?*'

'Well, she knew Kain.' Aric looked uncomfortable, like this wasn't a discussion he wanted to be having.

'This has something to do with your plan for revenge, doesn't it? You think Scarlett can confirm Roran's involvement.'

When Aric avoided my eyes, I knew I was right. 'Come on,' he said, taking my hand. 'Let's get out of here.'

I threaded my fingers through his, but I was still thinking of the way he'd smiled at Scarlett – as though she wasn't a royal, wasn't the patron of the Order of Masks, but just a girl. A very *beautiful* girl.

I forced those thoughts aside as we walked through the barracks, passing the armoury, mess hall and open living quarters with their lines of neat bunks. A guard nodded at us as we cleared the Order of Warriors residence and entered the peaceful gardens beyond.

Aric led me through the palace gates and down the cobbled Imperial Road that passed through the Higher Districts. The land sloped towards the docks, and I felt relieved when we turned away from the main harbour with the Imperial Fleet. Those ships would have been impressive, but in my current mindset, I wasn't interested in yet another demonstration of Ravalian power.

We paused on a small hill, overlooking the modest harbour below. It was a hive of activity: merchants loaded and unloaded their wares, while colourful boats bobbed merrily at the wharves. Children swam around them, shouts and laughter carrying on the breeze. I could almost pretend that nothing had changed, and we were still on Aldara, dreaming of entering the Trials and making a difference.

'Do you ever wish you could go back?' I asked, thinking of Lillian's bright smile and the life I'd left behind.

Aric lay back beside me, looking up at the darkening sky. 'I can't imagine I would have made a different decision, so it probably doesn't matter. It was always inevitable I would end up here.'

My fingers stretched over the grass, strands sweeping across my skin. Aric caught my hand in his, tracing my palm and lingering on my new callouses. He had once called my hands delicate, soft. They were still delicate, but they were no longer soft.

'It's not your fault, you know,' he murmured. 'What happened to you. To your mother.'

I thought of everything I had kept from her. My naive belief that I could protect us both.

Then I thought of Zandri's words, and the hard truth in them. *The moment you announced your candidacy for the Trials, you were both living on borrowed time. I merely sped up the inevitable.*

'I hate them,' I said. 'I hate all of them.'

'I know,' Aric replied, his grip tightening. 'I know, Mira.'

'I didn't understand what you meant, that night on Aldara.' My voice was low, so low that Aric leant in closer. 'But I do now.'

I'd told Aric that he was destroying his life, but if he was able to avenge Kain – wasn't that worth it? Vengeance couldn't bring back the dead, but maybe it could help them rest easier in their graves.

Aric was silent for a long moment. Then he said, 'Let me get revenge for us both.' His warm eyes met mine, filled with sincerity.

'Say the word, and I'll help you run. The Kalurians would shelter you, and perhaps you could do some good there. Help to heal the wounds Emperor Kalias inflicted on your home.'

'If I travelled to Kalure, I'd only bring war with me. Now that he knows who I am, Emperor Kalias will never stop hunting me.'

'But you can't stay.' Aric leant in. 'Surely you can see that. Even if you make it through the Trials, you'll always have a target on your back. Your only chance at a future is to disappear.'

I stared into his face, which was suddenly far too close. Like this, it was too easy to get caught up in his words, in the possibility of something else. Something more.

Would you leave with me? I almost asked, but I already knew the answer. If it came down to a choice between being with me and avenging Kain, I'd lose. He'd made that perfectly clear.

'My mother tried to run. Look where that got her.' I pulled my hand from Aric's.

'Mira—'

'No.' My voice was soft, but my words were sharp and definitive. 'No, my choice is already made. It was made the moment they killed her.'

I didn't know if I would survive the Trials, but I couldn't turn back now. Not even if I wanted to. As for Kalure – I would only be a burden there, a hunted half-Ravalian queen who had no idea how to rule a country. But if I killed Emperor Kalias, I would have done something to truly help them. And if I died in the process . . . well, I'd be a better queen to them dead than alive.

Aric was watching me sadly. 'I've changed my mind,' he said. 'I do wish I could go back.'

I almost told him that I wished the same. That I wished it with all of my blackened, broken heart. And maybe the Mira from Aldara would have cracked then, would have changed her mind and begged Aric to run with her – to choose love over hatred and death. But that Mira was dead. She'd died, the moment her mother's heart had stopped beating.

So instead, I stood and faced Aric with a spine like iron. I looked down at him and I wasn't sure who he saw in that moment, but whoever it was, I doubted it was anyone he recognised.

'I don't,' I told him, and walked away.

From my position on the wharf, I stared over the harbour. Rain dripped onto my shoulders, lightning splitting the night sky. In comparison, the black water was eerie in its stillness.

I didn't want to be here, but my dream was impossible to ignore. As I'd tossed and turned in my sleep, worried about the second Trial, I had seen my mother. The scene was one I had recognised instantly; it was the same vision I'd had after discovering the blood ruby on Aldara.

Celeste was dancing in a ballroom, with a diadem in her hair and a dress like rippling ice. But it wasn't just my mother I noticed: it was the man at her side, tall and handsome, with a fighter's athletic build and an easy smile. The resemblance between us was uncanny, and I knew I was looking at my father.

As I drank him in with desperate, reverent eyes, my mother turned. She smiled, her hand dropping to the necklace she wore. The locket with the wreathed crown.

'Return to the docks and enter the water,' she told me. Her voice was younger than I remembered, yet achingly familiar. 'The locket will find you.'

I stepped towards her, but Celeste was no longer looking at me. She had turned towards the entrance to the ballroom, where I could hear the distant sound of banging. The sound filled me with dread.

Every dream of my mother always ended the same way: with her death.

I watched, breathless and frozen, as my father handed Celeste a blazing lantern.

'Please,' I begged her. 'Please don't go. I can't do this alone.'

My mother held the lantern aloft, her face cast in the flickering light of the flames.

'You won't be alone,' she promised—

And let it fall.

Thunder boomed, jolting me back to reality. With a start, I realised that I was barefoot, balancing halfway down a rusted ladder. Water lapped at the rungs, and I couldn't see beyond its dark surface.

Swallowing, I descended the last of the steps. Before I lost my nerve, I unclenched my grip from the slimy rail.

The cold made me gasp, my heart racing as I broke the surface.

Return to the docks and enter the water. The locket will find you. What kind of instruction was that?

But I'd always trusted my mother, and I needed to trust her now. She wouldn't have told me to come here if it wasn't important – wouldn't have wasted those precious last moments together in the arena.

Teeth chattering, I kicked my legs even harder, trying to warm up. If I waited long enough, perhaps something miraculous would happen. The locket *was* magic, after all: maybe it would simply appear. Or maybe . . .

I closed my eyes and took a deep, steadying breath. *Don't look with your eyes.*

I was expecting a faint, almost imperceptible pull. The kind I had felt when aiming a weapon at a target or picking a correct card. Instead, I was pulled underwater: sucked further and further down by a force beyond my control.

My eyes flashed open, but they might as well have remained shut. Everything was black and freezing. Something brushed past my face – a tendril of kelp, probably – but my chest tightened with panic, imagining a circling shark.

How far was it to the bottom? I had no idea how deep this water was, and I was already desperate for air.

I tried to struggle against the pull, but it was useless. I was caught in a freefall, a relentless current dragging me into its malevolent depths.

What if I die down here?

Just as I had the thought, my feet hit the sandy bottom. The force was enough to make my whole body shudder.

Though it shouldn't have been possible, a flicker of light pierced the inky blackness. The faintest gleam of gold.

I reached down into the sand, my fingers brushing something smooth and round.

Warmth and power surged into me. And as my hand enclosed around the locket, my arm was drawn upwards—

My entire body with it.

It happened quickly. So quickly that the sensation was nothing more than a rush of water until my fist broke the surface and air – beautiful, sweet, life-saving *air* – flooded into my lungs.

In a daze, I stared down at the locket nestled in my palm. It was glowing a muted red now, but still pulsing with warmth and familiarity. With welcome.

The feeling was almost too tender, too wondrous to be real, and tears pooled in my eyes. Somehow, this locket – my *father's* locket – contained a piece of my mother. Her essence, her being – whatever it was, it felt like I was holding my mother's beating heart in my hand.

And as I swam towards the ladder, surety enveloped me. No matter what happened, I wouldn't be alone. Even after death, my parents would be with me.

They would be with me always.

CHAPTER THIRTY-TWO

Mira

Nikolas didn't pull his punches, didn't break a sweat, and didn't show mercy. His opponent hit the ground and stayed down. Two Warriors hauled his unconscious body out of view.

I watched from the covered staging area where I had once waited with my mother, my locket now clasped tightly in my hand. Around me, the tension was almost palpable. Most of the candidates were putting on a brave face, but only a handful were truly confident. Odessa, unfortunately, was one of them. She'd already faced Rae – who hadn't even lasted ten minutes.

But I didn't care about Odessa or Rae. I only had eyes for Aric, who was fighting a muscular boy whose name I'd forgotten.

I'd wished him luck before his match, but I still felt guilty about the way we'd left things. We had the same goal, and yet somehow, it felt as though we were inexorably drawing apart.

At times, I had to look away, fearing the worst, but Aric was too fast to be caught, attacking efficiently but remaining out of his opponent's grasp. When the other boy began to tire, Aric seized his chance, launching himself into a carefully coordinated attack. They grappled for about a minute before Aric swept his opponent's legs out from underneath him. In a flash, he had his knee braced against the boy's chest and his arms restrained. No matter how much the other boy thrashed, Aric held firm.

The emperor had no choice but to declare Aric the winner. His opponent was escorted from the arena, and even from a distance, I could see his disappointment.

'It's time,' Scarlett said, striding over.

My stomach clenched as I wondered who I would be paired with. It was supposed to be determined according to skill level; the other Mask candidates had been paired with each other. But each of them had already faced the arena – which left me.

'Do you know who I'll be facing?'

'No. It's different for everyone, of course, but for you . . .' Scarlett paused. 'It's bound to be harder.'

'A nice change then,' I said dryly. The princess didn't respond to my sarcasm.

Aric entered the staging area and flashed me one of his crooked smiles. A smile that said our conversation from the night before was forgiven. 'How are you feeling?'

Scarlett gave us some space, but Odessa glanced in our direction. She was probably too far away to eavesdrop, but I lowered my voice anyway.

'Like I'm balancing on a knife's edge,' I said, 'and if I fall, I die.'

Aric's eyes were serious, but the smile didn't leave his lips. He leant in and murmured, 'Don't fall.'

I barely had the chance to nod before the trumpet sounded. *My turn.*

I strode out of the shade into the bright afternoon sun. The stands were packed, the crowd waiting to see what I could do. Expecting to see me fail.

In the royal box was the emperor, his expression remote. Ivalene and the two princes were at his side, their faces unreadable. I noticed that Cassius wasn't lounging on his throne this time; he was sitting up straight, like he was interested in the outcome of my match. He was probably eager to watch me die – execution was the punishment for stealing from a prince.

But I didn't intend to die today.

'For our final match,' Emperor Kalias announced, 'I have something special planned: a traditional Ravalian duel, fought to the point of yielding or death. I present to you our next candidates: Kasmira Volaris and Nikolas Atwood.'

A murmur went through the stands. Nikolas had already faced his opponent; it was unorthodox for him to fight again. But he was a crowd favourite, and he'd fought without weapons earlier. Now, the crowd would get to watch him compete like a true arena fighter.

My throat went dry as I accepted a sword and dagger from a nearby Warrior. I'd practised for a sparring match, not a Ravalian duel. But perhaps it could work in my favour; I was quick and slight, and at least I wouldn't be trapped in a small circle with Nikolas. I would have room to move.

I glanced at Nikolas, who was swaggering towards me without a hint of concern. When my gaze locked with Aric's, he gave me an encouraging smile. But it didn't reach his eyes.

If even *Aric* didn't believe I could beat Nikolas, what chance did I have?

'I'll let you concede now, if you want.' Nikolas's full lips upturned in a mocking smile. 'I'd hate to mess up your pretty face.'

I forced myself to meet Nikolas's gaze, thinking of the night he had followed me back to my tent. Of what he had tried to do – of what he had felt *entitled* to do, all because he was a noble and I was a nobody. Or so he had believed.

The old anger rose quickly to the surface, and I clung to it with everything I had.

'I can't say the same,' I retorted. 'I'd quite enjoy messing up your face.'

He looked surprised. Hadn't expected me to fight back, had he?

He should have known better.

Nikolas shook his head. 'Always so arrogant. You're going to wish you stayed on Aldara.'

I smiled, although it felt more like a snarl. I wasn't going to make this easy for him. I had given up too much, come too far, to be defeated now. Nikolas was more experienced than I was, but he didn't have as much to lose. He was only fighting for himself; I was fighting for my mother. For vengeance.

We faced the royal box side by side, waiting for the emperor's signal. At his sharp nod, we started to circle.

There was no warning before Nikolas transferred his dagger to his left hand, his right fist barrelling towards my face. I was a second too late to avoid the blow, which sent me sprawling to the ground. But he didn't move in for the kill. He was confident in his victory; he wanted to draw this out, to make it a show.

I climbed to my feet, ignoring my aching jaw. *I can do this. I have to do this.*

'Scared, are you?' Nikolas taunted as I backed away, circling from a distance.

'Not even a little,' I snapped back. 'If you're so sure you can beat me, why don't you come closer?'

Nikolas responded to my challenge, closing in with his sword raised. I barely blocked the strike in time, panting through clenched teeth as my shoulder protested. He was much stronger than I was, and it was only a matter of time before I faltered.

He knew that, too. Nikolas was expecting me to fall back, to buckle against his onslaught. He wasn't expecting me to kick out at his legs, landing a lucky blow to his shin – a blow that made him stumble.

Before he could recover, I shifted to the attack, stabbing with both blades and dancing out of reach. I needed to keep him distracted; as soon as I slowed, as soon as I went on the defensive, it would be all over.

But my strength was decreasing at an alarming rate.

Nikolas's keen eyes noticed my tiredness. 'You're dead, Princess,' he said, spitting the title like a joke. 'Just like your mother.'

I lunged forwards, intending to run him through—

Steel screeched against steel as his blade parried mine, and while I was focused on his sword, his heel slammed into my stomach.

And then the pommel of his sword descended.

Pain erupted in the back of my head, and I crumpled instantly, tasting sand and blood as I hit the arena floor.

I was too stunned to move. To *breathe*.

Where was the girl from Aldara, who had been so determined to beat Nikolas in the arena? I needed her now. I needed her belief, her determination.

I needed her *fire*.

But when I reached for her, all I found were ashes.

Through half-closed eyelids, I saw Nikolas approaching. He was taking his time, basking in the crowd's roaring approval. I needed to get up. *Now*.

My body didn't respond. The temptation to close my eyes was almost overpowering, to let myself descend to a place where I would feel no pain. No emotion. Nothing at all.

But just as I shut my eyes, I remembered the locket.

The moment my desperate fingers brushed it, all the anger and conviction I'd forgotten flooded back. The emotion was fuel, waiting to be ignited. Waiting for me to reach out and *use* it.

Adrenaline burst through my veins, lending strength to my aching muscles. My eyes snapped open and I rolled, right as Nikolas's blade slashed towards me, hitting the arena floor instead. The impact tore the sword from his hand, sending it clattering to the ground.

On my feet, I stared Nikolas down with hard challenge.

Nikolas paused, confused by the sudden change. The entire atmosphere of the battle had altered in the blink of an eye, and I knew the Mira facing Nikolas now wasn't the same Mira who had walked out into the arena.

But Nikolas was still confident. He still thought he could win.

I waited, letting him come closer. It didn't even occur to him to collect his sword; his brute strength was his advantage, which meant that the closer he was, the easier it would be to overpower me.

But while Nikolas had strength, I had *speed*.

He couldn't match it. Couldn't stop me as I sliced with my dagger, opening small, stinging wounds that penetrated his dark leather. He hadn't wanted to make my death quick, so I wouldn't give him the mercy of a quick defeat either.

I whirled and struck and darted away again, moving like Zandri had done – like my feet barely needed to touch the ground.

A dance. That was what this was – a beautiful, deadly dance.

It was Nikolas's turn to panic. He wasn't suited to this style of fighting: he needed his sword, needed the order and structure of the formal duels he was so practised in. But I wasn't fighting like a typical Warrior.

I was fighting like a Mask.

By the time I broke away again, circling at a distance, Nikolas was dripping blood onto the ground and I was smiling.

Whatever was left of his composure disintegrated. He charged – desperate to get his hands on me, to squeeze the life from my lungs.

Exactly as I had anticipated.

The crowd erupted as I sprinted towards him – shouting, screaming, standing from their seats. It looked like we were about to collide: two bodies hitting in a clap of thunder and destruction.

At the last moment, I dropped to my knees and skidded across the floor, knocking Nikolas's legs out from underneath him—

And sending him careening face first into the sand.

I was on him in one quick movement. And there was nothing Nikolas could do – absolutely *nothing* – as I slashed his right hamstring with my dagger.

An agonised scream burst from his lips – more animal than human. It did nothing to diminish my sense of satisfaction.

Hobbled and gushing blood onto the sand, Nikolas crawled away from me – towards his sword. I watched him struggle, wondering if this was what I had looked like when I fought Roran.

Pitiful. *Broken.*

The roar of the crowd swelled to a crescendo as I kicked Nikolas onto his back, pressing the tip of my sword into his exposed throat.

Then silence fell. I didn't need to look up to know the spectators were watching with shock – the same shock that was reflected in Nikolas's wide, pain-glazed eyes.

'I'll let you concede now, if you want,' I said, taunting him with his earlier words.

Nikolas stared at me mutely, his face dark with hatred.

I pressed my sword more firmly into his neck, drawing a thin trickle of blood. *Give me a reason,* I thought. *Just* one.

'I yield,' he gritted out.

Emperor Kalias's expression was cold as he announced me the winner. To my surprise, the shocked silence of the crowd gave way to something else: cheers.

It took me a second to make sense of the individual sounds, to realise what they were shouting.

My name.

And when Nikolas was carried away by two Warriors – when I strode from the arena, the bloodied dagger still in my hand – the other candidates parted for me, like I'd earned their respect.

Or their fear.

CHAPTER THIRTY-THREE

Mira

In any crowd, in any place, Aric always drew my attention. Tonight, he was dressed in an embroidered doublet and fitted black pants, the fabric contouring beautifully to his form. But my gaze lingered on the statuesque girl at his side, her head thrown back in a laugh.

Candlelight played across the golden snakes emblazoned on the bodice of her ebony gown, and it was impossible not to notice the panels cut out at the waist, showing a daring amount of skin. Black diamonds sparkled as she moved, woven into her wine-red hair. As always, she looked beautiful – and deadly.

When her ice-blue eyes met mine from across the banquet hall, I could have sworn they gleamed with challenge.

Most of the royal family were already in position at the high table, servants bringing out steaming dishes. But knots of courtiers and candidates stood in front of the banquet tables, waiting to be seated. A glint of gold caught my eye as I approached a group of noblemen exchanging coins. They eyed me consideringly; no doubt my odds had gone up since defeating Nikolas in the ring.

I kept my eyes forward and my chin high, doing my best to discourage conversation. I didn't want to be anything to these people, but perception was everything in this court.

Apparently, Aric had learnt that lesson as well. *Too well*, I thought as Scarlett strode over with him in tow.

'There you are,' she said, a hint of admonishment in her voice. 'I've been looking for you.'

'Oh?' I asked, unsure what to expect.

'Your friend visited the palace this afternoon. The girl from Aldara – Lillian.' Scarlett smiled – a pleased, self-satisfied smile that put me on edge. 'Apparently, she's been looking for work in Ravalis, hoping to reconnect with the two of you. When she told me Aric was her brother, I offered her a position in the palace. It's dependant on you becoming a member of the Order of Masks, of course – but if you do, then Lillian can serve as your personal attendant.'

I stared at Scarlett. Lillian had been safe on Aldara, but if she came to work at the *palace*—

'I realise it's not a prestigious position, but in time, Lillian could rise to become a palace dressmaker.' A trace of defensiveness entered the princess's voice as she added, 'Lillian seemed thrilled by my offer.'

Opposing desires tugged at my chest. I wanted Lillian to be safe – but I also desperately missed my friend. And though I hated to admit it, Scarlett was right; a position like this could lead to the kind of career Lillian had always dreamt of.

I glanced sideways at Aric, who shot me a cautioning look. Clearly, only one response was appropriate.

'Thank you,' I said reluctantly. 'That's very kind.'

'You're very welcome,' Scarlett replied, but her gaze was already scanning the hall. 'I'd like to introduce Aric to some people,' she said. 'You don't mind, do you?'

Before I could respond, Scarlett linked her arm through Aric's. He shot me a rueful look but allowed the princess to guide him away. I knew Aric was only using Scarlett for information about Kain's death, but the sight was still painful. They looked good together – too good.

The sound of Scarlett's purring laughter was more than I could take, and I left the banquet behind. After climbing the grand staircase, I approached one of the deserted balconies, seeking solitude and fresh air.

Up here, the evening was peaceful. The city was a distant constellation of pinpricks of light – candles and oil lamps burning in the windows of the pitched-roofed buildings. It was a beautiful view, but to me, its beauty was tainted. After seeing the divide between the Higher and Lower Districts, after experiencing the emperor's cruelty for myself—

I wanted to tear it all down. Brick by luxurious brick.

'Do you know how painful it is,' a hard voice commented, 'to have healers work on you for close to four hours? To realise that even with their assistance, you might never be able to walk properly again?'

I turned slowly, annoyed at the intrusion. 'You shouldn't be here, Nikolas. Tonight's celebration is just for candidates.'

And you're not *one. Not anymore.*

'I am still a noble, which means something around here.' Nikolas moved closer, and I noticed that his right leg – the one I'd slashed with my dagger – had a pronounced limp. Frankly, it was miraculous he was standing at all.

'I've already proved that I'm capable of besting you in a fight,' I warned, holding my ground. 'You don't want to provoke me, Nikolas.'

'But that's *exactly* what I want to do.'

He lunged forward, ramming his shoulder into mine—

The wind muffled my scream as I teetered over the railing. Only instinct saved me as I grabbed for the one thing that would stop me from falling to my death: Nikolas himself.

Panic clawed at me as I clung to him, my fingernails sinking into his forearms. *No,* I thought frantically. *Not like this.*

'Don't worry.' This close, the triumph in Nikolas's face was highlighted in terrible, unforgiving detail. 'It'll be quick. So quick you'll barely feel a thing.'

My grip tightened even further, as if clinging to Nikolas could somehow save me. He smiled, an amused flash of white teeth, and I tasted bile.

All I needed was a distraction. It wouldn't take much – if he shifted even slightly, then maybe I could regain my balance. But Nikolas knew he had me trapped. He wouldn't be baited into giving up his advantage—

Until he glanced reflexively over his shoulder.

I didn't know why, and I didn't care. I moved quickly, kicking

Nikolas's legs out from underneath him. He fell heavily onto the tiles, and I used those precious seconds to step away from the edge. Before he could retaliate, the knife I carried – hidden in a thigh holster beneath my dress – rested against Nikolas's neck.

The fear on his face was glorious, almost as thrilling as the sight of his pulse pounding beneath his skin. Tempting me to apply more pressure, to—

'Your Highness!' Nikolas cried out. 'She's trying to kill me!'

My heart sank as I followed Nikolas's gaze. It wasn't a trick; the youngest prince was standing at the balcony entrance, taking in the scene with unnerving calm. His dark clothes blended in with the shadows, but the gleam of his golden hair was unmistakable.

I gripped the knife even tighter, trying to decide between two bad choices: killing Nikolas and running or backing down and accepting my fate. If I let Nikolas live, it would be his word against mine, and Cassius had no reason to take my side.

But Cassius didn't call for the guards. He only raised a blond eyebrow as he moved closer, his gaze briefly shifting to Nikolas. 'And what would you like me to do about it?'

Nikolas hesitated, his expression incredulous. 'Your Highness,' he protested, 'she is in direct violation of the laws of the empire. Surely she should be punished for it. She drew a weapon—'

'From what I saw, she didn't actually use it. So really, there's no harm done – unless Kasmira decides to kill you.' Cassius took a sip from the goblet in his hand. 'If you do survive, you can take it up with my father. But I wouldn't advise it. You've made enough of a spectacle of yourself today, and you're only here as a courtesy to the Aldarian governor.'

Nikolas's face flushed with rage.

'I think it best that you release him, Kasmira,' Cassius continued conversationally. 'And that you return to the banquet, Lord Atwood,' he added in a silken tone, which did nothing to disguise the order.

Nikolas clambered unsteadily to his feet, cutting me a cold glare as I reluctantly withdrew the knife. Then he turned wordlessly towards the hallway, his hands clenched into fists at his sides.

'There's no need to look so concerned,' Cassius said as I straightened. 'I come in peace.'

'Somehow, I doubt that.'

A small smile quirked his lips. 'I do enjoy your honesty. Not many people dare to be so open with me.'

His tone was pleasant, but his warning rang in my ears: *You don't want to play games with me, Kasmira. They usually have deadly endings.*

The prince strolled languidly towards me. I'd forgotten how tall he was, and how lethally attractive: like a panther in human skin. My stomach dipped as I remembered the last time we had been on a balcony like this one – and the hot press of his lips on mine.

Cassius smiled as if he knew exactly what I was thinking. And not one of his devious half-smiles, but a real smile, designed to dazzle. He continued all the way to the railing, his body brushing against mine.

'That's twice now you've helped me.' It came out sounding like an accusation. It *was* an accusation.

'Are you worried I'm keeping count?'

'I'm wondering *why*. After what happened during the first Trial—'

His low chuckle interrupted me. 'Have you considered, Kasmira, that's the *reason* I helped you?'

No. No, I certainly hadn't.

'No one challenges me.' His voice sharpened. *'No one.'*

Our gazes locked, and I felt his stare like a brand across my skin. His eyes were a deeper blue than usual, and the shadows within them only added to my sense of impending danger.

'I didn't do it to win your attention,' I said warily. 'Or your approval.'

'No? Maybe you should have. The people down there—' he jerked his hand in the direction of the banquet hall— 'desire my approval very much. To become a part of this court, you need allies. And I could be a *very* good ally,' he added, his voice midnight-soft. The kind of voice that promised other things.

My mind flashed back to the memory of his tongue on my skin.

Heat rushed through me, too much all at once, and I backed away from him. 'You don't know anything about me.'

'I know enough,' he said softly, holding my gaze intimately. 'Though I'm sure there's more to discover. You're strangely unpredictable, Mira.'

I blinked up at him, unnerved both by his comment and his use of my preferred name. 'Is that supposed to be a compliment?'

'I haven't decided.'

There was something ominous about that statement, like it could turn into a threat. But I refused to be intimidated. 'So – what? I stole from you and now you're intrigued?'

Cassius only smiled. 'Something like that.' When the silence lingered between us, he asked, 'Did you really try to kill Nikolas?'

He phrased it like an idle question, as if the answer was of little consequence. It irritated me.

'Nikolas attacked *me*,' I said, meeting the prince's stare with a burning one of my own. 'He tried to push me over the balcony.'

'Ah.' Cassius leant against the rail, casually folding his arms. He didn't seem surprised in the slightest. 'Well, I suppose that makes sense. He was cut from the Trials because of you.'

'How easily you justify attempted murder,' I said bitterly. 'It's not like I killed Nikolas in the arena.'

'No,' Cassius agreed. 'You just humiliated him.'

'Are you really turning this back on me? *Nikolas* was the one who—'

'I'm not saying what Nikolas did was smart,' Cassius interrupted, something hard and dangerous entering his voice. 'His strategy was flawed, at best. But you were foolish to put yourself in this position. If you want to survive here, you have to know who your friends and enemies are.'

'Which are you?'

'That depends,' he said slowly, 'on your answer to a very simple question: what do you want?'

'Pardon?'

'I think we both know your ambitions extend far beyond these Trials. The fools inside might believe otherwise, but I'm not naive enough to think that your motivations are so simple.' Cassius's expression turned serious. 'This is your chance, Mira, to convince me that you're worth backing.'

'You already know the answer, don't you?' I said as he pushed off from the railing. 'You've known what I want all along.'

Cassius smiled, but it was a strange smile. The blasé pose was gone, the nonchalant prince discarded just like another mask.

'If you make it through the third Trial, Mira, perhaps we can help each other.' His voice was low and very, very dark. 'If we struck a bargain, you and I, I could give you everything you desire.' Cassius stepped closer, until his breath tickled my ear: 'I could even give you my father's head on a platter.'

CHAPTER THIRTY-FOUR

Scarlett

I should have been relieved that Mira had survived the second Trial, that my plans were still in motion. Instead, I found myself searching the banquet hall for Severin.

He hadn't attended the Trial, which wasn't a surprise – his talents were always in demand – but I'd hoped he would be here tonight. Everyone else had taken time off from their usual duties – why couldn't he have done the same?

Beside me, Odessa picked at her nails, bored now that Cassius had left the high table. Despite their antagonistic relationship, both had an appreciation for court antics – and a keen mind for ferreting out secrets. It had proven mildly entertaining to eavesdrop on their conversation, but I still would have preferred to spend the evening as Sabine. Perhaps I could even have occupied the empty seat next to Aric.

I watched him from a distance, conversing easily with the other candidates. A few had left, but the majority had stayed to enjoy the desserts being brought out from the kitchens: fruit puddings, savoury pies and bowls of fresh cream.

'I don't know how you do it,' Odessa said with a superior little sigh. 'How you always seem to come out of things unscathed.'

I didn't bother to conceal my irritation as I turned to face her. 'You'll have to be more specific. I have no idea what you're referring to.'

'I'm referring to the governor, of course.'

I blinked in surprise. The truth was, I'd almost forgotten about Governor Halvor.

I was a second too slow to hide my reaction. Odessa smiled mirthlessly. 'That poor man never stood a chance, did he?'

'The governor made his own choices,' I retorted. 'It's not my fault he's rotting in the cells.'

'Maybe not. But it's your mother's fault that he's going to be executed.'

'. . . What?'

'You didn't know.' Odessa's smile held an edge of cruelty. 'Zandri convinced the emperor to make the governor's death a part of the final Trial. Thought it would be *dramatic*.'

I shouldn't have been rattled. But I was.

'I spoke to him a few times,' Odessa continued. 'While you were busy ignoring him, the governor was asking about *you* – trying to discover ways of making you happy.'

The words hit home, but I shoved my guilt aside. I focused on anger instead.

'You're just resentful,' I snapped, 'because Cassius couldn't care less about you. But at least you're engaged to a royal. Marrying my brother gives you everything you've ever wanted: status, luxury, power—'

'—not safety,' Odessa corrected. 'Not love.'

That gave me pause. Since when did *Odessa* worry about safety or love?

'So what?' I asked. 'Safety is an illusion for people like us, and love . . . well, love is hardly a useful emotion.'

For a moment, it seemed like I'd stunned Odessa to silence. 'Isn't there anyone you love?' she asked, sounding almost sad. 'Someone who you would sacrifice everything for?'

I thought of my mother, with her cool face and hard eyes. My father and brothers, who were willing to cast me aside in the name of power. Then I thought of Severin. If I loved anyone, it would be him. But what Odessa described . . . I couldn't fathom the feeling.

No, I almost said. *There isn't.*

And yet—

'Excuse me, Your Highness.' The low, melodic voice made me turn too quickly; the contents of my goblet overflowed, spilling onto the table. 'I believe we have a conversation to finish.'

Severin's eyes glittered down at me, as if in amusement. *You're welcome*, they seemed to say.

'I believe we do,' I replied, and for the first time all night, my smile was genuine.

Together, we left the hall behind. It was strange walking with Severin: it felt so familiar, but there was an element of uncertainty there, too.

'I haven't seen you for a while,' I said cautiously. 'Not since . . .'

'Since the night Zandri's servant fell to her death,' Severin finished, an ironic twist to his lips. He paused at the bottom of the stairs, forcing me to stop as well. 'How convenient that you've been impersonating Sabine ever since.'

I held his stare with an effort. It had been too much to hope that Severin wouldn't realise what had happened to Sabine. Most likely, he believed that Zandri had murdered her – disposed of her for the sake of convenience.

But before I could decide what to say to fix this – if this even *could* be fixed – my eyes dropped to a dark stain on his vest.

'You're bleeding,' I said, reaching for him instinctively.

He pulled back before I could make contact. 'It's not my blood.'

With a shiver, I understood. I had heard about the arrival of a boat packed with wounded soldiers from the Western Lands – but I hadn't made the connection until now.

During the months I had spent on campaign with my father, Severin had often been summoned to the tents filled with wounded men. I had observed him from a distance, pausing beside their pallets, his eyes closed as he gazed into their futures. Most often, he would shake his head and move on, taking the healers with him.

It made sense, in a cold way. The healers couldn't treat everyone effectively, and even assessing the severity of wounds took precious time. In a situation where men were dying all around, it was useful to have an Artisan directing resources.

I followed him up the staircase in silence, but when we turned the corner to my chambers, I stopped in my tracks. My usual set of guards were gone.

'How did you . . .' I didn't bother to finish the question, not really needing to know the answer. It was enough that he had found a way for us to be alone.

Severin pushed open the bronze doors and I brushed past slowly, not wanting to take my eyes off him. Having him here, in my rooms, was impossibly dangerous. But, oh, how I wanted him.

Warm light filtered down from the candlelit chandelier, illuminating his ebony hair and casting dappled shadows across his bare arms. Secretly, I liked him best like this: when he was dressed in the Western-style clothes he preferred – today, a cherry-red vest with veins of golden thread, and tan pants made from a light, airy fabric I didn't recognise.

Under normal circumstances, I would have ripped his clothes off by now. But these weren't normal circumstances.

I couldn't stop thinking about those soldiers, gasping out their last breaths, and Severin, forced to decide their fates. How had he endured it? Was it easier or harder to hold their lives in his hands, knowing they were responsible for killing his own people?

Severin crossed the receiving room slowly, his footfalls loud against the tiles. The sound echoed – everything echoed in here, like my chambers were as hollow as I sometimes felt.

His keen eyes took note of my careful distance. 'You don't need to worry, Scarlett. I don't hold you responsible for your father's deeds.'

'What about my mother's?'

Silence fell between us, tainted by everything I couldn't say.

I wanted to tell Severin the truth about Sabine's death, and my role in it. I wanted to trust him with the deepest, darkest parts of me. But if I did, how could I expect him not to run?

'He's going to be executed during the third Trial,' I said, unthinkingly.

Severin went still. 'The governor, you mean?'

'Yes.' I closed my eyes. 'Apparently, it was my mother's decision.'

My mother, who hated the Kalurians for turning against her. Who never missed an opportunity to strike back at her enemies.

'Can you intervene?'

I had the odd urge to laugh. There I was, dreading sitting through this execution – and yet I hadn't, not once, considered *doing* anything about it.

But Severin didn't look at me like Odessa had, with such resentment and disdain. He looked at me like he had when he'd found me spread out on that ice: as if I was a miracle, a girl more innocent and delicate than I ever had been.

'No,' I said heavily, thinking of my mother. 'I can't intervene.'

I won't *intervene.*

Though his expression didn't shift, I knew that I'd disappointed him. 'I understand you want Zandri's approval, but—'

'This isn't about her *approval*. It's about surviving this damn court.'

'You can do that on your own.'

'Is that your professional opinion? Because last I checked, you haven't been able to tell me anything concrete about the future, *except* when you said I was about to become a contender. And that's with Zandri's help.'

Severin took a step towards me, then seemed to think better of it. He shook his head. 'Not everything is about power.'

'Maybe in other places,' I said, more gently this time. 'But the Ravalian Court is all I know.'

'It doesn't have to be.'

I raised an amused eyebrow. 'Running away? Is that what you're suggesting?'

'It could allow us to be together,' Severin said softly. 'It might be the only way you have the freedom to make your own choices.'

'I make my own choices now.'

Severin said nothing.

His silence infuriated me. I lifted my chin so that my eyes were almost level with his. 'Not everything I do is about Zandri. She's my mother, not my puppet master.'

'Isn't it possible she's both?' Before I could snap something back, Severin continued, 'I have served Zandri for a long time. She isn't selfless, Scarlett. Every task she's given me has been motivated by self-interest.'

'That isn't true.' I exhaled. 'What about the night I drowned? Zandri sent you to help me – she was worried about my safety.'

Severin tilted his head. For a second, I glimpsed something like pity in his eyes. 'Scarlett, my orders had nothing to do with ensuring your safety. Zandri *wanted* Roran to drown you.'

I barked out a laugh. 'That doesn't make any sense.'

'It does.' Severin paused, as if he was willing me to make the connection. 'Think like Zandri. What does she value, even more than having a daughter?'

I refused to respond, but my mind answered his question all the same: *having a daughter with power.*

And my power over death had appeared after—

'No.' I shook my head firmly, as if I could shake away the implication. 'Zandri is my mother. She wouldn't risk my life.'

'Wouldn't she?' Severin regarded me knowingly. 'I told her what I'd Seen. She had every opportunity to stop Roran, and she chose not to. I'm sure she thought it was a relatively safe bet – that the magic in your blood would save your life, and you would find yourself changed for the better. But that outcome was only one possible future. I warned her there was a chance you wouldn't survive.'

I shivered. That was what I remembered most clearly: the cold. Worse than my desperate, primal urge to breathe. Worse than the thud of Roran's boots against the ice, his footsteps growing fainter as I sank deeper into the icy water.

Through bloodless lips, I said, 'Zandri ordered you not to intervene.' *And you listened.*

All this time, I'd thought Severin alone had tried to help me. That he, out of everyone at court, had cared whether I lived or died. But he had stood there, watching and waiting while I suffocated beneath the ice . . .

'I wanted to help you.' Severin's eyes were filled with tenderness.

'I would have, if I wasn't trapped by Zandri's orders. There was nothing I could do until you saved yourself.'

And I had. Against all the odds, I had survived – had returned from death, and brought some strange ability back with me. But I could have stayed dead, and my mother had known that. Had gambled with my life, because she had decided it was better to have a dead daughter than a daughter without blood magic.

I stiffened as Severin pulled me into his arms, but I allowed the embrace, leaning into him like I had so many times before. His chest was hard and warm against mine, and he smelt like sandalwood, familiar and comforting.

'I never intended to tell you any of this,' Severin murmured against my hair. His arms tightened around me, as if he could protect me from the truth. From the pain of it. 'At first, I kept Zandri's secrets for my own sake. But then . . . I couldn't bear to hurt you.'

I pulled back to look at him. 'So why did you?'

'Because Zandri isn't the person you want her to be. And one day soon, you're going to see that.' Severin's jaw tightened, the tattoos on his cheeks becoming more pronounced: a smile and a snarl. 'I'd rather that day come sooner. For all our sakes.'

CHAPTER THIRTY-FIVE

Scarlett

It was still dark when I woke from a fitful, uneasy sleep.

I immediately turned to look for Severin, but he was gone. He had stayed until I'd fallen asleep, though he had kept a careful distance. If he had been hoping for a romantic rendezvous, he shouldn't have admitted that he had allowed me to die.

What was I supposed to *do* with such an admission? It almost didn't matter that Zandri had ways of ensuring Severin's obedience. I had begun to think of Severin as someone who was wholly mine, and now I had to face the truth: he didn't belong to me any more than these chambers did.

Everything I had could be taken away – by my father, my brothers, my mother – and even the *belief* that I had control was just an illusion.

Standing abruptly, I crossed the room and opened my wardrobe. I took little notice of the gown I selected, stepping into it and fumbling for the clasp. It would have been easier with Aella's help, but I wanted as few witnesses to my late-night excursion as possible.

Closing my eyes, I visualised the outside hallway. All I needed to do was ensure that the guard saw nothing except what should be there: the white and gold of the walls, the crimson tapestries. All I had to do was believe.

The door opened silently on well-oiled hinges, affording me a view of the guard's profile. He appeared attentive, but I noticed the boredom in the small ways he shifted in place, the tiredness in his posture.

He wasn't expecting to see me at this hour, or anyone else. And people's minds often overlooked what they didn't expect.

I didn't need to reach for his hand, so temptingly close. I didn't need to brush his skin, not when I had a blood ruby coiled around my arm. *White and gold and crimson,* I thought, picturing the walls and tapestries. *White and gold and crimson.*

I shut the door silently behind me and inched past the guard, who didn't react to my presence. I made my way slowly down the hallway, barely daring to breathe. Though I was quite proficient in my illusions, there were some things I hadn't tried before. Invisibility was one of them.

Only when I was out of sight did I allow myself to relax. Only then did I allow myself to focus on what I was going to do. Because there were always choices to be made.

And while I might be a contender for the throne, I didn't have to become a monster in the process.

As it turned out, accessing the dungeons was easy.

I had anticipated a challenge, but none of the guards noticed as I slipped silently past. Tonight, it seemed, I was little more than a wraith.

I followed the winding steps down into the dimness. There was no sign of life – only the damp and the cold, a few tiny weeds growing in stone crevices. *Survivors,* I thought to myself. *There are always survivors.*

Was that what I was? A survivor?

I hadn't thought of myself that way before, but I liked it. Yes, I *was* a survivor – and I was determined to take control of the life I had fought so hard for. No matter what Odessa thought of me, I wasn't my mother. And I didn't have to make the same choices.

If the prisoners were awake, they were very quiet. The rows of cells were little more than distant shapes in the blackness, and I gave them a wide berth. Staying close to the middle of the long corridor, I focused on the only cell that mattered.

I had never used his first name, but I remembered it all the same. 'Søren?'

A figure stirred in the darkness. When he stood, I tried not to flinch: his clothes were covered in dried bloodstains, his proud face gaunt. If I'd seen him under different circumstances, I might not have recognised him.

The governor moved slowly over to the bars, until he was illuminated in the firelight. There was something fearful about the way he looked at me, as if he was expecting me to strike him.

'It's alright,' I said, in the gentle tone I usually reserved for children and small animals. 'I'm not going to hurt you.'

He didn't react at first, and I wondered if he was too afraid to speak. Then he asked, 'Are you really here?'

With a rush of pity, I understood. He wasn't afraid of me after all. He was afraid of himself.

'Yes,' I murmured. 'Yes, I'm really here. I'm real.'

His expression remained wary. Many prisoners went mad down here in the dark, and to the governor, insanity was probably the most realistic explanation for my presence. Why else would I be here – in the middle of the night, without a guard – when I'd made no secret of my dislike towards him?

'You once told me,' I said slowly, 'that we didn't need to be at odds. At the time, I thought that was impossible. But since you will no longer be my husband, I have no reason to work against you.'

The governor's measured gaze rested on mine. 'What are you saying?' he asked quietly, his cultured voice rough from disuse.

It was difficult seeing him like this, brought so low. A pitiful shell of the man I remembered.

I thought of the kindness he'd shown me, and I knew I was doing the right thing. Even if it meant weathering Zandri's anger.

'I'm here to offer you a chance. The final Trial begins tomorrow – and with it, your death. But there is another way,' I told him, leaning closer. 'Pledge your loyalty to the empire, and you can be spared. At the very least, my father will reduce your sentence. You're a political prisoner; you were only supposed to be imprisoned. I'm sure my mother convinced the emperor you were too dangerous to be left alive.'

I had anticipated a reaction. Relief, disbelief, confusion – *something*. But the governor said nothing. Did nothing.

'Didn't you hear me? All you have to do is pledge your loyalty, and—'

'I won't betray my queen.'

For a moment, I could only stare at him. 'Pardon?'

Steeliness entered his face, as if a measure of his old strength had been restored. 'I will not betray my queen,' he repeated. 'As I served her father before her, so too am I loyal to his daughter. To the true heir of the Kalurian throne.'

Anger pulsed inside me, but I forced it down. What was the *point* of such obstinance? He was no use to his country if he was dead. He was no use to anyone.

'Mira isn't a queen,' I said with fraying patience. 'She is a girl who knows nothing of Kalure, and only desires vengeance for her mother. *Zandri* is your queen.'

His grey eyes were clear and certain as they met mine. Unafraid. 'Zandri will never be my queen. And neither will you.'

I stepped back from the bars. Copper flooded my mouth as my teeth sunk into my lower lip.

I remembered asking him whether he would serve me as loyally as his previous king. Then I remembered his amused smile. The way he had looked at me – as if I was a precocious child who had done something vaguely endearing. Someone who was to be indulged but never given any real power.

Just like my father.

Now here I was, trying to save his life. Here *I* was, while Mira was nowhere in sight.

And still he didn't see me. Still, he didn't treat me seriously.

See? Zandri's satisfied, gloating voice echoed in my mind. This *is what mercy gets you.*

'Suit yourself,' I told him coldly, turning on my heel. 'If you love your queen so much, you can die for her.'

CHAPTER THIRTY-SIX

Mira

'It is my pleasure to announce that the Trials will conclude tonight.'
The emperor's voice was low but powerful, carrying effortlessly over
the gardens. 'After the completion of one last task, I will invite the
most talented of our sons and daughters into our three Orders.'

The applause from the assembled courtiers and candidates was
enthusiastic and polite. Unlike the lavish celebration the night before,
today's gathering was an intimate affair, but no less intimidating. I
shaded my eyes as I gazed up at the imperial pavilion, its crimson
Ravalian flags flapping in the afternoon breeze.

'Since the Artisan candidates didn't compete in the second Trial,'
the emperor continued, 'they will face their private testing today.
Each will be invited to meet with me individually and share a prediction or insight about myself or the court. If I deem their response
acceptable, they will progress to the final trial.'

Aric tensed at my side, and I wondered if he was thinking of
Sabine. We'd spent plenty of time together since the first Trial, even
though I wouldn't have blamed her for keeping her distance. But
Sabine hadn't seemed to mind publicly aligning herself with us,
cheering Aric and I on from the sidelines and feeding us snippets of
information about the other candidates.

As my gaze drifted over Emperor Kalias's advisers – instantly
recognisable in their stately robes – I caught a glimpse of brunette
curls from inside the imperial pavilion. Sabine's closeness to the royal
family surprised me – until I saw the person she was standing next to.

As if Severin felt my gaze on him, he turned, his mismatched eyes meeting mine.

I quickly looked away.

'Some of you,' Emperor Kalias was saying, 'are already known to me, and have proved your loyalty through decades of family service.' Ahead of me, I saw Brutus and a few other Warrior candidates exchange smirks. 'But for the rest of the candidates, this final trial is my opportunity to ask questions of you. Those who prove their loyalty will be welcomed into the Ravalian Court.'

With that, the emperor returned to his seat, and the festivities began anew. A group of musicians began preparing their instruments while a young man strummed at his lyre, the soft music barely audible over the sound of laughter and clinking glasses.

'Mira,' Aric said, touching my arm. 'You should try some.'

I glanced over to see a servant carrying a platter of farmed oysters, octopus and smoked fish cakes from the royal kitchens. Aric's enthusiasm suddenly made sense; this was the kind of food that was common in the Elusive Isles. But thoughts of the final Trial made eating impossible.

'It'll be fine, Mira,' Aric murmured, taking hold of my arm. I shot him a quizzical look as he led me across the manicured lawn, but he only smiled. 'Care to dance?'

And indeed, the musicians had struck up a lively tune – too cheerful for the cloud of worry pressing in on me.

'I'm not sure this is the right time—'

'It's *exactly* the right time.' Aric spun me and I went with it, twirling back into his arms a little too forcefully. He grunted and I laughed.

Just like that, the tension was broken.

'You're right,' I agreed, savouring the music and the moment. 'This is exactly the right time.'

Various lords and ladies joined us, all infinitely more graceful than we were. But the formal dances were reserved for the inside of the palace, and out here, no one seemed to care about two Trial candidates enjoying what might be their last hours together.

Aric's arm tightened around my waist. 'Whatever happens, Mira—'

'No.' I looked determinedly up at him. 'No goodbyes. We're going to survive the third Trial, and we're going to become Order members. *Both* of us.'

As the song drew to a close, I turned the emperor's words over in my mind, searching for anything sinister. I couldn't find anything: it really did seem as simple as he made it sound. Stand in front of the emperor and answer a few questions . . . I could do that. All I needed to do was tell him what he wanted to hear.

From the pavilion, Cassius's dark blue eyes locked with mine. Though his expression was unreadable, I had the sense the prince knew exactly what I was thinking. The barest hint of a smile upturned his lips as he shook his head.

And I knew that I was wrong. Despite what it might appear, this Trial wasn't simple or harmless at all.

I retreated to my chambers soon afterwards, tense and taut as a wire. Aric had asked me to stay, but I suspected he intended to use the opportunity to cosy up to Scarlett, and it would be easier for him to do that without me.

I brightened when a knock sounded at my door, thinking that Aric had changed his mind.

But it wasn't Aric who slipped inside.

Sabine was already dressed for the final Trial, in a frothy peach dress that made her seem deceptively young and innocent.

I glanced down at my strapless gown. It was black, matching the glittering dark jewels dripping from my ears, and it was the closest thing to my fighting leathers that I had been able to find. I couldn't have looked any more Sabine's opposite if I'd tried.

'Expecting someone else?' Sabine asked, with a knowing quirk of her lips.

'Why would you say that?'

'You looked disappointed to see me,' she said, without any trace of offense. 'And you left Aric behind at the celebrations. Did you two have an argument?'

'No!' I said, with a little too much vehemence. I'd forgotten how nosy Sabine could be.

And candid.

'I see,' Sabine said, amusement thick in her voice. 'Well, it's better like this anyway. I was hoping to catch you alone.'

'I suppose you're here to congratulate me?' I asked, turning back towards the oval windows.

That was all anyone had done since I'd beaten Nikolas. Even my attendants had murmured their congratulations while they helped me dress. As if I had survived the Trials already.

As if I wasn't terrified about tonight.

'Actually, I wanted to wish you luck,' Sabine said, crossing the receiving room to stand at my side. Sunlight lightened her eyes, and for a second, I could have sworn they were almost blue. Then I blinked, and they were their usual moss green. 'For the final Trial.'

I let out a pent-up breath. 'Most of the candidates seem to believe it's a formality.'

'Most of the candidates,' Sabine retorted, 'are here by choice. You and I . . .' She trailed off, and in her pause, I heard everything she couldn't say.

I almost asked her if my suspicions were correct: if she had been born with magic, and as a result, the emperor had forced her to participate in the Trials. But I didn't want to make her feel uncomfortable, so I held my tongue.

'It's different for us,' she said at last.

'Yes,' I murmured. 'It is.'

For a moment, we stood in companionable silence. Aside from Aric, Sabine was the closest thing I had to a friend here. It was a strange realisation, but not an unwelcome one.

I felt a sudden pang of guilt. With all my own worries, I had completely forgotten about the Artisans' private testing.

'How was it? Your second test – with the emperor?'

'Challenging,' Sabine said with a shrug. 'But I passed, so I must have said something right.'

I studied Sabine, unsure whether to believe her blasé attitude. I knew how intimidating the emperor could be, and I wondered if Sabine had sought me out because she was more unsettled than she let on.

'Of course, I had help.' Sabine smiled faintly at my obvious surprise. 'Severin,' she clarified. 'He's quite protective of the members of his Order. He isn't like General Tiran or Zandri. He really cares.'

My feelings about Severin were complicated, to say the least. But I supposed he had tried to warn me – and he'd led me to the locket, which had allowed me to defeat Nikolas in the arena. If it had been left behind on Aldara—

I pushed aside the thought. 'Do you have any . . . intuition or fore-sight, about this next Trial? Anything that might help us prepare for it?'

'All I know is that it's more dangerous than it seems. I overheard Emperor Kalias discussing it with Zandri.'

'Zandri?' My head jerked up at her name. 'She's involved?'

'I think so. The emperor needs a way to ensure our answers are truthful – otherwise, what's the point? I suppose Zandri will enchant us somehow.'

My stomach sank. 'Do you think you can do it? Tell him that you're loyal?'

Sabine considered this in silence, perhaps trying to decide how much she could trust me.

At last, she said, 'Sometimes magic is used to interrogate prison-ers. Most of the time, it's very effective. But I've heard of prisoners who have learnt ways around it. I think that if you convince yourself it's not a lie, then you can speak it like a truth. But that's a difficult skill to learn, and you only have a few hours.'

'What about you?'

Sabine smiled. A small, sly smile. 'I've had longer than a few hours.'

Hope stirred at her words. 'Can you teach me?'

'I'm not sure that I need to. Aric told me that you were a performer with a circus. Performers take on many different roles – and the key to the best performance is to believe it yourself. Have you ever watched an actor who was so convincing that you believed they *were* their character?'

Instantly, I thought of my mother. When I was younger, I didn't realise that we were running from someone. It must have occurred to me that it wasn't exactly normal, moving so quickly from one place to the next, but I didn't question it. That was just how life was.

And my mother had been so good at making it fun. She never looked happier, more vibrant or alive, than right before we started over somewhere new. To her, the moments before the choice were magical. In those moments, we could be anyone. The possibilities were endless.

More often than not, she selected the place and chose the people – shaping their personalities, their backstories, like an artist might shape a painting. Then she would sit me down and tell me a story of who we were going to become. As a child, I'd thought the characters my mother described really existed. Given breath by my mother's stories.

Oh, my darling, Celeste had said, *they are real. We give them life.*

Of course, such a thing wasn't really possible. I knew that. But the game I had once played with my mother was a game no longer.

It was now my best chance at survival.

I looked up to see Sabine watching me closely. 'I think you'll be just fine,' she said, turning towards the door.

'Wait,' I called after her.

She glanced back at me, an eyebrow raised.

'Thank you. For warning me.'

'Don't thank me yet,' she returned, sassy as ever. 'You still have to survive the Trial. We both do.'

CHAPTER THIRTY-SEVEN

Mira

My entire body stiffened as I entered the throne room. A crowd was already gathered in front of the dais, where Emperor Kalias sat on his heavy stone throne. Zandri loomed at his side, and behind her were the other members of the royal family: Empress Ivalene, Roran and Cassius. All three looked predictably bored and uninterested, though in Cassius's case, I knew that boredom was feigned.

He might be the only royal who *wanted* me to survive this task. Except, perhaps, Scarlett.

I searched the room, but there was no sign of her distinctive red hair and pale skin.

My gaze darted back to Emperor Kalias, lingering on the dagger strapped to his side and the sharp points of his bone crown. This was his last chance to kill me before I became a full-fledged Order member. Somehow, I didn't think he was going to waste it.

'Don't look at him,' Aric murmured. 'Look at me.'

I did. Aric's brown eyes were steady, grounding. I couldn't help but compare them to Cassius's midnight-blue ones: unpredictable, dangerous, as likely to be cruel as they were to be kind. Out of the two of them, I knew who I trusted. I was also acutely aware of my limitations *without* the prince on my side.

But none of that mattered right now. My focus needed to be on surviving this Trial – not what came next.

'We'll be fine,' Aric said, though he didn't sound convinced. 'Thanks to Sabine, we've had some forewarning.'

I thought of the measly three hours we'd had to practice, after I'd tracked Aric down and relayed everything Sabine had told me. Aric had done well, fielding my questions with carefully chosen portions of truth. But if the emperor asked him a question he *couldn't* avoid—

Aric's fingers laced through mine. I squeezed his hand as the first three candidates approached the dais, all from the Order of Artisans. Sabine led the way, confident and poised. I tensed when she reached the emperor, but he presented her with the final token without asking a single question. Her two companions followed: a tall, dark-haired boy and a petite blonde girl, who scurried up the steps like she was afraid Emperor Kalias might change his mind.

He didn't. Nor did he question the other Artisan candidates, leading me to suspect that the emperor had already established their loyalty during their private test – or perhaps Severin had vetted them for him.

All too soon, the Warrior candidates were approaching the stage. I let Aric's hand fall from mine, but my eyes were glued to him as he climbed the steps. This was how Kain must have looked: strong, capable and honourable, the very definition of what a Warrior should be.

Half of their number had been cut during the second Trial. Most of the remaining candidates were legacies like Brutus, or of noble birth. They greeted the emperor with a confidence born of familiarity, and I heard a few mentions of family members and vows of service. The emperor allowed them to pass without question, their words blurring together: *I am honoured to serve the Ravalian Empire . . . I vow to serve you as loyally as my father before me . . .*

And then it was Aric's turn.

Before Aric even reached the throne, Emperor Kalias inclined his head.

Zandri extended her forearm. The moment Aric took it, red tendrils encircled them both. Those tendrils didn't penetrate the dark leather Zandri wore, but they sank into the exposed skin of Aric's arms, drawing blood.

Anger rose up in me like tempered steel. But it was quickly eclipsed by fear as I wondered what would happen to Aric if he lied – and whether those tendrils were strong enough to cut through bone.

Emperor Kalias's voice echoed through the hall as he asked, 'Why did you fight against my son in the arena?'

Panic clawed at my insides. This wasn't a question we had practised, and I cursed myself for not thinking of it.

At Aric's hesitation, the tendrils cut in deeper. It must have hurt, but his face remained expressionless.

In a steady voice, he replied, 'Because Roran was going to kill a girl as she reached for her sword.'

'And that bothered you?'

This time, there was no hesitation. 'I believe all Warriors should possess a code of honour. At the very least, an opponent should have the opportunity to fight back.'

Emperor Kalias considered that for a moment. 'A nice sentiment,' he said finally, 'but would you have intervened for a different girl? One who wasn't your personal friend?'

'Yes,' Aric replied, his voice clear and resolute. 'I would.'

The emperor drummed his fingers against the armrest as he appraised Aric. I expected him to question Aric's relationship with me, but instead he asked, 'Why do you want to become one of my Warriors?'

Aric's composure didn't falter as he said, 'I want to make a difference. My brother was a proud member of the Order of Warriors, and he's the reason I'm standing in front of you today.'

I tensed at the mention of Kain. I hadn't warned Aric about his brother's ties to the resistance, hoping that ignorance would keep him safe. But there was no way Emperor Kalias didn't know.

I braced myself for the emperor to ask a more direct question about Aric's loyalties, but perhaps he was wary of doing so in such a public setting. No doubt he would instruct Zandri and maybe even some trusted Warriors to watch Aric closely. Still, he seemed satisfied with Aric's answer – satisfied enough to hand a golden pin to Zandri.

She pierced it through the dark material of Aric's shirt and released the magic. The red tendrils dissolved as if they had never existed.

My racing heart refused to slow, even as Aric joined the other Warriors. Safe.

For now.

The interrogations continued until only the Mask candidates were left. I followed Odessa and Danica up the steps, my legs leaden. Dressed in a golden gown that left little to the imagination, Odessa didn't seem the slightest bit concerned about facing the emperor or the court. She curtsied to Emperor Kalias, pledging her loyalty in a soft, breathy voice. Danica went next, smiling demurely as she received her final token.

My turn.

Zandri's cool fingers took hold of my bare arm as I reached the throne, but I didn't shift my gaze from the emperor. Not even as I felt Zandri's power surge between us – and the sting of those red tendrils sinking into my flesh.

'Do you blame me for your mother's execution?' the emperor asked, his tone conversational.

'I blame myself.' The red tendrils tightened – as if they sensed this wasn't the whole truth. But it wasn't a lie, either.

'Very clever,' Emperor Kalias murmured, so only I could hear him. More loudly, he said, 'I could ask you any number of questions, but in this case, I believe a simple statement would be far more effective. I assume you heard the pledge of loyalty that Odessa Tiran just made?'

Those damn tendrils tightened, prompting me to answer. 'Yes.'

'Good,' Emperor Kalias said, sounding satisfied. 'I would like you to repeat it.'

My teeth sank into my lower lip as I recalled Odessa's exact words. *I pledge my loyalty to you and your crown*, she had said to the emperor. *I swear to protect the Ravalian Empire to my last breath, and to serve my Order with valour.*

Even a *loyal* candidate might not have been able to say that and mean it. And I was far from a loyal candidate.

'If what you say is a lie,' Emperor Kalias continued, 'then Zandri's magic will detect it, and you will bleed out in front of me. But if you decline, I will consider you to have failed this Trial.'

And I would be executed, just like my mother. My gaze darted past Zandri – to where Roran stood, his hungry gaze fixed on me. Whatever happened, I wouldn't let him be the one to kill me.

I would rather let those tendrils shed my blood.

Closing my eyes, I called up the persona I had created after Sabine's visit – inspired by my mother's early life, but without her conscience. A selfish girl, desperate to do whatever it took to survive. A girl who had no love for anyone except herself.

I sank deep into my own mind, until an image formed in front of me: the Mira Tundra I might have been if I had grown up alone in Ravalis, eking out an existence on the streets and stealing from others to survive.

A girl with no parents, no friends, and no real future.

A girl whose loyalty could be bought by the man in front of me.

It was that Mira Tundra who addressed the emperor now, eager to take advantage of the lifeline he offered. It was that Mira Tundra who pledged her loyalty, swearing to protect the empire that would also protect her. It was that Mira Tundra who vowed to serve her Order with valour, because she was thrilled to enter the Order of Masks, where her skills for survival and deception would be valued and appreciated. Where she would finally be welcomed into a family of her very own.

When I finished speaking, there was silence. Stillness.

I glanced down at the red tendrils encircling my skin. Around me, I knew that everyone in the throne room was doing the same: waiting for those red tendrils to cut into my skin and spill my blood all over the dais.

But I hadn't lied. In that moment, when I had made my pledge, every word had come from a place of truth.

It just hadn't been *my* truth.

'She's passed,' Zandri said, and severed the connection.

I stumbled back from her, rubbing my bloody arms. Already, the cuts were beginning to heal – at a significantly faster rate than should be natural. I felt a stab of tiredness and dizziness.

Slowly, I raised my head to look into Emperor Kalias's cold face.

'Such devotion,' he said, his grey eyes locked on mine. 'It's almost difficult to believe.'

A shiver raised the hairs on my arms, even though the room was unpleasantly warm. Perspiration beaded on my forehead as I waited for Emperor Kalias to present me with the third token.

Instead, his cruel mouth curved into a smile. 'There's just one last thing,' he said smoothly. 'As much as I appreciate your pledge of loyalty, saying a few words doesn't change the facts of your parentage. For you to truly prove your loyalty, for you to ascend to the Third Order, you have to choose: Ravalia or Kalure.'

He nodded to one of the black-garbed Warriors, who disappeared for a moment and then returned, dragging a chained man into view.

I went still. Though I'd only met this man once, I recognised him immediately.

Governor Halvor.

My eyes lingered on the dried blood staining his clothes, the bruises marring his skin. Perhaps those things should have been my first clue. But I didn't want to see. I didn't want to understand.

And then he spoke, saying the words that damned him. That damned us both.

'Your Majesty.'

A gasp went up from the audience. The Warriors pulled back on the manacles, jerking the governor to his feet. Their grip must have been painful, but he didn't flinch. He was watching me, as if I was the only person who mattered.

Your Majesty. The words sounded powerful, murmured in his deep voice. They sounded like the person I wanted to be. Except I could barely save myself, let alone save a country. My time in the arena had shown me my talents, and they had nothing to do with leading. I was good at breaking things, not putting them back together.

I felt the heavy stares of the crowd, waiting to see how I would react. What I would do.

Which country are you loyal to, Princess? Emperor Kalias had asked me once. *Ravalia or Kalure?*

Because you can't be loyal to both.

'This man,' the emperor continued with a mocking smile, 'could have married my daughter, and ruled Kalure as a provincial governor. Instead, he chose to conspire against us.'

A Warrior walked over, a silver blade in his hands – a ceremonial dagger used by the Order of Masks.

'Your final Trial,' Emperor Kalias told me, nodding to the dagger. 'All you need to do is take that blade and kill him.'

My eyes went to the unarmed prisoner at my feet. The Kalurian governor who had looked at me with such reverence. The man who had laughed with my mother like an old friend. Who had offered the use of his ship.

Who had called me his queen.

It was a cruel, terrible choice. Refusal meant failure – and failure meant death. But what kind of person would I be if I killed this man, all to save my own life?

On the other side of the dais, Aric's face was pale, his lips bloodless. He looked at me like I was already dead. He didn't think I could do it.

But if I threw this blade down and walked away, the emperor would execute the governor anyway. And then he would execute me. I wouldn't make it a single step before the Warriors descended. And if Aric tried to help me, like he had during the Choosing Ceremony, he would die too.

I stared down at Governor Halvor. Did he have family waiting for him back in Kalure, loved ones who would curse me until the end of my days?

I wondered if he'd known my father. I wondered if he would still have tried to help me and my mother if he'd known how it would end. Would he have looked at me with such hope if he'd known that his queen would become his executioner?

'We don't have all day,' Emperor Kalias drawled from his throne. 'What's it going to be, Princess? Ravalia or Kalure?'

If I could have died to save this man's life, I might have. I might have walked away and let the Warriors kill me, knowing he would live. Instead, I clutched the blade tighter in shaking hands.

When I glanced up at the emperor, I realised that he still didn't think I was going to do it. But he didn't know the vow I'd made.

One day – in a month, a year, even a decade from now – I will make you pay for what you did. I will make you bleed, like you made her *bleed.*

The thing about vengeance was this: you had to be alive to get it.

My eyes locked with Cassius's. He had promised to help me destroy the emperor, but only if I survived this Trial. I could almost hear him saying the words: *This is your chance, Mira, to convince me that you're worth backing.*

The prince nodded once, as if in encouragement. He was probably the only person in the entire crowd who thought I could do this.

My whole body was trembling by the time I reached the governor's kneeling form. His face was upturned, his eyes staring into mine. They were calm, steady; they reminded me of my mother's eyes.

'What's your first name?' I whispered, crouching at his side. I couldn't explain why it was so important for me to know, only that it was.

'It's Søren,' he said, giving me a sad smile. A smile I didn't deserve.

I slowly straightened. The emperor shifted impatiently on his throne, and his guards tensed. In contrast, the rest of the audience was too still, too quiet.

'Do it,' Søren urged, and his conviction was somehow worse than if he'd hated me. *'Do it.'*

He didn't say those two words again, but I saw them in his eyes. *Your Majesty.* My queen.

His devotion almost broke me. Somehow, he still looked at me with reverence – even now, as I aimed a dagger at his chest.

'Fight for them, Kasmira. Promise me.'

Tears dripped down my face and onto his, like rain. And I knew that the image of his face would stay with me for as long as I lived.

'I promise,' I said—

And stabbed him through the heart.

Blood spilled onto the ground as he collapsed limply to the floor. For a moment, I could have sworn I saw it twice – that I saw my mother fall too, red spreading across the volcanic sand of the arena. For a moment, my own scream echoed in my ears.

I didn't scream this time, and I wasn't sure which was worse. Shock and horror – or the absence of it.

It was physically painful to look away from his body. To raise my gaze to the throne and beyond, where the entire royal family watched.

Let them doubt my conviction now. Let them try to kill me *now*.

'I choose Ravalia,' I said, in a voice like death.

The world was taking on a hazy quality, a kind of dreamlike unreality. I'd just killed someone so I could live. I'd killed one of my own people, and I should be crumbling. I should be breaking, like I'd forever broken him.

But when I met the emperor's cold eyes, when I heard him pronounce me a member of the Order of Masks, I felt nothing.

Nothing at all.

CHAPTER THIRTY-EIGHT

Mira

'Take it,' Scarlett said, offering me the mask. 'You've earned it.'

I shifted my gaze from the Order of Masks atrium to my hands, stained red with Governor Halvor's blood.

I expected the mask to feel heavy, weighed down by what I had done. But it was cool and delicate, beautiful and unnerving all at once. In the firelight, the ornate detailing seemed to come alive; it shifted beneath my touch, rearranging into patterns I'd seen once before: ancient beasts prowling, barbed vines snaking around the outline of dark eyes.

'Can you see them?' I asked, glancing up at Scarlett.

She shook her head. 'Those symbols are just for you. They represent the aptitudes you have.'

'Aptitudes?' I repeated, turning the mask over with curious fingers.

'My mother can't change *you* – it's impossible to make someone magical if they aren't already. But she can enhance the abilities you already possess. That's why the Trials are so important. Warriors must already be strong and fast to be granted increased strength and speed. Artisans need an innate intuition, to be turned into seers.' Scarlett tilted her head, the sunset setting her red hair afire. 'Masks are more complicated than the others, because we use more than one kind of magic. As a result, whatever powers you're granted by Zandri will be temporary, designed to suit the mission you're being sent on.'

I knew better than to ask Scarlett what her symbols were. Instead, I thought of my mother's mask. Of spiderwebs and flowers concealing bloodied thorns, stunning and sinister. What had her aptitudes been? And what price had she paid for them?

As if she could read my mind, Scarlett said, 'Adalyn was legendary, you know.'

At the mention of my mother, I went very still.

'Zandri told me she was a thief from the Lower Districts, before she competed in the Trials. No one expected her to succeed, but she was extremely talented. After she was initiated into the Masks, she was sent on all the most challenging assignments – she probably saw more of the empire than anyone.'

I closed my eyes, imagining my mother as she was then. Imagining the kind of iron-clad determination she must have possessed to come so far – and wondering what her real motivations had been. Because I didn't believe she would have sold out for wealth and status, forgetting about Darius and her friends in the Lower Districts.

'What happened,' I asked softly, 'between her and my father?'

It was a dangerous question, and I half expected Scarlett not to answer. But she only considered me in silence for a moment. 'Arioch was a popular king,' she said after a pause. 'He didn't have many weaknesses, but he loved his first wife very much. When she died, Zandri sent Adalyn to infiltrate the Kalurian Court, to prey on that vulnerability.'

I smiled mirthlessly. That sounded like Zandri – using people's emotions against them.

'But she fell in love.'

'Yes. Adalyn betrayed her Order and made a life for herself in Kalure. She probably thought she could keep Arioch safe.' Scarlett looked at me with pity. 'A sleeper Mask completed Adalyn's mission and tried to kill her, too – but she was Zandri's protégée, and she knew how to disappear.'

Until me. Until I'd decided that I wanted to compete in the Trials, that I was tired of running.

Pain squeezed my chest. I forced it away, avoiding the princess's keen gaze.

Scarlett turned towards the metal staircase, then paused. Her expression was unguarded as she considered me, and for a second, I could have sworn she looked at me with something close to tenderness. 'Mira, I—'

A gong echoed from below, cutting off her words.

I glanced down, then back at Scarlett. What had she been about to say?

'Come on,' the princess said, not quite meeting my eyes. 'We shouldn't keep Zandri waiting.'

She said nothing more as she led me far below the atrium. The onyx hall was every bit as disconcerting as I remembered; even with the faint flicker of fire, the entire space was dark and uninviting.

Danica and Odessa were already in position, dressed in the same clothes they had worn during the third Trial. Zandri was standing across the hall, her reflection silhouetted in a dozen mirrors.

'Speak the values of your Order,' she instructed.

Infiltrate. Exploit. Destroy.

Our voices melded together, until it was impossible to make out any individual sounds. Even when we stopped speaking, I could hear those three words echoing around us, entrancing and ominous.

'Now,' Zandri said, 'I want each of you to approach and speak your name. You first, Mira.'

I stepped forward until my face was bathed in the light of the fire. It was so bright that I raised a hand to my eyes, only to see a small slip of parchment appear in my palm. I felt the brush of something mystical, raising the delicate hairs on my arms.

'Mira,' I said, the paper taking on a reddish glow. As I stared down at it, riveted, four letters burned themselves into the parchment: *MIRA*.

Zandri nodded once, her eyes glittering. 'Now feed it to the fire.'

Fighting back rising trepidation, I held the paper up to the light. The letters of my name were crisp and clear. *Mira*. It was the name of the girl who had dreamt of a life with Aric. Who had wanted to become a Warrior and live by a code of honour.

It was the name of a girl who didn't exist anymore.

I let the paper fall. There was a soft hiss as it disappeared into the flames, the fire burning hotter and brighter. I imagined the letters of my name turning to ash and sinking down, never to be seen again.

Zandri moved closer. Something gleamed in her hands: a thin, stiletto blade. 'It won't hurt for more than a second,' she told me. 'I'll prick your finger, and then this will all be over.'

I extended my hand, palm up. There was the faintest of stings as it pierced my finger.

A drop of blood welled, vivid red.

As I looked on, lips parted, the drop of blood started to levitate. It rose higher and higher until it was level with my eyes, and then it began to swell.

It took me a moment to make the connection, to recognise what it was transforming into—

A blood ruby.

CHAPTER THIRTY-NINE

Scarlett

I had never asked my mother about the cost. But I knew there was one, because nothing in this world came without a price. Especially magic.

'What are you going to do with it?' I asked, staring down at the jewel pulsing in Zandri's hand.

Though I kept my voice level, I knew my question stemmed from concern – genuine concern for my cousin, who I had nearly confessed everything to only an hour earlier. What had I been *thinking*?

For a moment, I had allowed myself to get caught up in the ruse, to forget that my friendliness wasn't real. Couldn't be real.

Zandri braced her arms against the bench top, leaning too heavily to be natural. Her skin was paler than usual, another subtle sign of her fatigue. 'I'll put it in the cavern with the others,' she said, and my eyes flickered towards the stairwell at the far side of the tower.

I'd never been down there before, to the catacombs that concealed the true power of the Ravalian Empire. But I could imagine it well enough: hundreds of blood rubies filling the space with their unearthly glow.

Something like envy stirred in my chest. My mother was powerful enough to be connected to all that magic: so long as she was close enough, she could channel it for her own use. Even a single blood ruby amplified my abilities – what would it be like to draw on them all?

'Finally,' Zandri commented. 'I've been waiting years for you to show an interest.'

It wasn't that I *hadn't* been interested in magic. But my interest had always been tempered with wariness, much like my relationship with my mother. The difference was that I could no longer afford ignorance.

I folded my arms as I studied Zandri. I wanted to hate her. I *should* hate her – for her lies, her betrayal, her willingness to sacrifice me like a piece on a chessboard.

But no matter how hard I tried, I couldn't do it. Anger – oh, that came readily enough. But never hatred.

'Severin told me your private test went well.' Zandri smiled wryly. 'Apparently, Kalias believes Sabine has a bright future as an Artisan.'

I didn't smile back. 'I can't take credit for that. Severin told me what to say.'

'Still, keeping the guise of Sabine alive was your plan,' Zandri said, oddly magnanimous. 'And your illusions made it possible. It seems they're more useful than I thought. In fact, they might have given me the perfect idea for how to kill your father.'

I waited for Zandri to elaborate, but she didn't. 'Aren't you going to tell me what that is?'

Zandri waved a dismissive hand. 'I will. In time.'

She didn't even bother to look at me, more focused on the blood ruby pulsing in her hand. I watched as she tilted it to the candlelight, examining Mira's blood ruby with an admiration she had never shown me.

'It seems you have everything thought out.' The bitterness in my voice was obvious.

That bitterness caught Zandri's attention. She slipped the blood ruby into a hidden sheath. 'What do you want from me, Scarlett?'

'I want to know that you think of me as a daughter. Not a pawn.'

Zandri smiled faintly as she approached me. 'I've never thought of you as a pawn,' she said, brushing my hair back from my face. 'Always a queen.'

It was impossible to doubt her conviction. Her dark eyes speared into mine, filled with truth.

But I leant away, refusing to be won over so easily. 'Then why were you willing to sacrifice me? You had the opportunity to stop Roran. You chose not to.'

'I might not be a conventional mother,' she said, 'but everything I've done has been for *you*. To make you stronger, and to give you the best chance at survival.'

In other words, she had taken a calculated risk, based on the information Severin had provided.

A risk that had paid off.

But what if it hadn't? I wanted to ask. *What if I had died instead?*

I swallowed down the words. I already knew the answer. It just wasn't the answer I needed.

'I've always known what I want, Scarlett.' Zandri's voice was soft, but it wasn't weak. 'Every decision I make is in service of that goal. The question is: what do *you* want?'

In that moment, all I wanted was to hurt my mother. To find a way of cutting into her unfeeling heart.

But what left my lips was: 'I want to be empress.'

'Then you will have to risk everything, in order to gain so much more. Just as I did when I allowed Roran to drown you in Kalure.'

She tapped a sharp fingernail against the bench top, and a bird soared through the open window. Settling on the table, the raven folded its wings and fixed me with its luminous dark eyes.

My mother stroked the raven's feathers, her gaze never shifting from mine. 'When you manage to harness your death magic, resurrection will be the least of what you can do. My hope is that you might eventually be able to kill with touch – and when you can, you won't need to be afraid of your enemies. They will be afraid of *you*.'

I felt the pull of her words. More than anything, that was what I wanted: to never feel powerless or trapped again.

But I crossed over to the arched windows, staring unseeingly out over the palace grounds. Soon enough, they would belong to me – *everything* would belong to me. And to Zandri as well.

Would Zandri be any better than the emperor? Than Roran or Cassius?

Does the answer matter? a lilting, seductive voice replied – and the voice was mine. *As long as Emperor Kalias lives, you will never be free. As long as he lives, you will never amount to anything.*

And I realised that voice was right. *I* was right.

An alliance with Zandri was my best chance for a future free of my father and brothers. A future in which no one would ever look at me the way Governor Halvor had – like I was nothing. *Less* than nothing.

If I couldn't win the court's respect with mercy, then I would win it with fear.

The raven flew past me, so close that it ruffled my hair. As I watched it soar across the moonlit sky, something tugged at my chest. A distant, unexpected sense of exhilaration.

There was nothing I wouldn't risk, I decided, if it meant I could feel the way that bird did. If it meant a chance at that same, thrilling sense of freedom.

CHAPTER FORTY

Mira

One month later

'You're covered in blood.'

I didn't answer, twisting to remove my dark fitted armour. It resembled Zandri's, though without the feathered mantle. And much grimier, thanks to the messiness of my spy missions.

'Is it yours?'

'No.' My voice was flat. 'No, it's not mine.'

Aric chewed on his bottom lip, the way he always did when he was upset. 'What did they ask you to do?'

'I can't tell you that,' I said, unzipping my boots. 'Order business.'

He glared at me – downright *glared*. 'Since when do you care about following the rules?'

I looked at him blankly. He was trying to bait me, just like he'd been doing for weeks – trying to draw out some emotion in me, if only anger and frustration. He hadn't succeeded so far, and he wouldn't succeed now.

'Zandri's pushing you too hard,' Aric said darkly. 'It's like . . .' He paused, searching for the right words. 'Like she's trying to turn you into a machine.'

'It's not Zandri's fault.'

Aric didn't look like he believed me, but it was true. It wasn't Zandri's fault – it was mine. I was the one who wanted to be worked hard, and if I transformed into something cold and mechanical in the process, all the better. I would be one step closer to achieving my revenge.

He shook his head, his jaw clenched tight. 'Even guards have rest days, time to ourselves.' There was a fierceness to his expression, something burning and angry. 'What happened to you, Mira? How did you become . . . *this*?'

'Am I truly so unrecognisable?'

Aric averted his gaze, as if he couldn't bear to look at me. He motioned vaguely in the direction of the dressing room. 'See for yourself.'

Then he turned and strode off, slamming the bronze behind him. I had a brief glimpse of the Warriors outside before I was alone once more.

Billowing steam drew me to the bathing chamber, where my attendants had already prepared a bath – gloriously hot and perfect for my aching muscles. I took a breath as I sank into the claw-footed marble tub, revelling in the lack of *people*. If there was one thing that exhausted me more than anything else, it was unnecessary interaction. I didn't have the time or energy for it, and Aric was by the far the hardest to interact with. But I never had the heart to turn him away. Maybe I never would, even though we were on two separate paths – paths that would probably get us killed.

When I was done, the bathwater was pink with blood and my skin was clean. I couldn't say the same for my conscience. Today had been particularly awful – a brave rebel, who had refused to cooperate even under torture. Zandri had ordered him put down, and while I had done it quick and clean, the hatred on his face was burned into my memory. As was the knowledge that I had killed someone whose only crime was fighting for what was right.

Just like I should have been doing.

As I stepped into the outfit my attendants had prepared, I glanced in the mirror. Everything about me was sharper and harder, from my flinty eyes to my deliberate posture. But the dress was beautiful. Lillian's designs always were.

A soft knock sounded as she stepped inside. 'What do you think? I know you wanted black, but—'

'But the rest of the court consider today a celebration,' I finished for her. 'And I have to look the part.'

Lillian's clear blue eyes searched mine. 'It's not how we thought it would be, is it?'

I didn't answer. I didn't need to.

She adjusted my crimson dress with careful fingers. Then she pinned my hair so that it fell over one shoulder in dark, glistening waves. 'You look beautiful, Mira.' Her words were kind but tinged with sadness. 'I'm working on something new,' she added with a tiny smile. 'I hope you'll be impressed.'

'I'm sure I will,' I replied. So far, Lillian had exceeded even my expectations.

I hadn't told her about the vow I'd made after my mother had died, or the man I'd murdered during the third Trial. Most likely, Lillian knew it all anyway. I was infamous now, but it wasn't in the same way I once was. It was an admiring kind of infamy, the kind that resulted in people searching for me at public gatherings, curious to catch a glimpse of my face.

Either way, Lillian didn't dress me like the girl I once was. She dressed me as the person the court saw me as, a true member of the Order of Masks. My wardrobe consisted of sleek outfits of black and red, with hidden compartments and sheaths for weapons.

'You're brilliant, you know,' I said, trying to lift her mood. 'The best friend a girl could have.'

Lillian met my eyes in the mirror. Her own were suspiciously bright, as if she was holding back tears. 'I love you, Mira,' she said softly. Then she added haltingly, 'Don't go down to the docks today. Stay with me instead.'

The smile slid off my face. I turned away without answering, ignoring the expression on her face – the sheer, naked *hurt*.

A sea of red and gold.

That was my first impression of the Imperial Fleet, proudly assembled in the harbour. Each ship carried a hundred soldiers, and as I stared at the gathered ships – over one hundred strong – I had to fight back rising nausea. The governor's death had been the catalyst for yet another Kalurian uprising, and the emperor intended to make them pay dearly for it.

I swallowed as The *Drakkar* caught my eye, the lettering bright and unmistakable in the midday sun. This was just another piece of Emperor Kalias's calculated pageantry: anchoring the governor's abandoned ship in full view of everyone, where it seemed sad and shrunken.

Emperor Kalias was standing to one side, allowing Roran to direct the proceedings. The crown prince was already dressed for battle, and his cruel face looked eager. *This* was what he was suited for: battlefields and brutality. I could only imagine what Ravalia would look like with him on the throne.

He held up a hand for silence and the crowd instantly stilled. Like his father, Roran knew how to use appearances to his advantage; flanked by five of his most seasoned generals, their experience and authority seemed to transfer to him.

'My father has tasked me with ending the unrest in Kalure,' Roran announced, his jade-green eyes glinting with satisfaction, 'and this time, there will be no negotiation. The Kalurians will either bend, or they will break.'

That last word sounded too harsh to be real. People cheered, but I barely noticed. I was staring at Roran, whose hand rested impatiently on the pommel of his sword.

The sword that had killed my mother.

And now he was going to sail across the Azure Sea, to kill my father's people. *My* people.

Even my training couldn't shield me from the horror of all this. The eager crowd, hungry for bloodshed. Children looking on excitedly from under their parents' arms, not comprehending the tragedy about to unfold.

My hand enclosed around the locket I wore. It was hidden beneath the bodice of my dress, a dangerous secret.

What would my parents think, if they could see me now? Would they be as disappointed in me as I was in myself?

My father . . . I would never have the chance to know him, but surely he would want me to stop this. And my mother . . . in her last moments, she had spoken of me as a ruler, strong and brave enough to free my people.

I wasn't sure I could lead anyone or anything. But I felt the weight of that responsibility now, more heavily than I ever had. During the Trials, I had been focused on staying alive. But after I'd killed the governor . . . something had shifted.

Fight for them, Kasmira. Promise me.

Somehow, I had to keep my vow to the governor. I had to find a way of destroying Roran, of protecting the only home I had left. The Kalurians had no advocates here in Ravalia. No one willing to fight for them.

Except for me.

Cassius was watching the Imperial Fleet too, but there was a hungry gleam in his eyes. And when he looked at his brother . . . his expression turned heavy, calculating. He had no love for Roran either.

If we struck a bargain, you and I, I could give you everything you desire. I could even give you my father's head on a platter.

What better way to weaken the Ravalian Court than by giving the youngest prince exactly what he wanted?

I narrowed my eyes as I watched my mother's murderer board the flagship. I kept watching long after the fleet had faded from view, the image of Roran's hateful face burned into my mind – because this wasn't goodbye. This wasn't the end.

Not even close.

Let Zandri shape me into the perfect member of the Order of Masks, I thought viciously. *Let Cassius plot and scheme and believe he can control me. I'll use every scrap of knowledge and power to my own advantage. To* Kalure's *advantage.*

After all, that was what the Order of Masks was created for. Three words, designed to bring down empires.

Infiltrate. Exploit.

Destroy.

CHAPTER FORTY-ONE

Mira

Rhythmic drumbeats reverberated through me as I entered Caleah Fortress, the overhead lanterns casting everything in a scarlet haze.

It felt like stepping into my dance from the first Trial, except infinitely more primal. Shadows of performing acrobats ghosted across the walls, and I looked up to see half-clothed men and women suspended from the ceiling, their bodies contorted within golden hoops. Red cloth hung down around them, rippling in time with their movements.

Cassius was holding court in the centre of the ballroom, a crow-beaked mask concealing his features. Scantily dressed sycophants and masked nobility surrounded him, a far cry from the preening courtiers I had seen the last time I'd been here. From what I'd heard, he often held parties like this – for his amusement, I suspected, but also to increase his influence and uncover secrets. Most of the younger nobles attended regularly, preferring Cassius's darker brand of entertainment and debauchery to the stuffy functions at the palace.

Right now, his eyes were on one of the dancers. To anyone else, his attention might have been mistaken for keen male interest – but I saw the boredom in his posture. He was sprawled across his throne, his chin cupped in his hand. His other idly stroked a woman's long hair, a gesture similar to that of a master patting its pet.

'Wishing it was you up there?'

Even if Odessa hadn't been wearing the mask of a beautiful maiden, I would have recognised her. Everything about her was meticulously perfect, from her elaborate periwinkle gown to her flawless porcelain skin. Her sheet of blonde hair was so light it resembled snow.

'I'm perfectly happy where I am, thank you.'

Though I kept my expression blandly polite, she didn't believe it for a second. Odessa's instruction as a Mask was very different to my own; it was all about strategy, seduction and politics, using her access within the court to test loyalties and gather information. I supposed it only made sense she would be suspicious of my motives.

'My betrothed is off limits,' Odessa said coolly, not bothering with subtlety. 'You would do well to heed my warning where he is concerned.'

'Worried about keeping your man?' I retorted, a taunting smile curving my lips.

Odessa moved closer, the silk sleeves of her dress brushing my arm. 'It doesn't matter how many Trials you win,' she said, 'or how many people you butcher to prove yourself to the emperor. I know what you really are. Yet another rat, scavenging for scraps.'

I met her stare evenly. 'I hate to break it to you, but I don't care what you think of me.'

Her lips tightened into a thin line, the only sign of her irritation. 'Do you think you're the only one who has tried to seduce the prince?' she asked, her sharp nails enclosing over my wrist. 'Cassius has had his fair share of lovers, and it's never ended well for a single one of them.' She released me abruptly, smiling a disconcerting smile. 'But do enjoy the party. It's important to savour every moment; you never know which might be your last.'

With that, she turned and wove her way through the hot press of bodies. I stared after her, marking her every movement.

'If looks could kill,' a smooth voice drawled from behind me, 'poor Odessa would already have one foot in the grave.'

I shifted to face Cassius, who removed his crow-beaked mask. For once, he had forgone his usual black – opting for a tunic the same shade of dark red as the wine in his hand. He took a sip, absently adjusting his jagged high collar. Given the various stages of undress around me, it seemed strange he was so well put together.

'You don't sound concerned about your fiancée's welfare,' I observed.

Cassius shrugged. 'Odessa and I have a complicated relationship. Neither of us are what I'd describe as *sentimental*.'

I suppressed a smile. It was impossible to imagine Cassius being the sentimental type.

But my smile quickly faded, thinking of the last time we had spoken – down at the docks, after Roran and the Imperial Fleet had sailed off into the distance. There was a great deal riding on this alliance, and while Cassius's terms had been impossible to resist, I had the unsettling feeling I had strayed too far from the path of good sense.

'I'm glad you finally decided to accept my offer,' he continued. 'After a week with no contact, I was beginning to wonder. You know, it's considered rude to keep a prince waiting.'

I didn't dignify his comment with a response. Instead, I said, 'And yet the Warriors let me through without question. Apparently, they had standing orders to grant me entrance, any time of the day or night.'

A faint smile upturned his full lips. 'I live in hope, it seems.'

Cassius steered me through the crowded ballroom, until we were surrounded by gyrating couples, their hands and lips ghosting over each other's skin. Two bare-chested men pressed in closer, with an ease born of familiarity.

'Care to join us?' one asked Cassius, his skin glistening with gold paint. I flushed as his partner ran a teasing finger across my collarbone.

The prince smiled, utterly at ease. 'Not tonight.'

His arms wound assertively around my waist, and the various couples fell away before us, though I felt their eyes boring into the back of my head. I hesitated when we reached the central staircase, acutely aware that he was taking me in the direction of his chambers – and doing so in full view of everyone.

'Perhaps you could be a little less obvious,' I said, raising an eyebrow. 'Or do you *want* to put a target on my back?'

He smirked. 'Scared, are you?'

'Of Odessa? Hardly.'

But Cassius's expression turned serious. 'You shouldn't underestimate her. She's been playing the game as long as I have; she might surprise you.'

'You seem pleased by the possibility.'

'Quite the contrary,' he said, but I didn't know whether to believe him. There was an unsettling gleam in his eyes, as if he enjoyed the thought of Odessa and I pitted against each other.

We reached the end of the hallway and entered the set of rooms where I'd stolen his crown. Heat rushed to my cheeks as my gaze landed on the bedchamber, with its four-poster bed and mountain of satin pillows. The last time I had been here, he had pushed me back against those very pillows—

'You know,' Cassius said, watching me closely, 'our arrangement doesn't have to be purely professional.'

'I don't see how it can be anything else,' I said, looking up at him. 'Your family are reprehensible – I should hate you on principle.'

'*Do* you hate me, Mira?' he asked, his lips suddenly against the shell of my ear. 'Because it didn't feel that way last time we were here.'

'That was—'

'An act?' Cassius finished, an edge of amusement entering his voice. 'I don't think so. I felt the way you responded to my touch. I can feel the way you're responding to me now.' His smile curved against the sensitive skin of my neck, sending a shiver down my spine. 'Maybe a part of you hates me, but hatred isn't all you feel.'

As if my silence was permission, he removed the pins from my hair, sending it tumbling down my back. At first he ran his hands gently through the strands, but then his grip tightened, drawing my chin upwards. Baring my throat to him.

Cassius's midnight-blue eyes glittered as he pressed his lips to my neck, directly above my pounding pulse. As he pulled back to look at me, I could almost hear his smooth, ironical voice: *You* hate *me, do you, Mira?*

And maybe it was the pulsating beat echoing from the ballroom, or the memory of those couples writhing in each other's arms, but my traitorous eyes dropped to his lips. Those full, arrogant lips that I *should* hate, but instead—

Cassius kissed me like he was staking a claim. Powerful and sure, stoking the fire between us.

His touch cut through my defences, and in that moment, I didn't care that he was a ruthless Ravalian prince. Even though it was dangerous and wrong, I craved the distraction he offered.

My eyes fluttered closed as Cassius pressed me against the wall, only to flash open again when his clever fingers started undoing the laces of my gown. A distant, logical part of me warned that this was escalating too quickly, and that I should *stop*.

I opened my mouth to say as much, but he took my parted lips as an invitation, kissing me until I was breathless and aching. When he released me, I found myself leaning into his strong arms for support, even as I braced myself to pull away.

But why should *I tell him to stop?* a mutinous part of me murmured. Cassius was the perfect distraction: attractive, discreet, and seasoned in meaningless flings. Unlike Aric, there was no chance of him demanding more from me than I had to give.

All rational thought left my mind as Cassius undid my bodice, my nipples hardening in the cool air. His fingers brushed over the sensitive skin of my breasts, toying with a peaked nipple before his mouth—

A gasp left my lips at the sensation, at the way his mouth and tongue worked in tandem, until I felt like I was burning on a fuse for him. Impatient, I reached for him, but he merely smiled, sliding a hand down my stomach, my abdomen, and then lower, parting the material of my dress until—

I arched convulsively in his hold, my bare shoulders hitting the wall. A soft, feather-light laugh met my ears.

As his fingers trailed up my thighs, slow and explorative, I reached for his high-collared tunic. Soon the buttons were undone, and I was running my hands across his lean, muscular chest. Cassius stiffened when my hands brushed his neck, but it wasn't until I saw the scar that I understood.

'Who did this to you?' I breathed, tracing the raised red line with my eyes. It started at the base of his throat and continued up the left side of his neck, snaking around to the base of his skull. It reminded me of the criminals I had seen whipped on Aldara, but those wounds had never come up *this* high—

Cassius stepped back, absently touching his scar as he did. 'Father often asked Roran to punish me as a child – considered it a good lesson for us both. But Roran was always a little too enthusiastic.' He smiled thinly.

I swallowed, watching as Cassius did up the silver buttons of his tunic. It had never occurred to me that the high collars he wore were a kind of armour. Not until now. 'You don't have to—'

'I don't want your pity, Mira.' His voice was calm, but in the space of a few heartbeats, the entire mood had shifted. 'I never intended to take things too far anyway. I just wanted to prove a point.'

'What *point*?' I asked, some of my sympathy dissolving.

Perhaps that was what Cassius intended, because when he smiled at me, there was no trace of his earlier vulnerability. Only masculine satisfaction – and arrogance. 'That you want me,' he murmured, reaching over to tighten the laces he had loosened.

The silken invitation in his voice – and the knowing edge to it – infuriated me. I slapped his hand away.

Cassius laughed but let his hand fall. 'Back to business, then,' he said. His attention didn't stray from my face as I secured the bodice of my dress. 'I trust you remember the bargain we struck?'

'Of course.'

'Well,' he continued, 'in order to help *you*, there's something I need you to do for me.'

'And that is . . . ?'

'Nothing too difficult, I assure you.'

His comment didn't inspire me with confidence. I followed anyway as he entered a library filled with floor-to-ceiling book-shelves, moving to stand over a table filled with miniature figurines.

They were divided into sections, each inhabiting a particular area on the map.

'I thought it was time we discussed strategy.' Cassius nodded at the board. 'The red pins represent my father's armies. The others I'm sure you recognise.'

My gaze landed on the miniature wooden figures. One of them, clearly the emperor, wore a crown of spikes. The figure beside him had long hair and a delicate circlet. There were others, too – imitations of Cassius, the two other royal heirs, and the generals. Behind the figure of the emperor were clusters of red pins. The continent was dotted with them, but there were others too.

'What do the black pins represent?'

'Ah.' Cassius smiled, as if he'd been waiting for me to ask. 'Those are the people loyal to me. Nobles and soldiers, a few Warriors.'

I took in the map with new interest. There weren't as many black pins as red, but they were still substantial. I turned to look at him, my unspoken question obvious.

'I make a habit of formulating my own alliances. They're all committed to my rule, ready to support me in taking the throne.' He paused, then added, 'As you can see, my father is very well protected. But not even an emperor can account for every eventuality – and now that my father has sent Roran to Kalure, we have the opportunity to strike.'

I stiffened at the casual mention of Roran, but Cassius didn't notice my reaction. He was tracing one of the figurines with his finger – a man standing at the emperor's right-hand side.

'General Tiran,' he said slowly, 'is the main obstacle in my way. It would be very difficult to get to my father while he's around.'

'And what about Odessa?'

He shrugged. 'We were betrothed since before we were born. It's a union meant to demonstrate strength – a merging of the emperor and the military. But Odessa and her father are in my way. If I intend to take the throne, they will need to be removed.'

'You mean . . .' The words stuck in my throat. Despite my dislike of Odessa, I didn't wish her family dead. 'You'd kill them?'

'There's no need for me to do that. Not when I have your help.'

'My help?'

'Yes, Mira.' His voice turned indulgent. 'As a member of the Order of Masks, you have access that I don't. You can help me discredit General Tiran, leaving the path open for me to take my father's place.'

I stared at him, my heart pounding so hard that I felt sick.

'And what happens to his family?'

'Nothing final,' Cassius assured me. 'Though I don't know why you'd care. Odessa isn't your friend.'

'I know. It's just . . .'

There's been too much death already.

A frown pulled at his mouth. 'Don't tell me you're still feeling guilty about the third Trial. Dozens of Kalurians die in skirmishes each day. What does one more matter?'

I stiffened, my hand tightening on the table. The prince noticed the movement and his smile turned hard, almost cruel.

'Oh, sorry,' he said offhandedly, 'does that bother you?'

'You told me,' I replied with careful calm, 'that once you took the throne, you would give them their freedom.'

'And I will,' Cassius said, the brief flicker of cruelty gone as quickly as it had appeared. 'As agreed, you will be the Queen of Kalure. But don't forget – *I* will be the ruler of the Ravalian Empire. I need you to remember that.'

I said nothing. I didn't like the idea of relying on Cassius's word or trusting a Ravalian prince to be merciful. But what other choice did I have?

The prince seemed to find my silence satisfactory. His hand brushed my cheek, his expression abruptly softening. 'You did what you had to. There's no shame in that.' He smiled faintly. 'You're a lot like me, actually.'

'I'm nothing like you,' I retorted.

Cassius tilted his head, his striking eyes intent on mine. When he spoke, his voice was filled with certainty. 'You are, Mira,' he said, pressing something cold and heavy into my hands. 'You just haven't recognised it yet.'

I ignored the stares as I descended the central staircase, weaving my way through the wild party and into the tranquil gardens.

'You're in a hurry.' I whirled to face Sabine, who was sitting on a moonlit bench, her turquoise dress pooling elegantly around her crossed ankles. 'Didn't you enjoy the party?'

'Not enough to stay all night.'

'Fair enough,' she replied. 'These things can be tiresome.'

'Yes, they—' I stopped as something occurred to me. 'How did you get past the Warriors at the entrance?'

'I *am* an Order member now, same as you,' Sabine reminded me. 'Perhaps I was invited.'

'*Were* you invited?'

'Well . . . no.' Sabine flashed me an impish smile. 'But the guards aren't much of an obstacle for me. I can get in almost anywhere, no invitation necessary.' She raised an eyebrow. 'Don't you remember from last time?'

Last time. During the first Trial.

'It seems like a lot of trouble to go to,' I said. 'Even with your illusions.'

She shrugged. 'I was curious. The prince's parties have a reputation for being . . . interesting.'

'Right.' I stared at her, wondering if there was more to this than she was letting on. It should have been easy to read her, but as hard as I tried, I couldn't even guess at her motives. 'Well, I was just leaving—'

'Because you're about to complete whatever task the prince gave you?'

That gave me pause. 'What are you talking about?'

'I like to observe people, Mira. Particularly interesting people – which, by definition, means you and the prince.'

'And what exactly,' I asked cautiously, 'do you think you know?'

Sabine's green eyes locked with mine. Past the amusement, there was a deep intelligence there that unnerved me. 'I know enough. You didn't listen to any of my warnings, did you?'

The prince plays games with people, and they rarely end well.

'It doesn't matter,' I told her firmly, glancing quickly around the garden to make sure we weren't being observed. 'I know what I'm doing with Cassius.'

'That's debatable,' Sabine said, standing. In her heeled sandals, her eyes were level with mine – and uncharacteristically serious. 'Listen, Mira – whatever task he's given you to complete, whatever deal you've made, there are other ways to achieve your goals. *Better* ways.'

'I don't know what you're talking about,' I said. General Tiran's seal burned a hole inside my dress.

Sabine's gaze shifted to the concealed panel of my dress, as if she knew exactly where it was – and what it was hiding. Though she had never spoken outright about her feelings towards the Ravalian Empire, when she looked up at me, there was a rebellious glint in her eyes. One that reminded me of Aric and Darius.

'I could help you, Mira. If you let me.'

Her offer sounded sincere, and I hadn't forgotten how Sabine had helped me before the third Trial. It was thanks to her that I was still alive. But she was also right about Cassius – our plans were dangerous. *Treasonous.*

It was one thing if Cassius and I were discovered and killed. We knew the risks, and we'd made our peace with them.

But I wasn't willing to risk Sabine's life.

'Thanks,' I told her, 'but I don't need any help.'

A shadow crossed Sabine's face. Without her usual airiness, she seemed older and harder. Unfamiliar.

Then the moment passed, and her smile returned. 'Maybe I came to you too soon.'

Sabine turned, her brunette curls bobbing behind her. But before she reached the path, she glanced back over her shoulder.

'We made a good team during the Trials,' she reminded me. 'Just imagine what we could accomplish now.'

CHAPTER FORTY-TWO

Scarlett

I had expended a great deal of effort keeping the guise of Sabine alive. It was infuriating to realise I might have done it all for nothing.

Infuriating to realise that Mira had chosen Cassius over me – and she hadn't even known who I was. Everything about Sabine had been carefully crafted. Every word choice, every gesture and mannerism – it had all been meant to draw Mira in.

And I had failed. Abysmally.

Perhaps I should just kill Sabine off, I thought, gazing outside the arch windows of the royal parlour. Too much of my time was dedicated to maintaining this masquerade, and I was relying heavily on the information Severin fed me.

'I believe I asked you a question,' Lady Tiran reminded me, her voice sharp.

'Of course, My Lady,' I replied, turning away from the window. 'My apologies. Focusing on something else helps sharpen my visions.'

Lady Tiran looked doubtful, and she was right to be. I'd been lying through my teeth ever since Empress Ivalene summoned me to the royal parlour, and I would have to keep lying until her ladies were satisfied with my responses – or until they finally tired of me.

That moment couldn't come soon enough. After two hours of answering their inane questions, I was beginning to wish I had brought some poison with me.

'I see bloodshed in your husband's future,' I informed Lady Tiran, leaning across the table like I was sharing a secret. 'I suspect the emperor will send him on another campaign before the month is out.'

This was a guess – not an official vision from Severin. But given the situation in the Western Lands, it was only a matter of time before my father sent his best general to deal with the rebellions.

Lady Tiran raised a hand to her coifed white-blonde hair – a nervous gesture, since it was perfectly in place.

No doubt she was worried about her husband's safety, but I felt no sympathy for her. She despised me and my mother on behalf of the empress and had done her best to turn public perception against us. It was thanks to her influence I had never been accepted amongst the ladies of the court.

I glanced behind me, where Ivalene was reclining on a divan with her other ladies. After the first hour, when they had bombarded me with questions, their interest in my predictions had tapered off – and they had reverted to their favourite pastime: snacking on freshly baked honey cakes while exchanging court gossip.

I overheard snatches of their conversation every now and then, usually nothing of note. But I paid greater attention when I heard Antonia Seneca's name.

'—and I told Antonia, if she's going to wear last season's fashion, then she shouldn't be surprised when people wonder about her financial affairs.'

'I heard about this too,' another lady chimed in. 'My husband told me that they withdrew a suspiciously large sum from their accounts last month. They claimed it was for some poor relative of theirs, but there was no paper trail. Perhaps they have gambling debts.'

'Are you attempting to sharpen your visions again?' Lady Tiran commented, her voice dry.

I reluctantly returned my attention to my lone patron. 'Is there something else?' I asked, tapping my fingers impatiently against the table. 'My Lady,' I added, as a clear afterthought.

Lady Tiran's lips thinned. 'I'm afraid there is. What can you tell me about my daughter's future?'

I was far more interested in the *Senecas'* future. For some time, my mother had suspected that a noble family was financing the resistance, but without proof, the emperor had been reluctant to act.

The Senecas had always been above reproach – *suspiciously* above reproach, my mother had told me. They had no debts and no vices, aside from the husband's proclivity for taking lovers. But this development might convince Kalias they were worth further investigation.

If the information was accurate.

'Is there anything in particular you want to know?' I asked Lady Tiran, confident that whatever it was, I could make something up.

'Odessa joined the Order of Masks recently.' She hesitated. 'While it's an honour,' she continued, clearly choosing her words with care, 'their missions can be dangerous, and . . . well, quite frankly, it wasn't the life I wanted for her. I had hoped she would focus on her marriage to Prince Cassius.'

I'd never thought much about Odessa's motivations to become a Mask; the Orders were prestigious enough that plenty of nobles wanted to join. But it did seem like an odd choice for someone set to marry into the royal family. Then again, I couldn't blame Odessa for wanting a life of her own, independent from my brother.

'This vision isn't so clear,' I said, furrowing my brow in thought. 'It's more of a feeling than anything else.' I felt like the worst kind of charlatan, but judging by Lady Tiran's eager expression, she was buying into my ruse.

'Yes?' she prompted.

'I have a strong sense that Odessa will find her purpose in the Order of Masks. And there's something else, too – a sense of warmth. Connection.'

'It's not . . .' Lady Tiran's throat bobbled. 'Not romantic, I hope?'

'I See a girl with her,' I said, thinking of Odessa's friendship with Danica.

'Ah.' Lady Tiran was suddenly stiff. 'Thank you for your time,' she said, standing a little too quickly. And then, more softly, 'I would appreciate your discretion.'

I frowned. Clearly, I had stumbled onto something Lady Tiran hadn't wanted me to.

I couldn't imagine any reason for Lady Tiran to be bothered by Odessa's closeness with another girl – unless Odessa liked *women*, or perhaps men and women both. Ravalia was an open country, and same-sex couples were widely accepted – though they were less common in the royal family, with its obsession on having natural-born heirs.

Perhaps Odessa and I had more in common than I'd thought – both trapped by obligation to our families and the rules of the court.

It was an unsettling realisation.

But Lady Tiran's dismissal had given me the opportunity I had been waiting for, and I quickly forgot about Odessa. After a brief curtsy for the empress and her ladies, I left the royal parlour behind and went to find my mother.

Thunder echoed off the Archasian mountains as the storm hit. Lightning split the sky, but down below, the Warriors continued to practise. Storms like this were a common occurrence, clouds rolling in with the late afternoon breeze.

'You're watching her again.'

'I'm watching all the sparring matches,' I corrected, though this was a lie.

My attention was always drawn back to Mira, whether or not I wanted it to be. There was a certain symmetry between us, one that unsettled and intrigued me in equal measure.

'It's a shame,' I mused, 'that Mira doesn't know we're cousins.'

Zandri cast me a cold glance. 'You like her.'

I shrugged. 'It doesn't matter what I think of her. She's a means to an end.'

Zandri came to stand at my side, the wind rustling the feathers on her shoulders. Perched on the very edge of the battlements, she resembled a dark bird poised to take flight. 'Perhaps it's time you exploited that family connection – used it to form a stronger bond with the girl. Her hatred for the emperor needs to be carefully directed, which requires a certain level of influence. I would prefer that influence came from us rather than your brother.'

I agreed with Zandri's reasoning, but it wasn't that simple. 'Cassius will have spies watching Mira now that they're working together. He'll try to eliminate me if he believes I'm a threat to his plans.'

'She's a Mask. It's natural that you should have some interaction with her – particularly when I'm sending you on a mission together.'

I glanced up in pleased surprise. 'Evander Seneca?' At my mother's nod, I smiled. 'What abilities will you grant her?'

'Nothing that can be used against you. Some minor illusion magic, mostly to disguise her features. But you will be in charge, Scarlett, which means I need to trust you to do what must be done.'

I willed steel into my voice as I clarified, 'You want me to interrogate them.'

'You've seen me interrogate prisoners enough times; I have no doubt that you're perfectly capable of replicating the process. No, I'm referring to what comes *afterwards*.' Zandri smiled faintly at me. 'Kalias doesn't want more prisoners. My instructions are to establish the Senecas' guilt, discover the names of their contacts, and then clean house.'

'*Your* instructions?' I folded my arms as it began to drizzle. 'Does my father even realise I'm involved?'

'You know how Kalias feels about sending you on active missions.' Zandri waved a dismissive hand. 'He made you royal patron thinking the title would be ceremonial. But *I* am the head of the Order of Masks, and if I believe you're the best fit for a particular mission, then I will use you accordingly.'

'How sentimental of you,' I muttered. 'Is this so I can get closer to Mira?'

'I also want you to watch her. If she has any remaining connections with the resistance, this mission should expose them. It would be useful to know what state they're in, and what their plans are.' Zandri's lips curved. 'Not that they've ever been more than a bunch of discontents. But there will be period of instability when Emperor Kalias dies, and I don't intend to give the rebels any opportunity to take power.'

'Fair enough,' I said, turning to leave. 'I'll take care of them.'

Before I could take a step, cool fingers enclosed around my wrist – around the bracelet I wore. The blood ruby within warmed at Zandri's touch, and I knew my mother was already channelling some of its magic.

I had seen her do this before, mostly with other Masks, but I had never experienced it myself. There was something mesmerising about the dark red tendrils that extended from the blood ruby, writhing through the air like snakes.

'You know what to do,' Zandri said impatiently.

Slowly, tentatively, my lips parted. The tendrils swarmed – and I forced myself to inhale, welcoming them into my body. Embracing them.

But when I tried to let out the breath I was holding, I couldn't. My lungs wouldn't exhale, wouldn't cooperate—

And then the feeling of fullness subsided, and I doubled over, coughing and gulping down the crisp air. My eyes darted past Zandri, to where Aric was watching across the battlements, out of earshot but close enough to have witnessed everything. His body tensed, like he was preparing to run to my side.

When I regained control of myself, I shook my head at him. Personal guard or not, I didn't want to find out what Zandri might do if Aric intervened.

'What magic did you give me?' I asked, looking up at my mother.

'Something to help you dispose of the bodies.' There was an edge to Zandri's voice, and I knew what this mission really was: a test. 'I need to know that you're capable of doing this, Scarlett. You already failed once. With Governor Halvor.'

I swallowed down unwise, frustrated words. Twisted though it was, I wanted my mother to be proud of me – to think of me as a partner and an equal.

'I won't fail again,' I promised. 'I'll deal with the resistance – and I'll find a way to disrupt Mira's partnership with Cassius.'

Zandri turned away from me without responding. In her mind, I should have done that already. I should have done more.

Always more.

CHAPTER FORTY-THREE

Scarlett

Aric was a familiar presence at my side as I descended from the battlements. He had been serving on my security detail these past weeks, and I'd come to like him. He had an admirable strength to his personality, a fierce resolve that drove him like it did me.

And he was loyal. I could respect that.

I hadn't forgotten the way he'd stepped in front of Mira in the arena. He had been willing to fight for her – and die for her – without a second's hesitation. That kind of devotion was as rare as it was valuable.

When the Order residences came into view, Aric spoke for the first time. 'Your mother seems . . . intense.'

'That's an understatement.'

Aric glanced sideways at me. 'If you ever want someone to talk to . . .'

'I appreciate that.' Before he could say something else, I asked, 'How is Lillian?'

His expression brightened. Requesting Lillian's presence at court had been just another way of earning Aric and Mira's trust. But she meant so much to Aric that it was difficult not to take an interest.

'She's enjoying her new position in the palace.' Aric's voice was warm and open. 'It means a lot to me that you invited her here, and that you assigned her to Mira. I still feel like I should do something to thank you.'

My lips curved into the gentle smile I reserved for Aric. 'There's really no need.'

It was obvious Aric disagreed, but he didn't press the matter. He was careful to keep a professional distance during our public interactions, though the boundaries between friendship and duty were becoming somewhat blurred, thanks to the hours we spent swapping stories about Kain.

Though my carefully chosen recollections were false, Aric was hungry for every detail. I could probably win Mira over through Aric, but I hadn't cultivated him for that purpose. He was a weapon – and at the right time, I would tell him what I knew about Kain's death and use him against Roran.

But not until then. If Zandri had taught me anything, it was the importance of timing.

Crossing through the training barracks, I searched for Mira amongst the sparring Warriors. It didn't take long to find her; she was striding back towards the ring of onlookers, having disarmed her previous opponent.

'It looks like you need another partner,' I called, ignoring Aric's surprised glance.

Mira's ponytail whipped through the air as she turned. Her dark eyes narrowed as they fell on me; there was power in that single glance, a fire that warmed even my icy skin.

'If you can keep up,' she challenged.

'Let's see, shall we?'

Though my words were even, I knew she would see the steeliness in my posture – and that steeliness would appeal to her competitive spirit.

It did. Mira crossed into the sparring circle, ignoring the gathering spectators. It was rare for a royal to fight publicly, against anyone except the captain of the guard, and several Warriors paused their own matches to watch.

'Good luck, Your Highness,' Aric said, handing over his sword.

I took it and strode over to where Mira was waiting.

For a moment, we sized each other up. Then she leapt at me in a blur of motion.

I countered instinctively, blocking her sword and breaking away. But Mira didn't give me space to circle and formulate a strategy. She twirled around me like a dancer rather than a Warrior, impressively fast.

Teeth gritted with effort, I searched for an opening. But while my technique was better than Mira's, she was a worthy adversary, forcing me to concede step after step. I pushed back – and yet, no matter how forceful my attacks were, how creative or even unpredictable, she anticipated my every move.

Time became meaningless as we exchanged blows, my focus narrowing to our two blades. We were evenly matched, but I couldn't compete with Mira's endurance. I wouldn't be able to keep this up much longer.

There was another distant clap of thunder. The clouds released their rain in a warm, drenching torrent.

Whirling to the side, I impatiently slashed at Mira. It was a clumsy attack that she lithely avoided, teeth flashing in a fierce grin. As if she'd been waiting for this, Mira twisted—

And brought her sword up to my throat.

The instant the metal touched my skin, I went still. If this was a real battle, Mira could end my life right here and now. We stared into each other's eyes, neither of us blinking despite the moisture running down our faces.

Then Mira released me. As she did, I became aware of our clapping audience.

'Good match,' I said, inclining my head in respect.

Mira hesitated but returned the action. 'Good match,' she agreed. 'You fight well with a sword. How come I never see you sparring with the Warriors?'

'I don't like to advertise what I can do. I prefer my enemies to underestimate me.'

Mira's surprise was obvious. 'Enemies?'

I half-smiled. 'You'd think monarchs have so many children to ensure succession, but *I* think it's because they enjoy the entertainment of pitting us against each other. The sport of it.'

Mira cast me a wary glance. 'Surely your brothers wouldn't dare—'

'Wouldn't dare what, exactly?' I looked at her, all humour wiped from my face. 'Protect their claim to the throne by killing me?'

I could see Mira riddling this out, trying to determine whether there were any lines that the princes – or perhaps *one* prince in particular – wouldn't cross. There was something conflicted about her expression, and I resisted the urge to roll my eyes. Even with Mira's hatred of the Ravalian Court, Cassius had still managed to charm her.

'Be careful with my brother,' I warned. 'He makes all kinds of promises, but he doesn't always honour them.'

I was still smiling as I turned and walked away, the image of Mira's doubt branded into my mind.

Let her think about that.

Hours later, I found myself pacing the onyx chamber below the Order of Masks atrium. My reflection prowled around me, displayed in the dozens of mirrors encircling the space.

For once, I looked more like Zandri than my father. The black fighting leathers she'd provided even had a feather mantle like her own. I supposed we were about to find out if I really was my mother's daughter.

I'd spent the past fifteen minutes sharpening my blades and practising with the magic Zandri had given me. With one touch, I had disintegrated an entire pile of papers, and I could only imagine what would happen if I focused that magic on a body. *Bodies*, I corrected myself. By the end of tonight, I would be responsible for multiple bodies.

Footsteps rang out as Mira descended the metal staircase. Zandri must have told her what to wear, because she was dressed to blend in with the clientele at Evander Seneca's favourite tavern – though the proud set of her shoulders was sure to set her apart.

'You hold yourself too much like a Warrior,' I told her. 'You walk like it, too. Most ladies take smaller steps. They're more focused on grace than efficiency.'

'I prefer efficiency.'

'I said the same thing once.' A smile tugged at my lips. 'To my etiquette teacher. It didn't go down very well.'

'You have to study etiquette?' Mira eyed me curiously. 'What other lessons do you have?'

'Less than you might think,' I replied, trying to conceal my bitterness. 'I used to have tutoring sessions in history and battle strategy. But after my engagement was announced, my father cancelled them all. Except etiquette.'

'I'm sorry,' Mira said softly, and I remembered that she was technically a princess too – though our experiences were so different.

I forced a smile, irritated by how much I had given away. 'It's fine. At least I still have my duties in the Order of Masks.'

'Do you often go on missions?' Mira asked as she paced the hall.

'It's rare,' I admitted, trying to keep my tone light. 'I suppose it has something to do with being the princess. But this mission should be simple enough. A quick interrogation – nothing more.'

Mira stiffened. It was an almost imperceptible change, but it told me enough about her true feelings. 'Who's the target?'

'His name is Evander Seneca. Zandri suspects that he's connected with the rebels in the Lower Districts.' I watched Mira closely, but her expression was unreadable. Offhandedly, I added, 'I believe you've had some interaction with them before?'

'You could say that.'

Her tone didn't welcome further questions, and I decided against pushing her. I would find out what I wanted to know by observing Mira during the mission.

'My mother,' I continued as if I hadn't noticed her mood shift, 'wants you to gain access to Seneca Manor. How you do this is up to you, but Evander Seneca has a weakness for young women – and I know the tavern he will be at tonight.'

Mira glanced pointedly at the dress she wore, complete with delicate, high-heeled sandals that wound up her toned legs. 'It seems I can make that work,' she said, deadpan.

'Good.' I smiled, amused despite myself. 'He also has a weakness for blondes.'

'Is that your way of asking me to dye my hair?'

'Nothing so mundane. I assume Zandri channelled magic to you from your blood ruby?'

'Yes, but she didn't show me how to use it.' Mira's tone was cautious. 'What will I be able to do this time?'

Rather than answering with words, I moved in front of one of the full-length mirrors. I kept my attention on my reflection as I visualised the illusion, willing my hair to lighten to white-blonde and my icy eyes to warm to amber. It was easier than normal, probably because I had been staring at Odessa's mother all afternoon.

When my face was heart-shaped, and my mouth full and mocking, Mira came to stand at my shoulder, her eyes wide. I held the illusion for another minute, then allowed it to waver and distort, until the mirror no longer reflected Odessa's features – but my own.

'Consider this your first lesson,' I said. 'I can talk about infiltration all I like, but it's far more educational seeing this kind of magic in person. Don't you agree?'

Mira tilted her head, still studying my face. 'It was very convincing.'

'The best illusions always are.' Amusement entered my voice as I continued, 'It helps if you know the person you want to imitate. If you don't, it takes more time and effort to craft an illusion. But that's what the mirrors are for – so you can practise.'

'Then the other Masks – they have this ability too?'

'Most have an aptitude for illusion, but few can do what I can,' I said, skirting around the truth: that illusion was magic I had been born with, and not magic I had to channel from a blood ruby.

Mira's eyes narrowed in concentration. At first, nothing happened. Then a strand of her hair lightened – from black to a light chestnut.

I resisted the urge to laugh, knowing that she had been going for blonde. 'It's a start,' I said, feeling inclined to be generous.

'We have to leave for the tavern in an hour.' Tension was obvious in Mira's voice – and so was determination. 'Do you think I can learn how to master illusion by then?'

'I doubt it,' I said. 'Mastering any kind of magic takes a great deal of practice. Though I wouldn't worry too much. For this mission, all you need to do is change your features slightly.'

'How do you do it?' Mira asked, glancing over her shoulder at me.

It had been a long time since I'd thought about that – probably since my childhood lessons with Zandri. 'For me,' I answered, 'it isn't just about the illusion itself. It's important to visualise what you want others to see; the visual has to feel real to *you*, otherwise it won't convince anyone else.' I considered for a moment, then said, 'You have to shape your character, to give them motivations, backstories, likes and dislikes. Only then can you truly become them.'

Fleetingly, I thought of Sabine. I had never known the Artisan candidate, but Sabine felt like a real person to me – a distinct character, yet shaped by aspects of myself. The kind of person I would like to be if I had a choice.

Mira looked at me oddly, and I remembered that I had once given her similar advice – before the third Trial.

When I was *Sabine*.

It was too easy to let everything blur together, and I cursed myself for my carelessness. But Mira seemed to shake off the thought as I said, 'Here. Let me help you.'

It was strange to watch Mira's dark hair lighten. Even stranger to realise it was a combination of what Mira and I had imagined – blonde through the ends, and a light brown through the roots.

I focused again. When I was done, Mira was completely blonde—

And I could no longer stop myself from laughing.

Mira stared at her reflection. 'It looks . . .'

'Blonde really isn't your colour,' I agreed. 'It might be best if you keep to the dimmest parts of the tavern tonight. And if you wait until Evander has a few drinks before making your move.'

Mira glowered at me, but a smile tugged at her lips. 'Thanks for the support.'

'You're very welcome.' I reached for some hairpins I'd stored in a hidden sheath. Then I helped coil Mira's hair on top of her head, like Aella sometimes did for me. 'There,' I said stepping back to survey the result. 'I think that's as good as it's going to get.'

For a moment, we stood next to each other facing the mirror. It occurred to me that if we had grown up together, we might have shared many similar moments. There had been a time when I had desperately wanted a sister. I wondered how different things might have been if Mira and I could have filled that role for each other.

But my misguided warmth drained away as I thought of other things. Mira's wariness as she looked at me. The way she had dismissed my offer of alliance even when it had come from Sabine.

Mira turned away from the mirror, but then she paused. 'Thank you,' she said with a hint of vulnerability.

'Just try not to die,' I replied, with some of Sabine's sassiness. 'Or fail,' I added, lightening my voice so she would understand I wasn't entirely serious. 'That would be even worse.'

Mira nodded and strode towards the stairs. I waited a few seconds before following, trying to put some distance between us.

It was too easy to get close. To become so caught up in our inter-actions that I forgot I was playing a role at all. But Mira had made her choice – Cassius over Sabine.

And I had made mine. To win – no matter who I had to sacrifice in the process.

But as I left the onyx hall behind, there was the slightest twinge in my chest. A dull ache that felt an awful lot like regret.

In another life, Mira and I could have been friends.

CHAPTER FORTY-FOUR

Mira

Leaning against the stone wall of the tavern, I watched my target. Evander Seneca was clearly a noble: he was too richly dressed to be anything else, and so were his raucous companions, already deep in their cups.

Imitating Odessa, I looked up at him from beneath my lashes. A seductive, practised expression.

His gaze met mine. Like most nobles, he thought that his title gave him an invisible bubble of protection. It did, but that protection didn't extend to me.

'I've been watching you,' I said as he approached, striding over with a confidence that bordered on arrogance. Annoyingly, his confidence wasn't unfounded; a few serving girls took notice of him as he passed, admiring the fit, lean lines of his body and the jet-black hair curling at his temple.

'And what have I done,' he asked smoothly, his pale eyes glinting, 'to capture the attention of such a beautiful lady?'

I glanced away, wondering whether he would be so bold if he knew who I really was. 'I've heard rumours of you, sir,' I said sweetly. 'Maybe I wanted to find out if they're true.'

Evander seemed caught between amusement and intrigue. He extended his arm to me, winking. 'Care to find out?'

I took his offered arm, maintaining my shy smile. No one seemed interested as we left the tavern, stepping into the cool night. The city streets were busy, packed with people.

'Perhaps we could go somewhere a bit more private?'

'Of course,' Evander replied. 'My family has a small manor house not far from here, if you prefer?'

'That would be perfect.'

He nodded to a driver, who climbed into one of the gilded carriages. 'Ladies first,' he said, and I stepped inside. He followed, handing the driver a few bronze coins. 'Seneca Manor.'

Soon the public buildings transformed into stately manors. Golden carriages glinted in the moonlight, drivers ferrying their rich clients to and from their ostentatious homes. As we pulled up against the kerb, I saw copper turrets peeking out from behind a set of iron gates.

'This is where you live?' I asked, feigning awe. 'It's incredible.'

Evander shot me a superior smile. 'Wait until you see the inside,' he said, his voice lowering in a way that was probably meant to be seductive.

I giggled, like the foolish and eager girl he thought I was. It didn't even need to be particularly convincing. He'd already made up his mind about me. People weren't hard to fool, not really. They saw what they wanted to see.

He didn't offer me his hand as I climbed down from the carriage. Instead, he threaded his arm covetously around my waist.

The butler who opened the door didn't speak, but I saw how he looked at me as I entered the marble foyer – like I was the kind of opportunistic woman who heard the Seneca name and hoped to profit from it.

'Do you mind if I freshen up a bit?' I kept that preening, false smile on my lips. 'I won't be a moment.'

'There's a private chamber down the hall,' Evander said, already disappearing into his suite. 'Don't take too long.'

I turned down the hall and carefully opened the door to his study. A room I was definitely not supposed to enter.

The floorboards creaked as I crossed over to the mahogany desk, which was strewn with papers. I took care to remember their order so that I could replace them exactly as they were. Just as I picked up the first sheet – some sort of financial report – heeled footsteps rang down the hall.

I stilled. The wife wasn't supposed to be home, but clearly she was. And she was coming closer.

I did the only thing I could; I stepped away from the desk and closer to the door – just as it opened, displaying a glamorous older woman with auburn hair and assessing eyes.

'And who might *you* be?' she asked in a severe voice.

'I'm so sorry, My Lady,' I said quickly, dropping my gaze to the floor. 'I tried to follow Lord Seneca's directions, but I lost my way.'

Antonia Seneca looked me up and down, her lips pursing. 'Another of my husband's conquests, I assume.'

I kept my eyes lowered, barely daring to move. Or to breathe.

'Very well,' she said coldly. 'Go back to Evander and have your fun. But if I find a single jewel missing – or *any* indication that you're lying to me – I will go to the crown's Warriors with my suspicions. And, as I'm sure you know, the sentence for thievery is the arena.' She paused, eyeing me significantly. 'Do we understand each other, girl?'

I nodded, stepping past her and reaching for the door. My hand had just closed around the handle when I felt movement behind me. I quickly twisted, only to come face to face with Lady Seneca – who was holding a letter opener to my throat.

My gaze flickered towards the desk – to the sheet of paper that had fallen to the floor.

'Give me one reason why I shouldn't slit your throat right now,' she said, the blade pressing against my skin.

'Because if you do,' I said, barely daring to move my lips, '*she'll* kill you.'

Lady Seneca's gaze left mine and shifted to the far corner of the room, where Scarlett was standing in front of the open window. I watched her turn pale as she took in Scarlett's dark feather mantle, the mask obscuring her features.

'There must be some mistake.' The letter opener clattered to the floor. 'I don't know whose orders you're following, but—'

'You know exactly whose orders I'm following.' Scarlett moved into the light, the icy planes of her face fully visible. 'And my mother doesn't make mistakes.'

Lady Seneca opened her mouth to say something else, but she never had the chance. The dagger slashed her throat and she collapsed to the floor, blood soaking the expensive white rug.

I stared down at Lady Seneca's body in silence, taking in the sight of her glassy eyes and blank face. It had happened so suddenly that it didn't feel quite real.

'Next time,' Scarlett said to me, 'don't make such obvious mistakes. You were supposed to interrogate the husband, not search for clues.'

'What if the intelligence was wrong?' I asked, looking up at Scarlett. 'Isn't it better to make sure?'

'Would you call this *better*?' she challenged, gesturing to Lady Seneca. Despite Scarlett's cool tone, I noticed the faint tremble of her fingers.

'You didn't need to kill her.' My voice sounded dead even to my own ears. 'When she saw you, she let me go.'

'I did some investigating of my own,' Scarlett said, her words clipped. 'It was the wife who was financing the resistance, not the husband. He's culpable – no doubt about it – but Antonia Seneca was the mastermind.'

Her eyes were intent on mine as she said this, and I willed my face to go blank. But my mind was churning with possibilities. If the Senecas had been financing the resistance, that meant there was something *left* to finance. They hadn't given up after Darius's capture.

Scarlett's finger brushed the woman's pale cheek. It was a gentle gesture, almost tender, and for a second I was confused. Then Lady Seneca's face started to turn grey, her skin peeling off in flakes – until her entire body was nothing more than ash.

Scarlett scooped up the remains, stalked over to the window, and tossed them out onto the breeze. 'This is nothing,' she said when she caught me staring. 'Once you've completed your training,

Zandri will send you on missions that require advanced magic. The kind of magic you can use to advance the empire's interests – or your own.'

There was something strange about the way she said that, and I wondered about her agenda in all of this. But I knew better than to question her further.

Instead, I asked, 'So is that it? We hand the evidence over to the emperor and we're done?'

Scarlett looked at me with pity. 'No. We're not done at all.'

I searched through the papers while Scarlett interrogated Evander Seneca. His distant shouts made my stomach twist into knots.

At first glance, the papers didn't seem dangerous. There were some financial details that Zandri would be interested in; correspondence with individuals who didn't use their real names. Then I noticed a letter with a symbol at the bottom: two swords intersecting in an X.

The symbol of the resistance. The same symbol I'd seen on the door to Darius's headquarters.

This was my chance. The opportunity I'd been waiting for.

Reaching into a hidden panel in my dress, I withdrew the seal matrix Cassius had given me. The letter I held was suspicious enough, but once I'd made an impression of General Tiran's seal, it was damning.

The turning of the door handle alerted me to Scarlett's presence a second before she entered the room – just enough time for me to add the incriminating document to the pile and hide the seal matrix inside my dress.

'I have a name,' she told me impatiently. 'Are you coming?'

'What about these?' I asked, pointing at the papers.

Scarlett shrugged. 'The Warriors can go through the rest of the house. We don't have much time.'

I struggled to keep up as I followed Scarlett in the direction of the Lower Districts. My dress and heels had fulfilled their purpose tonight, but I found myself enviously eying her fighting leathers and feathered mantle.

The princess didn't slow, and she didn't glance over her shoulder to check on my progress. Even by Scarlett's standards, her brusqueness was surprising – but she had told me that she wasn't usually sent on active missions. Maybe she was more unsettled by Lady Seneca's death than she wanted to let on.

Or maybe I was imagining a conscience that wasn't there.

I followed her to the top of a nearby building, where we could observe the dark streets from a decent vantage point. I'd expected that we would confront the contact, and Scarlett's choice surprised me – at least until she handed over a crossbow.

There was no need to confront the contact, I realised. Not if they were already dead.

Two people came into view. One of them was a man, a servant dressed in Seneca colours. The other was a woman – a very familiar woman, her fitted vest baring the lean muscles of her arms. Even in the darkness, her braids gleamed, woven through with silver.

Jadis.

My heart pounded. That afternoon in the docks . . . she had allowed me ahead of her on the gangplank, even though she'd known it might cost her life. Jadis had proven that was willing to die for her cause. But I really didn't want to be the one who made that happen.

'Take the man out first.' Scarlett's voice was loud in the stillness. 'Then the contact.'

The crossbow was heavy in my hands, and I adjusted my aim carefully, making sure that I had the target in my sights. Perhaps I should have felt guilty about killing this man. His goal coincided with mine: taking down the emperor. But mercy wasn't a trait I could afford.

I closed my eyes, waiting for that familiar *pull*. When I felt it, I released the bow.

Scarlett didn't praise my accuracy as the target fell. All she said was, 'Now the other one.'

I raised the crossbow again, training it on Jadis. Jadis, who was searching for the shooter with her keen eyes. Though she couldn't recognise me in the shadows, I could see the resignation on her face. She was out in the open, exposed; there was no way I could miss.

I drew the crossbow back, preparing to shoot. I knew exactly where I needed to aim: straight for her heart.

My eyes closed almost against my will. When I opened them, Jadis was on the ground.

But there was no pool of blood surrounding her. Her body wasn't motionless, lifeless.

She had flattened herself against the cobblestones to avoid the bolt, which had skimmed over her head and thudded into the side of a nearby building. Jadis glanced up again, her confusion obvious. Then she turned and ran. If she was smart, she would return to her people and warn them. She would let them know that the Senecas had been compromised.

Scarlett looked at me, aware that I shouldn't have missed that shot. Her glacial, assessing eyes considered me for a handful of seconds.

But she said nothing.

CHAPTER FORTY-FIVE

Mira

'Do you have a moment?'

Aric paused, turning away from the Warriors he'd been speaking with. His expression was guarded as he looked at me, but he nodded slowly. 'Give me a minute,' he said to the others.

We made our way past the greenhouse and deeper into the gardens, the cultivated hedges and flowers giving way to leafy trees and chirping birds. The trickle of running water drew me to a curved bridge that spanned a small stream. Acres of greenery extended all the way to the towering iron gates and reflective white walls that encircled the palace grounds.

I gazed at the view. It was easier than looking at Aric, but there was only so long I could avoid facing him.

When I finally turned back, Aric was studying my outfit with a frown.

'You don't like it?' I glanced down at my leather bustier and matching pants. 'It's one of Lillian's designs.'

'I don't think it's you.'

'Well, I'm pleased with it.' I regretted my sharp words immediately. I'd come here to lessen the distance between us, and already I was doing the opposite. 'Let's talk about something else,' I said, making an effort to soften my voice. 'What's it like, being a Warrior?'

Aric hesitated, watching me closely. I couldn't decipher the look in his eyes.

'I'm not—' My breath came out in a frustrated sigh. 'It's not a calculated question, if that's what you're wondering. There's no alternative agenda. I just – it occurred to me that both our circumstances have changed since the Trials, but I've been wholly focused on my own life. I wanted to take more of an interest in yours.'

The dappled light played across Aric's face as he moved closer, a trace of surprise – perhaps even hope – colouring his expression. I found myself caught up in his golden-brown eyes, warmer and kinder than I probably deserved.

'I didn't think I was going to like it so much,' he replied after a brief pause, 'but I do. I think it's mostly down to the other palace guards.' Aric's posture relaxed further as he spoke of them, and I felt a pang of loss, remembering how that same ease had once existed between us. 'Even the ones from noble families aren't so bad, not when you spend hours a day training with them in the ring.' He cocked his head. 'We should spar together sometime. You won't believe the things I can do.'

'Like what, exactly?'

'Everything we imagined and more. Speed, strength – *reflexes*.' So fast his hand was little more than a blur, Aric plucked a gold pin from my hair.

I watched him roll it in his palm. 'I look forward to it,' I said. 'Though I have to warn you, I have been practising. And Zandri makes for a very exacting teacher.'

The moment I mentioned Zandri, I expected the mood to turn strained. But rather than retreating from me, Aric moved closer.

I went very still as his fingers hovered above my lips. A breath from making contact.

'All I've wanted is to see you smile again,' Aric murmured. 'To see you *happy*.'

I swallowed. Though Aric wasn't touching me, the way he looked at me . . . he was looking at me like I was his entire world, and as I stared up into his face, I remembered that he had once been my entire world, too.

But—

'I don't think I'll ever be happy again. I don't think I can be – not truly.' Even the word tasted like ash in my mouth.

Aric's brow furrowed, and I could see how much that pained him. 'Maybe happiness is too much to hope for, but anything is better than . . .' He trailed off, then said carefully, 'Seeing you suffer has been torture. It's been torture for Lil, too. We lov—'

'No,' I interrupted. 'No – don't. Please don't.' I stepped away, feeling claustrophobic and unsettled. 'I can't hear it.'

Aric let his hand drop. 'Listen,' he said, 'the last thing I want to do is push you. I know you're trying to cope with what happened during the third Trial.' He paused, his voice soft and almost pleading. 'But whatever you're doing . . . it isn't healing you, Mira. *It's killing you.* And you're the only one who can't see it.'

'You're one to talk. How can you preach to *me* about happiness when you're choosing revenge?'

Aric was silent for a while. Then he said, 'I was wrong. I realised it after I watched you kill the governor.' I flinched, but Aric continued relentlessly, 'Life is for the living, Mira. And we're wasting ours.'

Before I could react, his lips descended on mine. He kissed me like he might never get another chance, pulling me to his muscular chest. The charged tension between us transformed into something passionate and heated and unstable.

And suddenly I was kissing him back, not caring that it was dangerous. Not caring that Aric had the power to hurt me in a way that Cassius never could.

In that instant, nothing else mattered. All I knew was Aric. All I *wanted* to know was him.

His hands, one on my lower back, the other squeezing my hip. His mouth, devouring mine until I was breathless and aching. His knee, coming to rest between my thighs.

I had dreamt about him touching me like this. Somehow, the reality was better.

My hands tangled through his soft chestnut hair, needing him even closer. When I inhaled, I breathed in his familiar, woodsy scent – a scent that instantly transported me to balmy nights on Aldara.

More. I didn't know whether I thought it or said it, but it was an urgent pulse in my blood. *More, more, more.*

Then Aric pulled back, and reality slammed cruelly into me. His conflicted gaze met mine; I could see the same fiery passion echoed in his face, but it was slowly replaced by heart-wrenching sincerity.

'I'll turn my back on all of this, Mira,' he told me, 'if it means we can have a life together. If you ask me to, I will leave Ravalia behind.'

I searched his face for hesitation but found nothing except resolve. He would do it. He would really do it.

It was all I'd wanted for him, for *us*, only now it was too late. Now I was the one who couldn't walk away.

Not even for him.

I swallowed heavily. 'I can't.'

A brief flicker of *something* crossed his face. Maybe it was disappointment. Maybe it was anger. I had no idea, and I couldn't afford to care. Running with Aric would mean giving up my revenge, and my best chance to help the Kalurian people.

There's no future between us anymore, I thought, even as my eyes drank him in. *It's better that we face the truth. Pretending otherwise will only get us both killed.*

I forced myself to walk away. But as I crossed the bridge, his voice called me back.

'I'm leaving soon. With some of the other newly initiated Warriors,' Aric said. 'We're being sent to deal with a rebellion in the West. A few guards are going as well, since the emperor needs more men.'

Shock hit first. Then fear. As a royal guard, I'd thought Aric would be safe. That he would stay far away from battlefields. And the Western Lands . . . that was where Kain had died. The thought of Aric being sent there . . .

I acknowledged the emotions but forced them back down. Clinging to the coldness, the numbness, until it settled deep into my bones.

'Stay safe,' I said. The words sounded inadequate, even to me.

Aric's lips twisted in a bitter smile. 'Thanks.'

Silence descended between us, heavy and stifling. I didn't want to hurt Aric, but I had. And, for once in my life, I had no idea how to fix it.

I tensed as he strode towards me, half expecting – half *hoping* – that he would take me in his arms again.

Instead, he said, 'You look beautiful,' and kept walking, away from the bridge and away from me.

I stayed there for a long time, staring out over the water.

For once, I had nothing to do and nowhere to be. Odessa and Danica were probably practising in the training hall. As for Scarlett – well, I didn't know where Scarlett was, and I had no desire to see her. Things had been tense between us since the other night. We both knew I'd missed that shot to save Jadis's life.

It was a foolhardy choice. Even *if* Jadis had filled Darius's position as leader of the resistance, their funding had been cut and they were under observation by the Order of Masks. And yet even now, I was tempted to seek her out. To venture back to the headquarters Darius had once taken me to, in the hopes of making a deal.

But I had already made a deal – with Cassius. I couldn't risk jeopardising that, especially for such an uncertain reward.

I was so deep in my thoughts that I didn't notice the Warrior until he spoke.

'His Imperial Majesty has requested your presence,' he said. 'If you would follow me, please.'

He said nothing else as he turned and crossed through the gardens, his armour gleaming in the sunlight. I followed a few paces behind, ignoring the curious glances from various Order members and court ladies.

My first thought was that this was it. Scarlett had turned me in, and now I was walking to my execution. But if the emperor sentenced me to death, so be it. There was nothing I could do to convince him otherwise.

We passed the decorative fountain at the palace entrance and entered the main hall, with its soaring marble columns and ornate ceiling. Before we reached the landing, four soldiers came into view, escorting a group of prisoners down the stairs, their expensive clothes rumpled and torn.

Recognition seared through me as a female prisoner looked up. Even like this, there was no mistaking Odessa Tiran.

My gaze swept over her companions. Lady Tiran had the same pale skin and white-blonde hair as her daughter. The familial resemblance wasn't as obvious with General Tiran, who was muscular and tanned from years of outdoor campaigns. But there was a certain steeliness in his gaze that Odessa had inherited.

'Keep walking,' one of the soldiers instructed, and I realised that Odessa had stopped.

We stared at each other in silence. Her amber eyes were glassy with tears, but she kept her head held high, her expression carefully blank.

Despite myself, I felt a glimmer of respect for her. I knew what it felt like to have your life torn apart.

The soldier yanked on her chains, forcing her to keep moving. Odessa passed me on the stairs, close enough for me to smell her flowery perfume, but she was gone before I could think of anything to say – not that there was anything good enough. Nothing could make up for what I had done.

Continuing along the hallway, I noticed two Warriors guarding a towering set of gold-plated doors. My eyes dropped to the filigree doorknobs, shaped like roaring lions.

The emperor's personal chambers.

This must have been where Odessa and her family had come from. I wondered if Emperor Kalias had intended for me to see them being taken away in chains. It seemed like something he would delight in.

Before I could brace myself, a servant bowed and opened the doors.

My first impression was one of darkness and strength: obsidian floors, marble columns, and carved furniture upholstered in rich, dark shades. A set of rooms designed for intimidation.

Three figures stood at the far end of the spacious parlour. They were silhouetted against the large windows, making them even more imposing.

Emperor Kalias regarded me dispassionately, ominous in robes the exact colour of congealing blood. 'Well,' he said, 'you've certainly kept us waiting.'

'I was in the gardens, Your Majesty. As soon as the Warrior told me you were waiting, I came straight here.'

The emperor studied me. At his side, his wife's cold eyes were narrowed, hatred in the icy planes of her face.

Cassius was the only person in the room who seemed relaxed, sinking into a nearby chair and crossing his legs. 'Are we going to get on with it?' he asked. 'I do have plans this evening.'

The emperor's stormy eyes didn't so much as flicker towards his son.

'You are a problem,' he told me, low and sharp. 'You have been a problem from the moment you were born. The only reason you're still alive, much less a Mask, is because there's a chance you might prove useful to me.'

The ruthless certainty in his face left no room for doubt, and hopelessness engulfed me. I'd thought I was being so clever, using a law to manipulate him into keeping me alive . . . when all along, he had been planning to use me for his own ends.

But I refused to let him see how afraid I really was. How desperate to live – not for my own sake, but to see my plans through. To finally watch him bleed.

'The Kalurians,' he said, 'are an increasing annoyance. Loyalists in the Wilds continue to fight against the regime I have painstakingly put in place. *Your* notoriety has inflamed them even further, and now, the entirety of the Western Lands has been tempted into rebellion.'

It was a struggle to conceal my surprise. I hadn't heard anything about the loyalists since Roran was sent to Kalure, and I'd assumed that meant he had put a stop to their attacks. And the West . . . was the emperor suggesting that was my fault, too? That Aric was being sent to deal with fighting I was responsible for causing?

'You might think,' Emperor Kalias said, lethally soft, 'that this is a good thing. Perhaps you might even be pleased.' He held up a hand to stop me as I opened my mouth to protest. 'It doesn't matter to me either way. The point is, the Kalurians are outnumbered and outmanoeuvred, fighting a war they cannot hope to win. However,' he continued, 'there is a way you can help us, and limit the loss of life in Kalure at the same time.'

Whatever the emperor wanted from me, his wife clearly didn't agree. Her lips were curved into a sneer, her face set in an expression of severe displeasure.

'The girl is descended from a line of usurpers,' Empress Ivalene interjected. 'She should be executed like her traitor of a mother. There can be no exceptions.'

Emperor Kalias held up a hand, and she subsided into sullen silence. 'I believe,' he said slowly, 'that in this case, allowances can be made.'

Somehow, his mercy was more unnerving than his threats. I didn't know how to interpret the gleam in his eyes, the new way he considered me – like I was suddenly worthy of his interest.

'As my son is already aware, his betrothal to Odessa Tiran has outlived its usefulness. Whereas you . . .' he paused, his gaze intent on my face, '*you* can give me Kalure.'

I stumbled back a step, suddenly claustrophobic in the grand room. Cassius's face was unreadable, but there was no trace of surprise in his eyes. He'd known exactly what was coming. He'd *orchestrated* it, using me to incriminate General Tiran and ensure Odessa wasn't fit for a royal marriage.

My hands tightened into fists. All along, Cassius had wanted Kalure – and I'd just given it to him.

'I realise this is a lot to take in,' the emperor said, but I didn't trust the new gentleness in his voice. 'I am offering you the opportunity to stand at Cassius's side. The . . . unfortunate circumstances of your past need not define you.'

I understood perfectly. Through my marriage to his son, Emperor Kalias would gain legitimacy and full control of Kalure. He could command the North for the cheap price of a wedding, minimal military casualties required – and Roran, his heir and future emperor, would still be free to make an advantageous marriage with some foreign princess or queen. Though I doubted Cassius had any intention of letting that happen.

'You may continue to serve in the Order,' Emperor Kalias continued, 'at least for now. But I will organise a suitable date for the wedding, before the end of this month.'

Maybe this will be a good thing, I tried to tell myself. *I'll be closer to the emperor; it will make killing him much easier. And Cassius . . .*

Cassius was dangerous, but he'd promised to help me – and the Kalurian people. A betrothal only solidified that arrangement, didn't it? But then I remembered his ruthless comments about Kalure. *I will be the next ruler of the Ravalian Empire. I need you to remember that.*

'And if I decline?'

'Declining,' the emperor said, 'would be unwise. Right now, I am offering you a generous deal. But if you don't marry Cassius, then you're no longer useful to me. I think you know what happens then.'

A crown or a coffin. That was what he was offering me.

Emperor Kalias took a seat, leaning back in his chair. 'So, Kasmira, will you be useful?'

My throat tightened, like my body could feel the chains the emperor was wrapping around me.

'Yes,' I said coldly. 'I will be very useful.'

The emperor smiled in victory, but I wasn't looking at him. I was looking across the room, at Cassius. For the first time, I noticed that he was twirling something in his fingers. A ring.

He stood smoothly and walked over to me, until we were almost close enough to touch. Close enough that I could smell his scent: cedarwood and leather, like he had just come from a hunt. It occurred to me that all along he had been hunting me – and now he'd caught me.

I braced myself for what came next – for him to drop to one knee – but his deep blue eyes remained on mine as he slid the ring onto my finger. Slowly and deliberately, as if giving me the chance to change my mind.

I stared down at the square-cut black diamond. Then back up at Cassius.

He was watching me shrewdly. He'd already known what I was going to choose. Regardless of the emperor's threat, he didn't think there was any limit to how far I was willing to go to assure my own survival. To get my revenge.

Maybe he was right. Maybe there wasn't one.

CHAPTER FORTY-SIX

Mira

I woke up to Lillian's pale, tense face. To delicate hands, shaking me awake.

'You need to get dressed,' she told me quickly. 'The court has been summoned to the arena.'

'It's not . . .' It was a struggle to form a coherent sentence. '*I'm not . . .*'

Lillian seemed to understand. She shook her head, blonde curls bouncing. 'No! Sorceress no, Mira. You're safe.'

I let out a ragged breath. Steeling myself, I climbed out of the four-poster bed and crossed over to the vanity beyond.

Taking a seat in front of the mirror, I met Lillian's worried eyes. I didn't want to know, but I had to ask. 'Who is it?'

'I'm not sure,' she hedged. 'It must be someone important, for the emperor to go to all this trouble.'

As Lillian fussed over my hair, my gaze went to the black combat outfit hanging in the wardrobe. There would be no dresses today, no extravagant jewels, and I realised that she was right. Whoever we were about to watch die was *someone* to the court.

Anxiety rushed through me as I thought of the arena, trying to imagine sitting placidly in the stands while—

'Breathe, Mira,' Lillian instructed. 'You look like you're about to be sick.'

'I'm fine,' I forced out between clenched teeth.

But we both knew I wasn't fine. Not even close.

She pinned the last of my thick braids without meeting my eyes. But I saw the way her gaze lingered on the ring Cassius had given me – the trace of resentment darkening her sweet features. It was horrible to realise that I had no idea what to say to her, how to fix this. She was my best friend in the world, but right now, there was a yawning chasm of distance between us.

'All done,' Lillian announced with a tight smile, rolling the remaining pins in her palm. It was a nervous gesture, and I had the sense she was debating whether to tell me something. At last, she said, 'After your wedding, I'm going to leave the palace.'

It felt almost as if she'd struck me. 'But . . . I need you. I need you *here*.'

'You've made it quite clear that you don't, Mira,' Lillian said. 'I can't wait around for months or years, hoping for you to see reason. I've put my plans on hold long enough.'

'What would you do?'

'I'm going to open my own shop. I have enough funds stored away by now; if there's one good thing about the palace, it's that it pays well.'

'I could offer you a position in the court,' I said, twisting to face her. 'You could become one of the noble ladies you used to admire. Or I could make you the official dressmaker – you'd have your own staff, your own quarters, and when you did eventually open a shop . . . people would flock to you from far and wide.'

'You're trying to *buy* me?'

'I told you I needed you here, but that didn't seem to matter. So now I'm trying to negotiate.'

Lillian stepped firmly away. 'None of those things are yours to offer. Only the empress can make those kinds of decisions.'

'Maybe I'll be the empress soon enough,' I retorted, standing as well.

It was the wrong thing to say.

'What kind of deal did you make with him?' Lillian asked, raising a horrified hand to her mouth. 'What did you *do*, Mira?'

I folded my arms against my chest. 'What I had to.'

She took another step back, as if she was afraid – afraid of *me*. 'Aric was right. I don't know who you are anymore.'

'I'm the same person I've always been,' I protested, hating the feeling that I was *pleading* with her. 'I'm your friend.'

Lillian looked at me sadly. It had always been easy to read her thoughts, but right now, I wished I couldn't see them so clearly.

'You might look like the Mira I knew,' she said, 'but you're not her. Not really. Revenge is twisting you into a person I can't recognise, someone who uses other people and doesn't care about the consequences.'

Anger surged through me, bitter and corrosive. 'Don't *you* think they deserve to pay? What would you have done if it was your mother they murdered?'

'My mother wouldn't have wanted me to destroy my life,' Lillian answered quietly. 'Neither would Kain or Aric. They would have wanted me to find some measure of peace and happiness, to put the past behind me.'

I laughed, but there was no humour in the sound. 'Do you know what my mother told me before she died? She said, "You would have made an excellent Warrior, Mira. You would have made an even better ruler."' My eyes bored into Lillian's pale blue ones. 'That doesn't sound like someone who would have wanted me to give up.'

To her credit, Lillian didn't flinch back from the bite in my voice. 'Yes,' she said, 'but is *this* the kind of leader she was talking about? You're not plotting to liberate your people, Mira. You're plotting to destroy your enemies.'

'The Ravalians are *their* enemies too,' I argued. 'I'm doing this for them as well as myself.'

The doubt was clear on Lillian's face. 'Are you, Mira? Are you really doing it for them?'

I didn't know the answer to her question. Or maybe . . . maybe I did.

I wasn't sure which was worse.

Lillian's posture was stiff as she moved towards the door. Then she hesitated, glancing over her shoulder. A flicker of vulnerability entered her eyes as she murmured, 'I love you, Mira. I wanted you to be my sister one day.'

For a moment, I imagined a different ring on my finger – smaller, lighter, easier to bear. A different future – one based on love and trust, with Aric and Lillian filling the void my mother had left behind.

But already Lillian was slipping out of the door – and as it closed, I felt that future close along with it.

I didn't have the chance to tell her that if our circumstances were different, I would have wanted that too.

It was fitting that my new life should begin with an execution.

In some ways, it felt like coming full circle. Except, instead of me down there, helpless and afraid, I was now one of those monstrous people watching from the stands. The ones who had cheered for my mother's death, not so long ago. Who had cheered for mine.

Even the Warrior who ushered me through the massing crowds looked familiar, like he might have been one of the men who had escorted me from the dungeons. My eyes darted towards the lower section of the arena. I couldn't see the cells from here, but I knew they were there.

Today of all days, it was crucial that I appeared calm. Obedient. Unaffected. But every step felt like walking over hot coals. Fighting in the Trials was one thing. Coming here like this . . . it was horrifying.

Then another thought occurred to me. What if it was *Darius*?

No. No, that wasn't supposed to happen until after my wedding. The emperor hadn't wanted to taint the excitement, and no one cared too much about the death of one criminal from the Lower Districts.

'Make way,' a guard shouted. 'Make way for the princess!'

I turned to see Scarlett approaching: a gleam of red in an ocean of black. She caught sight of me and paused, her gaze darting to the sparkling circlet resting on top of my dark hair. The physical embodiment of my new status.

'Come with me,' Scarlett said. 'We are almost sisters, after all.'

I took Scarlett's offered hand. Her skin was cold; it burned like ice.

'There's no need to look so concerned,' she commented as we walked, people ducking their heads as we passed. 'You should be pleased.'

I cast her a sideways glance, wondering if I'd misheard. 'Pleased? That we're about to watch someone die?'

Scarlett's smile was difficult to read. 'We're about to watch a *Ravalian* die. If I were you, I'd be pleased.'

I didn't know how to respond to that, so I didn't try. But something twisted low in my gut. Was that the kind of person I'd become, if I spent long enough trapped in this court? Someone who delighted in blood and pain and death – so long as it was Ravalian? So long as it wasn't *mine*?

With the guards clearing a path through the stands, it wasn't long before the royal box came into view. It was easy to recognise Cassius even from a distance, his golden hair gleaming in the sunlight. He looked like he was attending a party rather than an execution, resplendent in a midnight-blue tunic that matched his eyes.

'You seem to make a habit of dressing for battle,' he said by way of greeting. 'Maybe you should be down there.' A nod towards the arena floor, where I caught a glimpse of the executioner's formidable figure. I quickly averted my gaze, not wanting to look too closely at the sword strapped to the man's side.

'I think I've spent enough time in that arena,' I said cautiously.

'I suppose you have.' Cassius's nonchalance was disconcerting. 'Either way, the royal box is much more comfortable.'

Nobles turned at our approach, stepping out of the way and bowing deeply. A few glanced at the black diamond on my finger, and I heard some murmurs about the Lapian mines, about the rarity and the expense. I hadn't realised the ring was anything out of the ordinary, and I cast a questioning glance at Cassius – but his attention was focused ahead. He didn't seem to notice the whispers and scrutiny, or perhaps he simply didn't care.

The emperor was seated in the centre of the royal box, murmuring something to his wife. He didn't acknowledge our presence.

Scarlett brushed past without speaking, claiming the vacant seat next to the empress. Two other throne-like chairs were situated to the emperor's left; Cassius slid into the one closest to his father, and I reluctantly took the other, waving away a platter of dried fruits offered by an over-eager attendant.

Cassius plucked a few sugared figs from the platter, his sapphire cufflinks sparkling in the midday sun. I would have liked to believe his carelessness was feigned, or that he was simply *used* to events like these. He wouldn't be the only one; around us, the crowd was already cheering, the arena amplifying the sound until it reverberated in my ears. But as Cassius took hold of my hand, his finger running lazy circles across my palm, I realised it was more than that.

He was *enjoying* himself.

'Who is it?' I asked.

'Hmm?' Cassius said. But I was certain he'd understood the question perfectly.

'Who are we about to watch die?'

'You'll see,' he replied with a small smile. 'I'd hate to deprive you of the surprise.'

A sick feeling built in my stomach. I started to press him further, but was cut short by the sound of a trumpet blaring. Hundreds of eyes turned towards the arena below, where three Warriors escorted a chained prisoner into view.

Stunned silence swept through the stands at General Tiran's approach. He was still wearing his military uniform, but it was covered in dirt and grime. Even from high above, I could see the way he blinked – struggling to adjust to the bright sunlight, after so long spent in darkness. I remembered the feeling.

Then my gaze went to the woman following just behind him, and my heart sank. Horrified, I leant forward, trying to get a better look.

I could have been staring at Odessa a few decades older, though

Lady Tiran's head was bowed in a way her daughter's never would have been. Her pale hair obscured her features from view, hiding her face from the crowd. That was a temptation I remembered, the urge to shield myself from the audience's vicious scrutiny.

My nails sunk into the plush armrests. This was a nightmare. This was – it was—

It's all my fault.

I barely heard the emperor's booming voice announcing the general's crimes. The crowd booed but all I could think of were Cassius's assurances, his promises that the general and his family would be granted mercy. That they would be spared.

The crowd roared even louder, hungry for blood. General Tiran kept his head straight ahead, facing the emperor. At his side, his wife was openly sobbing.

Was Odessa somewhere close, watching the deaths of her parents from the staging area where I had once waited with my mother? Or was she still down in those dungeons, screaming and clawing at the bars?

'You promised,' I said through bloodless lips, tearing my gaze away from the executioner. He was already advancing towards the shackled prisoners; they had minutes left to live, if not seconds. 'Nothing final.'

Cassius's expression was dispassionate as he watched the scene unfolding below. There was no apology in his face as he glanced at me. No trace of remorse.

'I lied.'

The execution was over. The bloodlust satiated – for now.

Cassius steered me through the exiting crowd without speaking. His arm wound around my waist, keeping me close to him – scandalously close.

I didn't need to look at the audience to know they would be whispering. But Cassius's presumptuousness served another purpose, and with inches between us, we could talk without being overheard.

'You used me,' I said numbly. 'This was what you wanted all along.'

'Of course it was,' he replied. 'You can give me a country. What use was Odessa in comparison?'

'She was your *fiancée*. Was it necessary to do it this way? To destroy her life?'

'Don't tell me you're feeling sorry for her,' he drawled, raising a blond eyebrow. 'She would have done the same to you, if she could. She would have done worse.'

I shook my head in disgust – with him, with myself. 'What's going to happen to her now?'

'She'll remain in the dungeons until her trial. Despite what you think, I'm not entirely heartless; I argued for a reduced sentence on her behalf.'

'And if the emperor had decided to execute Odessa along with her parents? What would you have done then?'

His silence was answer enough.

'Don't look at me like that,' he said, his grip tightening until it became almost painful. 'You're the one who planted the general's seal in Lady Seneca's home. I don't recall you being concerned with Odessa's welfare *then*.'

The accusation in his voice made me pause mid-step, and only Cassius's strong hold kept me moving. My pulse was racing so fast that I wondered if he could feel it.

'Let me give you some advice.' Cassius's voice lowered into something dangerous. 'In my court, either you play to win, or you lose. There is no in-between.'

'It's not *your* court yet,' I retorted.

He smiled darkly. 'It will be,' he vowed. 'And you're going to help me get it.'

We reached the bottom of the steps, and my gaze went to the bodies of the general and his wife, the sand around them dark with blood. It was a gruesome tableau, and even as the Warriors prepared to cart them away, I knew their efforts were in vain. Death stained this monstrous place, and nothing would ever make it clean again.

'Don't worry,' Cassius said, his lips shifting to my ear. 'Our terms still stand. Once we're married, I am prepared to be very generous.'

His fingers trailed down my neck and across my collarbone in slow, soothing strokes.

His touch should have been intimate, but it was possessive instead. It made me feel caged. Trapped.

In less than a month, I will be Cassius's wife.

The thought was like a bucket of icy water. All my plans to avenge my mother's death, to find a way of helping Kalure . . . I had been so focused on those goals that I hadn't considered – hadn't *allowed* myself to consider – what marrying Cassius would really mean. It wasn't a love match, but he would still want to consummate it. To have heirs.

And while I had once considered a dalliance with him . . . this would be permanent. *Inescapable.*

Staring up at the man who was going to be my husband, I swallowed down apprehension. He was giving me a promise, but how much was a promise really worth?

In Odessa's case, it hadn't been worth anything at all.

CHAPTER FORTY-SEVEN

Scarlett

The past few weeks had been filled with an endless string of court events, all requiring my attendance. No two occasions were the same, but one outcome was: Cassius and Mira were impossible to avoid.

They attended formal dinners, public events, even council meetings. And in the rare moments they weren't around, their engagement was all the court could talk about. I might not have minded if there was some outrage mixed into the gossip, but even the sharpest-tongued courtiers had lost their edge. Everyone believed this was the perfect solution to the fighting in Kalure, and now that Mira was set to become a *Ravalian* princess, her rebellions were forgotten. Instead, stories of her successes in the Trials were recounted with unsettling fondness.

It was infuriating. They hadn't even had their engagement ball yet, and somehow, Cassius and Mira's combined popularity had eclipsed Roran's. I almost wished he was back from Kalure, just so I could see his expression – and whatever brutal reprisal he came up with.

But I had my own problems. My father's success with Mira and Cassius had given him an appetite for matchmaking.

I remained a careful two paces behind the emperor as we strode through the jasmine-scented gardens. It was a romantic setting, and I wondered if he had chosen it deliberately, thinking it might soften me.

If so, he had severely miscalculated.

'You can't be serious,' I said, my voice brittle. 'We can conquer

Maesteri whenever we like. There's no need to consider a betrothal—'

'And their king knows that, which is why he offered such generous terms to acquire you for his son.'

Acquire – as if I were an object. A *thing* to be bought and sold.

Emperor Kalias slowed. 'I assure you, daughter, I did not make this decision lightly. Maesteri offered us a fleet of ships and an obscene amount of gold in exchange for your hand. This marriage will greatly benefit the empire.'

'And what of my other suitors?' I demanded, not bothering to keep my voice down.

A few promenading nobles turned to stare, only to quickly avert their eyes. Through the windows, I caught glimpses of the revelry unfolding in the ballroom. Everything was elaborately arranged; unlike the announcement of my betrothal to the governor, which had been a dinner like any other, no expense had been spared for Cassius and Mira's special evening.

'There will be no other suitors,' my father replied. 'It's already been decided.'

Anger rose, colder than ice. Sharper than steel. 'You made me a promise.'

'I know I said four months.' The words were utterly unapologetic. 'But Maesteri will be sending a delegation for Cassius and Mira's upcoming wedding. I've already informed King Damirian that you will be sailing back with them, where you and the prince can begin preparations for your own nuptials.'

Lengthening my stride, I cut in front of him. 'Is this how we do business now? Kowtowing to the demands of foreign nations?'

'Careful, daughter.' Kalias didn't raise his voice, but the threat was clear.

I stepped aside, but didn't lower my gaze. Once, I had looked at my father and seen a ruler to admire. Now, I saw a hypocrite – a man who clung to the trappings of power, despite his claims of ruling like the austere Northern kings. A man willing to sell his daughter for his own gain.

Blood-red robes trailed behind the emperor as he swept down the path. He didn't bother with guards; had no need of them, his every movement powerful and controlled. But he could no longer control *me*.

Whatever he believed, I had no intention of going through with this marriage – and every intention of taking his life.

And his throne.

The towering doors of the grand ballroom creaked open ahead of us, and a trumpet blared as the herald read out my father's long list of titles.

Kalias paused at the threshold and turned back towards me. 'Prince Adomas is handsome, mild-mannered and accomplished. He's also set to inherit his father's title, which will make you a queen one day. Don't fight the match. It's as much for your benefit as it is mine.' He brushed his thumb across my cheekbone, a gesture that was probably intended to be affectionate. But his gaze was already straying towards his makeshift throne and waiting advisers. And I knew that I had been forgotten.

A path opened up as he made his way through the circulating nobles. I drifted through the hall in his wake, feeling curiously light and insubstantial. Untethered. As if I was even more separate from the court than usual.

Plucking a glass of wine from a servant's tray, I stared down at the red liquid. My mind was consumed with plans that had once been vague outlines, and now began to sharpen into something firmer and clearer.

'You must be so pleased, Your Highness,' Lady Verne said, sliding into a perfect curtsy. 'Truly, the entire kingdom celebrates your brother's upcoming marriage.'

A handful of beautiful ladies accompanied her, all wearing exquisite gowns and carefully unreadable expressions. Empress Ivalene's ladies.

They dropped into similarly polished curtsies. I sipped my drink, forcing them to hold their curtsies as Lady Verne had once done to me. They were far more skilled than I was; they barely even wobbled.

I nodded for them to stand and turned a bland smile on Lady Verne. There was little chance that her comment was genuine. She had barely tolerated me during her etiquette classes, and her choice of company tonight said enough about her true feelings. Few courtiers despised me more than Ivalene's ladies.

I tossed back the rest of my drink, delighting in Lady Verne's appalled expression. After handing my goblet off to a passing servant, I said, 'Your celebrations are premature. Engagements are tenuous, breakable things; just look at what happened to Governor Halvor.'

I turned my back on her with a thin smile, striding towards Mira, who was the only person here who truly mattered. But my eyes narrowed as I noticed the way Lillian had shaped Mira's hair on top of her head like a crown. How she had taken inspiration from Zandri, turning Mira's outfit into a showstopping spectacle, with black feathers criss-crossing from her shoulder to the fitted bodice of her gown, where they spilled down the left side of her crimson skirts like a waterfall of ink.

A queen. That was what Mira looked like – what Lillian had dressed her as. Like the queen Cassius no doubt intended her to become.

Just as I reached Mira, a herald made the announcement I had been dreading all night.

My younger brother strode into the gathering with magnetic confidence, his charcoal-and-black ensemble standing out amongst the bright tunics and dresses favoured by the court. He had come without an entourage, and didn't seem concerned with his lateness; his apathetic face conveyed his disinterest in the nobles who parted before him, like sheep before a wolf.

His eyes searched the crowd before settling on me. 'I warned you not to trust Father's promises,' he murmured in my ear.

I didn't ask how he knew. Cassius's influence – made up of bribes, deals and threats – infected the rest of the court like a disease, and that disease had only spread now that the balance of power had shifted in his favour.

Cassius's gaze went over my shoulder. His voice was the epitome of silken threat as he said to me, 'I don't suppose you'll mind if I borrow my fiancée, Sister.' Without waiting for an answer, he offered Mira his arm.

She hesitated but took it, and he flashed me a darkly amused smile. Confident in the belief that he had finally outplayed me.

I watched my brother lead Mira onto the deserted dance floor. Every pair of eyes was on them, and I hoped that Cassius had miscalculated for once. Perhaps he hadn't seen the pitiful display from Mira and Aric in the palace gardens, which had hardly constituted as *dancing*.

The plucking of a single harp transformed into the commanding sound of a full string orchestra as musicians sprang into action. I recognised the melody; it was one of the formal dances characteristic of the court.

And it was far too ambitious for a beginner.

While it began slowly enough, it was the kind of dance that required one to be in tune with its ebb and flow. I expected Mira to miss the fluid turns and subtle nuances of the dance, but with Cassius leading, her fast reflexes and performer instincts kicked in. There was something engrossing about the way the music drew them together and pulled them apart, the way their eyes remained riveted on each other.

A few murmurs told me I wasn't the only one who had noticed the charged intensity between them, or how impressive their combined skill was. They presented an undeniably striking image: a whirlwind of red and black, twisting around the ballroom like a dark flame. Cassius's blond hair and dark blue eyes glinted under the light of the chandelier; he looked like an angel, if a fallen one. With her olive skin and dark hair, Mira was his opposite – together, they were two sides of the same coin.

And I realised I had been wrong. Cassius had not miscalculated at all.

Applause rang out as he bowed to Mira, lightly kissing the back of her hand. The very image of a handsome, dashing prince.

I saw the shiver she couldn't quite hide, and the envious way the court ladies watched her – as if being shackled to Cassius was a triumph. But I noticed what they didn't: the way Cassius held her too close, as if he was worried she might slip away. And I felt my brother's stare lingering on me as I left the ballroom behind.

I had suspected it would come to this, from the moment Cassius had first shown an interest in Mira. But it was one thing to suspect, and another to have those suspicions confirmed.

And now I would have to do what I had been dreading, ever since I had first learnt that Mira was plotting with Cassius.

I would have to destroy them both.

Two hours later, ways of dealing with Cassius and Mira continued to circle in my mind. It was quite annoying, because I was trying very hard not to *think*.

'Am I boring you, Princess?' Severin asked, gazing at me from where he'd been kissing his way up my thighs.

'No,' I said guiltily, breathing in the familiar, floral warmth of the greenhouse. 'I'm just a little . . . preoccupied tonight.'

'Would you like me to stop?'

That was an easy answer. 'No. Never.'

My body quivered in anticipation as he gently pushed me back onto the divan, relishing the sensation of his strong hands against my skin. Wordlessly, Severin parted my thighs and resumed kissing his way slowly up, up, up—

I arched against the cushions with a breathy sigh. Let my head fall back, his mouth making me warm and delirious with pleasure.

When I was achingly close, he stood and began removing his clothes. I watched him, admiring the lean lines of his chest, the hardness of his body. I *really* didn't want to think about my brother right now.

If Severin can live in the moment, then so can I.

Not for the first time, I marvelled at the irony. An Artisan who could see the future wanted nothing more than to live in the present. With me.

And yet . . .

'If I asked you to See into the future for me, would you?'

Severin's hand tightened on my shoulder, too hard to be fully comfortable. He relaxed his grip with what seemed like an effort, shifting so that he was poised over me – shirtless and magnificent, his mismatched eyes intent on mine.

'My whole life,' he said slowly, 'has been about the past and future. All I want to do is be with you right here, right now. Isn't that enough?'

I considered that in silence. *Was* that enough for me, to be with Severin – *just* Severin, without his powers as an Artisan?

I supposed the answer depended on what had attracted me to him in the first place. After Roran's attempt to drown me, when I'd struggled to understand my changed body, the magic pulsing beneath my skin . . . Severin had been there for me. And, in time, I had wanted other things from him. I had wanted—

A distraction.

The word felt cold. Callous. It had become more than that, hadn't it? I desired his company, missed him when he was gone, worried for his safety when he was sent away. But he had spoken of emotion that went beyond simple desire or concern.

Isn't there anyone you love? Odessa had asked me once. *Someone who you would sacrifice everything for?*

No, I had almost said. *There isn't.*

I had hesitated, though. Had thought of Severin and wondered whether it could be more, if I ever felt safe enough to truly let down my guard. Or perhaps I was just heartless enough to give him false hope, to draw out our dalliance as long as possible.

If that was the case, then I really was as unfeeling as the icy water that had claimed my life. My mother thought I was.

And if I was going to have the strength and cunning to claim the Ravalian throne . . . I would have to be.

But I didn't want to give him up – his unpredictability, his touch, the way he made my pulse race like no one else.

Was that love, or possession?

I tilted my head to meet Severin's penetrating stare. He saw the future so clearly, but did he see *me*?

I stroked a hand across Severin's muscled back. Even now, his closeness stoked a fire in me: I wanted nothing more than to stop talking, to feel his fullness inside me. So I smiled playfully, like this was all a game.

'No,' I breathed, bringing his face closer to mine. 'What interests me is the future.'

Severin didn't smile. He didn't pull away, either. 'You're too ambitious for your own good.'

Maybe I was.

'I can't help it,' I admitted, my words weighed down with finality. 'I am Zandri's daughter, after all.'

The sun was setting when Severin finally left the greenhouse. I raised a hand to my lips – still flushed and sensitive from his kisses.

As I stood, my gaze fell on the outline of another. Someone who had been standing amongst the plants, watching my tryst from the shadows.

The young man stepped forward into the dappled light and smiled. 'For what it's worth, I can see the appeal.'

Panic made my heart race – for a moment, words were beyond me. How long had he been there? How much had he *seen*?

'I can explain,' I said hurriedly, knowing that I didn't sound like I needed to: like a non-guilty person, someone calm and in control. 'It's not what you think. Whatever you saw—'

'Oh, I know what I saw.' Cassius's face was filled with vicious triumph. 'Don't worry, Sister. Your secret is safe with me.'

CHAPTER FORTY-EIGHT

Scarlett

I wasn't sure when the hammer would fall, but I was certain that it would. Cassius wasn't the sort to let a chance to strike at his enemies slip through his fingers, and that was what circumstance had made us.

But I knew how methodical my brother could be, and I doubted he would act immediately.

Which gave me some time. Not much – but some.

The stench of death greeted me before I entered the infirmary, a small stone building attached to the Order of Warriors residence. Inside, it was crowded with healers and wounded alike. The sights, sounds, and smells slammed into me with the force of a battering ram.

I stepped out of the way as two Warriors carried in another stretcher. A man's limp arm hung off one side, unnaturally pale. When I breathed in, I regretted it: the smell of blood and human filth clogged my nostrils.

Holding my sleeve to my nose, I continued down the narrow corridor between the occupied beds. Disguised as Sabine, no one paid me any attention. Even if they had, what was one more Artisan, sent to look into the futures of the wounded?

I followed the healers from bed to bed, staying out of their way as much as possible. The sleeve helped a little, but there was nothing I could do to block out the sound of the Warriors' anguished moans.

How do the healers stand it? I wondered, careful to avoid the dark puddles on the floor.

I usually gave the infirmary a wide berth, but everything Zandri had told me – about what I could achieve if I managed to master my death magic – had drawn me here. What better opportunity to explore my abilities than an influx of dying Warriors from the Western front? I had never been around so much concentrated death before. It made me oddly hopeful.

That hope died along with the men around me. As I lingered by the bedsides of men with fatal wounds, I felt nothing. No magic or emotion rose up inside me – except frustration. I had spent weeks experimenting with dead animals in my chambers, testing the limits of my blood. But if my blood was only good for reviving rats or mice, then I had suffered beneath that ice for no reason at all.

I glanced away from a man missing his forearm – and blinked as my gaze settled on Mira. She had replaced her extravagant dress with fighting leathers and the mask she had been given during Initiation. That mask was probably the reason why no one tried to stop her as she walked amongst the beds. Searching – she was search-ing each of their faces.

'He's not here,' I said, stalking towards her. 'Aric, I mean. He's not amongst the wounded.'

Or the dead, I thought but didn't say.

Mira nodded, her lips pressed into a thin line. It occurred to me that there was a certain irony in us both being here, surrounded by death and horror, on a night that should have been a celebration. I wondered if she felt as trapped as I did. If tonight had felt like a betrayal to her – a betrayal of whatever she and Aric had shared.

'You were right,' Mira said softly. 'Everything you said – about working with Cassius. You were right.'

She paused at a Warrior's bedside, watching the healers applying bandages to his chest. Bandages that were already weeping blood.

There was something so sad about her expression – something so defeated – that my earlier anger disappeared, replaced by a strange urge to reassure her. But though I looked like Sabine, I wasn't Mira's friend. Not really.

'I should have listened to you when I had the chance,' Mira continued. 'And now . . . now it's too late.'

'It's never too late,' I said, and I wasn't sure if I was referring to Mira's circumstances or my own. Again, that shared sense of symmetry struck me. 'There's always another way. Another choice.'

Mira looked up at me, and even through the mask, I could see the way her eyes burned. No longer defeated – but resolved.

'Thank you, Sabine,' she said, her fingers brushing the dagger strapped to her hip.

I watched Mira stride purposefully away. 'Where are you going?'

'To make a choice,' Mira called without looking back. 'One I should have made a long time ago.'

There was no need to rush after her. I knew exactly where she was going.

In some ways, she was utterly predictable. Just like her mother, she had a soft spot for a lost cause.

I returned my attention to the wounded and dying – only to pause as I noticed Severin. He was murmuring something to a patient with a head wound. The boy didn't look much older than fourteen or fifteen. I couldn't overhear their conversation, but when Severin brushed a curl from the boy's face, the gesture was tender.

Severin stood, shaking his head at the senior healer. Just like that, they moved on to the next bed.

I took their place at the boy's side. Unlike many of the others, he was quiet and still. Almost peaceful.

'I'm going to die,' he whispered. 'Aren't I?'

There was no point in lying. 'I think so.'

His blue eyes – glazed with resignation – met mine. 'Will you stay with me?'

'Until the end,' I promised.

The boy smiled faintly, like that was all the reassurance he needed. But it felt sorely inadequate. If Severin was still here, he would say something far more eloquent and comforting.

I reached tentatively for the boy's sweaty hand, trying not to feel disgusted. He flinched back from my touch.

'Your skin.' He blinked blearily up at me, like he was struggling to focus on my face. 'It's like ice.'

Considering he was so close to death, his reaction seemed extremely oversensitive. But I forced my irritation aside and tried out a smile instead. It seemed to work; his fingers threaded through mine.

He's so young, I thought, studying his burned face and blistered lips. Not a Warrior, but most likely one of their attendants. It seemed a waste that his life should end like this.

'Does it hurt?' I asked, taking in the bloody bandage encircling his head.

'A little.' He coughed. A horrible, wet sound. 'I don't want to die.'

'Everyone dies.' My fingers tightened around his clammy ones. Before I could think better of it, I whispered, 'I died once. But I didn't stay dead.'

When he looked at me, his face filled with hope, I knew I'd made a mistake.

'Can you save me?'

What a good question, I thought, and wished I had an answer that could satisfy us both.

The boy's chest rose as he inhaled one last, laboured breath – and then went still.

My fingers clenched around his, but the boy's hand was limp in mine. Lifeless.

Even as I released him, though, I felt a connection I couldn't explain. Instinct drew me closer, and I reached out, as if I would touch the boy's face—

Then I noticed the blood under my nails.

I turned my hand to the light. Though I couldn't remember scratching myself, beads of blood welled to the surface of my skin, vivid against the whiteness of my wrist.

I stared down at them, mesmerised. The same instinct that had made me reach for the boy tempted me to keep my wrist where it was, to find out what would happen if my blood made contact with his skin.

Can you save me? he had asked, and I was suddenly certain that I could. Maybe it wouldn't be saving him, not really, but I could make his heart beat, and his brain work, and his body obey him. I could give him some semblance of life. Just as I had with the raven.

But what use would this boy be, really? The thought was harsh, but it gave me pause.

If even bringing back an animal drained me, it was logical to assume that resurrecting a person would weaken me further. And if even *Severin* had looked into this boy's future and decided he wasn't worth saving . . .

I moved my hand at the last moment, letting my blood splash harmlessly against the tiles. Every precious drop.

I looked down at the dead boy in front of me. If Severin had the power I did, he wouldn't have even considered the cost to himself. He would have looked at this boy and seen his humanity, his potential.

I had looked at him and seen a body. A pawn to be used for my own ends.

As I left the infirmary behind, I remembered that Severin had once called me selfish. But perhaps selfish was the wrong word for what I was.

Perhaps *cruel* fitted me better.

I raised my hood as I strode through the dim alleyways of the Lower Districts, shielding Sabine's youthful face from view. There was nothing to fear – with my illusions and my weapons training, I was confident I could deal with any attackers – but I saw no reason to court trouble.

Shadows shifted in the alleyway nearest to me. Two hooded figures – thieves, most likely, looking for an easy mark.

Twirling a dagger in my fingers, I pinned them with a heavy stare as I passed. Perhaps they sensed the predator I truly was, because they slunk back into the darkness.

I allowed myself a smile at the minor victory – and at the sight of a brightly lit tavern up ahead. Raucous, drunk laughter echoed from within, instantly familiar. If memory served me, I had first seen Mira and Darius about a block from here.

I slowed my pace, scouring the buildings around me for the magical door they had once walked through.

I hadn't told Zandri that Mira had spared a member of the resistance. I couldn't be sure how my mother would react, and I preferred not to bring her into this. If I did, things could get very messy – and the resistance might yet prove useful.

Especially since Mira had left the infirmary to seek them out. I was almost certain of it – that *this* was the choice she had referred to.

After another few minutes of searching, I found it. A perfectly unremarkable section of wall.

Remembering Darius's actions, I raised my fist to knock—

A wooden door materialised in front of me, blazing with the symbol of the resistance.

Opening it, I stepped through into darkness. With the blood ruby coiled around my arm, my illusions were my best protection – and I used them to cloak myself from view.

I climbed the steps slowly and without a sound. Noise drifted from above – whispered voices and the creak of floorboards.

A promising start. I hadn't been sure if the resistance still used this place for their headquarters; it seemed logical that they would have vacated after their leader was taken into custody. But they seemed to have returned, confident in the knowledge that neither Mira nor Darius had given up their location.

When I reached the landing, I went still. A dark-haired man was in front of me, holding a blade to a young woman's throat.

'Was that really necessary, Jadis?' Mira asked, rubbing her neck as the man withdrew his knife.

'What are you doing here?' Jadis demanded without responding. The man moved to her side, the resemblance between them so striking that I realised they must be siblings. Perhaps twins.

'I want to help you,' Mira replied. 'I know the Senecas were compromised; I was there, the night a Mask shot their footman. I'm the reason you escaped with your life.'

'Of course you were.' Jadis sighed, but all she said was: 'Look around, Mira. There's no one left to help.'

Mira and I took in the large, mostly empty space. Flickering candles illuminated battered tables and threadbare curtains. Mira's disappointment was obvious, and I couldn't blame her. The resistance certainly didn't seem like a thriving operation.

'When I heard about the Senecas,' Mira said, a trace of accusation in her voice, 'I thought you were using that money for something meaningful.'

'I was,' Jadis said shortly. 'I've spent the past month increasing our numbers and stockpiling weapons. But ever since Darius was captured, people are scared to act. I don't blame them.'

I could tell this wasn't going the way Mira had hoped, but she switched tactics readily enough. 'You didn't seem surprised earlier, when I told you I saved your life. If you know I'm a Mask, then you know I have connections in the palace. With my access, I could help you strike back against Emperor Kalias. All you have to do is contact your people—'

'They're not my people,' Jadis interrupted. 'We answer to Darius, and you're the reason he was imprisoned. No one is going to risk their life based on a rousing speech from a girl of – how old are you, exactly? Eighteen?'

Reaching into a hidden sheath, Mira withdrew a knife. Before Jadis could react, she flicked her wrist—

The knife thudded into the table leg next to Jadis's foot.

'My abilities could prove very useful to your cause,' Mira said, her voice firm. 'You know where I'll be if you change your mind.'

She turned on her heel without waiting for Jadis's response. I raised an eyebrow, impressed by the display. But when I caught a glimpse of Mira's unguarded face, I saw that her eyes were bright – not just with anger, but with unshed tears.

I felt a brief pang of pity. Clearly, she knew what I did: right now, the resistance was broken, and nothing she said could change that.

But as I followed Mira out onto the street, it occurred to me that perhaps Darius could. When he had first been captured, I'd wondered how much he was worth to the resistance – and now I finally had my answer.

He was worth a great deal to them. Which meant I had access to something they desperately wanted.

Perhaps tonight hadn't been a complete waste after all.

CHAPTER FORTY-NINE

Mira

I was so absorbed in my thoughts that I didn't sense anything amiss. Not until I was even deeper within the twisting labyrinth of the Lower Districts.

The glint of metal was my only warning before a masked figure stepped out of the shadows.

I expected a sword, but was met with two daggers. I ducked down, lightning fast, and kicked my opponent in the ribs. She recovered quickly and aimed a slash at my stomach, her serrated blade cutting through my fighting leathers without nicking the skin. A relief, since most Masks coated their blades in poison.

I struck with my dagger, and while my attacker was distracted, I wrenched the mask from her face. Danica's honey-blonde hair and delicate features stared back at me, but before I could press my advantage, she was gone – reappearing a few metres away and smoothly loading her crossbow.

Only it wasn't directed at me.

There was no time for shock. No time to wonder how or why Sabine was here, not as I heard that familiar *twang*—

I threw myself at Sabine, knocking her to the ground and shielding her body with my own. Glass shattered as the bolt pierced a window behind us, raining down on my lowered head. A handful of shards sliced into my face, but I barely felt the sting.

Grabbing hold of Sabine, I pulled her into a nearby alleyway. For a moment, we stayed very still, listening for the sound of approaching footsteps. When none came, I turned my attention to the most pressing threat: Sabine herself.

'What are you doing here?' I demanded, keeping my voice low. 'How did you find me?'

Sabine's moss-green eyes darted down to my hand, clenched tightly around the dagger I carried. I released my grip, but the damage was done. Now, both of us had reason to be suspicious of the other.

'I followed you from the palace,' Sabine replied, her voice surprisingly steady. 'I wanted to warn you – Zandri's Masks have been tailing you.'

'I guess that explains Danica, then.'

Sabine's lips formed into a thin line. 'I'm not sure Danica is acting on Zandri's—'

It was only instinct that saved me as I rolled, barely evading the bolt that would have sliced through my abdomen. Adrenaline flooded my body as I rose to my feet, facing Danica, who had somehow materialised directly in front of us.

I grabbed Sabine's arm. 'Run. *Now*.'

We sprinted through the Lower Districts, hoping to lose Danica in the twisting alleyways – but she always kept pace with us, aided by Zandri's magic and her possession of a long-range weapon.

And then I made a fatal mistake.

Thanks to my Mask training, I was familiar with this kind of magic – and had done my best to choose wider streets and alleyways with multiple entrances and exists. But this alleyway only had one entrance and one exit.

When Danica materialised ahead of us, her crossbow already drawn, I knew it was over.

'Come on,' Sabine said, her fingers digging into my forearm. 'We have to—' The moment she turned, Danica reappeared behind us – covering the exit. Penning us in.

No matter which way we ran, we weren't leaving this alleyway. Not while Danica was alive.

I cast a careful eye over my surroundings. All the doors and windows were boarded up, and the walls were too high to climb. No cover – except for a few piles of wooden debris.

What do you do when there are no good options? Zandri had once asked me.

You change the paradigm, I had replied.

'Why are you doing this?' I shouted, trying to keep Danica distracted. 'We're in the same Order. We're on the same side.'

'Not from what I saw tonight,' Danica replied, training her crossbow on me. 'But this isn't about my duty as a Mask. It's about what you did to Odessa.'

'I never meant—'

'It was obvious what you were after,' Danica continued, her voice icy and merciless, 'from the moment you competed in the first Trial. And now they've just *given* it to you.'

I frowned, not understanding. 'It?'

'The crown,' Danica clarified. 'That's what you always wanted, isn't it?'

Danica didn't give me the chance to respond. The next bolt missed my body by a handful of inches as Sabine pulled me down behind a pile of timber.

I leant back against the filthy wall as I considered my options. *I might have a chance against Danica, but someone like Sabine, who had never trained in combat . . .*

'When I tell you to,' I said, low and urgent, 'I want you to run. *I'm the one Danica wants dead—* '

'I don't think Danica is acting on Zandri's orders,' Sabine interrupted, finishing what she had started to say earlier. 'Danica might want *you* dead, but I'm a witness now. She'll have to silence us both.'

She was right, of course, and that knowledge made me stiffen. But all I said was: 'It's going to be fine, Sabine. I promise.' I peered around the timber, a dagger clenched in my white-knuckled hands.

'If you're planning to kill Danica with *that*,' Sabine said dryly from behind me, 'then I've seriously overestimated your intelligence.'

'I have something else in mind.' I straightened before Sabine could ask what that was.

And then I was stepping into full view, like that was a perfectly sensible thing for me to do.

My gaze shifted to Danica, whose crossbow was already raised. We'd practised with this very weapon during training, and I had seen her accuracy for myself. With the additional magic Zandri had granted her, Danica was undeniably lethal.

But I didn't need to rely on magic from Zandri. Thanks to my mother, I had magic of my own.

The desire to run was still there, but I moved forwards instead, towards the danger. I let out a frustrated sigh as Sabine followed, twisting to cast her a withering glance – a glance that told her exactly how foolish I thought her decision was.

'Stay behind me,' I instructed, and reached for my mother's locket.

I had never tried to consciously summon the magic before. Both times had been accidents – desperate miracles. But Zandri had told me what was needed. Magic thrived on emotion.

And I had plenty of emotion to choose from. Fear, hope—

Rage. Bottomless, all-consuming rage.

Danica's next bolt disintegrated in a blast of black fire. The same black fire that danced in my hand.

Her lips parted in wordless shock. And her eyes – I had never seen them so wide. So afraid.

I liked the sight of her fear. Somehow, it didn't matter to me that Danica wasn't Emperor Kalias or Zandri; she was a threat, and I was tired of threats. Tired of bowing down and biding my time and taking orders.

I brought my hand up to my lips. And I *blew*.

The flames burst out in front of me – a vicious, crackling wall that licked at the wooden buildings and blasted me with heat. Boards fell in a groan of sparks. Glass followed a few seconds later, and despite the sudden drizzle falling from the sky, my fire spread, jumping from building to building—

Danica stumbled back, like she might run. *Too late*.

Her howls of pain were more animal than human. A horrible smell rent the air.

The smell of burning flesh.

I remembered my mother's words at the circus. *Breathe, Mira. Focus.*

I tugged on the magic, trying to call it back, but it was beyond my control – and so were my own emotions. The flames tunnelled higher, licking and biting and consuming. Exhilaration filled my veins, panic following close at its heels.

There was nothing I could do to stop the horror unfolding before me. My legs were leaden, my arms dead weights. I couldn't move, couldn't shout, couldn't run. All I could do was watch.

And listen.

Then silence descended. No screaming, nothing except the crackling of the flames, searching for anything to consume. But all that was left in front of me was a path of death and destruction.

The cost of my survival.

When the fire waned, I realised that I was hunched over, breathing heavily. Danica had been a threat. She would have killed me and Sabine. I'd done what I needed to. I had—

Sabine's voice was oddly hesitant. '. . . Mira?'

I looked up. In her wide eyes, I could see my own reflection. Illuminated by the full moon overhead, with flames still dancing in my eyes, I looked unfamiliar and powerful.

Monstrous. I look monstrous—

At least until the flames guttered out in my eyes and I stumbled, collapsing unconscious to the ground.

CHAPTER FIFTY

Scarlett

After checking Mira's pulse – strong and steady – I approached Danica's body. The stench alone should have repulsed me, but I breathed past it, not thinking of fried hair and sizzling skin. I needed to make sure she was dead.

Not that I expected otherwise. No one could have survived that, and those screams . . .

I shuddered, recalling what Mira had done. Her mother was powerful, but if Zandri was correct, Mira had the potential to become even more so. I suspected that was why Zandri was being so cautious with Mira's training. She didn't want to make the same mistake she'd made with Adalyn, turning her into both a weapon and a threat.

From what I'd seen tonight, it was already too late for that.

Crouching at Danica's side, I took in her charred fighting leathers and shrivelled hair. What little I could see of her face was blistered, her mouth open in a silent scream. At least she was no longer a problem.

But no – that wasn't quite true. Soon Danica's body would be discovered. I needed to make sure her death couldn't be tied to us.

Which meant the mask had to go.

I gagged as I prised it free, along with strips of skin and a hot layer of fat. Danica's face – I couldn't look at what was left of her face. But the instant my hand brushed her skin, black veins started to wind up my arms.

I stared at them with a mixture of shock and fascination.

With every second that I maintained the connection between us, my skin grew colder and darker. As if ice was flowing through Danica and into me. Ice, in the place of blood.

No, I thought dimly to myself, my eyes fluttering shut. *Not ice.* Death.

It flooded into me, and even though it was cold, I welcomed it like an old friend.

I thought of the girl I had seen when Roran had drowned me, with her snow-white skin and glacial eyes. Even though I resembled her now, I knew what she truly was. Death and rebirth wrapped into one.

And every time I embraced her, I came closer to unlocking my true potential. To becoming strong enough to defeat my brothers, kill my father, and claim my place as empress.

When I finally severed the connection, Danica's eyes were empty husks and I was smiling.

I felt no fear when the soldier burst into view, his sword already drawn. I watched him take in Danica's body, the debris and destruction around us. And I watched him open his mouth, preparing to call out for assistance—

I moved to meet him, unable to risk him bringing a whole platoon down on us. His first strike was easy enough to evade, but I didn't even try to avoid his second.

Instinct drove me to grasp his sword with both hands, stopping the metal a few inches from my heart.

'Surrender,' he told me. 'Surrender, or I'll run you through.'

The black veins surged in response, moving *through* me and into the sword. Darkening the silver to black.

The man's grip loosened and his face contorted – the first vestiges of pain and cold infecting him.

But he hadn't noticed the veins crawling up his arms. Not yet.

'What are you?' he asked, staring into my face – into my eyes. *'What are you?'*

I had no answer. Even *I* wasn't sure what this power made me – but I didn't care. All I felt was a cold certainty, the knowledge that soon, those black veins would reach his heart.

When he finally saw them, he reached in panic for another weapon. But not to attack me.

To attack *himself.*

When his screaming finally stopped and his chest went still, I became aware of a presence behind me.

I turned slowly, already knowing who it would be.

'Your eyes,' Mira whispered, backing away. She stumbled, tripping over the uneven ground.

I raised a hand to my face, only to pause. Admiring the black veins.

'It's alright,' I murmured, approaching Mira like I might a skittish animal. As I did, I wrapped an illusion around myself: covering the veins with normal skin, and transforming my eyes back to their usual blue.

Mira stared up at me, her lips parted, her skin white as paper. And then she turned and fled.

Running – from *me.*

I tracked her through the Lower Districts, my steps slow and unhurried. No one tried to stop me, and even the few animals I saw – two dogs and a cat – bolted at my approach.

Animals weren't so easily deceived. And I suspected they could see the truth my illusions concealed.

Because my eyes were identical to the corpse I had left behind. Two inky black husks—

Filled with death.

CHAPTER FIFTY-ONE

Mira

Sabine looked like a wraith. Long, dark curls nearly covered her face, but they couldn't hide her eyes. They were bright and luminous and *alive*, nothing like the terrible, inky black they had been earlier.

Was it possible that I had imagined it? That her eyes hadn't changed colour at all?

The thought made me hesitate. Sabine *had* pulled me out of the way of a crossbow bolt, after all. It seemed ridiculous to be afraid of her. But then I remembered how she had just *stood* there, watching that soldier cut into his skin—

'Mira?'

Sabine inched closer. She had always been graceful, but now that gracefulness seemed sinister.

'Don't come any closer,' I warned, holding up a hand.

Sabine paused. 'But we're friends,' she said, with a playful pout. 'I even saved your life.'

I considered her warily. I had so many questions – why Sabine had followed me, what she had done to that soldier, how she was so calm about the magic I had used . . . and yet I already had my answers. Because her eyes – those icy blue *eyes*—

'You're not Sabine.' The words left my lips with heavy finality, cleaving the air between us like a sword.

For a moment, it seemed like she would protest. But then she shrugged and said, 'What gave it away?'

'Sabine's eyes were green. Yours are blue.'

'Such an obvious mistake.' She shook her head, smiling ruefully. And as she came closer, her features wavered, until I wasn't looking at Sabine at all.

I was looking at—

I stared at Scarlett, who was dressed in black fighting leathers like mine, her hair snaking down her shoulders in deep, wine-coloured tendrils. The most obvious difference wasn't her pale skin or icy stare, but the way she held herself: with a haughtiness that didn't suit the girl she had been pretending to be.

At least now it made sense how she had killed that soldier. No doubt Zandri had given Scarlett some morbid kind of magic to protect herself. But her illusions . . . Gods, it should have been so *obvious*.

I didn't want to give away how deeply her betrayal stung, but I had to know: 'Was any of it real?'

'It was real to me,' Scarlett replied, her eyes intent on mine. 'All of it.'

I wasn't sure if I believed her – but I *wanted* to, and that was utter madness. 'Why? Why would you pretend to be someone else?'

'Isn't it obvious?' Scarlett asked, leaning against a nearby wall and folding her arms. 'I did it to keep you alive.'

I couldn't help it – I laughed. 'You expect me to believe that?'

'It's the truth.' Scarlett said nothing for a moment. When she did, her voice was very quiet. 'As the emperor's illegitimate daughter, I'm an outsider too. I have a target on my back, same as you. I thought perhaps . . .' A hint of vulnerability softened her face as she said, 'I thought we could help each other.'

'Did you?' I said, not bothering to hide my scepticism. 'Most part-nerships aren't based on a lie.'

'You lied to my brother when you stole his crown,' Scarlett pointed out. 'Cassius still found a way to look past that.'

'This isn't about Cassius.'

'It is,' Scarlett said, her voice measured, 'but I'll get to that in a moment. You want to know why I lied to you – well, what would you have done if you were me? I wanted to help you survive the Trials, but I couldn't expose my involvement. The only way was to disguise myself as another competitor.'

'But *why* did you want me to survive? The first time we met—'

'I saved you. From that archer at the docks.'

'You didn't save me,' I said bitterly. 'You kept me alive for my execution.'

'I *delayed* your death,' Scarlett corrected. 'I showed you as much mercy as I could, under the circumstances. As for what I said to you . . . we were being observed by my father's Warriors. I couldn't admit the real reason I intervened.'

'Which was . . . ?'

Scarlett leant forward, until her face was bathed in the moonlight. 'Mira, Zandri was King Arioch's sister. She's your—'

'Aunt.' The word tasted sour in my mouth, like even the syllable was poisonous. 'She's my aunt.'

Which meant that Scarlett . . .

I turned away abruptly. My only surviving family, and one of them was responsible for killing my father, while the other – *my cousin* – was standing here, asking me to trust her.

As if it was that simple. As if trusting the wrong person wasn't a death sentence.

'Zandri doesn't like to advertise her past – not in Ravalia, at least. And she has no particular love for family. But I've never wanted us to be at odds, Mira.' Scarlett's voice was soft, almost tentative. 'I hope you can believe that.'

Reluctantly, I allowed myself to look at her – searching for the resemblance that should be there.

'I used to look more like you,' Scarlett said, guessing my thoughts. 'I was born with your olive skin and eyes that were almost hazel. When the court visited Kalure a few years ago, Roran tried to drown me. I survived, but I found myself . . . changed.'

I didn't want to empathise with Scarlett, but I did. 'I thought you were exaggerating. When you spoke about the threat your brothers presented.'

'I wasn't.'

'But your father . . .'

'The Ravalian Court values strength above all else. If I die, I will have proven myself weak enough to be defeated, and therefore unworthy.'

Silence fell between us as I digested that. What would it be like, living with siblings who plotted your downfall at every turn?

Not that different to a lifetime of running, I realised, thinking of my own childhood. A childhood spent looking over my shoulder.

Scarlett started walking and I followed, remembering the moments we had spent together. To my surprise, the truth didn't change them much. Now that I knew what to look for, I could see glimpses of Sabine in Scarlett, and I suspected that she had crafted Sabine from parts of herself.

'You could have told me,' I said finally. 'During the Trials—'

'During the Trials,' Scarlett interrupted, 'I needed you to trust me. If I had told you who I really was, that trust would have dissolved – and then where would you have been? You wouldn't have even made it through the final task.'

'And after the final task? Why didn't you say anything *then?*'

'I almost did,' she murmured. 'After you were initiated. But then I discovered you were working with my brother.'

'Something you did your best to discourage,' I said, thinking of Sabine's warnings – and Scarlett's.

'For your sake as much as mine,' Scarlett replied. 'Cassius tried to kill me recently; I know exactly how ruthless he can be.' She smiled at my surprise, but her smile held no humour. 'I couldn't help you openly, Mira. But whether as Scarlett or Sabine . . . I *have* been helping you.'

That much I knew to be true. But—

'What about Aric?' I asked. 'How does he fit into your plans?'

'I promised Aric that I would find out what happened to Kain – and whether Roran was involved in his death.'

'And was he?' I asked carefully.

'Yes. But I think you already know that.' Scarlett tilted her head, sending red waves tumbling over her shoulder. 'I understand why you wanted to keep it from him. Revenge is all-consuming.'

Exhaustion seeped into me, turning my limbs heavy. Scarlett was right. The further I travelled down this road – the closer I came to my vengeance – the more I suspected it had no end. I didn't want that for Aric. He deserved to move on – to have a life of his own. Not one consumed by tragedies of the past.

'You don't have to tell him.' The words left my lips before I could think better of them.

Scarlett shook her head. 'I already told Aric everything, and I promised to help him when the time is right.' She paused, debating, and then said, 'I could offer you both the chance to destroy Roran. I have a feeling that's something you might want as well. Or am I wrong?'

Not wrong, perhaps, but presumptuous.

And unnerving.

'You don't have to decide now,' Scarlett said softly. 'But I hope you'll consider working with me. Unlike Cassius, I want to rule differently to my father and build friendships with other countries. I'm even willing to deal fairly with the Ravalian resistance.'

I kept my face expressionless, wondering whether she had seen me enter their headquarters earlier. Wondering how much she knew. 'Those are easy promises to make.'

'What if I could prove that I mean them?' Scarlett tilted her head as she considered me. 'Darius's execution date is coming up. With my illusions and some additional assistance, I could help him escape.'

'You would do that?'

'I would,' Scarlett replied. 'As a show of good faith – for the rebels, and for you.'

Scarlett slowed to a stop, and I was surprised to realise that we had made it all the way to the palace grounds. Reflected in the light of the fire braziers, Scarlett no longer seemed so cold and aloof. I wasn't sure what to make of her – or our new relationship.

'Why Ravalia?' I asked suddenly. 'You're Kalurian – or half Kalurian, like me. You have a claim to more than one throne, and yet you're so focused on beating your brothers. I don't understand it.'

'Don't you?' she said with a brittle laugh. 'I would have thought you knew exactly what it felt like to want to prove yourself. And to want revenge on the people who wronged you.' Our eyes met, and I knew the same shadows I saw in Scarlett's gaze were echoed in my own. 'As for Kalure . . . the Kalurians despise my mother for the same reason you do. They seem determined to view my rule as an extension of hers. That's why I kept it from you. I thought that if you learnt the truth . . . you would come to hate me. Just like Cassius and Roran.'

There was something raw about her words, and it was impossible to doubt her sincerity. For a moment, we just stared at each other. How strange it was to begin the day with one view of Scarlett and end it with something entirely different. Strange – but not unwelcome.

'Think about it,' Scarlett said again. 'That's all I ask.'

I hesitated, but then I nodded. 'I will.'

Scarlett touched my arm as she moved past me. Beneath the chill of her touch, I felt that kinship I hadn't been able to explain. Until now.

'That locket,' she said, and my hand rose protectively to the necklace I wore. 'I didn't see you wearing it when you were brought to the palace.'

'I . . . Aric gave it to me,' I said quickly – too quickly.

Scarlett smiled, just the slightest twitch of her lips. Clearly, she didn't believe me.

'Your mother stole something once,' she said, her tone conversational. 'Something valuable.'

I said nothing.

'I'm not sure how much you know about blood rubies, but they're powerful magical objects – so powerful that Zandri usually keeps them under lock and key. The guards searched you and your mother in the cells, but they never found the blood ruby that Adalyn stole.'

I met Scarlett's stare without blinking. Cousin or not, there were some secrets I was unwilling to trust anyone with. 'My mother probably hid it somewhere. Or maybe she sold it.'

Scarlett's smile widened, as if the thought of selling a blood ruby was ludicrous. But all she said was: 'Do you remember what I told you once, about the kinds of magical aptitudes Adalyn possessed?' When I didn't answer, she said, 'You demonstrated one of those aptitudes tonight. Her aptitude for *fire*.'

Those icy eyes glittered as Scarlett studied me, then the locket around my neck. She reached out and picked it up, rolling it in her palm. An arctic chill emanated from her skin.

The moment lingered until it became uncomfortable. Then Scarlett released the locket.

'Yes,' she murmured, stepping back from me. 'Perfectly ordinary.' But the twist to her lips said otherwise. 'Regardless, I think it best that you keep the locket out of sight from now on.'

Her eyes met mine, and the warning in them was clear.

She didn't wait for a response as she strode off. I watched her go, feeling more conflicted than ever. Family or not, I didn't trust Scarlett much more than I trusted Cassius. Which meant I was playing a very dangerous game – with Scarlett and with her brother.

It occurred to me that I was now in the most precarious position possible: caught between two warring heirs who hated each other.

And my survival depended on backing one of them in their bid for the throne.

But which one?

CHAPTER FIFTY-TWO

Scarlett

From the balcony of my chambers, I watched the gilded carriages make their way from the docks to the palace. There were so many that they resembled a golden snake, each carriage packed with officials and aristocrats.

The palace was filling fast, and still, there were more to come – provincial governors and royalty from the countries beyond the Azure Sea, all eager to witness Cassius and Mira's wedding. To strengthen their relations with the Ravalian Empire.

They were fools, believing that distance and political promises would protect them. But I knew my father. He would see their fine clothing and jewels, would hear stories of their lands and their luxuries, and plot to take those things for himself.

Which was precisely what I planned to do. Only my target was closer to home.

And I would need to act fast, because the Maesteri delegation had already arrived. I'd met with their ambassador this morning, who took great delight in presenting me with a portrait of Prince Adomas. For once, the nobles were envious of me; the prince was undeniably handsome, with turquoise eyes, nut-brown skin and hair the colour of volcanic sand. But I had no intention of marrying him – or allowing Mira to marry Cassius.

If it had been up to my mother, I had no doubt that Cassius would have met a convenient end already. But Cassius would be expecting me to try something – and if I failed, he would tell the emperor about my relationship with Severin.

No, I needed to be smart. Careful.

'You summoned me, Your Highness?'

Lillian joined me on the balcony, which was bathed in bright sunshine. No doubt she believed I had chosen the location to enjoy the nice weather.

I wondered how she would react if she knew the real reason. Probably with the horror Aella and the other servants had tried to hide, marching in like grim-faced soldiers each time they had to remove the cages of dead animals from my rooms. But with the windows flung open and a breeze carrying the sweet perfume of flowers through my chambers, there was little danger of Lillian smelling the underlying scent of decay.

I took a seat on a carved chair, and watched Lillian do the same, arranging her skirts primly around her ankles. Her elegance would have impressed the court ladies, but it didn't endear her to me. Quite the opposite.

And I was impatient, too. Eager to discover the answers I needed and deal with Cassius once and for all.

But I smiled, matching Lillian's demureness. 'Shall I call for tea?'

'No thank you, Your Highness.'

'Down to business then.' My smile widened as Lillian folded her hands in her lap, a tiny indication of her unease. Perhaps it was petty of me to take delight in such things, but I had such little power within the court that I had learnt to savour it where I could. 'I've grown quite fond of your brother,' I said, tilting my head to enjoy the warmth of the sun on my face. 'And, I suppose, of Mira as well. Though I haven't spent as much time with her.'

Lillian shifted uneasily. 'I'm sure they feel the same.'

'I must admit,' I said, ignoring Lillian's comment, 'I was distressed to hear about Mira's engagement to Cassius. I had the impression that she and Aric cared for each other.'

Lillian's nimble fingers plucked at the stitching of her gown. It was white and gold, like all house servants' attire. 'They're friends. That's all.'

I had anticipated Lillian's reluctance to talk. But it still irritated me.

'You can speak openly,' I told her, leaning forward. 'My only concern is Aric. I was close with your eldest brother, Kain, and I suppose I feel a sense of protectiveness because of that. If Mira wants this marriage, I won't stand in her way. But if she and Aric do care for each other, perhaps I could intervene on their behalf. Speak with the emperor.'

'You would do that?'

'I would,' I lied, holding Lillian's gaze. 'I couldn't tell my father the real reason, of course – the emperor would never agree to a marriage between Aric and Mira. But there would be hope for their relationship, at least, without Cassius between them.' I smiled, allowing my face to soften even further as I confided, 'A secret relationship isn't ideal, but it's better than nothing.'

'It sounds like you speak from experience.'

'Perhaps I do.'

Lillian considered me thoughtfully. 'You're not what I expected, Your Highness.'

'I'll take that as a compliment,' I said, with a slight laugh.

'You're right,' Lillian said suddenly. 'My brother loves Mira. He always has.'

'And Mira? How does she feel about him?'

'She loves Aric.' Lillian lifted her chin. 'I'm certain she does. She just refuses to acknowledge it.'

No matter how certain Lillian seemed, it was still just her opinion. But I had observed Mira and Aric's interactions for months, and all I really needed was confirmation of my own suspicions.

'I'll see what I can do,' I said, standing.

Lillian followed suit. 'Thank you, Your Highness.' She hesitated. 'But I don't want to put you in a difficult position with your brother—'

'Don't worry about it. I have little love for Cassius, and he has even less for me.'

Lillian frowned, like she found this difficult to comprehend.

'Mira is lucky to have you both,' I said, wondering what I might have been like, if I'd grown up with friends like Aric and Lillian. 'She seems to inspire nothing but loyalty – the Kalurians haven't even met her and they're willing to lay down their lives in her name. Even you and Aric are willing to sacrifice everything for Mira after knowing her for – what? Two years?'

Lillian said nothing.

I released a sharp breath as I thought of the Governor of Kalure, so determined to die for a girl he barely knew. Even the court, who regarded me with nothing but scorn, had come to respect Mira. And she had won herself enough influence that even my father had been forced to take her seriously.

'How does she inspire such loyalty?'

Lillian's eyes were intent on my face. I wondered how much those eyes saw. How much they guessed.

'Mira has the fiercest heart of anyone I've known. She fights for the people she loves – for what she believes is right.' Lillian's mouth twisted. 'At least she used to.'

'Perhaps she will again,' I said, seized by a strange impulse to clear the bitterness from Lillian's face.

Lillian smiled, but it was polite and unconvincing.

We walked through my chambers in companionable silence. I watched Lillian take in the sparseness of the space. There were no colourful cushions or embroideries to be seen, and no personal items on display. The one indulgence I allowed myself was the potted plant in the corner of the drawing room – a rare carnivorous variety that I had bred myself. I followed Lillian's gaze to the window above the plant, which was obscured by vines.

'I wanted to let it grow wild,' I said, in response to her unspoken question. No matter how unruly the vines became, I refused to allow the servants to touch them.

Lillian tilted her head, buttery curls cascading across her face. She looked at me curiously – as if she was reassessing prior assumptions. And I realised that I had underestimated the seamstress, too. I could see why Mira liked her. Perhaps, under different circumstances, I could have grown to like her as well.

But if I cared for nothing, then nothing could be taken away from me. I had learnt that lesson and learnt it well.

And I had already made that mistake with Severin.

I dismissed Lillian curtly, my focus returning to the plan solidifying in my mind.

It was time to deal with my brother.

CHAPTER FIFTY-THREE

Mira

The muscles in my arms burned as I ran through a series of practised movements. I pivoted and struck at an imaginary attacker before whirling around, sidestepping and—

'You're improving.'

I completed my final strike and lowered my sword. 'I had a good teacher,' I replied, slowly turning to face him.

Aric's hair was longer than I remembered, his muscles more defined, and the sun had deepened his skin to an even richer golden-brown that matched his eyes. But what really stood out to me was the way he held himself. As if he had become a true Warrior in the time he'd been gone.

He was watching me closely, too. His expression softened as we stared at each other, and he moved towards me, as if he felt the same pull I did.

The sounds of the training barracks – the clash of steel, the conversation of Warriors watching from beneath shaded arches – faded to nothing as I stared up into Aric's face. In that moment, a shared understanding passed between us.

And I knew that he had missed me as much as I had missed him. That we both regretted the way we had left things.

My fingers rose, itching to run through his hair. I didn't care about our audience, or the consequences. I wanted to bring his lips down to mine. Wanted to show him how I felt without words coming between us.

But Aric's softness disappeared as his gaze dropped to my hand – to the ostentatious ring on my finger.

'I heard rumours, but I didn't actually *believe* them.' He stepped back from me, a bitter smile twisting his lips. 'I suppose I should have known better.'

'You don't understand,' I said quickly. 'I don't love Cassius. It's not like that. He's—'

'—a means to an end?' Aric finished. 'Another way of getting closer to his father, to your revenge?'

'Not entirely.' I took a breath. 'It wasn't my choi—'

'I didn't expect to return and find you'd come to your senses,' Aric cut in, anger bringing a flush to his cheeks. 'But this . . . *this* is going too far, Mira. Even for you.'

'The emperor suggested the marriage. What was I supposed to tell him? *No?*'

'You can't have it both ways!' he snapped, ignoring the Warriors who looked in our direction. 'If you want to be with the prince, then *be* with him. I can't stop you. But I'm not going to watch it happen.'

He turned to leave, but I was already blocking his way.

'*Move*, Mira.' Low and dangerous.

'No,' I said, planting my feet. 'I let you leave once. I'm not making that mistake again.'

Aric took hold of my shoulders, and I had the sense he wanted to shake me. His grip tightened instead. 'I've given you plenty of chances. If you felt even a fraction of what I feel for you, we wouldn't be having this conversation.'

I sucked in a painful breath. 'That isn't fair.'

'Maybe not. But it's true.' Aric released me abruptly. The hurt in his face almost broke me, but I refused to let him make me the villain.

'Have you forgotten everything I had to do to get here?' I demanded. 'I have blood on my hands, Aric. Innocent blood. *And I can never get it off.*' Silence fell, broken only by my heavy breathing. 'You have no idea. *No idea* what I've sacrificed.'

'Don't I?' Aric's eyes blazed with molten fire. 'I've returned from battle, where I've seen men cut down by the hundreds. Some of the insurgents I killed were even younger than I am, and they had families too, loved ones who mourn them like I mourned Kain.' His jaw clenched, so tightly it looked like it might break. 'You're not the only one with blood on your hands, Mira. Both of us have had to sacrifice to fit into this monstrous place.'

'I don't want to *fit in* here,' I hissed at him. 'I want to destroy it. Every inch of it.'

'Well,' he said sharply, 'I'm sure that justifies everything. I'm sure that makes it all worth it.' He looked like he was going to say something else, but then his gaze shifted over my shoulder.

I swung around to see Cassius stride into view, accompanied by two guards. Rather than a tunic, he wore fitted black leathers. Fighting leathers, I assumed – until I took in his shiny black riding boots.

Calculating dark blue eyes raked over us, and I knew it looked bad. My face was flushed, and Aric and I were standing too close together; it looked like we'd been interrupted doing something more passionate than talking. I moved hastily away from Aric, trying to regain my composure.

'There you are,' Cassius said, no inflection in his voice. His gaze lingered on Aric before returning to me. 'I had thought you could accompany me on a hunt.'

'A hunt,' I repeated slowly.

The prince smiled, but it didn't reach his eyes. 'Yes. Unless you're otherwise occupied?'

'No,' I said immediately. 'Of course not.'

I crossed over to Cassius's side, expecting us to leave. But he was still watching Aric.

'The Warrior too,' he announced, his tone setting off warning bells in my mind.

Cassius turned on his heel and I reluctantly followed. As I did, I risked a glance in Aric's direction.

But he refused to meet my eyes.

*

The Warriors were already waiting at the stables, sitting astride hulking black stallions.

Cassius strode over to one of the stable hands, conversing in a low voice and motioning to Aric. The servant darted off, returning with another horse and saddle. His hands trembled as he tightened the straps, and I wondered if he was afraid of the prince or just nervous in the company of nobles.

'Your steed, Your Highness,' a young boy said to me, bowing deeply.

'Thank you,' I said, running a hand over the horse's soft mane.

With the boy's assistance, I climbed into the saddle. I'd ridden horses before, but never a creature such as this. The Zigilian stallions were huge, and though I was in awe of them, their size unnerved me too. Not only were they fast, but they had a reputation for being temperamental.

'Don't worry,' Cassius said. 'I've been assured that your horse has cantered this track many times. All you have to do is hold on to the reins.' He twisted in his saddle, his attention shifting to Aric. 'Since it's your first hunt, no one expects much from you. Just do your best to try and keep up.'

While the words were polite, I heard the challenge in them. So did Aric.

'Thank you, Your Highness,' he said, his face hardening, 'but that won't be a problem.'

Cassius raised a blond brow. 'You're a confident rider, then?'

'Confident enough.'

The prince smiled. 'Then perhaps you'd be interested in a race?'

Again, I tried to catch Aric's attention. But he was focused on Cassius, and the glint in the prince's eyes made me very, very nervous. 'What do you propose?'

Cassius waved a gloved hand. 'Nothing too dramatic,' he said easily. 'How about this: whoever reaches the herd of wild boar first wins.'

It sounded like a terrible idea. I was about to say so, but Aric beat me to it.

'Deal.'

'Good,' Cassius said, still smiling. He raised his voice to address the guards: 'Stay back. I don't want anyone interfering.'

A horn sounded as the dogs were released into the woods. Then Cassius and Aric urged their horses forward, and the race was on.

The Zigilian stallions moved like the wind. I quickly lost sight of Aric and Cassius as they burst into the forest, the Warriors and their mounts thundering behind them.

I galloped alone over fallen logs and along well-used paths, the baying of the hounds growing closer. My horse carried me faithfully through the trees, moving at a breakneck pace that made my heart race in exhilaration.

'Faster,' I cried, spurring the stallion on. 'Faster!'

I bolted into a clearing and the howling became deafening. I had a glimpse of Aric up ahead: he had beaten Cassius to the herd. But my pride was short-lived as a huge, tusked male launched itself at his leg.

Aric's stallion reared and his saddle lurched to one side.

I didn't even have the chance to scream before he fell, his head smacking the ground as he rolled to avoid the stallion's pounding hooves. I wanted to do *something* – to dismount and run to him, anything to help Aric as he shuffled backwards, trying to put some distance between himself and the grunting boar.

'Stay in position!' someone shouted.

It took all my willpower to remain where I was. My desperate gaze went to Cassius and the two other Warriors, each with spears in their hands. What were they waiting for? And why hadn't Aric been given a weapon? He was a Warrior too. Had it been because he was new to hunting, or—

Cassius threw his spear. It struck the first boar through the heart, and it fell quickly. I twisted to search for the others, but the guards were already taking aim, their spears launching through the air.

Once the animals were dead, I dismounted and raced to Aric's side. As hard as I'd tried to push my emotions down, to leave my past behind, it clearly wasn't enough. Because right now, my heart was screaming at me.

'Are you alright?' I asked frantically. 'Are you hurt?'

He blinked up at me dazedly. 'You look like an angel,' he said, and went limp in my arms.

CHAPTER FIFTY-FOUR

Mira

I'd thought I was beyond fear after the third Trial, beyond caring about anyone except myself. I was wrong.

Watching Aric fall was one of the worst moments of my life. Feeling him go still and limp in my arms – *that* was agony. It was torture almost beyond endurance.

He was left to recover in a private section of the infirmary, looked after by Cassius's personal physician. I knew that was supposed to make me feel better, a demonstration of the prince's regard. Somehow, it fell short.

Aric's shoulder was dislocated; he was lucky it hadn't been worse. According to the healer, a fall like that could easily have killed him. As it was, he was left with concussion and a recommendation for bed rest.

It was deemed an accident, and even I wasn't sure how it could have been anything else. So Aric hadn't been given a weapon – that could have been a simple oversight. And no one could have anticipated that he would fall out of his saddle. But still, I wondered.

'How are you feeling?'

'I'm fine,' Aric said, flustered. He could charge into battle and race against a prince, but he baulked at being fussed over. 'Mostly, I just feel foolish.'

'You should,' I said, sitting on the edge of the bed. 'What were you thinking, racing Cassius like that?'

'I wasn't,' he replied. 'Thinking, that is.'

'And you call *me* impulsive,' I said, trying to lighten the mood. Aric didn't smile.

Before I could say anything else, there was a faint knock on the door. Lillian peeked around the corner, her face filled with concern.

'Do you feel as bad as you look?' she said anxiously, taking in the bandages around Aric's shoulder.

'It's barely a scrape,' he reassured her. 'I keep trying to tell the healer that I'm fine, but she refuses to—'

'You're *not* fine,' Lillian said sternly, 'and the best thing for you right now is rest.' She paused, her gaze shifting to me for the first time. Her tone was frosty as she said, 'Do you mind giving us a moment, Mira?'

It would have been kinder if she'd yelled. Her strained politeness was horrible: in it, I heard everything she didn't say. Every second of Aric's pain that she held me responsible for.

I stepped out into the corridor, shutting the door and leaning against it.

As I did, I heard Aric say, 'That was harsh, Lil. It wasn't Mira's fault.'

'You wouldn't have been on that hunting trip if it wasn't for Mira, so I disagree,' she said sharply. 'I know you want to help her, but I think it would be healthier if you were away from the palace for a while.'

'I can't leave court. You know that. I'm one of Scarlett's guards—'

'If you asked the princess to reassign you, I think she would. Scarlett cares about you, even if you're too blind to see it.' Bitterness crept into Lillian's voice. 'She cares more than Mira seems to.'

'Mira has been through a lot,' Aric countered, but the words sounded flat even to me.

'It's time to stop making excuses for her,' Lillian said. 'A drowning person will pull you under if you try to help them. And Mira is drowning.'

'You're talking like she's a lost cause.'

'Maybe she is.' Lillian's voice turned pleading. 'Aric, I've already lost one brother. I've lost someone I considered a sister. I can't lose you, too.'

Closing my eyes, I let their words sink in. Let myself understand exactly how much I'd hurt the people I loved most.

I backed away before I could hear Aric's response. I'd already heard more than enough.

Court dinners were always tedious, but tonight was worse than usual. I silently endured all four courses, barely resisting the urge to follow the empress's example and drown myself in wine. I wondered if I was looking at my own future, a few years from now: a beautiful, empty shell, shackled to the emperor's side.

When I couldn't take it any longer, I stood. A few nobles glanced over from the banquet tables, but their focus quickly returned to eating, drinking, and socialising. No one else seemed to notice; Cassius and the emperor were in an intense discussion with the generals, and the empress was deliberately ignoring me.

I slipped carefully out of the banquet hall and into the small court-yard beyond. I couldn't face all those colourful, beautiful people, with their cold, assessing stares.

I especially couldn't face the prince.

I'd known I was risking a lot with Cassius, but Aric was right: this time, I really had gone too far. If I married him, he would have closer control of Kalure – with no reason to honour his word and give the Kalurians their independence. Not to mention what he might do to me. Cassius wouldn't have batted an eye at Odessa's execution, and they'd been betrothed since they were infants. He would care even less what happened to me if I played the game . . . and lost.

A flicker of movement drew my gaze across the courtyard, where Scarlett was watching me. 'I heard what happened to Aric,' she said, an edge to her voice.

'It was a hunting accident. I'm sure those happen often enough.'

'A hunting accident.' Scarlett's lips twitched. 'Let me give you some advice, Mira. Where royals are concerned, there are no such thing as accidents.'

'What do you mean?'

'I looked into it. The stable boy who saddled Aric's horse fled the castle immediately afterwards. Why would he do that unless he had something to hide?'

I would have liked to believe that Scarlett was wrong. That she'd made a mistake. But I felt the truth of her words in my bones. Cassius was the possessive type.

And in five days, I would be married to him.

What would happen to Aric *then*? Even if we stayed away from each other, would that be enough to protect him? Gods, if anything happened to Aric because of *me*—

I stopped the thought before it could form, refocusing on Scarlett. My *cousin*.

If I was going to escape Cassius's reach, if I was going to have any chance of getting free of this monstrous place, I would need to trust someone. And I wanted to trust her. I wanted to believe I had a family member I could rely on.

'You asked me to think about your offer,' I said, moving further into the courtyard. As I did, the sounds of the hall faded, leaving just me and Scarlett, and the soft trickling of a fountain. 'I'm ready to accept it. With a few alterations.'

Scarlett raised a brow. But she sank onto a stone bench and motioned for me to join her.

'I want to escape the court with Aric,' I said, perching on the edge of the bench. 'And for that, I need your help.'

The princess blinked. 'That's not exactly what I had in mind—'

'I don't care,' I said firmly. 'No more scheming and playing politics. I'm done. But this can still benefit you. You mentioned that you want Roran dead; if you help me get to Kalure, I'll take care of him for you.'

'You won't simply sail off into the sunset with Aric?' she asked dryly.

'I can't. I have the Kalurian people to think about, and I know a part of Aric will always want to avenge his brother. At least this way, we can deal with Roran together.'

'It's an interesting proposition,' Scarlett said at last, 'but it's not what I want from you. I want—'

'You want the same thing Cassius does. To use me to win yourself a throne.' When Scarlett didn't deny it, I continued, 'My absence can still help you do that. I'm sure it would suit your purposes just fine if Cassius's fiancée were to suddenly disappear – making him look like a fool to the court and ensuring he doesn't get his hands on Kalure. The less power he has, the better it is for you.'

Scarlett considered me in silence. 'And once Roran is dead?'

'I'll take my rightful place as Queen of Kalure,' I replied. 'Ready to make an alliance with the future empress of the Ravalian Empire.'

It was impossible to tell what Scarlett was thinking. For a moment, the only sound was the flowing fountain and the distant, muffled buzz of music and conversation.

Then Scarlett looked at me, and I knew I had her. But she held up a hand. 'I have a condition of my own. I would like you to speak with Darius. I think he can convince the resistance to strike against the palace.'

'As a diversion, you mean? So that Aric and I can make it out?'

'Not everything is about you,' she corrected with a small smile. 'An attack will increase your chances of escape, and Darius's. But more importantly, it will give me an opportunity to deal with my father and brother.'

I stared at her. 'Are you sure? That's quite a risk to take.'

'No risk, no reward,' she said, reminding me of the motto of the islanders who had entered the Trials.

Even so, the dangers didn't sit well with me. If Scarlett was discovered, she would be killed.

But it's her choice to make.

I pushed my complicated feelings aside. 'The resistance won't like this. They don't trust any members of the royal family.'

'Neither do you,' Scarlett said with a faint smile. 'But if you can be convinced to work with me, I feel certain the resistance will follow suit. At least for now, we all want the same thing.'

The princess didn't wait for a response. She strode through the courtyard and into the revelry beyond, leaving me staring after her.

It was risky, making a deal with a royal. Hadn't I learnt my lesson with Cassius?

But Scarlett's plan was more than tempting. It was also my best chance to get out of this mess.

It's my only *chance.*

CHAPTER FIFTY-FIVE

Mira

Victory sometimes required bold moves. Dangerous ones.

Adopting a confident stride, I rounded the corner and approached the two guards at the entrance to the dungeons. 'I'm here on Mask business,' I said, my heart pounding.

They looked me over, taking in my fighting leathers and ornate mask. Then the senior of the two shook his head.

'I wasn't informed of any official visits.'

'Do you really want to question Zandri on this?' I challenged. 'She won't be pleased to know one of her operatives was detained.'

The guards exchanged a look. Just as I'd hoped, the risk of Zandri's displeasure was enough to make them hesitate.

'Make it quick,' the older guard instructed.

I didn't thank him. I strode past without acknowledgement, thinking that even Zandri might have been impressed by my haughty demeanour.

The dungeons were dank and cold, the cells windowless and dim. I shivered as I passed each one, darting a quick glance inside. None of the figures looked up at my presence, and none of them was Darius.

Each step into the darkness made me increasingly uneasy. The longer I took, the more suspicious the guards would become. I needed to make this a quick trip, but down here, surrounded by criminals the world had forgotten, it felt like time had ceased to exist.

I quickened my pace. The sound of my boots against the stone caused some of the prisoners to stir, but none seemed lucid. I couldn't imagine what it must be like for them, being left to waste away for months or years. I didn't *want* to imagine.

'Wait.' The word was quiet, so faint that I could almost have imagined it. 'Please.'

I turned slowly towards the sound. A young woman climbed to her feet and wrapped her hands around the bars of her cell.

'Please,' she said again.

I knew who that voice belonged to. Even hoarse from disuse, there was a quality to it – a richness that only nobles could possess. Although I never would have expected to hear Odessa Tiran beg.

'Kasmira.' Her eyes were red from crying, though there was no trace of tears now. There was only desperate, heart-wrenching hope. 'What happened to my parents? No one will tell me. No one will tell me anything.'

'They . . .' I swallowed, feeling like my throat was filled with glass. The hope guttered out in Odessa's eyes, leaving them blank and empty. 'It was quick,' I said, the only comfort I could give her.

Odessa nodded, but it was the automatic action of someone whose mind had gone somewhere very far away. She released her hold on the bars, sinking to her knees. Her white dress pooled around her; even coated with dirt and grime, she managed to maintain her dignity.

'I'm so sorry,' I breathed.

'I laughed,' Odessa whispered, and for an instant, I feared that her mind had snapped. Then her eyes met mine, filled with unexpected gravity. 'I laughed, during your mother's execution. My friends were talking about something else, and I . . . I barely noticed. Not until you started screaming.'

I stared at her, unsure what to say. What *did* you say, to something like that? Odessa had callously watched while my world was ripped apart – and now I was responsible for destroying hers.

'It doesn't matter now,' I said firmly, unsure which of us I was trying to convince.

Odessa smiled, but there was no warmth there. Only resignation. 'Does it ever go away?'

I knew what she meant. The pain. The grief. The *anger*.

'No,' I admitted. 'It doesn't.'

To my surprise, the smile stayed on Odessa's lips. It was sad, but it was real. 'Thank you for stopping.'

Those words – and the gratitude in them – nearly broke me. They nearly made me confess everything that I'd done, every terrible outcome I'd been responsible for.

Instead, I forced myself to keep walking. I made it a few steps before her voice called me back.

'The only thing worse than being irrelevant to Cassius,' Odessa murmured, 'is being of interest to him.'

I paused, surprised by the warning. And in that moment, I thought I understood.

'You're scared of him.'

Odessa's face was little more than a shadowy outline in the gloom. 'Only a fool wouldn't be. You don't see it now, but you will.'

I already did, but I didn't say so. A chill that had nothing to do with the cold snaked down my spine. Even as I left Odessa's cell far behind, her warning lingered. Reminding me why I was here – and what I had to lose if I failed.

The tunnel widened into a larger cavern. It was clearly built for a singular purpose, with tools of torture laid out on iron tables.

I avoided looking at them as I approached Darius's cell. His shoulders stiffened at the sound of my approach.

'Darius?'

He looked up, drinking me in like a man starved of human contact. When he moved towards the bars, I heard his breath rattle in his lungs, as if he'd been left in the cold and damp too long.

'You can't be here,' he said, every word an effort. 'It's too much of a risk.'

'Let me worry about that.'

Even as I said it, though, unease ate at me. I'd been hoping to be back in ten minutes, but I'd spent five walking here and five with Odessa. I was already out of time.

'I have a proposition for you,' I continued, trying to keep the worry off my face.

The barest hint of a smile curved Darius's mouth, some of that old confidence entering his expression. 'I'm all ears.'

'I want to escape on the governor's ship, along with you, Jadis and Elian.' I lowered my voice even further. 'But I need the resistance to stage a diversion while we make our move. And I need your contacts to get a message to the Kalurians, to tell them we're coming.'

Darius considered me for a moment. 'The odds of success aren't high,' he said at last. 'It's more likely you'll end up in an adjoining cell.'

I folded my arms. 'I'm going to try either way. At least this way, you have a shot at survival, too.'

He smiled a little, as if at my daring. 'You've done well to get this far. Still, there's a world of difference between sneaking into the dungeons and helping a prisoner escape.'

He hesitated, and I could see him scrutinising my masked face. My Ravalian-style clothing.

'They killed my mother,' I said in a low voice. 'I'm not one of them, and I never will be. This is the last chance for all of us to be free.'

Finally, he nodded. Wetting his lips, he said, 'I'll give you a coded phrase, so Jadis knows this order is coming from me. But you'll have to trust her to coordinate this. We'll need more people if we're going to succeed.'

It should have been good news, but the more people who were involved, the more that could go wrong. And no matter their goals, the resistance was made up of criminals – men like Wyatt, who had betrayed us to the emperor's soldiers.

Darius's long-ago words came rushing back to me: *How much is a promise from a criminal really worth?*

Perhaps he saw my doubt, because he asked, 'Can you think of a better alternative?'

'No,' I said, after a pause. 'No, I can't.'

'Well then,' Darius said with a sly quirk of his lips. 'I guess we'll just have to trust each other.'

CHAPTER FIFTY-SIX

Scarlett

Though I took no satisfaction in Aric's pain, he would live, and his accident had finally convinced Mira to sever her ill-fated alliance with Cassius.

No matter how I looked at it, his hunting accident had been a stroke of genius.

But it left me with one last mess to clean up.

I strode through the streets, relaxed and unhurried. Thanks to my mother, I had been able to track the stableboy's purchases – though I had covered most of the Higher Districts by now. I rolled the coin in my palm as I changed course, entering the Lower Districts. Sure enough, it began to warm as I drew near one of the pleasure houses.

He's certainly made the most of his newfound wealth, I thought dryly. At least his final hours had been satisfying ones.

Entering the brothel, I did my best to keep the distaste from my face. Plenty of my father's Warriors and nobles visited establishments like this on a regular basis, but I had never thought that I would be one of them.

'Are you looking for a male or female?' a bored woman asked, not glancing up from counting coins. Beside her, a guard stood watch.

'Both,' I replied, finally capturing her attention.

She took a swig from the goblet in her left hand and focused her heavy-lidded eyes on me. 'That will be an additional cost,' she warned.

Frankly, I would pay to be rid of her – and this place. 'How much?'

I watched her debate, taking in the fine clothing I wore – though not so fine as to arouse suspicion.

'A silver piece,' she settled on, licking her thin red lips.

I handed it over without hesitation, suppressing a smile as the madam shifted on her feet. Clearly, she was regretting not asking for more – though one silver piece was more than generous. Especially considering the death magic in my veins, and the destruction I could cause if I decided to take what I wanted.

'I'm meeting a friend here,' I said, providing a brief description. 'He should already be with someone.'

'We don't usually—'

Another silver piece silenced her protest.

'A pleasure doing business with you,' she said, and nodded to the guard, who escorted me through the brothel – past shadowy cavorting shapes on the other side of the thin curtains, with their guttural moans and breathy sighs.

The guard parted a strip of purple linen, and I recognised the stableboy's sandy hair, his gangly figure intertwined with a female one. I moved inside, conscious of the curtain falling into place behind me.

I saw the exact moment the boy realised who I was. He straightened with a yelp, reaching for his discarded trousers.

'Leave us,' I told the girl. 'I've paid for this time. Your services are no longer required.'

With one last glance at the stableboy, she scampered from view.

I waited until the boy was dressed before turning. 'You couldn't have spent my coin on something else?'

He must not have heard the amusement in my voice, because he looked terrified.

Good, I thought with some satisfaction. *You* should *be terrified of me.*

'I did what you asked.' His voice was strong, but his hands were trembling. 'I loosened the saddle—'

'You did very well,' I said gently, removing my hood.

His tremble worsened as I dropped the illusion of Sabine's face. When I had visited the stables, I had disguised my features.

But I wasn't hiding now.

'Y-Your Highness.' He looked wildly around him, searching for a way to escape. 'I won't tell anyone. I swear I won't. I'll book passage to the Elusive Isles, and—'

I reached for my coin purse. Despite his fear, his eyes were drawn to it – and the greed in them was tiresomely predictable.

'To cover your travels,' I said, holding out a gold piece.

He didn't even pause before reaching for it, his hand brushing mine. Touching my skin.

I closed my eyes as the black veins surged, revelling in the sensation of them moving from me and into him. When it was done, I felt warmer – and emptier. This time, there was nothing left. No death magic, no comforting ice. I had used up everything I had taken from Danica.

But that was fine. Now that I knew I could invite death into me, I was sure I could find another body somewhere – but there was no rush. I didn't need death magic to kill my father.

The boy's voice was little more than a gurgle, but it was enough to make me open my eyes.

Dispassionately, I noticed that he was on his knees. His skin was so dark that it looked charred – a bit like Danica's body, after it had been consumed by Mira's fire. It was strange to realise that our methods of killing had that much in common.

What a force we could have been, I thought with a trace of regret. If Mira hadn't decided to run and had just accepted my deal, then perhaps everything could've been different.

'H-help—'

I stepped towards him. One step, but it silenced him like a blade to the throat. 'Don't try to talk,' I told him, taking hold of his shoulders and laying him back. 'It's almost over.'

I stayed with him until he stopped breathing, and the veins disappeared, leaving smooth, unblemished skin. For all intents and purposes, he appeared untouched.

Perhaps the madam would believe he'd died of natural causes. Either way, it didn't matter. She wouldn't want to make a fuss over his death; it would be bad for business.

I left the brothel behind, my mind already on what was to come. Zandri had wanted to use Mira to kill the emperor and then discard her afterwards – but so much of that plan relied on Mira's cooperation, and there were too many moving pieces: Aric, Lillian, Cassius, even the court itself.

My plan was so much better, and I had no doubt Zandri would agree. During the wedding, not only would I be able to deal with Emperor Kalias, but I would deal with them all: Mira, Cassius, and the resistance. Everyone who could possibly threaten my rule – except for Roran, but he was in the North and out of reach.

For now.

I turned resolutely away from the Lower Districts, striding back towards the palace and my birthright.

The moment Mira had decided to reclaim Kalure and become a queen, she had left me no other option than to destroy her – as thoroughly and ruthlessly as I would my father and brothers. I would never allow her so much power. Never trust in vague promises to protect my throne – and my life – especially when I knew how much Mira despised the Ravalian Empire.

No – there could only be one queen, and it was something of a relief to face that truth. To stop pretending there could be anything more between us than blood and death.

It was always going to come down to this, I told myself as I walked. Mira or me.

And no one's life meant more to me than my own.

CHAPTER FIFTY-SEVEN

Scarlett

I was drawn to the battlements. From this height, it was easy to imagine that the palace and city below belonged entirely to me.

Soon enough, there would be no need to imagine.

'I thought I might find you here.'

The melodic voice was instantly recognisable, but I didn't turn. The moment I did, I would have to face the consequences of my decision. A decision that could cost me my life, and would definitely cost me *him*.

'I've been thinking about what you said.' The words tasted acidic in my throat. 'About endings.'

Though our conversation had happened long ago, I knew he hadn't forgotten. Whatever he'd Seen had rattled him – it must have, otherwise he wouldn't have mentioned it. When it came to me, I had the sense that he feared thinking about the future at all.

And now that I had decided to act, I understood why he would be rattled. I might not be able to see the future, but there were a thousand ways my plan could go wrong. Even if it didn't, bloodshed was a certainty.

Severin moved closer, his sandalwood scent drifting to me on the faint breeze. 'And what did you decide?'

'I wish there was another way,' I said, finally turning to look at him. 'There isn't.'

Severin studied me for a moment. Though his expression didn't shift, I knew I'd disappointed him. 'Is this you talking, or is it *her*?'

I didn't answer. I didn't want to admit the truth – that this wasn't Zandri's plan. It was *mine.*

For a moment, we simply stared at each other. The breeze ruffled his dark hair, the setting sun playing across his exposed skin. He was as devastatingly handsome as always; I should have known something so perfect was never meant to be mine.

'I know you've met with Zandri multiple times this week,' Severin continued. 'The guards talk.'

'She's my mother. That's hardly unusual.'

'It is when she makes you so uncomfortable.' His voice was soft, contemplative. 'You used to avoid her whenever possible. And after everything I told you . . .'

'It doesn't matter,' I said, more sharply than I'd intended. 'Circumstances change. *People* change.'

'Yes,' he murmured. 'They do.' His tattooed face hardened. 'Aric could have died.'

I closed my eyes briefly. With his Sight, I'd known this was a possibility, but I'd still hoped to avoid this conversation.

'I told Mira it was Cassius.'

'I know.' His voice was lethally quiet.

'I did it for *you.*' I reached for Severin, but at the last moment I thought better of it and let my hand fall. 'Cassius saw us together in the greenhouse. If he'd exposed our relationship, you could have been executed. Didn't you See any of this?'

'No,' Severin said dangerously, 'because you'd already decided to act. All I Saw was you bribing that stableboy.'

I tried to summon some remorse. It didn't come.

What I had said to Severin was true – but it wasn't the whole truth. I had done it for myself as much as him, and it was difficult to regret my choice when it had destroyed Mira and Cassius's partnership.

Severin pulled me to him, his face suddenly inches from mine. His gaze was intent – searching.

And then his lips descended on mine.

Our bodies melded together with a passion I had never experienced with anyone else. When Severin kissed me, when he touched me, it was like he was trying to hold on to something precious and intangible – like smoke slipping through his fingers.

He poured everything into that kiss – not just emotions, but memories. I tasted the first time we met on the ice, slow and tentative and sweet, and then the times after that, when he became my protector, my confidant. The kiss grew more familiar, more heated. My fingers hooked around his vest, drawing him closer – like I had a hundred times before.

Except this time felt different. *Final.*

Just as I had the thought, he pulled back. His gaze was intense, and his breathing was uneven, just like mine. His kiss had been devouring, and I could still taste his love, his fear, his desperation.

'There's always another way, Scar. *Always.*'

Any doubt I felt dissolved, replaced by frustration. He'd once spoken of contenders – well, he could be a contender if he wanted. He could be fighting at my side for real power, using his abilities to help rather than cautioning me at every turn.

'What would you have me do, Severin? Remain a pawn, to be sold into marriage and shipped away to some insignificant island kingdom?'

'Those are your choices to make,' he said. 'But you once asked me what kind of ending I saw. And Scarlett, I saw a bloody one.'

My hand brushed the necklace he'd given me. *It's not a ring,* he'd said, *but perhaps you can think of it as a promise. Because I want to be with you, Scar. There's nothing I want more.*

Except that promise was meaningless, because I would lose him either way. And if I didn't go through with this plan, I would lose far more than just Severin. I would lose my mother, my freedom, and any chance I had at the throne – at the power and respect that came with it.

I wrenched my arm from his, hardening my heart against the temptation he presented.

'No revolution happens without bloodshed,' I said coolly. 'It isn't my fault you don't have the stomach for court politics.'

Severin regarded me in silence. I had always seen a better version of myself reflected in his eyes.

Right now, I saw my mother.

With as much confidence as I could muster, I swept past him. This time, he didn't try to stop me.

Zandri was as striking as the blood-red sunset, and equally unforgiving. Her features seemed sharper than usual, cosmetics deepening her crimson lips and black, bottomless eyes.

'Are you nervous about tomorrow?' she asked, entering my bedchamber and locking the door behind her.

'A little,' I admitted, turning back to the vanity mirror. A soft breeze played through my hair, like a lover's caress. *I don't want to disappoint you*, I thought but didn't say.

Zandri had been so pleased when I told her my plan. The way she had looked at me in that moment, the fierce appreciation burning in her eyes . . . it was the closest she had come to looking at me with true affection.

For the first time, I had truly believed that my mother was proud of me – for who I was, rather than who I *could* be.

'You're ready,' Zandri said, crossing the room. 'I'm certain of it.'

'And if I fail?'

'You won't,' she said – an assurance and a command.

I wished I could be so certain, but my mother seemed to take my silence for agreement.

Zandri moved closer, the black silk of her gown rustling. She rarely attended court functions, but tonight she would go in my place – making my excuses while I finalised last-minute details with the resistance. They had been surprisingly receptive to my plan – and my involvement. It almost seemed a shame that tomorrow would end with them dead or captured.

'I have waited so long for this moment,' she said at last, her voice thick with emotion. 'For almost two decades, everything I've done has been in service to you. To teach you how to survive – and to give you the life that you deserve. But I've always known that in the end, you would have to be the one to claim your crown. And I truly believe you will.'

Zandri gathered me into a surprisingly warm embrace. When she pulled back, the intensity of her belief was almost frightening. Her dark eyes glittered with a fanatical certainty I had never seen before.

'All you need to do, Scarlett,' she murmured, gently cupping my chin with her hand, 'is reach out and take it.'

I glanced down at my bracelet, the blood ruby vivid and gleaming in its centre – like it was eagerly awaiting the bloodshed to come.

You once asked me what kind of ending I saw. And, Scarlett, I saw a bloody one.

For a moment, I wished I was noble enough to turn and walk away. I wished I could tell my mother that I didn't want to rule over a court of monsters and death. I wished I could lie.

But I couldn't. And I didn't.

Instead, I nodded and stood. As if it was a signal, the raven flew through the open window and perched on my bare shoulder. It blinked at me in the mirror, almost like it was waiting for an instruction.

And my mother smiled.

CHAPTER FIFTY-EIGHT

Mira

'Are you going to tell me what we're doing?' Aric asked, keeping pace with me as we left the Higher Districts behind.

I swallowed down sudden apprehension. I had visited Aric often over the past few days – at the infirmary and afterwards, when he was released back to the Order residences. Trying to show him how much he meant to me without bombarding him with plans and declarations. But now that it was the eve of my wedding, I was out of time.

'You told me once,' I said softly, 'that you would run, if it meant having a life together. That you would leave all of this behind.'

Aric went very still. 'What are you saying?'

I looked around, but no one was watching us. Focusing my attention back on Aric, my eyes went to his bandaged shoulder. He would make a full recovery – *this* time. But next time he might not be so lucky. No one would last long in the court if a royal wanted them gone, and if Aric stayed, I would lose him. *Lillian* would lose him.

Unless I could give him a strong enough reason to walk away.

'I'm saying that if you still feel that way, I'd like to leave with you – and Lillian too.' I paused, then admitted, 'I've already spoken to her, and she's willing to come with us. But only if we all leave together.'

Aric studied me intently. If he was looking for hesitation, he wouldn't find any. I meant every word.

'What changed your mind?' he asked finally.

'When I watched you fall . . . I can't lose you, Aric. You or Lillian.'

You're my family, I wanted to say. *You're my family, and I love you.*

Maybe he saw that thought in my face, because the guardedness left his own. A slow smile upturned his lips, thawing whatever ice lingered between us. He reached up, tucking a strand of hair behind my ear.

'*There* you are,' he said, his voice low and intimate. 'I've missed you, Mira.'

I leant my forehead against his in answer. But all too soon, Aric was drawing back and returning his attention to our surroundings.

'Since we're all the way out here,' he said, his gaze sweeping over the dimly lit streets, 'I assume you have a plan?'

I filled him in, explaining about Scarlett's offer, my ambitions for Kalure and my recent interactions with Jadis. Aric's face hardened when I mentioned visiting Darius in the dungeons, but he said nothing except, 'Are you sure Jadis didn't name a location to meet?'

'I'm sure. All the note said was: *Lower Districts, midnight. We'll find you.*'

We approached a row of dim, cramped shops. When I dared a glance inside the apothecary, I saw all manner of strange concoctions and lethal-looking knives. Faint light filtered in from underneath a door near the back, where plants crawled across the wall.

As I turned away, I caught a glimpse of someone watching me. Aric stiffened at my side, his hand dropping to the hilt of his sword. I reached for my dagger but stopped when the woman removed her hood, revealing sharp eyes and braided dark hair.

'Took you long enough,' Jadis remarked. 'I've been following you for two blocks.'

'Why didn't you approach us earlier?'

'I wanted to wait until you were deeper in the Lower Districts, somewhere we wouldn't be observed.' Jadis's eyes flicked to the dark apothecary. 'Madam Mandrakes isn't the kind of place you should be so interested in. It has a bad reputation, even under new management.'

'Who said I was interested?'

Jadis only snorted. 'If you want to get rid of someone, there are better ways of going about it. Safer ways.' Her attention slid to Aric, appraising his fighter's build and stance. 'Kain spoke about you often. Glad to have you with us.'

Aric tensed at the mention of his brother, but he nodded politely back at her. 'Glad to be here.'

It was hard to keep up with Jadis's swift pace as she strode through the streets, and sometimes, we came close to losing her entirely. But then she stopped in front of a smooth section of wall and raised her fist to knock.

Aric looked perplexed, at least until he saw the door materialise. Then his expression transformed into awe.

We climbed the steps in silence. It was surreal being back here, and for a second, my mother was vivid in my mind: laughing with the Kalurian governor, a dagger twirling casually in her fingers.

And there was a female figure sitting in her place, opposite the grim-faced Elian. But it wasn't my mother.

Scarlett looked up at our arrival. Even in the dim glow of the lamps, her wine-red hair and luminous blue eyes were unmistakable. 'No trouble, I trust?'

'A court Warrior was tracking them,' Jadis replied, 'but I lured him away easily enough.'

'A court Warrior?' I repeated, shocked.

Scarlett leant back in her chair. 'Cassius has had you followed for weeks now. Meeting in person was always going to be a risk, but I suppose it can't be helped.'

Jadis eyed the princess warily as she claimed the seat next to her brother. Aric and I followed, sitting opposite each other.

'Is anyone else coming?' Aric asked.

'I don't trust anyone else to know the details,' Jadis said. 'But don't worry – we've been working on infiltrating the wedding ever since Mira reached out. When it comes time to act, all our people will be in position.'

'You want to act *during* the wedding?'

Amusement softened Scarlett's face. 'There's no need to look so worried, Mira. You won't actually have to marry Cassius.'

'The princess is right,' Jadis broke in. 'The plan is for you and Lillian to leave before the ceremony starts. You'll need to get ready together so the attendants aren't suspicious, but we'll organise an escape route from the palace to a carriage. Aric will wait for you there.'

I knew Aric wouldn't like that even before he said, 'Surely I'd be more help elsewhere. You're going to need all the muscle you can get.'

'You're still injured,' Jadis said, in a tone that left no room for argument. 'It's best that you stay by the carriage. When Mira and Lillian arrive, the driver will take you safely to the docks and away from the action.'

'And what about Darius?' Aric frowned. 'I don't see how a break-out of that magnitude is possible. The dungeons are a fortress.'

'It's already planned,' Jadis said evenly. 'I'll subdue the guards while Elian looks after Darius. With Scarlett's magic and the diversion in the throne room, it shouldn't prove too difficult.'

Aric opened his mouth, probably to question some other aspect of the plan, but I spoke before he could. 'I want to break Odessa out, too.'

'Odessa *Tiran*? The general's daughter?'

'Yes.'

Jadis's brows drew together. 'How do you know she's sympathetic to our cause?'

'I don't,' I admitted. 'But her parents were executed in the arena. I doubt she has any love for Cassius or his father.'

Scarlett looked as though she thought me very simple-minded. 'Do you really think Odessa would do the same for you, if your roles were reversed?'

No. No, we both knew that she wouldn't. And maybe that made me a fool, but—

'I won't leave her behind.'

Jadis studied me for a long moment. Then, finally, she nodded. 'In this instance, I think that an exception can be made. But *only* in this instance.' Her dark eyes lingered on mine, filled with warning.

I nodded, and Jadis released her stare.

'How do you plan on getting past the soldiers at the docks?' Aric asked. 'Even the merchant ships are heavily patrolled.'

'We've bribed the men we need and replaced the others. All I need from you,' Jadis said, eyeing me and Aric, 'is to stick to the plan. The last thing we need are any unexpected surprises.'

'I think we can manage that,' Aric replied, and Jadis's gaze settled on me.

'Yes,' I agreed, though I had no intention of following her directive. 'No surprises. I promise.'

It was late by the time I returned to the palace, my last-minute purchase heavy in the hidden folds of my dress.

I'd been worried that I wouldn't have the opportunity to slip away, but that wasn't the case. It had come together perfectly: Aric had suggested we take separate routes back to avoid suspicion, and the others had been too busy with final planning to tail me, leaving no one to try and stop me when I doubled back to Madam Mandrakes. No one to try and talk me out of what I was planning to do.

Turning the corner to my chambers, I nearly stopped in my tracks. Aric was there, standing right in front of the bronze doors. I blinked, wondering if I was imagining it. But no – I couldn't even *imagine* something this foolhardy.

'Your Highness,' he said, with a secretive smile. If he noticed my lateness, it didn't show.

I only nodded back, not trusting myself to speak in case servants were nearby. Servants that could easily report Aric's presence to the emperor – or to Cassius. What was he *thinking?*

The doors closed behind me, blocking my view of Aric. But he remained at the forefront of my thoughts as I crossed through to my bedchamber, already knowing that sleep would prove impossible.

My attendants had lit the candles, casting everything in a flickering glow. I settled on a divan near the gauzy curtains, which were fluttering lightly in a floral breeze. A book was discarded on the low table – one of many Cassius had gifted me, about politics and history. I stared at the words, but couldn't take them in. My mind was consumed with the dangers and possibilities that tomorrow would bring.

After a while, I gave up and approached the canopied bed, where my attendants had laid out a long nightgown of white silk. The balmy night air played across my skin as I removed my street clothes and stepped into it.

I was so preoccupied trying to do up the laces that I didn't notice the door open. Only the soft footfalls made me turn, squinting through the semi-darkness—

A warm, calloused hand brushed my shoulder blades. 'Let me.'

My heart leapt into my throat at Aric's touch, and my swallow was audible. I was suddenly very conscious of his presence behind me, his fingers pressing against my neck and leaving goosebumps in their wake.

'You can't be here.' The words left my lips like a gasp as he did up the laces – laces that he could easily undo, sending the flimsy silk falling to the floor. 'It's too risky. If you're discovered—'

Taking hold of my arms, Aric turned me so that I was facing him. Staring up at him.

The candlelight turned his golden-brown eyes molten, making it difficult to think. To remember why this was a terrible idea.

'They'd kill you,' I breathed, as his hands rose to cup my face.

'I don't care,' he said, and kissed me.

At the first touch of his lips, my body came alive. He was gentle, almost tentative, and I sensed the question in his kiss. It was a question with only one right answer.

My hands threaded through his soft hair, drawing him to me. Every brush of his hands, every breath, was achingly familiar.

But I pulled away, folding my arms across my breasts, barely covered by the sheer material of the nightgown. My stomach was twisted into knots. What would Aric say if he knew my plans? If he knew the full reason I wanted to run?

He studied me intently, reading me far too well. 'What is it?'

'I'm just nervous about leaving,' I said, not meeting his stare.

'It's more than that.' Aric's gaze sharpened as he looked at me. 'What are you up to, Mira?'

'Who says I'm up to anything?' I retorted, forcing a smile that he didn't return.

'If you're considering backing out of this, I need to know. It's not just our lives at stake, Mira. It's Lillian's, too.'

'Lillian won't be in any danger,' I said, but I felt a shiver of anxiety at the thought. 'By the time the ceremony starts, she'll be out of harm's way. Jadis promised she would be.'

'Mira,' Aric said firmly, 'I know you want revenge against the emperor. I know a part of you doesn't want to give that up. But you have to tell me right now: are you really willing to walk away?'

'I want to be with you,' I said, which wasn't quite the same thing.

He didn't press further, but I could tell he wanted to.

'I love you,' he said instead. 'I love you so much it hurts.'

He had never said those words to me before, though I knew he would have professed his love sooner, if I'd let him. If I'd been able to hear it.

All those months we'd lost to revenge . . .

Suddenly, a dam of emotion was unleashed. I hadn't cried since I'd killed the governor. I hadn't thought I was capable of it.

But I was crying now.

Aric reached for me wordlessly. He held me as my body shook, as I clung to him with clawing, desperate hands.

'I'm so sorry,' I gasped, and I didn't know what I was apologising for – only that I had to say the words, that I had to get them *out*—

'It's okay, Mira.' Aric's embrace tightened, holding me even closer. Holding me together. 'Everything is going to be okay.'

And, for the first time in a long time, I thought that maybe it would be.

I didn't know what expression I wore when I finally met his gaze, but whatever it was, it made Aric go still. He looked at me with such intensity, such tenderness, that I felt like he was seeing into my soul.

Tentatively, reverently, he wiped a tear from my cheek. For a second, we only stared at each other.

Then my eyes dropped to his lips. He'd kissed me earlier, but this felt different. If I closed the distance between us now, I knew there would be no going back.

I was standing on the edge of a cliff, and it was up to me to decide whether to jump.

As if from a lifetime ago, my mother's words returned to me. *That kind of love . . . I hope you experience it one day, Mira. But perhaps it's better if you don't. It can be a curse.*

I threw caution to the wind—

And hurled myself off the precipice.

There was something euphoric about free-falling. I surrendered to the sensation, losing myself in the feel of Aric's lips, his hands, his body.

His closeness was exhilarating. Maddening.

Not enough.

It wasn't anywhere near enough.

I unbuttoned his tunic and pushed it off his shoulders, exploring his muscular chest, glistening golden in the dim light. Running my hand down across his stomach, I undid his leather breeches and watched as Aric stepped out of them.

My breathing went ragged – from adrenaline, not nerves. Whatever nerves I might have felt were gone, extinguished by the passion in Aric's eyes. No one had ever looked at me the way he did – like I was everything to him. Like I was his entire world.

Without breaking eye contact, I lifted my nightgown over my head. I watched him swallow. Take me in with a burning gaze.

And I watched him lose patience with just *looking*.

Pulling me down onto the bed, Aric trailed scorching kisses along my throat. Then he shifted on top of me, the warmth and hardness of his body pressing against mine. His hand ghosted up my thigh, explorative at first, until—

He swallowed my gasp with his lips. My back arched and I pressed against him, filled with a kind of desperation I had no name for. And still he kept touching me, filling me with a fire that kept building, building, building—

It was torturous when he moved his hand. I was aching, burning, *wanting*.

I wanted him *now*. I wanted him more than I'd ever wanted anything.

'Aric,' I breathed, as I wrapped my legs around his back. Drawing him more fully against me. Into me.

He was gentle – so, so gentle, allowing me time to adjust, to become used to the sudden feeling of fullness, the brief pinch of pain. I could see how difficult it was for him not to move, but he kept his eyes on mine, watching my reactions.

'More,' I told him, moving my hips.

My head fell back as he obliged, the pain transforming into something else. Rapture.

And as our bodies fused together, becoming one, I was filled with a surety I'd never experienced before. A rightness.

I love you, too.

I wasn't sure if I thought the words or said them, but they were deafening in my mind. They were echoed in every caress, every loving touch of our lips, every laboured breath.

Every beat of my racing heart.

CHAPTER FIFTY-NINE

Scarlett

The gown was a masterpiece. With a fitted bodice and crimson tiered skirts, it made me feel like the empress Zandri had always intended me to be. Tilting my head to admire the seamstress's work, I was reminded of the old stories – back when the Sorceress roamed the earth, enchanting and punishing mortals as she desired.

And I would have to be every inch the ruthless Sorceress today, if I had any hope of seeing this through.

'I finally managed to get you out of black,' Lillian said appreciatively.

'And into Ravalian colours,' I said, with a practised twist to my bottom lip – as if the red and gold bothered me.

'Well,' Lillian said with forced lightness, 'it's not for long.' The seamstress motioned towards the vanity mirror with a delicate hand. 'Take a seat. I'll fix your hair.'

I followed the instruction, fighting to conceal my impatience. Every second I remained in Lillian's presence was a risk – albeit a calculated one. Thankfully, I had spent months observing Mira. So long as I took care with my words and expressions, there was no reason for Lillian to become suspicious.

Still, it was hard not to react to the oddness of seeing Mira's features reflected back at me in the mirror.

The top half of my dark hair was twisted into a bun, the rest straight down my back. Though the attendants had done a decent job, they had left out one crucial detail.

I tensed when Lillian reached for the hair stick, cursing myself when she paused. The seamstress frowned at the object in her hands, which was more like a blade than simple ornamentation. But she slid the hair stick through my bun without further hesitation.

'Stunning,' Lillian pronounced. 'The court would have been envious.'

I nodded but didn't reply. I crossed over to the window without speaking, relieved to leave my cousin's reflection behind. It brought up too many memories – uneasy reminders of what could have been.

But it was too late for doubts now. I had already ensured that Aric would be at the wedding – and that Mira wouldn't. *There's been a change in plans,* I'd told her – a lie I'd practised until it sounded natural even to me. *The breakout is going ahead sooner than expected; Jadis wants you down at the docks. Aric and Lillian are there already.*

Mira hadn't even questioned it. Somehow, that was the hardest part – how easily she had put her trust in me.

'You're doing the right thing,' Lillian said, in that irritatingly earnest voice of hers. 'I know it might not feel like it, Mira, but you are. And I'm so proud of you.'

My shoulders stiffened as I gazed in the direction of the city – where colourful crowds would be packing the streets, waiting eagerly to hear the wedding bells toll.

'We should leave now,' Lillian continued, 'before someone comes to check on you. It's almost time for the ceremony to begin.'

'I know,' I said, but I didn't turn. 'Go to the carriage and wait with your brother. I'll be right behind you.'

'We agreed to leave together.'

'There's one last thing I have to do first.'

'For *once*, Mira,' Lillian pleaded, 'just keep things simple. We don't have time to—'

A knock sounded at the door. Before either of us could say, 'Come in,' it opened.

The prince presented a striking image, his crimson outfit contrasting perfectly with his light hair and solid gold crown. Lillian acknowledged his arrival with a deep curtsy, but he ignored her. His dark blue eyes were fixed on me. For once, they were absent of the petty hatred I associated with my younger brother.

Because this wasn't my brother.

Lillian shot me a worried glance, but the moment I threaded my arm through Zandri's, my nerves disappeared. As we made our way through the halls and down the central staircase, I felt the stirrings of triumph. *This* was what it felt like to be united with my mother – this thrilling sense of certainty. Of power.

And I knew that together, we could do the impossible. We could claim an empire.

The towering doors groaned open, and there they all were: the nobles who had sneered at my face and whispered behind their hands. The throne room was filled with my father's sycophants, all eager to watch his latest victory unfold.

Instead, they would bear witness to mine.

Amongst the gathered resistance soldiers, I caught a glimpse of Aric – his horrified gaze fixed on me and Lillian. I tensed, wondering if he would do something noble and idiotic – like try to stop the wedding.

But Aric believed that Jadis had trusted him with a monumental responsibility: coordinating the diversion that would allow Darius to be freed from the dungeons. He wouldn't risk the entire operation, and Mira and Lillian's lives, by acting impulsively. No – even now, I could see him recalculating, turning to murmur something to the rebels around him.

I would just have to hope that Aric waited to act – long enough for me to do what was necessary.

I watched as Lillian reluctantly took her place on the dais, alongside the other bridesmaids. I hadn't intended to involve her in any of this, but Lillian's presence added further legitimacy to my masquerade. Once this was done, no one would have reason to doubt Mira's treason – and I couldn't afford even the slightest shred of doubt. Mira had become my enemy the moment I had donned her face, and she would have to be dealt with as ruthlessly as anyone else who posed a threat to my survival.

Trumpets rang out, announcing our approach. Zandri's grip tightened on my arm, filled with unspoken warnings. Both our lives hung in the balance now.

Still, I found myself smiling as I passed the Maesteri delegation, instantly recognisable in their fine blue-green tunics. I wondered how many of them – if *any* – would survive the carnage and return home to their prince. The prince I would never have to marry.

All too soon Zandri and I were climbing the dais steps, to where the emperor stood in front of his throne.

'We are here,' he began, 'to witness a joining between my son, Prince Cassius Valerian, and his fiancée, Princess Kasmira Volaris. A marriage that will unite not just man and woman, but also Kalure and Ravalia.'

I knelt in front of the throne and angled my head down. Bowing before my father one last time.

Emperor Kalias was still speaking, but his voice was unimportant. White noise.

I didn't pay attention until I heard the final word: *rise*.

I straightened, staring into my father's cruel face. He had allowed me to keep his name, but he hadn't done it out of kindness. He had never valued me – not as anything more than a way of controlling Zandri and securing a useful alliance through my future husband. But I had learnt from him all the same. I had always been a better student than his sons.

Kalias reached for my hand, as the ceremony dictated. For a brief, sentimental moment, I allowed the contact, imagining that the touch was one of affection.

Then I took my father's wrist and *twisted*.

With a howl of pain, the emperor fell to his knees. In a single, lightning-fast action, I removed the hair stick from my bun—

And stabbed him through the neck.

I had hoped for clarity to enter his eyes. For him to look past Mira's face and into mine, finally understanding everything I was capable of.

But there was only shock. Only blood gurgling from his lips as he raised a hand to try and stem the tide of blood—

Someone screamed. And then the entire crowd was screaming, panic spreading through the onlookers like a forest fire.

'The emperor!' The shout rang out from the guards. 'Protect the emperor!'

It was too late. I knew that already, even before I tore the thin knife from my father's carotid artery. Blood splattered across my face as he collapsed against the tiles. An emperor brought down by a hair piece.

It was almost laughable.

The emperor's personal guard launched themselves forward – only to be met by Warriors loyal to Cassius. Zandri had recruited many of the prince's supporters for this, and his men were butchering her a path through the gathering. I saw my mother – still disguised as Cassius – lingering to ensure that I followed safely. Her eyes glittered, revelling in the carnage.

I took a step towards Zandri when one of the emperor's guards broke through our defences.

His approach was too quick, too unexpected – there was no time to reach for a weapon, and I had no death magic left to save me. Ten metres away, Zandri's lips parted in wordless shock.

'*No!*'

Blonde hair whipped across my face as Lillian pushed me to the side. There was an instant of dizzying pain as I hit the tiles. Glancing down, I expected to see blood darkening my bodice, but I was unharmed. Somehow, I was unharmed.

I looked up in time to see the Warrior drive his sword, hilt-deep, into Lillian's stomach.

Rushing to Lillian's side, I caught her and almost crumpled under her weight. I lowered her to the ground, frantically pressing my hands against the wound – a useless attempt. Red soaked the front of Lillian's golden dress, spreading rapidly.

'Hold on,' I pleaded. 'Just hold on.' I looked desperately around me for Zandri, but I couldn't see her amongst the chaos.

Lillian coughed blood, shivered, but tried to smile. 'I love you,' she whispered. 'Mira.'

Her eyes fluttered closed.

It was Lillian who had died, but somehow, I was the one who couldn't breathe.

Guilt was such a messy, unpleasant emotion.

'She's gone. There's nothing you can do for her.'

Tattooed hands tried to tug Lillian free, but I didn't let her go.

'Scarlett,' Severin said again, firmer and more insistent, 'you can't stay here. Zandri's forces have cleared a path through the hall, but it won't hold.'

Those words were enough to make me raise my head. But rather than focusing on the protective ring of steel that had formed around us, my eyes locked with Severin's. Part of me couldn't believe he was here. I hadn't been sure whether I would see him again after our conversation on the battlements, and now . . .

'I never wanted this to happen.' My words came out like a plea. A plea for him not to hate me.

Severin didn't answer immediately. 'I met Lillian on Aldara. She shone as brightly as a flame.'

The ending he'd spoken of. The one he'd Seen during his time at the Elusive Isles . . .

'You knew,' I realised. 'You *knew* that Lillian would die to save me—'

'I warned you there would be deaths.' His voice was soft but not gentle. 'Beyond that, I've learnt not to try and actively change the things I See. Often, it leads to even worse consequences.' Severin frowned slightly, and I wondered whether he'd Seen me die, if Lillian hadn't intervened. He reached for Lillian, scooping her body into his arms – just as the clash of swords drew closer. A glance past him showed me that our Warriors were still holding, the path to the exit still clear. *For now.* 'I'll make sure she receives a decent burial.'

'No,' I said, and my voice was sharp. 'Take her body to the crypt.'

'Scarlett—'

'I don't want to hear your warnings.' I reached for the knife that had killed the emperor, clutching it with bloody hands. 'Consider this an order from your future empress.'

Severin nodded, but his face remained serious. 'Remember, Scarlett,' he said, before turning to descend the dais steps, Lillian's body still cradled in his arms. 'Some fates should not be changed – and all magic has a price.'

CHAPTER SIXTY

Mira

Three hours earlier

I stared out of the carriage window, unexpectedly calm. For perhaps the first time in my life, I knew that I'd made the right choice.

It still felt strange, walking away from the vengeance I'd desired for so long. After meeting with the resistance, I had been so *sure* of my next move – I'd returned to Madam Mandrakes to buy a thin blade that I could smuggle into the wedding, intending to strike when I reached the altar.

I'd reasoned it all out. Aric and Lillian had a solid plan to escape; they should be free and clear before they realised what I'd done. And by murdering Emperor Kalias, I would have finally done something to help the Kalurians.

But killing the emperor didn't guarantee their freedom. And vengeance wouldn't bring my mother back.

Aric was right: life was for the living. And I was done wasting mine.

It was surreal to step out of the carriage, knowing that I was about to see Aric again. Surreal, because I was finally ready to say those words back to him.

I love you, too.

I felt suddenly shy, though there was no reason to be. Aric had slipped out of my rooms before the guard rotation had changed, but I'd seen how hard it was for him to leave. It was impossible to doubt his love for me. Not after everything we'd been through.

And everything we're about to risk.

I forced the thought aside, striding through the harbour. The docks were peaceful this morning, and as I listened to the water lapping against the ships' hulls, it occurred to me this visit was very different from my last. With any luck, it would remain that way. Facing down arrows once was enough for a lifetime.

The *Drakkar* came into view as boots thudded against the cobblestones. I turned, catching sight of a strange collection of people running towards me: two hooded figures with blades glinting in their hands; a dark-haired prisoner, chains encircling his wrist; and a richly dressed lady, who despite the dirt on her clothes, could have come straight from the palace ballroom.

I glanced around the docks, but there was no one else in sight. 'Where are Aric and Lillian? Are they already on board?'

'No,' Jadis said tightly, removing her hood. 'We couldn't locate them. They weren't where they were supposed to be.'

'But Scarlett told me they were with you!'

'Well, I didn't see them.' Jadis glanced at her brother, but Elian shook his head too.

Panic surged through me. If something had happened to them—

'I have to get back to the palace.' I looked wildly around for a carriage. *'Right now.'*

'Mira.' Jadis's voice was sharp. 'You can't. We've just extracted a high-profile prisoner from the dungeons; the emperor will order his Warriors to investigate. And what happens if Aric and Lillian return while you're gone? You need to trust them to handle themselves. They know what's at stake.'

I bit my lip, conflicted. 'But if Scarlett betrayed us—'

'We don't know that. Maybe she was given some misinformation.' Jadis stared me down. 'Either way, we need to be ready to sail at a moment's notice. Give Aric and Lillian time to reach the docks.'

Jadis was right, but that didn't make her words any easier to hear.

She strode towards the ship without waiting for a reply. Her brother followed, half supporting Odessa over one shoulder. Darius looked dazed and exhausted – possibly drugged – but he possessed enough awareness to follow.

I remained on the deck, pacing back and forth in rising distress. The distant tolling of a bell made me flinch and I glanced towards the palace, just in time to see a familiar figure step lithely onto the wharf. The sunlight lit up Cassius's golden hair.

'Going somewhere?' he asked conversationally.

His nonchalance was unbelievable – even for him. Then I realised that only I was visible: he couldn't see Jadis and the others inside the cabin, and he must not have heard about the breakout. If he had, he would have brought Warriors with him.

'Yes, actually,' I said, matching his blasé tone. 'So, if you don't mind, I should be on my way.'

Just as I'd hoped, Cassius strode down the gangplank. He wasn't wary at all; it hadn't occurred to him that this could be a trap.

The prince was dressed handsomely for our wedding, in a crimson and gold tunic and fitted black dress pants. He eyed my plain clothes with dissatisfaction as he approached. That dissatisfaction darkened as he noticed that I was no longer wearing my ring.

'When my informants told me you were here alone,' he said, his attention still on my hand, 'I had hoped to bring you to your senses. Most girls would be thrilled to marry a prince.'

'Feel free to marry one of them, then,' I said. 'Because I have no intention of accompanying you back to the palace.'

The moment Cassius reached the deck, I made my move. He barely had the chance to flinch before my dagger was at his throat.

His eyes flared with impotent anger. 'We both know you're not going to kill me,' he gritted out.

'I wouldn't be so sure.'

He searched my face, but I didn't soften. I didn't waver. And then I heard the loud creak of the cabin door.

Cassius's eyes darted over my shoulder – and widened. I turned but didn't release my grip on the dagger.

'In,' I told him, motioning towards the cabin with my left hand.

Cassius, of course, didn't move. He was studying Jadis and the others, his expression calculating. 'How long have you been working with the resistance?'

'You're not in a position to be asking questions.'

As if to enforce my comment, Elian moved forward – and tightened a pair of cuffs around the prince's wrists.

In an exasperated tone, he asked, 'Is this really necessary?'

It was Jadis who replied. 'We're not taking any chances.'

'Am I along for the journey, then?' Cassius said pleasantly. 'Or will you let me leave once you cast off?'

That was a good question. I glanced sideways at Jadis, who didn't meet my eyes. A prince, after all, was a useful hostage.

I wasn't sure how I felt about that, but now wasn't the time to decide. 'Take him below deck,' I said, releasing the dagger from his throat.

Cassius didn't try to struggle as Elian took him by the shoulder, but I saw the flicker of fear that he was too slow to hide. He was no longer in control, and we both knew it.

The prince tried to catch my eye as Elian escorted him away, but I ignored him. Instead, I moved over to the rail. There was still no sign of Aric or Lillian, and I could hear trumpets blaring in the distance.

With the ceremony about to start, they were cutting it dangerously close. Soon, people at the palace would notice that Cassius and I were missing. When that happened . . .

'Mira,' Jadis said softly, 'I'll give them as long as I can, but we can't stay here indefinitely.'

I didn't reply. I wasn't willing to contemplate leaving without them. I wouldn't *need* to leave without them.

Aric had promised he would be here, and he always kept his promises. He would find a way.

I have to believe he'll find a way.

Midday.

As impossible as it seemed, it was midday. And still, they hadn't come.

Jadis was growing impatient, but I kept my gaze fixed on the palace. The Warriors must have started looking for me by now, and it was likely that the dungeon breakout had also been discovered. How long until the emperor's Warriors reached the docks, the most obvious place to search? How long until they descended on the *Drakkar* with their swords and arrows?

My heart hammered as I recognised the unmistakable sound of hoofbeats on cobblestones. A mixture of excitement and terror speared through me.

Jadis reached for my arm. 'Mira—'

But I was already scrambling towards the docks. Towards the young man dismounting from his horse.

'Aric!' I shouted.

He didn't show any sign that he had even recognised me, though his gaze met mine. I shuddered as I noticed the emptiness in his eyes – and the blood staining his armour. His *dented* armour.

'What happened?' I demanded as he approached. 'Where's Lillian?'

'Don't pretend.' Aric stepped onto the gangplank. 'Don't *lie*.'

I stared at him in bewilderment. 'What are you talking about?'

'I saw what you did. I saw Lillian's body cut down because of you.'

'Lillian's—' I broke off, feeling like I was going to be sick. *No. No, it can't be true.*

'My sister loved you. She *died* for you.' His voice cracked. 'And it is only because of that, Mira, that I'm here right now. That I'm willing to let you leave.'

I shook my head back and forth. 'There has to be some kind of mistake. I don't know what's happened, Aric, but—'

'Do you deny buying a blade from Madam Mandrakes? Plotting to kill the emperor?'

'No,' I spluttered, 'but I didn't go through with it! I swear – I would never do *anything* to hurt you or Lillian!'

Aric didn't appear to be listening. 'You as good as admitted it to me last night,' he said, almost to himself. 'I knew you were planning something, and I – I was so *blind*.' He let out a rough laugh. 'Lillian was right. You destroy everything you touch.'

I stumbled back, but he kept advancing.

'I never want to see you again, do you understand? From now on, you're nothing to me.'

My tears overflowed. 'You don't know what you're saying.'

'What I *know*,' he said, 'is that my sister is dead and you're responsible.'

My whole body was trembling; I felt like I was about to shatter apart. He must have seen that too, but he turned decisively on his heel. As if he meant every cruel, heartbreaking word. As if I really was nothing to him.

'Please.' It was all I could think to say. 'Aric, please . . .'

His shoulders tensed, but he kept walking.

'If you leave now,' I shouted after him desperately, 'when will we ever see each other again?'

Aric paused to look back over his shoulder. 'You'd better hope we don't, Mira,' he said coldly. 'Because if that day comes, there will be a reckoning.'

It would have hurt less if he'd struck me. He watched me collapse to my knees with pitiless eyes.

Then he strode away from me – towards the Warriors galloping down the hill on Zigilian stallions. Towards the young woman leading the charge, the emperor's bone crown gleaming on top of her red hair.

The gangplank was pulled back, our ship sailing away from Ravalia for what could be the last time.

I waited for Aric to glance back, even just once—

He didn't.

CHAPTER SIXTY-ONE

Scarlett

The crypt was eerily still, the air stale. The darkness was so thick that I couldn't see the alcoves around me, filled with hundreds of stone coffins. There was only the seamstress's body, faintly illuminated by the oil lamp in my hand.

'You ordered the Warriors to take Lillian.' Aric's voice sounded dull, like some part of him had died along with his sister.

'I thought it best,' I said gently.

Aric's gaze went past me – to his sister. Lillian was laid out on a marble slab, her golden hair spread out like a halo. She looked so peaceful that she could have been sleeping, if it wasn't for the unnatural paleness of her skin and the blood staining her dress.

'You would bury her here?' Aric asked. Though he was trying to be stoic, tears glistened on his cheeks. 'In the royal crypt?'

I moved towards him. This close, I could smell his aftershave: musky and familiar, thanks to his time spent guarding me. It was a scent I had come to appreciate – or perhaps I had simply come to appreciate *him*. 'I didn't bring Lillian here to bury her, Aric. I brought her here to offer you a choice.'

Aric looked up at me, his confusion obvious.

This was my last chance to hesitate. To change my mind.

Some fates should not be changed.

An Artisan's warning was not something to be ignored, but I liked the idea of embracing my powers and saving a life. Particularly one that might prove useful to me.

'I can help Lillian,' I murmured, keeping my voice soft. Inviting. 'If you ask me to.'

'You could . . . but she's dead.' His voice broke. 'She's beyond anyone's help.'

'Not mine.'

Aric stared at me, and I saw a desperate shred of hope burning in his eyes. Oh, he would love me for this – *if* I could accomplish it.

'What are you saying?'

'I can bring her back,' I said. 'I can make her whole again, Aric. For a price.'

He shook his head, as if he was certain he must have misheard. Misunderstood. But then he whispered, 'A price?'

And I knew I had him.

'There's always a price. I wonder . . .' I cast him a curious glance, 'are you willing to pay it?'

'For Lillian? Anything.'

I smiled and stepped forward. The knife was already in my hand – the thin, stiletto blade that I had used to kill the emperor.

'You have to cut me,' I instructed, passing him the knife. Then I extended my palm so that it was directly above Lillian's body.

Blood welled, vivid against the whiteness of my skin, but I didn't feel the sting.

As it dripped onto Lillian's upturned face, I braced myself for pain, for dizziness, a more extreme version of my reaction after resurrecting animals with my blood.

All I felt was numbness. An absence of feeling.

I knew I should feel disappointed – this was, after all, the same failure I had experienced with Sabine – but instead of disappointment, something strange began to build beneath my skin. A kind of pressure I had never experienced before.

When I glanced down at my hand, the veins had turned black – as black as the blood rolling down Lillian's cheek. Like an inky tear.

A chill breeze suddenly raced through the hall. The oil lamp flickered uncertainly and went out.

Though my eyes were open, they might as well have been closed. In the absolute darkness, every inch of me felt alert, my previous numbness dispelled. Touch, smell, hearing . . . they were all heightened, taut and tense. My breathing was loud in my ears, ragged. Beside me, I could hear Aric's, too. Neither of us dared speak.

And then I heard something else. Silk rustling against skin.

I jerked back, my hip striking painfully against the stone slab. *There's nothing to be afraid of,* I told myself, trying to calm my racing heart.

But when I tried to move my arm towards Lillian's body, I couldn't. I was frozen with fear, terrified of what I might feel if I did. Terrified that Severin had been right, and I had made a terrible mistake.

I took a deep, steadying breath—

And reached into the blackness.

Resurrecting Lillian felt like a dream. One that I would wake up from at any moment.

But it had been an hour, and still, Lillian's heart was beating. Still, her face was flushed with warmth and *life*.

Not some unnatural, undead thing, but the seamstress, exactly as I remembered her. Every bit as alive as she had been a day ago.

And entirely dependent on me for her continued survival.

The awareness had come on slowly, but now it was inescapable. Even when Lillian was out of sight, I could *feel* her – sense her through whatever magical tether connected her life to mine.

A tether that I could snap with a single thought.

'Lillian,' I said gently, 'could you give us a moment?'

It was clearly torturous for Aric to loosen his grip on Lillian's hand. To watch Lillian step away from him with a soft smile.

'I'll be right outside,' she reassured him.

I perched on the edge of the stone slab, wincing as I did. Aric frowned with concern, his brown eyes canvassing my face. This close, it would be impossible for him not to notice the blue tinge to my lips, the way my red hair transitioned to white on the ends. I had no idea whether they were permanent changes, but for now, I felt as if I had escaped lightly.

'When it comes to magic,' I told Aric, 'there's always a price –
both for the recipient and the wielder.'

Aric's frown became more pronounced. 'I thought I was the only
one who had to pay the price.'

I believed him, but I doubted it would have mattered if he had
known. Aric would have damned the whole world to hell if it could
have saved his sister. His depth of feeling was something I admired
about him.

'It was worth it,' I said, and meant it. 'To have something good
come out of all this.'

Aric knelt before me, his face upturned. 'How can I ever repay
you?'

I considered him for a moment. What I wanted was his devotion – the devotion I had envied ever since I first saw it directed at
Mira. My rival.

My enemy, now.

'For all intents and purposes,' I said slowly, 'Ravalia is mine. But
before I can officially become empress, Roran will need to be dealt
with. Not to mention Mira and Cassius.'

My casual mention of Mira was a test, but Aric didn't flinch. I had
done my work well – isolating her from her closet allies with a single
strike. I thought back to the devastation on Aric's face when he had
laid eyes on Lillian's body. Devastation that had shifted into something darker and harder when I mentioned Mira's clandestine trip to
Madam Mandrakes the night before.

Aric hadn't even held his dead sister before leaving to intercept
Mira at the docks. And though he had let her escape with her life, I
doubted he would offer her that same mercy again. After everything
he believed Mira had been responsible for – killing the emperor,
scheming with Cassius, costing Lillian her life – he must wonder if he
had ever known her at all.

That kind of betrayal was a good start, something I could work
with. And when I was certain of his loyalty . . . I studied Aric, thinking of how his trainers had described him: a talented Warrior with a
mind for battle strategy. Honed by experience, those skills would

make him invaluable. I had no illusions about the task ahead: war was coming, and my father's generals and advisers were sure to throw their lot in with Roran. I would need to replace them with people I could trust.

People I could *control.*

I brushed a finger across Aric's jawline. He shivered at the sensation, and I smiled. 'What I need from you, Aric, is to fight for me. And in time . . . to lead my army. That's my price.'

'I'm with you, Your Highness,' he said, without hesitation. 'Whatever you need.'

'Scarlett,' I murmured, my eyes inches from his. 'It's Scarlett, to my friends.'

'Scarlett,' he repeated, equally soft. I liked the way he said my name: like it was something precious and delicate.

I was still smiling as I said, 'I think you'll make a wonderful general.'

'And you,' Aric told me, kissing my hands, 'will make a fearsome empress.'

My laughter was a very distinctive, very unexpected sound.

Like ice cracking.

CHAPTER SIXTY-TWO

Severin

I shut my eyes as the cool wind buffeted my face. I had Seen this moment play out so many times that I could visualise it effortlessly: the glowing lights of the city below, the austere beauty of the battlements, and *her*.

She always came to me in the end, her face flushed with triumph. Victory.

Because all of this . . . it was *her* victory. Not her daughter's.

'I didn't think it would be so easy to get you alone,' Zandri said, the sharp sound of her heeled boots stalking closer.

'You make it sound like I was trying to avoid you,' I replied, 'when nothing could be further from the truth.'

'Or perhaps,' Zandri continued, her voice lethally soft, 'you were waiting for someone else.'

And there it was. The secret that was never really a secret, the game that was about to come to its inevitable conclusion.

There was only one way this ended. I had always known it, and had fallen in love with Scarlett anyway. But now that Scarlett was Zandri's ticket to power, I had become an inconvenience. More than that – I had become a threat to her plans. She wouldn't allow anyone else to influence the future empress.

'Always the puppet master, aren't you?' I said, finally twisting to face her.

I would much rather have been looking at the city – drinking in its night-time splendour as opposed to Zandri's harsh features. But, as usual, she was impossible to ignore.

'You should be careful how you speak to me.' She tilted her head to one side, an avian gesture that had once unnerved me.

But that was a long time ago. Back when I was plucked from my war-torn home and told that I was lucky. *Lucky* to be liberated from my own country, to serve the empire that had destroyed everything I held dear.

'We both know I'm not going to survive this meeting,' I said evenly. 'Nothing I say can change that.'

There was only one way that Zandri dealt with loose ends. She killed them.

My only regret was that I wouldn't see Scarlett one last time, but she was occupied with her new kingdom – she finally had a real-life chessboard of her own, where she had claimed the only piece that mattered: the queen.

Except there were two queens. And only Mira held the throne in her own right.

Zandri fixed me with a calculating stare. In many ways, she had been as much a mother figure to me as she had been to Scarlett, teaching me the ways of the court, showing me how to develop my magic. Many orphans inducted into the Orders served her with genuine devotion.

I might have been one of them, if my abilities didn't allow me to See everything much more clearly. Zandri had never cared about anyone beyond their usefulness to her.

'If you know how this ends, why didn't you run?' She stepped closer, raising her voice as the wind picked up. 'Aren't you supposed to be a seer?'

I didn't answer immediately. The moment I did, this conversation would be over. Her curiosity was keeping me alive, and even that was tenuous.

'First, I have a question.'

I could have asked her about the future. Even Artisans had their limits, and I couldn't See past my own death. The moment I had decided to come here, all the futures that had once been so clear and bright to me had disappeared, like stars blinking out of existence.

Zandri would probably share her plans – what reason would she have to lie to a dead man? But there was only one thing I wanted to know, and it had to do with the past.

'I saw you plan it all out. Every last detail – from Scarlett sending Mira to the docks so she could take her place, to ensuring Cassius went after his fiancée, allowing you to impersonate him. Lillian was an unfortunate complication, of course, but Scarlett never intended for her to be hurt.' I paused. 'But how did you convince her to betray Mira?'

It had bothered me, ever since I'd touched Lillian's hand in the Elusive Isles and Seen the events leading up to her death. This was one outcome, but there had been another, with Mira and Scarlett working together to reshape their respective worlds. Not enemies, not at odds . . . but at peace.

Glimpsing the future wasn't an exact science. Often it was muddled and confused, particularly when there were diverging paths. I couldn't be sure if that second vision had ceased to exist the moment Scarlett killed the emperor, or whether there was still a slim chance for it to come to pass.

Amusement crinkled the fine lines beneath Zandri's hateful eyes. 'It was Scarlett's idea to frame Mira, not mine. Perhaps your feelings for my daughter have blinded you to her true nature.' A thin smile. 'Now it's your turn. If you knew you weren't going to survive this meeting, why are you here?'

'Because,' I replied, echoing the words I'd said to Scarlett, 'some fates shouldn't be changed.'

Shouldn't. Not *couldn't*.

I allowed myself a second to take in Zandri's incredulous expression, her lack of understanding.

She thought she had won and I was a fool, but there was one way – one slim, desperate way – that she could still lose. Because I knew Scarlett better than anyone – and I knew that she loved me.

No matter what lies Zandri decided to tell about my absence, Scarlett would one day discover the truth for herself, and that knowledge would cut through their relationship like a fault line. A crack that could shape the course of nations.

I looked into Zandri's face one last time, but I wasn't seeing her cold features.

I was seeing her daughter's.

I allowed myself to imagine Scarlett's red hair, proud face and beautiful smile. And her eyes. Those aquamarine eyes I knew as well as my own.

In that moment, there was no fear. There was only hope. Gratitude. *Love.*

Filled with peace, I lunged sideways—

And hurled myself from the battlements.

CHAPTER SIXTY-THREE

Mira

The ship lurched violently, throwing me against the railing as it pitched downwards.

My stomach dropped as I gripped the rail with numb fingers, clinging on for dear life. Icy water sloshed across the deck as another wave propelled us up again, the screaming wind threatening to shred the sails.

Terror warred with nausea. Nausea won.

I leant over the side and retched, shutting my eyes against the stinging onslaught of saltwater.

We're not going to die. I repeated those words over and over as I tried not to think of Aric. He had been in my dreams enough as it was. Before the storm had hit, the nightmares had dragged me from sleep. Most often, they featured his face. Or Lillian's.

'Hold on,' Jadis shouted as we tilted sideways.

I screwed my eyes shut as I tightened my grip even further. Maybe I deserved to drown out here. It had been my idea to try and escape, after all. If Aric was right, and I was somehow responsible for Lillian's death . . .

But no. I'd made the right choice, turning against my plans for revenge. Aric would come to see that. He had to. I hadn't recognised the man on the docks. He had been insensible, consumed by grief.

And yet . . .

Irrational though it was, it felt like the Tempest Sea was seething with Aric's anger. Like it, too, wanted to punish me.

Like it didn't want me to reach Kalure.

*

Dawn was breaking on the horizon when the winds finally died down and I had my first view of our destination: thick forest spanning as far as the eye could see, with snow-capped mountains in the distance. After everything I'd survived, it was like glimpsing paradise.

Wrapping my furs more tightly around my shoulders, I thought of my mother. Wondering how differently everything might have turned out if we had made this journey together.

But I'm here now, I thought as I looked over the sapphire bay. My hand enclosed around the locket, which warmed at my touch. *I made it.* We *made it.*

Darius came to stand at my side as we drew closer to the beach, facing the line of warriors who had received our message. With the capital city of Taiga under Roran's control, it had been too risky to land anywhere close to the main ports, but he'd claimed we would be safe enough in the Wilds – the untamed lands to the west of the mountain range.

I wasn't so sure. The Kalurians didn't appear friendly, dressed in chain mail armour with unsheathed weapons and long braided hair. Northerners had a reputation as fierce fighters, and all these men and women radiated the same warlike intensity.

Maybe Darius noticed the way my hand clung to the rail, like we were still caught in that raging storm. 'These are your people,' he reminded me. 'They're here for you.'

Swallowing, I nodded. The instant our shallow-draft vessel grounded on the shore, Darius jumped off the bow and motioned for me to join him. I lowered myself into the clear water more cautiously, my legs wobbly. After three days at sea, I was unused to solid ground.

As we waded towards the beach, I was very grateful for Jadis and Elian. Regardless of Darius's assurances, neither of their hands left their swords.

The six of us stood shoulder to shoulder, facing the assembled Kalurians, who stared me down without warmth. None of them spoke, and I felt my skin flush. What had I expected? Welcoming smiles? *Bows?*

'Come with us,' one said in a heavy Kalurian accent, and with a gesture from Darius, the rest of our party came ashore.

The warrior led us between gnarled, windblown trees and through a meadow filled with wildflowers. A damp chill enveloped me as we entered the thick forest beyond, its emerald canopy blocking out the sun. Animals darted in and out of sight with flashes of colour, trumpeting our presence with urgent calls.

And as we delved deeper into the forest, the glow of lanterns drew my gaze upwards. To—

'Incredible,' I breathed, staring at the dwellings above. They were built artfully into the trees – multiple buildings on top of one another, all connected by wooden bridges.

I paused, squinting at the intricate homes with their carved doors and balconies, many of them lit in a golden glow.

A village.

I was staring at a Kalurian village.

'Welcome to the Wilds,' the warrior told me, his expression softening as he followed my gaze.

Odessa was focused on the vibrant world in the treetops too, watching forest dwellers cross the boardwalks high above. It was impossible to tell what she was thinking, but she seemed reluctant to leave the village behind.

The clink of manacles alerted me as Cassius strode up to my side, the mottled light playing across his wan face and dishevelled tunic.

'You've made your point,' he said, extending his bound hands in front him. 'You've proven that you're in control. You can release me now.'

I blinked at him. And then I laughed. 'Are you serious?'

'It would be in your best interests, Mira, for us to work together. I don't want my sister to rule Ravalia any more than you do.'

I didn't ask how he'd put it together. He had probably overheard me telling Darius and Jadis what I had seen before we set sail: Scarlett riding towards the docks with her father's crown on her head. I still wasn't sure exactly what had happened the day I was supposed to marry Cassius, but I knew Scarlett had given me false information – and there was only one way she could have taken that crown.

What a fool I'd been. How many times had I reminded myself that I couldn't trust anyone in the Ravalian Court?

'I've tried making deals with you before,' I said dismissively to Cassius. 'I won't make that mistake again.'

Apparently, Cassius was done with diplomacy. He leant closer, his eyes narrowing. 'One day, you're going to need me. And when that day comes—'

Lightning fast, Odessa stepped in front of the prince. 'You're in no position to make demands,' she snapped. 'In case you haven't noticed, you're surrounded by people who want you dead. If I were you, I would focus on remaining useful and *quiet*.'

Cassius tilted his head, considering the retinue of Kalurian warriors around us. But when he looked back at Odessa, it was with an assessing stare. 'You can't be pleased about this,' he said in a low voice, 'not when you fought so hard to maintain your position as my fiancée. To become a *Ravalian* princess.'

'Don't try to imply that you *know* me.' Her face was hard as she regarded him, no softness to be seen. 'I did that for my family, not for ambition. And certainly not for *you*.'

Odessa strode to the front of the group with her head held high. I had the sense that her dismissal aggravated Cassius more than anything else. He scowled as she walked away, but his expression turned impassive as he noticed me watching.

'I could tell her everything, you know,' Cassius said. 'I wonder how cooperative she would be *then* – if she knew that you framed her father.'

I went still. 'You'd be exposing yourself, too.'

He shrugged. 'That only matters if I have something to lose.'

I didn't dignify that with a response. Following Odessa's example, I quickened my pace, leaving the prince behind.

Time was meaningless in the forest. Only the hunger gnawing at my stomach suggested that we'd been travelling for hours. My breath started to come more heavily as the land sloped upwards, opening out into a clearing.

With a start, I realised there were people everywhere. They lined both sides of the path, standing in front of rickety structures with thatched roofs.

'Refugees,' Darius told me. 'Displaced from their homes, and desperate for food from the temple stores.'

My hunger and tiredness were instantly forgotten, replaced by queasiness.

Roran. Roran was responsible for this, for all these *people* . . .

'Keep moving,' Odessa hissed, and I realised that I'd slowed to a stop. Her clammy hand tightened urgently around mine.

It didn't take long to understand the reason for her nerves. Hard stares were directed at the Ravalians, lingering longest on Cassius. Even with the retinue of warriors escorting us, we could easily be overwhelmed by sheer numbers.

I stayed close to Darius, conscious of the refugees pressing in tightly on either side. They followed as the path inclined steeply, drawing up towards an imposing structure built into the base of a mountain. Rising above it was a domed temple, hewn from basalt stone – much harder, darker and denser than the surrounding sandstone.

And in front of it were even more people. Men and women with thin faces and threadbare clothes. Warriors guarding the landing of the temple, stopping the crowd from coming any closer.

But as we approached the well-worn steps, the mass of people suddenly pushed forward. Just as I reached for the dagger at my side, the ranks of warriors parted, revealing an equally intimidating woman.

She glided towards us with purpose, her braided hair highlighting an angular face decorated with silver tattoos. Unlike the women who followed behind her, dressed in white, fur-lined cloaks, her slender body was covered by material so fine it was almost sheer, as if she didn't feel the cold at all. It fell to the ground in slitted midnight-black panels.

The moment she raised her hand, absolute stillness swept over the gathering.

'I am High Priestess Velanthe,' she said in a voice that carried effortlessly over the throng. 'Be welcome in my domain, Princess Kasmira, daughter of King Arioch.'

Rumbling broke out, and I wondered what these people saw. Did they see the leader my mother had envisioned, or was I as unremarkable as Emperor Kalias had always thought I was?

I couldn't be sure. Their expressions varied from wary to curious, but there was none of the tentative warmth the high priestess had shown me.

What right did I have to come here? To ask them to accept me as their leader?

None, their cold faces replied.

'Come, Kasmira,' Velanthe said gently but firmly, striding towards a towering silver door.

Darius and the others climbed the steps without further prompting. I started to follow, but then I paused. Something about these people – their distrust and pinched faces – held me immobile.

I couldn't turn my back on them. Even when the weight of their stares threatened to make me crumble.

'I've lived my whole life in the Ravalian Empire.' The words left my lips before I could think better of speaking. Men, women and children stared at me, so silent I could hear the faint rustle of the trees. My heart was pounding, but I forced myself to continue: 'I don't know Kalure, but I know Ravalia. I've seen their injustices and their cruelty. I was there when the emperor ordered Roran to crush your rebellion with brute force. I watched my mother beheaded for loving King Arioch, and a good man sacrifice himself for your cause.'

Perhaps it was only my imagination, but I could have sworn the Wilds went still: like the trees themselves were listening in anticipation.

I took a deep breath, and as I exhaled, I knew what I needed to do.

I slipped the furs from my shoulders, revealing the fighting leathers underneath.

And then I unsheathed my dagger.

A few of the people nearest to me drew back, and the warriors visibly tensed. They relaxed as I sank to one knee.

'Søren Halvor,' I said strongly, my voice amplified by the temple wall, 'loved Kalure. He gave his life so that I could fight for you. *With* you.' For the first time, saying his name didn't fill me with guilt, but a sense of rightness. 'And that's exactly what I intend to do. If you'll have me.'

I extended the dagger in my palms. My offering.

My vow.

The silence held for another, mortifying minute. Then, with great reverence, the high priestess bowed her head. In unison, the warriors followed her lead, until everyone had their gazes angled to the ground.

But it wasn't their gestures that moved me.

It was the feeling of someone tugging on my arm. A little boy, in ragged clothes, helping me to my feet. In an instant, he was joined by others: a crowd of people lining the temple steps.

I had been afraid of these people before – afraid of their numbers, their potential for violence.

I wasn't afraid now.

I walked between them, hand in hand with the little boy. And as I passed, their fingers brushed my hair, my shoulders, the hem of my skirts.

It was humbling. Tears welled in my eyes as I embraced the sudden connection to my father's people.

A connection that I had never allowed myself to hope for or imagine.

When I reached the temple landing, a rhythmic thudding met my ears. The warriors below, pounding their shields against the ground.

As I stared out over the glade, my mother's words came back to me: *You would have made a brilliant Warrior, Mira. You would have made an even better ruler.*

I had made so many mistakes. I had more regrets than I could count, but I was determined to live up to that belief.

I ascended the remaining steps, my eyes on the entrance to the temple complex, where the high priestess waited. Darius and the others stood respectfully to one side, but Cassius tried to follow, only to have two warriors bar his way. His face paled slightly – then hardened when he realised the Kalurians were looking at me. Awaiting *my* orders.

'What are your instructions, Your Majesty?' one of the warriors asked, his voice strong and deep.

Velanthe's black eyes met mine, but she inclined her head. Deferring to my judgement.

I considered for a moment, thinking of everything Cassius had done – and what he had threatened in the forest.

'If you think you're safe here, in this backwater,' Cassius said quickly, 'you're wrong. There's a reason both Scarlett and I fear Roran. Without my help, Mira, you're going to get yourself and your people killed.'

The conviction in his voice gave me pause, but I refused to let him rattle me.

'Lock him up,' I told the warriors – my first official order. Cassius had been content to let Odessa rot in the dungeons; it seemed only fair that I returned the favour.

'Wait!' The desperation in Cassius's voice made me glance over my shoulder. As the warriors seized his arms, I saw real, undiluted panic on his face. 'You need me, Mira. You can't do this without me.'

I met his gaze with a resolute one of my own. And I felt nothing but satisfaction as I said, 'Watch me.'

Dimly, I heard Cassius yelling, 'You're making a mistake! Mira! *Mira!*'

But then he was dragged away, and I heard nothing more.

The faint rustle of silk alerted me as the high priestess came to stand at my side. Together, we faced the life-sized carving of the Sorceress, which dominated the massive door leading to the temple complex.

My ancestor. The very woman whose legend had intrigued me as a child.

But unlike the woman I'd once seen on my mother's card, *this* Sorceress didn't resemble a trickster. Her beautiful face was hard and cold, not an ounce of levity to be seen.

'The Sorceress could do all sorts of incredible things, Kasmira,' Velanthe murmured, following the direction of my stare. 'You can't possibly imagine the scope of her power.'

'I can imagine better than you might think,' I said, flashes of black fire dancing before my eyes. 'I've used magic before – channelled it from a blood ruby.'

Velanthe's answering laugh was soft. 'Whatever magic you think you've used is but a fraction of what you're capable of. As a descendant of the Sorceress, you're born with natural magic of your own – and the ability to wield blood magic. In time, I will share with you the Sorceress's old grimoires – forbidden texts I keep hidden even from the other priestesses. When you have read them, I have no doubt you will become as devout as I am.'

Her conviction made me uneasy. After my interactions with Zandri, I was wary of magic – and I wasn't sure that I wanted to worship the memory of a being who had lived over a century ago.

'Is that what you want? For me to become a part of the Temple?'

Perhaps Velanthe heard the wariness in my tone, because she smiled faintly. 'No, Kasmira. My plans don't involve making you into one of my acolytes.'

'Then what do they involve?'

The high priestess pushed open the silver door, her eyes glittering. When she spoke, her voice was filled with religious fervour.

'Making you a queen.'

Scarlett

I took the precious stone from Zandri, turning it over in my fingers. This blood ruby was the brightest of them all, glistening a vivid, brilliant crimson.

There were hundreds just like it, each brimming with inner fire. Many more filled the shelves of the cavern, from decades past. But the others had darkened to the reddish black of congealed blood, their fire long since burned out.

'I don't understand,' I said coolly. I had been in the middle of combing the palace for Severin, and didn't appreciate being pulled away from my search – particularly when my mother phrased her request like an order. 'You brought me here to admire your treasure trove?'

'Of course not.' Zandri's tone was dismissive. '*This,*' she said, her arms widening to indicate the cavernous space around us, 'is how we take Kalure.'

An answering hunger rose up inside me, but my eyes narrowed. 'You already had the chance to strike a blow against Kalure. You were supposed to stop Mira before she set sail – that was the plan.'

'Yes,' Zandri agreed mildly. 'It was.'

'So why—' I took a step closer— 'is Mira still breathing?'

Zandri regarded me with a cool, assessing gaze. Something stirred behind her dark eyes – a power that made my chest constrict. Then she looked away, and I could breathe normally once again.

'Mira is still alive,' Zandri continued, 'because she is still useful. It would be a waste, not to take advantage of her unique position. Not only will she draw the loyalists out, but she'll finally allow me to deal with the Temple.'

I said nothing for a while, weighing her words. No matter Zandri's justifications, letting Mira leave still seemed like a dangerous risk. 'But she's a threat to my rule,' I protested. 'She's a threat to everything we've worked towards. And now she's gone – out of our reach, far from our control.'

Zandri merely smiled, her eyes lowering to the blood ruby she had given me. Against my skin, I could feel the faint vibrations of a pulse: the distant thump of a heartbeat. It warmed at my touch, the fire inside the ruby growing brighter.

'Mira is right where we want her.'

Acknowledgements

The Order of Masks is the story my younger self wanted to read, filled with fierce female protagonists and morally grey characters. It is absolutely surreal to have it out in the world, and I am thrilled to be able to share Mira and Scarlett's stories with you.

I wouldn't be here without my incredible editors, Molly Powell and Claire Craig. From the bottom of my heart, thank you for falling in love with this world and its characters. Your keen editorial vision has taken this story to new heights, and I am forever grateful to you both for your support, encouragement and passion.

To the phenomenal Hodderscape and Pan Macmillan Australia teams: thank you so much for championing *Masks*, which couldn't be in better hands. Belinda Huang, your notes are a treasure, and Sophie Judge, I really appreciate your quick responses and ability to accommodate last-minute edits. To Lily Cameron, Chloe Patterson and Dave Cain, your enthusiasm and forward-thinking ideas make promotion fun. Thank you also to my copy editor Helena Newton, proofreader Sharona Selby, map artist Barking Dog Art, and Marcela Bolivar, who created the spectacular and dramatic cover of my dreams.

Josh Adams and Christabel McKinley, I am incredibly fortunate to have you as my agents. Thank you for your great advice and for finding this book such wonderful homes! Christabel, your 'cauldron-brewed magic' truly works wonders.

To my writing friends and first readers, Julie Eshbaugh and Samantha Sainsbury: thank you for your belief in me, your feedback, and your supportive Zoom calls and emails. Sam, your inspiring editorial report still hangs on my study wall. And Julie, I eagerly look forward to the day when I can travel to the US and give you a well-deserved hug.

Like many writers and readers, I found myself in books, and some of my earliest memories are of making up stories in my family's bookstore (and reading them to customers, much to my parent's amusement). Thank you to Mostly Books, Dymocks, Matilda and other local bookstores and libraries, for being my magical portals to fantastical worlds.

Even though writing can be a solitary pathway, I am never alone. To my furry writing companion, Scamp: you inspire me every day with your feisty terrier spirit. And to my human friends (writers and non-writers alike): you know who you are, and I value each of you deeply.

Mum and Dad: you recognised my potential as a writer long before I did. Thank you for always being in my corner, supplying endless cups of tea, hugs, and unwavering support. And a massive thank you to Dad, who, despite not being an avid reader, has read every draft I've written. I love you so much.

Aunt Jeanette, Uncle Roy, and my cousins Deb and Renee: I am blessed to have you in my life. A special mention to my grandmother Audrey, who nurtured my imagination as a child and remains forever in my heart. And to my grandfathers Les and Wally, who I never had the chance to meet but whose strength is always with me.

Finally, to you, dear readers, thank you for joining me on this incredible journey. Your support and love fuel my writing, and as I prepare to immerse myself in the sequel, know that your eagerness for what comes next is my biggest motivation.

With love,
Alina